Soviet law

Butterworths' Legal Systems of the World

EDITOR: PROFESSOR W. E. BUTLER

Soviet law

Second edition

W. E. Butler MA, JD, PhD, LLD
Professor of Comparative Law
in the University of London
Director, Centre for the Study of
Socialist Legal Systems, University College London

London
Butterworths
1988

United Kingdom	Butterworth & Co (Publishers) Ltd, 88 Kingsway, LONDON WC2B 6AB and 61A North Castle Street, EDINBURGH EH2 3LJ
Australia	Butterworths Pty Ltd, SYDNEY, MELBOURNE, BRISBANE, ADELAIDE, PERTH, CANBERRA and HOBART
Canada	Butterworths. A division of Reed Inc., TORONTO and VANCOUVER
New Zealand	Butterworths of New Zealand Ltd, WELLINGTON and AUCKLAND
Singapore	Butterworth & Co (Asia) Pte Ltd, SINGAPORE
USA	Butterworths Legal Publishers, ST PAUL, Minnesota, SEATTLE, Washington, BOSTON, Massachusetts, AUSTIN, Texas and D & S Publishers, CLEARWATER, Florida

© Butterworth & Co (Publishers) Ltd 1988

First published 1983

All rights reserved. No part of this publication may be reproduced or transmitted in any form or by any means, including photocopying and recording, without the written permission of the copyright holder, application for which should be addressed to the publisher. Such written permission must also be obtained before any part of this publication is stored in a retrieval system of any nature.

This book is sold subject to the Standard Conditions of Sale of Net Books and may not be re-sold in the UK below the net price fixed by Butterworths for the book in our current catalogue.

British Library Cataloguing in Publication Data

Butler, William E. (William Elliott), *1939–*
 Soviet law.——2nd ed.——(Butterworth's
legal systems of the world, 0264-8636)
 1. Soviet Union. Legal system
 I. Title
 344.707

 ISBN Hardcover 0 406 56261 X
  Softcover 0 406 56264 4
 ISSN 0264-8636

Typeset by Colset Private Limited, Singapore
Printed in Great Britain by Billing & Sons Ltd, Worcester

Preface

Butterworths' *Legal Systems of the World* is a series devoted to single-country or, when appropriate, multi-country studies of the principal contemporary legal systems of the world, reflecting a high level of scholarship but suitable for a broad audience. Each study treats briefly the historical development of the respective legal system and its place in the larger family of legal systems or legal tradition in which it originates or by which it has been significantly influenced, the structure and organisation of legal education and the legal profession, the principal institutions involved in the administration of justice and dispute settlement, the sources of law, the constitutional or State system, the basic elements of the principal branches of law, including attention to conflicts of law and foreign relations law, and an analytical bibliography of the principal official gazettes, court reports, and other relevant materials. The studies are designed to serve as a basic reference tool for the particular legal system and to be suitable as primary or supplementary reading for courses in international or comparative law, a resource for practitioners, executives, and government legal advisers engaged in legal transactions with the country concerned, and background for area students and specialists who require an introduction to the legal orders of their area of concern.

In the case of Soviet law, there has been no comprehensive introduction for decades. Harold J. Berman's masterful interpretation of justice in the USSR coincided with the end of the Khrushchev period. The late Edward L. Johnson's introduction to the Soviet legal system, based on public lectures delivered in 1963–65 at the Faculty of Laws, University College London, was intended primarily for those concerned with Soviet affairs who were not trained lawyers and has long since been overtaken by developments in the law.

The present volume presupposes no knowledge of the Russian language. Footnotes have been kept to a minimum in the interest of narrative. Citations are given to legislation only when the enactment concerned is not readily available in English in one of three collections: W. E. Butler *The Soviet Legal System: Legislation and Documentation* (1978), which contains the state of the law just prior to the adoption of the 1977 USSR Constitution; W. E. Butler (ed. and transl.) *Collected Legislation of the USSR and Constituent Union Republics*, a multi-volume looseleaf service for current legislation published since 1979, updated regularly, and available in libraries of consequence; and W. E. Butler *Basic Documents on the Soviet Legal System* (1983; 2nd edn, 1988), issued in a student edition. All are published by Oceana Publications Inc, Dobbs Ferry, New York. For other references, see chapter 21.

The volume draws upon lectures delivered since 1970 at the Faculty of Laws, University College London, in the first such university course offered in the realm as an LL.B. option, 'Introduction to Socialist Legal Systems'; the LL.M. course presently entitled 'Soviet, East European, and Mongolian Law'; and the M.A. course on 'The Soviet Legal System' offered at the School of Slavonic and East European Studies.

The second edition incorporates the principal changes affecting the text since June 1983, drawing on materials as of 1 March 1988. The chapters on economic law, labour law and criminal law have been significantly expanded, as has the chapter on foreign relations law to take account of the restructuring of foreign economic relations and the introduction of joint venture legislation, and a new chapter has been introduced on the law of taxation. Errors in the first edition that came to my attention have been rectified and the text throughout altered as appropriate to reflect recent developments.

An enormous debt to Harold J. Berman, with whom I have been privileged to study and collaborate, and to John N. Hazard, who has been so supportive over the years, is gratefully acknowledged, together with that owed to dozens of Soviet jurists and institutions with whom in the course of more than thirty-five visits spanning three decades I have had occasion to discuss Soviet law or pursue research.

The transliteration of Russian follows the Library of Congress/British Library System.

March 1988   W. E. Butler

Contents

Preface v
Table of principal Soviet legislative acts xi
Table of cases xxi
Abbreviations xxii

Chapter 1 Soviet law in comparative legal studies 1
Comparative law in the Soviet Union 7

Chapter 2 The pre-revolutionary heritage 9
Kievan Rus 10
Mongol subjugation, 1240–1480 12
Muscovite law, 1480–1648 14
The Russian Empire, 1649–1917 17
Continuity and change 25

Chapter 3 The ideological foundations of Soviet law 27
Marxist-Leninist theory of State and law 27
Theory of State and law in the Soviet era 30

Chapter 4 Sources of Soviet law 41
Legislation 41
Acts of social organisations 48
Acts of State Arbitrazh 50
Acts of military commands 50
Court judgments and guiding explanations 51
Doctrine 53
Custom 54
Rules of socialist community life 55
International treaties 56
Publication and entry into force of legislation 57
Translation of enactments into indigenous languages 59
Techniques of law reform 61

Chapter 5 Soviet legal education 64
Modern legal education 68
Reforms in legal education 74

Other types of legal education 75
Legal research 76

Chapter 6 The Soviet legal profession 80
The advocate 80
Jurisconsults 90

Chapter 7 The administration of legality in the Soviet Union 96
Ministries of justice 96
The judicial system 98
Procuracy 107
Notariat 116
Registry for Acts of Civil Status 120
State Arbitrazh 121
Administrative commissions 126
People's control commissions 130
Citizen initiative 132
Police agencies 133
Comrades' courts 136
People's guards 139
Social centres for the protection of order 141
Arbitration 141

Chapter 8 The constitutional foundations of the Soviet legal order 143
Continuity of constitutional development 145
Socio-political and economic structure 146
The State and the individual 149
Soviet citizenship and equality of citizens 150
Basic rights, freedoms and duties of citizens 151
National and State structure of the USSR 153
The electoral system 154
Legislative and executive agencies 155
Arms, flag and anthem 162
Constitutional amendment 162

Chapter 9 The Communist Party and the legal system 163
The Party 163
Legal status 167
Party members 169
Party guidance of law and the legal system 171
International legal status of the CPSU 173

Chapter 10   Civil law   175
Contemporary civil law   177
Copyright, discoveries and inventions   197
Inheritance   199

Chapter 11   Family law   203
Current family legislation   207

Chapter 12   Labour law   221
Contemporary regulation of labour   223

Chapter 13   Economic law   242
Economic law or civil law   242
Economic management from NEP to 1965   244
Economic management from 1965 to 1987   245
The concept of economic law   252
Restructuring economic legislation   255

Chapter 14   Collective farm law   261
The modern collective farm system   263
State and Party guidance of collective farms   264
Inter-collective farm enterprises and associations   272
Other co-operative organisations   273

Chapter 15   Natural resource law   274
Soviet 'ecological law'   275
National economic planning and natural resources   276
Natural resource regulation   277
Institutional enforcement of natural resource legislation   279
Sanctions against breaches of natural resource legislation   280
Restructuring and Soviet environmental policy   281

Chapter 16   Taxation   284
Compulsory payments to the State budget   284
Fixed payments (rents)   286
Residual profits   287
Deductions from profits   288
Turnover tax   288
Other payments to State budget   289
Income tax on collective farms   290
Income tax on co-operative and social organisations   291
Income tax on individuals   291
Tax on bachelors, single citizens, and citizens with small families   294

Agricultural tax 294
Vehicle tax 294
Local taxes 295
State and customs duties 295
Recovery of unpaid taxes 296

Chapter 17 Criminal law 297
Criminal law: the General Part 298
Criminal law: the Special Part 311
Other union republic criminal codes 317
The rising generation of criminal codes 318

Chapter 18 Criminology and correctional-labour law 323
Criminology 323
Correctional-labour law 325
Application of correctional-labour legislation 332
Criminal punishments not connected with correctional-labour 333

Chapter 19 Civil and criminal procedure 334
Civil procedure 334
Civil procedural rights of foreign citizens and stateless persons 348
Criminal procedure 350
Trial 358
Presumption of innocence 360
Appeal and review 362
Restructuring and the law of procedure 364

Chapter 20 Foreign relations law 366
Legal status of foreign citizens in the USSR 366
Foreign economic relations 378
Public policy (ordre publique) 394
International treaties 395
Relationship between international treaties and Soviet law 397
Territory 398
Diplomatic and consular law 399

Chapter 21 Note on additional reading 403

Index 415

Table of principal Soviet legislative Acts

Enactments are ordered chronologically with references where appropriate to readily accessible English translations as follows:

BD W. E. Butler *Basic Documents on the Soviet Legal System* (2nd edn, 1988; 1983, Dobbs Ferry, N.Y., Oceana Publications).
BQ H. J. Berman and J. B. Quigley *Basic Laws on the Structure of the Soviet State* (1969, Cambridge, Mass., Harvard Univ. Press).
CL W. E. Butler *Collected Legislation of the USSR and Constituent Union Republics* (1979-, Dobbs Ferry, N.Y., Oceana Publications).
SLS W. E. Butler *The Soviet Legal System: Legislation and Documentation* (1978, Dobbs Ferry, N.Y., Oceana Publications).

		PAGE
1917		
26.X	RSFSR Decree on Peace	25
26.X	RSFSR Decree on Land	261, 298
29.X	RSFSR Decree on the Procedure for the Confirmation and Publication of Laws	25
24.XI	RSFSR Decree No 1 on the Court	80, 98, 108, 116, 335
18.XII	RSFSR Decree on Civil Marriage, on Children, and on Keeping Books for Acts of Civil Status	203, 204
19.XII	RSFSR Decree on the Dissolution of Marriage	204
1918		
15.II	RSFSR Decree No 2 on the Court	80, 98, 108, 297
19.II	RSFSR Decree on the Socialisation of Land	261, 274
22.IV	RSFSR Decree on the Nationalisation of Foreign Trade	378
10.VII	Constitution (Fundamental Law) of the RSFSR	145, 149, 298, 368
20.VII	Decree No 3 on the Court	297
23.VII	RSFSR Provisional Instruction on Deprivation of Freedom as a Means of Punishment and the Procedure for Serving Such	326
16.IX	RSFSR Code of Laws on Acts of Civil Status, Marriage, Family, and Guardianship	120, 204, 205, 217
30.XI	RSFSR Statute on the People's Court	297, 335
9.XII	RSFSR Code of Laws on Labour	221
1919		
14.II	RSFSR Law on Socialist Land Tenure and on Transition Measures to Socialist Land Cultivation	261
12.XII	Guiding Principles of Criminal Legislation of the RSFSR	298, 326

xi

xii *Table of principal Soviet legislative Acts*

		PAGE
1920		
21.X	RSFSR Statute on People's Courts.................	81
15.XI	RSFSR Statute on General Places of Confinement.....	326
1922		
25.V	RSFSR Code of Criminal Procedure................	350
[not later than 31.V]	RSFSR Criminal Code.........................	298, 326
4.X	RSFSR Statute on the Notariat....................	116
30.X	RSFSR Labour Code............................	222, 236
31.X	Civil Code of the RSFSR........................	176, 178, 184, 191, 193, 199, 243
1923		
15.II	RSFSR Code of Criminal Procedure................	350, 362
7.VII	RSFSR Code of Civil Procedure...................	335, 336
12.XI	Statute on USSR People's Commissariat for Foreign Affairs..	366, 400
1924		
31.I	Constitution (Fundamental Law) of the USSR........	108, 145, 298, 368
29.X	USSR Fundamental Principles of Court Organisation..	99
31.X	USSR Fundamental Principles of Criminal Legislation	298, 306, 326
31.X	USSR Fundamental Principles of Criminal Procedure..	350, 351
16.XI	RSFSR Correctional-Labour Code.................	326
1926		
14.V	USSR Decree on the Basic Principles of Organising the State Notariat.................................	116
20.VIII	USSR Statute on Military Tribunals and the Military Procuracy	99
19.XI	Code of Laws on Marriage, Family, and Guardianship of the RSFSR..................................	204, 208, 211, 212–214
22.XI	RSFSR Criminal Code..........................	298, 300, 305, 306
1927		
30.III	RSFSR Decree on Jurisconsults of State Institutions and Enterprises and Co-operative Organisations and the Supervision of Their Activity.....................	91
30.X	RSFSR Statute on the Agriculture Co-operative.......	262
1928		
5.XI	RSFSR Decree on Conciliation Procedures in the Struggle Against the Custom of Blood Vengeance......	317
1929		
12.VI	USSR Decree on Financial Responsibility of Workers and Employees for Damage Caused by Them to Employer......................................	319
1932		
27.II	RSFSR Statute on Collectives of Members of Colleges of Defenders..................................	82
1933		
1.VIII	RSFSR Correctional-Labour Code.................	327

Table of principal Soviet legislative Acts xiii

PAGE

1936
5.XII   Constitution (Fundamental Law) of the USSR........   34, 37, 43, 44, 55, 82, 100, 109, 145, 157, 159, 177, 182, 184, 195, 298, 336, 351, 368 [BQ, SLS]

1938
16.VII   Law on Court Organisation of the USSR and the Union and Autonomous Republics......................   44, 82, 100, 336, 351

1939
16.VIII   USSR Statute on the Advokatura..................   82, 91

1941
21.XI   USSR Edict on Taxation of Bachelors, Single Citizens, and Citizens with Small Families..................   294

1943
30.IV   USSR Edict on Income Tax from the Populace........   291–293

1944
8.VII   USSR Edict on Increasing State Assistance to Pregnant Women, Mothers With Many Children, and Unwed Mothers, Strengthening the Protection of Motherhood and Childhood, On Establishing the Honorary Title 'Mother-Heroine' and the Order of the 'Glory of Motherhood' and the Medal 'Motherhood Medal'.....   206, 209, 212, 214

1947
16.XII   USSR Edict on the Procedure for Relations of USSR Institutions and Their Officials with Institutions and Officials of Foreign States.......................   400 [CL]

1951
12.III   USSR Law on the Defence of Peace................   149

1954
10.VII   USSR Statute on Correctional-Labour Camps and Colonies of the Ministry of Internal Affairs...........   327

1955
24.V   Statute of Procuracy Supervision in the USSR.........   109 [BQ, SLS]

1957
12.II   Statute on the USSR Supreme Court................   52 [BQ]

1958
8.XIII   USSR Statute on Correctional-Labour Camps and Colonies   327
25.XII   FPCrimL ....   135, 298–311, 321, 398 [CL, SLS]
25.XII   FPCrimP.......................................   350–364 [CL, SLS]
25.XII   FPLCOrg ....   83, 100 [CL, SLS]
25.XII   USSR Law on Crimes Against the State..............   298 [CL]
25.XII   USSR Law on Military Crimes.....................   298 [CL]
25.XII   USSR Statute on Military Tribunals................   106 [CL]

xiv Table of principal Soviet legislative Acts

PAGE

1959
14.V Decree on the Procedure for the Entry into Force, Promulgation, and Publication of Decrees and Regulations of the Turkmen SSR Council of Ministers 58

1960
17.VIII Statute on State Arbitrazh attached to the USSR Council of Ministers .... 122 [BQ]
27.X Criminal Code of the RSFSR .... 54, 171, 193, 298, 301, 305, 311–318, 321 [BD, CL]
27.X Code of Criminal Procedure of the RSFSR 87, 351–364

1961
8.XII FPCivL .... 56, 147, 177, 192, 193, 195, 198, 200, 219, 242, 243, 246, 249, 281, 336–349, 372–374, 394, 398 [CL, SLS]
8.XII FPCivPL .... 398 [CL, SLS]

1962
20.XII USSR Statute on the Party-State Control Committee ... 131 [BQ]

1963
18.VII Civil Code of the Ukrainian SSR 197
18.VII UkSSR Code of Civil Procedure 337–349

1964
5.V Customs Code of the USSR .... 44, 398, 400 [CL]
11.VI Civil Code of the RSFSR 54, 178–202
11.VI Code of Civil Procedure of the RSFSR 56, 141, 337–349

1965
10.IV On Income Tax from Collective Farms 290
30.IX RSFSR Statute on Supervisory Commissions .... 329 [CL]
4.X USSR Statute on the Socialist State Production Enterprise .... 245–250 [CL, SLS]

1966
23.V Statute on Diplomatic and Consular Representations of Foreign States on the Territory of the USSR 401, 402
11.XI Statute on Fixed Payments to Budget 286

1967
14.II Instruction on the Procedure for Applying Compulsory Treatment and Other Medical Measures to Mentally Ill Persons Who Have Committed Socially Dangerous Acts 309
10.VII General Statute on Ministries of the USSR .... 46 [BQ, CL, SLS]
12.X Statute on Permanent Commissions of the Soviet of the Union and the Soviet of Nationalities of the USSR Supreme Soviet .... 155 [BQ, CL, SLS]
18.XI RSFSR Statute on Social Educators for Minors 333

Table of principal Soviet legislative Acts xv

PAGE

1968

12.IV	USSR Edict on the Procedure for Considering Proposals, Applications, and Appeals of Citizens............	133, 134 [BD, BQ, CL, SLS]
3.VI	RSFSR Statute on Labour Colonies for Minors........	327
27.VI	FPMarL......................................	207–220, 394, 398 [CL, SLS]
17.IX	Merchant Shipping Code of the USSR..............	44, 54, 394, 398 [CL]
13.XII	FPLL..	275 [CL, SLS]
19.XII	Statute on People's Control Agencies in the USSR.....	131 [SLS]

1969

11.VII	FPCorL......................................	325–333 [CL, SLS]
11.VII	USSR Statute on Preliminary Confinement Under Guard.......................................	354 [CL]
17.X	RSFSR Instruction on the Procedure for Registering Acts of Civil Status.............................	218
28.XI	Model Collective Farm Charter....................	262–263 [CL, SLS]
19.XII	FPPubH.....................................	398 [CL]

1970

15.VII	FPLabL......................................	223–241 [CL, SLS]
22.XI	USSR Statute on Entry into the USSR and Exit from the USSR....................................	369 [CL, SLS]
10.XII	FPWL.......................................	275, 276 [CL, SLS]
23.XII	USSR Decree on Improving Legal Work in the National Economy.....................................	62, 92 [CL]

1971

26.V	Statute on the All-Union Scientific Research Institute of Soviet Legislation.............................	77
9.XII	RSFSR Labour Code...........................	228, 234

1972

21.III	Statute on the USSR Ministry of Justice.............	96 [SLS]
22.VI	General Statute on the Legal Section (or Office), Chief (or Senior) Jurisconsult, and Jurisconsult of a Ministry, Department, Executive Committee of a Soviet of People's Deputies, Enterprise, Organisation, or Institution...................................	92 [CL, SLS]
20.IX	USSR Decree on Measures to Further Improve Nature Conservation and Rational Utilisation of Natural Resources....................................	275 [CL]
29.XII	USSR Decree on the Intensification of Nature Conservation and Improved Utilisation of Natural Resources....................................	275 [CL]

1973

2.III	General Statute on All-Union and Republic Industrial Associations..................................	250 [CL]
19.VII	FPPubEd.....................................	398 [CL]
19.VII	USSR Law on the State Notariat..................	116, 401 [BD, CL]

xvi *Table of principal Soviet legislative Acts*

		PAGE
21.VIII	USSR Statute on Discoveries, Inventions, and Rationalisation Proposals................................	198, 199, 374 [CL]
1974		
18.I	Statute on State Arbitrazh attached to the USSR Council of Ministers................................	122 [SLS]
27.III	USSR Statute on the Production Association (or Combine)..	250 [CL]
20.V	USSR Statute on the Procedure for the Consideration of Labour Disputes...............................	233
20.V	USSR Model Statute on Voluntary People's Guard Detachments for the Protection of Public Order..........	139, 140 [BD, SLS]
19.VI	RSFSR Statute on the Section (or Bureau) for the Registry of Acts of Civil Status of the Executive Committee of the District Soviet of People's Deputies..............	120 [SLS]
2.VIII	RSFSR Law on the State Notariat..................	116 [CL]
12.IX	Statute on the USSR Chamber of Commerce and Industry..	387 [CL]
1975		
25.IV	Statute on Payment for Labour of Advocates..........	86
30.VI	Statute on Turnover Tax.........................	288, 289
9.VII	FPML...	275, 398 [CL, SLS]
29.XII	USSR Statute on the Procedure for Awarding Academic Degrees and Conferring Academic Titles............	73 [CL]
30.XII	USSR Statute on the Scientific-Production Association	250 [CL]
1976		
28.V	Statute on the Production Association in Agriculture...	250, 272 [CL]
25.VI	Consular Statute of the USSR.....................	378, 400, 401 [CL]
13.VII	USSR Statute on Material Responsibility of Workers and Employees for Damage Caused to an Enterprise, Institution, or Organisation.......................	236–239 [CL]
29.X	USSR Law on the Protection and Use of Monuments of History and Culture.............................	185 [CL]
30.XI	USSR Edict on Legal Transactions with Currency Valuables on the Territory of the USSR..............	376
1977		
—	Rules for the Internal Order of Correctional-Labour Institutions	326, 327, 329,
11.III	RSFSR Statute on Comrades' Courts...............	137–139 [BD, SLS]
23.V	USSR Statute on the Procedure for Opening and the Activity in the USSR of Representations of Foreign Firms..	394 [CL]
17.VI	FPFL..	275 [CL, SLS]
4.VIII	USSR Instruction Concerning Payment for Legal Assistance Rendered by Advocates to Citizens, Enterprises, Institutions, and Organisations.....................	80, 342 [CL]
7.X	Constitution [Fundamental Law] of the USSR........	36, 41–46, 55, 56, 83, 122, 131, 145–

Table of principal Soviet legislative Acts xvii

		PAGE
		162, 168, 170, 183, 195, 207, 266, 271, 277, 312, 314, 339, 366, 368, 379, 395, 399, 404 [BD, CL]
1978		
14.II	USSR Decree on the Procedure for Signing Foreign Trade Transactions...............................	392 [CL]
12.V	USSR Edict on Income Tax from Foreign Natural and Juridical Persons.................................	291 [CL]
31.V	USSR Statute on the All-Union Economically Accountable Foreign Trade Association Within the System of the Ministry of Foreign Trade......................	383–385 [CL]
5.VII	Law on the USSR Council of Ministers...............	45, 159 [BD, CL]
6.VII	Law on the Procedure for the Conclusion, Execution, and Denunciation of International Treaties of the USSR...	56, 156, 174, 395–397 [BD, CL]
1.XII	Law on Citizenship of the USSR....................	150, 299, 367, 368 [BD, CL]
1979		
1.III	USSR Edict on Income Tax from Co-operative and Social Organisations............................	291
17.IV	Reglament of the USSR Supreme Soviet.............	43, 157 [CL]
29.VI	USSR Edict on State Duty........................	296, 343 [CL]
30.XI	Law on the Advokatura in the USSR................	83 [BD, SLS]
30.XI	Law on State Arbitrazh in the USSR................	50, 122 [BD, CL]
30.XI	Law on the Procuracy of the USSR.................	55, 56, 109, 111 [BD, CL]
30.XI	Law on People's Control in the USSR...............	131 [BD, CL]
30.XI	Law on the USSR Supreme Court...................	52, 53, 55, 56, 105 [BD, CL]
—	USSR Statute on Procedure for Distributing Profits (Plan and Above-Plan) of Production Associations, Enterprises, and Organisations of Industry.............	287
1980		
19.VI	Statute on Post-Graduate Studies at Higher Educational Institutions and Scientific Research Institutions.......	72
25.VI	USSR Law on the Protection of the Atmosphere.......	275 [CL]
25.VI	USSR Law on the Protection and Use of the Animal World...	275, 277 [CL]
25.VI	RSFSR Statute on Social Centres for the Protection of Order...	141 [CL]
28.VIII	USSR Decree on the Procedure for the Conclusion, Execution, and Denunciation of International Treaties of the USSR of an Interdepartmental Character........	396, 397 [CL]
9.X	Statute on the Maritime Arbitration Commission......	142, 392 [CL]
23.X	FPAdR..	127, 354, 370, 398 [CL]

xviii   Table of principal Soviet legislative Acts

		PAGE
28.X	Statute on Class Ranks of Workers of Procuracy Agencies of the USSR..........................	110 [CL]
20.XI	RSFSR Statute on the Advokatura................	88 [CL]
1981		
26.I	USSR Statute on Recovery of Overdue Taxes and Non-Tax Payments...............................	296
26.I	Statute on Local Taxes..........................	295
18.V	Statute on the Procedure for Compensation Caused to a Citizen by the Illegal Actions of Agencies of Inquiry, Preliminary Investigation, the Procuracy, and the Court..	193 [CL]
24.VI	Law on the Legal Status of Foreign Citizens in the USSR	218, 348, 366–378 [BD, CL]
9.VII	USSR Decree on the Further Improvement of Co-operation of USSR Ministries and Departments, Associations, Enterprises, and Organisations With the Respective Agencies, Enterprises, and Organisations of Other COMECON Member Countries in Science, Technology, and International Specialisation and Production Co-operation...........................	387
1982		
13.I	Rules of Procedure of the Maritime Arbitration Commission..................................	142, 392 [CL]
6.IV	USSR Statute on the Import, Export, Transfer, and Sending From and To Abroad of Soviet Currency, Foreign Currency, Other Currencies, and Other Valuables..	377 [CL]
29.IX	USSR Statute on Trade Representations of the USSR Abroad.......................................	382 [CL]
24.XI	Law on the State Boundary of the USSR............	135, 371, 398, 399 [BD, CL]
25.XI	Model Statute on the Agro-Industrial Association......	252, 272 [CL]
1983		
15.III	USSR Statute on the Procedure and Conditions for Executing Criminal Punishments Not Connected With Correctional-Labour Measures of Influence on Convicted Persons................................	333 [CL]
11.V	Air Code of the USSR...........................	44, 370 [CL]
26.V	USSR Edict on Procedure for Effectuating Activity on Territory of USSR of Joint Economic Organisations of USSR and Other COMECON Member Countries.....	388, 389 [BD]
17.VI	USSR Law on Labour Collectives and Raising Their Role in the Management of Enterprises, Institutions, and Organisations.............................	147, 224, 225 [CL]
4.VIII	Edict on Procedure for Issuance and Certification by Enterprises, Institutions, and Organisations of Copies of Documents Affecting Citizens' Rights.............	117
29.IX	USSR Decree on Incomes of Citizens Not Subject to Income Tax...................................	293
22.XII	Law on Agricultural Tax........................	294
1984		
17.II	Statute on Procedure for Disciplining and Rewarding Procuracy and Investigative Personnel..............	110

Table of principal Soviet legislative Acts xix

PAGE

1985

16.V	USSR Edict on Intensifying Struggle Against Drunkenness..................................	324

1986

23.V	USSR Edict on Intensifying Struggle Against Deriving Non-Labour Incomes..........................	186, 277
19.VIII	USSR Decree on Measures Relating to Improvement of Administration of Economic and Scientific-Technical Co-operation with Socialist Countries..............	379, 389
19.VIII	USSR Decree on Measures Relating to Improvement of Administration of Foreign Economic Relations........	379
19.XI	USSR Law on Individual Labour Activity............	186, 187, 241
22.XII	USSR Statute on All-Union Economically-Accountable Foreign Trade Organisation (or Association) of Ministry or Department....................................	383
22.XII	Model Statute on Economically-Accountable Foreign Trade Firm of Scientific-Production or Production Association, Enterprise, or Organisation............	385

1987

13.I	USSR Decree on Procedure for Creation on Territory of USSR and Activities of Joint Enterprises with Participation of Soviet Organisations and Firms of Capitalist and Developing Countries............................	379, 389
13.I	USSR Decree on Procedure for Creation on Territory of USSR and Activities of Joint Enterprises, International Associations, and Organisations of USSR and Other COMECON Countries..................	389
5.II	USSR Decree on Creating Public Dining Co-operatives	239–241, 273
5.II	USSR Decree on Creating Co-operatives for Production of Consumer Goods.............................	239–241, 273
30.VI	USSR Law on Discussion by Whole People of Important Questions of State Life.......................	147
30.VI	USSR Law on Procedure for Appealing to Court the Unlawful Actions of Officials Which Impinge Upon Rights of Citizens..............................	161, 338
30.VI	USSR Law on State Enterprise.....................	224, 225–260 277, 286, 386
17.VII	USSR Decree on Restructuring Financial Mechanism and Enhancing Role of USSR Ministry of Finances Under New Economic Conditions...................	255, 286, 287
14.XII	Statute on Arbitration Court attached to USSR Chamber of Commerce and Industry................	142, 392

1988

5.I	USSR Statute on Conditions and Procedure for Rendering Psychiatric Care..............................	309–311
7.I	USSR Decree on Fundamental Restructuring of Nature Conservation in the Country......................	282, 283
8.II	USSR Decree Approving Recommendations on Procedure for Electing Labour Collective Councils and Enterprise Directors............................	225
11.III	Reglament of Arbitration Court of USSR Chamber of Commerce.....................................	55, 142, 392

		PAGE
14.III	USSR Edict on Taxation of Citizens Working in Co-operatives for Production and Realisation of Products and Rendering Services..........................	292
21.III	USSR Edict on Taxation of Owners of Means of Transport and Other Self-Propelled Vehicles and Mechanisms.................................	294
25.III	Model Collective Farm Charter....................	263–273, 386
—	Law on Co-operative Societies in USSR............	241, 273, 388

Table of cases

Abramenko v Ramensk Registration Bureau.................................345
Banque des Marchands de Moscou (Koupetschesky, Re) [1957] 3 All ER 182..........53
Bulguchev, Case of..317
Davies v TASS 181
Kazarian, Case of...341
Krajina v TASS [1949] 2 All ER 274......................................181
Leushkins, Case of..346
Radchencko, Case of..88
State Farm 'Molodinskii' v Karpacheva...................................342
Yessenin-Volpin v Novosti, 443 F Supp 849 (1978)........................181

Abbreviations

COMECON	Council of Mutual Economic Assistance
CPSU	Communist Party of the Soviet Union
FPAdR	Fundamental Principles of Legislation of the USSR and Union Republics on Administrative Responsibility
FPCivL	Fundamental Principles of Civil Legislation of the USSR and Union Republics
FPCivPL	Fundamental Principles of Civil Procedure Legislation of the USSR and Union Republics
FPCorL	Fundamental Principles of Correctional-Labour Legislation of the USSR and Union Republics
FPCrimL	Fundamental Principles of Criminal Legislation of the USSR and Union Republics
FPCrimP	Fundamental Principles of Criminal Procedure Legislation of the USSR and Union Republics
FPFL	Fundamental Principles of Legislation of the USSR and Union Republics on Forestry
FPL	Fundamental Principles of Legislation
FPLabL	Fundamental Principles of the USSR and Union Republics on Labour Legislation
FPLCOrg	Fundamental Principles of Legislation of the USSR and Union Republics on Court Organisation
FPLL	Fundamental Principles of Land Legislation of the USSR and Union Republics
FPMarL	Fundamental Principles of Legislation of the USSR and Union Republics on Marriage and the Family
FPML	Fundamental Principles of Legislation of the USSR and Union Republic on Minerals
FPPubEd	Fundamental Principles of Legislation of the USSR and Union Republics on Public Education
FPPubH	Fundamental Principles of Legislation of the USSR and Union Republics on Public Health
FPWL	Fundamental Principles of Water Legislation of the USSR and Union Republics
MAC	Maritime Arbitration Commission
MFER	Ministry of Foreign Economic Relations
MShC	Merchant Shipping Code of the USSR

NEP	New Economic Policy
RSFSR	Russian Soviet Federated Socialist Republic
SFEC	State Foreign Economic Commission
SU RSFSR	*Sobranie uzakonenii i rasporiazhenii RSFSR*
SZ SSSR	*Sobranie zakonov i rasporiazhenii SSSR*
UkSSR	Ukrainian SSR
USSR	Union of Soviet Socialist Republics
VTsIK	All-Russian Central Executive Committee
VTsSPS	All-Union Central Trade Union Council
ZAGS	Registry for Acts of Civil Status

Chapter 1

Soviet law in comparative legal studies

The nature of and the reasons for studying the Soviet legal system have elicited a broad spectrum of opinion during more than seven decades of debate by comparative legal scholars. Few have doubted, whatever their philosophical disposition, that the Soviet public order contains 'law' among its constituent elements. Rather it is the uniqueness of the legal system which has given rise to lively debate, sometimes within the narrow confines of Soviet legal studies and more frequently in recent years within broader dialogues about the objects of comparative law generally.

Some dismissed Soviet law as a field of inquiry for lack of venerability. In an introduction to the world's principal legal systems published in 1968 the editor omitted Soviet law because Soviet juridical doctrines were felt to '. . . lack the depth given by undisputed maturity.'[1] Others held that the Soviet legal system was but an extension with ideological encrustations of the European Germano-Romanist civil law system.[2] The late Professor Albert Ehrenzweig maintained that if the Soviet legal system could be segregated as unique in the traditional realm of private law, he would have been obliged '. . . to abandon the philosophical pattern of two and one-half millenia and the comparative concern of a thousand years.' Whatever innovations may have been wrought in public law, he believed that the 'essentially civilian structure' in the law of the family, property, succession, contract, and tort remained unchanged, and he perceived only minor developments in old European patterns of criminal law and procedure.[3]

Perceptions of continuity and change in the classification of foreign legal systems depend in part on developments within our own. Those who in the interwar or early post-war era were impressed when studying the Soviet legal system by differences in economic order between East and West find in the 1980s that the enlarged State sector in Western economies and greater decentralisation and recourse to economic

---
1 J. D. M. Derrett *An Introduction to Legal Systems* (1968) p xiv.
2 See F. H. Lawson, cited in the preface to J. N. Hazard, W. E. Butler, P. B. Maggs *The Soviet Legal System* (3rd edn, 1977) p xvi.
3 See Ehrenzweig's review of J. N. Hazard *Communists and their Law* (1969), in California Law Review LVIII (1970) 1005, 1007.

accountability in socialist economies has reduced what seemed to be a distinction of principle to one of degree.[4]

Much, of course, depends in this exercise on to what one attaches significance and weight when asserting or dismissing claims for uniqueness. Soviet law codes of the 1920s did draw expressly upon those in Germany, France, and Switzerland; several of the Soviet draftsmen had participated in pending reforms of Imperial Russian law prior to the Revolution, and even though Imperial law was formally repealed by the Soviet authorities, the draft·Russian codes, in some instances the most forward-looking in Europe, were consulted. Moreover, the NEP period in which the codes were drafted was one of mixed economic and legal policies containing capitalist and socialist elements. The legal changes attendant upon the socialisation of the economy were reflected willy-nilly in the codes of that era. The more considered codifications of the 1960-70s raise the issue of innovation and uniqueness on a far more profound level. Roman law, one should add, was restored to the Soviet law curriculum in 1943 after two decades of disgrace following some harsh words by Lenin, who criticised the early draft 1922 RSFSR Civil Code for being too Romanist. It continues to be taught because, whether Soviet law be unique or not, Soviet jurists believe a knowledge of Roman legal concepts sharpens the analytical skills of their students. A feeling of security in revolutionary achievement has enabled the reintroduction of those elements of the past which have a useful role to play in the present.

Claims to uniqueness, moreover, are not eternal. All legal systems are constantly changing and developing; yester-year's novelty may be widely imitated in other systems or cast aside as inappropriate. The Soviet model of the State monopoly of foreign trade introduced in the early 1930s, for example, and widely received in other socialist legal systems, was sharply altered during the 1970-80s in Eastern Europe and China, and in 1986 the Soviet Union jettisoned its approach in favour of the East European-Chinese version.

Soviet law appears not to have been taught in law faculties and schools of the Anglo-American world during the interwar era. The rise of Soviet legal studies as an object of sustained serious concern came in the aftermath of the Second World War when the international status of the Soviet Union changed abruptly from that of a medium power to a major power. As an area of research, however, Soviet legal studies has been with us since 1918, studied principally in the interwar era as the legal system of a large country whose legislation and institutions, however imperfectly understood, were a part of the corpus of foreign law. To proponents of changes taking place in the Soviet Union, the legal system

---

4 Contrast, for example, René David's perceptions: David *Traité élémentaire de droit civil comparé* (Paris, 1950) p 224; David and Brierly *Major Legal Systems in the World Today* (3rd edn, 1985).

contained much of possible interest to law reformers abroad; for governments and commercial firms it was essential to know the rules applicable to transnational transactions. Language remained a formidable barrier, and except for a tiny handful of Russian emigré lawyers, the number of individuals in the common-law world suitably trained to engage in serious comparative study was virtually nil.

Comparative legal studies in general before 1939 were dominated by the conviction that a principal task was to identify or develop general or common principles of law in all the major extant legal systems. Harmonisation and unification figured prominently in the thinking of the time; to those who viewed the Soviet legal system as a variant of the Germano-Romanist civilian tradition, the Revolutions of 1917 posed no insuperable barriers to the continued development of unification. To the extent, however, that one credited Soviet claims to represent a qualitatively new and higher socio-economic, political, and legal order, the base for possible harmonisation and unification, even in the most congenial international political climates, had narrowed considerably.

For a time after the Second World War that base appeared to have vanished completely. The ambit of what we now call the family of socialist legal systems had expanded from the Soviet Union, the Mongolian People's Republic,[5] the Chinese Soviet Republic,[6] and a brief episode with the Hungarian Soviet Republic to embrace all of Eastern Europe and eventually China as a whole. An era of intense political hostility and confrontation transpired which, while it had the lamentable result of substantially cutting of meaningful contacts, acted as a long overdue stimulus for area and disciplinary studies of the region. Comparative studies had before them not merely a different legal model, but one which was being received, transplanted, absorbed, assimilated into countries of widely varying legal cultures, languages, revolutionary experiences, values, and traditions.

In this era Soviet legal studies to an appreciable degree were a part of the 'know thine enemy' syndrome: to comprehend how he lives, to facilitate means of understanding and communication so as to avoid miscalculation, to identify and clarify opposed positions and values. Professor Harold J. Berman observed in the introduction to his interpretation of Soviet law: '. . . a legal system expresses in a most vivid and real way what a society stands for. It represents both what is preached and what is practised.'[7] This was an era in which many of the cherished designs of comparative lawyers in the interwar period had to be abandoned, for meaningful harmonisation of law or legal systems on a world scale had become quite inconceivable, as had the prospect of locating or developing general principles of municipal law common to the principal

5 W. E. Butler *The Mongolian Legal System* (1982).
6 Butler (ed) *The Legal System of the Chinese Soviet Republic, 1931-34* (1983).
7 H. J. Berman *Justice in the USSR* (rev. edn, 1963) p 3.

legal systems. Yet it was an epoch in which specialists in the field came to appreciate more fully an enduring quality of Soviet legal studies: the need to study law in the larger context of the basic philosophical, historical, sociological, and political premises of the foreign legal system in comparative studies, and hence indirectly those of our own legal system. Architects of programmes in Slavonic and East European studies were quick to appreciate that some knowledge of law and legal institutions would be essential to an understanding of Soviet society; most who specialise in Soviet law maintain close links to Slavonic studies as part of the infrastructure of their area of concentration.

During the past three decades western students of Soviet law have followed closely and with absorbing interest the legal reforms within the Soviet Union and very recently the incipient development of a 'socialist community law of economic integration,' to which Soviet legal concepts have contributed. Access to Soviet legal materials has improved, partly due to more enlightened distribution policies in the USSR but principally by reason of the prodigious labours of western specialists in translating Russian texts. It is no exaggeration to say that the western law student has more materials available to him in English translation concerning the Soviet legal system than for any other continental European jurisdiction.

As Soviet society has matured and the concerns of comparative law grown, so too have the reasons for studying Soviet law. To be sure, an improved knowledge and understanding of the Soviet Union continues to be important. Avoiding miscalculation in times of political tension is a vital consideration, but the legal issues posed when relations improve can be even more daunting. Closer relations ordinarily involve greater interaction in transactions of a practical character, whether interpersonal, commercial, or intergovernmental, and consequently there is a greater need to come to grips with legal rules and institutions that genuinely are obstacles to understanding or intercourse.

Lawyers, especially in North America, comprise a significant source of personnel in the private and governmental sector who deal with counterparts abroad. They may represent or negotiate on behalf of clients who maintain commercial links with the USSR or who have some other personal matter requiring disposition, or they may be recruited into the civil service in either a legal or non-legal capacity to represent the interests of their government. Their general background and special expertise are likely to be more proficient if they have a basic grasp of the law and legal institutions of the countries with which they are concerned. One responsibility of comparative legal studies, including Soviet legal studies, is to train national elites to deal effectively with their overseas counterparts.[8]

8 J. A. Cohen 'On Teaching Chinese Law' American Journal of Comparative Law XIX (1971) 655.

Soviet law offers virtually the same scope of comparative enquiry as other continental European systems, yet offers in addition fundamentally different and challenging approaches or views for the student's contemplation. It presents the concept of a legal system within a single national entity, within a federated system of national units, or within a cluster or family of legal systems. As a society with an explicit ideology and multiplicity of languages, a nation with an elaborate, specific, and articulate concept of what law is, why it exists, how it develops, and where it will go, the Soviet Union introduces the variable of cultural context in comparative legal studies in a highly instructive way.

Whereas one may examine the impact of revolution upon a preexisting legal and social order in several societies, including the English, American, and French, the effects are most immediately and significantly to be seen in the Soviet legal order, the more so since the revolution occurred in the industrial age. In the 1980–90s another radical revolution is promised with a view to eradicating the pernicious influence of inertia, bureaucracy, and excessive State control upon the development of society. The tension between revolutionary change and the need for order, stability, and predictability are manifest not merely in the substance of law, but in the nature and role of the legal profession, in the sources of law and schemes for its systematisation and codification, and in the types and functions of State and social organisations engaged in the 'administration' of socialist legality. The relationship between the State and the individual is to be seen not merely in the domain of individual liberties but likewise in the educational role postulated for socialist law in connection with theories of ideal personality and of institutional responsibilities, both State and social.

But in modern times the Soviet legal system has become more than a watering place to be frequented when seeking to develop a comprehensive theory of law. It serves as an historical and contemporary model for other legal systems in the socialist and third worlds and, as a system of the industrial and post-industrial ages,[9] can have positive and negative experience which is instructive for other advanced western legal systems. Socialist legal systems in Eastern Europe, China, Korea, Vietnam, and elsewhere are expected to pass through the same basic developmental stages as the Soviet legal system; one of the constant debates within the family of socialist legal systems relates to which facets of the model are mutable and which are absolute prerequisites. The same applies to third world countries of a 'socialist orientation.'

The legal aspects of the planned economy in the Soviet Union are of practical relevance to western lawyers and to third world countries. The planned economy affects concepts of ownership (and therefore sovereign immunity); techniques for allocating the possession, use, and alienation of

---

9 F. J. M. Feldbrugge 'The Study of Soviet Law' Review of Socialist Law IV (1978) 201–214.

property, including land, water, forests, minerals, enterprises, and the like; the obligations arising out of delicts, especially when State bodies or officials are concerned; the relationship between law and plan; the legal status of State-owned corporate entities; and the traditional distinctions not merely between public and private law but likewise between civil and economic law. In the realm of administrative law one encounters a range of offences and penalties which have no equivalent in the common law, whereas in the criminal law one finds a distinctive and sometimes disappointing equation of public and individual rights, a system of investigation and adjudication more akin to continental jurisdictions than our own, and the existence (or non-existence) of offences peculiar to a socialist planned economy and a Soviet concept of public order.

Comparative issues of this nature and magnitude help us to rethink crucial social and economic questions which confront our own legal system, the historical bases of our law, and the appropriate role(s) for law in society. Soviet legal studies, just as the study of other legal systems, offers a convenient backdrop, an analytical screen, for approaching our own problems with a fresh and perhaps unique perspective.

For the legal practitioner these considerations acquire a different dimension. Commercial transactions especially have required adaptations or the creation of special institutions to facilitate trade with the Soviet Union. Notions of public policy, of sovereign immunity, and of principles for the settlement of commercial disputes are areas which reflect the nexus of contact between East and West and are familiar areas of concern for the harmonisation and codification of law. The introduction in 1987 of joint enterprises owned by Soviet and western participants requires that western companies transact not merely *with* the Soviet Union, but *within* the Soviet legal system in its entirety on a collaborative and sustained basis to produce agreed goods and services.

However, the value of Soviet legal studies transcends the traditional realm of comparative law. Soviet State practice in the form of foreign affairs legislation in the broadest sense contributes to the development or clarification of international law. That contribution may be assertive in the sense of postulating a claim on a matter not wholly regulated by international law, or reinforcing in the sense of expressing a concordant view shared with other states, or receptive in the sense of transmitting to the municipal level rules of conduct prescribed at the international level. In all three instances and others the Soviet legal system interacts with the international legal order, and for international lawyers a basic understanding of at least the principal families of legal systems has become indispensable.[10]

---

10 W. E. Butler 'International Law and the Comparative Method' in id (ed) *International Law in Comparative Perspective* (1980) pp 25–40; id 'Comparative Approaches to International Law' Recueil des cours CXC (1985) 9–89.

The Marxian socialist states have developed an international legal vocabulary deeply indebted to the philosophical, socio-political, economic, and legal tenets of their respective societies. Domestic legal institutions are a key to understanding those terms which appear in an exceptionally extensive range of international negotiations. The Soviet international lawyer himself is a product of his municipal system of legal education; his concepts of law, the matter and style in which he reasons and expounds his views, are deeply indebted to the domestic legal milieu in which he was trained. Also formed in this municipal legal context is the international lawyer's notion of what role(s) a lawyer has in giving counsel to his employer or client.

On a larger scale, the effectuation of international legal arrangements can depend upon the effectiveness of, or obstacles within, national legal systems. Those who draft international arrangements must have regard to not merely the municipal formalities for approving international agreements but likewise to the municipal legal context in which they will operate. These are but a few of the concerns to which comparative legal studies, including Soviet legal studies, can make an indispensable contribution to improving our understanding of international law.

Comparative law in the Soviet Union

Although our concern here is with the Soviet legal system, our impression of the place and value of Soviet legal studies would be incomplete without a few words about comparative legal studies in the USSR, for attitudes towards comparative law there have had some impact upon the nature and direction of our own endeavours. The study of foreign law goes back to the earliest days of formal legal education in Russia, not least because most of the professors were of foreign origin. The Byzantine and European origins of Russian legislation were explored by early Russian legal historians; Roman law was taught at Moscow University from its founding in 1755. A comparison of Russian and Roman law published by G. A. Artem'ev in 1777 may have rightful claim to being the first printed Russian work on comparative law. Foreign legislation, especially Swedish, was studied and adapted by Peter the Great. Catherine II read Beccaria, Blackstone, and Montesquieu, among others, and ordered them to be translated into Russian in order to further her legislative reforms. M. M. Speranskii and his associates were well-schooled in French law when they prepared their draft codes under Alexander I and were sufficiently attracted by the ideas of Jeremy Bentham to translate his major work on codification into Russian.

In the late nineteenth century a few Russian scholars, notably M. M. Kovalevskii and Ia. Ia. Iakushkin, pioneered studies of primitive law in the spirit of Sir Henry Maine; Kovalevskii in particular produced a work on the usefulness of the comparative method in studying Russian law.[11]

During the 1920s, several Soviet legal scholars produced interesting comparative legal studies, but by the end of the decade comparative legal research was reduced either to contrastive self-justification of Soviet law in contradistinction to 'bourgeois' law or to purely descriptive, albeit often excellent, accounts of foreign legal systems. A more enlightened view began to emerge in the early 1960s. It has come to be recognised that, first, the comparative method is indispensable for studying the Soviet legal system itself, the law codes of the 15 union republics. The Uzbek SSR Academy of Sciences has played a leading role in this regard, encouraging the comparative study of legislation in the Central Asian republics. Second, comparison has become essential to investigations of the family of socialist legal systems, a need more keenly felt as COMECON has pressed measures requiring the harmonisation or unification of law and consequently a detailed knowledge of what the law is in its member countries. Third, the exigencies of enlarged international contacts and domestic law reform have produced some serious detailed comparative studies of western and third-world legal systems which transcend the rhetoric and ritual of contrastive comparison. Soviet legal research establishments have impressive numbers of specialists on branches of foreign law. To date, however, neither the academies of sciences nor the universities have formed sectors or chairs expressly devoted to the pursuit of comparative law.

In the 1980s bilateral symposia with Soviet legal scholars, especially from the Institute of State and Law of the USSR Academy of Sciences, were arranged with greater frequency and on a long-term planned basis. A direct link between the Institute and the Faculty of Laws, University College London, generated collected papers on comparative law and legal system, comparative justice law, comparative labour law, law, policy, State administration, comparative environmental law, legal history, international trade, and public international law (see chapter 20, below), striking new ground in legal research with Soviet specialists. The American legal profession has sent thousands of attorneys to the Soviet Union through continuing legal education programmes, and law teachers and political scientists in the United States have held bilateral symposia on local government and criminal law. Individual American and Soviet scholars are producing a multi-volume study of contract law in the USSR and the United States.

11 M. M. Kovalevskii *I storiko-sravnitel' nyi metod v iurisprudentsii i priemy izucheniia russkogo prava* (1880). Although he left no works in Russian especially devoted to the comparative method, Sir Paul Vinogradov is regarded as having based all his works on the comparative method. Vinogradov was professor at Moscow University from 1884–1903 and then became the Corpus Professor at Oxford University when he was forced to emigrate from Russia. See A. A. Tille and G. V. Shvekov *Sravnitel' nyi metod v iuridicheskikh distsiplinakh* (2nd end, 1987) p 57.

Programmes such as these are laying the base for collaborative research on a scale never attempted in East-West legal relations. 'Intertypal' comparative studies have been endorsed in principle[12] and, once the descriptive and empirical prerequisites have been established and access to data on the implementation and effectiveness of law is secured, students of the subject will be well placed to advance the quality of comparative generalisation significantly.

---

[12] V. A. Tumanov 'On Comparing Various Types of Legal Systems' in W. E. Butler and V. N. Kudriavtsev (eds) *Comparative Law and Legal System* (1985) pp 69–78.

Chapter 2

The pre-revolutionary heritage

Soviet law and the Soviet legal system are comprehensible only against the background of their past: what was rejected, what was transformed, what has endured. The 1917 October Revolution proclaimed in the exuberance of its triumph a complete break with the past, and in 1918 there followed a formal repeal of Imperial legislation. But law is not merely the statute book at any given moment of time; it represents an accumulation of historical experiences, values, terminology, attitudes constructed in the course of human affairs over many centuries, elements which cannot be wholly dispensed with by any functioning society irrespective of how drastic a revolution it may undergo.

Reconstructing the pre-revolutionary legal heritage in the Soviet Union is no easy task. Records for the early period are exceptionally sparse, and for latter centuries, hardly touched by legal historians. Moreover, within the frontiers of the Imperial Russian Empire and of the Soviet Union today there were dozens of legal systems operating simultaneously: customary law of various tribes and peoples, Islamic law, Baltic law, canon law, Georgian, Armenian, Azerbaidzhani, Judaic, and others, side by side with Russian law enacted by the central authorities. The development of Russian law itself was affected by foreign law: Byzantine, Roman, Tatar, Polish, Swedish, German, French, English, Italian, among others, sometimes by precept, more often perhaps by deliberate adaptation.

Kievan Rus

The importance of legal materials for an understanding of early Russian history may be simply stated: virtually all of the few surviving documents from the Kievan period are legal texts of one kind or another. The earliest are in fact international legal documents, three peace treaties concluded in the first half of the tenth century between the Kievan Prince and Byzantium, which offer insight into penal practices, the status of foreigners, the law of shipwreck, and the ratification of treaties. With the conversion of Kievan Rus to Christianity (circa 988), a channel was created for the reception of canon law and perhaps too the means for readily reducing to written form either the enactments of the princes or the customary rules applied.

There is a strong supposition that the Slavic peoples inhabiting the lands of what became Kievan Rus had fashioned definite rules for interpersonal and interclan or intertribal behaviour long before the Kievan princes consolidated their authority. Whether the earliest surviving compilations of Russian laws, the *Pravda Russkaia*, represented a creative codification of law or a reduction to writing of customary law continues to be debated. So too does the extent to which the substance of the *Pravda Russkaia*, which contains striking parallels with aspects of Frankish and Anglo-Saxon law, was the result of mutual influence or of the independent development of peoples at a similar stage of societal development. The surviving redactions pose internal obstacles to understanding as well. Their obsolete terminology and grammar have given rise to interminable debates about the true meanings of terms. Most of the texts available for study were copied centuries after the original was allegedly composed; the *Expanded Pravda Russkaia*, for example, attributed on the basis of internal evidence to the eleventh or twelfth centuries, survives in only three texts prior to the fifteenth century and 92 texts of the sixteenth to eighteenth centuries.[1] The *Short Pravda*, believed to antedate the Expanded version, is known to us only in manuscript versions that were transcribed after the earliest manuscripts of the Expanded redaction.

The initial *Pravda Russkaia* is believed to have been composed in the reign of Iaroslav the Wise (1015–54).[2] It began with the rules of the blood feud, which the Expanded version tells us was abolished by Iaroslav's sons and replaced by a system of monetary compositions; the latter contained provisions treating various forms of stealing, interest, storage, suits for money, shipwreck, beehives, succession, oaths, slavery, and ownership.[3] The versions of the Pravda suggest that the prince's court played a minor role in prosecution and litigation. The system relied upon party initiative; there were no permanent judges, merely officials who presided over the proceedings, and ultimate judgment was decided by kissing the cross or by ordeal, later augmented by numbers of witnesses. So far as is known, there was no possibility of appeal, no system of courts, no legal profession, no legal commentary on the princely legislation or judicial judgments. Nor can we judge with any

---

1 D. H. Kaiser *The Growth of Law in Medieval Russia* (1980) p 18. Kaiser gives an excellent account of the manuscript sources and the problems they pose for the legal historian. .
2 G. Vernadsky (transl.) *Medieval Russian Laws* (1947).
3 On land ownership, see F. J. M. Feldbrugge 'The Law of Land Tenure in Kievan Russia' in W. E. Butler (ed) *Russian Law: Historical and Political Perspectives* (1977) pp 1–28.

certainty the territorial extent to which even within Kievan Rus the provisions of the Pravda were applied.

It does seem clear that the Pravda did influence local legal texts in regions north and west of Kiev. Again international legal documents are a key: the treaty negotiated by Novgorod with Gotland (circa 1189-99) and the Smolensk treaty of 1229 in its Gotland and Riga redactions. Both texts contain provisions that can be traced to the Pravda concerning criminal law and commercial matters.

The sources of legal rules in these early documents must have been several. Customary rules, princely decisions, borrowings from Byzantine, German, Scandinavian, Slavic, or other peoples—all are plausible candidates. But Christianity brought an undisputedly imported body of canon law whose texts have survived principally in the form of the Book of the Pilot (*Kormchaia Kniga*).[4] The collections, varied in content, generally encompassed church canons, epistles, sermons, selections from Byzantine secular legislation, versions of the *Pravda Russkaia*, and princely statutes. Canon law was important throughout the entire pre-revolutionary era, for it contained provisions regarding marriage, divorce, and the family, for example. In dispossessing the church of its powers in 1917, the Soviet Government was not merely eliminating a rival source of influence; it was also asserting for the first time in perhaps ten centuries secular authority over certain facets of interpersonal relations. In the Kievan period, ecclesiastical courts came to exercise jurisdiction over certain classes of the populace.

The Book of the Pilot often included portions of Byzantine law, notably the *Ecloga* in the eighth century and the *Procheiros Nomos* of the ninth. A Bulgarian compilation of Byzantine law, the *Zakon sudnyi liudem*, was quite extensively disseminated in Kievan Rus and later manuscript versions sometimes incorporated the *Pravda Russkaia*. It is the Byzantine heritage in these forms which has led one observer to suggest that Roman law provided Russia and the West with a common legal vocabulary, a common set of legal distinctions, and a common concept of legislation.[5]

Mongol subjugation, 1240-1480

In the mid-thirteenth century there thundered across the Eurasian steppes the most powerful armed adversary Europe had ever confronted. For nearly two and one-half centuries the Golden Horde exacted tribute from Russian cities and episodically laid waste to pockets of resistance.

---

4 On the origins and status of the Book of the Pilot, see P. I. Zuzek *Kormčaia kniga* (1964).
5 H. J. Berman *Justice in the USSR* (rev. edn, 1963) p 189.

Kievan Rus, which in its prime had flourished as a centre of civilisation with familial and commercial links ranging from England and Scandinavia in the North, to Spain and France in the West, Byzantium, Persia, and India southward, and China to the East, was devastated by the Mongol advance, never to rise again. The Mongol subjugation of Russia is unanimously, it would seem, regarded as the principal reason for Russia's failure to keep up with the pace of legal development in Western Europe. Had Kiev survived, in the course of time universities might have opened, law might have been systematically taught, commentaries compiled, a legal profession formed, and the Russian legal system might have come to resemble others of the Romanist tradition more closely.

The Mongols were not a sedentary people. It was not their pattern to conquer and then permanently occupy territory. Rather, they preferred to introduce a tributary structure, often relying upon local Russians who appeared to be loyal, and to extract horrible retribution when the tributary obligations were not observed. So far as the legal system was concerned, the Mongols were content that it should operate quite normally; but they imposed a style of autocracy and public administration which many observers believe left an indelible imprint on subsequent Russian styles of State leadership. Nor, it should be added, did the Mongols in principle oppose commercial or other intercourse between Russian cities or principalities and western Europe. Why then could not law in Russia, or at least private law, have continued to develop under European stimulus?

There is no persuasive answer, but it may not be amiss to suggest that something other than the Mongol presence needs to be taken into account. It is incontestable, and paradoxical, that the number of manuscript copies of Russian legislation during the period of Mongol subjugation is much larger than for the earlier period and that several medieval Russian legal texts actually originated in the Mongol era, for example, the Charter of Dvina Land (circa 1397), the Charter of the City of Pskov (1397-1467), and the Charter of the City of Novgorod (1471). During the Mongol period, the Book of the Pilot continued to proliferate in redactions which more fully reflected Russian legal rules. This period saw the appearance of another collection of legal texts called the Just Measure (*Merilo Pravednoe*); it too owed its origin to the Russian Orthodox Church and included secular and clerical texts. The stages of amalgamation of these texts into successive manuscript collections remains controversial, but the process of consolidation and codification during this era is incontestably in evidence.[6] Nevertheless, the substance of these enactments had developed only marginally beyond the *Pravda Russkaia*.

---

6 See Kaiser, note 1, above, pp 26-27.

Muscovite law, 1480–1648

Factional rivalries within the Mongol Empire led in due course to its decline and destruction. In central and western Russia the Grand Duke of Muscovy gradually asserted his authority over neighbouring princes and fashioned a centralised State which ultimately threw off the surviving remnants of Tatar bondage and then militarily eliminated serious threats to Muscovite lands from that direction. As the Grand Prince's authority extended over newly acquired provinces, charters were issued to confirm the relationship to Muscovy or to grant special privileges to certain communities. The most important surviving text of this nature is the Beloozero [White Lake] Charter of 1488, which defined, inter alia, the powers of the Grand Prince's judges and laid down judicial procedures and penalties.[7]

The Charter was followed nine years later by what has been called the first national Russian Law Code, the *Sudebnik* of 1497. This and the *Sudebnik* of 1550 are the two major legal monuments of the period under consideration. Both *Sudebniki* concerned themselves primarily with the technicalities of judicial procedure. The extent to which they created new rules of procedure or reflected pre-existing patterns is much debated; the evidence of judgment charters prior to 1497 would seem to indicate the transition to a vertical system of justice with a hierarchy of courts and judges was a gradual process rather than an innovation in 1497. The Grand Prince had the right to act as judge in first instance or at final appellate instance in all cases, if he chose. The right to the personal justice of the ruler was an esteemed privilege in Muscovy which many subjects had secured to them by charters of grant. Certain categories of the populace—the clergy, servitors and peasants of priests and monasteries, some categories of peasants, guild merchants, foreigners present in Muscovy as merchants or military personnel, among others—were exempted from the ordinary courts and were dealt with by departments (*prikazy*) more responsive to the central authority. The majority of cases, however, came to be heard by regional vice-regents endowed with judicial powers in certain types of cases. Notwithstanding charters of grant and the usual judicial channels, subjects retained the right of direct petition to the Grand Prince to redress wrongs, which ultimately led to the creation of a department specially charged to handle these. The *Sudebniki* would appear to reflect a realisation that the personal dispensation of justice by the Sovereign had become too complex; accordingly, a hierarchy of agents came to perform these functions. Some of the charters of grant even provided for this possibility. But the

---

7 Translated in H. W. Dewey *Muscovite Judicial Texts 1488–1556* (1966) pp 3–6; commentary in Dewey 'The White Lake Charter: A Medieval Russian Administrative Statute' Speculum XXXII (1957) 74–83.

judgment charters contain no conclusive evidence of a fixed judicial hierarchy; on the contrary, some court officials appeared to have different degrees of authority and sat on the same case on appeal two or more times.[8]

Litigation in Muscovy seems to have been open to anyone, from princes to slaves, women, children, clergy, and bondsmen. Representation and substitution were allowed at trial, even among witnesses and on appeal. Witness testimony was the form of evidence most frequently used; documentary evidence was less common and of great variety, ranging from charters of grant, to purchase deeds, land-exchange or property division instruments, marriage settlements, promissory notes, or rent receipts. Witnesses unable to appear are known to have sent depositions containing their testimony. Extracts from land registry books were employed, and some parties even submitted default judgments. Forgeries were not unknown, and especially in land cases the court would personally verify or authenticate the documentary evidence. Divine justice also might be invoked. An icon or piece of turf might be carried during boundary inspections and the appropriate oath taken. Kissing the cross also appears on the judgment charters as a means of confirming evidence or independent means of proof. A judicial duel might be invoked, usually by one of the parties but sometimes by initiative of the judge. Yet another method of divine justice was the casting of lots. Foreign visitors to Muscovy have left two descriptions of judicial duel and one foreigner an account of his own involvement in a trial resolved by casting lots (overdue freight account).[9]

In many cases the Muscovite judge merely prepared a trial record (*doklad*) of the proceedings and submitted this to a higher instance, which read the record and then questioned both parties to the dispute. The trial record could be challenged for inaccuracies and further evidence submitted. The higher instance would then come to a decision and instruct the inferior judge accordingly. Precisely when and why this procedural device was used is not disclosed by legislation or the judgment charters.

On the whole, the Muscovite lawsuits of this period have impressed scholars as an adversary-type proceeding in which the two parties had primary responsibility for initiating the case, presenting the evidence, and adducing the arguments. The courts rarely summoned witnesses; judges seemed to have refereed the proceedings by ensuring that each party had full opportunity to present its case. Occasionally, the court would carry out on-the-spot views and seek the submission of additional

---

8 The roles of judges and sundry authority they exercised are described in A. M. Kleimola *Justice in Medieval Russia: Muscovite Judgment Charters (Pravye Gramoty) of the Fifteenth and Sixteenth Centuries* (1975) pp 10–21.

9 See Butler 'Foreign Impressions of Russian Law to 1800: Some Reflections' in id (ed) *Russian Law: Historical and Political Perspectives* (1977) pp 77–78.

evidence. On the other hand, litigants did not employ professional counsel. We have no evidence of a nascent legal profession. The judge did ask questions but, the records suggest, mainly to ensure all evidence was presented. Cross-examination or interrogation evidently was not practised.[10]

Judicial corruption was punishable under both the 1497 and 1550 *Sudebniki*. Contemporary accounts by foreigners reported official corruption to be commonplace. Appeals could be lodged by litigants on the ground of deliberate miscarriage of justice, violation of procedural rules, bribery, and an unjust decision. Appeals on the grounds of corruption appear not to have been unduly frequent, however, and one western scholar who has examined the ratio decidendi of judgment charters of the period has concluded that the judges did base their conclusions on the evidence.[11]

In the realm of public law, the impact of the Mongol heritage has remained speculative, but many observers believe the centralist autocracy which came to characterise Muscovite administration was the consequence of Mongol despotism. Ivan the Terrible destroyed the power of the hereditary nobility and abolished the right to pass in service from one lord to another without loss of patrimonial property. The nobility became bound to the Tsar by service, and in turn the peasants were bound to their landlord, gradually being prohibited from leaving their estates and likewise becoming indirectly the servitors of the Tsar. Towards the end of the sixteenth century other progress was to be noted. Trial by ordeal became uncommon, and trial by combat was formally abolished in 1556. But in criminal proceedings investigation of allegations was by torture, a practice which endured well into the eighteenth century. Evidence and proofs collected in this manner were then sent to Moscow, where they were reviewed and, if the party was deemed guilty, punishment assigned.[12]

From Byzantium, Muscovy had received Christianity via Kievan Rus, and with the fall of Constantinople in 1453 and the marriage of the Tsar to Sophia, the niece and heiress of the last of the Byzantine Emperors, Muscovy assumed the mantle of the 'Third Rome.' The Mongol tradition of tolerance for religious faiths was supplanted in Russia by intolerance for the non-Orthodox. But the Tsar's dual role as head of State and Church contributed, many believe, to an attenuation of some of the harsher features of the Mongol autocratic tradition being adapted by the Muscovite rulers.

---

10 Kleimola, note 8, above; the 1497 and 1550 *Sudebniki* are translated in Dewey, note 7, above. Examples of judgment charters, petitions, bailiff documents, deeds, antenuptial agreements, charters of manumission, donation charters, wills, and surety bonds are translated in Dewey and Kleimola *Russian Private Law in the XIV-XVII Centuries* (1973).
11 Kleimola, note 8, above, p 90.
12 On punishments, see Butler, note 9, above, pp 81-85.

The Russian Empire, 1649-1917

The period 1648-50 was a watershed in Russian legal history as consequential as the Peace of Westphalia was for European diplomacy and the law of nations. Within that two-year span in Russia, two major law codes, unprecedented in size and scope, were approved and printed for distribution (the first to be printed in all of Russian history) and the substantial German work on the art and laws of war by J. J. Wallhausen (1615-17) was translated into Russian and printed in 1647. The latter was the first printed work treating the law of nations in the Russian language.

Although we have referred principally to the 1497 and 1550 *Sudebniki* for the Muscovite period, there were hundreds of supplemental enactments issued in the later sixteenth and early seventeenth centuries.[13] By 1649 the morass of legislation required a new compilation, and in just over two months during 1648-49 the Zemskii sobor or Land Assembly prepared the most substantial and important achievement of medieval Russian law, the *Sobornoe ulozhenie* of 1649. Whatever doubt there may be about earlier Russian enactments constituting 'codes', the *Ulozhenie* indisputably qualified. Consisting of 967 articles divided somewhat haphazardly into 25 chapters, the *Ulozhenie* consolidated provisions drawn from the *Pravda Russkaia*, the *Sudebniki*, the *Litovskii Statut* (1588) or Lithuanian Code, and sundry individual decrees, and introduced some new provisions. Widely regarded as the benchmark in the transition of Russia from feudalism to absolutism, the *Ulozhenie* in any event came to represent a distillation of the past and the point of departure for Imperial Russian codification. It was printed at once in the Russian language and promptly found a translator in the person of Baron von Mayerburg, who provided a Latin text in the narrative of his diplomatic mission to Russia, published circa 1680.

Legal historians debate to this day the extent to which the *Ulozhenie* represented a reception of Polish-Lithuanian and even Byzantine law in Russia. The scope of the *Ulozhenie* embraced sacrilege, deference due to the Tsar, the Tsar's household, forgery and counterfeiting, jewellers, goldsmiths, and coiners, passports, military service, the ransom of prisoners, customs duties, legal procedure, trials of various classes of the populace, oaths, land law, succession, land tax, serfs, robbery, capital crimes, the Cossacks, and liquor licensing. Criminal penalties were especially severe under the *Ulozhenie* and became the object of repeated comment in foreign observations about Russia. The gradual enserfment

---

13 Texts of 345 enactments survive and have been collected and annotated in N. E. Nosov (ed) *Zakonodatel'nye akty russkogo gosudarstva vtoroi poloviny xvi-pervoi poloviny xvii veka* (1986). These offer rich data on the legislative process of the period and will stimulate reinterpretations of the Russian legal process during the late Muscovy era.

of the peasantry was confirmed and consolidated by the *Ulozhenie*, which forbade peasants to leave their landlords' estates for any reason whatever.

Ecclesiastical jurisdiction remained virtually intact under the *Ulozhenie*, and the Church immediately set about producing a modern redaction of the Book of the Pilot. This was approved by an ecclesiastical council and printed in 1650 and, with revisions, again in 1653. For the remainder of the Imperial era, this ecclesiastical 'code' continued in effect with minor modifications introduced in the late eighteenth century. Here were preserved tenets of Byzantine and early Russian law. In 1656 the Patriarch Nikon acting through the Novgorod ecclesiastical court, ruled on the extent to which a widow's dowry was liable for her late husband's debts by applying the relevant provisions of the *Ecloga* preserved in the Book of the Pilot.[14]

The systematisation and codification of law accomplished so expeditiously in 1648–50 in the reign of Tsar Aleksei Mikhailovich, father of Peter the Great, is perhaps undeservedly overlooked as part of the process of the 'westernisation' of Russian society accelerated under Peter. If the 1649 *Ulozhenie* did draw significantly upon the Lithuanian Code of 1588 for example, this represented a reception of European law. Peter's modernisation of the Russian State and elimination of the patriarchate as an alternative repository of power had implications more for Russian administrative law, and indeed it was here that Peter's chief claim to law reform lay. He acknowledged the need for continued systematisation of Russian legislation and appointed no less than three commissions between 1700–20 to attend to the matter. None progressed very far.

It was Peter's reforms of the State apparatus and military law that give him claim to the title of law reformer. The Russian government was reorganised with close account being taken of Swedish and German practice. Recent archival research has disclosed that Peter sought and obtained data on both the law and practice of Swedish institutions even while at sword's point during the Northern War[15] and modelled his collegial reform of 1718 on the Swedish practice. Foreigners were extensively recruited to operate the system until Peter could produce sufficient Russian trained personnel. In 1722 Peter established the Procuracy, perhaps also adapting Swedish institutions, to act as the 'eye of the Tsar' and watch over the conformity to the law of actions of local officials and bodies. Military and naval law were fundamentally reformed by the enactment of a Military Statute (1716) and a Naval Statute (1721), both drawing upon European models, including German, French, Swedish, Dutch, and English, remaining in effect with minor modifications for

14 Cited in E. L. Johnson *An Introduction to the Soviet Legal System* (1969) p 13.
15 C. Petersen *Peter the Great's Administrative and Judicial Reforms* (1979).

more than a century, and extending to certain civilian matters.

These were natural areas of concentration for a ruler intent on modernisation and at war constantly during his reign. Had he lived, one may only speculate what changes might have been wrought in private law. In some senses, Peter deserves to be classified as a comparativist: he personally drafted or revised many of his enactments; it was he personally who instructed that foreign laws and legal experience be assembled and it was he who read or had specially translated these materials for his own edification. Whatever reception of foreign law may have occurred at earlier stages of Russian history, Russia herself had never before reached so insistently and assertively for foreign legal experience.

Peter's immediate successors did not pursue his pace of reform; however, within less than four decades a foreigner came to the Russian throne whose enlightened attitude toward law and law reform rapidly earned her the title 'the Great.' Catherine II set about immediately to bring Russia up to the standard of eighteenth-century Europe.

Peter I had set in motion the measures required to found the Academy of Sciences in Russia, which opened shortly after his death in 1725. Law was among the sciences to be pursued, and the Academy of Sciences was to serve simultaneously as a research and a teaching institution, an Academy and a university. The first appointee in law, J. S. Beckenstein from Germany, offered lectures on natural law and politics but attracted no students and left in 1735. C. F. Gross lectured at the same time on moral philosophy, using the Russian translation (1726) of Pufendorf's *De officio hominis et civis* made at Peter's behest. Beckenstein's successor appointed in 1738 was F. H. Strube de Piermont (1704–90), who published at St Petersburg in 1740 a major study on the origins of natural law, in the French language; a revised edition issued at Amsterdam in 1744 was reprinted several times with emendations. Under the 1747 Statute of the Academy a sharp distinction was drawn between the academicians and the professors; the latter offered lectures in the physical, mathematical, and humanitarian sciences, law falling within the latter, and Strube was appointed to offer them. In 1756 Strube delivered a lecture on the origins of Russian law that was published in both Russian and Latin.

Three chairs of law were initially established within the Law Faculty of Moscow University founded in 1755; the notable professors were P. H. Dilthey, K. H Langer, I. A. Tret'iakov and S. E. Desnitskii. The latter especially merits our attention. Desnitskii was the first Russian law professor. Sent abroad in 1761 to read law at Glasgow University, he and Tret'iakov completed the full course of study at what was then Britain's leading university. Desnitskii published several works upon his return to Russia, acquainting his countrymen with the ideas of Adam Smith and John Millar, and at Catherine's instruction translated into Russian volume 1 of Blackstone's *Commentaries*, published at Moscow in 1780–83. He offered courses on the history of Russian law, on Justinian's *Pandects*, on a comparison of Russian and Roman law, and on the English language.[16] Since he and Tret'iakov, also appointed at the University, could lecture in Russian, the number of law students increased appreciably. Z. A. Goriushkin introduced the practice of teaching Russian law through mock trials and actual proceedings.

Catherine II's own enduring contribution to Russian law occurred in 1767 when there was published a Nakaz composed by herself with extensive borrowings from leading Enlightenment thinkers, notably Beccaria, Montesquieu, and Voltaire. Although the Nakaz was never enacted, its translation into the major European tongues and issuance in more than 20 editions made it the single piece of Russian legislative material best known abroad. An English version appeared at London in 1768. The Nakaz and perhaps Catherine's administrative reforms of 1775 and 1780, also published widely in Europe, were her major legal achievements; she too appointed codification commissions, but to no effect. However, the intellectual climate and institutions which she fostered, despite later apprehension about some of their implications, laid the base for an emergent Russian legal elite in the nineteenth century. Foreign perceptions of Russian law had altered dramatically. No longer the epitome of arbitrariness and cruelty, Russia was praised in print and public law lectures abroad for having set inspired examples which other nations might profitably emulate in their law reform undertakings.[17]

An indigenous legal literature began to complement translations into Russian of foreign works. Pufendorf and Blackstone have been mentioned; Bielfeld, Justi, Nettelbladt, and Montesquieu, among others, were translated, as were extracts from Diderot's *Encyclopédie* relating to law. Strube de Piermont, Dilthey, and Langer all left significant works. V. T. Zolotnitskii published the first original Russian work on natural law in 1764. N. I. Novikov, M. D. Chulkov, and others began through their compilations to introduce the Russian public to original texts of their early legal heritage. By the end of the century collections of and indexes to Russian legislation began to appear, essential raw material for teaching Russian law to students.

Russia embarked upon the nineteenth century with a new Emperor, Alexander I, in a liberal frame of mind, determined to modernise the State apparatus and bring order to the chaotic state of Russian legislation. In 1801 the tenth codification commission since Peter I was instituted. The Commission looked initially to Europe for ideas. The works of Jeremy Bentham were translated into Russian (1805–10) and the

---

16 A. H. Brown 'The Father of Russian Jurisprudence: The Legal Thought of S. E. Desnitskii', in Butler, note 9, above, pp 117–121.
17 Butler, note 9, above, pp 88–90.

Code Napoléon closely followed in the preparation of the initial drafts. But imposing intellectual or foreign schemes for systematisation did not ultimately find favour with Alexander I; codification work fell into desuetude, to be revived in the 1820s in the spirit of Savigny: Russia would look to her own historical experience and legislation to fashion a new code of law.

Alexander I also introduced a ministerial reform to supplant the collegial model of Peter the Great. Modelled upon the French scheme, the administrative reform was accompanied by an expansion of the education system and a transition to a system of civil service recruitment based on examination performance rather than exclusively hereditary links. 'Jurisprudence' was among the subjects examined; it encompassed natural law, Roman law, private law, criminal law, and the State economy. New universities were founded and faculties of law formed. Foreign law professors had to be recruited in the early decades, but preference was given to Russian candidates and in the course of time Russian graduates came to fill the majority of posts. Moscow University continued to offer legal training in both the general law subjects and in the procedures and arts of advocacy in Russian tribunals. With the accession of Nicholas I in 1825, codification work resumed at an accelerated pace. Drawing upon the talents of a small group of lawyers at St Petersburg University, M. A. Balugianskii and M. M. Speranskii brought to completion the most ambitious and comprehensive systematisation of legislation attempted in Europe. First to appear was the Complete Collected Laws of the Russian Empire (*Polnoe sobranie zakonov Rossiiskoi imperii*), a chronological collection of Russian legislation (more than 30,000 enactments) commencing with the *Sobornoe ulozhenie* of 1649 to 1825. Published in 48 massive tomes (1830), this collection formed the base for the next stage: a Digest of Russian Laws (*Svod zakonov*) published in 15 volumes in 1832. Both collections survived with continuations until the end of the Empire. A second series of the *Polnoe sobranie* was published annually from 1826–81, and the third series, from 1881–1916. From time to time the *Svod zakonov* would be supplied with supplementary volumes and reissued at intervals in a complete revised edition. This pattern of systematising legislation was taken over by the Soviet Government and continues to be used.

Speranskii's account of preparing the collections offers much insight into the administration of law and justice in that day. Few enactments had been printed. No chancellery had a complete register of enactments, and those that existed were badly organised. A full record of the law did not exist, and much of what did exist was inaccessible, not to say unknowable by official and citizen alike. Systematisation, Speranskii said, was an absolute prerequisite for the development of a legal system:

> It is not therefore from the Roman Law, nor yet from the isolated efforts of our lawyers, that we can expect to construct a solid foundation for a systematic study

of the laws. It must be based upon a body of the laws, and will date its commencement from their publication. Until this is done, it would be useless to devise commentaries and prescriptions calculated to develop the science of national legislation.[18]

Although the model of the Digest may appear to be Justinian, the precepts for its compilation were drawn from the writings of English jurists, Sir Francis Bacon and Jeremy Bentham, especially the former, as Speranskii makes unequivocally clear.

Administrative reforms, expansion and improvement of legal education, the publication of comprehensive law collections, a trained civil service—the gradual implementation of these measures in the nineteenth century contributed mightily to legal professionalisation in Russia.[19] The precise origins of the legal profession remain obscure. It is probable that litigation in medieval Russia was conducted by the parties themselves, although some contemporary accounts referred cryptically to 'attorneys.' In the eighteenth century it is evident that laymen experienced in the ways of courts often interposed themselves between party and judge and acted as a kind of advocate on behalf of their client. Lord Macartney described them as '... in general very sharp and expert ... they will undertake to spin out any cause for a term of years, on payment of a certain sum agreed on...'.[20] Judges depended for their livelihood upon a percentage of monetary compensation awarded; contemporary accounts provide conflicting evidence on the extent of judicial bribery and corruption in Russia, but there is ample evidence of public opinion, including Peter I, Catherine II, Alexander I, and Nicholas I, profoundly distrustful of judges and lawyers. By the third quarter of the nineteenth century legal professionalisation and legal values were beginning to leave their imprint within the State administration and without. Many observers believe that these were among the factors which contributed to the great nineteenth century reforms of Russian law: the emancipation of the serfs in 1861 and the judiciary reforms of 1864.

The emancipation of the serfs, quite apart from ending an intolerable social injustice, set in motion reforms of land, family, and inheritance law that required several decades to gestate. Reforms of local government, the introduction of the zemstvo system, in 1864 and 1870 gave the peasants greater involvement in self-government. The judiciary reform, which originated within the councils of the Tsar, wholly restructured the court system and officially established an organised legal profession. English influence was to be seen, including the intellectual genius of Bentham. The judiciary was made independent of administrative

18 M. M. Speranskii (W. Wall, transl.) *A Summary of Historical Sketches on the Formation of the Body of the Russian Laws* (1841) pp 89–90.
19 R. Wortman *The Development of a Russian Legal Consciousness* (1976).
20 G. Macartney *An Account of Russia* (1767) p 103.

officials, with rights of appeal, and no removal of judges except for malfeasance in office. *Volost'* courts were retained for the peasants, but otherwise courts based on class were abolished. The English 'justice of the peace' nominated by local zemstvos was introduced to handle minor offences. The complicated system of written pleadings characteristic of Russian procedure was replaced by oral proceedings and trials were to be open, again on the English model. Jury trial was available for serious criminal offences. French influence was to be seen in the creation of two cassational instances in the Ruling Senate (civil and criminal) to review cases when appeal had been exhausted. But although many features of the common law had been adapted and although medieval Russian trial practice had been akin to an adversary-type proceeding, the continental type of inquisitorial proceeding in criminal cases was received, many aspects of which survive in modern Soviet criminal procedure. A professional Bar was instituted, and all parties to civil and criminal proceedings were accorded the right to professional representation.

The last half-century of Imperial rule has been called the 'Golden Age' of Russian law.[1] The Russian legal profession flowered, producing distinguished practitioners, judges, and legal scholars, successfully challenging in several celebrated jury trials an absolutist autocracy bent upon eradicating political dissent and pluralism. Even to the revolutionary, the legal profession in Russia had its attraction as a channel for effectuating political and social change. Lenin read law at Kazan and St Petersburg Universities and passed to the Bar precisely for these reasons. In the course of time the reforms came to be attenuated by subsequent legislation. Judicial independence was circumscribed; the jurisdiction of class courts was somewhat enlarged, trial by jury was precluded in a growing number of instances, opportunities for imposing administrative sanctions were increased, the jurisdiction of justices of the peace was narrowed, the openness of trials was limited, and court martials were used increasingly to try civilians.

Pressure for social and legal reform intensified early in the twentieth century. The Revolution of 1905 brought a constituent assembly, the State Duma, and a form of constitutional monarchy. Political parties became active; attempts at enacting far-reaching economic and social reforms were made. A serious but belated effort to reshape the Russian socio-economic and political order was begun. Russian jurists were busy with civil and criminal law reform. A draft criminal code of 1903, based on several years of deliberations, was approved only in part, but as a whole it represented the most advanced statement of criminal jurisprudence in Europe. A draft civil code compiled in 1910–13 achieved the same standard of technical and substantive proficiency. Both were drawn upon in the Soviet period by those who crafted the RSFSR civil and criminal codes. The legal profession played an increasingly prominent

---

1 S. Kucherov *Courts, Lawyers and Trials Under the Last Three Tsars* (1953).

role in Russian political life; many members of the State Duma were people with legal background or education, from all parties. But reform could not keep pace with the demands for societal change. In 1917 the Imperial order collapsed under the pressures of war and revolutions.

We already have alluded to the multiplicity of legal orders operating simultaneously within the Empire to govern the affairs of more than 200 ethnic groups. Definitive studies of these systems, the relationship they enjoyed with and their influence upon Russian law, and their precise fate in the Soviet period have yet to be made.

Armenia and Azerbaidzhan, for example, were annexed in the early nineteenth century. Armenian codes dating to the twelfth century were influenced by Byzantium and customary rules. Unlike the *Pravda Russkaia*, these laws dealt in much greater detail with matters of civil, family, and criminal procedure law. Azerbaidzhan law was based on Islam and custom. The Baltic regions came under Russian domination in the eighteenth century but continued to enjoy a distinctive legal status and be governed only partially by Russian legislation. In 1864 a Baltic Civil Code was enacted, drawing upon customary law, Roman law, and German law. Applicable legal rules differed even within cities: in Reval (Tallinn) the legal formalities of drafting a will varied from the lower town to the upper, and from class to class. The Russian judiciary reforms of 1864 were not extended to the Baltic provinces until 1889, and then in modified form.

Georgia became a Russian protectorate in the eighteenth century largely at its own initiative and by 1878 found itself wholly absorbed into the Russian Empire. Several written laws were composed in the fourteenth and fifteenth centuries and a major Law Code (267 articles) in the first quarter of the eighteenth century. The latter regulated a wide range of civil transactions, including a minimum interest rate of 30 %, and imposed an elaborate scheme of compositions for criminal and civil wrongs.

Legal relations in Russian Central Asia, populated chiefly by peoples of the Islamic faith, were governed by Islamic written law and local custom. The Kazakhs compiled a written Code in the early eighteenth century based largely on customary rules with some Persian influence. Bride-price was provided for, and some civil law transactions (sale, loan, carriage) were mentioned. Penal sanctions were severe and blood vengeance sanctioned.

In those areas conquered or annexed by Russia, it was generally the practice to introduce the Russian administrative system, to eliminate some of the worst local practices (slavery, blood vengeance), and to allow local legislation or customary law to otherwise continue to operate. Full introduction of Russian law would have required a political and military commitment to russification of non-Russian minorities beyond the strength of the Empire. Tolerance of customary rules, however, was in the mainstream of Russian practice with respect to the Russian populace itself. Land relations and succession amongst the rural Russian populace were based chiefly upon local customary rules enforced by the peasant courts. It was commonplace to speak of 'peasant customary law.'[2] Amongst the nomadic tribes of Siberia, Russian legislation came gradually to play a larger role, especially through the Code of Steppe Laws of the Nomadic Peoples of Eastern Siberia, but on the whole local customs remained the basic source of law of these peoples.[3]

Continuity and change

Whatever of the pre-revolutionary heritage may have endured after the October 1917 Revolution, consciously or unconsciously, has engaged the attention of dozens of observers. Bolshevism arrived in the initial expectation that a world revolution was imminent and rapidly found itself obliged to contend with the formidable natural limitations of the Russian Empire itself: its size, its vulnerability, its languages, its standard of industrialisation, its illiteracy and poverty; its hunger for peace and land reform; its ethnic diversity; its historical, religious, and political experience; its economic order. After a Revolution engendered in Russian experience, it was unavoidable that some responses to problems would draw upon Russian patterns.

The forms of pre-revolutionary legislation were adopted at once. Decrees were cumulated into chronological collections which later served as the base for systematic compilations and digests. Whereas Decree No 1 was 'On Peace,' Decree No 7 dealt with the publication of laws. Habits of neglecting systematisation and codification, and of allowing legislation to fall into an appallingly chaotic state of confusion and inaccessibility, unfortunately persist; only in the 1980s did the *Svod zakonov* of the USSR and union republics come to fruition.

On the institutional plane, the Soviet Procuracy owes much to the pre-revolutionary model, more perhaps to the original concept in the Petrine era than the anaemic adaptation of the nineteenth century. Some scholars have found intriguing analogies between the pre- and post-revolutionary periods in the structure and functions of ministries and patterns of collegiality in state administration.[4] The concept of a Bar independent of the State with fees paid by clients has been retained. The collective farm household (see chapter 14), so deeply rooted in the

---

2 R. Beermann 'Pre-revolutionary Russian Peasant Laws' in Butler, note 9, above, p 190.
3 V. A. Riasanovskii *Customary Law of the Nomadic Tribes of Siberia* (1938) pp 61–62.
4 G. P. van den Berg 'Elements of Continuity in Soviet Constitutional Law' in Butler, note 9, above, pp 215–234.

Russian peasant mentality, was preserved as a legal concept in Soviet agricultural organisation and civil law.

In the realm of substantive law the early Soviet draftsmen looked to the progressive elements of Russian law just as to continental codes for form and system. And although all legal systems look in some measure at the miscreant as a person, Soviet law seems to convey something of a traditional Russian attitude in the degree to which it requires a court to take account of the totality of the individual offender and his relationship to society.

These are examples of conscious adaptations of the past. Many believe the Imperial pattern of autocracy, intolerance, russification, bureaucratism, backwardness, and absence of a modern western legal tradition left its own burden upon post-revolutinary Russia. Resistance to political pluralism and religious freedom, difficulties in instilling regard for socialist legality or rule of law, a suspicion of legal rationalism, arbitrariness during the Stalin era represented by purges, executions, disappearances, a reluctance to subject the political system itself to legal intervention—these too impress foreigners as part of an historical legacy which the Revolution has not fully transcended.

But continuity and change in law is not a mechanical exercise in identifying what seem to be analogous institutions, rules, or practices. Context is of the utmost significance, nor should one lose sight of the fact that both eras of Russian experience relate to the larger western and eastern legal traditions. Similarities and differences may owe their explanation or their more plausible hypotheses to legal developments or traditions beyond the Soviet Union.

Chapter 3

The ideological foundations of Soviet law

The fundamentals of Marxism-Leninism today, as they have for over seven decades, comprise the starting point in the USSR for university-level studies in all disciplines. Courses in political economy, historical materialism, dialectical materialism, history of the Communist Party, and basic principles of Marxism-Leninism are required in the first and second years of higher education to create what the Soviet authorities consider to be the proper ideological and philosophical base for the further acquisition of knowledge. The Soviet jurist of whatever specialty in the law has undergone that training, and whether he be a convinced Marxist-Leninist or not, of whatever disposition, his concepts of law, its origins, role, and purpose, have been affected by this intellectual framework. It is therefore essential to examine the main points of that world outlook and some of the contending theories which have emerged in the post-1917 period.

Marxist-Leninist theory of State and law

Marxism-Leninism postulates the primacy of economic relations in society. The history of human society falls into five socio-economic 'formations' or levels of development. The first was 'primitive communalism.' The family or clan was the key unit of societal organisation. Gradually there emerged a system of clans, tribes, and even alliances of tribes, said to have been the case among Slavic peoples, for example. Within the family or clan there existed purely a natural division of labour between man and woman. The male protected and hunted, the female cooked and worked at home: 'The domestic economy was conducted on communist principles.'[1] The development of productive forces led eventually to the break-up of primitive communalism and to a social division of labour, as some tribes took up livestock herding or land cultivation. As cultivation implements improved, labour productivity increased. Gradually metal crafts emerged, and so on. Families and tribes began to produce for exchange, and this led to the formation of a class not engaged in producing, the merchants: a 'parasitic class' which interposed itself as middlemen between two producers and exploited each of them.

---

1 Quoted from K. A. Mokichev (ed) *Teoriia gosudarstva i prava* (2nd edn, 1970) p 54.

The desire to produce wealth greater than consumption needs led to the enslaving of prisoners in order to enlarge the labour force; slave-owning itself became a form of wealth. The land began to be divided among individual families. Private ownership came to supplant collective ownership of the means of production. Differences between free and enslaved, rich and poor, were exacerbated. The heads of tribes used their power and influence to acquire wealth. The family or clan system outlived itself. Economic changes led to its downfall and the emergence of private ownership and the division of society into classes with irreconcilable contradictions.

Slavery was the first form of exploitation, the first form of class oppression according to Marxism-Leninism, and gave rise to the first State and law in human society. The origin of the State occurred in different forms at various periods: Engels postulated three methods of class struggle, the Athenean, the Roman, and the Germanic. Public authority and a concept of territoriality distinguished the State system from the family or clan system. Class struggle had led to the formation of the State, the political organisation of the economically dominant class and perforce politically dominant class. The origin of class society and the State, Soviet jurists are taught, was one of the turning points in the development of human society.

Law originating with the State is an expression of the will of the ruling class, according to Marxism-Leninism, and the same reasons gave rise to the appearance of private ownership and of antagonistic classes. Law protected the interests of the ruling classes and reflected only their will. Observance of law was ensured by State coercion. A law of ownership developed. The division into rich and poor meant the disappearance of traditional customs and habits, some positive, others not. The law of succession, for example, is held to be an instance of a custom under primitive communalism which was transformed into legislation regulating inheritance from the standpoint of class positions. As society moved from one based on slave-ownership to feudalism and then to bourgeois society, the forms of exploitation and the exploiting classes holding State power changed, but State and law retained their exploitative character and were adapted to new circumstances and requirements in order to serve the ruling classes. In all types of society the majority of working people were oppressed by the economically dominant minority.

As general propositions Soviet jurists are instructed that any State ruled by exploiting classes will consolidate and protect private ownership, especially of the instruments and means of production, will coerce the oppressed working people in order to enrich the exploiters, and will resort to open military oppression and terror against those who side with the oppressed.[2] The precise attributes of feudal and bourgeois States

2 N. G. Aleksandrov (ed) *Osnovy teorii gosudarstva i prava* (1960) pp 62-64.

are much debated by Soviet philosophers, historians, and jurists. It is accepted that both types of State have experienced monarchies and republics and often have changed from one to another, with many peculiar distinguishing points. Always, however, the ruling classes seek to rule by concentrating their power in the military and police organs to enforce law that meets the requirements of the State. Law always will protect the integrity of private property in order to safeguard the interests of its owners.

Classes, State and law as thus conceived are dependent upon the mode of production in material life. Matter is the ultimate reality; Man is a product of that reality; his means of existence are a reflection of that reality. As the mode of production changes, so too do man's ideas, institutions, and laws. Economic activity is the base that determines the nature of society's superstructure. Law and State consequently are elements of superstructure, an ideological expression of economic relations at a particular point in time. Law, Engels wrote, is an 'economic reflex' rather than a body of a priori principles. Law is not without its impact upon economic relations. The precise reciprocal relationship between base and superstructure too is the subject of continuous debate, but in the Marxian view the base is ultimately determinative of the course of change.

Change in society, as change in all matter, occurs dialectically in the Marxist conception. A disharmony always exists at any given point in time, for matter is constantly in motion, following what seem to be laws of action and reaction, attraction and repulsion, thesis and antithesis, a constant struggle of opposites. Struggle eventually achieves a synthesis, but the synthesis comes into conflict with other forces or contains its own antithesis, or both. Perfect harmony is attained only when all opposites have been spent; if one perceives changes to be progressive, perfect harmony is possible at some ultimate point. Translated into societal terms, as the mode of production changes and the oppressed working class grows in strength, the ruling classes are obliged to resort to increasingly repressive measures. Temporary adjustments may be made, but quantitative changes cumulate and ultimately reach a point where a qualitative change is inevitable. The old order is overthrown and a new order emerges. Expressed as legal change, the property law relations fashioned to safeguard economic relations under a particular mode of production eventually come into conflict with that mode and operate as a restraint on the forces of production: the tension in a basic sense is resolved by social revolution. In the Marxian view, the course of human history shows these factors at work. Fundamental social revolution expressed in the transition from one level of societal development to another, from feudalism to capitalism, for example, or capitalism to socialism, is the product of the contradictions between changes in the mode of production and the futile efforts of those unable to preserve their power or accommodate the changes taking place.

It followed from these general tenets that social revolution could be next expected to transpire during the late nineteenth century in the most advanced capitalist economies of Western Europe, for there the contradictions between the oppressor and oppressed were most intense. So Marx and Engels confidently anticipated. Among Lenin's original contributions to Marxian thought was his analysis as to why the Revolution did not transpire where and when it was expected. Capitalism, Lenin diagnosed, had entered its highest phase—imperialism. The European proletariat was being 'bought off' by the ruling classes in the form of higher wages and rising living standards paid for by cheap raw materials and labour from colonial dependencies. The struggle had shifted for the moment, Lenin argued, to the third world. As undiscovered territories disappeared, the most advanced capitalist countries would fight one another for colonial possessions. Such wars were inevitable if Europe was to avoid domestic civil strife. The break-up of colonial empires would mean the hastening of social revolution in Europe, in Lenin's perception; hence the stress upon self-determination and national liberation for colonial dependencies. These were not ends in themselves but the key to European revolution.

Why revolution came to pass ultimately in one of Europe's less industrialised powers, nearly 90 % of whose populace was engaged in agriculture, and not where Marx and Engels anticipated, is attributed in Marxist-Leninist doctrine to human factors: organisation and leadership. Lenin and his associates were activist revolutionaries, contemptuous of the social reformism which in their eyes had captured all the mainstream of the European socialist movement in the early twentieth century. Conscious revolutionaries were capable of leading the unconscious, the politically unaware, proletariat to power and thereby accelerating the inevitable process of societal change. The Bolshevik Party under Lenin's leadership conceived itself to be a disciplined conspiratorial vanguard of the working class and dedicated itself to the cause of precipitating Revolution. Its role in Russia's first 1917 Revolution, in February, to overthrow the monarchy was virtually nil, but in the contest for power culminating in the 1917 October Revolution, considerable. The role and status of the Communist Party in the Soviet Union continues to be profoundly affected by Lenin's original perceptions of its role (see chapter 9).

Theory of State and law in the Soviet era

Marx and Engels had comparatively little to say about law in their writings, and what they did say appertained principally to their larger critique of contemporary society and explanation of societal change. Law in effect was explained away. Future society, it was supposed, would administer itself without need of legal rules. Those who came to power in October 1917, who confronted, as Marx and Engels had not, the need to govern nations, peoples, an economy, an Army, found no specific blueprint in the writings of Marx and Engels. There commenced the process of developing and adapting theories of revolutionary change to cope with a real revolution, a process which continues to this day, by devising substages through which a society is to pass in the course of transition to socialism and communism. These levels of societal development are closely linked to and dependent upon law and legal institutions. Intense and enormously important debates about the role or purpose of law have figured in Soviet policy dialogues on these issues; at various periods in Soviet history legal theory, or more properly, the theory of State and law, has contributed to these discussions both within the Party and without and, of course, duly reflected the ultimate decisions taken. Law is, inter alia, policy as well as politics, whether one speaks of law writ large or as a single legislative act; it is a product of political processes, it records a policy judgment or decision, and it transmits that decision to whomever it is addressed in the form of a normative or legally binding rule.

In his *Critique of the Gotha Programme* Marx spoke of a transition period between capitalist and communist society when the former would transmute into the latter. Politically the State during this period could be nothing, Marx said, other than the 'revolutionary dictatorship of the proletariat.' Lenin developed the notion in his *State and Revolution* (1917), suggesting that a proletarian State would be essential in order to crush the bourgeoisie but would commence the withering away process at once. Much of Soviet legal theory has since been devoted to the relationship between these contradictory processes and the relative weight to be accorded to each. Once power passed into their hands, the Soviet leadership fashioned a highly centralised form of government within a federated structure. Initial expectations that an untrained, often illiterate, proletariat and peasantry could simply step into a dismantled State apparatus proved illusory. Normative acts represented 'proletarian commands'; they were to be obeyed because they represented the will of the new ruling class. Philosophically, however, the Soviet leadership saw no long-term virtue in those legal rules and institutions governing the personal interests of citizens. These were to disappear during the transition period. The classics of Marxism were explicit with respect to the State and law of the old order: it was to be smashed; the power base of the old order was to be dismantled with all the legal institutions that supported it.

The dismantling and restructuring processes simultaneously at work during this early transition period are variously interpreted against the background of the NEP. Some have viewed the legal history of 1917–21 as an era primarily of dismantling the old Imperial order and experimenting ad hoc with the minimum legal measures required for transition.[3] To them NEP represented an unfortunate but essential tactical reversal of this process, a restoration of capitalist elements whose doom otherwise was sealed by initial proletarian legislation. Others have viewed the NEP as a logical continuation and development of the revolutionary measures. The NEP codifications, according to this view, were a consolidation and systematisation of revolutionary achievements and by no means a retreat or compromise; the NEP was a necessary next step in the class struggle to achieve socialism.

Soviet legal theory during the 1920s has been variously characterised as an era of considerable diversity and originality among Marxian and non-Marxian jurists seeking a new path on terrain uncharted by the Marxist classics, and as a period of sharp conflict between communist and non-Party theorists culminating in the eventual dominance of the radical theorists led by E. B. Pashukanis. Much of what was written attempted to draw upon certain strands of European legal philosophy and criticise them in the light of Soviet experience or Marxian tenets. In the absence of a cohesive Marxist theory of law for the dictatorship of the proletariat, it was easier to react against the ideas of others. Jellinek, Petrazhitskii, Duguit, Renner, and Kelsen were among those who had Marxist followers, albeit in a revisionist spirit, and whose pre- and post-revolutionary writings were subject to avid scrutiny in Soviet legal media. For all of the searching for a Marxist theory of State and law in the 1920s, however, no one seriously challenged the notion that law was expected to die away rapidly.[4] In the interim, law was an instrument for revolutionary social change. Legalism was decried as a 'bourgeois fetish'.

The Soviet jurist who developed original notions of the role for law in a society building socialism and of the rapid withering away of law and who came to lead intellectually the legal policies associated with the transition from NEP to national economic planning and collectivisation was E. B. Pashukanis. His ideas acquired considerable reputation in the West at the time through a German translation of his *General Theory* and enjoyed fresh reconsideration in the late 1970s. In Pashukanis' mind, law, while originating in class domination, was distinct from other means of class domination by virtue of its role in commodity exchange.

3 See J. N. Hazard 'Soviet Law: The Bridge Years; 1917–1920' in W. E. Butler (ed) *Russian Law: Historical and Political Perspectives* (1977) pp 235–257; Z. L. Zile 'Seizure of Power and War Communism (1917–21) in Soviet Legal Historiography' in W. E. Butler, P. B. Maggs, and J. B. Quigley (eds) *Law After Revolution* (1988) pp 1–34.
4 An excellent account of the development of Soviet legal theory is A. A. Plotnieks *Stanovlenie i razvitie marksistsko-leninskoi obshchei teorii prava v SSSR* (1978).

Those who purchase and sell goods in the market place rely on contract or other forms of legal transactions to define and enforce reciprocally their mutual economic relations. The participants identify themselves as juridical persons bearing particular rights and duties. The law of contract, to Pashukanis, is founded upon the intentional voluntary reciprocal conduct or consent of the parties giving effect, in this instance, to their economic relations, but the same consensual base underlies other branches of law: labour relations, between management and employee; family law, in the form of marriage and parent-child relationships; or even constitutional law, based on a social contract reflecting an alleged consensus to govern. All law consequently had an economic basis, in this case founded on commodity exchange.

Pashukanis believed he had accurately diagnosed the legal process in society, not law as an abstract idea but as a genuine operational element in human relations. Although law was to be found in every level of societal development after primitive communalism, its inherent individualism and contractual or consensual base led naturally to its apogee of development under capitalism. The dictatorship of the proletariat would avail itself of bourgeois law only insofar as the transition to a socialist economy required. With the introduction of Plan and elimination of a commodity-exchange economy, the legal superstructure of bourgeois law would die away.

Pashukanis and his followers enjoyed an opportunity rarely open to legal theorists: to practise what they preached. The introduction of national economic planning in 1928 brought a revolutionary offensive against law. The day of withering away was believed to have arrived, and the goals were not modest. Large-scale industrialisation required the planned concentration and allocation of resources and investment. Part of the rural labour force had to be released for the factories, and this could be accomplished it was believed only by mechanising agriculture on a large scale and eliminating the potential economic stranglehold of the middle and wealthy peasants over the nation's food supply. Moreover, the State intended to finance industrialisation partly through the export of grain and raw materials, which also required that the State have full control over agricultural production. Survivals of capitalism were to be abolished. By the end of the second Five-Year Plan antagonistic classes were to have disappeared.

The pace of change gave rise to vigorous debate about economic policy and the human capacity to effectuate short-term vast social change. Those who believed man was now fully capable of shaping his own destiny carried the day. A dynamic approach was preferred to the stability-mindedness of those who counselled caution. In the realm of law, Plan was expected to supplant the remnants of bourgeois law. The transition to socialism had accelerated; an adaptive socio-economic policy needed a flexible set of institutions and policies that would give effect to Plan not in terms of rights and duties but in terms of elastic revolutionary legality. As a means of social control, law would be superseded by Plan in economic relations. Codification and systematisation of legislation, at an advanced stage in 1929–30, were suspended for fear the forms of law would constrain socio-legal change. In the realm of interpersonal relations, civil law was relegated to a minor place in legal studies. Draft penal codes prepared by followers of Pashukanis consisted of broad principles and no Special Part, for Pashukanis had regarded pre-existing criminal law and its fixed penalties for offences as a kind of contractual relationship between society and the individual.

The actual dismantling of the legal system during the early 1930s is difficult to assess. Legal education experienced some cutback and expectations were high that by the end of the 1930s courts would be redundant. Other hard data is unavailable. The amount of legislation increased significantly, and new legal institutions were introduced, for example, State Arbitrazh and the maritime and foreign trade arbitration commissions. Administrative and police controls were expanded, and the role and authority of the CPSU enhanced. By 1936 it was apparent that the pace of imposed change could not be sustained. On the other hand, it was felt that the necessary threshold had been crossed. The 1936 USSR Constitution declared the Soviet Union to be a socialist society. Antagonistic classes had been eliminated. Those who counselled restoration of stability of laws came to the forefront, and those responsible for earlier policies of rapid change were purged and in many cases, including Pashukanis, executed. The State under socialism would not rapidly wither away. Socialism existed only in one country (the USSR) and was being built in another (Mongolia), neighbours surrounded by hostile capitalist powers, and for self-defence the State would be maintained and strengthened. For the State ultimately to disappear, Stalin said, it must pass through the dialectically contradictory stage of being stronger.

Since it is unclear to what extent legal institutions actually were in abeyance during the 1930s, so too is the measure of actual restoration ambiguous. But the change in attitude and policy was dramatic in many respects. Law had a formal stabilising role to play under socialism in the economy and in interpersonal relations. State Arbitrazh, for example, was enjoined to apply law to disputes and not economic policy. Personal property, including inheritance, was protected. For the foreseeable future, money and property concepts would survive. The family was strengthened. Russia became more conscious of itself as an entity and less disposed to be a transitional entity toward a world State. Many changes in attitude represented a reaction not against the early 1930s but a reversal of policy toward measures dating from 1917 or the mid-1920s. In the realm of legal theory, the lack of tolerance which Pushukanis and his followers had displayed toward their opponents became equally applicable to them. An insistence upon orthodoxy of views in a climate of physically eliminating those who had supported a contrary approach had a chilling effect upon Soviet jurisprudence.

A. Ia. Vyshinskii became the principal spokesman for legal theory under the period of stability of laws. Replete with invective against western legal thought and all earlier Soviet views, intensely defensive in tone, and reflecting the exalted personality cult of Stalin, Vyshinskii's writings nonetheless were the first sustained attempt to develop a theory of a permanent socialist law. The stage of socialism reached by the USSR was no dialectical aberration. That had been foretold in the Marxian classics and duly accomplished. Unexpected was the continuance of law, for all writers, including Vyshinskii himself in the 1920s, had predicted or assumed the disappearance of law under socialism. Orthodoxy of view in legal theory consequently was not only a handmaiden of authoritarianism under Stalin but a defensive mechanism to protect a new departure in socialist superstructure. Law does not reach its apogee under capitalism, Vyshinskii argued; this is attained under socialism. Nor can law be reduced merely to economics or to politics, as other Soviet legal theorists of the 1920s (Stuchka, Reisner, etc) would have done. Having staunchly defended the integrity and necessity of law under socialism, Vyshinskii was unable to offer a concept of law that transcended the instrumentalism of the 'will of the people.' Nor did the restoration of stability of law constrain the extra-legal persecution of individuals or their relations who were identified with the opposition. To the outside world the survival of law under socialism was for two decades paradoxically but inextricably linked with a regime of terror and authoritarianism such that many wonder whether and how legality could exist at all. Modern assessments of Soviet society during the late Stalin era believe that legality and terror existed side by side, in their respective realms so to speak, but the definitive answer is by no means available yet.

Socialist legality eventually evolved into a standard by which excesses of the Stalinist period came to be condemned and legal reforms to be effectuated in the post-Stalin era. The initial law reforms of the post-Stalin era amounted to an attenuation of the harsher political terror and the introduction of greater substantive and procedural guarantees. Stalin was accused of violating his own socialist legality and of betraying Marxism-Leninism in many of his policies. Following the XX Congress of the CPSU, most of the jurists criticised during the Stalinist era were rehabilitated; Pashukanis' _General Theory of Law and Maxism_ and other works finally were republished at Moscow in 1980. The relaxation in the post-Stalin era similarly brought an extensive preoccupation with western political and legal philosophy of all periods and orientations, both critiques and translations. The turning point in Soviet legal thought, however, dates from the XXI and XXII Congresses of the

CPSU in 1959 and 1961 respectively. At the XXI Congress Soviet society was said to have entered a higher phase of socialist development, the period of the 'expanded construction of communism.' A new Programme of the CPSU adopted at the XXII Congress called for completion of the first phase of communist construction by 1980, a timetable that quietly was shelved when the economic prerequisites proved too ambitious.

For a brief period the transition to this new level of socialist development refuelled the debate about the imminent withering away of the State. The 1961 Party Programme declared the Soviet Union to be a 'State of the whole people' or an 'all-people's State.' The dictatorship of the proletariat had ceased to be necessary. The all-people's State would rely less on coercion and more on persuasion and would commence the process of divesting its functions to non-State bodies such as social organisations. The comrades' courts and people's guards (see chapter 7, below) were introduced as social agencies to assume law enforcement functions. Criminal law reforms placed greater emphasis upon social measures to reform first offenders who committed minor crimes. A constitutional revision committee appointed in 1962 was to prepare a new constitution reflective of the new level of societal development. It may have been intended to reduce the numbers of lawyers; reports persist of an unpublished Party resolution circa 1963–64 calling for a reduction in the numbers of law students. Soviet jurists gave serious thought for the first time to mechanisms for social control in the first phase of communism as the State withered away. Customary law took on special interest in this connection and no longer was deemed to be inherently retrograde. Vyshinskii's definition of law was deemed unsuitable for the new stage of societal development. Debate was opened and continues to this day over a new definition of law and legality appropriate to the age.

The change of leadership in 1964 brought a new style and slight reorientation to the debate. The new codifications of civil and criminal law had been completed. Attention concentrated on economic reforms (see chapter 13, below) and upon making the middle and lower levels of State power and administration more democratic, participatory, and responsive. The all-people's State emphasised less the immediate divestiture of its functions and more the greater involvement of citizens in its affairs. The comrades' courts and people's guards were retained as proven quasi-legal institutions but modified to introduce better procedural safeguards. Legislation on local government was reworked thoroughly for the first time since the 1930s. For reasons not yet wholly clear, the new constitution was delayed until 1977. Its enactment signalled a full-fledged legislative acceptance of the all-people's State.

Soviet legal theory during this period has been preoccupied with the nuts and bolts of legal development. As legislation has become more detailed and comprehensive, the theorists have engaged themselves with the minutiae of legal institutions and rules. Larger questions, to be sure, are of concern. Soviet jurists, as jurists everywhere, confront the issue of distinguishing 'good' laws from 'bad.' State command, it is widely recognised, is not always sufficient to establish the 'legality' or the 'justness' of legislation. Various efforts to measure legislation against the larger goals of a socialist society building communism, or against communist morality, or against laws of societal development or analogous basic standards bring Soviet jurisprudence close to some sort of natural law position in the minds of many western legal philosophers. On the other hand, the inclination of many Soviet legal theorists to treat planning directives, certain acts of social organisations, or even the 'rules of socialist community life' as having a legal quality suggests that law may be deemed to have a long-term value to, and role in, future Soviet society; no longer is there preoccupation with the disappearance of law but rather its transformation into a social regulator of a new type.

On a similar level, there is some indication that the human rights discussions of the 1970s have made Soviet legal theorists aware that citizens' rights cannot always be reliably protected by the State but must be protected against the State. The full implications of this view have yet to emerge. Perhaps the trend of the 1970s in Soviet law to place greater reliance upon the courts to resolve disputes, to admit defence counsel to many administrative proceedings, and to enlarge Procuracy responsibilities for securing the rights of citizens are reflective of this concern, although these measures by no means resolve the matter.

On a more mundane but nevertheless vital level for the individual is the lively theoretical dialogue which developed concerning the nature and status of personal property. It is one of innumerable examples demonstrating the importance of debates about Soviet legal theory for an understanding of Soviet legal policy and legal change. The abolition of private ownership of the instruments and means of production, in the Marxian view, has always been regarded as an absolute prerequisite for any society to build successfully a socialist order and to consolidate the economic basis of its power against the antecedent system. Differences in the legal regulation of property constitute fundamental points of distinction when demarcating the transition of society from one stage of development to another. Soviet policy toward nationalisation, what should be taken by the State and when, and toward Plan and law were strongly influenced by these ideological axioms. But abolition of private property has never been understood to mean that all ownership would necessarily be eliminated. The *Communist Manifesto* expressly declared that '. . . the distinguishing feature of communism is not the abolition of property generally, but the abolition of bourgeois property.' The 1936 USSR Constitution restored the integrity of ownership as a useful conceptual tool to reinforce planning, discipline the execution of planning directives, and offer incentive for fulfilling planning targets. All private ownership was declared to have been liquidated, and a sharp terminological distinction drawn between 'private' and 'personal' ownership. The latter was admissible, even desirable, but the issue of principle remained. Would personal ownership too be fated to disappear under communism? Was it a necessary anachronism in a socialist society or an institution fully compatible with a society building communism? As the material prosperity of the average citizen grew, should any limitations be placed on personal ownership or, on the contrary, should an expansion of national economic growth see commensurate increases in the personal wealth of the individual? The task of legal theory was to develop an appropriate concept of personal ownership, and a lively dialogue continues among jurists as to its nature and ultimate fate as Soviet society develops.

The term 'ownership' is often used in two senses in Soviet legal doctrine: (1) as a category of political economy to designate a 'certain aggregate of material social relations not dependent on the will and consciousness of the people and constituting an integral part of the economic base of society,' and (2) as a legal concept, a 'phenomenon of the State legal superstructure embracing the realm of volitional and ideological relations.' Modern Soviet legal theory has accepted personal ownership as an integral part of an advanced socialist society, not an anachronism, by demonstrating that these two notions are not contraposed to one another, but were closely interconnected and developed in Marx's writings. The view that Marx concentrated almost exclusively on the first definition and ignored the second is challenged by many Soviet jurists; Marxian theory, in their view, similarly explains the legal forms in which ownership relations are to be expressed under socialism. Ownership, it is contended, cannot be reduced solely to an autonomous and independent link between a person and a thing. In all instances ownership is simultaneously a 'community' (*obshchenie*) between people, a relationship between the owner and non-owners, that is, a social relationship.

As a social relationship, personal ownership is held to be conditioned by and subordinate to interlinkages in the realm of social production. Many Soviet jurists have been influenced in recent years by the view which has gained currency among Soviet economists that 'nonproduction consumption does not lie outside the economy and that it forms the concluding phase of the regeneration process where special social relations are formed...'.[5] These economic conclusions are believed to provide a basis for regarding the interlinkage between the law and the relations of personal ownership as part of the general issue of the co-relation of legal institutions and production relations. It follows,

---

5 V. F. Maslov *Osnovnye problemy prava lichnoi sobstvennosti v period stroitel' stva kommunizma v SSSR* (1968).

under this reasoning, that in a socialist society the relations of personal ownership are one link in the system of ownership relations. Since the 1961 Programme of the CPSU and successive Five-Year Plans have accorded a high priority to raising the cultural, intellectual, and material level of the Soviet citizen, that is, non-production consumption in its social role, personal ownership is not a legacy of the past but an integral and essential component of the present and future. Consequently: (1) the significance of personal ownership itself in a socialist society is the reason and the basis for legally consolidating personal ownership; personal ownership is an integral part of Soviet ownership: State, cooperative, social, and personal; (2) the role of civil law is to provide the legal conditions necessary for citizens to participate in production relations related to consumption, that is, the legal capacity of a citizen to be a 'subject of the law of personal ownership;' and (3) the social role of law in regulating personal ownership is to provide maximum legal stability in order to create optimal conditions for the processes of personal consumption.[6]

There are variations of and embellishments on this theme in doctrinal writings amidst a general recognition that the entire subject requires further investigation. Overall, the disposition since the mid-1960s and consolidated in the 1977–78 Soviet constitutions seems to be to emphasise personal ownership as an integral, desirable, and essential part of modern socialist society. Personal ownership accordingly is in step with policies currently pursued with respect to the 'tasks, forms, and means' of meeting the requirements of individuals in a socialist society.

The XXVII Party Congress in February 1986 substantially revised the 1961 Party Programme and the Party Rules, introducing elements of style, realism, and substance that suggest the Congress will become a landmark in the development of Soviet legal theory equal to the XXII Party Congress. Unlike earlier benchmarks which demarcated a transition from one stage of societal development to the next, the XXVII Party Congress retracted the exaggerated timetable for effecting the fundamental transformations postulated in 1961 and commenced a searching reassessment of those forces and factors in Soviet society retarding the pace of social advance. In some instances (for example, economic management and the law of ownership) a certain reconceptualisation was deemed to be necessary. In others it would suffice to impart real meaning to statutory provisions already enacted or genuinely to implement legal standards in existence with some restructuring of legal institutions. The spirit of *glasnost'* that informed the ensuing discussion and dialogue has introduced a dynamic of its own and led, in the realm of law, to a spirit of candour startling in its contrast with earlier styles.

---

6 A. A. Rubanov *Grazhdansko-pravovoe polozhenie lichnosti v SSSR* (ed N. S. Malein) (1975) pp 53–59.

Further democratisation and accelerated socio-economic development are the principal domestic goals being pursued. Expanded public participation in State affairs and continued devolution of power and responsibility to local units of government, State enterprises, and social organisations are the main lines to be pursued. The administrative apparatus is expected to be reduced and made more responsive; in selected situations it may find its decisions subjected to suspension by social organisations. Within enterprises, the labour collectives and their councils will be given broader final jurisdiction over matters. Nationwide referenda are likely, and the practice of contested elections, introduced experimentally in 1987, has been favourably received. In matters of social justice the accent is on equality before the law, respect for the individual, equality of nations, and social welfare for the disadvantaged. But social justice is also being reassessed against economic presuppositions of the past. Incentives for excellence and quality are being increased, those who do not produce up to standard are being economically penalised, and those who exist on the proceeds of non-labour incomes are to be punished more severely. Increased incentives and earning differentials will lead to disparities in wealth requiring sensitive handling.

Soviet legal theory, legislation, and the legal system are at the heart of all these changes. They cannot be effectively dealt with outside the legal system or without the use of law and legal personnel. All branches of law have been called upon to further economic reforms, to control the relationship between labour expended and consumption, and to effectuate social justice. Legal services and personnel are likely to continue to expand, particularly law-enforcement personnel and jurisconsults. Legal education of laymen, and the involvement of laymen in judicial and other activities, is expected to be preserved in its diverse forms and new ones sought.

As these examples and the history of Soviet legal theory since 1917 suggest, the Soviet legal system differs markedly from the Anglo-American in the premium placed upon the interlinkage among theory, law, and policy, and this has been as true in periods of ultra-orthodoxy as in periods of relative permissiveness and diversity irrespective of whether legal dialogue aids policy-formation or merely rationalises the result. In most instances legal theory must perform both functions in the Soviet legal system.

Chapter 4

Sources of Soviet law

The 'seamless web' of the common law orginates in several sources—legislation, judicial decisions, even community custom—without ascribing priority of place to any one of them. The common lawyer, in contrast to his Soviet (and continental) counterparts, consequently has never attached particular significance to a formalistic hierarchy of sources of law, although in many constitutional democracies the written constitution imposes limitations on the power of the State to issue certain types of enactments or legislate in general on certain matters.

Soviet legal doctrine conventionally distinguishes between two meanings of 'sources of law.' In their 'fundamental' sense 'sources of law' are the socio-economic order of a particular society which gives birth to and shapes a distinctive political, economic, and legal superstructure. A socialist society, in this sense, is said to form and shape the substance of its socialist law and legal system. In their 'technical' meaning, which is the aspect we treat in this chapter, 'sources of law' are the rules or norms created or sanctioned by State agencies in a duly established manner. Not all State acts fall within this category; only those prescribing general rules of conduct, or *normative* acts, as they are often called. Non-normative acts appertain to individual specific matters and are based upon legal norms. The distinction between normative and non-normative is easier drawn in theory than in practice, and is one drawn in many different ways.

Legislation

The concept of separation of powers has been emphatically rejected in Soviet constitutional theory and jurisprudence. Because a socialist state is structured according to the principle of popular sovereignty and State policy is to originate from popularly elected representative bodies, a delegation of legislative power to non-representative organs, it is argued, would derogate from the very foundations of the socialist political order. Article 2 of the 1977 USSR Constitution establishes the co-relationship of popular sovereignty and legislative supremacy as follows: 'All power in the USSR shall belong to the people,' who shall '. . . exercise State power through soviets of people's deputies, which shall constitute the political foundation of the USSR.' All other State agencies shall 'be under the control of and accountable to the soviets of people's deputies.' Article 108 provides that the USSR Supreme Soviet shall be 'the highest agency of State power of the USSR.' Identical provisions are to be found in the constitutions of the union and autonomous republics comprising the Union of Soviet Socialist Republics. The Soviet judiciary, the Procurator General of the USSR, and what might loosely be called the executive branch of government—the agencies of State administration (union and autonomous republic councils of ministers, executive committees of local soviets of people's deputies)—are expressly accountable to agencies of State power. Some Soviet jurists have equated positively the extent to which a society relies upon legislation as a formal source of law with its level of societal development.[1]

Although legislation is the paramount source of law in the Soviet Union, the respective hierarchical relationships among acts containing legal rules (normative) are confused and confusing, a situation aggravated by the inconsistent and extensive use of more than 40 denominations for enactments.

Primacy of place is given to the law (*zakon*). Under the present constitutions in the USSR, the right to enact laws is reserved exclusively for the supreme soviets of the USSR and the union or autonomous republics or for 'all-people's' referenda. This includes the constitutions, which are themselves laws, whose position in the hierarchy of legislation in practical terms appear to differ only marginally from that of other laws enacted by the supreme soviets. The new Constitutions of 1977–78 in the Soviet Union were all adopted by the respective supreme soviets sitting in extraordinary sessions. Soviet doctrinal writings, however, frequently distinguish between constitutional or basic laws, on one hand, and current or ordinary laws. The USSR Supreme Court also reinforced this distinction in 1978, reminding lower courts that the right to counsel under Soviet law was a 'constitutional principle.'

The elevated status of the constitution vis-à-vis other laws enacted by supreme soviets appears to rest on two factors. All Soviet constitutions contain in their official titles the parenthetical expression 'fundamental law' (*osnovnoi zakon*), itself implying that their status is superior to other laws. Moreover, constitutional amendments (and the constitution itself) must be approved by a two-thirds majority of each chamber of the respective supreme soviets, whereas other laws require merely a simple majority vote.

To western eyes both factors seem to be somewhat technical distinctions. The Soviet Union has a single party system, and until 1987, the public record disclosed only unanimous votes cast in plenary sessions of supreme soviets. For all practical purposes, any legislation which reaches

1 See V. M. Chkhikvadze (ed) *The Soviet State and Law* (1969) pp 219–220.

the floor of a supreme soviet is likely to command overwhelming endorsement, be it consistent with the written constitution or otherwise. Moreover, there have been instances when the USSR Supreme Soviet or its Presidium enacted legislation in direct contravention of constitutional provisions without obtaining the formal technicality of an amendment. Two occurred in 1940, when the USSR Supreme Soviet increased the working day to eight hours and introduced tuition charges for certain levels of secondary and higher education. The discrepancy was repaired in 1947, when it was proposed to bring the Constitution into conformity with prevailing law. In 1966 a similar practice was followed in altering the representation of union and autonomous republics in the USSR Supreme Soviet. (It should be noted that the Supreme Soviet is 'supreme' in this domain and the guardian of its own constitution. There is no judicial review of the constitutionality of its acts, nor is the USSR Procurator General empowered to protest against unconstitutionality, though he may submit recommendations to the Presidium of the USSR Supreme Soviet on matters subject to resolution by legislation.)

The power to make laws (*zakon*) having been reserved to the supreme soviets of the USSR and the union and autonomous republics, all other enactments are classified as *podzakonnyi*, literally translated as 'sub-law' and hereinafter referred to as 'subordinate' acts or legislation. Note that we avoid the expression 'delegated legislation', for subordinate acts may be issued without delegation so long as they are 'on the basis of and in execution of' the acts of superior agencies or agencies at the same level as the issuing organs.

Even the supreme soviets adopt subordinate enactments bearing other designations. The USSR Constitution refers to 'laws of the USSR, decrees, and other acts . . .' (Art 116). The decree (*postanovlenie*) seems to be utilised in the following types of situation: (1) to fix the personnel complement of organs accountable to the USSR Supreme Soviet, its Presidium, the USSR Council of Ministers, the USSR Supreme Court, the USSR People's Control Commission; to appoint the USSR Procurator General; and to make recommendations for a new government; (2) to approve reports on the fulfilment of the State budget or to evaluate the activities of governmental bodies, for example in the foreign or domestic policy of the Soviet government; (3) to issue 'normative auxiliary acts' containing, for example, legislative instructions for other supreme soviets on the application of particular laws; (4) to deal with internal organisational matters of the supreme soviet, such as the membership of permanent commissions of the supreme soviets.

The USSR Supreme Soviet has also adopted a *Reglament* governing its internal procedures and a statute (*polozhenie*) concerning its permanent commissions. Finally, supreme soviets from time to time adopt appeals (*obrashchenie*), declarations (*deklaratsiia*), statements (*zaiavlenie*), and messages (*poslanie*) for other governments, legislatures, or peoples, especially in the domain of foreign policy. These are in no way legally binding and properly speaking are not sources of law, whatever their moral or political import, although in the early years following the October 1917 Revolution some appeals and declarations did contain normative provisions.

In quantitative terms the law-making activity of the supreme soviets is rather low. The constitutions at all levels require that they meet twice annually, although extraordinary sessions may be, and occasionally are, convoked. In the intervals between sessions, the sessions themselves usually being two to four days in duration, most of their powers are exercised by presidiums. Legal acts of presidiums are superior to those of all executive and administrative bodies, local organs or State power, judicial organs, and the Procuracy.

The USSR Constitution merely provides that the Presidium of the USSR Supreme Soviet 'shall issue edicts and adopt decrees' (Art 123) without specifying which type of act should be used for what purpose. The procedure for enacting them does not differ; the practice of the Presidium suggests that edicts are reserved for matters requiring the subsequent confirmation of the full supreme soviet and for the conferment of orders, medals, and honorary titles. Decrees are used for acts containing an interpretation of a law or edict, for matters of citizenship, and internal regulations of the Presidium itself.

Laws, edicts, and decrees are utilised to confirm a host of other all-union enactments bearing various appellations. The most important are the 'Fundamental Principles' (*osnovy*) laid down for certain branches of Soviet legislation. The 1936 USSR Constitution originally contemplated a substantial centralisation of legislation through the creation of all-union law codes. Drafts were prepared and discussed, though never published, but a 1938 Law on Court Organisation was the only one to be adopted. In 1957 the Constitution was amended to grant the union republics greater latitude in certain domains of legislation. Fourteen sets of all-union fundamental principles have been enacted since 1958, followed by union republic codes elaborating and adapting these principles to suit local conditions and peculiarities.

There are three all-union codes (*kodeks*): the Air Code, the Merchant Shipping Code, and the Customs Code. Other all-union acts of a code nature govern communications, railway transport, and inland water transport but bear the appellation 'charter' (*ustav*).

Statutes (*polozhenie*) are confirmed by organs at all levels of the State system, even within State enterprises and other economic organisations. This appears to be purely a matter of practice, and indeed the appellation is very broadly applied.[2] It is evidently expected that statutory

---

2 See D. A. Loeber 'Statutes *(Polozheniia)* of the Agencies of State Administration in the Soviet Union—An Unexplored Area of Codification' in D. D. Barry, F. J. M. Feldbrugge, and D. Lasok (eds) *Codification in the Communist World* (1975) pp 221–238.

provisions will conform to laws, edicts, decrees, decisions, regulations, and other legal acts issued by superior bodies.

In accordance with the USSR Constitution, the supreme soviets elect the government. Called the 'council of ministers' at the all-union and the union and autonomous republic levels, it is accountable to its respective supreme soviet or, in the interval between sessions, to its presidium. As 'agencies of State administration,' they, together with subordinate ministries, State committees, executive committees of local soviets, local branch agencies of administration (eg sections or administrations), and the like, adopt the vast majority of enactments in the Soviet Union, and it is this body of chiefly subordinate acts which gives rise to the greatest difficulties as regards sources of law.

Acts of the USSR Council of Ministers are issued 'on the basis of and in execution of laws of the USSR and other decisions of the USSR Supreme Soviet and its Presidium' (Art 133, USSR Const) and are binding throughout the territory of the USSR without further action by lower union or autonomous republic bodies. Since the competence of the councils of ministers extends to the entire State system, including the economy, the importance of their enactments will be readily appreciated. Article 133 of the USSR Constitution has been understood to mean that the Council of Ministers may enact new legal rules which conform to law and are within its jurisdiction. The relatively small number of laws (*zakon*) and edicts (*ukaz*) adopted by legislative bodies has given the councils of ministers broad scope to originate normative acts on their own. Acts of the USSR Council of Ministers are superior to all others adopted by agencies of State administration, and, paradoxically perhaps, even certain decisions of local soviets of people's deputies must conform to them on the ground that local soviets have some responsibilities for State administration.

The USSR Constitution provides that the councils of ministers shall adopt decrees (*postanovlenie*) and regulations (*rasporiazhenie*). Efforts to distinguish between them have occasioned much doctrinal controversy, and the failure to do so in practice has been of some consequence. The 1978 Law on the USSR Council of Ministers provides that decisions of the Council 'bearing a normative character or having important national economic and general significance' shall be issued in the form of decrees. Regulations shall appertain to 'operative and other current questions' (Art 31). In practice, both decrees and regulations contain normative prescriptions, and proposals to refine the legal terminology applied to governmental acts or to resolve the issue of publication on the basis of other criteria (eg the social importance of a particular act) so far have come to naught.[3]

---

3 For a thorough discussion of current typologies of normative acts and the implications for codification and systematisation of law, see S. V. Polenina and N. V. Sil'chenko

Enactments of ministries, State committees, and of ministers and similar officials raise analogous problems. The USSR Constitution (Art 135) empowers ministries and State committees to issue 'acts'; these ordinarily take the form of an order (*prikaz*) or instruction (*instruktsiia*) on the basis of and in execution of both laws and other decisions of the USSR Supreme Soviet and its Presidium and decrees and regulations of the USSR Council of Ministers. Moreover, the 1967 General Statute on Ministries of the USSR (point 17) authorises USSR ministers to promulgate, in addition, an instructive regulation (*ukazanie*) which is binding upon subordinate union republic ministries and upon enterprises, organisations, and institutions within the particular ministerial network. Union and autonomous republic constitutions contain analogous provisions with the addition of relevant superior bodies; eg the order of an autonomous republic minister must conform to all-union, union republic, and autonomous republic laws and other decisions of the respective supreme soviets, to decrees and regulations of USSR and union and autonomous republic councils of ministers, and to orders and instructions of union republic ministers.

USSR ministers are empowered to issue, and frequently do, joint orders and instructions with other ministers. The difference between an *instruktsiia* and an *ukazanie* is not at all clear in theory or practice, except perhaps that ministers cannot issue a joint *ukazanie*. As for orders and instructions, it would seem that orders may contain both normative and non-normative provisions, whereas instructions always are normative because they provide details concerning the elaboration of a particular law, edict, or governmental decree.

Other State bodies or officials occupying equivalent positions in the State hierarchy as ministries and ministers promulgate enactments; these are sometimes designated as orders or instructions but often bear other appellations. The State Committee of the USSR for Labour and Social Questions and the State Planning Committee of the USSR, for example,

Nauchnye osnovy tipologii normativno-pravovykh aktov v SSSR (1987). Can decrees of councils of ministers be considered a source of criminal law? The union republic criminal codes stipulate that the basis of criminal responsibility is the commission of a socially dangerous act provided for by law (*zakon*), that is, presumably a law enacted by a supreme soviet. The predominant view seems to be that councils of ministers cannot by decree define new types of crimes or fix punishments unless they act pursuant to dispositive provisions of a criminal law. The same applies to local governmental bodies. In 1964 the RSFSR Supreme Court held that rules promulgated by the executive committee of the Leningrad City Soviet could not establish criminal responsibility for the failure to return things taken on hire, as this would exceed its competence. See *Kurs sovetskogo ugolovnogo prava v shesti tomakh* (1970) I, p 157. However, departmental normative acts sometimes significantly influence the scope of the criminal law by defining, for example, the scope of admissible initiative for executive managerial personnel. See A. Iakovlev 'Vedomstvennoe ugolovnoe pravo?' *Izvestiia* 8 February 1988, p 2, cols 1–7.

issue decrees (*postanovlenie*),[4] but the State Committee of the USSR for Inventions and Discoveries issues the instructive regulation (*ukazanie*) or explanation (*raz"iasnenie*). The State Foreign Economic Commission, in an unusual formulation, has been empowered to take 'decisions in the form of regulations of the USSR Council of Ministers.' The procedure for adopting departmental enactments varies; the State Planning Committee of the USSR approves its decrees collegially, for example, whereas the heads of other State committees may do so alone or jointly with a deputy head.

Ministries and departments sometimes issue rules (*pravila*) or a *nastavlenie* which may extend to institutions and personnel of their own particular system or may be binding on all government bodies and individual citizens. In the latter case they clearly are normative in character.

Local 'agencies of State power,' the soviets of people's deputies at various levels below the supreme soviets, are empowered under the USSR Constitution (Art 148) to adopt decisions within the limits of powers granted them by legislation of the USSR and union and autonomous republics. Reference to the regulations (*rasporiazhenie*) has been deleted in the 1977 USSR Constitution and from all-union legislation amended in 1979 defining the powers of local soviets of people's deputies; nor is mention made in these enactments of the terminological designation to be used for the acts of local soviet executive committees and permanent commissions.

Other appellations for acts do arise in the course of local soviet activities. Decisions (*reshenie*) frequently confirm the statutes (*polozhenie*), provisional statutes (*vremennoe polozhenie*), or model statutes (*primernoe polozhenie*) of regulating organs attached to local soviets, and many local soviets have enacted regulations to govern their own internal procedures.

Some decisions of local soviets appertain to matters relegated to their exclusive jurisdiction by law (*zakon*), in which case the decision is an act independently operative within the soviet's territorial jurisdiction. The decision must conform to enactments of superior agencies of State power and administration. Other decisions are adopted on the basis of or in execution of acts of higher bodies. Acts of local soviets are not subject to Procuracy supervision (contra acts of their executive committees), although they can be repealed by superior soviets or suspended by the executive committees of superior soviets.

The acts of local soviet executive committees and of their departments, sections, and administrations are in all instances issued on the

4 Decrees of the USSR State Planning Committee are binding upon all ministries, departments, and other organisations. The chairman of Gosplan may issue an order or an *ukazanie*, but these are binding only upon organisations and institutions within the Gosplan network.

basis of or in execution of acts of superior bodies, the latter having the right to annul them and the Procuracy the right to supervise their conformity to law in force. Such acts may and do contain normative prescriptions, and the same evidently is true of orders (*prikaz*) and regulations issued by the heads of departments or administrations of local soviet executive committees. Doctrinal writings contain references to so-called 'obligatory decisions' (*obiazatel'noe reshenie*) of local soviets, ie normative enactments binding upon individual citizens and officials which must be published within a designated period after promulgation. Current legislation on local soviets does not, however, contain a terminological distinction of this nature, and it is possible the doctrinal references invoke a concept of legislation from the 1930s.

A local soviet itself has enterprises, institutions, and organisations within its jurisdiction whose directors are empowered to adopt orders and regulations. Depending on their hierarchical status, such enactments may be annulled or suspended by the local soviets if they are contrary to legislation.

Acts of social organisations

The concept of a 'social organisation' in the Soviet Union is a very broad one. It embraces voluntary combinations of citizens, ranging from the Communist Party of the Soviet Union, trade unions, the Communist Youth League, collective farms, philatelic societies, unions of writers, artists, musicians, bibliophiles, or composers, tourism societies, the Red Cross and Red Crescent, and the like. Their significance has increased appreciably in recent years with the emphasis on transferring State functions to social organisations as part of the transition to the all-people's State and eventually the 'self-administration' of a communist society.

Some social organisations are of interest in connection with sources of law because they have been empowered to issue normative rules, or may issue them with the sanction of the State. In all instances this right is founded on law, and consequently such enactments are classified as subordinate legislation which usually must be confirmed by or registered with competent State agencies or issued with their previous authorisation. Trade unions, for example, issue instructions, rules, and explanations in respect of the application of labour legislation with the approval or sanction of the USSR Council of Ministers, adopt normative acts independently in regard to certain aspects of social insurance or the administration of rest homes, and frequently adopt joint decrees together with the State Committee of the USSR for Labour and Social Questions. The decree (*postanovlenie*) is the principal designation employed for trade union enactments.

In 1988 the Fourth All-Union Congress of Collective Farmers adopted a new model collective farm charter, subsequently approved by joint decree of the USSR Council of Ministers and the Central Committee of the Communist Party, whose provisions are binding on all collective farms and farmers, and also on those State and social organs having legal relationships with them. Individual collective farm charters must conform to its provisions while adapting and elaborating them to their particular situation. When collective farms adopt acts pursuant to their charter (and therefore sanctioned by the State) on such matters as farm labour discipline, holidays, wages and bonuses, and work norms, these have legally-binding force and are regarded as a source of law.

The Central Union of Consumer Co-operatives issues, pursuant to 1924 legislation, legal acts independently without their being confirmed by State organs. These relate principally to the operations of the consumer co-operatives and include decrees, instructions, model charters, statutes and instructive regulations.

Some Soviet jurists are of the view that 'normative contracts' sanctioned by the State may serve as 'a form of expressing' sources of law. This is a carefully drawn formulation; they have in mind collective contracts concluded between the administration of an enterprise, on one hand, and the local trade union committee, which acts in the name of the labour collective. Such contracts are discussed at general meetings of the labour collective, formally signed, and registered with the nearest local soviet executive committee. Certain provisions of the contract relating to the payment of wages are of a normative character and arguably bear analogy with normative rules emanating from social organisations.

Enactments of the Communist Party raise special considerations in the context of sources of law. The Union of Soviet Socialist Republics is a single-party State, the Party being constitutionally designated as 'the guiding and directing force of Soviet society and the nucleus of its political system and State and social organisations' (Art 6). Party organs adopt or issue resolutions (*rezoliutsiia*), decisions (*reshenie*), decrees (*postanovlenie*), programmes (*programma*), rules (*ustav*), directives (*direktive*), appeals (*obrashchenie*), informational notifications (*informatsionnoe soobschchenie*), statutes (*polozhenie*), instructions (*instruktsiia*), circulars (*tsirkuliar*) and letters (*pis'mo*). Most of these are concerned exclusively with internal Party matters and are of no concern to us here. But Party programmes, resolutions, decisions, and decrees, although not per se sources of law because they do not emanate from the State, nonetheless provide programmatic context for State-enacted normative acts and frequently are expressly referred to in preambles of legislative texts. Manuals reproducing the texts of Soviet legislation often publish key Party documents as well, and at various times in Soviet legal history some jurists have recommended that the official systematisations of normative acts should be supplemented by a volume of programmatic Party documents to illustrate their political origins and context.

Some decrees are adopted jointly by the Government, Party, and on occasion, trade union organs. There are jurists who would elevate such joint decrees to a special status because they 'directly reflect the Party's role in the development of law.'[5] The predominant view seems to that joint Party-State decrees enjoy a symbolic significance but formally speaking are not superior to government decrees adopted by bodies at the same or higher levels. As State functions are transferred to social organisations in the 'all-people's State', the place of Party vis-à-vis formal governmental enactments doubtless will receive further consideration.

Acts of State Arbitrazh

State and departmental arbitrazh are networks of tribunals having exclusive jurisdiction over economic disputes between State, co-operative, and other social enterprises, organisations, and institutions. Under a 1979 Law, State Arbitrazh of the USSR Council of Ministers and union republic state arbitrazhes issue instructive regulations (*instruktivnoe ukazanie*); confirm special conditions (*osoboe uslovie*) for the delivery of particular types of consumer or production goods; issue instructions (*instruktsiia*) on the procedure for accepting products, rules (*pravila*) for considering economic disputes, and a statute (*polozhenie*) on an arbitration tribunal; and issue an explanation (*raz"iasnenie*) to ministries, State committees, and departments regarding the application of decisions of the USSR or union republic councils of ministers regulating economic activity. These are binding on the entities concerned and are regarded as subordinate acts whose effect extends throughout the USSR.

Acts of military commands

During periods of martial law, military councils or commands may be authorised to promulgate normative acts. In the Second World War Soviet military authorities were empowered to promulgate decrees (*postanovlenie*) and regulations (*rasporiazhenie*) on certain issues, and a State Defence Committee issued more than 10,000 decrees and regulations on general matters affecting the life of the country and the pursuit of the war.

---

5 K. S. Batygin (ed) *Soviet Labour Law and Principles of Civil Law* (1972) pp 10–11.

Court judgments and guiding explanations

The supremacy of the legislative branch in the Soviet Union and the absence of any power of judicial review over the constitutionality of acts means that, formally speaking, the courts are charged with the application of legislation to cases within their jurisdiction. Strictly speaking, Soviet doctrine denies that court judgments in individual cases, at whatever level of the judicial hierarchy rendered, are a precedent in futuro; consequently, they cannot be a source of law.

The objections raised against 'precedent' in Soviet doctrinal writings are several: it would diminish the role of legislation; it would give scope for judicial arbitrariness; and it would encourage a mechanical concentration on analogous elements in cases to the detriment of their individual distinguishing features.[6] But 'judicial practice' is not ignored in the Soviet legal system and in fact often plays a creative and unusual role in the development of law. Many appellate court judgments, rulings, and decrees are reported in supreme court bulletins and other law journals, often accompanied by specially printed cards reproducing the case headnote so that lawyers may keep their own files of judicial practice. There are annual surveys commenting on judicial practice in particular branches of law, and commentaries on codes of law contain references to individual reported cases. Procurators, judges, investigators, and policemen are enjoined to follow case reports in order to familiarise themselves with errors which higher courts correct when reviewing judgments. But the courts are regarded as interpreting and applying law in this regard, not 'creating' law, and hence Soviet textbooks generally discuss the effect of court judgments under the rubric 'interpretation of law.' Many common lawyers nonetheless will suspect that Soviet courts, just as many continental jurisdictions, will tend to hold their previous judgments in esteem even though in no way obliged to follow them. Soviet jurists on rare occasions actually have used the expression 'precedent' (*pretsedent*) with regard to cases whose outcome is looked upon as a highly desirable one.[7] Presumably this would mean merely that other

---

6 In the preface to an exhaustive index of reported cases involving criminal law and procedure decided by the USSR and RSFSR supreme courts the editors caution: 'However, it would be incorrect to consider rulings and decrees of superior courts as a standard or model for deciding other analogous cases. This would be recognition of the practice of "judicial precedent", which would diminish the role of legislation in the struggle against criminality and give scope for arbitrariness, would signify the mechanical carrying over of one decision, without taking into account individual peculiarities, to another which though analogous has its own specific features that must be considered in resolving it.' S. V. Borodin (ed)*Voprosy ugolovnogo prava i protsessa v praktike verkhovnykh sudov SSSR i RSFSR (1938–1969 gg)* (2nd edn, 1971) p 5.

7 P. Stavisskii 'Muzhestvo i zakon,' *Izvestiia*, 30 March 1971 p 3; translated in J. N. Hazard, W. E. Butler, and P. B. Maggs *The Soviet Legal System* (3rd edn, 1977) pp 466–468.

courts ought to find the result and method of reaching it a useful one to follow.

Comprehensive as they are, Soviet codes of law nonetheless are not exhaustive, and Soviet courts have acted creatively to fill 'gaps' in the law. The Soviet law of obligations, especially that portion we associate with the law of tort, was from the 1920-50s substantially shaped by decisions of the USSR and RSFSR Supreme Courts, which were then treated virtually as if part of the Civil Code and subsequently were introduced into the Code with no discernible difference in their actual operation.[8] The law of necessary defence owes much to court decisions and the guiding explanations of the Plenum of the USSR Supreme Court, which thrice since 1956 have altered the threshold and substance of that principle.[9] Under the 1957 statute and 1979 law on the USSR Supreme Court, the powers of the court to act creatively have been circumscribed, but Soviet jurists continue to debate actively the role of judicial practice in the process of law creation.[10]

The question of whether courts 'make law' in the Soviet Union also arises in a special context: the binding guiding explanations (*rukovodiashchee raz"iasnenie*) which the Plenum of the USSR, union republic, and autonomous republic supreme courts are empowered to issue 'concerning questions of the application of legislation which arise during the consideration of judicial cases' (Art 3, USSR Supreme Court Law). This formulation would seem to narrow still further the wording of the 1957 USSR Supreme Court Statute and dispose of once and for all any law-creating functions the supreme courts may have arrogated under pre-1957 legislation:[11] the classic instance was a lengthy 1943 guiding explanation augmenting the civil code provisions in tort; many cases could be decided only by looking to the guiding explanation for the applicable general rules. But even under the 1957 formulation there were complaints that the court was 'legislating' rather than interpreting and applying the law.[12]

Quite apart from the question of whether guiding explanations may

8 See B. Rudden 'The Role of the Courts and Judicial Style Under the Soviet Civil Codes' in Barry, Feldbrugge, and Lasok (eds) *Codification in the Communist World* (1975) pp 317-331.
9 W. E. Butler, 'Necessary Defense, Judge-made Law, and Soviet Man' in Butler, Maggs, and Quigley, *Law After Revolution* (1988) pp 99-130.
10 On the early debates see J. N. Hazard 'The Soviet Court as a Source of Law' Washington Law Review, XXIV (1949) 80-90. For the recent period, see S. N. Bratus (ed) *Sudebnaia praktika v sovetskoi pravovoi sisteme* (1975); D. D. Barry and C. Barner-Barry 'The USSR Supreme Court and Guiding Explanations of Civil Law, 1962-1971' in D. Barry, W. E. Butler, and G. Ginsburgs (eds) *Contemporary Soviet Law* (1974) pp 69-83; id 'The USSR Supreme Court and the Systematization of Soviet Criminal Law', in Barry, Feldbrugge, and Lasok (eds) *Codification in the Communist World* (1975) pp 1-22.
11 See I. B. Novitskii *Istochniki sovetskogo grazhdanskogo prava* (1959) pp 133-156.
12 I. D. Perlov (ed) *Organizatsionnoe rukovodstvo sudami v SSSR* (1966) pp 57-59.

contain new rules of law, Article 3 seems to mean that the USSR Supreme Court, as the highest body in the Soviet judicial system, is empowered, just as any other supreme organ, to issue normative acts binding within that system on lower courts. The binding effect of guiding explanations extends to lower courts, other agencies, and to officials who apply the law for which an explanation is given; since any person may have recourse to the courts, they therefore constitute a source of law.[13] The texts of guiding explanations, it should be added, are published cumulatively in book form; in the instance of the USSR Supreme Court, the volume contains texts from the period 1924 to date, amended as necessary, those items being omitted which have been repealed or replaced.[14] Guiding explanations are frequently cited by the courts, together with legislation, when deciding cases.

Soviet doctrinal writings also make use of cases, both published and unpublished reports, to illustrate, trace, or comment upon the development of the law.

Doctrine

The teachings and writings of jurists are not regarded as a source of law in the Soviet Union nor, so far as the present writer can determine, has it ever been the practice for a Soviet court to cite the published works of a Soviet jurist when issuing a decree or judgment. As trained lawyers, of course, Soviet judges are aware of doctrinal views and doubtless are influenced by them; indeed, Soviet advocates sometimes expressly refer to doctrine and commentary in their oral pleadings. At higher levels of the judicial system there exists a formal system of 'scientific advisory councils' made up of outside experts or jurists attached to universities, academies of sciences, law institutes, and other legal agencies. The scientific advisory council of the USSR Supreme Court, for example, consists of some 30 jurists who offer opinions and guidance on summaries of judicial practice and on draft guiding explanations to be issued by the court.

In 1957 the Chancery Division of the High Court in the United Kingdom accepted testimony, somewhat incredulously to be sure, from an expert witness to the effect that Soviet courts may construe legislation by reference to the writings and speeches of prominent leaders of the Soviet Union, in this case utterances by V. I. Lenin.[15] Although the present writer regards that incredulity as wholly justified and can find no reported case where such a practice has been followed, in the very

13 For this argument base on the 1957 Supreme Court statute, see O. S. Ioffe *Sovetskoe grazhdanskoe pravo* (1967) pp 54–55.
14 For example, *Sbornik postanovlenii plenuma verkhovnogo suda SSSR 1924–1983* (1984).
15 *Re Banque des Marchands de Moscou (Koupetschesky)* [1957] 3 All ER 182.

early days following the 1917 October Revolution, judges in remote regions of the country were instructed to fill gaps in the law by reference to the works of Karl Marx and V. I. Lenin as 'undoubted sources of law and justice.'[16]

Custom

Soviet attitudes toward customary law have been ambivalent. Under the Imperial Russian Government, customary rules had been widely applied in property, inheritance, family, and other legal relationships. Native courts and customs were supplanted in the early 1920s by Soviet courts and written legislation. Customs deemed primitive and reactionary were made illegal by many union republics. Chapter XI of the 1960 RSFSR Criminal Code, for example, still contains articles punishing the payment and acceptance of bride price, compelling or obstructing the marriage of a woman, concluding a marital agreement with a person under marital age, and bigamy or polygamy when such acts are committed in autonomous republics or other localities where the acts constitute survivals of local customs.

Contemporary Soviet legislation expressly sanctions the application of 'custom' only in two instances. The 1968 USSR Merchant Shipping Code allows the inclusion of contract clauses relating to the application of merchant shipping customs when the Code permits departures from its own rules (Art 15) or authorises recourse to 'international merchant shipping customs' if the law governing aspects of general average is 'incomplete' (Art 251). The RSFSR Civil Code stipulates as a general rule that obligations must be performed in the proper manner and within the prescribed period laid down by law, planning directive or contract, or, in the absence thereof, by 'customary requirements' (Art 168). The expression 'customary requirements' is understood to mean 'business usages' applied in the operations of Soviet industrial, trade, or other economic organisations, in the professional affairs of citizens, or in foreign trade transactions. The expression 'customary requirements' also appears in Article 245 of the RSFSR Civil Code in relation to the quality of articles sold, where it is construed by the commentators as meaning 'suitable for ordinary use.'

The 1968 Merchant Shipping Code further provides in Articles 134 and 135 for the application of periods or rates 'customarily applied' at ports in the absence of an agreement of the parties in respect of additional laytime, demurrage, or an award for loading a vessel ahead of schedule. Since as regards Soviet vessels these matters are regulated

16 I. B. Sternik 'V. I. Lenin i pervye sudebnye dekrety' Sovetskoe gosudarstvo i pravo, no. 4 (1976) p 112, fn 4.

either by law or plan and in actual fact are governed by the technical equipment used in ports, it is argued by some civilists that 'custom' in this instance amounts to technical rules sanctioned by legislation.[17]

To some customs the Soviet legal system is indifferent. A textbook example relates to recovery of a gambling debt: although such a debt is not recoverable at law, if paid voluntarily the law will not compel the recipient to reimburse the payer. In other instances traditional and local customs deemed compatible with the Soviet social order apparently are still applied to modify written codes. In the Carpathian region of the USSR it is said to be the custom for a daughter to continue to reside with her parents after marriage and a son to move to the home of his wife's parents, the object being to preserve the financial independence of the daughter. Her brothers are said to observe the custom by refraining from making claim to any share of inheritance to which they may be entitled by law.[18] There also is some evidence to suggest that traditional customs may be applied in family law matters within communities inhabiting the Caucasus or Soviet Central Asia by people's courts as part of an accommodation to local mores.[19]

The formation of customary rules and the relationship between law and tradition are attracting the renewed interest of Soviet jurists, who are increasingly concerned with the positive role customs may have in ordering modern society. Socialist traditions and rules, it is maintained, are in the process of formation and should be expected to have an enhanced position in a society wherein law ultimately will die out.

Rules of socialist community life

Although these rules are referred to in Soviet legislation, including the Soviet constitutions, they are still in the process of evolution, and their place in the legal system is much debated. They are commonly discussed under the rubric 'sources of law,' but the predominant view seems to be that such rules are not legal norms. Rather they are rules of social morality governing the conduct of individuals in their work and their daily life which are reinforced by public opinion and interact with and support legal rules. The meaning of 'rules of socialist community life' attracted much attention when the expression was introduced in Article 130 of the 1936 USSR Constitution. The same obligation of citizens '... to respect the rules of socialist community life' has been carried over to Article 59 of the 1977-78 Soviet constitutions. Similar provisions

---

17 Ioffe, note 13, above, p 53; 'Trade customs' also may be applied by the USSR Arbitration Court to disputes which it considers. See the 1988 Reglament of the Arbitration Court attached to the USSR Chamber of Commerce and Industry.
18 This example is given by M. N. Kulazhnikov *Pravo, traditsii i obychai* (1972) p 62.
19 'Crime and the Courts in Tadzhikistan' Central Asian Review, XII (1964) 185.

are incorporated in the 1961 all-union fundamental principles of civil legislation (Art 5); the 1964 RSFSR Code of Civil Procedure provides that inculcating respect for such rules is itself a task of civil procedure (Art 2); and the 1979 laws on the USSR Supreme Court (Art 1) and on the Procuracy of the USSR (Art 2) are among recent legislation incorporating reference to these rules.

The extent to which a duty to rescue may exist in Soviet law or to which compensation may be awarded for injuries sustained while rescuing human life has in considerable measure involved a discussion of the nature of the rules of socialist community life (see chapter 9, below). While some commentators believe that breaches of the rules of socialist community life may give rise to liability in tort, Soviet legislation more commonly provides that 'measures of social pressure' may be applied to offenders by social organisations specially empowered. Comrades' courts and people's guards were created in part for this purpose. Soviet comrades' courts consider, inter alia, cases involving such antisocial behaviour as the failure to observe labour safety rules, an unworthy attitude towards women or parents, drunkenness, and the like. The people's guard detachments assist, as a volunteer auxiliary police force, in securing enforcement of both the letter of the law and the rules of socialist community life. Since both the comrades' courts and people's guard are themselves social organisations, their actions in upholding rules of socialist community life are not regarded in Soviet doctrine as transforming these rules into legal norms ipso facto.

In the broadest sense rules of socialist community life embrace all rules of social behaviour, including law, morality, manners, traditions, and so forth. A partial enumeration of these is to be found in the Rules of the Communist Party of the Soviet Union (Art 59) adopted in 1961 by the XXII Party Congress.[20]

International treaties

The USSR Constitution (Art 29) and constitutions of the constituent republics provide that 'relations of the USSR with other states shall be built on the basis of . . . good-faith fulfilment of obligations arising from generally recognised principles and norms of international law and from international treaties concluded by the USSR.' The expression 'international treaties' embraces all such interstate, intergovernmental, or interdepartmental documents irrespective of their form and appellation (treaty, agreement, convention, pact, protocol, exchange of letters or notes) or other forms and appellations (see Art 1, 1978 Law on the

---

[20] The Rules of the CPSU are translated in W. E. Butler *Basic Documents on the Soviet Legal System* (2nd edn, 1988).

Procedure for the Conclusion, Execution, and Denunciation of International Treaties of the USSR).

The rule laid down in the various fundamental principles and union republic codes is that if an international treaty to which the USSR is a party contains rules inconsistent with Soviet legislation, then the provisions of the international treaty shall prevail. Edicts ratifying international treaties are regarded as special normative acts conferring internal legal effect on treaty provisions.[1] Both the USSR Supreme Court (Art 5, 1979 law) and the USSR Procuracy (Art 11, 1979 law) are empowered to settle questions arising out of international treaties of the USSR respectively if such questions are within their powers or competence.

Publication and entry of legislation into force

The publication and entry into force of legislation are usually two closely interrelated processes. Publication is associated with the 'presumption of knowledge of the law'; if an enactment has been brought to the information of the general public in a duly established procedure—ordinarily printing the act in a designated official gazette—no one may plead ignorance of the law as a pretext for failure to observe its prescriptions. Publication in printed form also may establish the official text of the enactment, provide a precise benchmark in time from which the enactment takes effect, and enable the legislator to communicate most effectively with those to whom his enactments are addressed.

The highest all-union and union republic agencies of State power and administration issue their own official gazettes. The USSR Supreme Soviet and its Presidium issue a weekly gazette, the *Vedomosti verkhovnogo soveta SSSR*, which appears both in the Russian language and in the languages of the union republics. The USSR Council of Ministers publishes its enactments in an irregular gazette, the *Sobranie postanovlenii Pravitel'stva SSSR*. The union republics have equivalent gazettes, combining them in a few cases into a single publication. Some ministries and departments issue their own gazettes, for example, the State Committee of the USSR for Labour and Social Questions and the State Committee of the USSR for Public Education. Since 1972, the *Biulleten' normativnykh aktov ministerstv i vedomstv SSSR* has existed as an interdepartmental gazette for departmental materials of more general significance. At the lower level the situation is less satisfactory. Soviets of people's deputies in a few large cities, such as Moscow and Leningrad, publish their decisions in bulletins. Most, however, rely on local news-

---

1 A. N. Talalaev *Mezhdunarodnye dogovory v sovremennom mire* (1973) p 64. Precisely how international treaties become a part of Soviet law has become the subject of renewed debate among both Soviet international and constitutional lawyers. For a comparative lawyer's view, see S. L. Zivs *Istochniki prava* (1981) pp 221–236.

papers to carry unofficial information about or texts of their decisions.

At the all-union and republic levels, certain newspapers have been officially designated as gazettes; the texts they publish have the same status as those which appear in *Vedomosti* or the *SP*. In cases of special urgency, acts may be promulgated by radio or transmitted by telegraph.

Most enactments, however, do not appear in the official gazettes described above. Either they are issued by organs which do not publish a gazette or they are deemed to be of narrow interest, albeit normative in character.[2] In these cases publication takes the form of circulation to the relevant departments and institutions, with the result that materials of general applicability or importance often are inaccessible to officials, jurists, or citizens who need knowledge of them. This practice is not easy to reconcile with the presumption of knowledge of the law. The criterion of 'normativity' is difficult to apply in any event, and acts published or distributed to a limited circle do not become part of the professional, scholarly, or ordinary dialogue and discussion essential to an effective evaluation of their wisdom or implementation, so vital to a democratic order. While some Soviet jurists claim that considerations of 'state or military secrecy' may justify restricting the publication or circulation of certain acts, there are no well-defined criteria or definitions for imposing this standard. The general position in Soviet doctrine seems to be that the absence of wide publication of a legal act does not affect its legal force or the significance of its prescriptions. An unpublished normative act is binding, but only on those to whom it is officially disclosed.[3] Some union republics have made express reference to 'secret' legislation in their enactments governing the procedure for the publication of legislation.[4]

Three different approaches have been followed in Soviet legal history with regard to the actual date of the entry of legislation into force. The first was the principle of immediate entry into force as of the date of publication in an official source. This meant that an act published in Moscow would be deemed to be in effect throughout the entire country irrespective of whether other areas actually had knowledge of the act. Dissatisfaction with this practice led in the early 1920s to the principle that enactments entered into force on the date they were officially received at the executive committee of the local soviet or similar institution. Depending on the frequency and reliability of the post, enactments

---

2 Some ministries have issued excellent collections, systematically arranged, of their own enactments. See O. Kulistikova 'Podgotovka sbornikov otraslevykh normativnykh aktov' *Khoziaistvo i pravo* no 9 (1987) pp 52–55. But lengthy delays are reported in the publication of materials in the *Biulleten' normativnykh aktov ministerstv i vedomstv*, such that sometimes vital enactments are obsolete before publication.
3 A. S. Pigolkin (ed) *Opublikovanie normativnykh aktov* (1978) p 35.
4 For example, the Turkmen SSR. See the decree of 14 May 1959 translated in Soviet Statutes and Decisions XII (1975/76) 214.

entered into effect on various dates throughout the country. 'Knowledge of the law' was more realistically observed under this practice, but courts experienced difficulty in knowing precisely what the state of the law was at any given time.[5] Current practice seeks to strike a balance between actual knowledge of the law and uniformity of legal regulation. Normative enactments of the USSR Supreme Soviet and its Presidium enter into effect ten days after their publication either in the *Vedomosti* or in the newspaper *Izvestiia*, whichever first occurs, unless the enactment provides otherwise. Other enactments enter into force on the date they are received by the relevant officials or departments, unless the enactment provides otherwise.

Governmental enactments follow a slightly different pattern. Normative decrees are published in the *SP*: unless they provide otherwise, decrees enter into effect when adopted. Regulations also enter into effect when adopted but are not subject to publication in the *SP*. Both decrees and regulations not published in the *SP* or the press may be published in other printed publications if appropriate authorisation is given. Irrespective of publication in any media, governmental decrees are circulated to a list of ministries and departments specially maintained. The publication of ministerial and departmental enactments, and those of local agencies of State power and administration, evidently is not governed by general legislation and, as noted above, ordinarily appears only in the departmental or local gazettes already mentioned, or in unofficial specialised departmental journals.

Translation of enactments into indigenous languages

As a multinational state containing more than 200 different national groupings, the Soviet Union confronts special problems in making legislation linguistically accessible to the populace. Many official gazettes during the 1920s were published in two or more languages, including Russian, although it is not always evident whether the Russian text represented a translation or was the original language in which the legislator worked.

A distinction is to be drawn between all-union and union republic legislation in this respect. From 1938-60 the *Vedomosti SSSR* was issued in Russian and all other union republic languages. Translations of the Russian text were made by a special department of the *Vedomosti* editorial board. From 1960-65 this pattern was modified; all-union acts translated into union republic languages were published in the union

---

5 Pigolkin, note 3, above, p 21; A. A. Tille 'The Publication of Normative Acts in the Early Years of Soviet Power (1917-1922)' Soviet Statutes and Decisions XII (1975) 10-28; R. M. Romanov 'Publication of All-Union Legislation: Experience of the Early Years' ibid, pp 51-74.

republic gazettes together with union republic legislation. This procedure raised problems. Some objected to all-union legislation being brought to general notice in the name of the republic and not of the USSR. Variant texts sometimes occurred which, in the absence of a simultaneously issued Russian text, gave rise to ambiguities and doubt as to when the act entered into force. Translation difficulties increased after responsibility for preparing the text had been transferred to the union republics. In 1965 the earlier system was restored with modifications: special editions of *Vedomosti SSSR* are issued for each union republic in the respective languages, each version having its own editorial staff and translators.

Acts of the USSR Council of Ministers and of ministries and departments are treated likewise. The general practice has been to issue these only in Russian, although in some union republics unofficial translations of individual acts may be published.

Most union republic official gazettes are issued in Russian and the principle languages of the people inhabiting the area.

The authenticity of the legislative texts in various languages seems to differ widely. In some union republics it is the custom to prepare draft legislation in the Russian language and then translate the draft into the union republic language so that the legislator may consider and enact both versions. Both texts in this case are considered equally authentic. Some jurists would go farther and argue, for example, that the translations of all-union acts into union republic languages also are equally authentic even though the translation takes place after the Russian text has been enacted, ie at the stage of preparation for publication. These jurists point out that the translations are prepared, edited, and 'visaed' by executive personnel of the Presidium of the USSR Supreme Soviet and then published in the official gazette in the name of the USSR Supreme Soviet.[6] Although they are correct in suggesting that no legal norm establishes the inequality of various language texts and in emphasising the constitutional requirement of the equality of nations in the USSR, the very difference in the process of preparing bilingual texts of legislation before or after enactment would seem to confer official status on those texts formally endorsed by the legislator as distinct from those subsequently translated by non-elected civil servants.

Discrepancies between the original language of an enactment and its translation do cause problems in the application of Soviet legislation. The Tadzhik translation of *tsennye bumagi* as 'currency' (*denezhnye bumagi*) narrowed the scope of Soviet legislation considerably; several Tadzhik translations confused 'duty' (*obiazannost'*) and 'obligations' (*obiazatel'stvo*). Translations into the Azerbaidzhan language rendered 'legal transaction' (*sdelka*) as 'agreement' and the 'termination of

6 Pigolkin, note 3, above, p 125.

marriage' as the 'dissolution of marriage'; there are numerous other examples.

Techniques of law reform

It will be apparent from our account of the sources of law in the Soviet Union, the inconsistent and extensive use of denominations for enactments, the exceptionally large number of entities empowered to 'legislate,' the need to distinguish between normative and non-normative enactments, and the problems of making enactments physically and linguistically accessible, that law reform has become a matter of priority and urgency.

The amounts of legislation involved are stupendous by any yardstick. Soviet law reformers in the early 1960s mentioned, for the USSR and RSFSR alone, figures in the order of 450,000–600,000 normative acts. A 20-volume chronological collection of prevailing legislation compiled for the Kazakh SSR for the period 1920–69 included 3,292 enactments. To reach this sum Kazakh law reformers reviewed 150,000 enactments, including 50,000 of all-union origin.[7] At lower levels of the hierarchy the number of enactments multiplies. In April 1975 the State Committee of the Estonian SSR Council of Ministers for Publishing Houses, Printing, and the Book Trade reviewed its own normative acts for the preceding 12 years and turned up 2,500 orders (*prikazy*) issued during this period. Structural sub-divisions of the State Committee had produced even more, and the review did not take in other *types* of enactments issued, such as instructions (*instruktsiia*).

Efforts to compile comprehensive systematic and chronological collections of all-union and union republic legislation originated in the early 1920s and, after periods of intermittent activity in the 1930–60s, were renewed in the late 1960s and 1970s. The principal impetus for this type of law reform—as distinct from substantive law reform, dealt with elsewhere in this study—has been the economic reforms of 1965 and their subsequent modifications (chapter 13, below), which have led to an enlargement of the legal profession (chapter 6, below) and attention to the state of the statute book: 'It is no accident,' as an early Soviet law reformer commented, that revolutionary legality arises out of economic necessity.[8] The devolution of a greater role in planning and more discretion in contractual relationships to State enterprises and institutions

---

7 S. B. Baisalov, V. M. Levchenko, and Kh. B Akhmetov 'K voprosu ob uluchshenii normotvorcheskoi deiatel' nosti gosudarstvennykh organov Kazakhskoi SSR' Izvestiia akademiia nauk Kazakhskoi SSR; seriia obshchestvovaniia, no. 3 (1970)
8 See W. E. Butler 'Toward a *Svod Zakonov* for the Union of Soviet Socialist Republics' in Barry, Feldbrugge, and Lasok (eds) *Codification in the Communist World* (1975) pp 89–111.

has been accompanied by an attempt to rationalise the general body of rules and directives which channel the exercise of that discretion, that is to rely increasingly upon law and the legal system—rules, procedural formalities, sanctions, and enforcement procedures—to make the economic system work. Among other things, this presupposes that competent legal advice is available at all levels of economic and State administration and that legal personnel have ready access to a comprehensive, well-ordered statute book.[9]

A basic USSR decree of 23 December 1970, 'On Legal Work in the National Economy,' followed by analogous union republic enactments, authorised the preparation and publication of a systematic *Sobranie* of all-union legislation in force and equivalent union republic collections. At the XXV Congress of the Communist Party of the Soviet Union in February 1976 endorsement was given to a *Svod zakonov* of the Soviet State, that is, to a 'Digest' of prevailing legislation in systematised and consolidated form. The all-union *Sobranie* has been completed in 50 volumes, and the *Svod zakonov* of the USSR, issued in a looseleaf format and completed in December 1986 in 11 volumes, is being followed by union republic *svody* of the same format. The *Svod zakonov* of the USSR is an official publication of the Presidium of the USSR Supreme Soviet and of the USSR Council of Ministers. Many of the enactments included appear in a consolidated format together with amendments and consequently represent the most current official text of a legislative act. However, the *Svod zakonov* is not exhaustive, even for the bodies which issue it. Included are 'legislative acts and the major joint decrees of the Central Committee of the CPSU and USSR Council of Ministers and decrees of the Government of the USSR of a general normative character.' Looseleaf supplements are irregular.

Although our concern in this chapter has been with contemporary sources of law in the Soviet legal system, there have been significant developments in attitudes towards sources of law. While legislation remains paramount, the tension sometimes evident in earlier decades to regard legislation and especially codification as a kind of intellectual transformation that contraposes traditional patterns of values and government against substantive innovation seems to have evaporated. Law as an instrument of social engineering, so fundamental to Marxian theories of law, is by no means neglected, but there is greater realisation that legal change requires not merely directives but also cohesion, system, rationality, and stability within the system of legislation. The concern of modern Soviet policy-makers and law reformers is not principally to remove the encrustations of obsolete legal norms as an invidious

---

9 Butler 'Techniques of Law Reform in the Soviet Union' Current Legal Problems XXXIII (1978) 207–225.

influence of the dead hand of the past upon the present but to make the legal system work, insofar as possible, responsively as a system to meet the demands being placed upon it. To the extent that in the short term there continues to be a disposition to transfer State functions to non-State bodies, custom as means of social regulation will in all likelihood be accorded greater attention. Sources of law in the Soviet legal system, or at least doctrines respecting them, are not immutable, but rather change in response to major and minor alterations in political institutions, social conditions, legal philosophy, and perceptions of the way legal institutions actually function in contrast to the manner in which they are supposed to function.

Chapter 5

Soviet legal education

The education or 'formation' of the legal profession in the Soviet Union is of great importance to an understanding of that country's legal system. It is in the law schools that the knowledge, skills, and values of the jurist are initially inculcated, often to be followed by a period of further training or 'apprenticeship' in a law office, enterprise, or legal agency.

To understand a lawyer from a foreign legal system, how he conceptualises law and reasons in juristic categories, one must have some familiarity with the way he has been educated to perform legal or other roles in society. The teaching of law in turn is influenced by considerations of the kinds of lawyer which educational institutions seek to produce and the values and skills they undertake to implant.

HISTORICAL BACKGROUND

Ideas about legal education were in turmoil during the early years following the 1917 October Revolution. Throughout 1918 university law courses continued to be taught essentially as they had been before the Revolution, presumably taking due account of the new government's dismantling of the Tsarist courts, laws, and legal order. The extent to which expectations of a rapid 'dying out' or 'withering away' of law may have affected early attitudes toward legal education is debatable, but there was no doubt in the minds of educational policy-makers that the instructional plans extant at the universities were obsolete and non-Marxian.[1] In August 1918 the Soviet authorities altered admission requirements to make university learning accessible to everyone, irrespective of their social status. For students of proletarian origin the reform was inadequate, since most were ill-prepared to undertake university work. By early 1919 it was decided to train legal personnel elsewhere for employment in Soviet institutions. The university law faculties were formally abolished and replaced by faculties of social sciences (FON), which offered, inter alia, courses for judicial and

---

1 Some were openly hostile to legal education per se. M. N. Pokrovskii commented, when the law faculties were abolished: 'the science of law was an attractive jacket which concealed the enslavement of hundreds of millions by tens of thousands . . . of course, for socialist Russia all such "sciences" are completely useless.' See Narodnoe prosveshchenie nos. 23–25, 31 (1919).

administrative personnel on Soviet law. The early teaching syllabi for the FON were prepared by the political-legal section of the Socialist Academy of Social Sciences, founded in 1918. The Academy itself offered advanced lectures in law during 1918–19 to some 400 evening students, of whom 50 were regular attendees.[2] In many places 'Workers' Faculties' (*rabfak*) were formed in 1919–20 to provide secondary-level education on a Marxist basis for students of proletarian background who aspired to higher education. In Autumn 1921 legislation was enacted to give children of proletarian origin preference in admission to educational institutions.

The FON offered courses on the history of State and law, the development of political and legal thought, State law of the Soviet Republic, social law, criminal sociology and policy, labour law and social policy, the history of international law and international relations, and social hygiene and sanitation. The introduction of the NEP in 1921 brought a partial restoration and adaptation of legal institutions previously known in Imperial Russia, such as the Procuracy, further stabilisation of the court system, and an urgent need for codifying and systematising legislation. As the demand for trained legal cadres within the State apparatus intensified, the Workers' Faculties and FON were supplemented by the widespread use of short-term (usually four to six months) courses on the basic principles of new Soviet legislation and codes.[3] The FON were officially abolished in 1924 (though some continued to operate until 1926) and their legal sections were superseded by Faculties of Soviet Law formed at the I Moscow University, Saratov, Irkutsk, eventually Leningrad, and later elsewhere in the country.[4]

The university law faculties offered a four-year course of study, including lectures on the basic principles of the Soviet constitutions, criminal law, economic law, land law, administrative law, court organisation, criminal procedure, international law, and the co-operative and trade union movement.[5] By 1928 there were some 15,000 Soviet jurists with a higher or secondary legal education.

At the end of the 1920s Soviet legal education was being profoundly affected by contending approaches to the Marxist theory of State and law. Those of the university teaching staff most antipathetic to the revolutionary order had left in 1918–19, and many other progressive but non-Marxian figures were screened out when the law faculties were reopened in 1924–26. There remained nonetheless a diverse, creative,

---

2 A. A. Plotnieks *Stanovlenie i razvitie marksistsko-leninskoi obschchei teorii prava v SSSR* (1978) p 114.
3 See E. I. Kel'man *O sisteme iuridicheskogo obrazovaniia* (1926).
4 M. M. Isaev 'O vysshem iuridicheskom obrazovanii RSFSR' *Sovetskoe pravo*, no. 6 (1927) pp 116–118
5 See S. Kucherov *The Organs of Soviet Administration of Justice: Their History and Operation* (1970) p 266.

and often original community of Soviet legal scholars excited by the prospect of revolutionary social engineering through law who represented a considerable range of non-Marxian, quasi-Marxian, and Marxian thought.[6] Among those a pre-eminent role on the 'theoretical front' was played by E. B. Pashukanis (see chapter 3, above). By the end of the 1920s Pashukanis and his adherents exercised a predominant influence over legal education by virtue of control over the drafting of teaching syllabi, the placement of teaching personnel, and the implications of his commodity exchange theory for the legal system itself.

The preparation of syllabi for law courses had been concentrated by 1929 in the Institute of Soviet Construction and Law of the Communist Academy, directed by Pashukanis. The new syllabi amounted to a fundamental and far-reaching reworking of earlier eclectic approaches to course syllabi, introducing the terminology and conceptual apparatus of the commodity exchange theory. There was an intense campaign against 'bourgeois' legal scholarship, an appraisal of the principal bourgeois legal institutions, and an examination of the theory of State and law as laid down in the works of Marx, Engels, and Lenin. The syllabus on the 'Doctrine of the Soviet State,' which stressed the political rather than the legal dimension of the Soviet State, and on 'economic and administrative law,' which contemplated the abolition of the civil law, especially reflected the notions of the Pashukanis school. The first-year law course on the general theory of law became, in effect, an exposition of the commodity exchange theory, and students studying law externally through correspondence courses, including Party activists, offered by the Institute of Red Professors (of which Pashukanis was Rector) similarly were imbued with this approach.[7]

While law students were absorbing the lessons of the commodity exchange school, the larger implications of Pashukanis' views were becoming noticeable in legal education. The imminent withering away of law boded ill for legal careers. Study of the purely 'legal infrastructure'—the constitution and State system—was being phased out of the curriculum, and law school enrolments dropped dramatically. In 1930-31 Pashukanis and his associates were obliged to modify their position that the State would rapidly wither away, but thoughout the early 1930s they continued to emphasise the 'flexible' and 'expedient' dimensions of the law as an instrument of revolutionary policy rather than its stabilising role.

The adoption of the 1936 USSR Constitution heralded a transition to

---

6 An excellent selection of writings from this period is given in M. Jaworskyj *Soviet Political Thought* (1967).
7 For a detailed account of these developments, see R. Sharlet 'Pashukanis and the Withering Away of Law in the USSR' in S. Fitzpatrick (ed) *Cultural Revolution in Russia, 1928-1931* (Bloomington, 1978) pp 169-188; id 'Pashukanis and the Rise of Soviet Marxist Jurisprudence, 1924-1930' Soviet Union, I (1974) 103-121.

a policy of 'stability of laws,' which in the realm of legal education meant a restoration and expansion of university-level law teaching and a substantial increase in numbers of law students. Pashukanis himself disappeared from the scene in January 1937 during the purges, to be succeeded in the leadership of the legal profession by A. Ia. Vyshinskii. Almost immediately after Pashukanis' arrest, civil law was restored to the law curriculum in place of economic law and a massive effort undertaken to revise course syllabi and prepare new textbooks.[8]

In 1936 the system of legal education was reorganised. The USSR People's Commissariat of Justice assumed principal responsibility for providing legal education, appointing the directors of law schools, and preparing the syllabi and textbooks for courses to be taught.[9] Four-year courses of legal studies were offered in juridical institutes and university law faculties. Special short-term courses of from six months to one year were established in outlying areas of the country to raise the proficiency of legal personnel in post. In addition, correspondence schools and three-month courses to train what today might be called paralegal and auxiliary legal personnel were introduced, and an advanced two-year course in law for higher level legal personnel at the All-Union Law Academy.[10]

Except for the early war years, legal education expanded from the late 1930s for nearly two decades. The course of law studies in universities was extended to five years in the mid-1940s, and pursuant to a decree of the Central Committee of the CPSU adopted on 5 October 1946 and a joint Party-Government decree of 30 August 1954, a number of steps were taken to improve the quality of legal studies. By the late 1950s, however, perhaps influenced by the transition of Soviet society to the stage of the building of communism and a concomitant emphasis on transferring State functions to non-State bodies, sharp reductions in law school enrolments were imposed. Between 1956 and 1963, the number of law graduates in full-time study declined by more than 50% (although night school and correspondence courses kept the total number of law graduates in 1963 at a higher level than in 1956). In the summer of 1964 a decree of the Central Committee of the CPSU (as yet unpublished) reasserted the need for better jurists and an expansion and improvement of legal education, a need more keenly felt after the economic reforms of

---

8 For a student perspective on Soviet legal education from 1934-37 recorded in contemporary correspondence and lecture notes taken at the time, see W. E. Butler (intro) *Law Student Life in Moscow: The Letters and Course Notes of John N. Hazard, 1934-1939* (1978); excerpts from the letters are published in D. Barry, W. E. Butler, and G. Ginsburgs (eds) *Contemporary Soviet Law* (1974).
9 For the period 1938-1945, see B. Osherovich and B. Utevskii *Dvadtsat' let vsesoiuznogo instituta iuridicheskikh nauk* (1946).
10 See J. N. Hazard 'Legal Education in the Soviet Union' Wisconsin Law Review (1938) 562-579.

1965. The economic reforms, inter alia, gave greater discretion and independence to economic units in concluding economic contracts, foreseeing at the same time that economic units would exercise their discretion within the constraints of the applicable law. It followed, of course, that economic units would require more and better advice in these matters from qualified legal personnel. A similar devolution of responsibility within the lower levels of local government also has been accompanied by a substantial increase in the number of jurisconsults employed.

The veritable explosion in the number of Soviet law graduates has had a dramatic impact upon the qualifications and quality of the corpus of legal personnel as a whole. In 1936, when the reversal of Pashukanis' theories commenced in earnest, less than 6.7% of Soviet judges had any formal higher legal education and more than 50% had no legal education whatever.[11] By 1980 virtually all judges and procurators had a higher legal education, and indeed today it is almost impossible to enter any branch of the Soviet legal profession without an educational qualification of this level.[12]

Modern legal education

At the present time law is taught as a specialisation at 48 Soviet universities, four law institutes, and 15 higher schools of the Ministry of Internal Affairs. In 1986 there were 16,900 graduates who qualified in the speciality 'Law', more than double the figure of 7,900 in 1970. In the academic year 1987-88, about 100,000 students enrolled in all law faculties and institutes, of which 29,100 were full-time day students and the balance were evening or external. Despite the enormous expansion in the institutions offering law and the enlarged enrolments in existing institutions during the 1970s, the numbers of law graduates fell well short of demand. Law enforcement agencies received only 60-65% of their requests for law specialists; agencies of state administration, only 33%. Remote areas of the country in 1985 still had judges and advocates with merely a secondary legal education.

As in many European countries, the Soviet Union has a State Committee of the USSR for Public Education which is responsible for the general direction of legal education throughout the entire country. It is the Ministry and not the universities which establishes chairs, fixes the numbers of students to be admitted in each specialty, works out the plan of study, confirms the syllabi, directs the preparation and publication

11 Data published in Ia. Berman 'O pravovom obrazovanii' SGiP no. 5 (1936) p 115.
12 D. D. Barry and H. J. Berman 'The Soviet Legal Profession' Harvard Law Review LXXXII (1968) 2.

of textbooks, organises legal research, arranges for the placement of graduates, and has responsibility for assessing the students and submitting the results for confirmation.

Within the law faculties, headed by a dean, the key structural units are the chairs of law created for particular branches or subjects of law. A chair is headed by a professor, around whom are grouped senior and junior university staff of a similar specialisation and the students who have chosen to major in that area of the law. Each chair has a 'cabinet' room where students may meet the teaching staff, diploma theses may be defended, and the affairs of the chair conducted. The number of chairs varies from one university to another, depending on the number of students and the quality and importance of the teaching staff.

ADMISSION

The rules for admission to an 'institution of higher education' are laid down each spring for the following autumn by the State Committee for Public Education. In Autumn 1987 an applicant for law was required to have completed a full ten-year programme of secondary education, to have at least two years' work experience, to have 'positively displayed themselves in social work, possess political maturity, be morally irreproachable', have a recommendation from soviet, Party, Komsomol, law enforcement, or military organisations, and to be under 35 years of age (for full-time study). Admission is highly competitive. Each successful law applicant must have passed entrance examinations in the Russian language (or local language in which teaching was done), Russian literature, history of the USSR, and possibly a fourth subject. Those who achieve the best results in the entrance examinations, most of them oral, and have excellent secondary school references are likely to be admitted. Tuition is free of charge, and most university and all institute students are given a stipend to cover living expenses, which may be increased for excellent marks. Students who complete their secondary schooling with distinction may have the two-year work requirement waived.

COURSE OF STUDY

The full-time course of study in law at a university requires five years; at an Institute, four years; and for night studies or by correspondence, six years. Since the period of secondary schooling is two years shorter than in England and the United States, much of the first year and part of the second is devoted to non-law subjects required of all Soviet university students: history of the Communist Party, Marxist-Leninist philosophy, political economy, scientific Communism, the principles of scientific atheism, and logic. A modern foreign language is compulsory, as is, often, Latin. Law students then commence their discipline in earnest, with required courses in: the history of USSR State and law, general history of State and law, history of political doctrines, Roman law, Soviet State law, Soviet construction (local government), State law of foreign socialist countries, State law of bourgeois countries and countries liberated from colonial dependence, Soviet administrative law, Soviet financial law, public international law, Soviet civil law, family law, economic law, Soviet civil procedure, Soviet criminal law, Soviet criminal procedure, criminology, correctional-labour law, Procuracy supervision in the USSR, criminalistics, court and justice in the USSR, Soviet labour law, law of social security, collective farm law, Soviet land law, nature conservation law, forensic statistics, forensic bookkeeping, forensic medicine and psychiatry, principles of legal cybernetics, and general and forensic psychology.

These subjects are intended to give the law student a basic grounding in all branches of legal science and legislation and in the basic skills required by a lawyer. Five weeks are given over to visits to legal institutions (third year) and 12 weeks to 'production practice' in the fourth and fifth years to enable students to become personally familiar with the workings of a particular legal institution. At the end of their third year law students select a specialisation within law and concentrate their efforts during the last two years of their law studies on special courses relating to that choice. In their fifth year law students must prepare and defend publicly before the chair a diploma thesis of some 100 pages or so. This is an independently researched 'term paper' intended to introduce students to the basic principles of legal research method and to encourage them to delve more deeply into their chosen branch of law.

TEACHING AND ASSESSMENT

The basic method of instruction has been the lecture. Soviet law students carry a heavy work load, some 26–30 hours of lecture per week, tapering off in the last two years. These are augmented by small seminars, study groups, or circles, and the like, to analyse and discuss matters or problems treated in lecture. During the fourth and fifth years the special subjects often take the form of seminars since the numbers of students involved are smaller. Many subjects require students to prepare short written or oral reports on selected topics. From time to time there has been experimentation in Soviet legal education with other instructional techniques. Some Soviet jurists were impressed in the 1920s with the American socratic case-method of teaching and with the 'Dalton Plan', used in the state of Massachusetts to encourage the students themselves to present materials to the class. The former evidently was never actually tried and the latter abandoned after a short time.[13] Pursuant to higher education reforms introduced in 1986 (see below),

13 W. E. Butler 'The American Case Method and Soviet Legal Education' The International Lawyer XI (1977) pp 206–209.

the numbers of lecture hours are to be reduced in favour of seminars and independent reading and research by about 18%.

Assessment is based on oral examinations administered by the teaching staff. Questions are drafted by persons designated within each chair and approved by the chair as a whole. The questions are then typed on individual slips of paper. When the student appears at the designated hour for his examination, he draws the questions by lot and then may sit for a quarter-hour or so to think about the answer. He is then summoned to a small table opposite the instructor where he gives a discourse on the question. The instructors may ask further related questions to probe the depths of the student's mastery. Failures are not common and resits readily granted. The diploma paper in the fifth year is submitted in writing and read by an instructor and a fellow student designated by the chair. Each acts as an official opponent. The examinee appears at a meeting of the chair, summarises the main points of his paper, followed by critiques from the opponents. The chair then votes whether to pass the diploma paper or not.

CAREER PLACEMENT

Graduates of a Soviet law faculty are regarded as trained jurists entitled by law to employment in their chosen specialisation. As a condition of receiving a higher education at State expense, each graduate has a duty to accept employment assigned by the State for three years following graduation. Rather than hunting for a job, the Soviet law graduate finds himself being 'distributed' by a special commission set up at his institution for this purpose. The commission acts on the basis of 'requests' for personnel submitted by ministries, departments, enterprises, and the like. If student preference for type and place of work can be matched with a request, those preferences will be taken into account; otherwise, the graduate is likely to be assigned to some of the developing areas of the country. Sometimes institutions will request particular students whom they have come to know through the fifth year 'production practice'; high marks are likely to attract offers and such intangible factors as family connections can be influential in placement. After the three-year period has lapsed, the graduate is free to alter his employment if he chooses or to apply for post-graduate studies. It will be evident that if education planning is optimal, this system hopes to accept and train the numbers of specialists in each discipline called for by the national plans for economic and social development.

POST-GRADUATE STUDIES

There are two post-graduate degrees in law in the Soviet Union: the candidate of legal sciences and the doctor of legal sciences. Equivalents with the Anglo-American systems of legal education are not easy to identify, particularly in the United States and Canada where the first degree in law is a post-graduate degree, but taking into account the respective national systems of education *as a whole*, the candidate of legal sciences degree would correspond roughly to the British PhD degree and the American MA obtained by thesis. The Soviet doctor of legal sciences would correspond to the highest degrees in Britain and the United States, respectively the LLD in Britain and the PhD or SJD in the United States.

Entry to post-graduate study in the USSR is open on a competitive basis to individuals who have completed their first university degree and, as a rule, worked for at least two years. Only the most exceptional students would be allowed to waive the requirement of two years' employment. Unlike Britain and the United States, post-graduate studies are supervised not only at universities but also within the academies of sciences and other research establishments or even enterprises which have been duly accredited for this purpose. The universities in fact supervise a minority of post-graduate students in the country.

Post-graduate studies may be either full-time or part-time. Full-time students must be aged 35 or less and part-time, 45 or less; either category must have completed the first university degree or its equivalent and have displayed the ability to do scientific research work. Applicants must successfully complete examinations, propose an area for research in consultation with a thesis supervisor, and satisfy competitive entry examinations in one foreign language, their chosen specialisation, and the history of the Communist Party. Full-time students receive a stipend; part-time students are granted paid leave by law from their employment for at least two weeks prior to post-graduate examinations.

Each post-graduate student carries on his studies on the basis of an individual work plan approved by the post-graduate studies council of his supervisory institution. Under the 1980 Statute on Post-Graduate Studies at Higher Educational Institutions and Scientific Research Institutions, the post-graduate student has a legal duty to take examinations in historical and dialectical materialism, one foreign language, and a special discipline, depending on his thesis subject; to submit and defend a candidate thesis; and to master Marxist-Leninist philosophy, modern scientific methodology, and the application thereof in scholarly research and analysis.

The principal result of study for the candidate degree is the thesis. Soviet legislation emphasises the close link which is to exist between thesis research and the frontiers of knowledge as defined in research plans of the supervisory institution. The thesis must be a finished piece of research containing a 'new resolution' of a consequential scientific problem, which has material significance for the respective branch of knowledge and displays the author's capacity to undertake independent scientific research and a profound theoretical knowledge of his discipline and specialised command of the thesis topic.

A doctoral dissertation must be an independent work based on the author's research in which scientific propositions are formulated and justified and as an aggregate can qualify as a new long-term orientation in the respective field or as a theoretical generalisation and resolution of a large scientific problem having important national economic, political, or socio-cultural significance. The work ordinarily will have been published in book or article form before submission.

The procedures for writing and defending the candidate's thesis and doctoral dissertation and for conferring the respective degree are determined not by the supervisory university or institution, but by legislation. It is the State which ultimately approves the granting of degrees through a body known as the Supreme Attestation Commission (VAK).

Within each university or institution authorised to supervise postgraduate studies a 'specialised council' is formed. Its membership consists of reputable scholars and is confirmed by the VAK. Only the councils may accept candidate and doctoral dissertations for defence within their respective designated specialties. As a rule, a dissertation topic should be linked with the basic scientific work plan of the supervisory institution and be confirmed by the council. Legislation also requires that a dissertation:

... be responsive to the tasks of the contemporary development of science and practice, the deepening of research on the laws of nature and society, the struggle for the development and purity of Marxist-Leninist theory, a reasoned critique of bourgeois ideology, the requirements of raising further the role of science in resolving urgent problems of the construction and material-technical base of communism, accelerating scientific-technical progress and the growth of production efficiency, raising socialist culture and forming a Marxist-Leninist worldview of the working people, and also reflect questions of the world economy and international relations, the world revolutionary and liberation movement, and the foreign policy of the Soviet Union.[14]

When the dissertation is ready for submission, the author prepares a thesis abstract, which is printed in 100 copies and circulated. In the case of law, the abstract would be sent to all law faculties in the country and leading authorities. Two official opponents are appointed to read the dissertation in full; a law faculty or legal institution may be chosen to submit detailed written comments on the thesis. The defence is a public occasion, often advertised in the press. Members of the specialised council hear the author outline his principal contentions and the views of the official opponents, to which the author may reply. Written comments submitted are read aloud to the council. When the defence is

---

14 Point 30, 1975 USSR Statute on the Procedure for the Awarding of Academic Degrees and Conferring of Academic Titles.

concluded, the council decides by secret ballot whether the dissertation conforms to the standard of the degree. The proceedings of the council are taken down in shorthand or tape-recorded. However, the ultimate decision to award the degree rests with VAK, which receives the recommendations and files of the specialised council.

Reforms in legal education

The restructuring of Soviet higher education generally in 1986 had immediate implications for the training of legal personnel. For the first time in Soviet history, the 1961 Programme of the CPSU, as amended in February 1986, singled out 'legal nurturing' as a basic orientation of ideological and educational work. The future of law seemed further assured by the provision in the November 1986 Decree of the Central Committee of the CPSU on socialist legality pointing to the need 'to be constantly concerned with the improvement of legal training for executive cadres and specialists, this being an essential condition for raising their skills.'

While numbers of law graduates are important, the emphasis is to be on quality. In the period 1990–95, education plans call for 12,600 graduates per year from the universities and law institutes with an increase in full-time day enrolment of 20 to 25%. The number of law faculties is unlikely to increase; the weakest may be phased out (73% of the law graduates at Kemerovo University were rated as 'unsatisfactory'). Per capita spending on library and equipment for law students, at 1/15 of the rate for science students, is to be raised. Emphasis in revising the syllabus is to be on inculcating habits of independent thought, improving comprehension of foreign legal systems and foreign languages, and more independent study. Seminars, practical exercises, discussion groups, computer and games modelling are to fill the hours released by reduced lecture obligations.

At the same time, law studies are to become more 'practical.' Specialisations are being introduced in the law faculties expressly for procuracy, investigative, judicial, and advokatura careers, with distribution being more tightly linked to manpower requirements and occurring at an earlier stage of legal training. Theses, dissertations, and papers are to be based on an analysis of practice, including direct links with law enforcement agencies. Practitioners of all types are to be encouraged to lecture occasionally or to teach part-time in the law faculties, and textbooks are to have increasing regard to the realities of practice.

Other types of legal education

Knowledge of Soviet law or of particular branches of the law is now regarded as absolutely essential for every Soviet citizen. An elementary course on the basic principles of Soviet law has been introduced into the secondary school curriculum. A special network of 'people's universities for legal knowledge,' more than 4,300 of them, has been formed with guidance from the USSR Ministry of Justice in order to instruct people's assessors, people's guards, people's controllers, and members of comrades' courts in the basic elements of law. More than one million individuals take part each year. In many communities these are augmented by special lecture series, schools, and courses, all part of what is known as 'legal propaganda.'

In university or other forms of higher education, Soviet law is a required component of the syllabus for engineers, economists, technicians, medical personnel, agricultural workers, journalists, transport personnel, and countless others. This remarkable expansion of legal education has spawned an equally extraordinary flood of basic law texts and instructional aids designed for the layman.

More advanced specialist law courses or subjects are offered at dozens of institutions, for example the Institute of International Relations, the Diplomatic Academy, the Academy of Foreign Trade, the Institute for the Management of the National Economy, the various army, navy, maritime transport, and fishery institutes, to single out merely a few. Senior Party members are required to study law as part of their course at the Higher Party School. Foreign students studying law in the Soviet Union often do so at the Lumumba University in Moscow.

The majority of law graduates actually complete their studies, either at night or by correspondence as external students, at the All-Union Correspondence Law Institute. The Institute granted its 60,000th diploma in 1979 and maintains faculties in 13 cities to supervise the studies of 20,000 external students, many of them already employed as legal personnel in the Procuracy, courts, Notariat, or industry.

For aspiring law students some universities have introduced 'junior lawyers' schools' that meet once or twice a month in local high schools. Intended to interest gifted students in the profession, they also provide an opportunity for informal recruitment. Leningrad University reportedly has used this technique since 1977. Those already in the profession are encouraged in a variety of ways to improve their skills through schemes known in the Anglo-American legal world as continuing legal education. Education plans up to the year 2000 call for a substantial expansion of the role of law faculties in this process, including for local government personnel. During 1986–90, five legal polytechnics are to be opened in the RSFSR and two in the Ukraine with a view to improving the legal skills of those who have a secondary legal education.

Legal research

Legal research in the Soviet Union enjoys, by Anglo-American standards, vast government support and is closely linked to themes singled out for priority in the Congresses and Programme of the Communist Party and in the State five-year plans for economic and social development. Unlike the United Kingdom or the United States and Canada, where legal research is highly individualised and carried on principally within the law schools and faculties, the Soviet Union draws a sharp distinction between 'institutions of higher education', such as universities, and 'scientific research institutions' such as the USSR Academy of Sciences. The latter employ thousands of jurists engaged exclusively in legal research. To be sure, Soviet university teaching staff also undertake legal research; they have the principal responsibility for preparing text-books and instructional aids and pursuant to their faculty research plan may undertake to produce scholarly monographs or articles. Scientific research institutions for their part, as we have seen, supervise post-graduate dissertations.

Legal research, just as research in the natural sciences, medicine, and other disciplines, is planned research. All the scientific research institutions are financed by the State budget and carry on their activities on the basis of commitments assumed under five-year plans for their respective institutions. Research plans make provision for what we would call pure and applied legal research, that is, research into aspects of legal theory, for example, and research on practical matters of concern, such as the causes of crime. Often particular topics for research will be commissioned by government agencies on the basis of research contracts, for which the research organisation will receive agreed remuneration. The Institute of State and Law of the USSR Academy of Sciences in recent years has, for example, prepared draft economic and criminal codes, a draft law on State planning, draft Fundamental Principles of transport legislation, assisted local governmental bodies and large enterprises in drafting legislation, and produced monographs on the law of the sea to aid those negotiating international maritime conventions.

A. USSR ACADEMY OF SCIENCES

The most important and prestigious scientific research institution is the Academy of Sciences. Several Academy institutes include law among their interests, but the principal body of the Academy for legal research is the Institute of State and Law in Moscow. The Institute has a staff exceeding 350, including technical personnel, more than one hundred of whom hold the title of professor. The roots of the Institute as the first autonomous legal research body in the USSR date to 1925 with the formation of an Institute of Soviet Construction within the Communist Academy. The Institute was merged in 1929 with the Section for the General Theory of State and Law of the Communist Academy and was renamed the Institute of Soviet Construction and Law. Several months later, in March 1930, the Institute absorbed the Russian Association for Scientific Research in the Social Sciences (RANION), which had functioned since 1920 attached to Moscow University. Other changes of name occurred from time to time, the present dating from 1960. Institute staff are organised into six departments for designated subject areas; each department is further sub-divided into sectors.

Legal research to the end of the century is programmed to emphasise four 'tasks': (1) the legal consolidation of economic restructuring; (2) the development of a political system appropriate to restructuring which stresses the expansion of democracy and self-government; (3) the strengthening of socialist legality; and (4) public international law. In an effort to link research theory with practice, the activity plans of State agencies are to be co-ordinated more closely and in advance with Academy research plans and there are to be more research contracts, joint working parties, legal consultancies, and legislative drafting projects. Links with law enforcement, judicial, and practitioner bodies are to be established or expanded and, when appropriate, integrated research programmes undertaken.

B. UNION REPUBLIC ACADEMIES OF SCIENCES

Two union republic academies of sciences have formed autonomous legal research institutes (eg the Ukrainian SSR, the Uzbek SSR) and others carry on legal research within sectors or divisions devoted to or combined with other disciplines. In Estonia, for example, legal research personnel are linked with the economists.

C. INSTITUTE OF SOVIET LEGISLATION

Attached to the USSR Ministry of Justice is the All-Union Scientific Research Institute of Soviet Legislation (VNIISZ) formed in 1963 as a consequence of reorganisation in the All-Union Institute of Legal Sciences.[15] Whereas the academies of sciences are principally concerned with legal theory, VNIISZ has devoted its energies to the drafting, systematisation, consolidation, and harmonisation of legislation and the study of foreign law. VNIISZ had primary responsibility for developing the Digest of Laws of the USSR, carries out empirical research to assess

15 For the Statute on VNIISZ, see Review of Socialist Law VII (1981) 379–382.

the effectiveness of legislation, studies questions of legal co-operation within COMECON, is extensively involved in developing techniques for legal propaganda amongst the populace, prepares thematic collections, manuals, and commentaries relating to legislation, and publishes its own series of scholarly papers and proceedings and abstracts or translations of foreign legislation. The Institute has nearly 300 professional jurists.

D. ALL-UNION SCIENTIFIC RESEARCH INSTITUTE FOR PROBLEMS OF STRENGTHENING LEGALITY AND LEGAL ORDER

This Institute too emerged from the reorganisation of 1963 and presently has about 250 jurists. From 1963–87 it was called the All-Union Institute for the Study of the Causes and Working Out Measures for the Prevention of Criminality. It publishes its own series of proceedings and scholarly papers. As its name suggests, the Institute is concerned with the techniques of crime prevention, including juvenile delinquency, criminalistics, forensic psychology, criminal investigation and procedure, criminal statistics, and the like and has concentrated on methods to assess the effectiveness of particular crime prevention measures. The Institute is attached to the Procuracy of the USSR.

E. OTHER LEGAL RESEARCH ORGANISATIONS

There are dozens of other legal research bodies, often quite sizeable, in the Soviet Union. The USSR Ministry of Public Health has the Central Institute of Forensic Medicine; the USSR Ministry of Internal Affairs administers the All-Union Scientific Research Institute for the Protection of Public Order; the Ministry of Justice, in addition to VNIISZ, has the All-Union Scientific Research Institute for Forensic Expert Examinations. Each of these has counterparts at lower administrative-territorial sub-divisions of the USSR and each publishes its own organ to disseminate the results of its investigations. The Serbskii Central Scientific Research Institute for Forensic Psychiatry is another quasi-legal research body which has received much controversial notice in recent years for its techniques of treatment.

Many Soviet ministries and departments maintain specialist legal research divisions to service their particular requirements. The USSR Ministry of the Maritime Fleet and the USSR Ministry of Fisheries, for example, each maintain legal departments of some 50–60 lawyers to study questions of relevance to their operations, translate foreign legislation, and advise on matters of international law. Each publishes its own series of learned papers.

In 1985 the number of Soviet legal research personnel was said to exceed 4,000, of whom about 600 had higher doctorates. Nearly 300 scholarly monographs on law are published annually; between 1984 and

1986 the union republic publishing houses issued a total of 226 on legal subjects, but these were unevenly distributed—56 appeared in the Ukraine and 18 in Belorussia.

Overall co-ordination of more than 50 legal research bodies is vested in the Scientific Council of the USSR Academy of Sciences which has a special section concerned with the development of the State, administration, and law.

Chapter 6

The Soviet legal profession

The expression 'jurist' (*iurist*) in the Russian language can be used in a very broad sense to encompass all who have a legal education and all who work in some capacity in a legal specialty, whether as judge, professor, arbitrator, procurator, investigator, notary, or whatever. In this chapter we examine two types of jurist who most closely approximate the narrower Anglo-American concept of the lawyer, solicitor, or barrister, that is those who principally advise citizens and legal entities or appear in court on their behalf. These in the Soviet legal system are the advocate and the jurisconsult.

The advocate

HISTORY

The continued existence of a group of professional people in the Soviet Union who may be retained on a fee basis by individual citizens comes as a surprise to many in the West who imagined that the employment of one citizen by another was no longer possible. The initial reaction of the Bolsheviks to the Advokatura, or 'Bar,' in Russia was antipathetic; it was dissolved on 24 November 1917 in Decree No 1 'On Courts.' The Petrograd and later the Moscow Bars refused to recognise the legality of the dissolution and continued to function for nearly a year. Lenin was himself an advocate in the Imperial era. Expelled from his law studies at Kazan University, he completed them externally at St Petersburg University, was admitted to legal practice, and actually appeared in court in several cases before devoting himself wholly to the revolutionary movement. He took a dim view in some of his writings about aspects of the Russian legal profession, but was never opposed to the legal profession in principle. It was Lenin who personally inserted clauses on defenders in the early draft enactments on criminal procedure.

Decree No 1 'On Courts' opened to every citizen who enjoyed civil rights the right to act as defence counsel,[1] and under this proviso many advocates of the Tsarist era continued to practice their profession. Although this right was retained in Decree No 2 'On Courts,' adopted

---

1 *SU RSFSR* (1917–18) no. 4, item 50.

15 February 1918, Lenin modified the draft to allow 'colleges' of individuals to be formed and attached to local soviets; college members might act for remuneration either as prosecutors or defence counsel.[2] The link between prosecution and defence proved to be incompatible and was abolished in May 1918. There followed a period of constant reorganisation of the provision of legal services for some four years. For the most part regulation of advocates was left to local soviets. Initially a fee system operated on the basis of a schedule fixed by councils within the colleges of defenders; then the colleges were reorganised and defence counsel became salaried employees just as judges and prosecutors. Into this new scheme of colleges passed many members of the Tsarist Bar in November 1918 when they resolved to liquidate their former organisations. In 1920 a dramatic new experiment was tried. Local soviets were obliged to confirm twice-yearly lists of individuals who were capable of acting as defenders in court; they were paid per diem from State funds. Individuals on the list found themselves pressed into the role of defender whether they wished to act or not. The system proved unworkable, and in the majority of instances defenders were appointed from officials of local justice organs attached to the respective local soviets.

The introduction of the NEP brought a full-fledged Statute on the Advokatura, adopted 26 May 1922.[3] Under the Statute, colleges of defenders for civil and criminal cases were formed and attached to *guberniia* justice sections. College members were confirmed by the Presidium of the Guberniia Executive Committee, but new members could now be admitted by the College itself with subsequent notification of the Committee. Members were precluded from holding simultaneously posts in State institutions and enterprises except for elective offices and law teaching positions. Defenders were free to negotiate their fees with the client except with workers of State and private enterprises or employees of soviet institutions and enterprises, for whom fees were regulated by the People's Commissariat of Justice. Indigents were exempted from legal fees by court decree. The defenders then paid a stipulated percentage of their remuneration to the College for overhead expenses. Defenders did not enjoy a monopoly position. Close relatives of an accused or a victim and authorised representatives of certain State and social originsations also might appear in court as a defender. Other individuals, however, required the special authorisation of the court.

The influence of lawyers from the *ancien régime* in local advokaturas evidently troubled many local party organisations. Should communists be allowed to join? The Central Committee of the Party on 2 November 1922 counselled affirmatively in a Circular to all regional and provincial

2 *SU RSFSR* (1918) no. 26, item 240.
3 *SU RSFSR* (1922) no. 36, item 425. Although entitled as a separate Statute, the enactment was in fact an amendment to Articles 43–49 of the Statute on People's Courts of 21 October 1920.

Party organisations; otherwise, the Committee said, the colleges would be taken over by elements hostile to Soviet power. But limitations were imposed. A communist was required to have the advance approval of a senior Party organisation before joining the College; communist advocates must not accept cases, especially civil cases, involving the defence of bourgeois interests in disputes against workers or State enterprises nor in criminal cases defend clearly counter-revolutionary or other impure elements.[4] Throughout much of the NEP period advocates worked as private practitioners, the fee arrangements being attenuated by legal consultation centres at factories or public places where workers might obtain legal advice free of charge. During the era of forced collectivisation in 1929–31, advocates in most places found themselves pressured to merge into voluntary 'collectives' of advocates. The arrangements varied from locality to locality; as a rule, clients contracted for services with a collective and fees were paid to the collective. Advocates were then remunerated on the basis of quantity and quality of work performed.[5]

Somewhat greater central guidance over the legal profession ensued with the creation of a Legal Defence Section within the RSFSR People's Commissariat of Justice by legislation of 20 July 1930. On 27 February 1932 the RSFSR People's Commissariat of Justice adopted a Statute on Collectives of Members of Colleges of Defenders, confirming that the notion of collectives in this realm was on the whole regarded as a positive development. The collectives worked under the direct guidance of the presidium of colleges of advocates, whereas the colleges received their 'general policy guidance and supervision' from the territorial, regional, and higher courts. The collectives admitted new members, subject to final approval by the colleges. Clients elected their own defenders from those available; fees varied depending on the qualifications, socio-legal work, and work-load of the advocate but were levied at rates worked out by the Presidium of the College and confirmed by the court.[6]

The 1932 Statute was enacted at a time when the need for a legal profession at all was being seriously questioned by the Pashukanis school. In the event, the importance of defence counsel was staunchly defended. Following the adoption of the 1936 USSR Constitution, the system of court organisation was remodelled and for the first time all-union legislation on the Advokatura was approved, on 16 August 1939, by the USSR Council of People's Commissars.[7]

---

4 Reproduced in EzhSIu no. 1 (1923) p 24; signed by V. M. Molotov.
5 The best account of the advocate in the 1920s is J. N. Hazard *Settling Disputes in Soviet Society* (1960) pp 247–300.
6 See M. V. Kozhevnikov *Istoriia sovetskogo suda 1917–1956 gody* (1957) p 237.
7 *SP SSSR* (1939) no. 49, item 394.

CURRENT LEGISLATION

The 1958 FPLCOrg returned responsibility for the Advokatura to the union republics, all of whom between 1962 and 1963 enacted their own statutes for their respective Advokaturas. Some central direction was felt to be necessary, however, and in 1976 work commenced on drafting an all-union enactment. The 1977 USSR Constitution (Art 161) provided for a new pattern of regulation—USSR *and* union republic legislation— and elevated the colleges of advocates to organisations of constitutional significance for the first time in Soviet history. On 30 November 1979 the USSR Supreme Soviet adopted a Law on the Advokatura in the USSR. In 1980–81 each of the union republics enacted a Statute in pursuance of the USSR law for their respective Advokaturas. Discussion continues about creating an Advokatura of the USSR to represent the profession as a whole.

As of 1988 there were nearly 25,000 advocates in the Soviet Union, more than half of whom were in the RSFSR. The City of Moscow had 1,100 advocates, Moscow Region circa 600, and Leningrad circa 600. In 1980 the Azerbaidzhan SSR had 420; the Lithuanian SSR, 260; and the Moldavian SSR, 245.[8] The ratio of advocates per capita of populace would be misleading if compared to Britain or North America, however, because the Soviet jurisconsult performs work which needs to be taken into consideration. There are also variations per capita among union republics. In the USSR as a whole there was one advocate per 13,000 people, but in the Georgian SSR the figure was one advocate per 6,000 people in 1987.

COLLEGES OF ADVOCATES

Advocates are organised into 'colleges of advocates,' defined in legislation as 'voluntary associations of persons who are engaged in advocacy activity.' As an 'association *of persons*,' the colleges avoid the tax liabilities of social organisations, although individual advocates are subject to income tax on their earnings. Advocates enjoy a monopoly on the practice of law but not on the right to legally represent someone in court. The 157 colleges of advocates in the USSR have as their principal task 'the rendering of legal assistance to citizens and organisations.' Each college is a juridical person. Colleges are formed either upon the application of a group of persons who have a higher legal education or upon the initiative of an executive or administrative agency of the respective local soviet. Moscow and Leningrad each have their own city and regional colleges of advocates, as do some autonomous republics and territories.

---

8 E. Huskey 'The Limits to Institutional Autonomy in the Soviet Union: The Case of the *Advokatura*' Soviet Studies XXXIV (1982) p 201.

MEMBERSHIP

The membership of each college is controlled principally by the members themselves. Sources of new members are essentially two: recent law graduates assigned by the distribution process (chapter 5, above) to colleges, or applications received from jurists in other branches of the profession seeking a change. Available data suggests the latter category may encounter resistance from the profession in large urban centres, where there has been a pronounced disposition to stabilise membership in the interests of economic viability, although the USSR Ministry of Justice is also blamed for discouraging the expansion of the profession. Current legislation allows part-time advocates to be recruited from other walks of life in rural areas where a full-time practitioner cannot be justified.

A higher legal education is not an absolute prerequisite for admission to a college of advocates. Some 95% of all Soviet advocates now possess that qualification, but not all of that figure have the full five-year university training or its equivalent. The profession as a whole tends to consist of older practitioners and has been under pressure for some time to alter that ratio. Change has been modest, and in 1980 only 25% of RSFSR advocates were under age 40. Women comprise about 40% of the profession, On average about 60% of the advocates are members of the Communist Party, which contrasts dramatically with the 1920s when communists wondered whether they should become advocates at all.

GENERAL MEETING

Unique in the Soviet Union as a self-administering profession, the Advokatura places ultimate responsibility for administering the affairs of the profession within the colleges of advocates on the 'general meeting' or 'conference' of the college. The number of delegates to the general meeting is based on a representation quotient fixed by the college; in the Moscow City College of Advocates, for example, one delegate is chosen for every three members. The general meeting elects the executive organ of the college (presidium) and an audit commission; decides the size of college membership, the numbers of administrative personnel, and financial estates; hears and confirms reports about the activities of the presidium and audit commission; confirms the work rules for the college by agreement with the trade unions; determines the procedure for payment of remuneration to advocates in accordance with government directives; and considers appeals against presidium decrees. Recent accounts based on archival research and personal interviews suggest these functions are actively exercised; Party nominees for the presidium are on occasion rejected and the other matters within the general meeting's competence are the subject of vigorous controversy.[9]

---

9 Ibid, for accounts of election and disciplinary practices.

PRESIDIUM

The presidium of a college of advocates, elected by secret ballot for a three-year term, has broad powers. It organises the legal consultation officers, directs their activity, appoints or dismisses the heads thereof, admits members to the college, assigns advocates to offices, organises probation for new or inexperienced advocates, performs a variety of tasks to assess and improve the work of advocates and the college as a whole and supervises the payment of fees to advocates.

LEGAL CONSULTATION OFFICES

Legal consultation offices are distributed throughout cities and the countryside. It is there that the Soviet citizen applies for legal assistance. The presidium of the college determines precisely where and how many offices should be formed and the number of advocates within each. Each consultation office has its own bank account. The expenses for operating the legal consultation offices and indeed the college itself, as well as State pension contributions, are covered from fees paid to the offices for legal services rendered by advocates. About 30% of the fee income is allocated for expenses of this nature.

Pursuant to the Comprehensive Programme for the Development of the Production of Consumer Goods and Services for 1986–2000, there is to be a substantial expansion in the numbers of legal consultation offices to reflect natural population growth and the increased demand and new opportunities for legal services.

LEGAL FEES

By Anglo-American standards, Soviet legal fees are extremely modest. The fee structure is laid down in detail in an Instruction confirmed by the USSR Minister of Justice on 4 August 1977. Certain categories of legal assistance are rendered free of charge, for example: for recovery of alimony; labour cases; suits of collective farmers against collective farms for payment of labour; for compensation for harm caused by mutilation or other impairment of health connected with work, or on behalf of dependants for harm caused by the death of a breadwinner which occurred in connection with work; and appeals against irregularities in lists of electors. In addition, specified categories of the populace may be given legal assistance free of charge, such as disputes of local soviets when they require legal advice on certain matters, or citizens petitioning for the assignment of pensions and benefits. Any legal fees may be waived by the presidium or head of a legal consultation office for reasons of financial hardship.

When fees are to be charged, a formal agreement is concluded between the advocate and the client specifying the services to be rendered, fees and expenses, and so forth. The agreement is signed by the advocate, the client, and the head of the legal consultation office. A deposit may be required from the client, refundable if the work cannot be completed or performed, less an amount for the work, if any, actually done. Fees may range from up to two rubles for drawing up legal documents or for legal advice to as much as six rubles for drafting a will or contract. For appearance in court in civil cases the fees are based on the value of the suit: up to five rubles is charged for cases valued up to 100 rubles, or up to 30 rubles for suits valued at from 501 to 1,000 rubles, for example. For representation in administrative agencies, a fee of up to ten rubles may be charged, rising up to 30 rubles in complex cases. These charges assume a one-day appearance in court. If a case extends beyond one day (most do not), a per diem charge is imposed at a declining rate. Soviet advocates have no financial incentive to drag out litigation.

In criminal cases fees are charged on a per diem basis for participating in the preliminary investigation, studying the file of the case, appearing in the court of first instance, drawing up appeal documents, and so forth.

Legal assistance is rendered by advocates to organisations, enterprises, and institutions on the basis of contracts concluded between the legal consultation office and the organisation. Nearly 65% of Soviet advocates engage in work of this kind, especially for organisations which do not have their own jurisconsults. The value of the contract may not exceed 50% of the post salary of a jurisconsult. Fees are established at special rates for organisations; for example, up to five rubles for drawing up a draft contract, or up to 30 rubles for conducting a case in State Arbitrazh if the value of the suit exceeds 1,000 rubles. In addition, when travel is involved, an advocate is entitled in every instance to reimbursement of expenses at rates fixed by legislation.

The low fee scale and substantial amount of pro bono work by advocates have a depressive effect on annual incomes. Earnings vary from city to country; on average it is believed that advocates may earn about 250 rubles per month. A ceiling of 350 rubles has been imposed by some colleges of advocates pursuant to the Statute on the Payment for Labour of Advocates confirmed on 25 April 1975. Nearly one-third of advocacy revenues come from legal services rendered to organisations. The economic reforms of 1987 have led to a strong case for revising the scale of advocates' remuneration, removing the ceiling on earnings, and reducing the incentive for illegal and unethical supplementary payments from clients.[10]

---

10 See F. S. Kheifets 'Printsipy oplaty truda advokatov' in V. M. Savitskii (ed) *Advokatura i sovremennost'* (1987) p 120.

SUPERVISION

Although independent of the State, the Advokatura is not exempt from supervision by State and Party organs. Regional and higher Communist Party committees have an administrative organs section with responsibility for overseeing the work of the college of advocates. Most of the supervisory functions are exercised by justice sections of local soviets or by the ministries of justice. The presidium of each college of advocates reports regularly on its activity. The justice sections must approve, inter alia, the location of legal consultation offices and the number of advocates working in them. Although colleges of advocates admit new members, a refusal to admit may be appealed to the relevant local agency of State power. These bodies may convoke the general meeting of the college of advocates, if necessary; register the formation of new colleges of advocates; or hear appeals against the imposition of disciplinary sanctions. A common form of supervision is the issuance of methods instructions to colleges of advocates, laying down in precise detail how certain matters are to be conducted. These may range from major policy matters, such as payment for services and model contracts for rendering legal assistance, to household matters, such as filing and indexing legislation and court reports. If colleges of advocates take decisions or adopt decrees contrary to law, these bodies may suspend the effect thereof and submit the enactment for new discussion. Supervision of this nature extends to the operation of the Advokatura as an organisation and may not intrude into the substance of individual cases handled by an advocate.

It is the practice that in cases investigated by the Committee for State Security (KGB), which are enumerated in the Code of Criminal Procedure, advocates are selected or assigned from a list by the chairman of the presidium of a college of advocates rather than by the head of the legal consultation office, although in principle any advocate can be authorised to represent a client in a case of that type.[11] Colleges of advocates involve other outside bodies in their activities through social Councils for the Affairs of Advocates. Although not formally supervisory organisations, these Councils are advisory and consist of representatives from local soviets, trade unions, komsomol, and academic institutions. They are empowered to discuss matters relating to advocates, make proposals to improve their work, participate in drafting normative materials, and the like.

LEGAL ETHICS

Difficult ethical and moral conundrums can arise for the Soviet advocate no less than for others. In 1923 the Kiev College of Defenders adopted

---

11 Y Luryi 'The Role of Defense Council in Political Trials in the USSR' *Manitoba Law Journal* no. 4 (1977) pp 307–311.

an instruction on professional ethics, and in 1925 the Moscow College of Defenders published a volume recounting presidium decisions relating to legal ethics.[12] The practice appears to have lapsed, and so far as is known, only the Lithuanian College of Advocates now has a written regulation on the matter. The Advokatura legislation of the USSR and union republics contains certain prescriptions governing the behaviour of advocates and provides some detail, elaborated in departmental instructions, about procedures in disciplinary proceedings. An advocate, for example, may not accept a commission to give legal assistance in a case where he is giving or has rendered assistance to persons whose interests are contrary to the person seeking aid, or if he has participated in the case as a judge, procurator, investigator, etc, or if a relative of the advocate took part in the investigation or consideration of the case. Nor may an advocate disclose information communicated to him by a principal in connection with rendering legal assistance or be questioned as a witness concerning facts which became known to him in connection with the performance of his duties as a defender or representative. While observing the requirements of legislation in force, the advocate has the duty to '. . . use all methods and means provided for by law to defend the rights and legal interests of citizens and organisations who have applied to him for legal assistance' (Art 16, RSFSR Statute on the Advokatura), although some lower courts have not understood the parameters of admissible defence.[13]

Disciplinary sanctions range from a reproof, reprimand, severe reprimand, to expulsion from the college. An advocate has the right to submit a written explanation and appear personally to explain his conduct. A remarkably brief statute of limitations applies: a sanction must be imposed within six months from the date the offence was committed. If a sanction is imposed and no new offence is committed within one year, the offence is expunged; by irreproachable conduct and a conscientious attitude toward his work, the advocate may have the record expunged before the year has lapsed. Expulsion from a college of advocates may be appealed in a judicial proceeding.

Advocates are expected to remain abreast of their field and may be subjected to 'attestation' by ad hoc commissions set up for this purpose. Failure of an advocate to maintain his qualifications can be grounds for dismissal from the college of advocates.

---

12 Hazard, note 5, above, pp 281-291
13 See the Case of Radchenko, in which the Judicial Division for Criminal Cases of the Ukrainian SSR reversed a special ruling against an advocate for shielding a defendant and 'defending a crime.' Translated in J. N. Hazard, W. E. Butler, P. B. Maggs *The Soviet Legal System* (3rd edn, 1977) p 79.

SCOPE OF ACTIVITY

Most advocates spend the greater part of their time giving legal advice and drafting documents. Current data suggests that advocates make court appearances in only about 10% of civil cases, although the figure is about 25–30% for labour and housing cases. Even in criminal proceedings advocates appear in court in only about 70% of the cases and perhaps one-third of the preliminary investigations. In the instance of criminal appearances, the figures represent an increase; Soviet courts have been construing more strictly the right to defence guaranteed by the USSR Constitution. Despite the brevity of civil and criminal court proceedings in the USSR as compared with Anglo-American proceedings and the limited occasions for Soviet advocates to become involved at the preliminary investigation stage of criminal proceedings (chapter 18, below), the demand for legal services by Soviet citizens has been increasing. Partly this represents population growth, but an important reason during the past decade has been a sustained legal propaganda campaign by the authorities informing citizens of their rights and encouraging people to use them. Under present legislation, advocates have received on an all-union scale the right to represent citizens before administrative agencies and in cases involving administrative sanctions, which may prove to be a significant source of work. Greater involvement in the preliminary investigation and opportunities to act in cases of judicial review of the illegal actions of officials under 1987 legislation are being cited as reasons to increase the size of the profession. There is no meaningful way to quantify the role of advocates in advising organisations except to say that this form of legal work has increased enormously and now comprises a significant share of most advocates' work-load.

FOREIGN CITIZENS

Several colleges of advocates in the Soviet Union maintain special legal consultation offices to handle civil cases for foreign citizens or organisations or to represent Soviet citizens and organisations in foreign legal matters. The best-known is 'Iniurkollegiia,' attached to the Moscow City College of Advocates. Iniurkollegiia specialises in inheritance, sale of property, insurance, patents, trademarks, property, and related matters, and will bring suit in the USSR or abroad on behalf of its clients. Its fees are not governed by the usual fee schedule for the colleges of advocates and are approximate to those charged by leading Anglo-American law firms. Foreigners may apply on the same basis as Soviet citizens to any legal consultation office for advice, although in civil cases Iniurkollegiia may have special expertise not readily available elsewhere. The enactment of joint enterprise legislation in 1987 has laid the basis for collaborative ventures between colleges of advocates and western law firms. Legal advice to joint enterprises is tendered on a fee basis by the Consultation Centre of the USSR Chamber of Commerce and Industry.

ALL-UNION ORGANISATION FOR ADVOCATES

Although the decentralisation of the Soviet Advokatura seems to be generally accepted, some advocates believe a national organisation would be helpful in consolidating the identity of the profession, co-ordinating activities, and promoting professional standards. Such a body has never existed in the Soviet Union. In 1950 and again in 1986 an All-Union Meeting of Advokatura Leaders was convoked by the USSR Ministry of Justice, and in recent years the Association of Soviet Jurists, sometimes called the Soviet Lawyers' Association, has become active. The last, however, encompasses the entire legal profession, not merely advocates, and exists primarily to further contacts with legal personnel abroad. Several colleges of advocates have created 'social scientific research institutes for forensic defence', utilising the services of more than sixty legal scholars to produce commentaries on legal practice and advocacy techniques.[14] A national association might draw these activities together, publish a journal especially for advocates, represent the profession on advisory legal councils (see chapter 7, below) or in public interest lawsuits, and in general act to raise the stature of the profession in the public mind.

Jurisconsults

Jurisconsults in the Soviet Union are the legal advisers to ministries, departments, local government units at all levels, State enterprises, associations and the like, State or collective farms, foreign trade delegations, and even large social organisations, cultural institutions, construction, scientific research, or design organisations.

HISTORY

A thorough study of the jurisconsult in pre-revolutionary Russia has yet to be made. It is evident that the term and position of jurisconsult existed in Russia in the late nineteenth century and that the term goes back at least to Petrine Russia to refer more generally to a jurist or lawyer. Jurisconsults appeared at once in Soviet people's commissariats and other governmental organs after the October Revolution and survived in a few of the large enterprises, where despite the early expectations of an

---

14 For an example of the work of these councils, see W. E. Butler 'Criminal Appeal Procedure and the Soviet Advocate' *Year Book on Socialist Legal Systems* II (1987) 372-390.

administered economy and society, their skills were provisionally required. In the categories of Soviet workers established in 1918 for wage scales, jurisconsults were included in category 1 of Group I, the highest classification.[15] By 1920 the need for legally-trained personnel had become desperate. On 11 May 1920 the Council of People's Commissars ordered all individuals with a higher legal education to register so that 'proper use of [their] specialised knowledge' might be made.[16] One week later the same organ created 'consultation subsections of justice' to be staffed by jurisconsults in the 'people's commissariats and all central institutions of the RSFSR'.[17] The Moscow College of Defenders in 1922 requested the Moscow City Soviet to authorise members of the College to jointly hold the post of jurisconsult and practise in the College, which was approved on 23 July 1922.[18]

The establishment of the Procuracy in 1922 led to a reorganisation of regulating the jurisconsult. Supervision over the jurisconsult vested in the People's Commissariat of Justice in May 1920 was transferred to the Procuracy, which was to register them and oversee their activity in justice agencies. Outside this commissariat, regulation of jurisconsults largely became a matter for the organisation employing them. In industry an all-union conference of jurisconsults was convoked at the initiative of the USSR Supreme Economic Council, which on 14 August 1925 enacted a statute on the jurisconsults subordinate to that Council. On 30 March 1927 the RSFSR Council of People's Commissars enacted a Decree 'On Jurisconsults of State Institutions and Enterprises and Cooperative Organisations and the Supervision of Their Activity.'[19] The decree confirmed the supervisory role of the Procuracy over the jurisconsult, which was broadened by subsequent legislation. Throughout the late 1920s conferences of jurisconsults were held on an all-union or lesser scale to exchange work experience, hear reports, and even adopt resolutions about organising and supervising the profession.

Unlike the advocates, however, jurisconsults have never formed a professional body that transcended ministerial or departmental lines. The transition from the NEP to the planned economy posed an initial threat to the jurisconsult because law was expected to rapidly wither away and be supplanted by Plan. The 1927 legislation on jurisconsults had become obsolete; in most branches of industry the 1927 decree was superseded de facto by commissariat statutes on jurisconsults from 1932–39. The supervisory role of the Procuracy diminished accordingly. The 1939 Statute on the Advokatura prohibited advocates from

15 *SU RSFSR* (1918) no. 48, item 567.
16 *SU RSFSR* (1920) no. 47, item 211.
17 *SU RSFSR* (1920) no. 51, item 221.
18 Luryi 'Jurisconsults in the Soviet Economy' in D. B. Barry et al (eds) *Soviet Law After Stalin* (1979) II pp 170–171.
19 *SU RSFSR* (1927) no. 36, item 238.

serving simultaneously as jurisconsults, but in 1941 enterprises which did not have the post of jurisconsult included in their personnel establishment were allowed to retain an advocate's services by agreement.

In 1957 Khrushchev initiated a major reorganisation and decentralisation of the administration of the national economy. These reforms were followed by local legislation on the jurisconsult endowing the post with widely varying duties and status. At the union republic level 'model statutes' on the jurisconsult were enacted to aid enterprises and organisations in fashioning their own. The Ukrainian SSR approved a model statute in 1959 and the RSFSR in 1963, among others.

CURRENT LEGISLATION

The 1965 and 1987 economic reforms in the Soviet Union (chapter 13, below) gave State enterprises greater responsibility for their contractual relations with other enterprises and expanded the scope of economic accountability. The enlarged discretion accorded to enterprise management required disciplining; law and contract were the chosen instruments and State Arbitrazh the principal forum. A massive increase in legal personnel was required, together with other legal improvements. Several tentative measures were taken, but the key document for the jurisconsult was the Decree of 23 December 1970 'On the Improvement of Legal Work in the National Economy.' The Decree, inter alia, required the enactment of a General Statute on the jurisconsult, the formation or strengthening of legal departments in the central apparatus and at all levels of economic administration, local government, and agriculture; the USSR Ministry of Justice was reinforced in its role of exercising methods direction over legal work in the national economy and improving the substance and systematisation of Soviet legislation; the admission of students to law faculties was greatly increased and measures were introduced to raise the qualifications of jurisconsults already in post.[20]

On 22 June 1972 the USSR Council of Ministers confirmed the General Statute on the Legal Section (or Office), Chief (or Senior) Jurisconsult, and Jurisconsult of a Ministry, Department, Executive Committee of a Soviet of People's Deputies, Enterprise, Organisation, or Institution. On the basis of this General Statute, ministries and departments draft and confirm their own statutes for their respective legal offices or legal personnel. Social organisations also were recommended to use this General Statute as a model when establishing a procedure for carrying on legal work within their organisations. Collective farms and inter-collective farm enterprises and organisations arrange their legal services pursuant to an Instruction confirmed jointly by the ministers of agriculture and justice on 3 January 1973.

20 J. Giddings 'The Jurisconsult in the USSR' Review of Socialist Law (1975) 171–211.

JURISCONSULT AS EMPLOYEE

Unlike the advocate, the jurisconsult is a salaried employee in the establishment where he works. The enormous expansion in Soviet legal education since the 1970s has rebounded primarily to the jurisconsult's benefit. There are now about 125,000 jurisconsults in the USSR, the largest segment by far of the Soviet legal profession. Jurisconsults are expected to have a higher legal education but may be appointed to office if they possess at least three years' work experience in a legal speciality or are completing the last years of legal education. The key to the concept of the jurisconsult's role in the national economy lies in his relationship to his employer. If the jurisconsult could be removed at will or ignored, his legal advice would be likely to be less than objective or to be disregarded. The 1972 legislation sought to raise the status of the jurisconsult in several respects. Although the jurisconsult is directly subordinate to the director of an enterprise or to the minister or deputy minister of a ministry, he may be appointed and dismissed only by the organisation superior to the enterprise or by the minister himself. Analogous provisions apply to jurisconsults of local soviets or collective farms. While protected against his immediate superior, the jurisconsult must 'visa' or attest the legality of legal documents before they may become valid. If the documents do not conform to law, the jurisconsult must refuse to visa them, indicate why, and suggest an alternative approach whenever possible. Should the director nonetheless sign the documents contrary to the jurisconsult's opinion, the jurisconsult is legally obliged to notify the superior organisation; otherwise, he bears liability personally, together with the director. Also, jurisconsults are now protected against being diverted to non-legal duties by their employer. The object of these measures is to make the jurisconsult the guardian of legality and not the instrument of management.

FUNCTIONS

The duties of the jurisconsult vary slightly, depending upon whether his employer is a ministry, or state enterprise, a local soviet, or a collective farm. In general the jurisconsult has responsibility for verifying and certifying personally that draft legal enactments conform to legislation in force; to supervise the conformity to law of similar enactments in structural sub-divisions of his employer; to prepare amendments for enactments, when necessary; to help draft collective labour contracts or other measures to strengthen labour discipline; to arrange work relating to, draft, and visa economic contracts; to organise and carry on claims work; to take part in discussions concerning the indebtedness of the enterprise; to supervise the procedure for accepting goods and products, to represent his employer in State Arbitrazh or court; to help prepare draft normative acts or opinions thereon; to give advice on the other legal questions which arise in the course of operations; and to prepare materials relating to wastage, theft, shortages, and the like for transfer to investigative or judicial agencies or to comrades' courts. The jurisconsult may be called on to advise other organisations connected with his employer such as the local trade union committee, comrades' court or people's guard. He has responsibility for keeping all normative acts received, informing others about them, and propagandising Soviet legislation in general.

The ministerial jurisconsult has less responsibility for direct economic operations and more work involving legislation, administration, and supervision of inferior structural sub-divisions or enterprises. In some ministries the jurisconsult may be heavily engaged in questions of foreign law or public and private international law. The ministries of foreign trade, fisheries, civil aviation, maritime fleet, and foreign affairs are examples. The jurisconsult of a local soviet deals extensively with the legality of draft normative materials and gives legal advice not only to the local soviet and its executive committee, but likewise to all the permanent commissions of the local soviet or even individual deputies.

Collective farms are serviced least adequately by jurisconsults. Only the largest and wealthiest are likely to employ a full-time jurisconsult, although a few actually employ two or more. Commonly collective farms pool their resources to share a jurisconsult or contract with a local college of advocates for legal services. Jurisconsults participate regularly in social consultation offices (chapter 7, below), giving legal advice free of charge to employees or citizens who apply.

METHODS ASSISTANCE

The USSR and union republic ministries of justice issue methods recommendations to jurisconsults. These may relate to matters of major policy, such as the procedure for drafting normative acts of ministries or departments, to procedures for using legal means to ensure the issuance of high quality products, or to registering and keeping normative acts. The more important of these are published in the *Biulleten' normativnykh aktov ministerstv i vedomstv SSSR*, published monthly since 1972.

The rise of the jurisconsult since 1970 certainly represents a concern for legality, but legality in this instance is supposed to produce economic dividends. Observance of economic legislation is expected to make the economy run more smoothly and efficiently. A major incentive for organisations and collective farms to employ jurisconsults, widely publicised in the Soviet press, is the improvement in economic performance, directly measurable in rubles, likely to accrue through proper prosecution of claims and penalties in court or arbitrazh. Countless stories have been related about hundreds of thousands or even millions of rubles saved by jurisconsults through the proper filing of claims or defences against suits.

In the long term, if the role of the jurisconsult survives, it may not be unreasonable to suppose that experienced jurisconsults may become a source for recruiting management personnel, in the past drawn chiefly from individuals with an engineering or technical background. The inservice training of the jurisconsult, albeit not the formal legal training, is emphasising a professional (ideal, of course) well-versed in the law, the economics of production, accountancy, basic production techniques, and managerial practices. He is expected to be familiar with all stages of production from receipt of the order to shipment of the finished good or service.

Chapter 7

The administration of legality in the Soviet Union

The expression 'administration of legality' is being used in a special sense in this chapter to refer to both State and non-State bodies directly concerned in the Soviet Union with the application and enforcement of the law, excluding the advocates and jurisconsults who have been discussed previously (chapter 6, above).

Ministries of justice

HISTORY

The Soviet ministries of justice in either their present or past forms have no exact analogue in Britain or North America. The first RSFSR People's Commissariat of Justice created the day after the 1917 October Revolution included among its functions the investigation of offences, the administration of prisons and camps, the administration of the separation church from State, and the codification of legislation, among others. In 1921 these were broadened to include supreme judicial control and in 1922 to embrace the Procuracy. The repeated reorganisations of the ministries need not detain us here, except to note that from 1963-70 they were abolished completely and their functions dispersed among other organs.

CURRENT LEGISLATION

Pursuant to a joint Party-Government decree of 30 July 1970, the USSR Ministry of Justice was formed as a union-republic ministry by an Edict of the Presidium of the USSR Supreme Soviet on 31 August 1970. The Statute of the Ministry was enacted 21 March 1972. The Ministry, either directly or through union and autonomous republic ministries of justice and the justice sections of local soviets, exercises 'organisational direction' over courts; that is, where they are to be located, structure, personnel establishment, hears reports on these matters by court chairmen, supplies equipment and furnishings. Judicial practice is studied and summarised together with the USSR Supreme Court. The Ministry organises the gathering of forensic statistics and sociological research with a view to crime prevention. A major function of the

Ministry since 1976 has been the preparation of the Digest of Laws of the USSR. As noted in the previous chapter, the Ministry has responsibility for 'methods guidance' of legal work in the national economy and since 1977 has collaborated with State Arbitrazh in publishing the monthly journal *Khoziaistvo i pravo*.

In the realm of 'legal propaganda' the Ministry also exercises 'methods guidance' by issuing methods recommendations and supervising the planning and execution of this work by ministries, departments, and social organisations. Special 'methods co-ordination councils' composed of representatives from outside organisations have been set up throughout the ministry of justice system. An enormously popular monthly journal, *Chelovek i zakon*, has been published for the layman since 1968 by the Ministry.

The Ministry's responsibilities for legal personnel are various. It takes part in drafting State plans for training legal 'cadres' and for distributing law graduates. Likewise, it has a voice in preparing the course syllabi for most law courses taught in the country and the publishing plans for legal literature of all types. Through its own scientific research bodies (chapter 5, above) it carries on legal research and co-ordinates its activities with the Academy of Sciences and other research institutes. A Scientific Advisory Council attached to the Ministry and composed of scholars and specialists makes recommendations for improving the organisation of justice agencies. The USSR Minister of Justice has the right to submit suggestions to the Plenum of the USSR Supreme Court for the issuance of guiding explanations.

The Ministry of Justice exercises 'State guidance' over three important legal institutions: the Advokatura (chapter 6), the Notariat, and the Registry for Acts of Civil Status; 'guidance' includes fixing fees which may be charged for legal services.

Finally, the Ministry maintains international links of various forms. It takes part in drafting relevant international treaties, such as legal assistance treaties, and represents the USSR in several COMECON bodies concerned with legal questions.

The union republic ministries of justice perform analogous functions, although they are not concerned with military tribunals or foreign relations. The RSFSR Ministry of Justice operates courses for raising the qualifications of justice workers and has a Central Methods Cabinet for New Civic Rites, which, for example, would deal with the formalities of marriage ceremonies. The RSFSR Ministry publishes jointly with the RSFSR Supreme Court a leading legal journal, *Sovetskaia iustitsiia*.

The judicial system

HISTORY

The Bolsheviks came to power determined to completely reshape the pre-existing judicial order. Revolutionary tribunals sprang up immediately, without legislative sanction, under various names. Cases were judged not on the basis of Imperial law but by their revolutionary consciousness; judgments were not subject to appeal. The first official legislative act creating courts was Decree No 1 'On Courts' enacted 24 November 1917. In place of the old court system the Decree created 'people's courts' presided over by a judge directly elected and two assessors, the latter being laymen who served on a part-time basis. Their jurisdiction was limited to civil cases of up to 3,000 rubles and criminal cases in which the punishment could not exceed two years' deprivation of freedom. Judgments could not be appealed but were sometimes subject to review by cassation. As a separate system of courts Decree No 1 established revolutionary tribunals consisting of seven persons elected by provincial or city local soviets. These tribunals heard cases involving serious crimes or counter-revolutionary acts; their judgments were not subject to appeal, and they administered what came to be known as the 'Red Terror.'

This relatively simple judicial structure was elaborated by Decree No 2 'On Courts' adopted 15 February 1918. Intermediate-level courts were organised in some provinces and a Supreme Judicial Control organ authorised but never actually instituted. The functions of people's assessors were given in greater detail, and the courts were officially authorised to allow persons to speak their native tongue in court. The powers of cassational instances were enlarged.

Decree No 2 said nothing of the revolutionary tribunals. These continued to be the object of special legislation; their numbers were reduced but their jurisdiction was broadened. The All-Russian Extraordinary Commission for the Struggle Against Counter-Revolution and Sabotage (VChKa) worked closely with the revolutionary tribunals as an investigative agency, possessing for some time the power to punish summarily without trial. New statutes on revolutionary tribunals were enacted on 12 April 1919 and 18 March 1920. The latter was viewed as a kind of unification act for the tribunals; procedural rules were clarified; cassation was strengthened; measures of repression had to be based on legislation. Outside this system there operated revolutionary military tribunals and revolutionary military railway tribunals on the basis of slightly different principles and their own legislation. In mid-1921 the entire scheme of tribunals was unified; the Supreme Tribunals attached to the VTsIK became the sole cassational and supervisory organ for the entire system and a court of first instance for especially important cases.

The people's courts too underwent modifications. They had jurisdiction over all civil and criminal cases except those within the competence of revolutionary tribunals. Most cases were heard by a judge and two people's assessors; especially grave crimes were heard by a college of the court consisting of the judge and six assessors.

At the outset of 1921 moves were underway to set up a single centre of judicial supervision for people's courts and revolutionary tribunals in the person of a body called Supreme Judicial Control; instead the people's commissariat of justice was given judicial supervisory powers, but only partial ones. The introduction of the NEP brought further changes for the judiciary: the VChKa was reorganised into the GPU; the Procuracy was founded; and criminal, civil, labour, civil and criminal procedure codes were enacted. The 'judicial reform of 1922' in the RSFSR instituted a uniform system of judicial institutions consisting of the people's court (in two guises), the provincial court, and the RSFSR Supreme Court, broadened the rights of people's assessors somewhat further, and clarified the competence of each level in the system. The other union republics enacted similar reforms in early 1923. The union republic reforms were hardly in motion before they were overtaken by the formation of the USSR (by treaty of 30 December 1922) and the creation in July 1923 of the USSR Supreme Court.

The details of the USSR Supreme Court of this period are beyond the scope of this study except to note a few distinctive features. The Court exercised several types of supervisory power: general supervision, constitutional supervision, and judicial supervision, as well as trying important cases at first instance. It issued guiding explanations to inferior courts on all-union legislation. The Procuracy was linked to the Supreme Court in the person of the 'Procurator of the USSR Supreme Court' until 1933, when the two were separated and the Court lost its responsibilities for general supervision over legality.

Several reorganisations of the judiciary ensued. On 29 October 1924 the USSR enacted Fundamental Principles of Court Organisation, followed on 19 November 1926 by a new RSFSR Statute on Court Organisation. Military courts were separately regulated by a Statute of 20 August 1926 on Military Tribunals and the Military Procuracy, but were considered to be part of the judicial system; the USSR Supreme Court exercised general guidance over them. Nevertheless, there persisted an inclination to create specialised tribunals. In 1930 'line courts for railway transport' were formed, followed in 1934 by analogous courts for water transport; both were served by the Supreme Court as a cassational instance. In 1934 a separate body was formed outside the judicial system, the Special Board (*Osoboe soveshchanie*) attached to the USSR People's Commissar of Internal Affairs. The Special Board was authorised to apply to persons deemed 'socially dangerous': (a) exile for up to five years under public supervision in localities listed by the

Commissar; (b) banishment for up to five years under public supervision and a prohibition to reside in capitals, large cities, and industrial centres of the USSR; (c) confinement in correctional-labour camps for a term of up to five years; (d) banishment of socially dangerous foreign subjects beyond the limits of the USSR. The Procurator might protest decisions of the Board, but no judicial review was possible under the Decree.[1] The Board was apparently free to decide who was 'socially dangerous' on any basis it chose without regard to substantive or procedural law. Countless Soviet citizens fell victim to this institution; it was abolished formally in 1958, but presumably ceased to function after Stalin's death in 1953.

The ordinary court system evidently functioned throughout this period in the normal way. The 1936 USSR Constitution transformed a number of established elements of judicial administration—electivity of judges, participation of people's assessors, national language in court proceedings—to the status of constitutional principles. The 1936 Constitution also 'federalised' a number of areas which had been shared between the central and union republic authorities. On 16 August 1938 the USSR Supreme Soviet adopted a Law on Court Organisation to replace the 1924 Fundamental Principles. The 1936 Constitution having proclaimed the disappearance of antagonistic classes in the USSR, the 1938 Law made provision for the equality of citizens before the court. The concentration of judicial supervision in the Supreme Court, however, while it contributed to uniformity of judgments and perhaps in some areas (the law of tort) to judicial innovation in the law, did complicate and prolong the judicial process. During the war, military tribunals assumed jurisdiction in areas proclaimed to be in a military situation; in areas under siege, the ordinary courts were simply transformed into military tribunals.

CURRENT LEGISLATION

In 1957 the USSR Constitution was amended to return responsibility for court organisation to the union republics to be exercised in accordance with all-union Fundamental Principles of Legislation. The FPL were enacted on 25 December 1958, replacing the 1938 Law, and union republics approved their own laws on court organisation in 1959-61. These FPL and union republic laws continue in force with slight amendments arising out of the 1977-78 USSR and constituent republic constitutions.

JUDGES

It is not easy to ascertain the extent to which the Soviet judiciary may resemble the civil service-type of judiciary in much of Western Europe

---

1 *SZ SSSR* (1935) I, no. 11, item 84.

or the Anglo-American judiciary appointed for life or a high pensionable age. Soviet judges are elected to office by secret ballot for five-year terms, directly at the lowest level of people's courts by the populace and at intermediate and highest levels by the respective legislative organ. The number of senior judicial posts is small compared to the numbers of lower-court judges, and there is no career-pattern data on the extent to which senior judicial positions may be filled from the ranks of experienced lower-court judges. In 1987, 29% of the people's court judges were elected for the first time, suggesting that some 2,500 judges had either moved into a superior court or found employment elsewhere in the legal profession or national economy.

Any citizen of the USSR aged 25 or above may be elected a people's judge. The candidacy for each judgeship in practice is limited to a single person, usually selected on the basis of his legal, political, and personal qualifications. There are, in all, about 15,500 judges in the USSR. In June 1987, 12,122 people's judges were elected. Of these an absolute majority had a higher legal education. 55.5% were men. The USSR Supreme Court presently consists of a chairman, two deputy chairmen, and 16 members. There are about 3,000 judges serving in the union republic supreme courts and inferior courts above the people's courts. Although the percentage level of higher legal education among judges is still lower than the Soviet authorities would wish, the figures represent a vast improvement; in 1941 only 6.4% of the judges had this qualification.

PEOPLE'S ASSESSORS

All Soviet courts in principle have original jurisdiction and therefore all have people's assessors because Soviet law requires that civil and criminal cases in all courts be considered collegially at first instance, that is, by a judge and two people's assessor. Any Soviet citizen aged 25 or above may be elected a people's assessor. In the 1987 elections held between April and June at collectives in enterprises, factories, military units, collective farms, and so forth 850,344 people's assessors were elected for a two-and-a-half-year term. Each assessor is called upon to sit in court for not more than two weeks per year. Of those elected, 44.7% were workers, 7.5% were collective farmers, 43.6% were men, 41.9% were members or candidate members of the Communist Party, 20% were under age 30, and 9.7% were members of the Communist Youth League. The USSR Supreme Court has a panel of 45 people's assessors elected by the USSR Supreme Soviet. People's assessors are expected to introduce a lay element into judicial proceedings. They each have an equal vote with the judge and on occasion are known to outvote the judge. Although few have legal training, most are likely to take part in elementary law courses offered by 'people's universities' (chapter 5, above) or seminars arranged by the legal profession, the court, or a local soviet. Many, of course, serve more than one term and accumulate experience. Their employer is obliged to release them from work with pay for the two-week period and they are reimbursed for expenses under certain circumstances.

RECALL

Both judges and people's assessors are subject to recall by the voters or agency which elected them. When performing their duties, neither may be brought to criminal responsibility, arrested, or subjected to administrative penalties imposed in an administrative proceeding without the consent of designated officials. Recalls are uncommon, but are known to occasionally occur. In 1986 some 76 judges were recalled and 837 subjected to disciplinary measures for various forms of incompetence. Judges and people's assessors are by law accountable to those who elected them and are expected to report at designated intervals on the course of their work.

COURT STRUCTURE

Under current legislation courts are divided into two categories: courts of the USSR (USSR Supreme Court and military tribunals) and union republic courts (all others, depending upon the administrative-territorial sub-divisions of each union republic). Although by reason of their gravity or complexity superior courts may hear civil or criminal cases at first instance, about 95% of all cases are decided initially by the district or city people's courts. Under the 1977-78 constitutions a people's court is being instituted in each rural or urban district (rather than sub-dividing districts into 'precincts' as previously). As a rule each people's court has several judges; from 50-75 people's assessors are elected per judge, depending on case-load experience in the court. Single-judge courts exist only in sparsely populated areas. The basis for allocating the case-load varies among districts with multi-judge courts. Some judges specialise and hear all cases of a particular type (family, labour, criminal); some specialise in 'zones' of the district, hearing all cases emanating from a territorial unit within the district; some use a mixed system, reserving criminal cases for the court chairman and dividing types of civil cases among the others by zone. People's courts decide other types of matters, for example, expunging of convictions, conditional release from places of deprivation of freedom, appeals of citizens against actions of officials or administrative agencies, and special proceedings (establishment of facts having legal significance, and others). Each court has a plan for social legal propaganda amongst the masses. This takes the form of periodic reports to the electors, required by law, and voluntary lectures on legal topics at factories, clubs, universities of legal knowledge and the like, and on radio and television. Some people's judges submit their special rulings in particular cases to collectives of working people for discussion.

The extent to which intermediate tiers of courts are interposed between the district or city people's courts and the union republic supreme court depends upon the administrative-territorial structure of the respective union republic. The RSFSR is by far the most complex: the RSFSR Supreme Court exercises supervision over 16 autonomous republic supreme courts, six territorial courts, 51 regional courts, five autonomous region courts, and five autonomous national area courts. The respective local soviet elects the court at each level from a list of candidates proposed by the RSFSR Ministry of Justice. Although the law does not include formal legal qualifications as a prerequisite for nomination, about 90% of the judges at these levels have a higher legal education and experience in legal work. In areas where national minorities are important, regard is had to nominating candidates who have some command of the language, customs, and morals of the local populace.[2]

The precise structure of each tier of courts varies slightly; as a rule, each is divided into divisions for civil and criminal cases and has a presidium. Each division has a chairman confirmed by the executive committee or equivalent thereto upon the recommendation of the court chairman. The court presidium is composed of the court chairman, deputy chairmen, and the number of members determined by the executive committee. The competence of each tier also varies slightly. Each tier may act as a court of first instance in cases designated by law or in cases deemed too complex for a lower instance; as a court of second or higher instance to consider cases on appeal or protest from inferior courts (judgments and rulings which have not entered into legal force); and as a court of supervisory instance to consider protests against judgments, etc, which have entered into force. The period for appeal and protest is uniform for all courts in criminal cases: seven full days from the date judgment is proclaimed or, for a convicted person under guard, from the moment he is handed the court judgment; and for civil cases, ten days. Civil cases which a superior court is likely to hear at first instance include: copyright, defamation, decisions twice reversed in cassation, and cases of great social significance. The court presidiums chiefly exercise supervisory powers, considering protests against judgments and the like; the officials who have the right to bring protests are many under Soviet legislation, but in practice the majority are brought by procurators at the respective level of courts. Prior to 1976 the presidiums exercised disciplinary powers over judges. Those functions

---

2 A. T. Bazhanov and V. P. Malkov (eds) *Sud i pravosudie v SSSR* (1980) p 152. The Tatar ASSR Supreme Court had a permanent staff all of whom had a higher education (not necessarily legal), 10 to 15 years of court work, and 60% of whom were Tatar.

have been removed and placed in the hands of disciplinary divisions of the said courts.

SUPREME COURTS

The union republic supreme courts are structured similarly to the intermediate tiers of courts, but with the addition of a plenum. The plenum consists of the court chairman, deputy chairmen, and all court members; it meets at least quarterly and adopts decrees by majority vote. The presidium is composed of the court chairman, his deputies, and court members in a number determined by the respective presidium of the union republic supreme soviet. In the RSFSR six court members, four deputy chairmen, and the chairman (11 in all) comprise the Presidium.

The competence of union republic supreme courts varies in practice from one to another depending upon the existence of intermediate tiers of courts. In those smaller union republics the supreme courts act more commonly at first instance in both civil and criminal cases (Estonia, Latvia, Moldavia, and others). Both intermediate and supreme courts hold circuit sessions frequently at factories, enterprises, or institutions. The great majority of criminal cases heard at first instance in the supreme courts are considered in advance at executive sessions of the court. Supreme courts of autonomous and union republics and the USSR Supreme Court all have the right of legislative initiative which is rarely, if ever, exercised.

The presidiums of supreme courts consider cases by way of supervision upon protests, hear reports concerning the work of judicial divisions and the court apparatus, and spend much time on surveys of judicial practice. It is the plenums of the supreme courts, however, which distinguish Soviet courts so dramatically from their Anglo-American counterparts; the plenums issue 'guiding explanations' to lower courts regarding the application of legislation on the basis of analyses of judicial practice, forensic statistics, court decisions, or proposals made by the chairman of the supreme court, minister of justice, or procurator. The importance of guiding explanations can not be overemphasised, for it is by this means that the supreme courts instruct inferior courts on how to understand and apply the law and ensure uniformity of interpretation and application. Guiding explanations, binding upon all inferior courts, are published in supreme court bulletins and raise lively debate about their role as sources of law (chapter 4, above). Most if not all supreme courts have formed scientific advisory councils to advise on the drafting of guiding explanations and other matters. The Scientific Advisory Council attached to the RSFSR Supreme Court consists of 49 persons, including leading scholars, judges, trade union personnel, and jurisconsults. In some union republics (Georgia, Kazakh) the supreme court plenum also acts as a supervisory instance to hear protests in specific cases.

Whereas the union republic supreme courts operate on the basis of relevant provisions in the union republic laws on court organisation, the USSR Supreme Court operates pursuant to both the 1958 FPLCOrg and the Law on the USSR Supreme Court of 30 November 1979. The distinction mentioned earlier between courts of the USSR and courts of the union republics is extremely important. The USSR Supreme Court exercises supervision over the judicial activity of the former (itself and the military tribunals), but over the latter only in certain situations. The USSR Supreme Court does not, under present legislation, accept cases which arise in the judicial agencies of union or autonomous republics unless the union republic supreme court already has considered them. The union republic supreme court is the final judicial instance for considering protests against judgments, decrees, and protests of the union republic supreme court unless they are contrary to all-union legislation or they violate the interests of another union republic. The freeing of the USSR Supreme Court from unrestricted powers of judicial supervision is intended to enable the Court to concentrate upon studies of inferior court practice and the issuance of appropriate guiding explanations. The inclusion of the chairmen of the union republic supreme courts ex officio as members of the USSR Supreme Court is believed to enhance the union republic role in 'principled' issues of judicial policy.

The USSR Supreme Court structure is analogous to the union republic supreme courts. The Court consists of 20 judges and 45 people's assessors. The total staff of the Court, including judges, consists of 201 people. Occasionally the Court hears cases at first instance and less often on circuit. Because the Court has responsibility for military tribunals, it consists of three judicial divisions: civil, criminal, and military. The Court's scientific advisory council is about the same size as the RSFSR Supreme Court but is divided into two sections: civil and criminal.

In addition to the protests already mentioned, the Plenum of the USSR Supreme Court may consider cases being reopened because of newly discovered circumstances and hear a variety of matters relating to activities of union republic supreme courts. When drafting guiding explanations, the Plenum submits the draft to its scientific advisory council; the practice has grown up also of circulating the drafts for comment to law faculties and research institutes.

Through its judicial divisions, the Court will resolve disputes between union republic courts about where a case should be heard, the issue of whether a court shall apply the procedural legislation of a foreign state when performing judicial commissions pursuant to international treaties, and protests against awards of the Maritime Arbitration Commission. As a court of the USSR, the Supreme Court has special powers with regard to military tribunals.

The USSR Supreme Court publishes a Bulletin six times a year containing the texts of guiding explanations, reports on judicial practice, and reports of individual cases disposed of by the Court. The decisions, judgments, and rulings of judicial divisions of the Court and decrees of the Plenum in individual cases are not binding upon inferior courts when analogous categories of cases are considered even when published in the Bulletin. Their publication is intended to help lower courts better understand the will of the legislator and contribute to the strengthening of a uniform notion of socialist legality.[3]

The personnel apparatus, as one would expect, consists primarily not of judges but of consultants and inspectors of various types to review judicial practice of other courts. Indeed, the USSR Supreme Court, despite its position as the supreme judicial instance in the Soviet Union, is not the largest court as measured by staff. That distinction belongs to the RSFSR Supreme Court.

MILITARY TRIBUNALS

The Soviet, and to some extent pre-revolutionary, tradition of having special systems of tribunals was largely abandoned by the mid-1950s in the USSR with the abolition of the special boards and the transport courts. Military tribunals, however, have survived for reasons not wholly, perhaps, convincing. The usual reason adduced is that military life has special features which require adjudication in tribunals composed of military personnel. Soviet military tribunals are 'courts of the USSR.' They operate on the basis of a statute as amended on 25 June 1980. Unlike the ordinary courts, military tribunals are elected by military unit and not on the basis of administrative-territorial sub-divisions. In other respects the basic principles of Soviet legislation in courts apply: electivity, people's assessors, social accusers and defenders, collegiality when considering cases, right to counsel, openness of trial, and substantive legislation. Only individuals on active military service may serve on military tribunals, but otherwise the same requirements for election apply. Despite the command principle of the armed services, judges and people's assessors of military tribunals are to be independent and subordinate only to law.

Military tribunals exist on three levels. At first instance only are the tribunals of armies, flotillas, formations, and garrisons. At cassational and supervisory instances and at first instance in some cases are courts of second tier: military tribunals of areas, fleets, force groups, and branches of the Armed Forces. The third level is the Military Division of the USSR Supreme Court. Military tribunals hear cases concerning all crimes committed by servicemen and reservists (while training), officers, etc, including members of State security agencies, and the command staff

3 Ibid p 203.

of correctional labour institutions, all cases concerning espionage, and crimes specifically designated by USSR legislation. Related civil suits also may be considered, and in exceptional situations where there are no ordinary courts, military tribunals may consider all cases. Military rank often will govern which level of tribunal hears a case at first instance. A superior military tribunal always has the right to remove any case at first instance from an inferior tribunal.

Supervisory powers are exercised by respective superior tribunals over inferior, the highest supervisory instance being the Plenum of the USSR Supreme Court. Protests by way of supervision may be brought by a number of designated officials. The judicial activities of military tribunals are taken into account just as those of other courts when summaries of judicial practice are prepared. The structure and personnel establishment of military tribunals are fixed by the Military Tribunals Administration of the USSR Ministry of Justice jointly with the USSR Ministry of Defence.

Procuracy

HISTORY

The Procuracy is very much a Russian institution. Its precise origins await definitive study. Peter the Great created the office of 'fiskal' in 1711 with certain supervisory functions in treasury matters and is known to have studied carefully Swedish institutions similar in nature. The classical Petrine model of procurator as an official independent of local influence to act as the 'eye of the Tsar' in supervising the conformity to law of all government departments, officials, and courts, including the Senate itself, was established by an Edict of 12 January 1722. Subordinate procurators were authorised to submit 'proposals' to local officials who violated the law and to present 'protests and reports' regarding violations to superior procurators. In the three years or so of operation until the death of Peter the Great in 1725, the institution reportedly enjoyed some success. Peter's successors reduced its importance; Catherine II revived the Procuracy in modified form, transforming it into an administrative office rather than a supervisory one. Alexander I in his government reorganisation of 1802 combined the Procurator General with the Minister of Justice and removed most remaining supervisory powers over State administration. The 1864 judiciary reforms ultimately eliminated these and required the procurators to confine their activities to the judicial department. Nevertheless, in the last half-century of Imperial government the procurators did participate as members of certain provincial committees, but without the right of supervision or protest. Prosecution of cases had become their principal function.

The pre-revolutionary Procuracy was abolished by Decree No 1 'On Courts' of 24 November 1917. The prosecution function was left initially to the public-spirited or aggrieved citizen. A College of 'accusers and defenders' was formed by Decree No 2 'On Courts', and revolutionary tribunals relied on their own colleges of accusers, to consist of at least three persons for each tribunal selected by the local soviets directly or upon the recommendation of its tribunal or the People's Commissariat of Justice. But these were makeshift measures and in the end proved to be unworkable. The supervisory functions of the pre-revolutionary Procuracy over justice matters was dispersed to organs of local soviets. One archival source of the period (1918) disclosed that the 'Commissar of justice is the representative of central authority in the provinces, replacing the former procurators.' Supervisory functions also were exercised by ancillary bodies, the People's Commissariat for State Control and later the People's Commissariat of the Workers'-Peasants' Inspectorate. These too were inadequate, and at Lenin's behest on 28 May 1922, following prolonged debate, the RSFSR instituted the State Procuracy.[4] The original model combined elements of the Petrine and Alexandrine versions: Peter's notions that the Procuracy was to be independent of all local authorities and that it would supervise the legality of acts of all government bodies, enterprises, and citizens through its powers of protest, proposal, and prosecution; Alexander's policy of placing the Procuracy within the People's Commissariat of Justice and making the Commissar simultaneously the Procurator of the Republic. The Procurator appointed all inferior procurators from candidates put forward by central and local authorities; a separate system of military procurators also was subordinate to the Procurator.

Under the 1924 USSR Constitution, an all-union Procuracy was created within the USSR Supreme Court with powers of constitutional, general, and judicial supervision; its powers were elaborated in a Statute of 24 July 1929.[5] In 1933 the Procuracy was reorganised; its role in constitutional supervision was abolished, but there remained the dual system of the USSR Procuracy and union republic people's commissars of justice acting simultaneously as procurators. The latter found themselves in a position of dual subordination: to the USSR Procurator and to the council of people's commissars of their respective republic. Ultimate centralisation of the Procuracy came in 1936 with the formation of the USSR People's Commissariat of Justice and separation of union republic procuracies from that commissariat at all levels. Curiously, this

4 *SU RSFSR* (1922) no. 36, item 424.
5 *SZ SSSR* (1929) no. 50, item 445. On the debates over the revival and powers of the procuracy, see J. N. Hazard *Settling Disputes in Soviet Society* (1960); G. Morgan *Soviet Administrative Legality* (1962); S. Kucherov *The Organs of Soviet Administration of Justice: Their History and Operation* (1970) pp 404–447.

centralisation was not followed by new unified legislation. Articles 113-117 of the 1936 USSR Constitution became the principal legislative definition of Procuracy powers and functions together with the 1933 Statute. Specialised procuracies for water transport and the railway underwent episodic restructuring in the 1930s, and on 5 November 1936 the structural sub-divisions of the Procuracy were reorganised. On 19 March 1946 the Procurator of the USSR was renamed the Procurator General of the USSR. After Stalin's death and the dismantling of the special boards, it was decided to reinforce rather than abandon the supervisory role of the Procuracy. A *Pravda* editorial of 12 April 1955 called upon the Procuracy to eliminate 'serious shortcomings' in its work and criticised the institution for having been 'insufficiently principled,' not fully using the 'rights granted to it by the USSR Constitution,' not uncovering violations of law at the time, and not stopping the 'anti-State activities of individual officials.'

The extent to which the Procuracy was a willing collaborator or pawn in special board proceedings (Procuracy participation was compulsory under the decree establishing the boards) has yet to be studied, but it is doubtful under the political climate of the time that the Procuracy could have effectively altered the course of events when the Party itself was unable to do so. On 24 May 1955 the Procuracy received its first comprehensive legislation in the form of the Statute on Procuracy Supervision in the USSR. The Statute enlarged the scope of general supervision by the Procuracy, empowered procurators to demand and obtain data and documents from officials, and elaborated the procurators' powers to make proposals, representations, and protests.

CURRENT LEGISLATION

The Procuracy is the most prestigious component of the Soviet legal profession and seems to attract the most able law graduates into its ranks. There are more than 18,000 procurators in the Soviet Union. In 1975 Procuracy sources indicated that 2.3% of the 4,008 city and district procurators were women. Communist Party membership among procurators is high, probably higher than for any other branch of the legal profession, averaging about 83%. Some observers place the figure higher. The qualifications for appointment as procurator are laid down in the 1979 Law on the Procuracy of the USSR: citizenship of the USSR, aged 25, higher legal education, and the 'necessary political, professional, and moral qualities.' Individual exceptions may be made to the requirement of a higher legal education, but 98% of all procurators presently have that qualification (compared with 10.7% in 1936). All procurators are appointed to office for a term of five years. Reappointments are evidently the rule, for a high degree of career continuity is characteristic for procurators. In 1973 more than 50% of the Procuracy had in excess of ten years of service.[6] It should be added that since 1933 only eight jurists have served as Procurator General, and of these only two in the post-Stalin era: A. I. Akulov, 1933–35; A. Ia. Vyshinskii, 1935–39; M. Pankrat'ev, 1939–40; V. M. Bochkov, 1940–43; K. P. Gorshenin, 1943–48; G. N. Safanov, 1948–53; R. A. Rudenko, 1953–81; and A. Rekunkov, 1981–.

True to its Petrine model, the Procuracy is a unified, centralised system of agencies. The Procurator General is appointed by the USSR Supreme Soviet and accountable exclusively thereto; he in turn appoints inferior procurators down to the level of regions, and confirms the appointment by union republic procurators of autonomous national area, district, and city procurators. Inferior procurators are subordinate to superior. The entire system is enjoined to enforce legality and exercise supervision notwithstanding local differences and regardless of local or departmental influences. Ranks within the Procuracy are governed by the Statute on Class Ranks of Workers of Procuracy Agencies of the USSR adopted 28 October 1980. The procedures for disciplining and rewarding procuracy and investigative personnel are regulated by a Statute confirmed 17 February 1984.

STRUCTURE

Procuracy agencies exist at each administrative-territorial level of the USSR and additionally there are military and transport procuracies. The USSR Procurator General is the head of the entire system. He has a first deputy and deputies appointed upon his recommendation by the Presidium of the USSR Supreme Soviet and works closely with a Collegium, of which he is chairman, consisting of his deputies and other Procuracy executive personnel. Chief administrations, administrations, and sections of a functional nature are formed at each level of the Procuracy; these are laid down in a Decree of the Presidium of the USSR Supreme Soviet dated 29 May 1980.

The Collegium considers the basic state and orientation of Procuracy work, personnel training and appointments, drafts of important institutions and orders, and reports submitted by various Procuracy personnel. The Procurator General implements Collegium decisions, but if there is disagreement, implements his own decisions and reports the matter to the Presidium of the USSR Supreme Soviet. Similar collegiums exist at lower levels of the Procuracy.

The structured sub-divisions of the Procuracy include the general supervision administration, the chief investigative administration, the personnel administration, the section for supervision over investigation in State security agencies, the section for supervision over the

---

[6] G. Smith *The Soviet Procuracy and the Supervision of Administration* (1978) p 25.

consideration of civil cases in courts, and a similar section for criminal cases, a section for the supervision over the execution of laws on transport, a section for supervision over the observance of laws in correctional-labour institutions, a statistics section, a letters section and others.

The Procuracy has a large number of investigators who carry out the preliminary investigation in cases relegated by law or by the Procuracy to their competence. Attached to the Procurator General are senior investigators and investigators for 'especially important cases;' lower levels of the Procuracy have investigators of the same nature.

Attached to the Procuracy are several institutions of a research or instructional nature. The All-Union Scientific Research Institute for Problems of Strengthening Legality and Legal Order explores the causes of crime and preventative measures (see chapter 5, above). Procuracy personnel are required to undergo periodic attestation and courses to improve their skills. These are conducted chiefly by the institutes for raising the qualifications of procuracy and investigative cadres. A 'scientific methods council' within the Procuracy, which includes well-known legal scholars from without the organisation, considers proposals to improve the organisation and activities of the Procuracy. The Procuracy publishes its own monthly journal, *Sotsialisticheskaia zakonnost'*.

BRANCHES OF PROCURACY SUPERVISION

The supervisory functions of the Procuracy are multifarious and collectively comprise that institution's claim to uniqueness among bodies with analogous objects in other families of legal systems. Present legislation demarcates four branches of Procuracy supervision. The first and most important is the Procuracy's power of 'general supervision,' that is, supervision over:

... the execution of laws by ministries, State committees, and departments, enterprises, institutions, and organisations, executive and administrative agencies of local soviets of people's deputies, collective farms, co-operative and other social organisations, officials, and citizens ... (Art 22, Law on Procuracy Supervision in the USSR)

so that acts promulgated by these bodies correspond to the constitutions and to other enactments of superior legislative and governmental bodies and so that laws are precisely and uniformly executed by officials and citizens. This formulation makes it clear that the Procuracy is not the supreme guardian of the law; it has no supervisory authority over acts of the all-union, union republic, or autonomous republic councils of ministers, nor over the supreme soviets or their presidiums. Its concern is to ensure that the Soviet bureaucracy and citizenry adhere to law and not that the highest agencies of State power and administration do so.

The powers of the Procuracy to give effect to general supervision are several. Chief among them perhaps is the procurator's right to demand copies of subordinate legislation and relevant supporting data concerning violations of law or the execution of legislation as well as, under amendments introduced in June 1987, information concerning the state of legality and measures taken to ensure legality. Departmental and non-departmental expert examinations may be carried out and information received or brought to the notice of the Procuracy may be verified. Officials and citizens may be summoned to give oral or written explanations regarding violations. Unlawful legislation may be protested, an instruction given to eliminate clear violations of the law (1987 amendment), and offenders prosecuted. If material harm was caused by a violation of law, the procurator may initiate civil proceedings for recovery. Recommendations may be made concerning the correction, elimination, or reasons for violations, which are binding upon those to whom they are directed.

In the realm of general supervision a procurator may protest against a normative or non-normative act as contrary to law to the issuing agency or official or the superior thereof and demand the act be repealed or brought into conformity with law, the illegal actions of the official be terminated, and the violated right be restored. The act is suspended until the protest is considered in certain instances; the agency or official receiving the protest has ten days to consider it and must notify the procurator of the results. A *recommendation* regarding a violation of law carries no time limit for consideration, merely 'without delay.' If the recommendation is considered by a collegial organ, the latter is to notify the procurator of the date of its session; the procurator has the right to be present and take part personally when the recommendation is considered. Specific measures must be taken within a month and the procurator informed of the results. If a violation of law justifies the initiation of a criminal, disciplinary, or administrative proceeding, the procurator renders a reasoned *decree* for these proceedings to be undertaken.

Under changes introduced in 1987, the Procuracy has the right to issue a written instruction (*predpisanie*) to an agency or official, or their superior, to eliminate a clear violation of a law that may cause material harm to the rights and legal interests of the State, an enterprise, institution, or organisation, or a citizen unless it ceases at once. The instruction must cite the relevant norm of law being violated and suggest corrective steps. Appeal may be made against the instruction to the superior procurator within ten days, but the appeal does not suspend the instruction, and the decision of the superior procurator is final. If the Procuracy learns that unlawful acts are at a preparatory stage on the part of an official or citizen, it may issue a written warning, which may also be appealed to the superior procurator, though no time limit for appeal is imposed. The Procuracy warning also may be notified to the individual's or official's place of work, study, or residence. If the warning is not observed, an appropriate measure may be taken to bring the person to responsibility.

The second branch of Procuracy supervision concerns the execution of laws by agencies of inquiry and preliminary investigation. The Procuracy's powers are vast and, to Anglo-American eyes, curiously anomalous in some respects, for the procurator is expected both to discipline and further, by himself if necessary, the investigatory process. The procurators are to ensure that when crimes are investigated, the legal requirements for a 'comprehensive, complete, and objective' investigation of all circumstances of the case are observed, both those incriminating and vindicating the accused, aggravating and mitigating circumstances, the causes of the crime, conditions furthering the crime, and measures taken to eliminate these conditions, that no one is detained, arrested, or prosecuted other than in the procedure provided for by law.

The sanction of the procurator for the arrest of a suspect or accused person is mandatory. The powers of the Procuracy to give effect to supervision over inquiries and investigations are numerous and encompass, among others, the right to verify all materials, give written instructions concerning the course of the investigation, personally take part in the investigation or wholly take it over, sanction specified investigatory actions, remove a case from one agency or investigator and transfer it to another, initiate or refuse to initiate a case, consent to termination of a case, confirm a conclusion or decree to indict, and send criminal cases to court.

The third branch of Procuracy supervision takes place in the courts when cases are being heard. Although the procurator is prosecuting the case on behalf of the State, he is nonetheless obliged by law to ensure that there is a comprehensive, complete, and objective judicial consideration of the case, that all judgments, decisions, rulings, or decrees rendered are legal, well-founded, and executed in a timely manner. The procurator may participate in the hearing of a case at all stages, from executive session of a court of first instance to all cassational and supervisory instances; he may file suits and applications in court, give opinions regarding the substance of a civil case as a whole, or, if there are grounds, refuse to accuse. Illegal decisions, judgments, decrees, and rulings are subject to *protest* by the procurator, who may also retract the protest before consideration thereof commences. Even if decisions, etc, have entered into force, a procurator may demand any case or category of cases from a court and bring a protest by way of supervision. Under certain circumstances the procurator may suspend execution of judgments, decisions, rulings, and decrees. Under a change introduced in 1988, those circumstances include a protest in a case concerning an administrative violation or a court case brought under the 1987 Law on the procedure for appealing unlawful actions of officials. The procurator's powers of judicial supervision extend to the highest levels of judicial activity. His participation is mandatory in the sessions of court plenums and presidiums; he has the right to make recommendations both for the issuance of guiding explanations to courts and for the failure of guiding explanations to conform to law. Under reforms introduced in 1987–88, the Procuracy is empowered to initiate suits in State Arbitrazh.

The final area of Procuracy supervision concerns institutions where individuals may be confined or detained, ranging from preliminary confinement to imprisonment or compulsory medical treatment. The procurator is to ensure that legislation regarding treatment of confined persons is observed by visiting places of confinement systematically and at any time, familiarise himself with relevant documentation, release immediately persons illegally confined, question detained or confined persons, and verify the conformity to law of orders, regulations, and decrees issued by the administrations of places of confinement. He also watches over the legal requirements applicable to the right of confined persons to submit appeals and applications to State agencies, social organisations, and officials, including the Procuracy itself.

The plurality of roles which the Procuracy sometimes faces can raise conflicts of interests, especially when the procurator must act as accuser on behalf of the State yet initiate objections to procedural or substantive violations by the court. To some extent conflicts are avoided by depersonalising the conflict. Protests against judicial decisions usually are brought by the Procuracy section specially charged with reviewing criminal or civil cases. Instances of procuratorial protests of this nature are frequently reported and the Procuracy has enjoyed a high success rate, approaching 80%.[7] Nevertheless, courts may and do reject Procuracy protests (as do State agencies and officials) if they do not concur with the reasons adduced on behalf of the protest, in which event the procurator may either acquiesce or protest on a higher level. The essence of the Procuracy function is to persuade agencies to correct their own errors; except in certain aspects of inquiries and preliminary investigations, the Procuracy itself has no administrative power to set affairs in order by itself.

The structure and powers of the Procuracy and its distinctive relationship to, or rather independence from, other branches of government have led many observers to characterise it as the fourth branch of government. Current legislation makes plain, however, that the Procuracy as the 'eye of the State' does not oversee the highest agencies of power and administration. Of all the agencies administering socialist legality, moreover, the Procuracy is perhaps most responsive to Communist Party guidance. This is not to suggest that Party organs directly administer the Procuracy, but rather that the Party influences more immediately than

---

[7] Ibid p 19. Published Procuracy protests have been extensively translated into English by G. Morgan and L. Boim in the *Law in Eastern Europe Series* vols. 13 (1966) and 20 (1978).

other legal bodies the concentration of Procuracy activity, especially in its powers of general supervision. Collections of Procuracy documents reproduce dozens of Party resolutions urging that greater attention be devoted to specified types of aberrant behaviour. Environmental legislation and economic violations have been among the areas singled out for emphasis. Campaigns against certain types of activity produce other forms of reinforcement in the form of press coverage, citizens' complaints, and signals of other types. These, accompanied by Procuracy verifications, are the principal reasons for Procuracy involvement in categories of activity by way of general supervision. Data from 1955-74 has suggested that the Procuracy in the 1970s was favouring the recommendation form of redress to the protest in exercising general supervision and concentrated upon economic violations. On an informal basis, Procuracy agencies enlarged their practice of sending informational memoranda to local Party organs about serious violations of law, principally crimes against State ownership, which commonly were accompanied by some kind of legal proceeding against the individual.[8] While individual citizens in the past have experienced difficulty in persuading the Procuracy to espouse their complaints, that may improve in the light of 1987 amendments to the Law on the Procuracy requiring that agency also to 'struggle against violations of laws which are directed toward ensuring the rights and legal interests of citizens.'

MILITARY PROCURACY

Supreme supervision over the execution of laws in the USSR Armed Forces is effectuated by the USSR Procurator General and the military procurators subordinate to him. The latter are independent of any local or military agencies. The Chief Military Procurator is appointed for a five-year term by the Presidium of the USSR Supreme Soviet upon the recommendation of the Procurator General. The sub-divisions of the military procuracy correspond to those of the military tribunals, and its basic functions include taking measures to prevent violations of law, military discipline, combat readiness, and State security; ensuring that USSR legislation is correctly and uniformly applied; protecting the rights and legal interests of military servicemen and their families, workers and employees of the Armed Services, and other citizens or military units, institutions, enterprises, and organisations. The supervisory powers of the military procuracy extend to ensuring that all military personnel execute the law when performing their duties; that military tribunals observe legality when considering civil and criminal cases; and that legality is observed in guardhouses and disciplinary battalions. The ability of military procurators to demand data and information is more

8 Smith, note 6, above, pp 103-104.

limited than their civilian counterparts, but they may obtain orders, instructions, and other acts to verify their conformity to law, conduct on-the-spot verifications, but only in connection with applications, appeals, or other information concerning violations, and demand explanations from officials, military servicemen, and other citizens.

Notariat

HISTORY

The Decree No 1 'On Courts' of 24 November 1917 omitted to mention the Notariat among the Imperial legal institutions being abolished. The Moscow Council of People's Commissars repealed on 23 March 1918 the 'presently prevailing Statute on the Notarial Office' and municipalised all notarial offices. Local practices varied, but the general pattern was initially for local city soviets to open notarial offices. A Circular of the RSFSR People's Commissariat to eliminate these and distribute their functions among other bodies was not implemented; instead notarial 'tables' operated in some cities attached to the judicial-investigative subsections of provincial justice sections or local people's courts. The exigencies of the NEP required some offices to certify legal transactions and verify their conformity to law. Despite some reluctance within the People's Commissariat of Justice, 'Theses on the Notariat' were published for discussion early in 1922, and on 4 October 1922 the RSFSR Statute on the State Notariat was enacted, superseded on 7 July 1923 by a new redaction incorporating elements introduced by the new RSFSR Code of Civil Procedure. Other union republics enacted similar but by no means identical legislation, which led to the adoption on 14 May 1926 of an all-union decree 'On the Basic Principles of Organising the State Notariat.' On 4 October 1926 the RSFSR introduced a new Statute on the State Notariat of the RSFSR, succeeded successively by statutes of 20 July 1930, 31 December 1947, 30 September 1965, and the present Statute of 2 August 1974, as amended. The latter statute and similar republic enactments operate within the framework of an all-union Law on the State Notariat adopted 19 July 1973.

CURRENT LEGISLATION

In 1975 there were 3,255 notaries in the USSR of whom 80% were women. Citizens of the USSR who have a higher legal education are eligible for appointment as a State notary, and in individual instances also persons who do not have that level of education.

Notariat activities are carried out on three, so to speak, levels. Each major administrative-territorial centre down to regions contains a 'principal' State notarial office capable of performing all notarial activities of whatever complexity. Other State notarial offices perform most notarial functions. In communities where there are no notarial offices, the executive committees of local soviets perform these functions, and overseas, Soviet consular officials. The notarial offices are under dual subordination: to the respective agency of State power and to the respective ministry of justice.

Notaries in the Soviet Union perform many functions which in the Anglo-American legal system would be done by lawyers or solicitors and commissioners for oaths. Since notaries are concerned with what some call the humdrum of legal life, the everyday non-contentious transactions of ordinary citizens, Anglo-American lawyers involved in Soviet legal matters are highly likely to encounter the Soviet notary. The Soviet notary is not a private individual, however, but a civil servant salaried by the State. Fees charged by notaries are fixed by the State and are paid into the State treasury. Nor is the notary concerned exclusively with the personal affairs of citizens who apply for assistance. Legislation on the State Notariat requires the notary to protect socialist ownership, strengthen socialist legality and the legal order, prevent violations of law, as well as safeguard the rights and legal interests of citizens and organisations.

Soviet law provides some guarantees that notarial activities remain secret. Information about such activities and documents are issued only to those on whose behalf or with regard to whom they were performed, but may at the request of a court, the Procuracy, or agencies of investigation or inquiry be released in connection with proceedings in criminal or civil cases. Wills, however, are protected until the testator's death. The secrecy proviso extends to all who become aware of notarial activities in connection with their official duties, including the typist. Criminal penalties apply to unlawful disclosure under the union republic criminal codes.

Notarial activities fall basically into three categories. The first concerns the certification of the accuracy of copies of documents: about 70% of all notarial activities are of this nature. If the notary is doubtful about the document, he is obliged to submit it for expert examination. If the document turns out to be false, it is to be sent to the procurator. So burdensome has this activity become, that on 4 August 1983 the Presidium of the USSR Supreme Soviet adopted an Edict 'On the Procedure for the Issuance and Certification by Enterprises, Institutions, and Organisations of Copies of Documents Affecting the Rights of Citizens' instructing those bodies to issue copies of documents emanating from them if the documents are required for resolving matters affecting the applicant. Certification is now done by the issuing agency, and indeed must be done unless legislation requires notarial certification.

The second category encompasses the certification of legal transactions, such as contracts, wills, powers of attorney, and others. Soviet law requires many legal transactions to be notarially certified before they may become legally valid, and the notary will not do so if the contract is contrary to law. A purchase-sale contract for a dwelling house or dacha, for example, or an automobile, or a loan contract must be notarially certified. Indeed, any contract may if the parties so desire be notarially certified. Notarial certification performs several functions. The notary acts as the guardian of legality in transactions between private citizens, refusing to allow unlawful transactions to proceed. A certified contract, on the other hand, constitutes prima facie evidence of the facts recited in the document and the identity and legal capacity of the parties. The notarial office also keeps one copy of the contract and can supply replacements if the others are lost or destroyed. When property is being transferred, the notary must verify both the right to sell and to purchase, for Soviet citizens are restricted in the numbers of dwelling houses and amounts of dwelling space they may own or in the prices they may legally charge:

Example. An RSFSR notary was asked to certify a lease for a dwelling erected without permission. Certification was refused on the ground that since a dwelling erected without permission cannot be lawfully owned, there can be no lawful right to dispose of the dwelling by lease, and the notary therefore may not certify the contract.

The Notariat also offers another service arising out of contractual relations when one party has not discharged his indebtedness. If there is no dispute between the parties as to responsibility for the debt and no issue requiring judicial settlement, and the contract falls among the list of documents subject to notarial execution, the creditor can secure a notice to pay from the notary which, if not contested or answered, can be followed by a notarial endorsement of documents of execution. These documents will be given to the court sheriff for execution in the same manner as a civil court judgment. As a simplified procedure for execution, this method is extensively used to recover sums due for rates, utilities, or other local taxes. The debtor has recourse to the courts against any notarial action if he has any defence against the failure to pay.

It is not known how extensively Soviet citizens avail themselves of the possibility for testate succession, but inheritance is a third major category of notarial activity. Wills to be valid must be notarially certified. Standard forms are widely used. The notary must verify the legal capacity of the testator, his identity and residence, and explain to him the relevant provisions of the civil law:

Example. A notary certified a will signed by two persons as spouses. The legal department of the local soviet instructed that the certification was void even if the spouses requested certification. Each must make a separate will.

There are no estate taxes or death duties in the Soviet Union, although an inheritance tax is under serious consideration, nor administrators or executors as in the Anglo-American legal tradition. When evidence of the right to inherit is necessary, it is obtained through a certificate concerning the right to an inheritance issued by the notary; this might be necessary, for example, to claim monies due under an insurance policy, recover debts, establish heirs, or divide property amongst heirs. Notaries in such instances explain to the heirs their rights and duties and may help to decide disputes between them, although the right to appeal to the court is always available against the notary's determinations. The issuance of an inheritance certificate attracts State duty under Soviet law depending on the value of the estate, ranging from one ruble, to 5% of an estate valued at from 500 to 1,000 rubles, and 10% of estates valued in excess of 1,000 rubles, although exemptions are granted under certain circumstances.

Soviet notarial legislation contains a lengthy enumeration of other types of notarial activities. These include taking measures to protect inherited property, certifying rights of common ownership, prohibiting the alienation of a dwelling house, certifying the accuracy of translations, certifying that a citizen is alive or in a particular place, accepting money, securities or documents for deposit or safe-keeping, performing maritime protests, and others.[9] Under the Comprehensive Programme for the Development of the Production of Consumer Goods and Services for 1986–2000, by the end of the century the demand for notarial services is expected to be 2.3 times the 1985 level.

In fact, notaries give a great deal of legal advice and assistance. They are required by law not merely to explain rights and duties; they must anticipate the consequences of notarial activities so that the lack of legal information cannot work to the detriment of those seeking advice. Often advice can transcend the legal formalities of the transaction. For example, an aged Soviet citizen in poor health and requiring constant care applied to a notary to certify a contract of gift, as he wished to give his house to his sole surviving relative. The notary advised after ascertaining the full facts that the Soviet citizen conclude a purchase-sale contract instead with his relative on condition of the seller being supported for life by the purchaser. The house would in any event go to the relative, but the seller would receive much-needed material assistance and support for the remainder of his days; the applicant accepted the advice.

---

9 J. N. Hazard 'Humble Guardians of Routines (Notaries and ZAGS)' in D. D. Barry, et al (eds) *Soviet Law After Stalin* (1979) III, pp 247–258. Collignon described the principal Moscow Notarial Office in 1971 as handling about 60 to 70 inheritance cases, 100 to 150 certifications of contracts, 10 to 15 registration of wills, three to four sale of motor vehicle contracts, one or two property transactions, and about 1,000 certifications of copies per day: J. G. Collignon *Les juristes sovietiques* (1977) p 268.

Foreign citizens, enterprises, organisations, and stateless persons have the right to apply to State notarial offices, other agencies which perform notarial activities, or Soviet consular institutions. Unless this would be contrary to Soviet sovereignty or security or beyond their competence, Soviet notarial offices will execute commissions on behalf of foreign 'organs of justice.'

Registry for Acts of Civil Status

HISTORY

In pre-revolutionary Russia vital statistics concerning birth, marriage, divorce, death, or adoption were kept chiefly by the ecclesiastical authorities. By Decree of 18 December 1917 these functions were entrusted to the local administrative authorities, many of whom formed special sections for the registration of acts of civil status (ZAGS). The activities of ZAGS were governed principally by the 1918 RSFSR Family Code and those family codes which supplanted it.[10]

CURRENT LEGISLATION

Vital statistics are registered in the Soviet Union either at ZAGS offices of district soviets or at the executive committees of settlement or rural soviets. ZAGS offices are under dual subordination: to the executive committee of the respective soviet and to the USSR and union republic ministries of justice. Although ZAGS officials are not normally individuals with a higher legal education, they often have some legal training. Their functions transcend the purely mechanical function of registering a birth, marriage, divorce, adoption, paternity, change of name, or death. In the case of birth and marriage, ZAGS officials are to ensure the solemnity of the occasion, often through rituals or rites that impress upon the parents or intending couple their civil obligations. They have the power to dissolve marriages under certain situations prescribed by family legislation, but are enjoined to counsel couples seeking consensual divorce and reconcile them if possible.

Fees are charged for some ZAGS services which go to the State budget. Failure to register a vital statistic is subject to a fine. Methods assistance is offered by the ministries of justice to ZAGS officials. In large cities ZAGS functions are performed in specially designed premises, 'marriage palaces;' the RSFSR Ministry of Justice has a section directly concerned with civic rites. Refusals of ZAGS officials to register a vital statistic or the improper registration thereof may be appealed to a court.

---

[10] The 1974 RSFSR statute on ZAGS is translated in Butler *The Soviet Legal System* (1978) pp 275–278.

The records kept by ZAGS supplement Soviet census data as a whole. They are evidence of population trends, social mores, or demand for public welfare and eventually are transferred to State archival repositories.

State Arbitrazh

HISTORY

The conviction that economic disputes between State-owned enterprises required special expertise to resolve and perhaps special procedures surfaced early in Soviet legal history. Even during the NEP, State arbitration commissions were established for this purpose, by a Statute of 21 September 1922; they functioned in each province, and in Moscow a Supreme Arbitration Commission was formed to decide appeals filed against awards of provincial commissions and hear certain disputes at first instance. In 1924 the USSR Supreme Arbitration Commission was created to take jurisdiction over disputes involving enterprises of all-union stature or enterprises from different union republics. The introduction of national economic planning rendered NEP-style arbitration obsolete. On 4 March 1931 the arbitration commissions were abolished; pending and future litigation between enterprises was to be transferred to the ordinary courts, which would assign two people's assessors employed in economic agencies to hear the case with the judge. For a brief spell unification was achieved in the Soviet judicial system, but it was short-lived. The ordinary courts proved to be wholly unsuited at the time to handle this type of dispute. On 3 May 1931 the modern system of State Arbitrazh was created as an integral system attached to each administrative-territorial level from region upwards.

Resuscitated when the Pashukanis school of economic law was influential, State Arbitrazh initially represented a kind of hybrid between arbitration and adjudication. Reconciliation of the parties was to be the primary object; the enterprise managers themselves often appeared around the table to arrange a settlement. Failing that, Arbitrazh was to resolve the dispute on the basis of prevailing economic plans and regulations, having regard to economic policy and expediency. Civil code provisions were but useful guidelines and not binding; for a time even jurisconsults were barred from the proceedings. On 19 December 1933, Arbitrazh jurisdiction was extended to precontractual disputes between socialist organisations; by the mid-1930s the restoration of 'stability of laws' had left its imprint; Arbitrazh was to apply relevant Soviet legislation to disputes, jurisconsults appeared on behalf of their management, civil procedure codes were used when relevant, and the arbitrator was required to produce a reasoned written opinion based on an accurate account of the proceedings. Economic expediency had become a supplementary consideration to be invoked when legislation or the contract itself did not dispose of all the relevant issues.

The 1931 decree was replaced on 17 August 1960 by a statute which broadened the scope of Arbitrazh activity, enlarged Arbitrazh control over the terms of economic contracts, and elaborated the rules of Arbitrazh procedure. The 1960 Statute was replaced on 18 January 1974.

CURRENT LEGISLATION

Pursuant to the 1977 USSR Constitution (Art 163), which elevated State Arbitrazh to an agency of constitutional stature, a Law on State Arbitrazh in the USSR was enacted by the USSR Supreme Soviet on 30 November 1979, followed by a new statute and set of procedural rules confirmed by the USSR Council of Ministers on 5 June 1980. On 18 February and 30 December 1987 the Law on State Arbitrazh was extensively amended with a view to restructuring the State Arbitrazh system. The debate which commenced in the early 1920s about the need for specialist tribunals as against a unified judicial system for the consideration of all disputes persists in modern guise but under present legislation has taken a different turn. Although not a part of the judicial system, State Arbitrazh possesses many attributes of a court and also of an agency of State administration; it most emphatically is not an arbitration tribunal, and hence it would be misleading to render the Russian term *arbitrazh* in this instance as arbitration. State Arbitrazh bears analogy with a court in that it settles disputes solely on the basis of law in accordance with simplified rules of procedure that incorporate the essential protection of the codes of civil procedure, including the right of the parties to be legally represented. Arbitrazh awards are subject to execution in the same manner as civil court judgments and are binding upon the parties. And since 1987, like the courts, State Arbitrazh agencies are under the subordination of the superior arbitrazh. On the other hand, arbitrators are not independent and subject only to law as are the judges. Proceedings are informal and not open to the public, and arbitrazh itself may initiate proceedings when it discovers cause to do so. Finally, arbitrazh commonly finds itself resolving a category of dispute inconceivable in Anglo-American law: a pre-contractual dispute, which arises when the parties are obliged by the Plan to conclude an economic contract but cannot agree on those terms which remain for the parties to negotiate. Some observers believe the Arbitrazh role in pre-contractual disputes is akin to administratively completing the formulation of a planning directive rather than adjudicating a legal issue.

Soviet doctrinal writings offer no definitive view on the question. The majority of learned writings seem disposed to treat State Arbitrazh as a sui generis system of specialised legal agencies or tribunals created to settle economic disputes between socialist enterprises, institutions, and organisations with the object of strengthening socialist legality, planning discipline, production efficiency, and product quality.

STRUCTURE

There are two arbitrazh systems: State Arbitrazh and departmental arbitrazh. The latter system is for disputes between enterprises which are both within the jurisdiction of a single department. Each departmental arbitrazh operates on the basis of its own statute. In principle the procedure for initiating cases, settling disputes, and executing awards is analogous to that of State Arbitrazh, on which we shall dwell.

Even though arbitrazh has never been part of the judicial system it is only since 1974 that arbitrazh agencies have comprised their own unified system. State Arbitrazh of the USSR heads the system and is a union-republic agency. Inferior State arbitrazh agencies exist at all administrative-territorial levels down to city. The Chief State Arbitrator, appointed by the USSR Supreme Soviet or its Presidium for a five-year term, is in charge of the entire system. Unlike the Procurator-General, however, he does not appoint inferior arbitrators; the latter are appointed by the respective agency of State power. USSR State Arbitrazh and union republic arbitrazhes have formed arbitrazh colleges composed of the Chief State Arbitrator, his deputies, and leading executive personnel. Similar to colleges elsewhere in the ministerial system, for example the Ministry of Justice, the arbitrazh colleges deal with personnel placement, guidance of inferior arbitrazhes, discuss draft normative acts or instructive materials being worked out by USSR State Arbitrazh, and study arbitrazh practice.

JURISDICTION

State Arbitrazh handled over 700,000 cases in 1981, including over 60,000 pre-contractual disputes. Some 10,000 cases were initiated by State Arbitrazh itself. The jurisdiction of individual levels of the arbitrazh system is prescribed by statute and depends upon the value of the suit, the location of the parties, and the complexity of the issues to be resolved. The highest all-union and union republic levels may take jurisdiction over any dispute. The role of arbitrazh, however, is not confined to the four corners of the dispute. Legislation requires that arbitrazh agencies be attentive to violations of law or State discipline which emerge when disputes are considered, make proposals to eliminate them, and take measures to initiate prosecution of the guilty and compensation for harm caused. To this end State Arbitrazh agencies issue to directors of enterprises, or to appropriate law enforcement agencies, notifications, which must be responded to within a month of receipt with indications of remedial measures taken. USSR State Arbitrazh is obliged to report the most serious violations to the USSR Council of Ministers.

Under the 1987 amendments, State arbitrazh agencies have been given a type of 'general supervision' right to establish whether enterprises, institutions, and organisations properly observe the legal requirements for concluding contracts, performing contractual obligations, applying sanctions for breach, and for submitting pre-contractual disputes to arbitrazh agencies. These powers also extend to ministries and departments with regard to data on contractual formalities and performance. Directors of enterprises, institutions and organisations may be given a binding instruction (*predpisanie*) by arbitrazh agencies to eliminate any violations uncovered and, where appropriate, to impose financial liability on those responsible. In the same spirit, State arbitrazh agencies are to verify the work of departmental arbitrazhes with the right to issue binding instructions to eliminate violations; the instructions must be executed within ten days and the results reported to the issuing arbitrazh.

Certain categories of disputes fall outside arbitrazh competence, for example any dispute to which a citizen, collective farm, inter-collective farm or State-collective farm enterprises are parties, disputes within the jurisdiction of departmental arbitrazh, and disputes regarding bank operations connected with financial control over the proper use of capital investments. As amended in 1987, State Arbitrazh jurisdiction extends to disputes between State, co-operative, and other social enterprises, institutions, and organisations, and between joint enterprises, international associations, and organisations of the USSR and other COMECON member countries; disputes between State enterprises and their superior agencies regarding compensation for losses caused to the enterprises as a consequence of the superior agencies improperly performing their duties in respect of the enterprises; and to applications submitted by State enterprises to deem void the acts of superior agencies that affect the rights and interests of the enterprise and that are *ultra vires* the superior agency or issued in violation of Soviet legislation.

Suits may be brought by an interested party only upon showing that it took necessary measures to settle the dispute directly with the defendant. Arbitrazh may itself initiate a suit, as may the superior agencies of a plaintiff. Under the 1987 amendments, other State agencies may have recourse to State Arbitrazh when authorised by legislation and the Procuracy may bring suit in Arbitrazh irrespective of whether the parties have endeavoured to settle the case directly. Arbitrazh sessions are held by an arbitrator and representatives of the parties in dispute. Representatives of the parties may be a director or his deputies, duly authorised workers, or jurisconsults. The arbitrator will endeavour if at all possible to persuade the parties to come to an agreement. If that approach fails, the arbitrator will decide the dispute himself, which he also must do if the parties come to an agreement that violates the law or financial, planning, or contract discipline. Social representatives or individuals representing the economic *aktiv* also may take part in the session. When the arbitrator makes an award, it must be in accordance with the law, well-founded, and exhaustive of the issues submitted for consideration. The arbitrator must report any serious shortcomings or violations which emerge to the State agency to which his arbitrazh is attached. If the case concerns the validity of an act of a superior agency, a procurator has the right to be present.

LEGISLATIVE FUNCTIONS

The extent to which the relationship of arbitrazh agencies to agencies of State power interferes with the concept of a unified State Arbitrazh system is not clear. Legislation on arbitrazh refers mostly to the duty of arbitrazh tribunals to report violations. Agencies of State power at the respective levels receive reports from State Arbitrazh, appoint the arbitrators and their deputies, and so forth. This obviously opens the possibility of involvement in arbitrazh operations on behalf of local interests, but the extent to which this is undesirable does not emerge from the legislation. There are no prohibitions against local influence as one finds in the case of the Procuracy.

USSR State Arbitrazh does have a number of functions unrelated to the settlement of disputes that strengthen the 'unified' dimension of arbitrazh. To an appreciable extent State Arbitrazh exercises a legislative function by drafting normative acts 'on the basis of and in execution of' Soviet legislation which are binding upon State enterprises; for example, Special Conditions for the delivery of types of consumer or producer goods; instructions on the procedure for receiving goods, model contracts, and others. Under the 1987 amendments, State arbitrazhes are empowered to issue instructive directives relating to contractual practices at enterprises; when ministries and departments issue enactments on the subject, the text must be agreed beforehand with the USSR on union republic State arbitrazh. USSR State Arbitrazh also issues 'explanations' to ministries and departments regarding the application of normative acts (statutes on deliveries, conditions for the delivery of export goods, and others). These introduce a measure of uniformity and detail into economic and legal relations and are, of course, enforced by State Arbitrazh when disputes are heard. In addition, USSR State Arbitrazh issues instructive directives regarding the application of USSR legislation in economic disputes which are binding on inferior arbitrazh tribunals and State enterprises and organisations. These are published for general guidance. On the basis of studies of arbitrazh practice, State Arbitrazh may submit proposals for the improvement of economic legislation.

APPEAL OF DECISIONS

Technically, an appeal does not lie against an arbitrazh decision. A review of a decision by way of supervision is possible upon the application of a party or its superior agency, a petition of a ministry, State committee, or department, a protest of the procurator, or the initiative of State Arbitrazh itself within one year from the date of the decision. The review is conducted either by the chief or deputy State arbitrator of the arbitrazh which took the decision or by the superior arbitrazh. Special arrangements apply for collegial supervision when the acts of a ministry, State committee, or department of the USSR are deemed void and in certain other situations. The decision may be left intact, changed, replaced, terminated, the entire case transferred for new consideration, or the suit left without consideration. Review also lies for newly discovered circumstances within three months from the date the circumstances were established. When an arbitrazh award is being reviewed by way of supervision, execution may be suspended until the supervision proceeding is completed.

EDUCATIONAL FUNCTIONS

Reference already has been made to the duty of arbitrazh agencies to report irregularities and violations to the proper authorities. State Arbitrazh to this end sometimes considers economic disputes on circuit at enterprises so that workers may learn from the proceedings. Economic legislation and experience are 'propagandised,' especially through the monthly journal *Khoziaistvo i pravo* in whose publication State Arbitrazh collaborates.

State Arbitrazh is thus more than a mere system of economic tribunals. It is conceptually part of the planned economy as an indispensable device for integrating and disciplining Plan and Economic Contract and enabling State enterprises and organisations to enter into and fulfil their legal obligations vis-à-vis one another.

Administrative commissions

Illegal conduct in the Anglo-American legal system is punished in accordance with the criminal law. Under Soviet legislation anti-social conduct may likewise be criminal or it may fall into a category unknown to the Anglo-American legal world: administrative offences. An administrative offence is an unlawful, guilty (intentional or negligent) action or failure to act which infringes the State or social order, socialist ownership, the rights and freedoms of citizens, or the established administrative order, for which administrative responsibility is provided by legislation. Administrative responsibility is in fact established by a bewildering variety of all-union and union republic, even local governmental, enactments. Basic principles governing the imposition of administrative responsibility are laid down in the 1980 FPAdR and union republic codes of 1982–83. Administrative sanctions which may be applied include a warning, fine, confiscation, deprivation of a right, correctional tasks, and administrative arrest. The agencies which likewise may consider cases of administrative violations are diverse, ranging from district or city people's courts or people's judges, internal affairs or State inspectorate agencies, and other agencies or officials duly empowered by law. A great number, if not the majority, are heard by administrative commissions attached to executive committees of local soviets or by commissions for cases of minors.

The administrative commissions exist purely to dispose of cases concerning administrative violations, which can number 1,500 or so per year each. They are composed of a chairman, deputy, secretary, and at least four members who are selected from among deputies of the local soviet and representatives of social organisations. Some local soviets have several administrative commissions. Unless the administrative offence is subject to a fine levied on-the-spot (jaywalking, for example), a protocol of the violation is drawn up and signed by the alleged offender and the drafter. The administrative commission hears the case on the basis of the protocol. The alleged offender has the right to familiarise himself with the materials of the case, give explanations, present evidence, make petitions, be represented by an advocate, and appeal the decree in the case. The case must be considered by the commission in the presence of the alleged offender, or in absentia if he fails to appear after timely notification. The case is considered openly, and the commission is obliged to ascertain when the violation was committed, whether the particular person committed it, whether he is subject to administrative responsibility, whether there are aggravating or mitigating circumstances, whether property damage was caused, whether there are grounds to transfer the case to a comrades' court, social organisation, or labour collective, and any other relevant considerations. The commission renders its judgment in the form of a decree, which may be appealed by the alleged offender or a victim to either the executive committee of the respective soviet of people's deputies or to a district or city people's court, whose decision is final. A procurator may protest a decree, which has the effect of suspending execution until the protest is considered. Published Procuracy protests have in the past contained significant numbers of protests concerning administrative violations, suggesting that this has been and probably still is an area in which irregularities in the application of the law occur with frequency.

Although administrative violations often relate to very petty transgressions, the sanctions imposed are intended to be more than perfunctory. The 'tasks' of legislation on administrative violations encompass '. . . the nurturing of citizens in a spirit of precise and undeviating observance of the USSR Constitution and Soviet laws, respect for the rights, honour, and dignity of other citizens and the rules of socialist community life. . . .' Language to this effect appears throughout the legislation regulating the administration of socialist legality. Here 'nurturing' is expressed in the structure of the proceedings themselves, the involvement of representatives from social organisations on the commissions and, inter alia, in the arrangement of circuit sessions of the commissions at enterprises and other public places to resolve five or six cases at a time. On the other hand, especially when the sanctions are minor, it is often the practice for offenders not to appear at all, allowing the decree to be rendered in absentia and the fine paid in due course.[11]

More serious categories of administrative violations (for example, petty hooliganism, petty stealing, petty speculation) are considered in the people's courts or, in the case of a traffic violation, by the State Motor Vehicle Inspectorate, or by police or inspection agencies. The basic procedures for considering the violation are the same, but the penalties can be far more severe, including administrative arrest for up to 15 days. An administrative offence is not a crime, and an offender who commits what otherwise would be a criminal act but is subjected to administrative responsibility does not acquire a criminal record. Even the record of an administrative offence is expunged within a year if a second is not committed. Neither, on the other hand, does an alleged offender have the full protection of criminal procedure law, experienced investigators, and a legally trained judge (except possibly on appeal).

Commissions for Cases of Minors operate in many respects just as the administrative commissions. They are attached to local soviets and consist of a chairman, deputy, executive secretary, and 6–12 members appointed by the soviets from among deputies, representatives of social organisations, educationists, and others who work with youth in some capacity. But the commissions for minors exist at each territorial-administrative level up to and including the union republic, and their mandate goes far beyond punishing juvenile delinquents. The commissions are concerned with child neglect or abuse, school-leavers, orphans, foster parents, child labour, adoption, guardianship, protection of children's rights and interests, leisure time, education, and reform schools of various kinds. There is almost no aspect of a child's being that in principle is not within a commission's purview. The commissions depend heavily upon public involvement in their activities: representatives from trade unions, the Komsomol (Communist Youth League), parents' committees, guardians, voluntary people's guard, and house

---

11 J. Giddings 'Administrative Commissions of Local Soviets' Review of Socialist Law III (1977) 74.

committees, and from among these 'activists' social inspectors and social educators are selected to work with individual minors.

The district or city commissions for minors normally deal with the minors themselves; commissions at higher levels verify and co-ordinate the work of lower commissions. The sanctions which a commission may impose on a minor who has committed a socially dangerous act range from making a public apology, to a severe reprimand, to the duty to make compensation, to a fine on a minor who has independent earnings, to being bound over to parents, social educator, or a collective under supervision or probation, to being placed in some type of reform school. Parents likewise may be punished by a public warning, duty to pay compensation, or a fine for various forms of child neglect or abuse. Cases are considered upon the initiative of the commission or citizens, the recommendation of trade union or social organisations, house committees, and the like, or of police, education, or State agencies. The commission chairman has broad latitude in deciding whether the case should be heard or not. When preparing and considering cases, the commission must establish the age, occupation, living conditions, and education of the minor, the fact of a violation, whether there were accomplices or instigators, and whether measures of pressure had previously been applied to the minor. Citizens and officials may be summoned to appear to give explanations. The procurator must be notified of commission sessions, but his participation is not obligatory.

The commission must consider the materials collected, hear explanations of the minor, his parents, the victim, witnesses, and come to a balanced decision either to apply sanctions, terminate the case, conduct a supplementary verification, or transfer the case to the Procuracy. The case record is brief and takes the form of a protocol signed by the persons presiding and the secretary. Commission decrees regarding a case are adopted by majority vote and must set out the essence of the violation, the evidence on which the decision was made, the measure of pressure assigned, and the reasons for assigning it. Appeal lies only to the executive committee of the respective local soviet within ten days.

Alcoholism by all accounts is a grave problem in Soviet society and believed responsible directly or indirectly for the majority of criminal offences committed. A number of measures have been introduced to alter consumption patterns, including drastic price increases, limited hours of sale, restrictions on quantities subject to purchase, administrative penalties, and more severe criminal sanctions. In 1972 Commissions for the Struggle Against Drunkenness were formed in the union republics to co-ordinate the activities of State and social organisations to prevent and suppress drunkenness. Just as the commissions for minors, these are created at all levels up to union republic and attached to the respective soviets, and they also draw heavily upon volunteers from the general public. Much of their activity is aimed at portraying the evils of alcohol and supervising the activities of agencies, medical and legal, which treat the symptoms of excess consumption. Since 1985, the commissions may impose certain administrative sanctions on individuals, and they may recommend compulsory treatment or petition a court to deem an individual to be of limited legal capacity.

People's control commissions

HISTORY

The system of people's control commissions does not, strictly speaking, fall within the class of agencies administering socialist legality as this class is defined in Soviet legal doctrine. Most Soviet jurists regard these commissions as a form of popular involvement in State administration rather than law enforcement. Socialist legality is a major concern of people's control, however, and for our purposes it is instructive to examine them in this connection.

Workers' Control agencies were formed by legislation of 27 November 1917 in industrial, trade, banking, transport, and other institutions in order to verify the production, storage, and distribution of products and raw materials. In January 1918 a Central Control Administration within the State Control Agency was established, which became in May 1918 the People's Commissariat of State Control, dedicated to eradicating bureaucratism, red-tape, and 'formalism' in State administration. The majority of commissariat staff were holdovers from the pre-revolutionary regime. By 1919–20 serious efforts were underway to unify all control groups under single direction and secure broad participation from workers and peasants. In early 1920 State Control had become the People's Commissariat of Workers'-Peasants' Inspection, which promptly set about recruiting volunteer members. The Workers'-Peasants' Inspection was unified in 1923 with a Party control agency, the Central Control Commission; the combined body operated with an enlarged mandate until 1934, when the Party-State link was severed and two organs formed: the Party Control Commission and the Soviet Control Commission, each with a reduced mandate. Soviet Control Commissions in particular were confined to verifying the actual fulfilment of important government decisions and no longer served as a guardian over bureaucratic efficiency. These commissions remained, however, under close supervision by the Party, which nominated members of the Soviet Control Commission for confirmation by the government. Citizen involvement was de-emphasised.

In the decade after Stalin's death, the Ministry of State Control, as it had been renamed, underwent minor reforms, becoming in 1961 a union-republic agency, but in 1962 the body was wholly restructured.

The Party-State link was restored and citizen participation greatly encouraged as part of the doctrine of the State of the whole people. The Statute on the Party-State Control Committee of 20 December 1962 embodied the reforms. On 9 December 1965 the commission was renamed the People's Control Commission, citizen participation ordered to be expanded yet again, and the hierarchy of people's control units from the all-union level to collective farms established. The Statute on People's Control Agencies in the USSR of 19 December 1968 elaborated the changes and confirmed that whereas public involvement in control functions was to be emphasised, the Party-State link again was to be severed. The Party would continue to direct the USSR People's Control Committee together with the government, but without formal attachment to the Central Committee. Between 1963 and 1982 the volunteer membership of people's control groups grew from under two million to more than ten million persons.[12]

CURRENT LEGISLATION

The 1977 USSR Constitution elevated people's control agencies to organs of constitutional stature. On 30 November 1979 the USSR Supreme Soviet enacted the Law on People's Control in the USSR. The 1979 Law undertakes to combine State and social control at enterprises, collective farms, institutions, and organisations through people's control agencies formed by soviets of people's deputies or elected by labour collectives. The link with the Communist Party remains severed, but the activity of the agencies is to be effectuated on the basis of both legislation and 'decisions of the Communist Party of the Soviet Union.' The agencies verify the execution of law and policy: fulfilment of State plans, efficient use of economic resources, observance of State discipline, elimination of localism, red-tape, and bureaucratism, and control over the observance of Soviet laws by officials when considering citizens' complaints. Their work is carried out in contact with local soviets, State agencies, the Procuracy, courts, and internal affairs, justice, and State arbitrazh agencies, but people's control agencies are not to become involved in work of those bodies connected with dispensing justice, Procuracy supervision, inquiry, preliminary investigation, or consideration of economic disputes.

The USSR People's Control Committee is formed by the USSR Supreme Soviet for a five-year period; the chairman is a member of the Government of the USSR. The network of people's control committees then extends down to district in city level, and at settlement or rural soviet level becomes a people's control group. The network then transcends the agencies of State power; people's control committees, groups,

[12] J. S. Adams *Citizen Inspectors in the Soviet Union: The People's Control Committee* (1977) p 152.

and posts are organised at enterprises, collective farms, institutions, organisations, and military units. The terms of office vary: five years to the level of autonomous republic and two-and-a-half years below, but two or three years for people's control groups or posts, where the collective elects by open ballot. People eligible for election at the lowest levels include workers, collective farmers, employees, school children, pensioners, and housewives.

Within the State levels of people's control, the structure and establishment of committees are fixed by the USSR or union republic people's control committees and financed by the State. Groups and posts conduct verifications, raids, and reviews, discuss the results, and raise questions. Committees may demand documents, materials, or necessary information and order audits. If a people's control committee discovers a violation of law, it may warn the appropriate officials, transfer the materials for discussion by labour collectives and social organisations, seek the repeal of regulations issued by officials which violate the legal interests of enterprises, collective farms, institutions, organisations or prejudice the rights of citizens and suspend clearly illegal regulations and actions of officials if they could cause material harm to State or social interests or to the rights of citizens. Sanctions subject to imposition by the committees are several: public exposure, reprimand or severe reprimand for guilty officials; monetary deductions on officials who have caused material harm to the State, collective farms, co-operative, or other social organisations on a basis determined by the Presidium of the USSR Supreme Soviet. For flagrant violations of socialist legality or State discipline and other dereliction of duties officials may be removed from office by the committees. Appeals lie within ten days to the superior people's control committee.

Only the chairman of a people's control group of an enterprise, collective farm, institution, or organisation is protected against dismissal or demotion as a form of reprisal, but opposition to or persecution of people's controllers in connection with the performance of their duties is an offence.

Citizen initiative

Individual citizens are involved as laymen in the administration of legality in a multitude of ways and capacities, as noted above. But purely in their capacity as citizens they are expected to be guardians of legality through a complaints procedure, the filing of 'proposals, applications, and appeals.' This is a form of 'citizen control' over the activity of State and social agencies protected by law under the 1968 Edict on the Procedure for Considering Proposals, Applications, and Appeals of Citizens in its 1980 redaction. The essence of the system is simple: citizens have the right to make written or oral appeals to all State and social agencies concerning the improvement of their activity, to criticise shortcomings, and to complain against actions of officials and of State and social agencies. These appeals must be received by and replied to within periods laid down by legislation for the agency or official to whom the object of the complaint is directly subordinate and within whose direct jurisdiction the resolution of a particular question falls. If there is no superior agency, appeal lies to the executive or administrative body of the agency and in some instances to a court. Regular office hours must be held to receive citizens personally. Reasoned decisions must be taken, and the pattern of complaints as a whole studied with a view to disclosing and eliminating the reasons for them. Newspapers, television, radio, and other mass media often act as conduits for appeals of all types. Many large organisations have permanent personnel or even departments exclusively engaged with this type of activity. People's control agencies and the Procuracy oversee the implementation of the Edict, which does not relate to appeal proceedings in civil, criminal, labour, inventions, communications, and other Soviet legislation. Millions of complaints are received annually pursuant to this Edict. In 1988 the Edict was amended to require that all complaints and appeals must contain the full name, address, and place of work or study of the citizen filing the complaint or appeal; in the absence of that information, the complaint or appeal is regarded as anonymous and will not be considered.

From 1 January 1988 citizens also may apply to a court if they have been illegally deprived of the opportunity to fully or partially exercise a right granted them by law or other normative act or if any duty whatever is illegally imposed upon a citizen by the actions of an official. Such appeals may be lodged after the citizen has utilised his right under the 1968 Edict or they may be filed at once with the court (see chapter 8, below).

Police agencies

Police functions are vested primarily in two agencies: the Committee of State Security of the USSR (KGB) and the Ministry of Internal Affairs (MVD).

COMMITTEE OF STATE SECURITY

The KGB performs both intelligence and police functions. The KGB USSR is a State Committee of the USSR Council of Ministers with branches at union and autonomous republic levels and local levels. As one Soviet commentator has noted, the activities of 'KGB agencies are of a clearly expressed political character.' They are 'political agencies implementing the line of the Central Committee of the Party and Soviet Government. . . .'[13] The organisation has experienced several changes of name and functions. It began as the VChKa in November 1918 with broad powers to administer the Red Terror in pursuit of counter-revolutionaries. The VChKa was abolished in 1922 and superseded by the State Political Administration (GPU) incorporated within the People's Commissariat of Internal Affairs of the RSFSR. With the formation of the USSR it was decided to unify the union republic GPUs under the Unified State Political Administration (OGPU). From 1934–41 the State security agencies operated as the Chief State Security Administration of the all-union and union republic people's commissariats of internal affairs (NKVD). On the eve of Russian involvement in the Second World War the USSR People's Commissariat of State Security (NKGB) was formed. That same year of 1941, the NKGB was merged with the NKVD again but separated ten years later. In 1946, the NKGB became the Ministry of State Security, supplanted on 13 March 1954 by the Committee of State Security attached to the USSR Council of Ministers and renamed on 5 July 1978 the Committee of State Security of the USSR.

In the popular image the KGB and its predecessors have always been linked with the most repressive features of Soviet life, and as an institution it was severely criticised by Party organs for abuses during the Stalin era. Party, State, and Procuracy control over KGB operations are said to have been strengthened.

The statute of the KGB, if there be one, has not been published. Soviet commentators say that the KGB is guided in its work by decisions of Party congresses, decrees of the Central Committee of the CPSU, USSR legislation, and other acts of 'Party and State agencies' relating to State security. From materials of this nature the basic functions of the agency are divined: unmasking the aggressive plans and subversive acts of imperialism which are a threat to the security of the USSR or other socialist countries, the prevention of espionage, terrorist acts, sabotage, and subversion by foreign intelligence services, protecting State secrets and the State frontier, struggle against subversive political and ideological acts directed against the USSR by foreign anti-Soviet centres and other hostile elements, and active involvement in crime prevention work.[14] The Party link to the KGB is stressed by the commentators. The KGB is said to be under the 'guidance' and 'constant supervision' of the Party.

---

13 Iu. T. Mil'ko, in A. E. Lunev et al (eds) *Sovetskoe administrativnoe pravo; upravlenie v oblasti administrativno-politicheskoi deiatel'nosti* (1979) p 78.
14 Ibid pp 83–84.

Some rights and functions of the KGB are defined by legislation. The FPCrimL (Art 28) and union republic criminal codes specify that the preliminary investigation for certain crimes against the State and military crimes are to be performed by KGB investigators. As guardians of the State frontier, the KGB has broad administrative powers relative to search and seizure laid down, for example, in the 1982 Law on the USSR State Boundary.

Although the KGB is a union-republic organ and structured accordingly, certain functions are centralised in a manner unusual for the normal union-republic State committee. The USSR KGB, for example, retains direct control at all levels over the selection and appointment of executive cadres, the implementation of measures to safeguard State security, generalisations of experience, operations directed against subversive activity, the border guard, and training institutions. KGB organs at lower levels are not sections or administrations of local soviets but are subordinate only vertically to superior KGB agencies. The chairman of the KGB is appointed by the USSR Supreme Soviet and his deputies, by the USSR Council of Ministers. Like other State committees, the KGB has a college composed of the chairman, his deputies, and certain other KGB officials. College decisions are taken on the basis of a 'businesslike discussion' of matters and promulgated in orders of the Chairman. This procedure seems not to allow for the College members or Chairman to appeal or report disagreements to the Council of Ministers.

INTERNAL AFFAIRS AGENCIES

The ordinary day-to-day function of protecting public order, crime prevention, and traffic control are performed by internal affairs agencies. The present scheme of internal affairs agencies consists of two sub-systems: central and local agencies. The central system comprises the USSR and the union and autonomous republic ministries of internal affairs. The internal affairs administrations of local soviets at all levels to district in city represent the local sub-system. The Statute of the MVD has not been published, but the general USSR legislation governing ministries extends to the MVD. The USSR Minister of Internal Affairs in particular promulgates orders and instructions regarding traffic and pedestrian safety that are of a general normative character. The Ministry has a College, a scientific-methods council, and functional sub-divisions for the protection of public order, criminal search, struggle against the stealing of socialist ownership and speculation, traffic safety, fire safety, and others. The headquarters of the USSR MVD is engaged in analyses and forecasting, working out long-term plans, drafting normative acts, and carrying out inspections.

The union and autonomous republic MVD agencies perform functions analogous to MVD USSR but also administer certain sub-divisions directly within their jurisdiction: the police (*militsiia*, sometimes translated as militia; it is not of course the army, but the ordinary constable or policeman in Anglo-American parlance), inspectorates for cases of minors, correctional-labour institutions, and therapeutic-labour institutions, among others. The union republic minister of internal affairs is simultaneously the head of the republic police; his counterparts at inferior levels hold the same dual posts. Dual subordination also prevails throughout the system to the superior internal affairs agency and the respective soviet of people's deputies. At the lower operational levels internal affairs agencies also are engaged in inquiry and preliminary investigation, internal passport service, State motor vehicle inspection, and affairs of minors. Great emphasis has been placed in the 1970s on the crime detection and prevention function of the MVD, which maintains a large network of training institutions to improve the skills of its personnel. In 1988 a Statute on political agencies within the MVD system was approved with a view to strengthening Party guidance of the agencies and raising the standard of law enforcement.

Comrades' courts

HISTORY

Informal community courts and councils have deep roots in rural pre-revolutionary Russia which helped lay the groundwork for techniques of dispute settlement in the post-revolutionary period. Comrades' courts appeared in some units of the Petrograd military district by December 1917 and by summer had been extended throughout the entire Red Army to deal with minor infractions of military discipline and untoward conduct. By 1919 'disciplinary comrades' courts' had been formed in local trade union sections at enterprises to punish minor breaches of labour discipline. Their jurisdiction was expanded in 1921 to embrace hooliganism, indecent conduct, and other offences, but their sentencing powers, which at one time included the assignment of prison terms, were curtailed somewhat. The expansion of the regular court system that accompanied the NEP and the introduction of procedural codes pushed comrades' courts into the background, but later in the decade they were revived with enlarged jurisdiction. Their formation was authorised not only in plants and in other State and social institutions (Industrial Comrades' Courts) but also in residential housing units and rural areas (Rural Social Courts). Some 45,000 comrades' courts were reported to exist in the RSFSR alone in 1938. Their number diminished dramatically during the wartime era. In 1951 a new Statute on Comrades' Courts in Enterprises and Institutions was enacted for the entire country, principally to deal with labour violations which no longer were punishable as criminal offences. By the late 1950s, comrades' courts had become associated with another dimension of social life: greater lay involvement in protecting public order by transferring functions to social organisations which had been reserved exclusively for State organs. In the 1950s and early 1960s the union republics adopted statutes, not identical, on comrades' courts.

A key ingredient in the original concept of the comrades' court was its status as that of an elective social agency (not a State judicial institution) entrusted with nurturing citizens 'in the spirit of a communist attitude toward labour, socialist ownership, and the observance of the rules of socialist community life. . . .' It did not 'punish' offenders, it applied 'measures of social pressure.' The language of the statutes referred to the offender, to misconduct or offences, to condemnation, rather than to the guilty person, crime, correction, and punishment, thereby accentuating the persuasive role of comrades' courts as against the coercive nature of regular courts. The balance between expeditious lay informality and expert adjudication by due process was and remains a difficult one, much debated in the Soviet Union and other socialist countries in the 1960–70s. In the USSR the lay element was retained intact in the comrades' courts, but efforts were made to give comrades' court judges basic training in the law through training sessions or courses and the publication of legal commentaries. Within a relatively brief period after their adoption, the union republic comrades' court statutes were amended in the direction of further procedural formality and given greater responsibility for criminal offences deemed too petty to be heard by ordinary courts.[15]

CURRENT LEGISLATION

On 11 March 1977 the Presidium of the RSFSR Supreme Soviet enacted a new Statute on Comrades' Courts containing changes intended to accommodate some of the principal difficulties with or objections to experience under the 1961 Statute as amended. The notion of comrades' courts as elective social agencies is retained; the courts are formed by general meetings of workers, employees, students, collective farmers, residents, and the like at places of work or residence. Any citizen who by his 'professional and moral qualities' can successfully serve on a court may be nominated by social organisations or individual citizens. Any nomination may be challenged with reasons. The jurisdiction of the courts is broad and includes cases concerning truancy or late arrival at work and other violations of labour discipline or safety requirements, loss of or damage to equipment as a result of an unconscientious attitude toward work or the unauthorised use of State, social, or co-operative ownership for personal purposes; drinking in prohibited places, intoxication in public, petty stealing of State or social property,

---

[15] On the development of comrades' courts, see H. J. Berman and J. W. Spindler 'Soviet Comrades' Courts' Washington Law Review XXXVIII (1963) 842–910.

petty hooliganism, home-brewing, petty speculation, and certain types of petty theft of personal property; insults, slander, or light beatings; child neglect or abuse or an unworthy attitude toward parents, family, or women; violations of rules for halls of residence, flats, and the like; the procedure for using structures commonly owned or distribution of collective farm household property; damage to trees and greenery; minor civil disputes up to 50 rubles in value; or administrative or other cases directly referred to comrades' courts.

An extensive range of institutions, organisations, and citizens may initiate comrades' court proceedings, including the court itself. The procedures for hearing a case have been tightened. Protocols of sessions must be kept and signed, and court decisions must be reached under circumstances 'excluding extraneous influences.' The decision itself must be formal and encompass personal data on the individual(s) before the court, the members of the bench who heard the case, the reasons for the decision and evidence on which it was based, and the period and procedure for appealing the decision. At least three comrades' court members, and always an uneven number, must sit on the case. The court must consider materials available, hear the explanations of the 'accused,' victim, witnesses, and any other parties. In coming to a decision, the court is to be guided by prevailing Soviet legislation and its social duty. Cases may be judged in absentia only if a proper summons has been served and the hearing has been twice rescheduled.

The 'measures of social pressure' subject to application by a comrades' court are various. Under present legislation a court may no longer suggest eviction from housing, but it may recommend, when appropriate, that an individual be deprived of bonuses due for annual production results. Other measures range from a public apology to a victim or the collective, to fines in certain instances of up to 50 rubles or even a recommendation in labour cases of demotion. Compensation for damage caused up to a specified amount, usually 50 rubles, likewise may be levied. When justified, a comrades' court may refer the case to an appropriate law enforcement agency.

An appeal lies within seven days to the executive committee of the local soviet or the local trade union committee, who may return the case for rehearing or terminate the proceedings if the decision is contrary to law or the facts of the case. Financial sanctions are executed by the court itself, which may apply for a writ of execution from a people's court. The people's court will verify the legality of the decision before issuing the writ. Comrades' courts may issue a kind of 'special ruling' notifying social organisations and officials about causes and conditions facilitating a breach of law that become evident when hearing a case. Those so informed must advise the court within a month of measures taken.

The direction of comrades' courts is essentially a matter for the local soviet executive committees and bodies to which the courts are attached.

An innovation under the 1977 Statute is the creation of Social Councils for the Work of Comrades' Courts attached to executive committees of local soviets or trade union committees. The councils organise and co-ordinate the courts' work, assist in arranging elections and annual reports to the electorate, help instruct comrades' court members in the law, publicise court activities, and propose rewards for honourable service.[16]

People's guards

HISTORY

Early experiments with the exercise of policing functions by ordinary citizens are linked to the antecedents of people's control agencies. From 1924 rural sheriffs recruited from volunteers aged 18–50 were appointed to assist with preserving public order, and from 1926 police assistance brigades were formed in urban areas. By 1930 such brigades were said to number 26,000 persons in the RSFSR. Following some reorganisation, the brigades in 1932 were placed exclusively under police control. The Ukrainian republic reportedly had 182,000 brigade members in 1958. Social organisations from time to time have assumed quasi-policing functions. The Communist Youth League, for example, organised patrols, detachments, and raiding parties to uncover violations of local retail trade regulations or similar offences, but activities of this character perhaps bear closer analogy to people's control-type operations than to police functions. Some local experimentation in the late 1950s with volunteer citizen police units, and the emphasis emanating from the XXI Congress of the CPSU on the devolution of State functions to non-State bodies, led to a series of union republic enactments during 1959–60 establishing voluntary people's guard units.[17]

CURRENT LEGISLATION

Despite some problems with the people's guard, ranging from abusive vigilante actions by the guards to citizen disrespect for the organisation, the notion of civic police has proved to be a durable one. By joint Party-Government decree a Model Statute on Voluntary People's Guard Detachments for the Protection of Public Order was confirmed on 20 May 1974. The Model Statute provided

16 Butler 'Comradely Justice in Eastern Europe' Current Legal Problems XXV (1972) 200–218; id 'Comradely Justice Revised' Review of Socialist Law III (1977) 325–343.
17 On the early experience with these, see D. O'Connor 'Soviet People's Guard: An Experiment With Civic Police' New York University Law Review XXXIX (1964) 579–614.

that people's guard detachments may be formed on transport, and at enterprises, construction sites, collective farms, State farms, institutions, organisations, educational institutions, housing offices and administrations, and similar places under the direction of local soviets. People's guards have become a familiar sight in Soviet streets and at public events, where they help with crowd control, police jay-walking, and curb drunkenness or hooliganism. Wearing red armbands and carrying appropriate identification, people's guards are Soviet citizens from all walks of life over 18 years of age who have volunteered to strengthen public order and 'struggle against violations of law.' They may act independently or directly assist internal affairs or Procuracy agencies or the courts. Their mandate extends to crowd control, traffic safety, educational work in labour collectives, child neglect and juvenile delinquency, rendering first aid, poaching, assisting the border guard in frontier areas, and preventing hooliganism, public drunkenness, property theft, speculation, and other breaches of the law.

Guard detachments must be founded by a group of volunteers. The Procuracy successfully protested against the director of an enterprise forming a detachment simply by inviting 30 persons to enrol by decree.[18] In the performance of his duties a people's guard has the right to demand that citizens observe public order and cease any violation. If a malicious violation of public order or law occurs in the absence of police officials or authorised persons, a people's guard may draw up a protocol and transmit it to his people's guard detachment head or commander. He has the right to demand the presentation of identity documents, to 'deliver up' to the police or people's guard headquarters individuals who have committed a violation of the law, or who otherwise could commit a violation, or whose identity cannot be ascertained, and to seize instruments used to commit a violation. He may enter public places to pursue an offender, suppress violations, or restore public order. Under urgent circumstances he may commandeer transport for persons who require medical aid, or use the telephone. With regard to traffic violations, he may demand to see a driver's licence and deliver up drunken drivers or persons without a licence to the nearest police agency. People's guard agencies liaise closely with the Procuracy and courts, but especially with internal affairs agencies. Links with the latter embrace joint exercises, instruction, and methods assistance. The Procuracy exercises supervision over the execution of laws by people's guard detachments.

Although people's guards are members of a voluntary force, they are now extended the protection of Soviet criminal legislation if assaulted in the course of their duties. Soviet courts have held repeatedly that people's

---

18 J. H. Hazard, W. E. Butler, P. B. Maggs *The Soviet Legal System* (3rd edn, 1977) p 20.

guard detachment commanders are responsible officials and both enjoy the protection and bear the responsibilities of that status.[19]

Social centres for the protection of order

Social centres for the protection of order are of recent origin. They exist to unify and co-ordinate the activities of the various bodies involved in protecting public order, including people's guards, comrades' courts, house, street, or rural committees, social inspectorates for the affairs of minors, social legal consultation offices, and others. All union republics have statutes governing the centre; the RSFSR Statute was adopted on 25 June 1980. The co-ordination is done through the centre council appointed by the executive committee of the respective local soviet. As a rule the centres are formed in urban areas within the confines of housing operation offices and in rural areas within the boundaries of settlement or rural soviets. The councils are composed of individuals recommended by social organisations, labour collectives, law enforcement agencies, or the agencies protecting public order themselves. They make proposals for improving the protection of public order and preventing offences, enlarging the exchange of experience, disseminate legal propaganda, assist State agencies and social organisations in uncovering persons who lead an antisocial, parasitic way of life and help such persons find employment or schooling, and are involved in the struggle against alcoholism and juvenile delinquency. Council decisions, however, are purely recommendatory.

Arbitration

Article 27 of the RSFSR Code of Civil Procedure and identical articles in the other union republic codes stipulate that in the instances provided for by law or by international treaties or agreements, a dispute which has arisen out of civil law relations may by agreement of the parties be transferred for consideration by way of arbitration. There are four possible alternatives for arbitration under Soviet law: ad hoc arbitration between citizens; ad hoc arbitration between State enterprises; the Arbitration Court attached to the USSR Chamber of Commerce and Industry, or the Maritime Arbitration Commission.

Ad hoc arbitration between citizens seems to be rarely used but can be invoked under Annex 3 to the RSFSR Code of Civil Procedure. Any dispute except labour or family relations may be transferred for

---

19 See Iu. D. Severin (ed) *Kommentarii k Ugolovnomu kodeksu RSFSR* (1980) pp 326–334.

consideration on the basis of a written *compromis*. One umpire may act or, if the parties prefer, several, including one chosen by each party. The arbitrators act free of charge and are not bound by the rules of civil procedure, except that they must hear the explanations of the parties. The award is set out in writing and signed; the file of the proceeding is transferred to a people's court for safekeeping. A writ of execution may be obtained if the award is not voluntarily executed, but when issuing a writ the judge will verify whether the award was contrary to law or not. Ad hoc arbitration following analogous principles may be arranged for disputes among State enterprises or organisations instead of applying to State Arbitrazh. Special legislation governs the proceedings.

The Arbitration Court attached to the USSR Chamber of Commerce and Industry operates on the basis of a Statute adopted 14 December 1987 and a Reglament confirmed in 1988. The Maritime Arbitration Commission also is attached to the USSR Chamber of Commerce and functions on the basis of a Statute of 9 October 1980 and Rules of Procedure confirmed 13 January 1982. Both are permanently functioning tribunals. Each maintains a panel of expert arbitrators from whom the parties may select a single arbitrator, or a tribunal of three may be formed. Awards are to be executed voluntarily, or otherwise in accordance with law and relevant international treaties. A principal difference between the two commissions lies in the appeal procedures. Awards of the Arbitration Court are final and not subject to appeal, whereas awards of the Maritime Arbitration Commission may be appealed by any party within a month to the USSR Supreme Court and the USSR Procurator General or his deputies may protest an award of the Maritime Arbitration Commission (see chapter 19, below).

Chapter 8

The constitutional foundations of the Soviet legal order

The Soviet Union is a country of many constitutions and, by Anglo-American standards, rather frequent constitutional revision. Since 1917 the sundry entities making up the Union of Soviet Socialist Republics have spawned nearly one hundred constitutions. At the moment, 36 constitutions are in force on Soviet territory.[1] We shall observe the customary practice of discussing these on the basis of prototypes.

The frequency of Soviet constitutional revision in itself suggests that the purpose of a constitution in the Soviet legal system differs markedly from the Anglo-American concept. Within Soviet legal doctrine, however, the scope of constitutional law is being actively debated. Traditionally, Soviet legal science has preferred the term 'State law' (*gosudarstvennoe pravo*), perhaps a legacy of the German *Staatrecht*, for what common lawyers understand to be constitutional law. This branch of law treated State sovereignty, authority, and structure, and the rights and duties of the citizen in respect of the State. Many Soviet jurists now prefer the term 'constitutional law' (*konstitutsionnoe pravo*) on the premise that the scope of the subject embraces the system and structure of authority in society as a whole, including the CPSU, and legal or social relationships that cut across all branches of law. The implications of the latter view have yet to unfold. Possibly it could lead to greater constitutional 'control' or supervision over the administration of legality.

Constitutions, written or unwritten, are associated in Anglo-American experience with the limitation of arbitrary power that has been or may be exercised by the State or by the 'majority' through the State. Limitation of State power has been a minor and extremely belated consideration for Soviet constitutional draftsmen. Soviet State structure proceeds from the unity of State power, for class rule was decisive in Marx's view, not the State per se. The State in the hands of the working class would be an instrument for suppressing antagonistic class elements and realising the ultimate transition to communism. Eventually, the State would wither away; its inevitable destiny, in the Marxian view, is to disappear as its functions become superfluous or are absorbed by non-State bodies. In the interim the State serves an instrumental purpose; the

---

[1] All are translated in W. E. Butler *Collected Legislation of the USSR and Constituent Union Republics* (1979-) with an introduction discussing their differences.

object of the draftsmen consequently is not to limit State authority during its temporary existence, but to fashion the optimal utilisation of the State in order to achieve an ulterior end.

This attitude of mind results not merely in the rejection of Anglo-American concepts of a constitution; it creates a profound mistrust of any constitution that undertakes to impose immutable or inalienable values of one generation upon another. American constitutional doctrine in particular, many Soviet jurists suggests, permits dead hands of past generations to unwarrantedly affect the adoption and execution of present and future policies. Apprehension about constitutional obsolescence extends even to Soviet constitutions. One Soviet jurist wrote: '... the strength of the Soviet constitutions lies in the fact that they correctly reflect things as they are. . . .' When events overtake the constitution, the latter, it follows, is to be amended or replaced; the constitution is not to restrain social change.

Soviet constitutions are not preoccupied with the present exclusively. They also contain programmatic elements for future accomplishments. Some western observers go so far as to call them a 'guide to action', a partial 'blueprint for a future society' intended to inspire people within the Soviet Union and without. At each stage of societal development, the constitution of the day is to record past achievements, present standards, and future intentions.

Finally, Soviet constitutions are in part a response to the pre-revolutionary heritage and a means of coping politically with issues that otherwise would prove to be intractable. Classical Marxism neither prescribed nor proscribed a constitution for a dictatorship of the proletariat or a socialist State. Lenin and his followers were well aware that the Russian revolutionary tradition had attached importance to constitutions and struggled for their enactment. Radishchev had found inspiration in the United States Constitution, as had the Decembrists, who actually dared to prepare a draft. The Basic Law of 1906 represented a 'constitutional limitation' upon the Tsarist autocracy, created the State Duma, and raised expectations of at least a transition to a limited monarchy if not outright parliamentary democracy. Even though that notion of democratic rule was anathema to the Bolsheviks, it would have been folly to ignore the attraction to Russians of all persuasions of a constitutional form of government.

The form of the Soviet constitutions has in some senses been regarded as an ingenious adaptation to the course of Russian history, for it enabled the Bolsheviks to offer tangible expression to their concept of nationhood and self-determination within a multi-national State. 'Federated in form, but socialist in substance' is the formula often posited by Soviet legal textbooks. The constitutions cement a structure and policy which otherwise would be quite inconceivable.

Continuity of constitutional development

There have been four developmental stages to date in Soviet constitutional history. The preamble of the present 1977 USSR Constitution refers to the 'succession of the ideas and principles of the first Soviet Constitution of 1918 (ie of the RSFSR), the 1924 USSR Constitution, and the 1936 USSR Constitution.' Two of the four constitutions (1924 and 1977) recount the characteristics of each stage in some detail. The 1918 RSFSR Constitution confirmed the dictatorship of the proletariat, a 'State of a new type,' to defend 'revolutionary conquests' and commence the 'construction of socialism and communism.' This document is said to mark a '. . . worldwide historical turning of mankind from capitalism toward socialism. . . .'

Civil war having ended in triumph and 'imperialist intervention' repulsed, the Soviet State turned to domestic reconstruction. Nationality policy, national defence, economic revival, and eventual unification into a single 'socialist family' were cited as the principal reasons for uniting the RSFSR, Ukrainian SSR, Belorussian SSR, and Transcaucasian SFSR into the Union of Soviet Socialist Republics under a new constitution. The 1936 Constitution signalled the transition of Soviet society from a dictatorship of the proletariat to a socialist State. Private ownership of the instruments and means of production and antagonistic classes had been eliminated. The primary threshold of socialism had been crossed; under the 1936 Constitution the construction of socialism was to be completed and the transition to the building of communism commenced.

Amendment of existing documents or constitutional growth by expanded interpretation were deemed insufficient or incompatible with Soviet legal style, although for both the 1936 and 1977 constitutions their drafting commissions originally were instructed to prepare amendments. The political inspiration, impetus, and programmatic substructure for constitutional revision in every instance has originated within CPSU programmes and resolutions. From the standpoint of societal development, these materials are the backdrop for constitutional change; once a constitution is enacted Party documents rapidly embellish, elaborate, and extend its provisions, eventually making it obsolete. The 1961 Programme of the CPSU marked the transition to the stage of a socialist society building communism in the USSR, not the constitution, and there are countless lesser examples of Party documents performing an analogous role.

The 1977 Constitution reflects the stage of 'developed socialism,' a society of 'mature socialist social relations,' a 'state of the whole people' formed on the basis of the 'coming together' (*sblizhenie*) of all classes and social strata and the 'legal and actual equality of all nations and peoples. . . .' This stage is said to be an 'objectively necessary' one on the 'path to communism,' for the 'ultimate purpose' of the Soviet State is postulated to be the 'building of a classless society in which social communist self-administration is being developed.' The principal tasks of the 'all-people's State' are to create the material-technical base of communism; improve socialist social relations and transform them into communist social relations; nurture 'communist man,' raise the material and cultural level of the people, ensure national security, and further the development of peace and international co-operation.

Socio-political and economic structure

POLITICAL SYSTEM

Marx and Engels left no detailed instructions for State organisation in a post-revolutionary society. This circumstance, the legacy of the Paris Commune, and the political heritage of the realities of Russia in 1917–18 contributed to the Bolsheviks deciding to combine ingredients familiar to the American and English traditions respectively: a written constitution and parliamentary supremacy, with a dash of popular sovereignty. The doctrine of separation of powers so central to American constitutionalism was rejected. The Revolution was to triumph, it was believed, through a unitary State system, initially directed to repress hostile classes and later to optimise the transition to a Stateless society. Popular sovereignty meant the sovereignty of the working people and peasantry, the proletariat, and the early constitutions restricted the franchise and the political and economic rights of other class elements. The 1977–78 constitutions vest 'all power' in the people, who are to exercise their power through soviets of people's deputies, the 'political foundation of the USSR.'

A principle central to Soviet State structure and Party organisation is accorded constitutional elaboration for the first time: 'democratic centralism.' Under this concept 'agencies of State power,' that is, elective State agencies, are all, from 'bottom to top,' to be elected, and be accountable to the people, and the decisions of superior agencies are binding upon inferior. The latter element is widely considered to be a constraint upon the criticism of decisions once taken by superior bodies, although the execution of decisions often is severely taken to task.

Socialist legality is treated under the 1977–78 constitutions as an integral part of the political system. The State, all its organs, and officials are required to 'operate on the basis of socialist legality,' to ensure the protection of the legal order and the rights and freedoms of citizens, and to observe the USSR Constitution and Soviet law. Although the Constitution is not the validating test for the legality of legislation by the highest organs of State power, this language is as close as any Soviet legal document has come to formally requiring subordination to law by the State itself and social organisations.

The enhanced role of the CPSU under the present constitutions is discussed elsewhere (chapter 9, below). It has been accompanied by greater constitutional emphasis upon the role of other social organisations—trade unions, the Komsomol, and the like—in assuming responsibilities for the administration of State and social affairs. Labour collectives are similarly endowed, and their rights and responsibilities are elaborated in the 1983 Law on the role of labour collectives in the management of enterprises, organisations, and institutions. This appears to be an extension of the direct democracy in the all-people's State called for by the constitutions: more citizen involvement in State and social administration, people's control, greater openness or 'publicity' for State affairs, taking account of public opinion, and, it is interesting to note, 'strengthening the legal basis of State and social life.' Soviet reforms of State administration during the 1980s have drawn upon this programme of action.

Article 5 of the 1977 Constitution in particular provided that the most important issues of State life are to be submitted for discussion by the whole people and even put to a vote through a referendum. The formal procedures for doing so were introduced by the Law on the Discussion by the Whole People of Important Questions of State Life, adopted 30 June 1987. These include draft laws, such as the 1988 Fundamental Principles of criminal legislation, originating at all levels of the State and the principle of broad *glasnost'* is to be secured. Subjects considered appropriate for discussion in this procedure include 'draft laws and decisions touching upon basic orientations of the political, economic, and social development of the country, the exercise of the constitutional rights, freedoms, and duties of Soviet citizens, as well as other major questions of State life. . . .'

ECONOMIC SYSTEM

The primacy of State ownership has been a stable feature of all four stages of Soviet constitutions. The 1977–78 constitutions accord unprecedented priority to the nature of the economic system. Following the 1961 FPCivL, the constitutions declare that socialist ownership comprises the basis of the economic system, there being three types: State, collective farm-co-operative, and trade union or other social organisations. State ownership is the highest of these and constitutes the common property of the whole Soviet people. In the exclusive ownership of the State are land, minerals, water, forests, the basic means of production in industry, construction, and agriculture, transport, communications, banks, and more. Socialist ownership may not be used for personal gain or other mercenary purposes.

Collective farms and other co-operative organisations are entitled to own means of production in order to carry out the objects of their charters. Land is allocated to them in perpetuity without charge. Ultimately, the constitutions stipulate, this category of ownership will amalgamate with State ownership. The ultimate fate of ownership by trade unions and other social organisations is not elaborated.

Personal ownership, as a separate category of property, receives greater constitutional protection than at any time in Soviet history. Personal property must be derived from 'labour income' and may be bequeathed to others. Land may not be owned by individuals, but the constitution does guarantee individuals the right to use land for subsidiary husbandry or individual housing in accordance with law. Property which is owned or used by citizens must not serve to derive 'non-labour income' nor be used to the 'prejudice of the interests of society' (see chapter 10, below). Labour, the constitutions add, is the source of economic growth. On the principle of 'From each according to his ability, to each according to his labour' the State exercises control over the measure of labour and consumption, including income tax, and has responsibility for labour productivity, production efficiency, work quality, and the dynamic, planned, proportional development of the national economy. The national economy is envisaged to be a single, interlinked complex directed on the basis of State plans for economic and social development (see chapter 13, below). Individual labour activity is permitted in handicrafts, agriculture, domestic services, and other areas, but all are subject to State regulation.

SOCIAL DEVELOPMENT AND CULTURE

Socialist legal systems are unique in making the State responsible for the 'social homogeneity' of society. Workers, peasants, and intelligentsia are said to be indissolubly allied as the social basis of the USSR. Differences between town and country, intellectual and physical labour, and nations and peoples are to be eradicated. Nonetheless, the constitutions appear to favour a libertarian concept of equality: the State is to make it possible for citizens to make full use of their creative powers, abilities, and talents. In the Soviet concept this entails a commitment to automation, transforming agricultural labour into industrial, wage levels based on productivity and performance, just distribution of social consumption funds, including public health, housing, public education and the moral, cultural, and aesthetic development of the individual.

FOREIGN POLICY

The 1977-78 constitutions devote a chapter to this topic for the first time. Principally a restatement of basic foreign policy aims, these provisions also contain normative elements. The prohibition of war propaganda, for example, is likewise expressed in the 1951 USSR Law on the Defence of Peace and union republic criminal codes. The reference to 'good-faith fulfilment of obligations arising from generally recognised principles and norms of international law and from international treaties concluded by the USSR' introduces at the constitutional level recognition of an international legal standard for Soviet legislation. The implications for Soviet acceptance of customary principles of international law remain to unfold. Elevated to constitutional stature is the Soviet commitment to economic integration and the international socialist division of labour, provisions reinforcing international obligations under international treaties and COMECON recommendations accepted by the Soviet Government.

DEFENCE OF SOCIALIST FATHERLAND

National defence under the constitution is regarded as a major function of the State. Universal military service is treated as a constitutional duty for those whom Soviet legislation deems subject to call-up.

The State and the individual

No portion of the Soviet constitutions is the object of closer and more sceptical scrutiny by foreign observers than the provisions treating the basic liberties of individual citizens. Soviet draftsmen avoided the omission of the founding fathers of the United States Constitution, who were obliged to amend their instrument at once to secure a Bill of Rights for the individual, and have always incorporated provisions concerning the basic rights of workers and peasants. In the 1918 RSFSR Constitution these provisions were placed at the very beginning of the document. But Soviet society has always struck a very different balance between the State and the individual as compared with Anglo-American principles. Soviet constitutions have stressed the State's role in granting and securing basic freedoms, whereas United States experience in particular has emphasised that rights must be secured against the State and not merely by the State. To Anglo-American eyes, the formulation of basic individual rights and duties in the Soviet constitutions often denies the individual the right to express himself in ways that may be inimical to the regime of the day but nevertheless fall well within the ambit of free expression and dissent tolerated, indeed encouraged, by western democracies because such expression is absolutely essential to the democratic process and an inalienable right which the State may not infringe. The Soviet formulation, which introduces the right to freedom of speech, press, and assembly, for example, that these rights are to be exercised 'in accordance with the interests of the working people and with a view to strengthening the socialist system,' to the western mind constitutes a denial of these rights rather than a guarantee. The Soviet practice of *glasnost*', however, has given greater credence to the freedom of expression and may suggest that tolerance of dissenting views can mature within the present constitutional framework.

Nevertheless, to dismiss these provisions of the Soviet constitutions as meaningless would be to overlook areas where the Soviet legal system has progressed and may continue to do so and to underestimate the importance that international arrangements securing human rights may have for domestic legislation. Like the United Kingdom but unlike the United States, the Soviet Union has ratified the international covenants on political and on social and economic rights. The covenant provisions have had considerable impact upon the 1977–78 Soviet constitutions, which treat the basic rights, freedoms, and duties of the individual in far greater detail than antecedent Soviet documents. The Soviet constitutions incorporate substantial elements of an international standard for conduct with respect to human rights. Although there is by no means universal consensus on precisely what the admissible range of conduct under the international standard may be, there is no longer disagreement about the existence of a minimum standard. Soviet citizens and foreigners in the USSR have both a constitutional formulation of their status as individuals and an international reference point to evaluate the substance of the formulation.

Soviet citizenship and equality of citizens

The USSR Constitution establishes a single union citizenship which Soviet citizens hold co-terminously with the citizenship of their respective union republic. The acquisition and loss of Soviet citizenship is governed by the 1979 Law on Citizenship of the USSR. Marriage and divorce of Soviet citizens with foreigners or stateless persons does not affect Soviet citizenship, nor does residence abroad by a Soviet citizen. Dual citizenship is not recognised. A Soviet citizen may not be extradited to another state. Citizenship is acquired by birth, naturalisation, or other grounds provided for by law or international treaties (see chapter 19, below).

Loss of citizenship may occur by virtue of withdrawal, being deprived thereof, or on other grounds provided for by law or international treaty. Loss of USSR citizenship automatically means loss of union republic citizenship. Withdrawal is based on application and must be authorised individually by the Presidium of the USSR Supreme Soviet. Deprivation may occur exceptionally by decision of the Presidium if a Soviet citizen '... has committed actions which discredit the high calling of a citizen of the USSR and harm the prestige or State security of the USSR.' Soviet dissidents have from time to time been deprived of citizenship on the basis of this provision. Soviet citizens who emigrate permanently commonly lose their citizenship with effect from departing the territory of the USSR. Deprivation of citizenship affects only the individual concerned and not a spouse or children. A person who has lost citizenship may petition the Presidium of the USSR Supreme Soviet to be reinstated.

The Soviet constitutions provide that all Soviet citizens shall be equal before the law irrespective of origin, social and property status, racial and national affiliation, sex, education, language, attitude toward religion, occupation, residence, or other circumstances, and that equality is to be ensured in all areas of economic, political, social, and cultural life. Women's rights include equal access to education, employment, and remuneration and a variety of special measures enabling women with children to combine work with motherhood. Racial and national equality under the constitutions precludes direct or indirect limitations or privileges based on race or nationality, but the realisation of these rights, while including the 'possibility to use' native languages, also embraces the long-term object of achieving the 'coming together' of all nations and peoples and the nurturing of Soviet patriotism and socialist internationalism.

Foreign citizens and stateless persons are guaranteed the rights and freedoms provided by Soviet law and equally are bound to respect Soviet law. The present constitutions preserve the right to grant asylum to foreigners who are persecuted abroad, a feature which dates back to the first RSFSR Constitution.

Basic rights, freedoms and duties of citizens

The Soviet constitutions devote 30 articles to defining the rights, duties, and freedoms of citizens. We already have noted some of the words of limitation which affect the exercise of political rights and the influence of the international human rights covenants upon the draftsmen. The Soviet constitutions are distinctive too for the great stress placed on economic and social rights: the right to be employed, to leisure, to health protection, to material security in old age or poor health, to housing, to education, to use cultural achievements, to be scientifically, technically, or artistically creative, and more. These rights are listed and elaborated ahead of political rights in the constitution. In some instances the rights are linked with specific obligations for the State; in others, the rights must be exercised 'in accordance with the aims of communist construction.' They are rights that in the Soviet concept can be realised only through the State or collective and do not depend upon a limitation of State power.

The political rights and freedoms are enumerated in much the same spirit. These include the right to participate in the administration of State and social affairs; to submit proposals to State agencies and social organisations for improvement of their work or to criticise shortcomings; the freedom of speech, assembly, and association, subject to the limitations described above; to unite in social organisations, in accordance with the aims of communist construction; freedom of conscience, which is defined as the right to confess or not confess any religion and to carry on atheistic propaganda; inviolability of the person and home; protection of the personal life of citizens and secrecy of correspondence, telephone conversations, and telegraph communications; and others.

Rights and freedoms are linked under the Soviet constitutions with duties. A Soviet citizen has a constitutional duty to work conscientiously and observe labour discipline, to care for socialist ownership, to safeguard and protect the Soviet State, to perform military service, to respect the national dignity of other citizens and their rights and legal interests, to support and nurture their children and parents, to care for the natural environment and cultural monuments, to develop friendship and co-operation with the peoples of other countries, to obey Soviet legislation and the rules of socialist community life, among others.

The manner in which political rights are to be exercised must be read not only in the light of some of the words of limitation which accompany them. The principles of democratic centralism and of popular sovereignty also affect their scope and substance. Some of the rights and freedoms enumerated have no precise counterparts in Anglo-American constitutional law; others are taken for granted or subsumed under more basic rights. There are omissions in the enumeration that seem bizarre in the Anglo-American tradition. Freedom of atheistic propaganda is widely tolerated under Anglo-American legislation as part of the freedom of speech, and whereas it is expressly protected under Soviet law, no such protection is granted to those who would propagate religious beliefs in the Soviet Union. On the other hand, *glasnost'* has brought greater tolerance of organised religion and an attenuation of some of the administrative constraints on religious activity introduced in the form of subordinate legislation. There are other examples of this nature one might mention, but it would be misleading to leave the impression that the Soviet constitutions place no limitations whatever on the State with respect to its citizens. Soviet legal theory in the 1970–80s has gradually come to acknowledge that there are certain bounds beyond which a State must not be permitted to extend its power over individuals. The philosophical bases of this view are still in gestation; some believe a variant of 'materialistic natural law' may emerge to justify something approximating inalienable individual rights. The 1977–78 constitutions contain language without parallel in earlier constitutions reflective of this type of concern: respect for the individual and the protection of rights and freedoms of citizens shall be the duty of all State agencies, social organisations, and officials; citizens have the right to appeal against the actions of officials and of State and social agencies; State and social organisations are obliged to observe the USSR Constitution and Soviet laws, among others.

National and State structure of the USSR

The Soviet State represents structurally an unusual amalgam of confederate and federal principles. The Union of Soviet Socialist Republics officially came into being on the basis of an international treaty concluded on 30 December 1922 by the RSFSR, Ukrainian, Belorussian, and Transcaucasian Republics, later joined by the other union republics. Each union republic is still regarded as a sovereign socialist State with the constitutional right to freely secede, to have its own constitution, to confer citizenship, to enter into relations with foreign states, conclude treaties, and exchange diplomatic and consular representations. Two union republics, the Belorussian SSR and the Ukrainian SSR, are members of the United Nations. These elements of confederation are more than balanced by elements of centralist federalism. The USSR Constitution carves out the jurisdiction of the USSR and leaves to the union republics those powers not reserved to all-union jurisdiction. Included within all-union jurisdiction are the establishment of general principles for the organisation and activity of all republic and local organs, ensuring the unity of legislative regulation in the country and enacting the FPL, national economic planning, State budget, including a uniform monetary and credit system, the revenue and taxation system, wage scales, management of branches of the national economy, ensuring State security, declaring war or peace, the conduct of foreign trade, and representation of the USSR in international relations. All the essential attributes of a unitary State are conferred on the all-union authority. Union republics through representation in all-union legislative and executive bodies and formal plenipotentiary representations in Moscow take part in all-union activities; their direct involvement in foreign relations has been limited, and for the greater part is of a symbolic character.

Four union republics contain within their frontiers 20 autonomous republics organised on the nationality principle. Sixteen of them are within the RSFSR. Although each has its own constitution and legislative, executive and judicial organs, their jurisdiction is considerably narrower than the union republics. Smaller national minorities are organised into autonomous regions (eight) and autonomous national areas. These provisions read together with others in the 1977/78 constitutions accentuate the forces of centralism and unity as a likely trend in Soviet nationality policy. The emphasis is upon the 'coming together' of nations and peoples, the emergence of a 'single union multinational State formed on the principle of socialist federalism,' and 'Soviet patriotism and internationalism.'[2]

The electoral system

The 1960–70s were a period in Soviet law of great emphasis upon improving and elaborating the powers of representative organs at all levels. Soviets as elective State bodies are the 'political foundation' of the Soviet Union, a 'unified system' of 'agencies of State power,' elected for a five-year term (all supreme soviets) or a two-and-a-half year term (all inferior soviets) by secret ballot on the basis of universal, equal, and direct suffrage. Candidates for deputies must be USSR citizens, 18 years of age, with full legal capacity, or 21 years of age to be elected to the USSR Supreme Soviet. Communist Party organisations, trade unions, the Komsomol, co-operative and other social organisations, labour collectives, and military units all have the right to nominate candidates. Although neither the Soviet constitutions nor election legislation so require, the accepted practice has been that only one candidate appears on the ballot for each position to be elected, representing a combined Party-non-Party choice. Enormous efforts are made to obtain near universal participation in voting through vast publicity, conveniently placed ballot boxes, organised transport for the infirm, liberal absentee ballot provisions, and the like. Well over 99% of the eligible voters turn out and usually only a fraction of 1% fail to support the agreed slate of candidates. The absence of a multi-party system and of contested elections has led many outsiders to look upon the Soviet electoral process more as an exercise in participatory solidarity than political choice. Citizens may not, *as a rule*, be elected to more than two soviets of people's deputies.

In the 1987 elections, as an experiment, multiple candidates were nominated in selected districts. The object was to encourage a more lively campaign, improve the standard of candidate, and reduce the passivity that has afflicted many deputies in local government. A thorough evaluation of the exercise has not been published, but all indications are that the results were positive and the experiment will be broadened at the next election.

---

2 See A. L. Unger *Constitutional Development in the USSR: A Guide to the Soviet Constitutions* (1981).

Legislative and executive agencies

What in Anglo-American practice would be called the legislative branch of government is known in the Soviet Union as the 'agencies of State power'; the executive branch is termed 'agencies of State administration.'

A. SUPREME SOVIETS

The highest agency of State power in the USSR and the union and autonomous republics respectively is the supreme soviet or parliament. The USSR Supreme Soviet has the power to decide all questions relegated by the USSR Constitution to all-union jurisdiction, including exclusive power to adopt and amend the Constitution, admit new union republics, and confirm State plans for economic and social development, the all-union State budget, and reports from accountable agencies. Union and autonomous republic supreme soviets decide matters relegated to their jurisdiction by the USSR and respective constitutions.

The USSR Supreme Soviet is bicameral, consisting of the Soviet of the Union and the Soviet of Nationalities. Each chamber is equal and contains the same number of deputies (750 at the 1984 election). The principle of deputy selection differs, however. The Soviet of the Union is elected by electoral districts having an equal population, whereas the Soviet of Nationalities is comprised of deputies chosen from each union republic, autonomous republic, autonomous region, and autonomous national area on the basis of representation norms fixed in the USSR Constitution.

Two features of the Soviet parliamentary system have caused most western observers to discount the importance of the legislative process. One is the single-party rule by the CPSU. Until recently all recorded votes in both chambers have been unanimous, and parliamentary debates impress outsiders as rubber-stamp approval for decisions taken elsewhere. Only since 1987 have difficult questions begun to be put to ministers by deputies. The other is the brevity of Supreme Soviet sessions, usually twice-yearly for two or three days. Compared with Her Britannic Majesty's Parliament or the Congress of the United States, the volume of law-making by the supreme soviets in the USSR is miniscule. Supreme soviet deputies are employed full-time in other positions; acting as legislator in formal session consumes but a tiny portion of their time. Recent western studies of the Soviet policy, however, caution against dismissing the policy role of the supreme soviets. If unanimity is the rule during formal sessions, the consensus is hammered out, it is believed, in the permanent or standing commissions or commissions of the USSR Supreme Soviet. Operating on the basis of a 1967 Statute wholly reworked in 1979, the permanent commissions seem to perform a real and active function in drafting legislation. Each commission has technical and service support and legal counsel at its disposal through the Presidium of the Supreme Soviet. As a rule, each permanent commission will draft or review a legislative act within its subject jurisdiction unless a special commission is set up. They have the right to request relevant information and solicit expert opinion. For substantial enactments a permanent commission often forms sub-commissions to work on certain sections or articles of a draft. In turn the sub-commissions or preparatory commissions may form working groups ad hoc, especially with a view to enlisting specialist assistance from outside the political milieu. A distinguished international lawyer, for example, chaired a working group formed by the Permanent Commission for Foreign Affairs when the 1978 Law on the procedure for the ratification of treaties was drafted. Specialists sometimes are invited to attend enlarged sessions of the permanent commissions. Circuit sessions may be held when required. Once drafts are ready for comment, the commissions often, if not usually, circulate them to specialists in academic institutes or legal agencies. Public meetings of specialists may be convened to obtain reactions on a draft or special conferences to exchange ideas and views. In recent years the advanced drafts of major enactments have been published in the press for general discussion. Comments and letters are tabulated as part of the legislative process and sometimes lead to changes in the draft. Permanent commissions also exercise a control function over ministries and departments to oversee the implementation of legislation, particularly with a view to learning whether further legislation may be required.

The right to propose legislation is vested by the USSR Constitution in each chamber of the supreme soviet, the Presidium, the Council of Ministers, the union republic supreme soviets, commissions of the supreme soviet and permanent commissions of its chambers, deputies of the supreme soviet, the USSR Supreme Court, and the USSR Procurator General, and social organisations in the person of their all-union agencies. Little data is available on the frequency with which each of these bodies exercises its right, but social organisations apparently are beginning to do so from time to time.

Since the supreme soviets meet only for brief periods in formal session, their functions in the intervals between sessions are carried out by a Presidium elected at a joint session of the two chambers. The chairman of the Presidium is the formal Head of State of the USSR. While the Presidium is accountable to the full Supreme Soviet, only certain of its actions require subsequent confirmation at regular Supreme Soviet sessions, to wit: changes in prevailing legislative acts, changes of union republic boundaries, the formation or abolition of USSR ministries and State committees, and the appointment to or dismissal from office of members of the Government. Actions which the Presidium may take independently, so to speak, are enumerated in 18 sub-points of Article 121 of the USSR Constitution. They encompass designating elections to and convoking sessions of the Supreme Soviet, co-ordinating the activity of permanent commissions of Supreme Soviet chambers, exercising constitutional control over union republic enactments, interpreting laws of the USSR, ratifying or denouncing international treaties, repealing decrees or regulations of the Government if they are contrary to law, establishing and conferring military and diplomatic ranks, establishing and awarding or conferring orders, medals, and honorary titles of the USSR, granting or withdrawing citizenship, granting asylum, issuing all-union amnesties and pardons, appointing and recalling plenipotentiary representatives and accepting credentials or letters of recall from foreign diplomats, appointing and removing the supreme command of the USSR Armed Forces, declaring martial law, a general or partial mobilisation, or, under specified circumstances, a state of war, and exercising other powers established by the USSR Constitution and laws.

The 1979 Reglament of the USSR Supreme Soviet elaborates in detail the procedures for the activities of the chambers, the Council of Elders, the Presidium, the commissions, the formation of the Government, and the People's Control Committee, the election of the Supreme Court, the appointment of the Procurator General, and the consideration of draft legislation and foreign policy matters, the exercise of control functions, and the publication of official materials.

The USSR Supreme Soviet is 'convoked' after each national election. Its convocations are calculated from the election of 12 December 1937 under the 1936 Constitution. The 1977 Constitution did not commence a new series of convocations. The present eleventh convocation was elected on 4 March 1984. The 1,500 deputies elected received 99.9% of the votes cast. Of the deputies elected, 32.8% were women, 71.4% were full or candidate members of the CPSU, and 51.3% were workers and collective farmers. These figures reflect, since 1937, an increase in the representation of women, some decrease in Party representation, and a considerable improvement in the educational standard. As measured by numbers of speeches by deputies, numbers of agenda items, numbers of permanent commission meetings, total enactments adopted, and changes in the State budget introduced by the Supreme Soviet, the USSR Supreme Soviet seems to have developed into something more than a 'rubber stamp.'[3] Students of Soviet affairs continue to differ widely about how much significance should be attached to evidence of this kind of change. From the standpoint of the legal process, the major

---

3 For a thorough account of recent trends and the state of the literature, see S. White 'The USSR Supreme Soviet: A Developmental Perspective' in D. Nelson and S. White (eds) *Communist Legislatures in Comparative Perspective* (1982) pp 125–159.

development lies less in representation patterns than in evidence of permanent commission influence in shaping legislative policy and more open and critical plenary debates.

B. COUNCILS OF MINISTERS

The highest executive and administrative agencies of State power in the Soviet Union are respectively the councils of ministers—the Government—of the USSR and the union and autonomous republics. Here the British parliamentary model has been adapted: The Government is formed by the USSR Supreme Soviet at a joint session of the two chambers. The Chairman of the council of ministers is the head of Government. At each newly elected Supreme Soviet the Government lays aside its powers and is reconstituted. The councils of ministers are accountable to the legislative branch and in the interval between sessions to its Presidium.

The competence of the Government is wide indeed and extends to all matters of State adminstration relegated to USSR jurisdiction and not, according to the Constitution, within the jurisdiction of the USSR Supreme Soviet or its Presidium. Among the constitutionally stipulated functions of Government are directing the national economy, the development of science and technology, rational use and protection of natural resources, the monetary and credit system, price policy, wage levels, social security, State insurance, organising the management of industrial, construction, and agricultural enterprises and associations, transport and communications enterprises, banks; working out and submitting to the legislature current and long-term State plans and the State budget; taking measures to defend State interests, socialist ownership, and public order, and the rights and interests of citizens; State security; general direction over the USSR Armed Forces and determining annual call-up quotas; exercising general direction over relations with foreign States, foreign trade, economic, scientific-technical, and cultural co-operation with foreign countries; ensuring the fulfilment of international treaties of the USSR, and confirming or denouncing intergovernmental international treaties, and forming needed committees, chief administrations, or other departments attached to the Government.

As the councils of ministers meet at least once a quarter, their lawmaking activity is much more extensive than the legislative branch. Nevertheless, each council of ministers also has a Presidium that gives particular attention to management of the national economy but also may deal with 'other questions of State administration.' The Administrative Office of each council of ministers prepares issues for consideration and takes part in verifying the implementation of Party and Government decisions.

Membership of the USSR Council of Ministers comprises the

chairman, the first deputy and deputy-chairmen, ministers of the USSR, the chairmen of USSR State committees, the chairmen of the union republic councils of ministers ex officio, and other heads of State agencies co-opted. The all-union ministries and State committees have responsibility for directing branches of administration within their jurisdiction or carrying out interbranch administration throughout the entire USSR either directly or through agencies of their creation. The union republic ministries and State committees do likewise but as a rule through their counterparts at union republic or inferior levels. The full competence of the Government and its Presidium and the procedure for their activities, relations with other State agencies, and a list of the all-union and union republic ministries and of the State committees all are elaborated in the 1978 Law on the USSR Council of Ministers, and the respective union and autonomous laws. The transference of the listing of ministries and State committees out of the constitutions has removed the greatest single source of constitutional amendment under the 1936–40 Soviet constitutions, for reorganisation of these bodies occurs with frequency. Each ministry and State committee is supposed to have its own Statute defining its competence and functions,[4] although in many cases the constitutive document is obsolete.

C. LOCAL AGENCIES OF STATE POWER AND ADMINISTRATION

The local soviets of people's deputies, from territories to rural population centres, are the agencies of State power and their executive committees, the agencies of administration. The Soviet constitutions give them jurisdiction over 'all questions of local significance.' They implement decisions of superior State agencies, direct inferior organs, take part in discussions of republic and all-union significance, direct State, economic, and socio-cultural construction on their territory, confirm local economic and social development plans and the local budget, direct subordinate State agencies, enterprises, institutions, and organisations, co-ordinate land use, nature conservation, construction, use of labour resources, production of consumer goods, and local domestic services and amenities. Detailed regulations governing each tier of local agencies are to be formed in a series of laws defining their basic powers.

Soviet legislation has since 1967 undertaken to improve the stature of deputies and permanent local governmental personnel. The rights of deputies to consult with officials and secure access to premises were strengthened, as was their right to obtain replies to questions submitted. Greater publicity is given to deputy efforts on behalf of reform or redress. Jurisconsults are increasingly made available to local soviet executive committees.

---

4 D. A. Loeber 'Statutes of Agencies with Ministerial Status in the USSR' Review of Socialist Law VIII (1982) 359–368; IX (1983) 182.

Both Soviet and western studies confirm, however, that 'passivity' has been a major problem in respect of local soviet deputies. The great majority of them, though exemplary citizens and model workers, have neither the experience, nor the confidence, nor the knowledge, nor the energy to play an active part in local governmental politics. Studies of the 1970s disclose that, although workers comprised about half of the total number of deputies, only about 10% actually spoke at soviet sessions. Those deputies who are elected to the executive committee of the local soviet tend to be re-elected for several terms, to be Party members, to have higher levels of education, and to be older.

There have been suggestions in the legal press and general media to alter the base unit of representation. At present the franchise is territorially based on place of residence. The nomination process, however, is territorially based sometimes and in other instances rests upon place of work. The suggestions are to make all, or virtually all, representation and franchise based on place of work. Labour collectives in places of work already enjoy constitutional stature and recently have begun to elect management personnel. Most individuals gainfully employed, it is pointed out, spend the greater portion of their waking hours at their place of work and often their true interest in local government matters is employment-related rather than residence-related, especially if their enterprise is subordinate to the local soviet. To date these continue to be merely proposals.

For the past three decades there has been a strong trend, despite certain reversals and interruptions, in the direction of broadening the revenue base and budgetary discretion of local government. Economic reforms furthering decentralisation of industrial management and enterprise autonomy in retaining larger portions of their net proceeds and directing them independently or within flexible limits to certain socio-economic or cultural purposes have had the effect of increasing substantially the amounts of revenues available to local government. Especially since 1971 city soviets have exercised greater control and co-ordination over all enterprises and organisations on their territories irrespective of the departmental subordination concerned. Under the 1985 restructuring reforms, the rights of local government vis-à-vis enterprises are being enlarged, and it is likely that local soviets will have a larger voice in the allocation of enterprise resources for housing, socio-cultural, and other municipal measures.

Despite the standard statutory base governing each tier of local government, analyses of Soviet local budgets disclose wide fluctuations over expenditure. The restructuring reforms are expected to encourage local soviets to generate local revenues, and this in turn will require some modifications in the local budgetary process itself. But negotiation between local government and enterprises on their territories about the joint use of funds for municipal amenities and housing will probably continue to play a key role in urban expansion.

D. JUSTICE, ARBITRAZH, AND PROCURACY SUPERVISION

Basic provisions on the courts, arbitrazh, colleges of advocates, and the Procuracy are found in all the Soviet constitutions (see chapter 7, above).

E. JUDICIAL REVIEW

Notwithstanding some early experience with judicial review of the constitutionality of legislative acts, until recently there has been great reluctance in the Soviet legal system to give Soviet courts the power to review either the constitutionality or the legality of acts of officials and State agencies. The provisions of Article 58, para 2, of the 1977 USSR Constitution guaranteeing that the 'actions of officials committed in violation of law, in excess of their powers, and impinging upon the rights of citizens may be appealed to a court' were not procedurally effected until ten years later. On 30 June 1987 the USSR Supreme Soviet adopted the Law on the Procedure for Appealing to a Court the Unlawful Actions of Officials which Impinge upon the Rights of Citizens, with effect from 1 January 1988. The Law itself experienced a stormy passage in the Supreme Soviet and had to be amended on 20 October 1987 to further strengthen its provisions.

Proposals are being mooted to extend the scope of judicial review. Some Soviet jurists favour allowing the Procuracy to apply to a court for redress against the adoption of an illegal decision by an administrative agency rather than issuing a protest, as presently, to the superior agency. Others would empower the USSR Supreme Court with the right to declare invalid the decisions of ministries and departments which violate socialist legality. During the 1920s the Supreme Court brought such issues to the Central Executive Committee Presidium, and reportedly two-thirds of all cases considered between 1924–28 by the USSR Supreme Court concerned the unconstitutionality of decrees and regulations issued by State agencies. While under the 1977 USSR Constitution the Presidium of the USSR Supreme Soviet is charged with ensuring that union republic constitutions and laws conform to those of the USSR, no procedures have been laid down for exercising such constitutional control.

Three variants are being discussed. One is a Constitutional Council to be created and attached to the USSR Supreme Soviet or its Presidium; the second is the formation of a separate Constitutional Court of the USSR; and the third is to endow the USSR Supreme Court with powers of constitutional control, with appropriate changes in its structure and composition.

Arms, flag and anthem

The USSR, each union republic, and each autonomous republic has its own symbols of statehood: State arms, a State flag, and a national anthem. The arms and flag are described in each constitution, and the procedure for using or placing each is elaborated in individual statutes.

Constitutional amendment

Soviet constitutions may be amended by the respective supreme soviet if a two-thirds majority of the deputies in each chamber favours the amendment. Constitutional amendments occur under the 1977–78 constitutions less frequently than under the antecedent constitutions. The 1977 USSR Constitution has as of 1988 been amended once. Given the single party system of the Soviet State, however, amendment is a routine formality very unlike the lengthy procedures required in the United States. Despite their status as the fundamental law, Soviet constitutions in the past have been overridden by subsequent legislation (see chapter 4, above).

Chapter 9

The Communist Party and the legal system

Few questions cause greater concern to the foreign lawyer than the role of the Communist Party of the Soviet Union (CPSU) in the Soviet legal system. Because the USSR is a single-party State, there is a widespread impression or apprehension that Party organs in fact administer the law behind the scenes, that the justice rendered is Party justice rather than justice administered by the State according to law. The CPSU does play significant roles in the Soviet legal system, roles not fully understood, but the data available on the Party-legal system relationship suggests a far more complex and subtle interlinkage than the caricature described above.

The Party

Broadly speaking, one may say that the Communist Party rules the Soviet Union but does not govern the Soviet Union. The Leninist concept of the Party's role in society was forged in the pre-revolutionary era. The Party represented in Lenin's view the vanguard of the working class, the most politically aware elements, and it operated as a clandestine disciplined core group whose destiny as a vanguard was to continue after the Revolution. Among Lenin's many precepts for Party organisation was the principle that the Party must lead the State but never become the State. That position now appears in Article 6 of the Party Rules: 'Party organisations shall not supplant State, trade union, cooperative and social organisations, nor allow the functions of the Party and other agencies to be mixed.' In the years that have elapsed the Party has grown in membership and reconceptualised aspects of its functions in a socialist society. In the Anglo-American understanding of the term, however, the CPSU is not a political party. It does not compete for political power with other parties, interest groups, or classes. Rather it endeavours to attract to its ranks the most capable of the Soviet professional, administrative, technical, rural, and intellectual elites, and most western Soviet specialists believe Party recruitment policy is on the whole quite successful in doing so.[1]

---

1 Western literature on the CPSU is substantial. See, among recent studies, J. F. Hough and M. Fainsod *How the Soviet Union Is Governed* (1979); L. B. Schapiro *The*

Official CPSU statistics disclose that as of 1988 the Party had a membership of 19,468,786 (including 715,592 candidate members), or 9.7% of the adult population. Of these 45% were classified as workers, 11.8% as peasants or collective farmers, and 43.2% as employees. Women comprised 28.8% of Party members; persons of Russian nationality, 59.1%, and of Ukrainian nationality, 16%.

The membership requirements and structure of the CPSU are laid down by the Rules of the CPSU confirmed by the XXII Party Congress, as amended by the XXIII, XXIV, and XXVII Party Congresses.[2] Party membership is open to Soviet citizens, who acknowledge the Party Programme and Rules, actively take part in the building of communism, work in one of the Party organisations, comply with Party decisions, and pay membership dues. The membership subscription depends on monthly earnings and ranges from a minimum of 1 ruble 20 kopeks per annum to 3% of annual earnings for those who earn more than 300 rubles per month. The minimum age is 18 years; individuals who join the Party at age 25 or under must do so via the Komsomol. Applicants for Party membership must have recommendations from at least three CPSU members of five years' standing. Decisions on applications are taken by the general meeting of the primary Party organisation; a two-thirds majority is required, as is subsequent confirmation by the district or city Party committee. Every applicant for membership must pass through a probationary stage called 'candidate membership' one year in duration. Candidate members take part in Party activities, but may not vote nor be elected to office or as delegate to Party conferences and congresses.

The organisational base of the Party is the primary Party organisations. In 1986 there were 440,363 such organisations. They ordinarily are formed at the places where Party members work—there must be at least three Party members—although in some rural areas they may become territorially based in villages or housing units. Depending on their size, primary Party organisations elect a secretary of a bureau to carry on the affairs of the organisation. The highest agency of a primary Party organisation is the Party meeting, which meets at periodic intervals, usually more frequently in smaller units. The largest primary Party organisations form Party committees elected for two or three year terms to run their affairs. In enterprises of all types, collective and State farms, scientific research or design institutes, educational, cultural-enlightenment, and treatment institutions the primary Party organisations enjoy the right of control over the activity of the respective administration. Communists are to play the vanguard role in the labour, socio-political, and economic life of these institutions. In ministries, State

---

Communist Party of the Soviet Union (2nd edn, 1971); J. N. Hazard *The Soviet System of Government* (5th edn, 1980) pp 13–38; R. J. Hill and P. Frank *The Soviet Communist Party* (3rd edn, 1986).

2 Transl. in W. E. Butler *Basic Documents on the Soviet Legal System* (2nd edn, 1988).

committees, and other central and local soviet and economic institutions and departments the primary Party organisations exercise control over the work of these bodies relative to the fulfilment of Party and government directives and the observance of Soviet laws. Except for those communists employed full-time in the Party itself, it will be apparent that most Party members act in a dual capacity: as Party members in the primary Party organisation and as employees or workers in their respective places of employment. Particular posts often are reserved for Party members.[3] It is this interlocking relationship between the CPSU and all other entities that ensures Party predominance in Soviet society.

The work of primary Party organisations is co-ordinated and directed at the administrative-territorial levels by republic, territory, regional, national area, city, and district Party organisations. In 1986 there were 14 union republic party organs (the RSFSR is not represented in the Party at this level), 6 territory, 151 regional, 2 city (Moscow and Kiev) Party committees equated to regions, 10 national areas, 891 city, 463 district, and 2,887 rural Party committees. Party organs at these levels spend much of their time on Party organisational matters: confirming new members, exercising *nomenklatura* powers in selecting or confirming leading personnel, ideological work with members, agitation and propaganda. Informed western observers believe, however, that Party organisations on these levels are deeply enmeshed in local decision-making. The Party Rules charge Party organisations and their committees to 'implement Party policy' within their respective territories, to 'organise the execution' of directives of the Central Committee, and to 'direct' local soviets and other bodies through the Party groups therein. This means policy leadership exercised through the right to fill key positions and authority through all officials who are Party members via the Party organisations. The Party role is not a passive supervisory one. Plan fulfilment by all enterprises, organisations, and institutions and the maintenance of political stability often require direct Party involvement in decision-making by non-Party bodies so that these objectives may be achieved.

The internal structure of Party organs at these levels follows the primary organisations. The plenary body is called a congress at the union republic level and a conference at inferior levels; these meet infrequently, usually once every two or three years, and therefore select a Party committee to act in the intervals between meetings. The Party committee in turn chooses an executive body of 7 to 15 full members called a politburo at union republic levels and a bureau at inferior

---

3 This is the practice of *nomenklatura*. There are two types: so-called ordinary *nomenklatura*, wherein the Party approves or confirms the appointment of personnel and often takes the initiative in proposing candidates; and *uchetnaia nomenklatura*, wherein the Party is kept informed about lower-level positions.

levels. In addition, the Party committee selects secretaries, one of whom is designated the first secretary, to serve as full-time officials assisted by apparatus staff to direct and service departments of the Party organisation. The size of the apparatus is related to the number of Party members at each respective level. Estimates vary, but it seems likely the number of full-time Party officials is approximately 100,000.

The highest organ of the CPSU is the Party Congress. Twenty-seven Party congresses have been held to date, the last in 1986, although not always within the five-year intervals which the Party Rules now prescribe. The Congress hears reports from the Central Committee of the CPSU, may amend the Party Programme or Rules, determines the Party line on matters of internal and foreign policy, and elects the Central Committee and Central Auditing Commission. In recent years the practice has been for congresses to coincide with the commencement of new Five-Year plans. Although the Party congresses no longer feature the outspoken political debate characteristics of the smaller gatherings of the 1920s, the more placid meetings of the post-war era do give evidence of some policy discussion and Aesopian dialogue. Party congresses have grown massively in size. The XXVII Congress (1986) consisted of 4,993 delegates, about 21% of whom were Party officials, 27% were women, and 76.5% were chosen for the first time.

The Central Committee of the CPSU is elected to function between congresses. The number of Committee members is to be fixed by the Party Congress; if full members leave the Committee, then places are filled from among candidate members elected by the Congress. In 1986, 307 full and 170 candidate members of the Central Committee were elected. The actual procedure for election and patterns for representation on the Central Committee remain obscure. Recent practices tend to suggest a consensus slate is fashioned with representation accorded to functional and territorial hierarchies. From 1965–82 the Central Committee tended to meet less frequently than formerly, thereby according greater significance to the executive body directing work between Central Committee meetings: the Politburo.

As of March 1988, the Politburo comprised 13 full and 7 candidate members. Its activities encompass the direction of highest policy, internal and foreign. Meetings normally are held weekly, and it seems probable that economic policies engage a major portion of the Politburo's attention together with foreign policy.

The General Secretary is the executive officer of the Central Committee and chosen by it; since the late 1950s the individual elected to that position has been the most powerful individual in the Soviet Union. Under the Party Rules, the General Secretary is responsible for the operation of the Secretariat, which is to select cadres and verify the execution of Party directives. However, the General Secretary is but one member of the Politburo. Even though acknowledged to be first among equals, it is not within his formal power to dismiss Politburo members from office. Collective leadership by the Politburo has remained the form, if not the substance, of Party governance in the CPSU. The secretaries of the CPSU also are elected by the Central Committee. They administer the Committee *apparat*, the Committee being divided into sections which correspond basically to branches of industry or specialist areas (Party work, information, and others). There are also miscellaneous sections dealing with housekeeping matters, publishing, retirement facilities, and the like. Some authorities estimate that the apparatus as a whole numbers about 1,500 persons. The Central Committee sections are further sub-divided into sectors, of which there are 150 to 175, staffed by instructors, inspectors, consultants, lecturers, research staff, and office personnel. The Central Committee elects the Party Control Committee as well, which verifies the conduct of lower Party officials and acts as the highest instance in deciding appeals against expulsions imposed by lower Party bodies.

In the interval between Party congresses, the Central Committee may convene an All-Union Party Conference to discuss questions of Party policy; this institution was reintroduced in 1966, having been abolished in 1941, and the first to be held was in June 1988.

The Central Audit Commission of the CPSU, consisting of 83 members in 1986, reviews the expeditious and proper handling of affairs in Party central agencies and in the bank and enterprises of the CPSU.

Party organisations in the USSR Armed Forces are directed by the CPSU Central Committee through the Chief Political Administration of the Soviet Army and Navy, which operates with the rights of a section of the Central Committee. Army Party organisations and political agencies at best liaise with local Party committees but otherwise are directed from the centre.

Operating under the direction of the CPSU but an independent social organisation is the All-Union Leninist Communist Youth League (Komsomol). Called in the Party Rules the 'active helper and reserve of the Party,' the Komsomol recruits well over 95% of all Soviet youth eligible to join. Komsomol members who join the CPSU must resign from the Komsomol unless they hold executive positions in the Komsomol organisation.

Legal status

Just as the precise structure and activities of the CPSU remain shrouded in mystery, so too is the legal status of the Party ambiguous. No legislative act defines comprehensively the role of the CPSU in Soviet society. The 1977 USSR Constitution mentions the Party in three places: the preamble, Article 6, and Article 100. The preamble refers to the Party as having led the 1917 October Revolution (para 1) and to the growth of the Party's 'leading role' as the 'vanguard of the whole people' (para 4). Article 6 is given over wholly to the Party, a change from the 1936 USSR Constitution which had mentioned the Party incidentally as the vanguard of the proletariat in the provisions on the freedom of association (Art 126). Article 6 provides:

The Communist Party of the Soviet Union shall be the guiding and directing force of Soviet society and the nucleus of its political system and of State and social organisations. The CPSU shall exist for the people and shall serve the people.
　　Armed with Marxist-Leninist teaching, the Communist Party shall determine the general perspective for the development of society and the internal and foreign policy line of the USSR, direct the great creative activity of the Soviet people, and impart a planned, scientifically well-founded character to its struggle for the triumph of communism.
　　All Party organisations shall operate within the framework of the USSR Constitution.

The more prominent positioning of the Party in the 1977–78 Soviet constitutions reflected a trend already underway in Eastern European constitutional draftsmanship of the early 1970s. The alteration in the vanguard role of the CPSU is significant. The Party is no longer the vanguard of the proletariat, in 1936 merely one segment of Soviet society, but has become the vanguard of the whole people, suggesting the legitimising of a monopoly political role underscored in Article 6 with references to being the 'nucleus' of the political system. The language about the 'guiding and directing' functions of the Party and about the Party's responsibility for the internal and foreign policy lines is indebted to the Party Rules. The third paragraph is wholly new in substance and spirit, and indeed was inserted into the USSR Constitution in the final stages of adoption. In 1986 it was incorporated into Article 60 of the Party Rules. The meaning and importance of the paragraph has provoked much conjecture amongst western observers, but there seems little doubt that the draftsmen intended to stipulate that the Party was not above the law and is directed to carry on its activities in accordance with the law. The Party, of course, has a major voice in initiating, drafting, approving, and enacting legislation, so the requirement is less a constraint on the Party organisations than an admonition to operate within the Party's own endorsed policies.
　　Juridically, the CPSU is a social organisation. This means that it is a non-State body, but presumably subject to relevant State regulations governing social organisations. Soviet jurists, however, have remarkably little to say about the application of legislation to the Party as an organisation. The author of a major treatise on Soviet administrative law wrote:

The State does not guide the Communist Party . . . [Its] activity, based on constitutional norms, is regulated first by the Rules and decisions of [this] very organisation.

That statement is highly misleading. Soviet legislation is replete with examples of Party organisations being expressly accorded particular rights and responsibilities. Article 100 of the USSR Constitution gives Party organisations the right to nominate candidates for deputies of soviets at all levels. That right also exists under other legislation with respect to candidates for people's judges and people's assessors, among others. Enterprises owned by the CPSU are taken into account in national economic planning and are exempted from the duty to pay income tax on balance-sheet profits.[4] On the other hand, no State legislation appears to govern the formation or termination of the CPSU as a juridical entity or define its external powers or jurisdiction. It is an open, but under Article 6, para 3 of the USSR Constitution by no means moot, question whether recourse to the State would be possible if a Party organisation acted contrary to Party Rules or decisions. Nor does it appear that the Party is required to register with the State as a social organisation. While the Party undoubtedly enjoys legal personality under Soviet law, it is unclear which Party unit bears that personality, which has the right to sue and be sued, or be answerable for liabilities out of Party assets.

Party members

Party membership in the Soviet Union represents a considerable achievement and opportunity for those who qualify. Access to positions of power and influence, effectively speaking, can be secured only through Party placement or confirmation, and many believe access to other facets of the better life likewise is enhanced through Party membership. The Party Rules contain a number of strictures for members relating to the legal system: to 'care for and increase social, socialist ownership,' to 'set an example in the fulfilment of social duty,' to 'observe the principles of communist morality,' to 'observe Party and State discipline . . .' among others. Although the Rules do not mention obedience to the law and the strengthening of socialist legality in so many words, Party manuals and resolutions make abundantly manifest that these are among the responsibilities of Party members.

Nevertheless, Party membership can raise unusual and sometimes difficult problems of principle in respect of the exercise of legal rights

---

4 D. A. Loeber 'On the Status of the CPSU within the Soviet Legal System' in W. B. Simons and S. White (eds) *The Party Statutes of the Communist World* (1984) pp 1–22.

and duties. Lenin once counselled, in the early 1920s, that Party members should be dealt with more severely by the courts if they committed a crime; since a higher standard of conduct was expected of them in their vanguard role, a greater measure of punishment should be imposed if they were found guilty. Soviet law does not so provide; on the contrary, under the 1977 USSR Constitution, all citizens are equal before the law. The fact of Party membership would be known to the court, however. Indeed, it is one of the first questions asked of an accused, after his name, address, age, and level of education. Courts could take Party membership into account therefore when assigning punishment, and this might serve to favour an accused or to subject him to sterner measures. Moreover, it would be admissible for a court to ask whether an accused Party member had been disciplined by his Party organisation for the alleged offence, a question which under Anglo-American procedures would be regarded as highly prejudicial since the constituent elements of acceptable Party behaviour may be very different from the constituent elements of a crime. The Party Rules (Art 12) provide that 'if a Party member has committed offences punishable in a criminal proceeding, he shall be expelled from the Party and brought to responsibility in accordance with the law.' The phrasing of the provision suggests the Party is to deliberate on the matter before criminal proceedings are instituted, reinforcing the impression shared by some that in practice '... a person on a sufficiently high *nomenklatura* list cannot be subject to criminal prosecution without Party approval.'[5] The practice must be fraught with dilemmas, for the Party may find itself protecting individuals who deserve to be prosecuted or prejudicing individuals when Party morality imposes higher standards than minimum legal conduct.

Similar conundrums can arise in other areas of the law. A Communist Party member has the legal right to file for divorce under Soviet family legislation but may find either the fact of or the grounds for divorce disclose conduct incompatible with continued Party membership. A classic textbook example arises in labour law if a Party member holding a *nomenklatura* post wishes to exercise his right under Soviet labour legislation to resign and take up other employment and his local Party organisation refuses to allow him to resign. The textbook answer to this conflict between Party discipline and legal right is that the individual may appeal the local Party decision to the next higher Party organisation. If the latter confirms the decision, the individual can still exercise his legal right but may suffer sanctions imposed by the Party, up to and including expulsion. On the other side of the coin, the dismissal of a Party member by management would be inconceivable without consulting the local Party organisation, *nomenklatura* post or not.

Although the CPSU is a non-State body, it is interesting that under

---

5 Quoted in D. D. and C. B. Barry *Contemporary Soviet Politics* (1978) p 117.

Soviet law even a Party official employed full-time in the Party apparatus could be held criminally responsible for violating duties which are a condition of his official position and have caused material harm to State or social interests or to the rights and interests of individual citizens protected by law (Art 170, RSFSR Criminal Code). Such a violation would constitute an 'official crime,' and an official for these purposes includes 'persons . . . temporarily or permanently exercising the functions of representatives of authority, and likewise who hold, permanently or temporarily, offices in . . . social . . . organisations . . . connected with the fulfilment of organisational-management or administrative-economic duties. . . .' The commentaries on the Criminal Code make clear that this language encompasses the administrative apparatus of 'social organisations fulfilling socially-useful functions.'[6]

Party guidance of law and the legal system

LEGISLATION

Reference already has been made (chapter 4, above) to the place of joint Party-State decrees in the hierarchy of sources of law. Although not law, Party resolutions are extremely important statements of policy which bind the Party membership and often serve as the basis or backdrop for subsequent legislation by State bodies. The extent to which Party organs, especially the Central Committee of the CPSU and its apparatus, themselves undertake to initiate and draft enactments of this nature or merely instigate State bodies to do so is unknown. Party resolutions doubtless are drafted within the CPSU apparatus, although the information and data on which they are based may be drawn from both State and Party sources. In earlier periods of Soviet history, especially the 1920s, there is evidence to indicate that Party organs in some union republics formally drafted or regularly vetted the drafting of most legislation as part of the legislative process. What little we know of the ordinary legislative process in the Soviet Union today suggests an interminable network of temporary drafting commissions and interdepartmental consultations with *interested* ministries and departments. The Party would seem more likely to play a guiding role rather than the implementing role in these matters, excluding perhaps those of greatest urgency and importance.

LEGAL SYSTEM

Soviet legal institutions are guided by Party policy just as are other institutions. Party membership among key participants in the legal

[6] B. V. Zdravomyslov, in Iu. D. Severin (ed) *Kommentarii k Ugolovnomu kodeksu RSFSR* (1980) p 326.

process is substantial: about 60% of defence counsel, 40–50% of judges, 40% of people's assessors, 90% of procurators (see chapters 6 and 7, above). The press is under strict Party control, as are police and investigative agencies. Legislation embodies Party-initiated or Party-endorsed policy. To imagine in the midst of all this that the CPSU apparatus needs to assume responsibility for deciding individual cases and instruct the courts accordingly flies in the face of what in reality is a far more complex and subtle system for the administration of legality. The CPSU has made it clear time and again in public utterances binding upon members that whereas Party organs have a responsibility to assess the general course of administering justice, they may not interfere in the disposition of individual cases. Local Party officials who have violated that injunction have been disciplined and publicly censured. In a Decree of the Central Committee published on 30 November 1986, that view was reiterated: while Party committees are to 'strengthen political guidance' and 'exercise control' over law enforcement agencies, they 'must not allow interference on the part of anyone in the investigation and judicial examination of specific cases'.[7]

The supervisory function of Party organs over law enforcement and the administration of justice is apparently not lightly assumed. Party committees bear full responsibility for the state of law and order in their respective level of jurisdiction. The Leningrad City and District Party Committees in 1969–70 reportedly considered 140 questions connected with strengthening legality and public order. One district Party committee was deemed to have overreached itself in 1969 when it invited to Party headquarters persons who led a parasitic way of life and in the presence of Party personnel and others undertook to arrange employment for them. This was regarded as involvement in the administration of justice and inappropriate for Party organs.[8]

Although Party organs are not to trouble, pressure, or interfere with the courts and law enforcement bodies, they are entitled to make inquiries (*zaprosy*) about matters. The Soviet newspaper *Izvestiia* investigated reports in 1977 that a model young worker had been sentenced to ten days for petty hooliganism. The investigation disclosed a careless police inquiry and a people's judge who acted on the basis of the police protocol. The judgment was reversed, of course, and the judge and

---

7 *Izvestiia*, 30 November 1986, p 1, col 3. The Central Committee of the CPSU is quoted as declaring that illegal interference by local Party organs in the work of courts '... undermines the authority of the court, disorganises the judges and pushes them into giving illegal decisions, violates the principle established by the USSR Constitution of independence of judges and their being subject only to law, deprives the procuracy and judicial agencies of independence, and makes them irresponsible'. V. P. Rad'kov *Sotsialisticheskaia zakonnost' v sovetskom ugolovnom protsesse* (1959) p 152, transl. in J. N. Hazard, W. E. Butler, and P. B. Maggs *The Soviet Legal System* (3rd edn, 1977) p 67.

8 S. E. Zhilinskii *Rol' KPSS v ukreplenie zakonnosti na sovremennom etape* (1977) pp 78, 80.

district procurator were all subjected to Party discipline by their District Party committee. The police investigator was dismissed from service. Malfeasance in office led for all three individuals to Party sanctions but apparently not to legal prosecution.[9]

Where corruption is widespread, involving Party and State officials alike, as occurred in Moldavia during 1985–86, local Party influence succeeded in stopping the Procuracy from prosecuting. Only when matters got beyond local control, were central agencies able to step in and redress the situation.

LEGAL EDUCATION

The enormous emphasis of the 1970–80s upon knowledge of the law by all Soviet citizens applied to Party personnel as well. Soviet law became a compulsory component for Party training schools. The Party worker's manual (*Spravochnik partiinogo rabotnika*), an indispensable source for key Party decrees and government decrees, especially prior to 1972 when the government gazette was not subject to export, has been augmented by dozens of basic texts and monographs on the basic elements of Soviet law for the Party member who is not a trained jurist. Party cadres are said to require legal training not merely as a body of knowledge, but so they know how to combat red-tape, so they better comprehend Party policy and the various mechanisms for regulating social relations. Party propagandists include legal materials in their lectures to Party personnel. All full-time and part-time Party training schools include Soviet law as an integral part of the syllabus at all levels of the system of Party education.[10]

International legal status of the CPSU

The relationship between Party and State in the Soviet Union on more than one occasion has caused legal complications on the international level. The CPSU maintains extensive links with other communist movements throughout the world, most of whom are in political opposition to the ruling governments. These links were maintained chiefly through the Communist International (Comintern), until its dissolution in 1943, and more loosely by its successor, the Communist Information Bureau (Cominform), wound up in 1956. Inexperienced diplomatic observers of the 1920s imagined that the Comintern actually governed the Soviet State. During the early 1930s some western governments, including the United States, sought to reduce Comintern support for revolutionary movements by invoking the principle of non-interference

9 *Izvestiia*, 26 January 1977, p 2, col 8.
10 A. S. Pavlov *Pravovoe vospitanie* (1972).

in internal affairs and holding the Soviet Government responsible for Comintern activities. This issue figured prominently in American recognition policy vis-à-vis the Soviet Union.

By the 1970s the concern had changed considerably. The General Secretary of the CPSU, whether or not he held the joint post of Chairman of the Presidium of the USSR Supreme Soviet, was regarded as the most powerful and influential individual in the Soviet Union. His signature on international treaties was felt to represent the true locus of influence and political commitment to honour their provisions. In a series of Soviet-American arms control and other agreements contracted from 26 May 1972 the late General Secretary of the CPSU, L. I. Brezhnev, signed on behalf of the USSR, symbolically underscoring the Party's endorsement of the agreements and the foreign policy line they represented. M. S. Gorbachev has done the same with respect to Soviet-American agreements in December 1987. Soviet law, it should be noted, does not endow Party officials with the right to conduct negotiations or sign international treaties without special powers issued by the appropriate legislative or executive agency nor in any way refer to the prerogatives of the Party in representing the State in such matters. Certain officials designated in the 1978 Law on the Procedure for the Conclusion, Execution, and Denunciation of International Treaties of the USSR may so act without special authorisation, but Soviet legislation falls well short of sanctioning expressly the practice envisioned in Article 7(1)(h) of the 1969 Vienna Convention on the Law of Treaties where the intention or practice of the State concerned may be decisive as to whether a person represented the State for such purposes.

Chapter 10

Civil law

'Civil law' is a term widely used in several senses. Civil law may refer to Roman law, or to the family of modern legal systems concentrated on the mainland of Europe which has developed on the basis of legal science fashioned after Justinian in the Romano-Germanic universities from the twelfth century, and to the legal systems elsewhere that have received the European civilist tradition. In a narrower sense civil law may encompass private law, that is, the branch of law regulating legal relationships between individual citizens. In the Soviet legal system civil law is a branch of law regulating 'property and personal non-property relations' in a socialist society for the object of creating the material-technical base of communism and in order to satisfy more fully the material and spiritual requirements of citizens. Anglo-American law has largely for historical reasons developed with divisions, concepts, vocabulary, and methods that draw but slightly on any of the aforementioned notions of civil law. Many of the advanced European socialist legal systems believe they are moving into a period in which civil law even as they have defined it is being or ought to be largely supplanted by a new branch of law called economic law (see chapter 13, below).

HISTORICAL BACKGROUND

Early Soviet civil legislation was largely concerned with eliminating or reshaping pre-existing civil relationships. Private ownership of the instruments and means of production gradually was abolished in key sectors of the economy, church property and large structures were nationalised, inheritance was abolished, obligations under stocks and bonds were annulled, many pre-existing debts were repudiated, copyrights and patents were monopolised by the State, as were banking, foreign trade, and insurance, and rail, sea, river, and air transport became wholly State-owned. Land, water, forests, and minerals all passed from private hands. For a time, private trade in foodstuffs was forbidden.

Comprehensive as these types of measures were, they represented neither the total extinction of private rights nor of private property. Actual confiscation of property often depended on the discretion of local authorities, and small enterprises employing as few as 5, 10, or

20 employees were allowed to continue. The countryside situation was chaotic; attempts to enforce decrees met with resistance or sabotage, and in many areas traditional patterns of land tenure continued in effect.

Economic collapse in the aftermath of civil strife led the Soviet leadership to introduce the NEP, under which land and the 'commanding heights' of the means of production would remain in State hands, but private commerce would be allowed to operate in small-scale industry and trade, and foreign private capital would be encouraged to invest in concessions and joint ventures. In the exchange of commodities the State assumed more of a regulatory than a proprietary role, although in some fields it intended to compete with the private sector. The NEP required legal reform and stability. On 22 May 1922 the RSFSR enacted a decree on basic private property rights recognised by the Russian Soviet Republic, ensured by the law and protected by the courts thereof[1] whose provisions presaged the approach of the impending RSFSR Civil Code. The decree denationalised certain structures and small enterprises, prohibiting further confiscations, and offered some basis for Soviet courts to enforce private rights, even some antedating the 1917 October Revolution. The RSFSR Civil Code followed in a remarkably short time, being confirmed by the VTsIK on 31 October 1922 and entering into effect on 1 January 1923.[2] As amended, the 1922 Code remained in force until the present act of FPCivL and civil codes were enacted in 1961–64.

Prepared in the course of four months, the 1922 RSFSR Civil Code drew upon continental European models, including Germany and Switzerland, and a draft Imperial Russian Code introduced in the State Duma in 1913. The eminent Soviet civilist, A. G. Goikhbarg, had a considerable hand in preparing both the 1913 draft and the 1922 Code. The obvious roots of the 1922 Code in Romano-Germanic experience led many western comparatists to look upon the Soviet legal system as a variant of, but firmly within, the civil law family of legal systems. Lenin was disquieted enough by early drafts of the 1922 Code to remind the draftsmen they were to apply to 'private law relations, not the *corpus iuris romani*, but our revolutionary concept of law.'

The 1922 Code was divided into four parts. The General Part treated the subjects of rights, legal transactions, and limitations. This was followed by a Part called the 'law of things' (ownership, buildings, and mortgages or pledge), a Part on the law of obligations, and a brief Part on inheritance. Family law, land tenure, and employer-employee relations were left for separate codification (see chapters 11, 12 and 15, below). Among the significant innovations introduced into civil law by the 1922 Code were the general confirmation that pre-revolutionary private rights

1 *SU RSFSR* (1922) no. 36, item 423.
2 Transl. in V. Gsovski *Soviet Civil Law* (1949) II pp 15–235.

had been extinguished, and the view that private rights acknowledged by the Code were conditional upon not being exercised contrary to their socio-economic purpose. Notarial control over contracts was extensive, and when State enterprises were involved, many contract provisions became imperative and not subject to party negotiation. A legal entity whose activities were contrary to State interests could be dissolved by the State. Unjust enrichment reverted to the State, especially if obtained in a contract concluded under duress or under extreme necessity. With regard to personal injury, the Code minimised and virtually did away with the element of fault. A variety of other provisions struck a balance between State and individual concerns usually in favour of the State. With the transition to national economic planning and collectivised agriculture, the Civil Code provisions affecting private commerce and rights were overridden by subsequent legislation, often without amending the Code. For a time in the early 1930s civil law seemed destined to be supplanted by economic and administrative law and Plan. State Arbitrazh looked principally to economic policy as defined in the Plan when deciding disputes. Courses and textbooks on civil law disappeared and were superseded by courses and texts on economic law.

The 1936 USSR Constitution redressed the balance somewhat in favour of the continued usefulness of civil law. The transition to planning and collectivised agriculture was confirmed, but civil law was seen to have a role to play in regulating the legal relationships of State enterprises and of non-State entities. Rights to personal ownership, succession, and intellectual property were affirmed. Economic accountability and legal personality were accepted as durable civil law concepts adaptable to the requirements of a completely socialised economy.[3] When the FPCivL were drafted in the late 1950s, debate reopened as to whether the civil law regulation of State enterprises might not be better placed in a separate branch of legal science and regulation (see chapter 13). The decision was to retain the pre-existing scope of civil legislation, which the FPCivL and union republic civil codes duly reflected.

Contemporary civil law

The union republic civil codes are organised in eight parts: general principles, property, obligations, copyright, discoveries, inventions, inheritance, and the civil law capacity of foreign citizens and application of foreign legislation and international treaties. The preamble to the

3 See Gsovski *Soviet Civil Law* (1949) II for details of the principal legislative developments and the chapters on civil law by O. S. Ioffe for a conceptual account of the period in id (ed) *Sorok let sovetskogo prava, 1917-1957* (1958).

1964 RSFSR Civil Code, which some Soviet commentaries do not even reproduce, relates the concepts of ownership and obligations in the Code to the planned economy and the task of building communism. Civil legislation is said to have an active role in shaping and developing forms of ownership, strengthening plan and contractual discipline, improving product quality, encouraging individual creativity, and harmonising individual and social interests.

A. GENERAL PRINCIPLES

The civil codes regulate property relationships and related or specified non-property relationships of three categories of persons: of State, co-operative, and social organisations among themselves; of citizens with such organisations; and of citizens among themselves. The civil codes have no application to vertical relationships between parties based on administrative subordination, nor to family, labour, or collective farm law. Civil rights and liabilities arise from civil law transactions provided by law, or, if not so provided, which are not contrary to law; from administrative acts, including certain planning acts; from inventions, discoveries, or rationalisation proposals; from causing harm to another or unjustly acquiring or retaining property; or as a result of events or activities to which the law attributes civil-law consequences.

The Soviet civil codes incorporate and extend the principle of the 1922 Civil Code that civil rights are conditional, that is, they are protected by law except for instances when they are exercised contrary to their purpose in a socialist society building communism. The commentators suggest recourse to this principle should be made only when other Code articles do not specify the purpose or object of a particular right. Examples include the use of a pseudonym, which is lawful, in a manner that infringed the social purpose of the right by disseminating false information in a *feuilleton* defaming a citizen, or playing a radio too loudly in order to disturb deliberately a neighbour's peace and quiet. Civil rights may be defended by seeking from a court or State Arbitrazh, and in some instances from a comrades' court, trade union, or other social organisation or in an administrative proceeding, either the acknowledgement of a right, or restoration of a right to the situation before it was violated, or specific performance, or a termination or modification of legal relations, and recovery for losses suffered and, when appropriate, contractual penalties. The civil codes specifically make provisions for a citizen or organisation to demand in court a public retraction of information defaming their dignity or honour unless the person who has disseminated such information proves it is true.

There are two categories of 'persons' under Soviet civil law: citizens and juridical persons. A distinction is drawn between legal capacity, that is the general capacity to bear civil rights and duties, which arises at birth and ceases upon death, and dispositive legal capacity, that is, the complete acquisition of the right to exercise legal capacity upon reaching legal age (18) or marriage (if earlier), unless restrictions have been placed on dispositive legal capacity by reasons of mental illness, drug addiction, or alcoholism.

Juridical persons are those organisations which possess separate property, may acquire property and personal non-property rights and bear duties in their own name, and appear as plaintiffs or defendants in court, State Arbitrazh, or mediation. The codes enumerate several types: State enterprises and organisations operating on the basis of economic accountability through basic capital and circulating assets allocated to them and an independent budget; institutions and other State organisations financed directly from the State budget but having an independent estimate and whose directors enjoy the right to dispose of credits; State organisations financed from other sources but having their own independent estimate and balance sheet; collective farms, and inter-collective farm and other co-operative and social organisations, and in some cases enterprises or institutions of those organisations and their associations which have separate property and an independent balance sheet; State-collective farm and other State-co-operative organisations; and other organisations as may be specified by Soviet law. Each juridical person operates pursuant to its charter or a general statute for organisations of a given type which defines the purposes for which the juridical person has civil legal capacity. Legal capacity commences with the adoption or registration of the charter or issuance of a decree forming the entity. A juridical person operates under its own name, is liable for its own obligations, and is not liable for obligations of the State nor of other juridical persons, and vice versa.

The lawful actions by which citizens and organisations establish, change, or terminate civil rights and duties are called legal transactions. They may be unilateral (for example, a will) or bi- or multi-lateral (for example, a contract). Soviet law is distinctive for the extent to which it regulates the form of legal transactions. In principle legal transactions may be performed orally or in writing. If the law imposes no specific form, they may be considered to be performed if the will to do so is manifest from the conduct of the person. Silence may represent such conduct only when the law so provides. Transactions performed at the same time they are entered into, for example, purchasing an item in a shop, may be oral unless legislation provides otherwise.

Except for the oral transactions mentioned above and certain other exceptions, all legal transactions of State, co-operative, and social organisations inter se and with citizens must be in writing and signed by the parties; so too those of citizens inter se in excess of 100 rubles or when the law requires the written form. The failure to observe the form required by law makes the transaction void only when the law so provides, but in the case of a foreign trade transaction the codes are categorical that failure to observe form or signature requirements invalidates the transaction. If a transaction must be in simple written form, the failure to observe this form deprives the party in the event of a dispute of referring to witness testimony in confirmation of the transaction and may result in its invalidity. Certain transactions must be notarially certified, for example, the sale of a dwelling house or an automobile. In all such cases the failure to observe this form results in the transaction being void, although if part performance has occurred and the transaction is not otherwise contrary to law, a court may declare the transaction valid.

Soviet law goes beyond observance of formalities, however, to look to the purpose of a legal transaction. If a legal transaction is performed for a purpose knowingly contrary to the interests of the socialist State and society and both parties had this intention and both have carried out the transaction, everything they have obtained under the transaction is forfeited to the State. If only one party had that intention, only that party is penalised, but in any event the transaction is void. The contrariness of a transaction to State or social interests may be judged either from the substance of the transaction or the purpose which a party desired to achieve, for example, ceding use of a land plot for payment or purchasing a house as a place for illegal prayer meetings. Other examples arising in judicial practice have been collective farms leasing land plots to citizens, or contracts between farms and citizens in which the latter engage in what in essence is private entrepreneurial activity. The courts also struck down on this basis a contract in which one citizen ceded part of his land plot to another in return for use of part of the latter's house built on the same land plot. This was deemed to represent a concealed purchase of part of the land plot.

Other grounds for invalidity of legal transactions include ultra vires, minority, legal incapacity, sham or pretence, inability to understand the significance of one's acts, fraud, coercion, threats, extreme necessity, collusion, and the like. Parts of a transaction may be deemed void if they do not affect other parts and the transaction would still have been entered into without including the void portion.

B. LAW OF OWNERSHIP

The Soviet constitutions distinguish between socialist ownership, which consists of State (all-people's), and collective farm-co-operative ownership, and likewise encompasses the property of trade unions and other social organisations. Personal ownership is a distinct but related category. Every owner, under Soviet law, has the right to possess, use, and dispose of property within the limits laid down by law.

(a) Socialist ownership. The State is regarded as the sole owner of all State property. In those instances when the State allocates a portion of

its property to State organisations, it does not relinquish ownership but places the property in the 'operative management' of that organisation, whose right of possession, use, and disposition must be exercised in accordance with law, the charter of the organisation, and the purpose of the property. State enterprises, buildings, and structures are transferred from one State organisation to another free of charge. Other disposition of State property is regulated in great detail by subordinate legislation. Except for certain articles, State property as a rule cannot be alienated to individual citizens. Circulating assets owned by State organisations may be disposed of more freely, but always in accordance with approved plans and the purpose of the particular assets.

Execution against State property is severely circumscribed under Soviet law. Enterprises, buildings, structures, equipment, and other property relegated to the category of basic assets of State organisations may be neither the object of a pledge nor be levied against in order to satisfy creditors. Other property may be levied against except as may be provided for in the union republic civil procedure codes or in other Soviet legislation. These constraints normally cause little difficulty in the Soviet Union. Enterprises commonly execute arbitrazh awards, for example, by presenting the award to the State Bank, for an award has the status of a writ of execution. In foreign transactions these constraints have given rise to difficulties. Soviet merchant ships have from time to time been arrested to satisfy civil claims against Soviet shipping or fishing companies. In recent Anglo-American practice the courts have accepted assurances from the Foreign Office or the Department of State that the vessels are State property and merely in the operative management of a particular company. Other cases, not so straightforward, have turned on the status of the Soviet organisation. The Telegraph Agency of the Soviet Union (TASS) has at least twice been held to be a department of the Soviet State, even though a juridical person, by English tribunals;[4] the Novosti Press Agency has been so characterised by an American court under the Sovereign Immunities Act.[5]

The property of collective farms, other co-operative organisations, trade unions, and other social organisations is similarly protected even though they are not State entities. They may possess, use, and dispose of their property pursuant to their charters and own the property specified in law. Execution may not be levied against trade union property, however, as follows: enterprises, buildings, structures, equipment, other capital assets of enterprises, sanatoriums, rest homes, cultural centres, clubs, stadiums, pioneer camps, or education-cultural funds.

---

4 W. E. Butler 'Immunity of Soviet Juridical Persons' Modern Law Review XXXV (1972) 189–193.
5 *Yessenin-Volpin v Novosti*, 443 F Supp 849 (1978).

(b) Personal ownership. The 1936 USSR Constitution drew a sharp distinction between 'private' ownership, which in the Soviet lexicon has come to be associated with private property in the instruments and means of production, and 'personal' ownership, which was accorded and continues to enjoy constitutional guarantees.

With the transition of the Soviet Union to a socialist State engaged in building communism postulated in the Programme of the CPSU (1961) adopted at the XXII Party Congress, debate reopened about the place of personal ownership in this process and whether any limitations should be placed on such ownership. That debate, the growing material prosperity of the average Soviet citizen, the expressed commitment of the Soviet leadership to increase that prosperity, the shortages of consumer goods and housing, and the continuous urgent need for agricultural products grown by individuals on personal plots have combined with other factors to give a special configuration to the Soviet legislation governing personal ownership. In recent years Soviet jurists have been disposed to look upon personal ownership as a social relationship conditioned by and subordinate to linkages in the realm of social production (see chapter 3, above).

The Soviet legal system offers no particular novelty with respect to who may own personal property. All citizens of the USSR possess in equal measure the legal capacity to own personal property, and foreign citizens or stateless persons likewise may be the 'subjects' of the right of personal ownership even though in principle the rights of an alien may be restricted by special decree of the USSR Council of Ministers in retaliation for limitations imposed by a foreign State upon Soviet citizens. Although a Soviet citizen's property is subject to confiscation under certain circumstances if an individual is convicted of a criminal offence, he may not be deprived of the *right* to own personal property but merely of the property owned by him when sentence is passed. Three subjects of personal ownership are specially regulated in Soviet legislation: the collective farm household (see chapter 14, below), the family farm, and the individual artisan or persons registered to engage in individual labour activity. The latter sometimes are treated as remnants of private property since their labour is not part of the social economy. Juridically, however, there seems no doubt they are subjects of personal ownership.

The key difference between the Soviet and western concepts of personal ownership often has been said to be one of degree, lying in the extent to which limitations are placed on personal ownership. No modern legal order gives full reign to personal property; all in some measure limit what may be owned privately or condition the possession, use, or disposition of private property. What distinguishes Soviet law in this respect is the conceptual relationship between personal and other social ownership and the reasons or alleged reasons for the limitations. The

1977-78 Soviet constitutions in fact give greater protection to personal ownership than their predecessors. The 1936 USSR Constitution provided: 'The right of personal ownership of citizens . . . shall be permitted by law.' The relevant provisions in the 1977-78 constitutions begin with the source of personal ownership (labour incomes), list some of the things which may be personally owned, and only then stipulate that the 'personal ownership of citizens . . . shall be protected by the State,' a more positive commitment than 'permitted by law.'

Soviet legislation does not attempt an exhaustive list of what may or may not be the object of personal ownership. The constitutions and civil codes mention '. . . articles of everyday use, personal consumption, convenience, and subsidiary household husbandry, a dwelling house, and labour savings.' Several qualifications must be placed on the definitions: first, the scope of the definition itself; second, the constitutional requirement that 'labour incomes' must be the basis of personal ownership; third, certain quantitative or other limitations imposed by Soviet legislation.

Whether an object may be personally owned is less a question of its natural properties than the actual nature of its use. An automobile, for example, may be owned by an individual in order to satisfy his material and cultural needs—a legitimate consumption purpose—but also used to convey passengers or carry goods for hire, which if systematically done without an appropriate permit would be contrary to Soviet legislation. Garden implements may be owned personally by urban dwellers to cultivate small kitchen-gardens on land allocated for this purpose by the local soviet, even though they are a 'means of production.' Bread or grain may be purchased for personal consumption, but may not be used as cattle or poultry feed. Actual use can be relevant when property of, for example, spouses is divided; judicial practice has taken into account such factors as personal use, profession, and even personal adornment.

Articles of 'subsidiary household husbandry' are expressly sanctioned in the Soviet constitutions as objects of personal ownership even though their purpose may extend beyond the production of agricultural produce for consumption needs to include items intended for sale to the State or in collective farm markets. The reason lies in the 'inadequacies in the sphere of organising social forms of the domestic servicing of the populace' or of distinctive living conditions in certain geographic areas, on State farms, or of teachers, doctors, mechanics, and others residing in a rural locale, of urban dwellers who enjoy or need to combine intellectual and physical labour, and of the inadequate development of social agricultural production. The precise articles of subsidiary household husbandry are laid down in union and autonomous republic legislation and, in some cases, by local soviet enactments. The dimensions of land plots allocated for use as gardens are stipulated by law and vary according to local conditions. The numbers and kinds of productive livestock (as distinct from working livestock, which usually are not allowed) are specified by union republic legislation. The intention is that such husbandry is subsidiary, that is, that able-bodied household members are to be gainfully employed and devote only their leisure time to such husbandry or else risk losing the right to own such property, unless pensioned, disabled, or unable to work.

The Soviet constitutions specifically mention a 'dwelling house' as an object of personal ownership. As a legal term it first appeared in the 1936 USSR Constitution but has never been precisely defined. The commentators find it instructive to reach back to the definition of 'house ownership' in the 1922 RSFSR Civil Code: '... house with appurtenant dwelling and auxiliary outbuildings.' As elaborated in departmental acts and instructions, 'house ownership' gradually came to be supplanted by 'dwelling house' and in theory and practice the terms became synonymous. A 'dwelling house' therefore is conceived of not just as premises but as an architecturally designed and constructed installation. The term refers to the building as a whole and, moreover, does not embrace so-called 'individual dwelling premises' produced by house construction combines and sold in unassembled form, nor does it extend to structures used for various other purposes, for example, leisure, hunting, fishing, storage. Ownership of a house must be authorised in the sense that the land on which the dwelling stands must be properly allocated by the local soviet, permission to build must have been obtained, and all requirements of size, design, and the like must have been observed. The penalty for violation can be draconian: demolition or confiscation of the house.

The citizen's constitutional right to own a house is circumscribed by other legislation which takes into account the housing requirements of the family. Spouses and minor children residing together may have only one house between them, whether owned jointly or by one family member. The union republic civil codes impose maximum dimensions for a dwelling house; in the RSFSR, for example, a dwelling house or part thereof personally owned by citizens may not exceed 60 square metres. Variations are granted for large families by the local soviet, but the standard applied is the same as that for persons who rent living premises in State housing.

Citizens may own an individual flat in a house belonging to a housing construction collective. Spouses residing together and their minor children are limited to one flat. The construction of this type of housing is encouraged by the Soviet authorities. Special legislation has been enacted to facilitate the formation of collectives in which each member invests his money and his personal labour. The flat itself is an object of personal ownership and the building as a whole is in the common ownership of the collective. For legal purposes the ownership of the flat is equivalent to the legal regime of personal ownership in an individual dwelling house.

Perhaps the most popular, and certainly from the legal point of view the most ambiguous, object of personal ownership is the dacha. Many Soviet citizens own dachas through inheritance, or through self-help have built them, or even have converted dwelling houses in a rural locality into dachas. Legislation is silent in most union republics as to whether an individual may own both a dwelling house and a dacha, and the commentators are divided. A dacha meets the criterion of a dwelling house, except that it is unsuited for year-round occupation and is used only for leisure, recuperation, or academic contemplation. For most commentators, this is sufficient to remove the dacha from the restrictions imposed on ownership of dwelling houses and assimilate it to other objects of consumption.

Soviet citizens may own 'monuments of history and culture,' that is, 'articles of antiquity, works of decorative and applied art, structures, manuscripts, collections, rare printed publications, and other articles and documents . . . of historical, scientific, artistic, or cultural value . . .' under the 1976 USSR Law on the Protection and Use of Monuments of History and Culture. Such materials are subject to State registration, and the sale, gift, or alienation thereof is allowed only if State agencies for the protection of monuments are notified beforehand. In the event of a sale, the State has a right of priority purchase. The collecting of antique documentary monuments, ancient paintings, and ancient applied art by citizens is allowed if special permits have been issued and registered in the established procedure. The difficulty with these provisions of the 1976 Law is determining what falls within the definition above and what constitutes a 'collection.' There are, for example, literally millions of philatelists, numismatists, and bibliophiles in the Soviet Union whose activities are encouraged and facilitated by all-union voluntary societies of collectors, but few would have collections worthy of State registration.

Certain articles may be acquired for personal ownership only by special authorisation. A list of these is confirmed by all-union and union republic legislation. Significance for the national economy, considerations of State security, or 'other reasons' are the grounds for inclusion on the list. Examples include weapons, aircraft, and highly toxic poisons. Gold, silver, platinum, and platinum-group metals in coin, ingot, and raw form, foreign currency, bills of exchange, cheques, remittances, and foreign securities may be acquired only in the procedure and within the limits established by USSR legislation.

Personal property under the Soviet constitutions and civil legislation may be not used contrary to its socio-economic purpose. Under the 1977–78 constitutions this civil law principle has been elevated to a constitutional principle. As already noted, the Soviet constitutions stipulate that labour incomes shall comprise the basis of personal ownership of Soviet citizens. They further require that personally-owned property should not serve to derive non-labour income nor be used to the prejudice of the interests of society. Individual labour activity is encouraged under the Law on Individual Labour Activity of 19 November 1986 in the sphere of handicrafts, agriculture, domestic servicing of the populace, and other forms of activity based exclusively on the personal labour of citizens and their family members.

Citizens engaged in such activity are required to register with, or acquire a 'patent' from, the local soviet, and this entitles them to obtain raw materials, tools, and other items on hire, from the customer, or by right of personal ownership, to use natural resources, and to acquire surplus or other property from enterprises, institutions, and organisations. Many thousands of applications have been approved by local soviets with a view to providing or improving consumer services.

'Non-labour income' is not defined in Soviet legislation, and the concept has posed both doctrinal and practical conundrums in Soviet law. Certain sources of income, even though not emanating from one's own labour, are lawful in the Soviet Union and not treated as non-labour income: inheritance, gifts, winnings from lotteries and premium bonds, interest on savings accounts, and rental income within the prescribed limits from housing and other personal property. In the realm of civil law, some have suggested that non-labour income should be viewed as a type of unjust enrichment: obtaining income without sufficient legal grounds but not as a result of any unlawful activity, and only as a part of civil 'turnover.'

Personal property held in excess of limits provided by law (productive livestock, dwelling space, number of houses, etc), revenues from hire or lease of personal property in excess of legally-established rates, misuse of personal property, such as employing it to commit a crime, failure to register ownership of property or transactions in property, or the failure to sell or exchange property through established channels are the principal situations in which non-labour incomes or unconscionable profit would be deemed to exist. Legal sanctions against non-labour income have been principally two: (1) seizure of the income obtained from the State or return of the income to the person at whose expense the defendant enriched himself; (2) seizure without compensation by the State of property which the owner used as the source of personal enrichment. Under the Edict of the Presidium of the USSR Supreme Soviet adopted 23 May 1986 'On Intensifying the Struggle Against Deriving Non-labour Incomes', administrative fines and other penalties were introduced for designated forms of deriving non-labour income.

Although as a rule an owner of personal property may dispose of his property as he chooses, including physical destruction, two objects of personal ownership are regulated in this respect: a dwelling house and cultural valuables. The failure to maintain these in a proper state, so that the destruction or damaging thereof is imminent, may serve as grounds for depriving the owner of the right to such objects and transferring them to State ownership. In these instances an owner is deemed to have a responsibility to combine personal wealth of this nature with its social value and significance; a dwelling house both accommodates its owner and contributes to solving the housing problem. Items of cultural value give aesthetic pleasure to their owner and also are part of society's cultural legacy. Confiscation of houses for this reason is extremely rare; the courts have required that it must be established that the owner consciously allowed the destruction of the house when it was fully possible for him to maintain it in proper condition. Soviet civil legislation does not define a 'cultural valuable;' the commentators suggest that a State organisation having responsibility for protecting or conserving cultural property might bring a civil suit against the owner.

(c) Artisans. Individual artisans come within the rules of Soviet civil legislation governing personal ownership so long as their activity is based on personal labour without the use of another's labour and unless otherwise established by law. Artisans are required to register with financial agencies and obtain an appropriate certificate in order to operate. A list of permitted forms of artisan activity has been confirmed by the RSFSR; they may be supplied equipment and raw materials or finished products in order to carry on their craft. The 1986 legislation on individual labour activity liberalises their situation somewhat.

Personal ownership under Soviet law has matured as a concept. The basic orientations for the economic and social development of the Soviet Union up to 1990 as endorsed at the XXVI Congress of the CPSU suggested that current policies are likely to be continued. The growth of material prosperity for Soviet Man remains a central consideration in economic priorities. In agriculture incentives linked to personal ownership are to be increased. Principal emphasis, however, continues to be placed upon 'strengthening the material and spiritual bases of the socialist way of life and forming a New Man,' and to this end personal ownership is relegated to a supportive role as against the predominance of the social consumption fund.

(d) Developments in the law of ownership. Reforms in the national economy and in foreign economic relations are contributing to the first profound reconsideration of Soviet concepts of ownership in half a century. The introduction of joint enterprises and other production entities has created either new forms of international socialist ownership (joint enterprises with other socialist countries) or socialist/capitalist ownership (joint enterprises with western and third world countries). The expansion in 1987 of the co-operative movement has implications for 'co-operative-collective farm ownership'. And within the category of socialist ownership, the notion of operative management has proved to be insufficiently flexible to accommodate the multiple legal relationships

and uses to which State property may be put under schemes of decentralised management and less directive planning of the national economy. Although many partial modifications have been introduced in the 1987 economic reforms—relaxation of restrictions on the disposition of State property, granting labour collectives more rights over enterprise assets, and the like—if the course of economic reform is sustained they will be inadequate. New models of socialist ownership are already under consideration.[6]

C. LAW OF OBLIGATIONS

The greater part of the union republic civil codes is devoted to the law of obligations, what in Anglo-American law roughly is encompassed by the law of contract and tort. A distinctive feature of Soviet law, however, is the fact that the greater portion of the law of contract concerns socialist organisations, and not individual citizens. Increasingly the principles of the law of obligations have been adapted to national economic planning and the special functions the law of contract performs among socialist organisations. The role of interpersonal contracts has diminished accordingly, and the principal area of civil contractual relations involving individuals concerns agreements between citizens and organisations, for example, for the purchase of goods and services, rental of housing, transport, and the like. Employment contracts are governed by labour law (see chapter 12, below).

(a) Contract. Many features of the Soviet law of contract unusual in the eyes of Anglo-American lawyers are commonplace to the continental European civil law systems.[7] A contract under Soviet law is predicated upon 'agreement' of the parties (not 'promise') on all essential conditions and, if the law so requires, reduced to writing and appropriately signed. Consideration is unknown to Soviet law. 'Essential conditions' are those that may be required by law or are necessary for particular types of contract, and any points which either party declares must be agreed. As has been noted, Soviet law does place considerable stress in comparison with Anglo-American law upon requiring contracts to be in writing and notarially certified, either when the contract value exceeds a certain sum or when a particular object is the subject of the contract. Offers may be made subject to a time limit for acceptance or not; in the latter case, an oral offer is subject to immediate acceptance and an offer in writing is deemed accepted if a reply is received within the time

---

6 See V. P. Mozolin (ed) *Razvitie sovetskogo grazhdanskogo prava na sovremennom etape* (1986) pp 77–114.
7 For a detailed parallel exposition of the two approaches, see E. A. Farnsworth and V. P. Mozolin *Contract Law in the USSR and the United States: History and General Concept* (1987).

normally needed to receive a reply. A delayed reply is treated as such only when the offeror immediately informs the other party that the reply was delayed, in which event the late reply is treated as a new offer. A reply varying the conditions of an original offer is treated as a refusal and simultaneously as a counter-offer.

When contracts are governed by Plan, as so many are between State enterprises and organisations, the content of the obligation is determined by the planning act. The parties may alter the substance of the contract only if the law or the planning act so allows or requires. Planning, if it is to be successful, requires that all components of the national economy perform their obligations to one another in a timely manner up to the standard stipulated in the contract, planning act, or legislation. Soviet law accordingly insists upon specific performance, and in a manner most economical for the socialist national economy. Unilateral repudiation or alteration of a contract, part performance, and early performance are admissible if provided for by law or in some cases by contract, planning act, or the nature of the obligation.

The Anglo-American concept of liquidated damages for non-performance of a contractual obligation does not exist in Soviet law. Rather a scheme of forfeits, fines, and penalties is employed. These are amounts of money determined by law or contract which one party must pay another for failure to perform or improper performance, usually delay. Normally they are expressed as a percentage of the value of the contract, although occasionally as a lump sum, and they accrue automatically irrespective of actual losses suffered by the injured party. In most cases the amount of forfeit is fixed by law and may not be agreed by the parties. In some instances the forfeit may arise from a planning act, for example, obligations for the delivery of export goods. Forfeits are no substitute for performance; they are intended as an automatic monetary sanction to encourage performance, and they are payable only if the defaulting party was at fault in the non-performance or improper performance of the obligation. Unless provided otherwise by law, losses in excess of a forfeit are recoverable, but there are situations where only the forfeit may be recovered, or where losses may be recovered in full over and above any forfeits paid, or where the injured party may choose either the forfeit or the actual losses. Moreover, if the forfeit is extraordinarily large in comparison with actual losses, a court or State Arbitrazh tribunal may reduce the forfeit, having regard to the extent of performance, financial status of the obligated party, or other interests which deserve consideration.

Specific types of obligations regulated by the civil codes include contracts of sale, barter, gift, delivery, State purchase of agricultural products, loan, hire of property, rental of housing, gratuitous use of property, independent-work contract, capital construction, carriage, State insurance, settlement and credit relations, commission, storage, joint activity, and competition. Many of these may be concluded exclusively by socialist organisations and not by citizens.

A contract of sale may be concluded by either citizens or socialist organisations. Under this type of contract the seller is obliged to transfer property to the ownership of the buyer, who is obliged to accept the property and pay a specified sum of money. If the buyer is a State organisation, it acquires the right of operative management over the property purchased. A contract of sale for a dwelling house or part thereof individually owned by a citizen or married couple may be sold if the owner has not sold more than one house or part thereof within three years unless the second dwelling was acquired on certain grounds, for example by inheritance. Sale contracts for a dwelling house or dacha must be notarially certified and registered at the respective local soviet. The sale of goods by State, co-operative, and social organisations must be at prices fixed by the State unless otherwise provided by legislation. Collective farms may sell their surplus produce not purchased by the State at free market prices, as citizens may likewise agree prices for items sold to one another, but in the latter instances such prices may not be speculative.

The seller must notify the buyer of all rights of third parties to the thing sold. Failure to do so entitles the buyer to demand a price reduction or repudiation of the contract and reimbursement. If ownership passes to the buyer before delivery, the seller must preserve the thing sold and not allow deterioration. When a seller fails to deliver a thing sold in breach of contract, the buyer may demand either delivery and reimbursement of losses caused by delay or repudiate the contract and require compensation for losses. The seller may do likewise if the buyer fails to pay for or accept the thing sold.

The quality of a thing sold must comply with the contract provisions or, if the contract is silent, with the 'usual requirements,' which the commentators understand to mean 'suitable for ordinary use or the use provided for by the contract.' Goods sold by a socialist trading organisation must meet the applicable State standard, technical conditions, or samples of goods of the particular type, unless the goods are being sold in a commission store or are reduced in price, and the like. Unless the buyer has given special notice of defects, the buyer has the option to demand: (1) replacement of the item by one of suitable quality; (2) a proportionate price reduction; (3) removal of defects by the seller at the latter's expense or reimbursement of the buyer for repairs; (4) repudiation of the contract with reimbursement of the buyer's losses. The first course of action is possible only if identical goods are available, which in the Soviet economy is not always the case. The second remedy would be appropriate if the goods even in defective condition were still suitable for use. The third alternative is widely used, but there is no time limit imposed on the seller to make good the product, and if the buyer arranges repairs himself, their cost may not exceed the price of the item. Under the fourth possibility, the buyer must return the goods and any income derived therefrom to the seller and is liable for any deterioration to the item caused by his fault. The seller is liable for transport expenses, if any, and for necessary and useful maintenance expenditures made by the purchaser. Detailed sets of rules issued by the Minister of Trade in each union republic elaborate and sometimes limit the procedures for exchanging goods or repudiating a sale contract. There are complaints that new regulations adopted in 1988 continue to favour the producer to the prejudice of the consumer. Claims as a rule must be made as soon as the defect is discovered and in any case within six months, unless a longer guarantee period has been provided.

Durable goods may be purchased on instalment credit at special retail trade stores. A down payment of 20–25% of the price is usually required. A list of goods that may be offered on credit is confirmed at union republic and lower levels. Purchasers of such goods are usually limited by regulation to workers and employees permanently resident in the city where the store is located or postgraduates studying in the same city. Collective farmers normally have credit facilities through a consumers' co-operative. Goods are sold at the price on the date of the sale, and ownership passes upon delivery, or as the law or contract stipulates, or upon registration, if the latter is required.

A dwelling house may be sold subject to a life tenancy on condition that the seller be supported for life by the purchaser, provided the seller by reason of age or state of health is unable to work. The seller receives support in the form of living space, food, care, and necessary assistance. Even if the house is accidentally destroyed, the buyer remains liable under the contract, although the house of course may be insured, and the buyer may not alienate the house during the seller's lifetime. If the buyer dies during the seller's lifetime, the contract terminates and the house reverts to the seller. Should the seller fully recuperate and become able to work, the buyer may seek termination of the contract and retain the house, but must continue to provide accommodation to the seller for the rest of the latter's life. Otherwise, the commentators suggest, a contract of this type might conceal a parasitic way of life; if that were so, the procurator also might bring a suit for termination of the contract in the interests of society.

(b) Tort. Early Soviet principles of tort were closely linked to social insurance. Liability was founded on causation, not fault, and judicial practice was prepared to go to some lengths in order to find causation as a means of protecting weaker parties. The courts were authorised by the 1922 RSFSR Civil Code to have regard when fixing damages to the respective financial status of the victim and the person who caused injury. While this policy had the advantage of favouring the less well-off

and personal exposure to losses was minimised by free medical care and expanded social insurance benefits, it did little to encourage an attitude of care on the part of tortfeasors, especially the worker. In an economy in which the State sector had absorbed the private sector, responsibility went hand in glove with morality: Soviet Man was to be aware of his duty to exercise care in all circumstances from which harm might arise. Deterrence of harm was as significant as compensation for injury. The change in policy was carried out almost entirely through judicial practice and guiding explanations. The key was the linking of subrogation and 'criminal act or omission.' If management had failed to adopt proper safety rules or observe them, the courts were quick to equate this with criminal behaviour even though a criminal prosecution was not brought. Social insurance came to be fixed at levels somewhat lower than full earnings, encouraging the victim to bring suit against the wrongdoer. The defendant avoided liability if he proved that he could not have averted the harm, or that he was empowered to cause it, or that the plaintiff himself was guilty of gross negligence or intended the harm to occur.

Another early and enduring principle of Soviet tort law was that of liability for 'heightened danger' or extra-hazardous activity. Liability was imposed on owners of all sources classified as 'heightened danger' in the belief that they should and could best bear the losses arising from their operations or activities. Automobiles continue to be a source of heightened danger under Soviet law even though the number of personally-owned vehicles increases annually. The State, or in the case of personally-owned vehicles, the State insurance company, is felt to be better able to assume the cost of accidents. Liability for extra-hazardous activity may be avoided only if the defendant proves the harm arose in consequence of insuperable force or the intention of the victim.

The 1961 FPCivL and union republic civil codes explicitly made fault the general basis of responsibility for causing harm: 'Harm caused to the person or property of a citizen, and likewise harm caused to an organisation, shall be subject to compensation in full by the person who caused the harm.' The person who caused harm is not responsible if it is proved the harm was caused not by his fault. Harm caused by lawful actions is subject to compensation only if the law provides, including actions taken in necessary defence, unless the limits thereof were exceeded, but not actions in extreme necessity. An organisation must compensate harm caused by the fault of its workers or employees in the performance of their duties, irrespective of whether the victim was an individual or another organisation or a person within or outside the organisation. The courts usually suppose the worker was performing his duties if the harm was caused during work hours unless the organisation proves the harm was caused, for example, for reasons of personal animosity. Suit in such cases must be filed against the organisation, which in turn may sue the guilty employee under the applicable labour code provisions.

The tort liability of the State developed along different lines. The Imperial Russian Government limited the responsibility of a 'treasury government establishment' or official to infringements of personal rights while acting as representative of the proprietary interests of the treasury. There was no liability when the establishment or official acted as an organ of public authority. Soviet law rapidly developed a functional test. The 1922 RSFSR Civil Code gave State institutions immunity, unless the law expressly provided otherwise, for harm caused by the actions of officials in the course of their duties. Enterprises engaged in economic activity were deemed to be outside this structure. The 1961 FPCivL reversed the formulation and made State institutions liable for harm caused to citizens by the improper actions of their officials in the domain of administrative management on the general grounds of tort liability unless provided otherwise by law. The commentators understand State institution to embrace any State entities, even enterprises, which ordinarily carry on or have been specifically instructed to perform activities in the realm of administrative management. An 'official' for these purposes is anyone encompassed by Article 170 of the RSFSR Criminal Code, and consequently a State institution is liable on different grounds for actions of its 'workers' or for acts of officials which are not within the ambit of administrative management.

Responsibility for harm caused by officials of agencies of enquiry, investigation, the Procuracy, and the court, under the civil codes, is governed by special legislation. For two decades implementation of the code provisions was awaited, finally achieving fruition in the 1981 Statute on the Procedure for Compensating Damage Caused to a Citizen by the Illegal Actions of Agencies of Inquiry, Preliminary Investigation, the Procuracy, and the Court. Compensation may be awarded for financial loss; reinstatement of labour, pension, housing, and other rights may be ordered, and other damage reimbursed if caused by an illegal conviction, prosecution, application of measures of restraint, or imposition of administrative arrest or correctional tasks. The following specifically may be compensated: (1) earnings and other labour income which is the basic source of assets for a citizen's sustenance and of which he was deprived as a result of the illegal actions; (2) a pension or benefit whose payment was suspended in connection with an illegal deprivation of freedom; (3) property confiscated by a court or converted to State revenue or seized by an agency of inquiry or preliminary investigation or subjected to arrest (including money, cash deposits and interest thereon, State bonds and winnings thereon, and other valuables); (4) fines recovered in execution of a court judgment, civil costs, and other sums paid by a citizen in connection with the illegal actions; and (5) amounts paid by a citizen to a legal consultation office for legal aid. Any earnings received by a citizen while serving punishment or correctional tasks are set off against his normal earnings. Property must be returned in kind or reimbursed by local financial agencies. The right to compensation if the citizen died passes by way of succession to his heirs and, if a pension or benefit is involved, to his family members. Detailed provisions govern reinstatement in employment and calculations of labour experience or pension rights, reallocation of housing, and the restoration of honorary titles, medals, and orders. If a citizen is acquitted, or if the case against him is terminated for absence of a crime or lack of evidence, the law enforcement bodies concerned must advise the citizen of his rights to seek compensation. Any information published in the press about the case must, upon request, be retracted within one month. The amount of damage suffered by a citizen must be calculated within one month of the citizen's application. Appeal against a refusal to compensate damage lies to a procurator or superior court. Suits may be brought at the plaintiff's election either at his own or the defendant's place of residence. The parties are exempted from court costs and State duty in cases of this type.

As a general principle, Soviet law authorises any person who has compensated harm caused by another to take recourse against the latter to the extent of the compensation paid unless otherwise provided by law. 'Person' includes insurance organisations for these purposes, but as noted above suits by employers against employees are governed by labour and not civil legislation. Parents, guardians, or trustees may not recover against minors or persons who lack dispositive legal capacity, the premise being that the harm would not have happened with proper supervision.

When awarding compensation for harm, a court may require the wrongdoer either to make good for the harm in kind by repairing the damaged article or replacing it with one of the same kind or quality or by paying in full for the losses caused, including expenses incurred, loss of or damage to property, and lost profits. Gross negligence by the victim that contributed to or aggravated the harm may be set off against or cancel any compensation due. In personal injury cases compensation is awarded for lost earnings or reduced earning capacity and medical expenses. No compensation is given for mental stress or pain and suffering. The procedures for compensation vary depending on whether the tortfeasor has a duty to pay social insurance contributions for the victim or not, whether the victim qualifies for a pension or social insurance benefit, and whether the victim is covered by social insurance at all. Future earnings are taken into account at the victim's level of skill at the time of the injury. Burial expenses are reimbursed if the victim dies. If an organisation liable to pay compensation for injury is liquidated or reorganised, arrangements are made for its legal successor or its superior organisation to cover the claims.

The measure of damages has caused problems when foreigners are involved. Soviet courts have been disposed to award recovery at price levels charged in the USSR for parts or treatment. If a foreigner elects to have repairs performed or receive treatment abroad, these costs are likely to be reimbursed by a Soviet court at the rate an equivalent Soviet organisation would charge for the same parts or services, or less if the foreign sum were lower.

(c) Duty to rescue. The assertion of a right to compensation for injuries sustained while rescuing or attempting to rescue the life or property of another date back in Soviet judicial practice to at least the mid-1920s. Suit was brought in 1926 against an electric power station by a widow for the death of her husband who perished while trying to save their son. When recovery was allowed in such cases, it was only on the general grounds. The 1936 USSR Constitution incorporated language which raised the hopes of jurists who advocated the duty to rescue. Every Soviet citizen, the Constitution stipulated, was obliged '. . . to execute the laws . . . to be honorably concerned with his social duty, and to respect the rules of socialist community life.' Another Article added the duty of each citizen to safeguard and strengthen social, socialist ownership. Taken together, many Soviet jurists and judges maintained these provisions had transformed a moral duty to rescue another's person or property into a legal obligation for which recovery should be awarded if injury were sustained. Judicial practice on the whole resisted this line of reasoning and continued to award recovery by a liberal application of the fault principle.

The draftsmen of the FPCivL succeeded in incorporating a chapter on 'obligations arising as a consequence of saving socialist property.' The obligation in this instance is an event to which the law attributes civil-law consequences. Harm sustained by a citizen when saving socialist property from imminent danger is to be compensated by the organisation whose property was saved by the victim. The commentators regard the provision as giving civil-law effect to Article 61 of the 1977 USSR Constitution laying down the duty of citizens to '. . . care for and reinforce socialist ownership.' While a citizen may evade rescuing socialist property, perhaps saying he did not perceive or comprehend the danger, if he does sustain an injury while acting to save it, he is entitled to sue for compensation. Several purposes of the obligation are stressed by the commentators: its educational purpose in nurturing the Soviet public in a concern for the safety and welfare of the public weal; its moral stimulant role in encouraging a citizen to act in the knowledge that his courage is both praiseworthy and legally protected.

The obligation is non-contractual, has no relationship to the actions of a tortfeasor, nor to unlawful actions of any kind, nor to notions of fault, and embodies no element of social censure or condemnation. Most commentators believe the obligation falls wholly outside those founded on principles of liability or responsibility and consequently reject the premises on which earlier Soviet judicial practice awarded recovery by analogy to acts involving the causing of harm. Some Soviet jurists prefer a theory of risk to explain the obligation, but the explanation ignores the fact that the victim is compensated for harm actually sustained and not his risk. If there is risk, it is the owner's risk for care of his property, the risk of the expense needed to avert danger to property or to combat such danger, and the risk is assumed even if the rescue measures are useless, inefficient, or ineffective.

Most commentators regard four elements or conditions as essential for the obligation to arise. First, there must exist a danger threatening socialist property, which some require be real and immediate and others would allow only the possible ensuing of harmful consequences as sufficient. If the rescuer himself created the danger, the general view is that no obligation arises for the owner organisation because the rescuer's efforts are in reality directed toward reducing his own liability. The law contains no such limitation, however, and there is doctrinal support for allowing recovery in such cases if the danger were to exceed vastly what a citizen would foresee while being slightly negligent and he courageously risked his person and property to avert the danger. Second, the citizen must perform actions directed toward saving particular socialist property and must act voluntarily, not in the performance of official or employment duties. This requirement precludes firemen, guards, watchmen, members of rescue services, and the like from recovering. Third, damage or injury must be sustained by the rescuer, whether of his property or clothing. Finally, there must be a causal link between the harm or injury sustained by the rescuer and his actions in saving socialist property.[8] But injury can result from related dangers. Recovery was allowed to a man electrocuted by a fallen wire while leading blinded cattle to safety from a burning shed and to a woman librarian who saved a lamb during a snowstorm but was attacked by wolves.

A rescuer may be any citizen, irrespective of age, nationality or citizenship, or legal capacity. Voluntary action is the key, and even voluntary members of fire brigades, people's guards, and similar bodies may qualify. Compensation has been awarded to a social fishery protection officer killed by poachers while protecting State property. Employees are in a more complicated position. The general view seems to be that workers or employees who voluntarily risk their life or property to save socialist property and are not employed specifically for this purpose will qualify for recovery; normal employment duties do not encompass this element of risk.

Possible extension of the right to compensation for the rescue of

---

8 For elaboration, see W. E. Butler 'The Duty to Rescue in Soviet Civil Law: Recent Developments' in *Hommage à René Dekkers* (1982) pp 443–458.

socialist property has given rise to interesting controversy, for example whether recovery may be had for injury sustained in protecting 'production interests' or larger 'State or social interests.' In general, the courts have been reluctant to allow recovery in the latter instance but have done so in the former. Greatest debate, however, has revolved around the right of recovery to rescuers who sustain injury while saving human life:

Example. While returning home from work, F answered the cries of a young child standing in a puddle of water with a live high-tension cable around her feet. F leapt and threw the child clear but was himself electrocuted, leaving a widow and three minor children. The electic power company refused compensation, and the Odessa Regional Court ultimately decided to award recovery by applying analogy of law. Noting that F perished while saving a child and the UkSSR Civil Code allowed recovery for injury sustained while rescuing socialist property, the Court considered even more compelling the argument for awarding compensation. The absence in the UkSSR Civil Code of an article regulating compensation for harm when saving a person cannot serve as a basis for rejecting the suit, which would be contrary to both general norms of civil law and principles of communist morality. Recovery was awarded against the electric power enterprise, having regard to the improper maintenance of the electric wires and the lack of secondary grounding.

When reporting the case in the press, one commentator extolled it as creating a 'legal precedent' because the Court 'for the first time expressly favoured compensation for harm sustained when saving the life of a person and applied clearly the analogy of law' in the absence of a special norm. On the protest of the deputy chairman of the UkSSR Supreme Court, the Judicial Division for Civil Cases struck out the reference to analogy of law and allowed recovery under the Code provisions governing extra-hazardous activity.

Copyright, discoveries, and inventions

Early Soviet legislation did not dispense with copyright and patent. Royalties were to be paid to authors, but on an objective basis of print run and type of work, rather than bargaining skill or sales. Under certain conditions works could be 'nationalised' by the People's Commissariat for Enlightenment. Patents likewise could be appropriated by the State if necessary and the inventor paid a stipulated sum; otherwise, the inventor was obliged to seek his own possibilities of exploiting the invention with a patent conferring an exclusive right of use. Copyright and patent protection terminated after the author's or inventor's death. The NEP briefly brought limited scope for private publishing, and by early 1925 a set of all-union fundamental principles on copyright law had been enacted, followed in due course by union republic acts; these were supplanted in 1928 by new legislation that was in turn not comprehensively revised until the 1961 FPCivL.[9]

Copyright extends to works of science, literature, or art, irrespective of the form, purpose, or merit of the work or of the method of production. Certain works are excluded, for example, official documents such as legislation, departmental instructions, judicial decisions, and the like. Formalities of registration are not required for copyright, for the act of creation automatically confers it. Neither is publication therefore a prerequisite. Publication is important, however, for determining when and whether other rules of copyright apply to the work. For works first published in the USSR or unpublished but located within the territory of the USSR in some objective form, copyright is acknowledged as belonging to an author or his heirs or legal successors regardless of their citizenship. Copyright in works published abroad is recognised for Soviet citizens, but for foreign citizens only pursuant to international treaties to which the USSR is a party. Copyright in photographic works or works obtained by analogous means is recognised only if the author, place, and date of publication are specified on every copy. A translator has copyright in his own translation.

Copyright is valid for the author's lifetime plus 25 years calculated from 1 January of the year following the author's death. The copyright passes by inheritance and is protected either by an executor whom he designates or by his heirs or the All-Union Copyright Agency (VAAP). An organisation enjoys copyright without limit of time. By special decree in each instance the State may exercise a power of compulsory purchase of copyright from an author or his heirs, and if copyright has expired, a work may be declared by the Government to be part of the public weal. The works of G. V. Plekhanov, Karl Marx, Friedrich Engels, and V. V. Makovskii are examples.

A discovery is defined in Soviet law as the establishment of previously unknown objectively existing laws, properties, or phenomena of the material world. An 'author' or person making such a discovery has the right to demand recognition of his authorship and priority in the discovery, which is confirmed by a diploma issued pursuant to the Statute on Discoveries, Inventions, and Rationalisation Proposals. Remuneration may be paid at scales fixed by the State, and the discoverer's right to a diploma and remuneration pass by way of succession. Geographic, archaeological, and paleontological discoveries are not included in the scheme, nor are discoveries in the social sciences. Those who find mineral deposits may qualify for remuneration on another basis.

A rationalisation proposal is a suggestion for improving existing

---

9 See S. L. Levitsky 'Continuity and Change in Soviet Copyright Law: A Legal Analysis' Review of Socialist Law VI (1980) 425–464; id 'The Beginnings of Soviet Copyright Legislation 1917–1925' The Legal History Review, L (1982) 49–61.

technology or equipment, products, production control, supervision, safety, and the like, or labour productivity, energy use, equipment, or materials. Certificates are awarded to the author by the enterprise or organisation which first implements them. Remuneration is based on a fixed scale and sometimes represents a percentage of savings effected over a prescribed period.

Inventors may seek at their option either an author's certificate or a patent. If an author's certificate is issued, the right to the invention passes to the State, which then has responsibility for exploiting the invention if it deems this to be expedient. Remuneration to the inventor under the certificate is based on the benefits or savings to the national economy and privileges accorded him by law. Soviet law defines an invention as the creative solution of a technical task which possesses material novelty and gives a positive effect. A patent is issued for a term of 15 years dating from the filing of application. In this event the inventor has an exclusive right to the invention. His consent is required for its use, and he may license use or assign the patent outright. However, any transfer of license or use abroad is allowed only in the procedure laid down by the USSR Council of Ministers. The formalities for issuing a patent are much more stringent than for an author's certificate, and consequently far more certificates are issued than patents.

All rights relating to or under a discovery, rationalisation proposal, or invention pass by inheritance.

Inheritance

In the eyes of the early Soviet leadership inheritance was closely linked with the perpetuation of private wealth in the instruments and means of production. A decree of 27 April 1918 drastically limited both testamentary and intestate succession. Except for families of a deceased working male which otherwise might be left destitute, all property left by individuals upon death passed to the State. Estates not exceeding 10,000 rubles in value and comprising a dwelling house, furnishings thereof, and an individual worker's means of production would pass to those relatives who resided with and were dependants of the deceased. Peasant households were treated similarly, but without any ceiling value. Local soviets undertook to provide for a surviving spouse, children, and ascending or descending relatives, drawing upon the excess value of the estate. The 1922 RSFSR Civil Code broadened the ambit of heirs but initially retained a ceiling on the value of estates. Property could pass by will only to beneficiaries within the statutory group of heirs, or to State or social organisations. Estates were distributed per capita with no right of representation. This liberalisation was tempered by a progressive inheritance tax up to 50%; when the ceiling on estates was abolished in 1926, the tax rate became up to 90%, although State bonds and later cash deposits held in banks were exempt from the normal rules of inheritance. In 1942 the progressive inheritance tax was replaced by a scheme of notarial fees levied for issuing an inheritance certificate. Further reforms were introduced in 1945 to liberalise succession. There are indications, however, that an inheritance tax may be reintroduced to reduce inequities in wealth arising out of the 1987 economic reforms.

The 1961 FPCivL and union republic civil codes have removed the restrictions on individuals to whom property may be left. Inheritance may be by operation of law or by will; it is the former when and insofar as it is not changed by a will. The property escheats to the State if there are no heirs by law or will, or if none of the heirs accepts the estate, or if all heirs have been deprived of the estate by will. The property which may pass by way of succession includes both rights and duties, that is, rights to personal property, to performance of obligations, to royalties, or to accept an inheritance, and likewise to debts of the deceased. Some rights do not pass, for example, the right to membership in a housing or dacha construction co-operative, to receive alimony or a pension, or a duty to fulfil an author's contract.

A will must be drawn up in writing, specify the place and time it was drawn up, be personally signed by the testator, and be notarially certified. In most cases the testator will simply apply to the Notariat for assistance in drafting the will according to established forms; the original is retained by the Notariat and a copy given to the testator. Wills of military servicemen certified by their commanding officer, or of citizens on Soviet-registered sea or river vessels certified by the master, or of citizens in hospital or other treatment institutions certified by appropriate doctors, or of members of Polar, prospecting, or other expeditions are equated to notarially certified wills. When certifying a will, the notary is required by law to explain the provisions of the Civil Code requiring a compulsory share in an estate for certain heirs and to make a formal notation that such explanation was given. A compulsory share is reserved for the testator's minor natural or adopted children and for children, a spouse, or parents (natural or adoptive) and dependants who are not capable of working, in an amount of not less than two-thirds of the share which would be due each if the estate were to pass by operation of law. The value of ordinary household property is taken into account for this purpose.

Unlike Anglo-American law, Soviet law makes no formal provision for the appointment of an executor or administrator of the estate, whether it passes by will or intestacy. Either the heirs or the Notariat performs these functions. The time of opening of an inheritance is the date of death or date specified in a declaration thereof. It is this date which determines the group of heirs, the composition of estate property, and the period for heirs to accept or reject the estate. The estate is opened at the last permanent place of the deceased or, if that is unknown, where the property or the major part thereof is situated. Heirs may be, in the absence of a will, citizens alive at the moment of the decedent's death and the decendent's children born after his death; by will, citizens alive at the decedent's death or conceived during his lifetime and born after his death. In the event of intestacy, the following take in equal shares: (1) first priority: natural and adopted children, spouse, natural or adoptive parents, and children born after the decendent's death; (2) second priority: brothers and sisters of the decedent and grandparents on the paternal and maternal side. The second priority is called upon to succeed only if there are no heirs of the first priority able or willing to succeed. Persons dependent on the deceased for not less than one year before his death likewise succeed in either priority. Grandchildren and great-grandchildren of the decendent succeed on intestacy, if when the estate is opened a parent of theirs who would have succeeded has died, equally to the share their deceased parent would have received.

A certain preference is accorded to heirs of whatever priority who lived with the decedent for not less than a year immediately before his death. Household articles pass immediately to them; the commentators suggest that valuable collections, antiques, original paintings, personal libraries used for professional purposes, and the like would not qualify as household articles.

If he so desires, a testator may appoint an executor in his will, who may or may not be an heir, to perform any actions needed to give effect to the testament. These may include determining and identifying the decedent's property, recovering debts, or satisfying creditors. The executor is not regarded as a representative of either the testator or the heirs; no remuneration is paid for his services, but he is entitled to reimbursement for actual expenses incurred to protect or manage estate property.

An heir may acquire an estate only when he has formally accepted it unconditionally by actually taking possession of the estate or filed a declaration of acceptance at the notarial office where the estate was opened within six months from the date of opening. This policy also favours heirs who lived with or near the decedent, although there are procedures for extending the period for acceptance. An heir who has taken possession or control of an estate before other heirs have appeared may not dispose of the estate until the six-month period has elapsed or a certificate of the right to an inheritance has been issued by the notary. Creditors of a decedent likewise must file claims to any obligations, whether due or not, within the same six-month period or lose their right to their claim. Protection of the decedent's property is the responsibility of the notarial office where the estate was opened until the estate is accepted by all heirs or the six-month period has expired. If the estate includes property requiring management, for example, a dwelling house, the notarial office may appoint a custodian or guardian over the property.

Heirs called to succeed apply to the notarial office for the certificate of the right to an inheritance. Ordinarily it will be issued when the six-month period has elapsed, but if the notary is satisfied there are no heirs other than those applying, the certificate may be issued earlier. State duty is payable for the issuance of a certificate of the right to inherit as follows: for an estate of up to 30 rubles (1 ruble), from 30 to 100 rubles (2 rubles), from 100 to 300 rubles (5 rubles), from 300 to 500 rubles (10 rubles), from 500 to 1,000 rubles (5% of the estate); and in excess of 1,000 rubles (10% of the estate).

The estate is divided by agreement of the succeeding heirs in proportion to their respective shares. In the absence of agreement, the matter is resolved by a court. Succession in a collective farm household is regulated differently (see chapter 14, below).

Soviet citizens may devise deposits in a State labour savings bank or in the USSR State Bank simply by instructing the bank to pay the deposit upon their death to any person or to the State. The deposit in this case is not part of the decedent's estate and involves none of the civil law procedures governing succession. If the depositor gives no instructions whatever to the bank, the deposit does form part of the estate and passes under the general principles laid down in civil legislation. A bank deposit disposed of by the depositor's instruction may be withdrawn at any time after the decedent's death, is not subject to the requirement of a compulsory share in the estate, may not be levied against for debts of the decedent, and, if a beneficiary of the decedent's will also was the beneficiary of the deposit, the deposit does not count in the division of the estate among the beneficiaries.

In dividing the estate, of course, due account would first have to be taken of a spouse's right to property by joint or common ownership.

Chapter 11

Family law

Prior to the 1917 October Revolution matters of marriage and divorce were left to the canon law of each religious denomination. A religious marriage ceremony was essential, and certain restrictions were imposed on the marriage of Christians with non-Christians or pagans. The State had been content to accept the practices of each religious denomination and give effect to their ecclesiastical judgments.[1] The Bolsheviks, intent upon breaking the authority of the church, secularised marriage and divorce even before formally legislating upon the separation of church from State and of school from church. The family in its bourgeois manifestation, as an economic and legal entity based on inequality of spouses and the dependence of the wife and children upon the husband, was to be transformed into a free association founded on the free will of its members. How precisely that transformation was to be realised proved to be a lively subject of debate in the early post-revolutionary years. Some urged a rapid transition to collective house-keeping and State-reared children. In the end more responsible heads prevailed. Consensual relationships came to be emphasised rather than the abolition of the family unit, formed in a secular context, with liberal opportunities for divorce and the emancipation of the wife and children. By the mid-1930s the pendulum had swung back. The family became important again as a legal and economic entity, a core unit of present and future society, and has continued to be so regarded. The 1961 Party Programme adheres to the original Marxian view that in the process of the development of communism 'family relations will ultimately be cleansed of material calculations and will be built on feelings of mutual love and friendship.' The family, in other words, is to survive as a key societal formation indefinitely.

HISTORICAL BACKGROUND

The Soviet authorities moved expeditiously to divest religious denominations of their authority over marriage and divorce. Two decrees were enacted within a day of one another. The first, 'On Civil Marriage, On Children, and On Keeping Books for Acts of Civil Status,' adopted

---

1 H. J. Berman *Justice in the USSR* (rev. edn, 1966) pp 330–333.

18 December 1917, proclaimed that the Russian Republic recognised only a civil marriage, entrusted the keeping of books for acts of civil status to Soviet agencies, and made equivalent the legal rights of children born within or out of wedlock. The following day the decret 'On the Dissolution of Marriage' placed divorce within the competence of local courts and marriage registry sections.[2] Neither decret offered much by way of detail, and on 16 September 1918 they were replaced by the RSFSR Code of Laws on Acts of Civil Status, Marriage, Family, and Guardianship.[3]

The Code, comprising 246 articles and some appendices, stipulated that only a marriage registered at a section for the registry of acts of civil status (ZAGS) would give rise to the rights and duties of spouses set out in the Code. Religious marriage had no legal effect unless registered in the established procedure.[4] The formalities of marriage were brief. An oral or written application was filed at the local ZAGS section with a certificate of personal identification and signed indication that the marriage was voluntary and there were no legal obstacles to marriage. The presiding official made the appropriate entry in the marriage register, read it to those being married, and declared the marriage to be concluded. A marriage certificate would be issued immediately upon request, but the entry in the marriage register constituted legal completion of the marriage. The requirements for marriage were: age (16 for females, 18 for males); sound mind; not married; no marriage to relatives in the direct ascending or descending line; and mutual consent. People of different religious faiths, monks, priests, or nuns, or persons who had taken a vow of celibacy all were expressly allowed to marry.

The draftsmen of the 1918 Code clearly wished to encourage registered marriages. Nothing whatever was said of de facto marriage in the Code, probably because that would have undermined the registration requirement. Section III of the Code, entitled 'Family Law,' however, seemed to introduce an element of inconsistency by providing that 'Birth itself shall be the basis of the family,' birth in the sense of lineage or ancestry. On this premise the Code declared there was to be no distinction between illegitimate and legitimate ancestry, and the provision was retroactive to births prior to 20 December 1917. The Code dwelt separately and at length on the rights and duties of spouses, on one

2 *SU RSFSR* (1917) no. 11, item 160; no. 10, item 152.
3 *SU RSFSR* (1918) no. 76–77, item 818.
4 Church and religious marriages concluded before 20 December 1917, the date of publication of the decret in note 2, above, were deemed to have the effect of registered marriages if performed with observance of the conditions and forms laid down in Articles 3, 5, 20–23, 31 or 90–94 of the *Svod zakonov* of the Russian Empire (1914 edn). Because Soviet authority was established at different times throughout the country, an official circular was issued fixing the date prior to which duly concluded religious marriages would be considered valid. For some regions, dates as late as 1925 are indicated.

hand, and the personal and property rights of children and parents, on the other. Among the latter was the right of the parents to agree to which religion their children under age 14 might affiliate; the agreement had to be in writing.

Divorce was readily obtained under the Code upon the request of either spouse without any statement of reasons. If both spouses consented, the ZAGS office granted the divorce. If only one spouse filed for divorce, the matter was decided by the local court.

Notwithstanding the Code's silence, people's courts began in certain situations to give some legal effect to de facto marriages. When the courts felt women had been taken advantage of in an unregistered relationship, they were prepared to award them a share of property acquired during the de facto relationship, or, on the basis of the decree abolishing succession, to give them a share of an estate. The RSFSR Supreme Court ruled in 1927 that people's courts under the 1918 Code often had treated registration as a procedural formality eliminating the need to prove the existence of a marriage by other evidence.[5] Some union republic codes had formally provided for the same view.

Preparatory work on a new family code began within the RSFSR People's Commissariat of Justice in 1923. A revised version produced in 1924 and submitted to the RSFSR Council of People's Commissars was discussed by a Special Commission together with another draft originated by the People's Commissariat of Internal Affairs. The former was preferred and submitted for confirmation in October 1925. The All-Russian Central Executive Committee (VTsIK) approved the draft in principle but deferred final acceptance pending public discussion of the draft. The public dialogue was extensive and lasted some months. A revised draft eventually was approved on 19 November 1926 after 'protracted and hot debate' by the VTsIK and entered into force on 1 January 1927. Other union republics adopted their own codes which differed in many material respects from the RSFSR model.[6]

The 1926 RSFSR family code extended formal acknowledgment to earlier judicial practice regarding de facto marriage. Under the Code, in the absence of registration the existence of a marriage became a matter of evidence and could be registered retrospectively. The RSFSR Code raised the marriage age to 18 for both males and females, an amendment inserted in the last draft of the act in the belief that early marriage could be harmful to the health of a mother and child and would deprive women of equal opportunities for education or vocational training, but several other union republics allowed females to marry at 16. In matters of

[5] Ruling of the RSFSR Supreme Court, No. 36188 *Sudebnaia praktika RSFSR* (1927) no. 5, p 16. For a contrary interpretation of the 1918 Code, see E. L. Johnson *Introduction to the Soviet Legal System* (1968) pp 171-172.
[6] The 1926 RSFSR Code is translated with comparisons to other union republic family codes in V. Gsovski *Soviet Civil Law* (1948) II pp 239-290.

matrimonial property, the 1926 Code departed from its predecessor and established that property acquired during marriage was community property whereas that acquired prior to marriage was separable. Freedom of divorce was maintained and placed entirely within the competence of ZAGS agencies. Despite a more flexible attitude toward registration, the formality was encouraged in order to facilitate the compilation of vital statistics and simplify the administration of inheritance. The courts even in the realm of succession allowed women in de facto relationships to inherit property. In one celebrated case the property of a man who simultaneously maintained a de facto continuing relationship with two women was divided between both women.

During the mid-1930s, the previous emphasis upon secularisation, freedom of divorce, and the liberation of women and children altered. The family began to be regarded as a permanent primary societal unit in a socialist and communist society. Family stability was essential, it was said, to the moral, legal, and spiritual awareness of every Soviet citizen. Individual enactments amended or superseded the family codes to give effect to this new approach. Motherhood was encouraged through limiting the grounds for abortion and introducing financial and other incentives for mothers of large families. Not insubstantial fees were introduced for the successive registration of divorces. Parents were made legally responsible for the delicts and crimes of their children.

Toward the latter stages of the Second World War, when it had become apparent that a substantial imbalance in the male/female ratio would persist for a generation and that casual wartime liaisons would require legal reinforcement if the family were to remain intact, the Presidium of the USSR Supreme Soviet enacted an Edict on 8 July 1944 reinstating the requirement that only a registered marriage would be given legal effect.[7] De facto marriages prior to that date could be registered retrospectively. Divorce policy tightened considerably. Only courts could grant divorces under the Edict, and before doing so they were obliged to attempt to reconcile the parties. If reconciliation were impossible, the case proceeded to the next instance for a new judicial consideration. The Edict specified no grounds for divorce. Courts construed the grounds narrowly, in effect forcing the parties to separate, form a new sustained unregistered relationship, and possibly have children therefrom. The fees payable to the State in connection with divorce proceedings increased significantly. Judicial practice liberalised somewhat in the 1950s in reference to divorce, and in 1965 family legislation was amended to do away with the double-tiered court proceedings. The decisions to grant a divorce, alimony, custody, and property division were all vested in the people's courts.

On 1 October 1968 the USSR Supreme Soviet confirmed the

7 *Vedomosti SSSR* (1944) no. 37 p 1.

Fundamental Principles of Legislation on Marriage and the Family (FPMarL), followed in 1969–70 by 15 union republic family codes.

Current family legislation

The union republic family codes are not divided into General and Special Parts. They consist of five sections: general provisions, marriage, family, acts of civil status, and the rights of foreigners.

A. BASIC PRINCIPLES

Under the 1977–78 Soviet constitutions, the family is under State protection. The State manifests its concern for the family by creating children's institutions and amenities, paying a birth allowance, granting other benefits and exemptions to families with many children, and other family allowances and assistance. State coercion, in other words, is child-orientated and mother-orientated, seeking to secure minimum standards of material security and enabling mothers to work. The ultimate Marxian objective of a family freed from all material calculations is reaffirmed in the preambles to the family codes. The 'remnants' of the unequal status of women are to be eliminated, and a 'communist family' is to be fashioned in which the deepest personal feelings of people find their complete satisfaction.

The specific tasks or purposes of the family codes elaborate the notion that family policy is to encourage: (1) a 'Soviet family' based on 'principles of communist morality'; (2) the structuring of family relations on a voluntary union free from material calculations; (3) raising children through organically combining family nurturing with 'social nurturing' in a spirit of devotion to the Motherland, of a communist attitude toward labour, and of training children to participate actively in constructing a communist society; (4) the fullest possible protection of the interests of mother and child and ensuring a happy childhood to each child; (5) eliminating once and for all harmful survivals and customs of the past in family relations; and (6) nurturing a feeling of responsibility toward the family. These purposes are related to specific code provisions, but Soviet courts sometimes find themselves using them as general guidance for deciding particular cases. Principles of communist morality in family life, for example, in the eyes of some judges might be incompatible with religious instruction in the family or with applications to emigrate. Some courts have queried whether minor children of a divorced mother should be allowed to emigrate with her or remain with a remarried father, since the children would not receive a communist upbringing abroad.

The equality of women and men in family relations is likewise a constitutional principle that dates back to the early period of Soviet power. Equality above all is understood to mean economic equality. Soviet commentators stress equal pay, equal access to education and vocation, and similar measures for women as reflective of the progress achieved. In family law equality is expressed in the right of spouses to choose their surname, occupation, profession, and place of residence when being married. All matters of raising children and family life are to be decided jointly by mutual consent; there is equal right to property, and a variety of other situations where when deciding family disputes the courts are required to proceed from the principle of equality or to compensate for actual inequalities by making adjustments appropriate to the situation.

B. MARRIAGE

The 1968 FPMarL introduced several reforms in family legislation, among them the requirement that a marriage be not merely *registered* in a ZAGS office but that it be *concluded* there. The ceremony or rites of marriage consequently became a matter of State concern. The new requirement was much debated, and its proponents stressed the State's interest in marriage went beyond the collection of vital statistics. Registration to be sure facilitated accurate projections of demographic change and protected the property and personal rights and interests of children. But it was pure formality and did nothing to enhance the solemnity of the relationship being concluded. ZAGS offices are now equipped with premises and amenities intended to do precisely that. In large urban centres special wedding palaces on quite an elaborate scale have been constructed. The presiding State official performs rites designed to be more than a perfunctory ceremony, reminding the intending spouses of their responsibilities toward one another, their future children, and society at large. Associated with this reform was another, a requirement that an application be filed at the ZAGS office one month in advance of the wedding. The waiting period may be reduced or extended by designated officials when there are 'justifiable reasons.' The object of the waiting period is simply to discourage marriages based on impulse. Examples of 'justifiable reasons' include the imminent departure of a future spouse for military service or arriving on leave for a brief period to register a marriage, the birth of a child, and the like. Filing an application to marry in and of itself creates no legal relations between the intending spouses and there are no legal consequences if it is withdrawn.

Soviet law continues to recognise religious marriages contracted before the formation or restoration of Soviet power and de facto marriages concluded under the 1926 RSFSR Family Code but before 8 July 1944. Under certain circumstances a de facto unregistered marriage before 8 July 1944 is still subject to being proved in a Soviet court; no statute of limitations ever was imposed. Cases sometimes are brought in order to establish a right to support, alimony, pension, or inheritance for a spouse or children of the relationship.

Religious marriage ceremonies may still be performed in the Soviet Union, but they have no legal effect whatever; only the civil ceremony at a ZAGS office would be legally recognised. The date of marriage would be the registration date at the ZAGS.

The legal requirements that must be satisfied for marriage are: (1) mutual consent of the intending spouses; (2) age 18, which in exceptional circumstances may be reduced to 16; (3) neither spouse already is legally married; (4) the spouses are not relatives in direct line of ascendance or descendance, full or half-brothers or sisters, or adoptive and adopted persons; and (5) neither spouse lacks dispositive legal capacity as a consequence of mental illness or feeble-mindedness, as determined by a court. Whether an intending spouse already is married, Soviet law determines by examining the time at which the previous relationship was formed. A religious marriage after 8 July 1944 in the RSFSR, for example, would not be recognised, but if concluded before that date the provisions concerning de facto marriages might apply.

C. PROPERTY OF SPOUSES

The FPMarL and family codes divide the property of spouses into two categories. Property acquired by spouses during a duly registered marriage is in their common joint ownership. If the marriage is not duly registered, the property relations would be governed by the ordinary rules of the civil law; spouses who are members of a collective farm or one-man peasant household are governed in this respect by the collective farm legislation (see chapter 14, below). Spouses in a de facto marriage before 8 July 1944 would be protected by current legislation for separation of their property. The property belonging to spouses before marriage or which they received during marriage by gift or inheritance remains respectively their personal property, although if the personal property increased in value during the marriage by reason of investments from common assets (house repair, rebuilding, etc) it may be deemed to be in their common ownership.

Certain articles for individual use, such as clothing, footwear, and the like, acquired from common assets of the spouses are deemed to be the personal property of that spouse who used them. Jewellery and other articles of adornment are an exception. In practice the courts look carefully at the quality and value of each article at the time the case is heard. Property initially acquired as adornment may no longer be fashionable; precious stones, rare plates and dishes, original works of art, antiquities, and the like are not normally viewed in judicial practice as articles needed to satisfy the ordinary requirements of citizens.

No reliance is placed on which spouse actually acquired property during the marriage or whether the spouses formally agreed to acquire property. There is a presumption that the actions of one spouse have been approved by and agreed with the other. Neither the nature of the property nor the time it came into possession matters. A spouse, for example, who bought a winning lottery ticket from their common assets, even though the drawing occurred after the marriage terminated, was obliged to treat the winnings as common ownership. The means of acquiring, whether purchase, exchange, or whatever, is immaterial. Gifts intended for both spouses, for example wedding or anniversary presents, likewise are common property.

Property under family law includes the earnings of spouses, other monetary remuneration (pensions, benefits, bonuses, royalties), articles, a house, dacha, car, clothing, household goods, savings accounts, letters of credit, State bonds, share accumulations in co-operatives, pawned property, hired or loaned property, and certain powers or rights, for example the right of demand or duty of execution. The children have no rights in the property of their parents unless they acquire the property by inheritance, gift, or other legal grounds. The spouses have equal rights of possession, use, and disposition over their common property. On more than one occasion the courts have declared void any agreement that would diminish the rights of one spouse to manage or dispose of their joint property. Although as a general rule the actions of one spouse with regard to managing and disposing of common property are regarded simultaneously as the actions of the other, there are circumstances under Soviet law, for example, the alienation of a house, when this is not the case and the signature of both spouses is mandatory.

Underlying the notion of common joint ownership of spouses is that each contributes through his labour to acquiring family property. In many if not most instances, both spouses are employed and have individual earnings. The family codes stipulate that even caring for the household and children is sufficient to give spouses equal rights to property. Should it become necessary to divide property in common joint ownership, the shares of spouses are deemed to be equal. If there is no dispute about what property goes to whom, the spouses merely draft a contract for the division of property and register it with the local Notariat or rural soviet.

Despite the provision for equal rights to common property, the family codes give the courts broad discretion to depart from the rule by taking into account the interests of minor children or one spouse. The share of one spouse may be enlarged if the other spouse avoided socially useful labour or expended common property to the detriment of the family's interests. Factors the courts weigh include, for example, the disability of one spouse, the spouse with whom minor children will continue to live, or drunkenness on the part of one spouse. Special considerations apply to the division of housing, shares in co-operative organisations, and bank deposits.

Property in the common joint ownership of spouses can be divided at the initiative of a creditor, as well as in the event of death or divorce, for a creditor may levy against the personal property of a spouse and his share of the common joint property. Execution also may be levied against property commonly owned by spouses in order to compensate for damage caused by a crime of one spouse if the trial court establishes that the property was acquired from assets gained through criminal means.

D. SUPPORT

Spouses have a duty to support one another from the moment their marriage is registered. Cohabitation without registration gives no right to support, whereas a separation of the spouses without divorce in no way alters the duty to support, irrespective of the length of the separation. If a marriage is declared null, no duty of support arises unless one spouse concealed a bigamous relationship from the other. A spouse who is not capable of working and needs material assistance, and a wife during pregnancy and up to one year after birth, may sue for alimony or support, which will be awarded if the other spouse is in a position to provide it. Even after divorce the right to support may continue. Spouses are protected against incurring a disability within one year after divorce, and if the spouse reaches age 55 (women) or 60 (men) within five years after divorce, the right to support likewise continues. These provisions extend the protection offered by the 1926 RSFSR Family Code, which afforded support only for one year after the dissolution of a marriage.

The duty to support a spouse may be removed or altered only by a court decision. A court will have regard to the short duration of a marriage or to the unworthy conduct of a spouse seeking alimony. Unworthy conduct must be proved by the other spouse on the basis of court decrees, references, and other evidence; it may have occurred before or after the marriage.

The amount of alimony payable to support a spouse is determined by the court as a monthly lump sum (not a share or percentage of earnings), taking into account the material and family status of each spouse, that is, the number of family members, their age and capacity to earn independently, and the like. Either spouse may petition a court to alter the amount of alimony as circumstances change. Remarriage or the disappearance of the circumstances which gave rise to the duty to pay support in the first place eliminates the right to support; however, support granted on other grounds, causing harm, for example, to a spouse would not be affected.

E. DIVORCE

The vicissitudes of Soviet divorce legislation, from the era of 'postcard' divorces for a nominal sum through ZAGS offices until the mid-1930s to the period of restrictive divorce after the 1944 edict, have been discussed above. The 1968 FPMarL brought a further easing of the restrictive approach by allowing spouses who have no minor children to dissolve their marriage by mutual consent at a ZAGS office. A three-month period must elapse before the application is formalised and a divorce certificate issued. A State duty of 50 rubles is payable to register the divorce. The ZAGS office under this procedure has no interest in the reasons for divorce. Consent and the absence of minor children are conclusive.

Under certain circumstances a marriage will be dissolved by ZAGS agencies upon the application of one spouse, for example, if the other spouse has been declared to be legally missing, or been sentenced to three or more years for the commission of a crime.

Otherwise divorce proceedings remain within the jurisdiction of the courts. The court is required to endeavour to reconcile the parties both at the stage of preparing the case for hearing and during the judicial session. Indeed, the USSR Supreme Court has decreed that the judicial procedure is to have great 'educational significance.' Both spouses as a rule must be present, and the reason for seeking the divorce must be specified and verified by the court. Soviet law stipulates no grounds for divorce. The codes merely provide the court shall dissolve a marriage if the further joint life of the spouses and preservation of the family has become impossible. Despite the suggestions of some Soviet jurists that a model list of grounds for divorce might be helpful in guiding courts, the draftsmen preferred a formulation which drew on long-standing court practice. Common grounds for divorce have included the abuse of alcoholic beverages by one spouse, non-cohabitation for a protracted period, or the inability of one spouse to conceive a child. Up to a six-month reconciliation period may be assigned by the court, a change from earlier legislation where no limit was imposed and courts in practice were assigning periods of from seven days to ten months or more.

Example. In a fascinating case, decided in 1985, which juxtaposed family law policy of the late 1940s against modern social and legal values, the full Plenum of the USSR Supreme Court dealt with a divorce action that received wide publicity in the press. During the war a senior military officer was wounded and fell in love with the young nurse who attended him. After the war the officer returned to his wife and two children, and in 1947 they had a third child. He told his wife about his affair with the nurse, whom he still loved, and this discussion led to a breakdown of the marriage. That same year, in 1947, he filed for divorce but his petition was rejected by the court. In 1949 he filed a new suit; the divorce was granted and the officer immediately went to the nurse and married her. His first wife appealed the divorce and the appellate court reversed the decision of the court of first instance, returning the case for rehearing. At the second hearing the divorce petition was rejected and the officer's marriage to the nurse was declared void. The officer appealed all the way to the USSR Supreme Court without success.

Divorce was exceptionally difficult to obtain during the late 1940s and early 1950s. To the court he appeared to be a family man with a wife and three children enmeshed in a battlefield romance—all too familiar a story and one which in the interests of family stability the courts wished to discourage. The officer, however, did not return to his family. His love for the nurse was genuine and he lived with her in an unregistered 'marriage' for nearly 40 years. Although 20 years younger, she cared for the officer through good times and bad. He was blind during their last eight years together and died at the age of 84. The nurse then sought the officer's military pension and was refused on the grounds that she and the officer were not legally married. The first wife also sought the pension and was refused on the grounds that she was not a dependant of the deceased.

The Plenum of the USSR Supreme Court ruled that the court of first instance in 1947 had been correct to deny a divorce, for there was reason to anticipate that the marriage might be saved, especially in light of the third child. However, the court which in 1949 granted the divorce also acted properly, for the two years which had elapsed showed that the battlefield relationship was not a casual liaison and that the marriage was unstable. The reversal of the 1949 decision and all subsequent proceedings were incorrect in that they failed to acknowledge the existence and stability of the battlefield relationship. Accordingly, on 3 April 1985, the Plenum reversed all previous proceedings in the case and reinstated the decision of the Tula Regional Court of 23 June 1949, which had granted the divorce. The nurse was awarded the officer's pension since the marriage was finally determined to be valid.[8]

The divorcing spouses are free to decide with which of them any minor children shall reside, but if agreement cannot be reached, the court will resolve the matter when dissolving the marriage by proceeding from the interests of the children and simultaneously will determine how much alimony is to be recovered for child support and from which parent. If the children are shared between the parents, the codes lay down a basis for adjusting the child support payment appropriately. At the request of an affected spouse, the court must determine when dissolving a marriage the amount of support payable to that spouse and must divide the common joint property of the spouses. State duty in court-decided divorces for issuing a divorce certificate is fixed by the court in an amount of from 50 to 200 rubles and may be levied against one of, or divided between, the spouses, or reduced or waived if financial circumstances require.

The family codes determine for the first time by way of legislation that a marriage is considered to be terminated from the moment a divorce is registered in the ZAGS register. If the divorce is by judicial decision, either spouse may register the divorce, and failure to do so means the divorce has not taken effect and remarriage is prohibited. A three-year statute of limitations applies for completing the registration.

8 See Biulleten' verkhovnogo suda SSSR, no. 4 (1985) pp 33–34; P. Feofanov 'Po zakonu znachit spravedlivo', *Izvestiia*, 20 April 1985, p 3.

A spouse who changed his surname when being married may either retain the surname or take his pre-marital surname when the divorce is registered.

F. NULLITY OF MARRIAGE

The 1926 RSFSR family code and other RSFSR family legislation said nothing about the consequences of violating the legal requirements for entering into marriage, although Belorussian and Ukrainian codes did make provision for this eventuality. The Plenum of the USSR Supreme Court filled the gap in 1949 by decree, and the 1968 FPMarL expanded upon the earlier practice. A marriage is deemed void if the conditions for concluding it were violated, or there were obstacles to the conclusion thereof, or if the marriage is fictitious. By fictitious marriage is meant the registration of a marriage without an intention to create a family but rather, for example, to obtain rights to a pension, dwelling space, or a residence permit, or to avoid State vocational distribution after completing secondary or higher education. Some codes allow the marriage to remain valid if one spouse had the intention to create a family, whereas others do not. If the circumstances precluding marriage have subsequently disappeared, the marriage may be deemed valid from the moment of their disappearance.

A judicial proceeding is required to declare a marriage null. The spouses, any persons whose rights were violated by the marriage, guardianship and curatorship agencies, or the Procuracy may bring suit to this end. A marriage deemed void is regarded as such from the moment it was concluded and no rights and duties arise from the marriage unless fraud were present. The rights of any children born of such a marriage are not affected by the nullity. Property relations between the spouses are governed by civil legislation and not the family code provisions on common joint ownership. But a spouse who entered a void marriage in good faith may be awarded support from the guilty spouse and the right of common joint ownership to property acquired during the marriage.

G. THE FAMILY

Present Soviet legislation returns to the principle laid down in the earliest family decrets, that blood relationship, the birth of children, is the sole basis for the rights and duties of parents and children. Both parents have an equal duty to nurture and support their child irrespective of what their own personal relationship may be, reversing the situation under the Edict of 8 July 1944 whereby if the parents were not in a registered marriage the father had no responsibility for the child. Rights and duties between parent and child arise from the moment of birth, but the relationship must be duly registered. If the parents are married, there is a legal presupposition that the father is the husband of the mother; accordingly, either parent may apply to register the birth. If the parents are unmarried, they file a joint application for registration of the birth at a ZAGS office.

Under the 1944 Edict paternity proceedings were abolished. The 1968 FPMarL restored them, although not retroactively, by providing that if a child is born of unmarried parents and the latter do not make joint application to register the birth, either parent may initiate a paternity proceeding in a court, as also may the guardian or curator of the child or the child himself when he attains legal age. The suit is brought against the putative father or, if the mother prevented the registration, also against her. If the putative father is deceased, the matter takes the form of a special proceeding to establish a legal fact. When establishing paternity, a court takes into account the cohabitation and keeping of a common household by the child's mother and the defendant before the birth of the child, or the joint upbringing or support for the child, or any evidence reliably confirming the acknowledgement of paternity by the defendant. The latter evidence may include witness testimony concerning statements by the defendant, blood tests, and the like. A person entered as the father or mother of a child has one year within which to contest the entry once the entry has or should have become known to him or her. If the individual was a minor when the entry was made, the one-year period runs from his eighteenth birthday.

In the event that paternity is not established or the mother refuses to name the father, the child is entered in the birth register under the mother's surname and whatever forenames she may choose. This obviates the embarrassing blank spaces that appeared in such cases under the pre-1968 legislation and disclosed the illegitimacy of the child. The mother does not qualify for paternity support, of course, but she is eligible for State grants to unmarried mothers and has the right to place the child in a children's home where his nurturing and support are entirely at State expense.

Children born out of wedlock have, under the law, the same rights and duties with respect to their parents and relatives as children born of married persons. Parents have a legal duty to nurture their children, be concerned for their physical and intellectual development, prepare them for socially useful labour, and raise worthy members of a socialist society. They act as legal representatives of their minor children and require no special authorisation to act in defence of their children's rights and interests. If the parents cannot agree on matters relative to raising their children, the guardianship and curatorship agencies will resolve the question.

Parental rights cannot be exercised contrary to the children's interests. If the parents do not live together, they nonetheless each have the right to help raise the children without obstruction from the other parent. Grandparents have a legal right to associate with their minor grandchildren and may not be obstructed by the parents. Guardianship and curatorship agencies may deprive a parent or grandparent from associating with a minor child for a specified period if such associations would impede the normal nurturing or exert a harmful influence on the child. Cruel treatment or neglect of a child, alcoholism, drug addiction, and amoral, antisocial conduct by parent(s) are all grounds for depriving the parent(s) of their parental rights, which may occur only in a judicial proceeding with the participation of a procurator. The RSFSR Supreme Court has held that if a parent fulfils his or her parental duties properly but does not achieve the desired result, he or she may not be deprived of parental rights. Guilty or blameworthy conduct is required. Some union republics use deprivation of parental rights as a penal sanction. The consequences of depriving a parent of parental rights are that all rights based on kinship with the child are lost, including the right to receive support from the child, but the duty to support the child remains intact. Having been deprived of parental rights, a parent who in derogation of the rules of socialist community life makes it impossible for the child to live together with him or her, and warnings and social pressure prove to be unavailing, may be evicted from the premises without alternative accommodation being provided.

The duties of family members to support one another are multifarious and mutually reinforcing. Parents have a duty to support both their minor children and those over age 18 who are not capable of working and require assistance. Alimony for child support, unlike support for a needy spouse, is based on percentage of income: for one child, 25%; for two children, 33⅓%; and for three or more children, 50% of the earnings of the parents. A court may adjust these percentages under certain circumstances. Even when children are placed in a children's home, the parents may be obliged to reimburse the State on the same scale. Children in turn must assist, upon reaching majority, their parents who are not capable of working and require assistance. Aid of this nature is determined in a monthly lump sum amount by a court. Step-parents must support their stepchildren and vice versa, likewise grandparents their grandchildren and vice versa if the parents in between are unable to provide. The same reciprocal principle extends to guardians and their wards.

Current legislation has tightened up considerably the procedures for paying alimony. Alimony may be paid voluntarily or withheld directly from earnings, pension, benefit, stipend, or other income. The management of an enterprise, institution, or organisation must withhold alimony if requested by an application in writing or by a writ of execution. Persons who maliciously avoid payment of alimony have a notation made on their internal passport by internal affairs agencies. Plaintiffs who sue to recover alimony are exempted from paying court costs.

On 1 January 1985 a procedure was established for assigning and paying temporary benefits to minors whose parents were obliged to pay alimony but had disappeared. These filled an important gap in the provision of support for minor children. The monthly benefit is payable until the child reaches age 18; once the defaulting parent is located, alimony in arrears is subject to immediate repayment plus a surcharge of 10% under a writ of execution against the parent's property or earnings, these sums being reimbursed to the social security administration.

H. ADOPTION

The 1918 RSFSR family code proscribed adoption in general for economic reasons. The draftsmen were apprehensive that adoption might be a screen for the exploitation of child labour. The 1926 code allowed adoption but permitted any citizen to seek to have an adoption made void if the interests of the child were not served. Current legislation allows a procurator or a guardianship and curatorship agency to challenge an adoption, but not other citizens. Allowing anyone to bring suit against an adoption, it was felt, could interfere materially with the rights of the adoptive and adopted persons.

Only minor children may be adopted, with the written consent of their parents unless the latter have been deprived of their parental rights. If the child is aged ten or above, his consent is required for an adoption and is obtained by the guardianship and curatorship agencies. The law is flexible with regard to equating adopted persons to relatives of adoptive persons. As a general rule, the adopted persons and their descendants are assimilated into their new family and lose their rights and duties in respect of their natural parents. Under certain circumstances, however, for example if only one spouse adopts a child, the latter may retain rights and duties toward his opposite natural parent.

The secrecy of an adoption is protected by law. Divulgence of an adoption is a crime in most union republics.

I. GUARDIANSHIP AND CURATORSHIP

The 1968 FPMarL was the first all-union enactment to define the purposes of guardianship and curatorship. Two categories of persons are affected: minors and persons of majority age who require assistance. Guardianship is the term reserved for minors under age 15 and for persons deemed by a court to lack dispositive legal capacity by reason of mental illness or feeble-mindedness. Curatorship refers to minors aged 15 to 18 and to persons who have attained majority and have dispositive legal capacity, but for reasons of health or because they are alcoholics or addicts cannot independently exercise their rights and duties or have been restricted by a court in so doing. The executive committees of local soviets from district to rural levels act as guardianship and curatorship agencies.

Guardians and curators are the legal representatives of individuals under their care and perform all necessary legal transactions in their name and interests or consent thereto. They are not obliged to support persons under their care, but in the case of minors they are obliged to live with them and care for them as parents.

J. FOREIGNERS AND STATELESS PERSONS

The principal acts governing foreigners and stateless persons with respect to marriage and the family are the 1968 FPMarL and union republic family codes as amended in 1979, the 1981 Law on the Legal Status of Foreign Citizens in the USSR, and Soviet citizenship legislation. Soviet law operates from the premise that, but for certain exceptions, a foreigner has the same rights and duties under family legislation as a Soviet citizen. In some cases these are modified by bilateral international treaties.

Foreigners who wish to register a marriage with another foreigner or with a Soviet citizen must comply with the Soviet legal requirements for contracting and registering a marriage. Two foreign citizens who marry one another in a foreign consulate or embassy in the USSR will, on the basis of reciprocity or international treaty, be recognised as lawfully married by Soviet law. A foreigner and a Soviet citizen may not be married in a foreign consulate on Soviet territory.

ZAGS offices are instructed to have regard to the fact that some States forbid their citizens to marry foreigners. Indeed, from 15 February 1947 to 21 January 1954 marriages between foreigners and Soviet citizens were prohibited. If foreigners in the USSR from such a country apply to be married, the ZAGS office will ask them to produce an authorisation issued by the competent agencies of the respective state. But if authorisation is not obtained and the individuals continue to insist upon registration, the ZAGS official must explain that their Soviet marriage will not be considered valid under the laws of that state, and if those who intend to marry remain resolute, the marriage is to be registered. Although in the end registration will be allowed, the Soviet authorities discourage marriages of this kind in the belief that they prejudice the rights and interests of the Soviet citizen in the marriage.

Under an Instruction on the Procedure for Registering Acts of Civil Status in the RSFSR of 17 October 1969, foreign citizens wishing to register a marriage must submit a residence permit and a national passport or merely the passport if it contains an authorisation to reside in the USSR. A seaman's passport is unacceptable. Persons previously married must submit documents confirming that marriage has terminated. The commentators suggest that for foreigners the one-month waiting period to register a marriage after application is usually extended to three months. Reductions of the period are said to occur when the sojourn of one party on Soviet territory is coming to an end or close relatives are arriving from abroad to attend the wedding, and the like.[9]

Marriages between foreigners outside the USSR are recognised by the Soviet authorities if they meet the requirements of the foreign legal system where they were contracted. A valid polygamous marriage contracted abroad between foreigners would be valid in the Soviet Union; to decide otherwise, the commentator suggests, would be to refuse to protect the rights of the second wife and children. In some cases a violation by foreigners married abroad of their own legislation might be disregarded in the USSR, for example, a marriage in violation of foreign legislation prohibiting inter-racial marriages. To give effect to the invalidity of such a marriage by applying foreign law in the Soviet Union would be contrary to the basic principles of the Soviet system (*ordre publique*).[10]

Divorce by foreigners in the Soviet Union proceeds on the same basis as for Soviet citizens. In the case of foreigners from countries where divorce is not recognised, the Soviet officials are required to explain to the applicants that the legal consequences of terminating their marriage in the USSR may not be recognised in their home state. A network of legal assistance treaties concluded by the Soviet Union with other socialist countries resolves a number of procedural issues, as do certain consular conventions concluded with western countries.

Alimony obligations of foreign citizens arise not infrequently in Soviet courts. In the absence of an international treaty, Soviet courts recover alimony for child support by applying Soviet law irrespective of the child's citizenship and place of residence, including situations where the parents are unmarried and paternity is established by joint acknowledgement or court decision. Under the FPCivPL the jurisdiction of Soviet courts over civil cases in which foreign citizens, stateless persons, and foreign enterprises and persons participate, and likewise disputes in which one of the parties resides abroad, 'shall be determined by USSR legislation . . .' (Art 60–1). The difficulty arises under this formulation when the defendant resides abroad and the child resides with a parent in the USSR. The Soviet court is competent to render a decision, but in the absence of treaty or reciprocal recognition, there is no means of enforcing recognition. Many Soviet commentators believe Soviet courts should accept cases for consideration on the basis of residence only when the decision rendered will be recognised and executed in the debtor's country of residence. When the debtor parent resides in the Soviet Union, Soviet courts have jurisdiction irrespective of citizenship or residence of the parents or child and will apply Soviet legislation. An

---

9 L. N. Galenskaia *Pravovoe polozhenie inostrantsev v SSSR* (1982) p 107.
10 S. N. Bratus and P. E. Orlovskii (eds) *Kommentarii k kodeksu o brake i sem'e RSFSR* (1971) p 225.

Estonian people's court, for example, recovered alimony for child support of a daughter in Sweden from the Soviet father in the amount of 25% of his earnings.

Foreign citizens abroad have the right to adopt a child who is a Soviet citizen and resides abroad, but the authorisation of the USSR or union republic Ministry of Enlightenment is required even if the adoption is performed in and under the rules of a foreign State. In deciding whether to grant authorisation, the ministry must examine both the interests of the child and whether the adoption conforms fully to Soviet legislation. The adoption of a Soviet child by a foreigner residing in the USSR likewise is permitted by law but on condition that the authorisation of the highest guardianship agency is obtained, usually an autonomous republic, territory, regional, or Moscow or Leningrad City soviets. This latter requirement is imposed exclusively on foreigners. The adoption of foreign children in the Soviet Union proceeds on the same basis as for Soviet children in the USSR; however, in practice the Soviet guardianship and curatorship agencies will whenever possible request consent to the adoption by an appropriate agency in the State of the child's nationality.

Chapter 12

Labour law

As one would expect in a social system whose revolutionary ideology and experience counsel the transition to a higher level of societal development through the formation of a workers' State, labour law is considered to be among the most important branches of Soviet law. The Soviet authorities and Soviet citizens measure social progress in terms of labour conditions, work norms, social security, benefits, and earnings to a considerable extent. To workers who live in a mixed economy these achievements and standards are held out as examples of what a socialist society has to offer.

HISTORICAL BACKGROUND

Early Soviet legislation dealt piecemeal with labour conditions and social insurance. An eight-hour work-day was introduced and the following year an annual two-week holiday, pensions were increased, unemployment, disability and sickness insurance introduced, and labour inspectorates reorganised. On or about 9 December 1918 the RSFSR Code of Laws on Labour was adopted.[1] Curiously, confirmation data by the VTsIK or its Presidium has never been found. The Code superseded all antecedent legislation and contracts contrary to its provisions and extended to all persons who worked for remuneration and to enterprises in both the socialised and private sectors. Every individual between the ages of 16 and 50, unless permanently disabled, had a 'labour duty,' that is, a duty to work, under the Code.

Temporary exemptions were granted to the ill and to pregnant women, the latter up to eight weeks before and after birth. Persons obliged to work but not engaged in socially useful labour would be compulsorily recruited for employment by local soviets. The Code allowed individuals to work in their particular specialty at the established rates; equal pay for equal work was proclaimed. Transfer, dismissal, work hours, labour productivity and labour safety also were regulated in the Code.

Soviet commentators attribute the strictness of the 1918 RSFSR labour code to the civil strife in which the country was embroiled. 'War

1 *Dekrety sovetskoi vlasti* (1968) IV pp 166–190; *SU RSFSR* (1918) no. 87–88, item 905.

communism,' as the period 1918–20 is often called, required, they suggest, a policy of labour enlistment rather than voluntary relationships. The introduction of the NEP brought a new labour code approved on 30 October 1922[2] and in effect as from 15 November of the same year which differed markedly from its predecessor. The chapter on 'labour duty' was supplanted by one 'On the procedure for hiring and providing labour;' labour relations were based on voluntary agreement. 'Labour duty' under the 1922 code was restricted to exceptional situations, such as coping with natural disasters or an inadequate labour force to carry out certain State tasks. Both collective agreements and individual labour contracts were provided for in separate chapters. Management and labour were accorded broad discretion to modify code provisions in labour contracts so long as minimum standards laid down by the code were met. Trade unions were expected to negotiate on behalf of the labour force on these matters within the discretion of the parties, for example, wage rates, quality standards, work rules, and the like. Labour disputes were relegated under the code either to people's courts or to price-conflict commissions, conciliation chambers, or mediation tribunals. The eight-hour workday was preserved and further limitations imposed on overtime.

In many respects the 1922 labour code resembled the labour legislation of western industrialised economies. When, however, different regulations were necessary for State and private industry in the USSR, State industry was favoured under the code. The transition to national economic planning at the end of the 1920s altered or eliminated many premises upon which the 1922 labour code had been conceived. The State sector became the sole employer of labour. Trade unions were transformed from an adversary bargaining entity into a component of economic management. Their task was to assist in meeting planning targets, improving economic efficiency and labour productivity, and, if necessary, accepting short-term reductions in employee welfare to achieve these larger objectives. Most collective agreements in labour relations ceased after 1934; they were declared to be institutions which had outlived themselves. Henceforth trade unions devoted themselves to administering social security and supervising the enforcement of safety regulations, assuming to some extent the duties of the People's Commissariat of Labour with which the Central Trade Union Council merged in 1933. Compulsory distribution of technical graduates was introduced in 1930 as part of manpower planning and industrialisation. Shop work rules increasingly gave way to legislative regulation. Unjustified absence from work for even one day could result after 1932 in instant dismissal. Disciplinary penalties introduced in 1938 for being late to work or leaving early became serious criminal offences under wartime legislation. Decrees enacted in the early 1940s made it a crime

2 *SU RSFSR* (1922) no. 70, item 903.

to resign one's job without management consent and allowed the State to transfer employees at will without their consent.

Collective agreements were formally reintroduced again in 1947, apparently acknowledging that their actual continuance after 1935 in both plant and industry levels showed they had a purpose despite their nominal abolition in 1935.[3] Wage rates increasingly came under centralised determination, although some local flexibility was allowed within minimum and maximum levels. Consequently, by the 1930-40s much of the 1922 labour code had been made obsolete by subsequent legislation. Texts of the code simply were no longer published. In the post-Stalin era some of the more draconian limitations on labour were removed. Workers were allowed to resign or to transfer jobs. New model rules adopted in 1957 relaxed the harsh requirements of wartime legislation. Work advanced on preparing Fundamental Principles of Labour Legislation (FPLabL) and new union republic labour codes. The draft FPLabL were published for discussion in 1959, but not enacted until 15 July 1970, with effect from 1 January 1971.

Contemporary regulation of labour

Many premises of earlier Soviet labour legislation have been given constitutional status. Wage rates and increases in real incomes are linked directly to the growth of labour productivity. Labour incomes are the basis of personal ownership of Soviet citizens. Among the basic rights, freedoms, and duties of citizens is the right to labour, defined as the right to guaranteed employment at wages of at least the State minimum in accordance with its quality and quantity, including the right to choose a profession, type of occupation, and work in accordance with one's vocation, abilities, professional training and education, but also with regard to the needs of society. The Soviet constitutions regard rights and duties as inseparable; accordingly, the right to labour is linked with the duty of every Soviet citizen capable of working to labour conscientiously in the socially useful activity which he has chosen and to observe labour discipline. The work-week is constitutionally fixed as not to exceed 41 hours, with paid annual leave, weekly days of leisure, and reduced hours for certain professions, trades, or types of worker. The State is constitutionally committed to reducing and ultimately abolishing arduous physical labour by introducing mechanisation and automation in all branches of the national economy, to improving labour safety and conditions, and to organising labour scientifically.[4]

3 See H. J. Berman *Justice in the USSR* (rev. edn, 1963) p 352.
4 See generally, W. E. Butler, B. A. Hepple and A. C. Neal (eds) *Comparative Labour Law* (1987); Butler, Hepple and R. W. Rideout (eds) 'The Right to Work under British and Soviet Labour Law' International Journal of Comparative Labour Law and Industrial Relations III, no. 3 (1987), 81-228 (special issue).

Under restructuring, the constitutional premises of labour law have acquired a somewhat different accent. While minimum standards continue to be fixed by law, reforms introduced in 1988 authorise the management of an enterprise, institution, or organisation to establish, jointly with the labour collective council and trade union, preferential conditions for its workers and employees that exceed legislative standards. These must be paid from the enterprise's own assets and may take any form not expressly prohibited by law, including cash increments, payment in kind, or additional leave. The earnings of each worker are to be determined by the *final* results of his work and his personal labour contribution, without any maximum limit being imposed.

A. THE LABOUR COLLECTIVE

In Article 8 of the USSR Constitution, added after the draft redaction was published, emphasis was placed upon the role of labour collectives in the discussion and deciding of State and social matters, in the planning of production and social development, in the training and placement of personnel, in discussing and deciding management issues of enterprises and institutions, in the improvement of labour conditions, in the use of assets earmarked for special purposes, and the like. These policies have been elaborated in the 1983 Law on Labour Collectives and On Increasing Their Role in the Management of Enterprises, Institutions, and Organisations, in the 1987 Law on the State Enterprise, and in the 1988 amendments to the FPLabL.

The labour collective is regarded as a basic component of socialist self-management in the Soviet economic system. Accordingly, the director and executive personnel of an enterprise, including all heads of structural entities, production units, shops, divisions, sectors, farms, and links, as well as foremen and brigade leaders, have become elected personnel, usually on a competitive basis. The director is elected for a five-year term by the general meeting (or conference) of the labour collective through secret or open ballot and is confirmed in his post by the superior agency. New elections are held if the superior organisation declines to confirm, but reasons must be given for its refusal. A director may be dismissed from office by the superior organisation before his term expires on the basis of a decision of the labour collective or its council. A similar procedure is applicable to lower-level executive personnel. However, the deputy directors and the heads of the legal and bookkeeping sections and of the quality control service are appointed and released by the director himself in the established procedure.

The labour collective is to meet at least twice a year. After some reluctance on the part of trade union sources, it was accepted that the labour collectives must elect 'labour collective councils' to function in the interval between plenary meetings of the labour collective. The councils ensure that decisions of the labour collective general meetings are fulfilled, hear management on how the plans and contractual obligations are proceeding, confirm the terms for the enterprise socialist competition together with Party, trade union, and Komsomol agencies, decide issues regarding improvements in management and in the structure of the enterprise and regarding the distribution of wages, take decisions concerning the use of all enterprise funds, the training of personnel, labour and production discipline, and perform a variety of other functions.

The council is elected by the labour collective for a two or three-year term by secret or open ballot at the general meeting of the collective. The collective determines how large the council should be, but management personnel may not exceed one-quarter of the council membership, and as a rule at least one-third of the council members should be replaced at each election. The council members are unpaid volunteers, but may not be dismissed or disciplined without the consent of the labour collective council.

Decisions of the labour collective council are binding upon management and members of the labour collective if they are within its competence and in accordance with legislation. If management disagrees with the council, the matter is referred to the general meeting of the labour collective. The latter's decisions are binding not merely upon management and its own membership, but also upon superior State and economic agencies so long as they are in accordance with legislation.

By autumn 1987 more than 30,000 directors of various ranks in industry and 6,000 in construction had been elected to office—about 1% of all such posts. Legislation does not specify in detail the procedures for electing labour collective councils and executive personnel. These are to be found in a set of Recommendations approved by the VTsSPS and the USSR State Committee on Labour. The Recommendations suggest that labour collective councils do not exceed 30 persons (although variations exist: in Kalinin one plant elected 360 persons, or 10% of the work force to the council). If a large council is chosen, it is suggested that a presidium of the council be formed. In large production associations, the bureaucracy of the labour collective can be formidable: one association contained 184 labour collective councils in all production entities and shops and 3,000 brigade councils made up of 22,000 individuals.

The Recommendations suggest that the labour collective councils not elect as their chairmen either the director of the enterprise or the heads of social organisations. An outstanding worker, specialist, or head of a lower structural link is preferable. Nonetheless, in practice there has been a strong preference for choosing executive personnel. Of 2,089 labour collective councils in the Moscow region in 1988, 1,830 chose executive personnel or directors as their chairmen. Even trade union chairmen have been chosen as heads of labour collective councils, although the Recommendations strongly condemn that practice as an improper combination of responsibilities.

B. COLLECTIVE CONTRACTS

The collective contract is one of the mediums through which the labour collective has a role in enterprise management. Collective contracts are governed principally by the FPLabL, the union republic labour codes, and the Statute of 28 September 1984 on the procedure for concluding collective contracts. Sub-contracts are concluded annually (not later than February) between the trade union committee and management. In large industrial, production, and scientific-production associations or combines the collective contracts are often concluded within each component thereof having legal personality.

The drafting process begins in April–May of the preceding year. Workers and employers are invited to submit proposals by the trade union committee for the draft contract, which by October–December is to be rendered in conjunction with the confirmed plan for the forthcoming year, together with trade union budget estimates and the State and social insurance budget. The draft is then discussed throughout the enterprise at all production levels and ultimately submitted for discussion and approval to the labour collective, general meeting or conference, whereupon it is signed by representatives of management and the trade union, enters into force as agreed, and is sent to superior economic and trade union agencies for registration within five days. Any disagreements between labour and management when concluding the contract are referred to the superior economic and trade union agencies who, with the participation of the parties, are to resolve the dispute within two weeks.

Each collective contract follows a format prescribed by the 1984 Statute. The collective contract begins with the formal undertaking of the collective to fulfil the State plan, and counterplan, if any, and socialist obligations. In this way the specific State planning targets for the enterprise become part of each worker's individual responsibility. Next are provisions regarding obligations under socialist competitions which the enterprise has assumed or responsibilities under the movement for a communist attitude toward labour. Both are movements which measure improvements and accomplishments of competing enterprises by prescribed indices and award large, sometimes enormous, bonuses to the best entrants. The clauses are followed by provisions for introducing technological innovations or inventions and progressive experience into production. Next come provisions governing wage rates and standards. These usually incorporate by reference tariff rates laid down by State agencies and agreed increments above those tariffs for specified levels of work. The collective contract then turns to specific ways in which workers and employees are involved in production management through consultations at particular times on stipulated matters and the like. Specific undertakings are made to improve the qualifications and general education of workers, to strengthen labour discipline, and to train young workers. Labour safety, social insurance, medical services, sanatorium passes, amenities for female employees and young children, housing, dining, and recreational facilities, and miscellaneous provisions conclude the collective contract, and it is in these latter arrangements that individual collective contracts are most likely to diverge one from another.

Some of these provisions, especially those affecting wages, work hours, rest time, incentive payments, and labour safety, are normative in character and enforceable at law if violated by either party provided they are not ultra vires. Some Soviet jurists believe collective contracts should be treated as a source of law (see chapter 4, above). The collective contracts differentiate between obligations assumed by the labour collective and obligations undertaken by the local trade union committee. By far the majority of obligations vis-à-vis management are assumed by the latter (see below).

Collective contract provisions may not be contrary to labour legislation. The provisions extend to all workers and employees of the entity concerned irrespective of whether they are trade union members. Once the contract is signed, it must be brought to the information of all workers and employees, and new employees must be familiarised with its terms. Periodically, reports are given by management to the trade union regarding fulfilment of the contractual terms, and at least twice-yearly the trade union and management hold a meeting with the labour collective to verify performance under the contract. At higher levels the process of concluding the contracts is directed by ministries and departments jointly with central and republic trade union committees through directive letters issued to each entity. The central trade unions likewise report by mid-April of each year to the All-Union Central Trade Union Council about all work carried on in respect of the fulfilment and conclusion of collective contracts. The collective contract has been moulded into a device representing ideally a harmony of planning, administrative, management, and labour interests; its object is to enlist worker support in giving effect to planning and to sublimate areas of conflict in the larger interests of a presumed community of labour-management concerns.

C. LABOUR CONTRACTS

The union republic labour codes speak of a 'labour contract' as an 'agreement' between the working people and the enterprise, institution, or organisation under which the worker is obliged to perform work of a certain specialisation, skill, or post and to be subject to internal rules for labour discipline, and the employer is obliged to pay a wage and ensure the labour conditions stipulated by labour legislation, the collective agreement, and the agreement of the parties. The Soviet law of contracts has no application to a labour contract and in actuality the terms of employment are governed in elaborate detail by legislation.

A labour contract may be concluded orally or in writing. Ordinarily the official hiring document takes the form of an order (*prikaz*) or regulation issued by management and delivered by registered post, but actually taking up employment is regarded as concluding a labour contract irrespective of whether the order has been formally sent. A worker who has been invited to transfer employment by agreement between the managers of the respective enterprises cannot, under the RSFSR Labour Code, be refused a labour contract, although Party members could find themselves with a conflict of interest (see chapter 9, above). Not all union republic labour codes contain this provision. Some union republics moreover require certain labour contracts to be in writing, for example, for work in areas of the Far North or localities equated thereto (UkSSR Labour Code).

Labour contracts are concluded for three terms: either indefinitely, or for a specified term not exceeding three years, or for a period to perform specified work. A probationary period may be agreed by the parties to ascertain whether the employee can do the work for which he was hired; normally, probation periods are from one week to one month in duration.

By arrangement between management and the employee or worker, certain terms of the labour contract or relationship may be modified. For example, if a worker works on a holiday or a day off, he may accept in lieu of overtime an additional day of leave or holiday or the overtime wage. Flexibility of this nature, introduced as part of restructuring, effectively alters the labour contract by removing constraints on the freedom of the parties to agree different terms. The overall level of constraints, however, remains substantial.

Most of the code provisions on the labour contract treat problems of transfer or termination. In the economic reforms of the 1960s many enterprises found themselves with a larger work force than was required, either because of overmanning or the introduction of new technology and automation. Wage costs and labour productivity became more prominent among the economic indicators of enterprise performance, but existing labour legislation, strongly enforced by the courts,[5] made it extremely difficult for planners and managers to redeploy the labour force. The 1970 FPLabL introduced somewhat greater flexibility to this end and this flexibility was enlarged in 1988. Transfer to other work was allowed only with the employee's consent unless the transfer were for a

---

5 See M. McAuley *Labour Disputes in Soviet Russia 1957-1965* (1969).

disciplinary infraction or by reason of temporary 'production necessity or stoppage,' the latter broadly defined to encompass industrial accidents, natural disasters, or replacement of an absent employee, among other factors. Under the 1988 changes an employee may be transferred without his consent on condition that he retains the post, skill-level, or specialty designated in his labour contract and that for two months he keeps his former level of earnings. As regards other imminent changes in his material labour conditions, the worker or employee being transferred must be given at least two months' notice. These requirements are intended ultimately to help the worker make his choice: accept the transfer or seek a new job. Dissolution of a labour contract by a worker or employee hired for an indeterminate period is admissible upon giving two months' written notice, unless there are justifiable reasons, in which case one month's notice is sufficient; contracts for a specified term may be dissolved before time if the worker becomes ill or disabled, if management violates labour legislation or the collective or labour contract, or for 'other justifiable reasons.'

Management may dissolve a labour contract if the enterprise is liquidated or if there is to be a reduction in the numbers or personnel establishment of the work force. In the latter event merely frictional unemployment is to transpire since workers released have a legal right and duty to work elsewhere and the general shortage of labour makes redeployment easier. Management must give notice in person to workers being made redundant for reasons of production necessity at least two months beforehand. Detailed provision is made in the 1988 amendments for provision of a new job or retraining, with retention of average earnings for two or three months, retention of work experience periods, and other types of compensation. Under the 1988 amendments, management may make workers redundant when they are entitled to a full pension for old age or, if management wishes, the ordinary labour contract with such individuals may be dissolved and replaced by a two-year contract subject to renewal. Management likewise may dismiss a worker whose qualifications or health render him unfit for the position held, or if the worker systematically and without justifiable reasons fails to perform duties under the labour contract or rules for internal discipline, on condition that disciplinary or social sanctions previously had been imposed, or if the worker is guilty of shirking without justifiable reasons or comes to work in a state of intoxication, or if by reason of temporary incapacity the worker does not appear for work for more than four months, or if an individual is reinstated in a position previously held. When workers are dismissed because of personnel reduction, those workers whose labour productivity and qualifications are highest have a priority to be kept on. If these factors are equal, account is taken of workers who have two or more dependants, to workers who have no other independent wage earners in the family, to length of service, to employees with production injuries, to those seeking to raise their qualifications and skills, and to disabled veterans.

In all cases of a dissolution of a labour contract at the initiative of management the prior consent of the local trade union committee is required unless USSR legislation provides otherwise. Failure to obtain consent is grounds for immediate reinstatement. By the same token, the trade union can demand that management dismiss executive personnel for violations of labour legislation or the collective contract or for bureaucratism and red tape. Appeal lies to the superior trade union organ, whose decision is final. Under certain circumstances a severance allowance of two weeks' wages is payable.

The restructuring of the national economy commenced in 1987 is especially directed against imbalances in manning requirements. The transfer of State enterprises to full economic accountability is intended to lead to reductions in the labour force where appropriate, with the risks of frictional unemployment on a larger scale being accepted as inevitable and even, by some economists, desirable. The State civil service is expected to slim down by 25% before the end of the century. Employment centres and retraining programmes are being rapidly expanded with a view to redeploying those released into the job market.

A Soviet citizen taking up employment must submit certain documents, among them his internal passport or appropriate identity document and his labour book. It is illegal for management to require the submission of documents other than those required by law. The labour book records the work experience of its holder at any enterprise, organisation, or institution exceeding five days, whether permanent, seasonal, or temporary, any incentives or awards for success at work, and the reasons for dismissal, with a precise reference to the title and article of legislation under which dismissal was carried out. When a worker leaves employment, the labour book must be issued to him together with any final earnings due. Violations of labour discipline are not recorded in the labour book.

Other aspects of the employment relationship are regulated in detail by the union republic labour codes: work hours, leisure time, wage scales, work norms, guarantees of a job and compensation for business trips, female and child labour, certain privileges and exemptions made available to workers who are studying while employed, and labour safety. Restrictions are imposed on overtime work. The schedule for workers and employees to take their annual leave is negotiated between management and the trade unions. Workers with outstanding records are accorded preference in obtaining housing and preferred holiday periods. Individuals who take up elective posts in State agencies, the CPSU, trade unions, Komsomol, co-operative, and other social organisations have a right to be reinstated in their employment when their term of office expires or to be offered equivalent employment. Workers performing State and social responsibilities, for example, called up for military service, acting as a people's assessor, serving as a delegate to sessions, plenums, and conferences called by State, Party and social organisations, voting, testifying, or serving in people's control agencies, are guaranteed both their position and average earnings when these responsibilities require time off from work.

D. BRIGADES

Although brigades have a history of their own in Soviet industry and agriculture, in their present guise they began to emerge in the mid-1970s and by 1988 encompassed more than 80% of the industrial work force. They function principally on the basis of the 1983 Law on Labour Collectives (Art 18) and a Model Statute confirmed by the State Committee for Labour of the USSR and the Central Trade Union Council, as amended 30 March 1984. Where introduced, the brigade has become the lowest production entity in the enterprise. The brigade contracts with management to perform production planning tasks, the latter no longer being issued to an individual worker. Workers are remunerated for their labour on the basis of the overall results of the brigade's work; and all members of the brigade take part in managing the brigade and in distributing the collective earnings.

The brigade is administered by a brigade leader appointed by management but approved by the brigade council. The leader's instructions are binding upon members. The brigade council is elected by the brigade for a one-year term and includes the brigade leader and trade union organiser within the brigade. The council is competent to discuss almost any aspect of brigade activity, and on issues of personnel and wages its decisions are binding. Although management continues to hire individuals under the labour contract, in practice it 'invites' a potential employee to join a brigade and if the brigade accepts the individual, an order to hire is issued by management. In effect, hiring requires consensus of management and the brigade council, and so does transfer of the employee. Judicial practice has sustained dismissals at brigade initiative when the grounds for dismissal under labour legislation were present.

Earnings are credited by enterprise management to the brigade as a whole. About 60% of brigade earnings are distributed on the basis of an individual's skills and seniority; the balance, treated as bonuses, is distributed at the brigade's discretion, having regard to quality of work, discipline, initiative, attitude, and the like. It follows that the brigade as a whole will suffer for the failure to meet standards, although individuals continue to be liable for disciplinary violations or material harm caused to the enterprise. If management violates its responsibility to the brigade, enterprise statutes commonly provide for an appropriate readjustment of the brigade plan, and the brigade keeps the entire wage fund calculated at tariff rates. However, if the brigade is at fault for failure to meet its production indicators, it is to be paid only for the work it has actually done with no incentive payments. If the brigade has caused loss to the enterprise by producing substandard products, compensation is due to the enterprise from the collective earnings of the brigade, which is then free when distributing its earnings to penalise those individuals within the brigade who were responsible for the loss.

Labour disputes between the brigade and a brigade member are normally first referred to the general meeting of the brigade for settlement. If there is disagreement with the decision, the normal channels for settling such disputes are utilised.

E. LABOUR DISCIPLINE

A combination of persuasion, incentives, social pressure, and disciplinary sanctions are used to ensure labour discipline, increase labour productivity, improve quality, observe technological discipline, safety regulations and industrial hygiene, and protect socialist property. Each enterprise, organisation, or institution has its own rules for internal order established by agreement between management and the local trade union committee on the basis of model rules created usually for each branch of industry but sometimes for certain categories of workers. A variety of incentives are available, from expressions of thanks to the awarding of medals, badges, and honorary titles. Disciplinary sanctions range from a reproof, to reprimand, severe reprimand, transfer to lower-paid work for a period of up to three months, and dismissal. Before a sanction is imposed, explanations must be sought from the offender, and the imposition as a rule must be within one month of the offence. If a year elapses without another disciplinary sanction having been imposed, the worker's original offence is expunged and he is deemed not to have undergone sanctioning. At management's discretion, a violation of labour discipline may be transferred to a comrades' court or social organisation (which for Party members could include the local Party unit) for consideration instead of imposing a disciplinary sanction.

F. LABOUR DISPUTES

A significant portion of the cases heard in people's courts concern labour law. The courts have proved to be zealous guardians of workers and employees, and the fact that court costs are waived and legal assistance must be rendered free of charge by advocates to plaintiffs in labour cases enhances judicial protection. When the numbers of jurisconsults were expanded so rapidly after 1970, one of the reasons adduced was the better advice management would receive in labour disputes. It was expected that the number of illegal dismissals would decline, and indeed many enterprises have reported that to be so.

Four bodies have jurisdiction over labour disputes: commissions for labour disputes organised at enterprises, organisations, and institutions with an equal representation from the trade union and management; the local trade union committees; the district or city people's courts; and for certain categories of workers, superior agencies in the hierarchy of the enterprise concerned. Unless jurisdiction over a labour dispute is expressly referred by law to the courts, the commissions for labour disputes are the primary compulsory instance for deciding the dispute. The details of a commission proceeding are regulated in the Statute on the Procedure for the Consideration of Labour Disputes. Applications are filed by an aggrieved worker or employee with the local trade union committee or organiser and must be heard within five days. The commission is to come to a decision on the basis of agreement between the representatives of management and labour, in which event the decision is binding. Failing agreement in the commission, the worker may apply to the local trade union committee, or appeal to that committee against an unsatisfactory commission decision, within ten days, whereupon the case of appeal must be heard within seven days (the procurator likewise may protest a commission decision to the local trade union committee, or to a people's court when that is the next instance, as contrary to law). If the worker does not concur with the trade union committee decision, he may then appeal to a people's court within nine days; management also may appeal, but only if it believes the decision is contrary to law. If the commission for labour disputes consisted of the enterprise manager and the trade union organiser, the worker may appeal directly to the people's court since there is no intermediate body of appeal.

In addition to acting as an appellate instance in all the examples mentioned above, people's courts hear labour cases at first instance concerning reinstatement against dismissal or amendment of the grounds for dismissal, in situations where there is no local trade union committee or organiser, and concerning suits filed by management against workers seeking compensation for loss caused to the enterprise. The courts also may hear disputes concerning the application of labour legislation already decided in a commission for labour disputes. Reinstatement is required when dismissal has been in violation of law or the procedures for dismissal, or if the worker was transferred illegally. Enforced absence or time spent in lower-paid work must be compensated at the level of average earnings for a period of up to three months. The official who is to blame for an illegal dismissal or transfer is personally liable to the employer for loss caused in connection with reimbursement of lost earnings provided that the dismissal or transfer was a clear violation of the law or if there was delay in reinstating a worker upon a court order or instruction of a superior organisation.[6]

Decisions in such cases must be executed at once. Summary writs of execution are obtainable even by a commission for labour disputes or a local trade union committee if its order in a dispute is not complied with by management.

Many millions of Soviet workers and employees, however, hold positions which appear on 'Lists No. 1 and No. 2'. These individuals by law may not apply to a trade union or a court against an unlawful dismissal or improper disciplinary sanctions applied under individual discipline statutes at their place of employment.

G. TRADE UNIONS

About 140 million Soviet citizens are members of trade unions, virtually every employed person in the country except military personnel and collective farmers. They are organised into about 31 trade unions structured along the same branch lines as the ministries. All the trade unions are members of and subordinate to the All-Union Central Trade Union Council (VTsSPS). The ministerial subordination of the worker's employer is decisive for union membership. Thus, the trade union for education, higher schools, and scientific institutions would encompass personnel at the Academies of Sciences from a full academician down to the beadle, whereas a legal researcher employed by the Ministry of the Maritime Fleet would be a member of the trade union for the maritime and river fleet. Senior management or administrative officials also belong to the trade unions, both at enterprise and ministerial levels. Commonly, senior ministers are elected to central committees of the respective trade unions or even their presidiums. Within each trade union, affairs are administered on an administrative-territorial basis, and the local trade union committees are organised at places of work. Senior trade union posts are in the *nomenklatura* (see chapter 9, above) of Party organs, and lower trade union officials must be confirmed by superior trade union committees.

Since the late 1920s and the advent of national economic planning, Soviet trade unions have given the impression of being the loyal servant of the State and Party rather than an autonomous force defending worker interests. Juridically, trade unions are social organisations exempted by law from registering with State agencies. Soviet citizens have a constitutional right to join trade unions, which must be exercised 'in accordance with the aims of communist construction.' Soviet legislation is completely silent about the right to strike. No such right is guaranteed, but neither are strikes per se unlawful. A Soviet trade union has never called a strike in modern times; when unofficial stoppages have

---

6 For a summary of recent judicial practice relating to such cases, see Soviet Statutes and Decisions XVI (1980) 340–351.

occurred, the usual practice has been to seek out the causes of discontent and dismiss the officials held responsible.

Trade unions are authorised by the FPLabL to represent the interests of workers and employees in the domain of 'production, labour, daily life, and culture.' At local, intermediate, and national levels, they have a voice in drafting and implementing State plans, deciding matters relative to the distribution and use of material and financial resources, involving workers and employees in production management, organising socialist competitions, and furthering production and labour discipline.

The VTsSPS, structured along functional lines which correspond to the basic responsibilities of trade unions, has considerable powers to adopt normative acts either alone or jointly with State and Party bodies (see chapter 4, above). Indeed, the VTsSPS publishes quarterly its own collection of normative decrees and resolutions. With regard to ordinary legislation, the trade unions frequently have representatives on drafting commissions or are asked to comment on drafts prepared by others. The VTsSPS also has a right of legislative initiative under the Soviet constitutions. The State Committee for Prices contains an official representative from the VTsSPS. At lower levels, trade union bodies often enact decrees jointly with ministries of State committees relating to labour matters. At plant level trade unions have assumed almost total responsibility for administering housing, sanatorium passes, State social insurance, and other cultural amenities or matters affecting the daily amenities of workers and employees. Their role in labour discipline and disputes already has been examined; they also oversee the observance of labour legislation and safety and hygiene rules together with special technical and legal inspectorates and other bodies.

Although Soviet trade unions minimise their adversary relationship with management, there seems little doubt that they exert some influence in protecting workers' interests and more in shaping policies affecting workers' interests. On debates regarding general wage policy, the trade unions on the whole seem to have favoured a more egalitarian policy, as opposed to those who would reward better quality and quantity of work by commensurate differentials. Soviet law extends protection to trade union officials in the performance of their duties vis-à-vis management. They may not be transferred to other work, or subjected to a disciplinary penalty, without the prior consent of the local trade union committee or, in the case of the committee chairman or trade union organiser, the consent of the superior trade union agency, which also must approve the dismissal of any trade union officials or organisers.

H. STATE SOCIAL INSURANCE

All workers and employees are subject to State social insurance, which under recent legislation has been extended to collective farmers (see chapter 14, below). Social insurance premiums are paid wholly by the employer and cover temporary incapacity to work, pregnancy and childbirth benefits, old-age and disability pensions, and loss of bread-winner. The trade union organisations administer the social insurance scheme, assign benefits, help prepare documents for assigning pensions, and make recommendations for pensions to the State social insurance agencies.

I. RESPONSIBILITY FOR DAMAGE CAUSED TO ENTERPRISE

Every Soviet citizen has a constitutional duty to protect and care for socialist property. Crimes against socialist ownership are punished under the criminal law, and civil liability attaches on the general grounds to those who cause intentional or negligent damage. Workers and employees in the socialist economy have socialist property placed at their disposal constantly throughout the working day; damage to such property causes harm not merely to the ultimate owner—the State—but also to the collective to whom the property has been entrusted and the collective's capacity to use the property to meet planning targets, earn bonuses, and maximise individual responsibility for every element of the production process. The 1922 RSFSR Labour Code allowed deduction of up to one-third of monthly wages from an employee as a penalty for the failure to observe labour rules which resulted in damage to the enterprise, but if the employer truly wished full compensation, a civil suit had to be filed in the usual way. With the advent of national economic planning and elimination of the private sector in industry, under legislation enacted from 1929–33 and in effect until 1 January 1977 the liability of workers and employees for damage caused to an enterprise was removed from the civil law. A limit was placed on employee liability except in special situations; if the employee agreed to the deduction and the amount, withholdings would commence automatically at once. If the employee disagreed, the matter was referred to a labour disputes commission or in specified instances to the courts. Only damage actually suffered, and not lost profits, was recoverable. Intentional or wanton spoilage of enterprise property could entail compensation of up to five times the damage inflicted. Many of these rules were conceptually linked to criminal responsibility imposed in the 1930–50s for labour violations.

The FPLabL and union republic labour codes laid down a new framework for employee compensation in such cases, the procedures for which were elaborated in the 1976 Statute on Material Responsibility of Workers and Employees for Damage Caused to an Enterprise, Institution, or

Organisation. The trade unions had a major role in drafting the Statute.

Cases of employee compensation are, as noted above, heard at first instance by people's courts. In 1978 the Plenum of the USSR Supreme Court indicated that such cases comprised 6% of the total number of cases decided in courts and 70% of all labour cases. Judgment was awarded to the plaintiff in 86% of the cases, but of those judgments appealed, nearly 25% were vacated or modified by higher courts. The Statute requires that compensation be made if a worker or employee is at fault in causing damage and if direct real damage is present. Damage arising from normal production or economic risk is not subject to compensation.

Example. A people's court denied recovery to a bauxite mine which sued a worker for 70 rubles, alleging that through his fault the strengthening of the face in the mine gave way during blasting operations, causing a slide and loss of 55 tons of ore. In denying recovery, the court noted that the ore had not been extracted, no monies had been spent by the plaintiff on extraction, and lost revenues were not subject to compensation under the law.

It is still open for a worker or employee to acknowledge his liability and voluntarily pay compensation, repair the damage, or transfer property of equal value to the enterprise. In practice, the legal requirement that management sue if the employee will not voluntarily pay compensation is resulting in enterprises writing off small losses in the belief that bringing suit is too costly in time and trouble. The employee remains liable for damage irrespective of whether he is subject to disciplinary, administrative, or criminal responsibility.

The Statute retains the basic guideline of limiting responsibility for damage caused in the execution of labour duties to 100% of the employee's monthly wage. Negligence resulting in the damage or destruction of materials, semi-finished products, or manufactures, tools, measuring devices, special clothing, and the like are subject to compensation at the same level of average monthly earnings. Officials bear the same level of financial liability for damage caused by their fault, up to their full monthly salary, and separately, as noted above, for illegally dismissing or transferring a worker, up to three month's salary. Full material responsibility for damage caused applies when the worker has expressly assumed such responsibility under a written contract, or the property was received under a special power of attorney or similar document, when the damage was caused by a criminal act actually prosecuted, or the damage was caused by shortages or intentional damage or destruction, or Soviet legislation specially provides for full responsibility, or the damage was not caused in the performance of labour duties. When the combination of labour duties performed by a worker makes it difficult to distinguish between full and limited material responsibility, eg a worker both uses and has formal custody over materials, collective or brigade responsibility may be utilised. Soviet courts have found it difficult to distinguish between the two categories in practice.

Example. A people's court recovered compensation from the manager of a medical storehouse for allowing meat to spoil in the amount of two-thirds of his monthly salary because the meat was regarded as a semi-finished product intended for consumption. The superior court imposed full responsibility because the manager was wholly liable for the safekeeping of the meat by virtue of his position.

Damage is assessed on the basis of balance sheet value or cost of production, deducting wear and tear at the established rates. If material valuables are stolen, missing, or intentionally damaged or destroyed, damage is assessed at State retail prices or by a procedure laid down by the State Price Committee of the USSR. Special procedures are invoked if actual damage exceeds nominal amounts. Unless the damage was caused by a crime committed for a mercenary purpose, a court may reduce the amount of damage subject to compensation by taking into account the degree of fault, specific circumstances, and the financial position of the worker.[7] The courts also need to have regard to the opinion of the labour collective or production brigade on the question of the worker paying compensation.

Proof of fault has caused difficulties in judicial practice where certain persons are presumed by law to be materially responsible for loss or damage, eg shortages or spoilage of material valuables. The courts allow in such situations the worker to prove that he was not at fault.

Example. A people's court granted recovery against a goods despatcher in the amount of 535 rubles for a shortage of products which occurred during transport. The trial court proceeded from the fact of the shortage and the contract of full material responsibility concluded with the despatcher. The defendant argued the shortage occurred not by his fault, but because the goods were shipped in unsuitable motor vehicles, one of which had overturned, and management, despite being notified, did nothing to protect the goods for 96 hours, and that because of damage to the overturned vehicle outside persons had access to the goods. The RSFSR Supreme Court reversed the decision and held the people's court must verify whether the defendant's arguments were correct, and if so, deny recovery to the plaintiff.

Despite the USSR Supreme Court's indication that cases for compensation are an appreciable percentage of all labour cases heard by courts, recent commentary by jurists argues that the 1976 Statute leans too far in the direction of the worker or employee. A principal object of the

---

7 Surveys of judicial practice in 1978 disclosed that the amount of compensation was reduced by courts in about one-third of the cases in which recovery was awarded. The Decree of the Plenum of the USSR Supreme Court of 23 September 1977 on the application of the 1976 Statute was amended precisely ten years later, on 23 September 1987, to tighten the procedures for hearing cases of this type.

legislation is to 'ensure an attitude of care by workers and employees toward socialist ownership' and improve enterprise profitability, yet management seems disposed to write off small claims rather than bring suit. The Procuracy has increasingly taken the initiative to bring suits for compensation and blames management for neglecting its legal duty to do so. With regard to suits filed against executive personnel for damage to State property, only 5% were filed by the enterprises and the balance presumably by the Procuracy. To be sure, this figure concerns executives, and it may well be that an enterprise management finds it easier to bring suit against workers and employees than against executive personnel. Nevertheless, there remains concern that a cost-effective approach to bringing compensation suits may undermine the educative role of law in inculcating respect and care for State property. Some jurists propose that compensation for small sums to which a worker does not agree be removed from court jurisdiction and placed in the labour disputes commissions, whose decisions a worker might appeal through the trade union in the usual way.

J. CO-OPERATIVES AND INDIVIDUAL LABOUR ACTIVITY

Involving under-utilised 'labour reserves' in the work force and improving the quality and availability of consumer goods and services are two objectives of restructuring which have led to a renewed emphasis upon the formation of co-operatives and the authorisation of individual labour activity. While both have been tolerated in the past, they were not encouraged and suffered under myriad legal restrictions. In 1987 legislation was enacted to encourage the creation of co-operatives for public dining, the production of consumer goods, the rendering of domestic services to the general public, the procurement and processing of secondary raw materials, the manufacture of confectioneries and pastries, and the sale of goods produced by co-operatives or individuals. The co-operatives as a rule are formed by citizen initiative, principally pensioners, housewives, students, and pupils, but a co-operative may hire individuals in their spare time who otherwise are gainfully employed in the national economy.

Co-operatives are eligible for long- and short-term credits to obtain circulating assets and may lease or be given rent-free premises and other fixed assets. The co-operatives are expected to be fully self-supporting, to work out their own plans for economic operations and submit them to the agency which created them, and to pay an income tax to the local budget at the prescribed rates. Local soviets of people's deputies register the charters of co-operatives and are instructed by law to assist them in various ways. Co-operative members may use their personal automobiles, premises, equipment, and tools to perform tasks for the co-operative and may be remunerated for doing so. State social insurance extends to co-operative members, and co-operatives are required to pay contributions at the same rates as State co-operatives.

A co-operative is defined as an 'organisation of citizens of the USSR who have voluntarily united on the basis of collective labour and self-management' to jointly perform designated tasks. At least three Soviet citizens aged 16 or above are required to form a co-operative on condition of contributing their own labour to its operations. A member has the right to work in the co-operative, to receive wages from co-operative revenues subject to distribution in accordance with the quantity and quality of labour invested, and to take full part in managing the co-operative. Each member has his own labour book kept exactly as it is for ordinary workers and employees.

The co-operative also may hire individuals under a labour agreement. The employment of these persons is regulated by Soviet labour legislation in the usual way and is remunerated at least once a month. Salary claims of those employed under a labour agreement take precedence over earnings due to co-operative members. The duration of the work day, days off, annual and supplemental leave, the minimum labour contribution required of each member, and other labour issues are governed for members by the Charter of the co-operative and the co-operative's internal labour rules. The general meeting of the co-operative is empowered to impose sanctions on those who violate internal labour rules; disputes concerning payment for labour, compensation for harm causing injury, impairment of health, or death of a bread-winner, or compensation for damage to the co-operative caused by a co-operative member are considered by a court. Other disputes of co-operative members arising in connection with their activities in the co-operative are decided by the co-operative chairman or the general meeting.

The general meeting—the highest organ of the co-operative—consists of all the members and meets at least twice a year. It adopts or amends the Charter; elects a chairman and auditor; admits and expels members; adopts the internal labour rules; approves the co-operative plan, expenditure estimates, processing norms, prices, remuneration rates, and deductions for the co-operative development fund; confirms the annual report; and winds up the co-operative, amongst other functions.

As of 1 January 1988 more than 15,000 co-operatives had been formed employing more than 150,000 persons. All types of activity and profession were represented—cafés, architects, photographers, handicrafts, bakeries, hairdressers, etc. They were slow to develop in rural areas, however, and often encountered obstacles and inertia from local government and ministries, or failed to draw upon proper resources when conducting their operations. On the whole, though, the reaction is a positive one and they are likely to continue to multiply.

In 1988 the entire scheme of Soviet co-operatives, including collective farms, was subjected to regulation by a general Law on Co-operative

Societies in the USSR. The Law substantially clarified and enlarged their rights, duties, and functions in furtherance of the 1987 economic reforms. The co-operative members and employees are governed by the 1983 Law on Labour Collectives as well as by the co-operative charter. No special authorisation is required to form a co-operative, but the co-operative charter, once adopted by the founding individuals, must be registered at the local soviet executive committee; the co-operative is legally in existence from the date of registration. The 1988 Law defines the relationships of co-operatives with State, Party, and economic agencies or enterprises, their right to engage in foreign economic activity, distinctive features of certain forms of co-operative, and the principles for co-operatives to carry on their economic operations (planning, prices, revenue distribution, taxation, finance and banking, and supply).

Whereas co-operatives amount to the expansion or introduction of labour activity not previously engaged in, the legislation on individual labour activity adopted on 19 November 1986 with effect from 1 May 1987 undertakes to regulate an area of human endeavour previously of considerable uncertainty. The key legal requirement is registration of all such activity with the local soviet except 'creative activities of citizens in the domain of science, technology, literature, and art, as well as the performance of paid work of a one-off nature and of work insignificant in amount or rate paid.' Individual labour activity may be authorised for persons in their spare time who are otherwise gainfully employed, housewives, disabled persons, pensioners, students, and pupils, or other persons not engaged in social production as appropriate. As in the case of co-operatives, local soviets are to assist individuals in obtaining raw materials, tools, premises, information, etc. Citizens are especially encouraged to contract to render such services to enterprises. Revenues from individual labour activity are subject to income tax; in some cases citizens may seek a 'patent' granting them the right to perform services. These are usually issued when the services are performed at various locations or times (taxi service, house repairs, photography). In this case the patent-holder pays an annual lump-sum fee to the local soviet for the right to operate and is exempt from income tax. Under 1988 amendments, the payment for the patent may be reduced or waived by local soviets.

The legislation on individual labour activity contains exemplary lists of approved and prohibited activities. Often the applicant will be required to meet minimum standards of education, training, or proficiency. A translator, for example, will normally need at least three years of higher education to be registered. Prohibited activities include the teaching of subjects or courses that are not included in the instructional plans of general education schools or of vocational-technical or secondary specialised and higher educational institutions of the USSR.

Chapter 13
Economic law

The quantity of legislation regulating the national economy in the Soviet Union is stupendous by any standard. It would not be implausible to say that the total number of normative acts at all levels concerned with socialist economic relations exceeds all other normative acts together. The pure bulk of legislation catalysed efforts in the late 1960s to consolidate and systematise all of Soviet legislation, culminating finally in the Digests of Laws (*svody zakonov*) of the USSR and each union republic issued in the 1980s. These law reform measures refuelled a debate about the relationship between law and the economy which dated back to the early days of the Soviet revolution, re-emerged in the early 1930s with the introduction of national economic planning, and was revived and seemingly put to rest in discussions preceding the 1961 FPCivL. In the late 1960s the debate centred on the drafting of an economic code as part of or prelude to the processing of economic legislation, but far-reaching issues of economic policy and reform implicit in these discussions led eventually to the decision taken at the XXVII Party Congress (1986) to restructure the national economy by further decentralisation of economic management.

Economic law or civil law

In 1917–18 Soviet policy-makers had little opportunity to reflect on the role of law in a future socialising economy. Some entertained naive assumptions about the rapid withering away of law and the legal system, but survival of the regime in the midst of civil strife and a hostile international community quickly took precedence over any grandiose transition to a new economic order. Morever, transformation of the private sector into a socialised economy was accomplished by law. Economic collapse required the mixed approach of the NEP, and as it happened gave an opportunity for economic analytical techniques such as input-output analysis to develop as tools for comprehending intersectoral relationships in the economy, so essential for economic planning. When the initial transition to planning was made during the late 1920s in the midst of prolonged debates about industrialisation strategy among Soviet economists, the group of Soviet Marxist jurists in the ascendancy, led by E. B. Pashukanis, counselled the rapid elimination of Romanist legal concepts—legal personality, contract, mutual rights and duties, ownership—associated with the NEP in the belief that vertical technical regulations based on Plan would suffice to manage the operation of production entities and the distribution of goods and services. Those views were rejected in the mid-1930s by the Soviet leadership and have played no evident role since.

Nevertheless, the legal and administrative structure that did emerge in the 1930s had produced, largely by separate legislation outside the 1922 RSFSR Civil Code, a body of planning, administrative, financial, property, contract, and enterprise law which many Soviet jurists believed in the late 1950s should be dealt with as a special branch of law outside the civil law. An intense debate broke out in connection with the drafting of the FPCivL. Those who favoured 'economic law' preferred a truncated civil law dealing only with the relations of citizens inter se and with socialist organisations. The civilists accepted the sui generis character of the planning and administrative aspects of relations of socialist organisations, but argued that these could be analytically distinguished from the civil-law dimension of these relations and that there was real merit in preserving the civil-law unity of horizontal relationships, whether between enterprises or citizens. So evenly drawn were the protagonists in the discussions that reportedly a formal debate was held before the late A. N. Kosygin by representatives of both views. The decision favoured the civilists, and the 1961 FPCivL seemed to have put an end to the issue by incorporating the horizontal regulation of the planned economy into the general body of legal rules governing interpersonal relations.

In fact, the debate had only begun. No sooner were the union republic civil codes enacted in 1963–64 than the issue re-emerged. By 1967 economic law was acknowledged to be a branch of legal science; textbooks were produced, economic law was officially approved as a specialisation in law faculties, and an economic law sector was formed within the Institute of State and Law of the USSR Academy of Sciences. The economic reforms of the post-Khrushchev era seemed to have injected a renewed vitality into the proponents of economic law. On 4 April 1969 the Social Sciences Section of the Presidium of the USSR Academy of Sciences authorised the preparation of a draft USSR Economic Code 'as a generalised law consolidating the new forms and methods of the economy and leading to a uniform system of normative acts for economic legislation.'[1] The draft, published for discussion in 1970, foreshadowed a number of economic measures enacted in the subsequent five years. As work proceeded on the Digests of Laws, the debate about an economic

---

1 See W. E. Butler (ed and transl.) 'Economic Code of the USSR (Draft of Basic Provisions)' Soviet Statutes and Decisions XII (1976) 433–483.

code intensified. The majority of Soviet jurists seemed to favour adoption. The legislator, however, was content to consolidate and systematise existing economic legislation. It remains to be seen whether the systematisation is a prelude to comprehensive codification or will suffice as an end in itself.

Economic management from NEP to 1965

The introduction of national economic planning was followed in the early 1930s by a series of measures intended to make State enterprises accountable for their activity and to enhance the powers of the planners over the allocation of resources. What has transpired since by way of 'reform' has largely represented an adjustment of the mechanism and not a fundamental reconceptualisation. In 1931 the essential attributes of legal personality in the form of economic accountability (*khozraschet*) were conferred on enterprises, each of which was to be responsible for its liabilities out of its assets and to conclude contracts in its own name. To guard against capricious use of their autonomy, the enterprises were subjected to sundry forms of supervision and control: contracts had to meet conditions laid down by planning agencies; funds and credit were disposed of through banks; local contracts came to be boiler-plate documents elaborating general contracts concluded by chief administrations of ministries, and as planning became yet more specific, the general and local contracts were supplanted by direct inter-enterprise contracts which only cosmetically strengthened enterprise autonomy. The Second World War brought an almost completely centrally directed economy operating on the basis of planning orders. In 1949 the pre-war scheme of general and local contracts was reinstated, but centralised planning continued to be pre-eminent.[2] Conceptually, the system of economic management encouraged the myth of the 'command economy' under which ideally the planners were able to comprehend all sectoral and intersectoral linkages and by concentrating resources, labour, and capital appropriately to stimulate industrial growth in those sectors accorded priority. In reality, the planners had no such command of the economy, and as the economy became increasingly large and complex, the conviction grew that a keener appreciation of economic efficiency for each entity was to be attained at lower levels than at the commanding heights. Vast ministerial empires administering branches of industry throughout the land found it cumbersome and inexpedient to develop interbranch, intersectoral, or territorial links with organisations under other ministries. Anecdotes abound of enterprises in remote areas of the Soviet

2 O. S. Ioffe 'Law and Economy in the USSR' Harvard Law Review XCV (1982) 1591–1625.

Union situated literally across the road from one another which were obliged to transact via Moscow with all the attendant delays and frustrations. For both political and economic reasons regional economic councils were introduced in 1957 to co-ordinate economic planning and policy within economic regions and replace the chief administrations of the economic ministries. The councils did not enter into general contracts, but the direct contracts reintroduced in their place continued to be along the 1930s model and planning, to be extremely detailed. Ministerial autarchy and localism was replaced by regional localism to some extent. Within each economic region, branch and functional administrations were formed, preserving elements of the old ministerial system. The bureaucratic process actually became prolonged in some respects, even though trade within each region was freed from branch departmental obstacles. The scheme as a whole was short-lived, and the councils were abolished in 1964.

Economic management from 1965 to 1987

In Autumn 1965 the Soviet leadership enacted a series of decrees intended to stimulate economic growth and streamline economic planning and management. Planning from the centre was to become simpler and more general. Indicators of economic performance were altered. Enterprise autonomy in planning, contract, and legal personality was to be enhanced, and the exercise of that autonomy was to be disciplined increasingly by the parties to contracts through recourse to State Arbitrazh, the agency with exclusive jurisdiction over economic disputes (see chapter 7, above). In order to exercise and defend their rights under economic legislation, enterprises were to have professional legal staff or to contract with advocates for legal services; hence the numbers of legal personnel were substantially enlarged in the 1970s and access to a cohesive body of economic legislation through systematisation and codification was believed to be a matter of priority. A key document in the 1965 reform was the Statute on the Socialist Production Enterprise. The late 1960s saw many branches of industry and services gradually brought within the scope of the 1965 Statute and placed on economic accountability.

A. PRODUCTION ENTITIES

Three features, one could say with certainty, distinguish a socialist economic organisation from an administrative body: economic accountability, legal personality, and property rights. As a method for organising economic activity, economic accountability means that when a production entity is created it is allocated basic and circulating assets by the State for the purpose of producing and selling goods or services for money in amounts sufficient to cover expenses and leave an 'accumulation' or 'profit.' The financial position of a production entity accordingly is dependent directly upon its performance, measured by such factors or indicators as production costs, prices, profits, profitability, labour productivity, and others. Unless for some overriding policy reason an enterprise is subsidised by the State or planned to make a loss, it must cover its costs from its revenues.

Each production entity operating on economic accountability with an independent balance sheet and with basic and circulating assets enjoys legal personality under the FPCivL and the 1965 Statute on the State enterprise. In March 1973 a further economic reform was initiated to encourage an amalgamation of production, construction, design, research, repair, and other entities under a single umbrella called an 'association.' There are various types of association, each of which has its own legal personality, but all contain within them some entities, such as production enterprises, which retain their own legal personality, and other entities which can act only in the name of the association as a whole. The legal capacity of each juridical person is defined in a charter confirmed by the creating agency. As in Anglo-American law, a Soviet juridical person may conclude those legal transactions which are within the scope of its charter purposes and subject matter. The State is not liable for the debts of juridical persons, and vice versa, nor for debts of other juridical persons unless assumed by contract, nor for the debts of the organisation to which the juridical person is administratively subordinate.

The property of a juridical person is within its 'operative management' and must be used in furtherance of the entity's purposes and in accordance with legislation. Soviet legislation imposes highly specific requirements upon the disposition of assets by a production entity, and upon the goods and services produced by the entity through plan and planned contracts. All dimensions of enterprise autonomy, consequently, have no independent raison d'etre; they exist conditionally to serve a larger economic purpose or function within the planned economy.

The 1965 reforms sought to strike a different balance between centralised planning and production entity independence. According to an oft-quoted remark uttered by A. N. Kosygin when the 1965 reform legislation was enacted, '. . . one must give up the habitual notion that in mutual economic relations between economic agencies and enterprises, the former only have rights and the latter, merely duties.' The new balance was reflected especially in the kinds of economic performance indicators to be fixed for a production entity by a superior organisation and in enlarged rights for the entity to determine its own operations. Among the plan indicators were the following:

(a) total sales volume to be measured in gross units produced (and not value) in order to encourage enterprises to cease producing items not in demand, improve product quality, increase sales, avoid surplus stocks, and plan production carefully;
(b) list of product types (*nomenklatura*) confirmed at planning, administrative, and enterprise levels with a view to ensuring the proper proportion of product types in the economy as a whole;
(c) wage fund and labour productivity, to be calculated by the enterprise within certain allocations fixed by superior agencies;
(d) profit, accumulated from reductions in production costs, labour productivity, increased sales, and fixed by the enterprise;
(e) profitability, the ratio of profits to basic and circulating assets, which was intended to encourage the disposal of surplus assets;
(f) budget payments and allocations. Stipulated percentages of enterprise profits were paid to the State budget as a return upon basic and circulating assets. The enterprise was encouraged to seek greater profit on a base of smaller production funds;
(g) introduction of new technology, representing the mastery and assimilation of new product types, automation, technology, and the like, usually on the basis of planning tasks.

Certain other plan indicators were worked out exclusively at enterprise level and need not be approved by superior organisations. Once planning tasks were confirmed, changes were supposed to be made by a superior organisation only as an exception, after preliminary discussion with enterprise management, and on condition that respective modifications were made in all interrelated plan indicators and budget accounts. Production technology was determined by the enterprise within the limits of confirmed plan indicators unless uniform standards are fixed for a particular industry. Modification was possible if quality would be increased or production costs reduced without adversely affecting quality or State standards. Goods exceeding quality standards could be issued if the customer consented. Enterprises could contract with design or other organisations to prepare modernisation designs or improve production either at their own expense or from bank credits.

Supply of raw materials and equipment became slightly more flexible. The 1965 Statute on the State enterprise introduced as an innovation a limited right of refusal for products allocated to it by giving timely notification. The supplying organisation was then free to direct the unneeded materials or products to other users.

B. PLAN

Under the 1965 reform national economic plans became less detailed. Prior to 1965, there were three basic methods of planning economic obligations. The first entailed the customers specifying their needs to the planning authorities, who then incorporated these in an appropriate plan and expected that those to whom the plan was addressed would conclude the requisite contracts with one another. This system was used most extensively for transport and the delivery of goods. The second method had the customer place orders directly with producing enterprises, who then incorporated these orders into the plan for the forthcoming year, and once the plan was approved, the appropriate contracts would be concluded. This method was used for certain types of consumer goods. The third approach involved the enterprise estimating consumer demand for the forthcoming period, but the estimates were not legally binding unless and until they were incorporated in the plan as a basis for concluding contracts. This method was used for construction investment, most of which was financed from the State budget, although enterprise-financed construction now may use the first or second method.

The economic reform legislation provided for greater application of the second approach. Once production levels were approved by planning authorities, having due regard to orders accepted, the enterprise worked out a final production plan and, for those products distributed on a planned basis, a supply plan. This approach required many enterprise managers to adapt to factors of fashion and demand in ways to which they were unaccustomed. In some instances the State found it easier to revert to more detailed planning.

C. CONTRACT

To the extent that detailed economic planning was curtailed after 1965 in the interests of enterprise autonomy and initiative, the role of contract, in this case, economic contracts, was enhanced. The expression 'economic contracts' is widely used as a general denominator encompassing civil-law contracts concluded between socialist organisations, eg contract of delivery, contract for the procurement of agricultural produce, capital construction contract, contract for the performance of scientific research and design work, and others. Most such contracts are concluded pursuant to a planning task, that is, are 'planned contracts' which the parties specified in the plan must conclude with one another within a specified period by agreeing the few conditions left to their discretion. If the parties cannot agree, a 'pre-contractual dispute' exists and is within the jurisdiction of State Arbitrazh (see chapter 7, above). Planning tasks issued by superior agencies to production entities were not sufficient to regulate inter-enterprise relations for several reasons: (1) the economic contract imparts specific detail to the planning task (quantity, assortment, quality, delivery dates and terms) which the planners cannot feasibly determine; (2) when concluding economic contracts, enterprises also have regard to their concerns as economically accountable agencies and presumably respond rationally to adjustments of their production and economic relationships in a manner that the planners could not; and (3) an economic contract enables enterprises to effectuate mutual control over contractual performance and take autonomous actions (filing suit, etc) in the event of breach. The FPCivL and civil codes, however, only regulate economic contracts in a basic sense. The provisions of economic contracts also are governed by a host of special enactments, for example, statutes on the delivery of consumer goods and of producer goods, transport statutes, model statutes for research contracts, and special conditions for the delivery of individual products or product-types. These enactments are incorporated into economic contracts by reference as boiler-plate clauses. The great dependence of economic contracts upon planning tasks and linkage with imperative legislation has led many observers to suggest they are not 'contracts' in the ordinary sense of the term but merely the ultimate extension of the planning task.

Certain sectors of the Soviet economy functioned with minimal or no planning tasks. In the absence of a planning task for goods or products exempted from such, an economic contract may be concluded by agreement of the parties. These are called 'unplanned' or 'non-plan' economic contracts, and they expose the producing enterprise to market demand for its goods. If an enterprise operating with unplanned contracts is to fulfil its performance indicators, it must produce and sell goods that customers demand and find the customers itself. Ideally, such an enterprise will have regard to consumer taste, fashion, needs, and even price.

The 1965 economic reforms introduced greater flexibility into contracts of delivery. Reference already has been made to the customer's right of refusal to accept all or part of his allotment of goods or products under a planning task by giving appropriate notice. State Arbitrazh practice sometimes has been willing to waive the ten-day notice period. The conditions of the delivery contract left for party negotiation were expanded as a concomitant of enhanced enterprise autonomy, and State Arbitrazh was granted enlarged powers to modify delivery contracts in the course of performance by reason of changed requirements.

Economic contracts are concluded in writing, signed by an authorised representative of each party, or by exchange of letters, cables, or confirmation of a customer order. In the case of contracts of delivery, the practice is widespread of parties accepting an allocation order under a planning task by simply allowing the period for reply to lapse. Economic contracts may be concluded for a specified period, usually one year subject to extension, or for a specific service. Usually the supplier or seller drafts the contract. If a planned contract, he is obliged to send the draft to the customer for signature within 20–30 days of receiving the planning task. In some cases delay in concluding a contract may entail penalties.

Although the commentators commonly say that economic contracts should contain all the requisite terms for mutual contractual relations (subject of the contract, a detailed description of the goods, quality and quantity, terms and procedure for performance, price and form of payment, liability for failure to perform), Soviet law provides no exhaustive list of such clauses, except for transport contracts, which are governed by an extraordinary morass of rules. Otherwise, contracts may contain such provisions as are not contrary to law.

The quality provisions must conform to State standards and technical conditions. Sets must be complete and guarantee periods designated. The law also lays down certain general requirements equally applicable to economic contracts: first, obligations must be performed properly and within the period prescribed by law, the planning task, or the contract. Penalties for late or improper performance are no substitute for specific performance; second, unilateral repudiation or modification of obligations is permitted only in exceptional situations, as for example the issuance of sub-standard goods or delayed deliveries; and third, when performing contracts each party must carry out its duties as economically as possible from the standpoint of the national economy and give all possible co-operation to the other party, for example, by refraining from delivering more expensive goods to the buyer. Sub-contracting is very common, but the enterprise concluding the basic contract is still responsible.[3]

Accounts are paid through the USSR State Bank or the Construction Bank. Obligations are considered to be performed on the date the products are shipped by the supplier or seller or on the date when a document certifying the completion of work is handed over to the customer organisation (usually in construction contracts), on condition that the provisions of law and contract have been complied with in full. Bonuses sometimes are paid for the completion or performance ahead of schedule of major economic contracts or rapid transport.

D. PRODUCTION ASSOCIATIONS

In 1973-74 further economic reforms were undertaken whose meaning is widely debated. The chief result of the reform was the formation of various types of 'production association,' a kind of umbrella economic entity integrating State production enterprises with other horizontal components of the production process: research and design, repair, construction, marketing, and others. The functions and jurisdiction of the associations were governed by the General Statute on All-Union and Republic Industrial Associations, the Statute on the Production Association (or Combine), the Statute on the Scientific-Production

3 On the 1965 economic reforms in action, see O. S. Ioffe and P. B. Maggs *Soviet Law in Theory and Practice* (1983) pp 190-224.

Association, and the Statute on the Production Association in Agriculture, among others.

The industrial associations act as administrative and co-ordinating organs for their constituent entities by setting planning targets and issuing instructions. To introduce economies of scale, they may centralise certain functions on behalf of all constituent entities, for example, construction, design, and research. The production associations within the industrial associations have legal personality and operate on the basis of economic accountability; they are comprised principally of various State enterprises, most of which retain their separate legal identity but nevertheless in some respects operate with reduced prerogatives assumed by the production association. The latter is empowered to centralise wholly or in part the performance of individual production and economic functions of independent enterprises and organisations comprising a part thereof. Under the 1973–74 legislation, the production association was conceived as the primary industrial entity in the Soviet Union.

Some observers interpreted the 1973–74 reforms as a complete reversal of those instituted in 1965:

The reform did not merely transfer legal and economic independence from one level to another ... The 1973–1974 reforms constituted a radical restructuring that moved the system back from economic independence to economic subordination.[4]

To the western student of corporate organisation, the 1973–74 reforms would seem to have merely integrated horizontal elements of production that the Soviet system for some peculiar reason had kept separated. The functions of enterprise independence were principally elevated to the production association or even the industrial association, and it was by no means evident that the virtues of economic decentralisation operated intrinsically better at production enterprise level as compared with a higher degree of horizontal corporate integration. If the 1974 reforms did represent a transition back to greater economic subordination, one would expect to find the evidence in the relationship between the planning and administrative organs, on one hand, and the industrial and/or production associations on the other. Although there is some indication of reverting to more detailed planning tasks on the part of administrative agencies, the evidence is to date inconclusive insofar as a complete retreat from the 1965 approach.

Judging the balance between reform and retrenchment, it should be added, was complicated enormously by other measures pursued by the Soviet leadership. Implicit in our discussion of legal personality and economic accountability was a sharp distinction between 'producer'

---

4 Ioffe, note 2 above, p 1623.

organisations that require these concepts to help regulate their economic operations and 'administrative' bodies that as State organs direct as best they can their subordinate entities in an administrative capacity. Since 1980 on an experimental basis the concept of economic accountability has been extended to a few ministries as such as a means of assessing their economic performance. Should that practice prove to be useful, the traditional distinctions between administration and production are likely to become more blurred, just as is the distinction between State and collective farm in the person of the 1982 agro-industrial associations.

The concept of economic law

Proponents of economic law find the present bifurcation of civil law governing horizontal relations and several branches of law (administrative, financial, budgetary, transport, and others) governing vertical relations extremely unsatisfactory. They seek a single code of law to integrate the regulation of both horizontal and vertical relationships. The traditional branches of law break up what in their eyes is a fundamental unity.

As developed in the 1970s, economic law encompassed all 'economic relations' arising in the process of directing and carrying on economic activities, having a planned character, and connected with the management of socialist ownership. The 'participants' in economic relations included enterprises, economic associations, so-called 'agencies of economic direction,' other socialist organisations, as well as the sub-divisions of an economic agency. Excluded were relations in which a citizen participated and relations between socialist organisations that fell purely under administrative law as distinct from those with a planning, organisational, or property element. Neither did economic law embrace budget, tax, land, water, mining, forestry, or foreign trade relations, nor collective farm relations arising out of their charters.

The traditional civil law concept of legal capacity, it was contemplated, would be supplanted by a new concept called 'economic competence,' by which was meant the aggregate economic rights and duties appertaining to an organisation or its sub-division. Those rights and duties might be acquired through legislation or as the result of performing specific legal actions. Most 'participants in economic relations' would be classified as 'economic agencies,' and the last might include entities superior to others (ie, not juridically equal). Agencies of economic direction could qualify as economic agencies for these purposes.

An economic agency would have the right of possession over property in its operative management or ownership, an independent balance sheet or estimate, the right to acquire and exercise economic rights and duties in its own name, responsibility for the results of its activities, and the possibility of recourse to defend its rights. Economic law would govern the procedure for creating them, confirming their statutes or charters, exercising their competence, and the representation, reorganisation, and winding up of all types of economic agency, whether State, co-operative, or social. All economic agencies would operate as independent subjects of law.

Agencies of economic direction would include economic ministries or departments, chief administrations, executive committees of local soviets, central organs of co-operative systems, and other economic agencies to which enterprises or associations are subordinate. They were to be distinguished from 'functional' agencies of economic direction—planning agencies, State Arbitrazh, State committees, and other agencies—empowered to issue binding instructive regulations to economic agencies without interfering in their operational activities and in the absence of a subordinate relationship. Such functional bodies were not deemed to be 'economic agencies.'

The property of economic agencies would be regulated along the general lines of constitutional and civil legislation prevailing in the 1970s with the addition of provisions governing rights to centralised funds and reserves and to the disposal of property according to Plan as distinct from the exercise of operative management rights. Detailed regulation was contemplated for the various production funds, finished goods, and circulating assets, but restrictions on enterprises would be relaxed for the distribution of several types of property. The enterprise in this respect would acquire, greater autonomy and opportunity to streamline its operations. Economic agencies would be granted the power to protect their property rights, including possession, against superior agencies of economic direction.

The proponents of economic law undertook to formulate the basic tasks and principles of planning, including the propositions that planning must be scientifically well-founded, proportional, stable, and must have regard for the independence of economic agencies. According legal stature to these principles, it was believed, would enable criteria to be developed for planning and the consequences of violations to be assessed. Even draft plans, under this approach, would take on a certain legal significance. Agencies of economic direction would be prohibited from notifying unbalanced plan indicators to enterprises, and an adjustment would be made if the plan indicator for a branch of the economy as a whole were unbalanced. Changes in plans would have to meet stricter procedural requirements before being introduced, and reciprocal duties to pay compensation arising out of plan modifications would be imposed on both agencies of economic direction and production entities. Supplementing planning tasks would be allowed only through modifying the basic plan. If the criteria for the legality of planning acts were violated, the recipient entity would be given the right to contest them before the issuing body and, if necessary, to appeal to State Arbitrazh. Until the planning act was formally declared void, however, the recipient agency would be obliged to execute it.

New categories of 'economic obligations' were developed to encompass obligations between socialist organisations regulated by civil legislation, intra-economic relations between sub-divisions of an economic agency, and economic-management relations formed when directing the economy. The delivery of a product, the performance of work, the rendering of services, or the performance of other economic activities by one economic agency for the benefit of another would be possible, as a rule, on the basis of an economic contract and exceptionally on a non-contractual basis.

Some imaginative ideas were put forward in respect of economic sanctions. Plan funds, for example, might be altered to the benefit of a prejudiced enterprise at the expense of the offending enterprise, for example, increasing the wage fund of the injured enterprise at the expense of the wage fund of the offender if the injured party incurred greater wage costs in consequence of the breach. Conditional recovery of losses was considered as a sanction to ensure that the implications of losses would be fully reflected in annual accounts. The elements of loss also would be expanded so that superior agencies would be liable to compensate losses of a subordinate enterprise in the interests of responsibility and economic accountability.

Although an economic code still has not commended itself to the Soviet legislator, the ideas and approaches developed by the economic lawyers in many cases did find favour.[5] The 1970 draft economic code provisions on economic associations foreshadowed the 1973-74 reform legislation. Many reforms in State Arbitrazh introduced in 1974, 1979, and 1987 were presaged by the draft code. Placing ministries and departments partly on economic accountability doubtless owed much to the economic law school, as does the view that enterprises should be able to engage in economic activities both directly relegated to their competence and all other activities not prohibited by legislation. But economic law accentuates centralised direction of the economy through Plan; the approach to restructuring the national economy chosen in 1986-87 accentuates an enterprise-oriented economy with less directive planning and greater reliance on competition, economic autonomy, and enterprise responsibility.

5 This discussion of economic law is based largely on the 1970 draft economic code. See note 1 above. In February 1984 the Presidium of the USSR Academy of Sciences authorised further work on a draft economic code. The leading theoretician of economic law, Academician V. Laptev, outlines his concepts in *Economic Law* (1987), but none of the restructuring reforms are taken into account.

Restructuring economic legislation

The programmatic case for restructuring (*perestroika*) the national economy adopted by the XXVII Party Congress (1986) followed years of legal and economic experimentation, mostly unpublicised, at individual enterprises. The key legal documents of the economic reform are the Law on the State Enterprise (or Association) enacted 30 June 1987 and in force from 1 January 1988, and ten decrees jointly adopted by the Central Committee of the CPSU and the USSR Council of Ministers on 17 July 1987.[6] The ten decrees affect the roles of, respectively, the State Planning Committee, the State Committee for Science and Technology, the State Supply Committee, the Ministry of Finances, the system of price formation, banking, statistics, material production, management at republic levels, and the State Committee for Labour and Social Questions. As of 1 January 1988, about 60% of Soviet enterprises began to operate under the new legislation.

(a) Concept of State enterprise. State enterprises, associations, and cooperatives are characterised as the basic 'link' of the national economy. They are to play the principal role in developing Soviet economic potential under the management of the labour collective in accordance with Plan and Contract on the basis of 'full economic accountability, self-financing, self-management, and the combining of centralised guidance and enterprise autonomy.' How precisely those words come to be construed in law and practice will in significant measure be the key to the success or failure of restructuring.

The initial impetus is strongly in the direction of enterprise autonomy and independence and a relaxation of planning controls. An 'enterprise' may exist in virtually all areas of endeavour—industry, agriculture, construction, transport, communications, science and scientific services, trade, material-technical supply, and services generally. Whatever its concern, the enterprise is to produce goods for consumption and render services for payment, and it is free to engage in several types of activity simultaneously even though such activities may cross over into several branches of industry.

The enterprise retains its civil-law identity as a juridical person 'enjoying the rights and fulfilling the duties connected with its activities, possessing a separate portion of the ownership of the whole people, and having an independent balance sheet.' The objectives of the enterprise are to satisfy the social requirements of the national economy and citizens for their products, work, or services at a high standard and with minimal expenditures, to enhance its contribution to the acceleration of socio-economic development, and on this basis to secure the well-being of its labour collective. To those ends the enterprise is expected to

6 See *O korennoi perestroike upravleniia ekonomikoi; sbornik dokumentov* (1988).

increase production efficiency and labour productivity, improve scientific-technical progress, conserve resources, and increase profits and revenues, while having regard for the full development of the collective and the principle of self-management.

In undertaking its economic operations, an enterprise is to confirm its own Plan and to conclude contracts with customers and suppliers, being guided in doing so by control figures supplied by superior agencies, State orders for goods or services, long-term economic normative standards and quotas, and customer orders. Economic accountability and self-financing mean that the enterprise must cover its material expenditures from receipts obtained through realising its goods or services. Profit revenue, in other words, becomes the general indicator for economic operations. Part of the profit or revenues is to be used to pay taxes and obligations to the State, the banks, or superior agencies. The balance is at the complete disposal of the enterprise, to be distributed as the labour collective determines.

Economic competition is expressly sanctioned by the 1987 Law on the State Enterprise as the most important way of meeting consumer demand and ensuring high quality, competitive products or services. An enterprise 'ensuring the production and realisation of the best product, work, or service at the lowest cost receives larger economically-accountable revenues and advantages in its production and social development and the earnings of workers.' The State is authorised to utilise methods of economic control, including planning, finance, credit, and prices, to encourage competition and limit a 'monopoly position' enjoyed by producers of a particular product or service.

(b) Protection of enterprise autonomy. The realities of enterprise autonomy lie in many areas, but three are of special importance. The first is the method(s) used for calculating economically accountable income. Two methods are authorised by the 1987 Law and in making its choice the enterprise must have the approval of its superior organisation. The first method is based on a 'normative profit distribution'; from gross profit there are to be deductions for the State budget and for the superior organisation, as well as repayment of interest on bank credits. The balance is at the disposition of the labour collective, which then makes allocations to certain enterprise funds (production development, science and technology, social development, material incentive, or others). Under certain circumstances the wage fund and the profit remaining after other funds have received their allocations may be merged. The second method is based on 'normative revenue distribution.' After production expenditures have been covered, appropriate deductions are made for the State budget, the superior agency, and interest payments. The balance, called the 'economically accountable revenue' of the collective, is allocated first to the various enterprise funds and only then

is available for distribution to workers as earnings. While the formation of certain funds by the enterprise is obligatory, the enterprise under restructuring has greater latitude in combining funds or moving assets from one designated purpose to another.

The second is the ability of the enterprise to protect itself against unlawful interference by superior agencies. In the past the most frequent offender against the integrity of the enterprise was the agency superior to the enterprise, often for reasons that from the ministry's point of view seemed perfectly sound. Although compensating adjustments should have been made when such interference occurred, in practice there was no method of enforcement. Under the 1987 Law, the superior organisation is required to respect the principles of economic accountability and self-financing in its relations with inferior organisations. The superior in particular has no right to impose on an enterprise control figures, economic normative standards, or quotas in excess of those confirmed by the USSR Council of Ministers on a List established for the enterprise. Moreover, a ministry, department, or other State agency may issue instructions to an enterprise only within the limits of their competence established by legislation. If such an instruction is ultra vires or contrary to legislation, the enterprise may bring suit in State Arbitrazh to have the act declared void in whole or in part. Losses caused to the enterprise as a result of performing an instruction issued by a superior agency which violate the rights of the enterprise or as a result of the superior agency not properly performing its duties with regard to the enterprise are subject to compensation by the superior and, in the event of a dispute, may be recovered in State Arbitrazh.

The third is the extent to which the labour collective can effectively and intelligently exercise the management prerogatives conferred on it. Summoning the entire labour collective in a large enterprise at frequent intervals to take decisions simply is not feasible, the more so if the enterprise operates on shifts. Accountability of management is pursued through the election of key management personnel by the labour collective, regular reports to the collective, mandatory submission of certain issues to the labour collective, and the formation of an enterprise labour collective council to function in the interval between meetings of the entire labour collective. While some were apprehensive that the creation of labour collective councils would detract from the powers of the labour collective as a whole, the trade unions resisted the creation of councils because they feared their own influence would wane. Eventually the 1983 Law on Labour Collectives authorised the councils, ratifying an emergent practice, and the 1987 Law on the State Enterprise enumerates (Art 7) their considerable powers in the enterprise. The principles of democratic centralism, one-man management, and labour collective democracy rest together uneasily, however, and much will depend upon how they develop at enterprise level in practice.

258 *Economic law*

(c) Planning. Under restructuring the State Planning Committee is to become engaged exclusively with long-term economic planning. The enterprise is to work out and confirm its own Plan, having regard to the long-term tasks of the branch and the integrated development plan for the territory where it is situated. In preparing its five-year Plan, an enterprise is to utilise certain base data: control figures, State orders, long-term economic normative standards, and quotas, as well as direct orders from customers. Each of these has a specific role to play:

(1) control figures express the social requirements for a product and the minimum levels of production efficiency. Not directive in nature, they merely give some notion to the labour collective of the latitude available for making decisions and choosing contract partners. Amongst the control figures are production indicators expressed in value, profit (or revenues), hard currency receipts, labour productivity, and others.

(2) State orders are intended to guarantee that certain social requirements are given priority and may be issued in the form of capital investment financed by the State to introduce modern technology or in the form of contracts for the delivery of certain products. They are issued by the agency superior to the enterprise and may be placed on a competitive basis. While they must be included in the enterprise Plan, the relationship is as between supplier and customer.

(3) long-term economic normative standards are intended to stabilise the interests of the State and the enterprise over the five-year planning period. Such normative standards include the amounts which each year the enterprise is to pay in to the State budget, the wage and economic incentive funds, and other aspects of enterprise activities.

(4) quotas establish the maximum State centralised capital investment available for developing interbranch production entities, new construction, assembly, or independent-work contracts, or the centralised distribution of material resources.

The enterprise drafts and confirms its annual Plan by proceeding from the five-year Plan and economic contracts concluded. The contracts for the production and delivery of consumer goods are to be concluded as a result of the free sale of the articles on the wholesale markets, and that demand is to reflect the quality of goods, assortment, and related factors. Depending on its level of subordination, each enterprise is to agree its Plan with the respective agency of State power on that level in respect of such matters as construction, use of labour resources and local raw materials, nature conservation and resource use, production of consumer goods or services, and development of the 'social sphere'.

(d) Prices and finance. In the view of western economists, the true test of fundamental economic reform in the USSR is the extent to which

price is allowed to fluctuate in accordance with supply and demand. The economic restructuring reforms of 1987 move some way in that direction. Prices and rents are being imposed by the State on resources, services, and amenities previously given free of charge or at a nominal price. Enterprises, for example, will be expected to reimburse State expenditure for retraining workers and to pay differential rent for the use of land, water, and minerals.

An enterprise is obliged to at least break even in its economic operations. Temporary planned losses may be financed by the superior agency, but otherwise measures are to be taken to eliminate loss-making activities. Isolated instances of enterprises going into liquidation already have been reported. The principle of economic accountability requires that an enterprise compensates for losses caused to another enterprise or to the State, and pays fines, penalties, and other sanctions established by legislation from its economically-accountable revenues. Likewise, compensation received forms part of economically-accountable revenues.

With few exceptions, most notably in the collective farm markets, prices prior to 1988 were fixed by the State Committee of the USSR for Prices. Under restructuring, the enterprise has primary responsibility for establishing prices in accordance with certain principles. Price is recognised as a means of reflecting 'socially necessary' expenditures for production and realisation of goods and services, their consumer appeal, quality, and effective demand. Price is to be used as an economic lever to raise production efficiency and quality and to reduce production costs. Three methods are employed to establish prices: centrally-fixed prices, prices negotiated with the customer, and prices established independently by the enterprise.

One concern is that an enterprise may fix prices too high. Unjustified profit as a 'result of violations of State price discipline' or the failure to observe State standards or technical conditions is to result in the profit being confiscated by the State from the economically-accountable revenues of the enterprise and excluded from report data on fulfilment of the Plan. In addition a fine equalling 100% of the amount confiscated is to be paid into the State budget. A customer has the right to dissolve a contract for delivery containing an excessive price.

Where prices are centrally determined or fixed by a ministry or department, the enterprise must observe them but is free to negotiate discounts or supplementary increments for extra orders or changes in customer requirements. 'Contract prices' may be negotiated directly between enterprise and customer for individual or one-off orders or new products and certain listed foodstuffs, scientific research or design work, agricultural products purchased by State farms and other State agricultural enterprises from the general public, products purchased by co-operative organisations, and other types of goods or services authorised by legislation. The enterprise may independently fix its own prices for consumer and production goods which are not subject to central price-fixing and for products or services realised within its own trade network or used for its own consumption. A State farm or other State agricultural enterprise may independently fix prices for part of its planned production and all of its above-plan agricultural production sold through its own trade network or on the collective farm market. As restructuring progresses, it is intended to enlarge the scope of contract prices and independent enterprise pricing.

(e) Wages. Although labour and wages are properly a part of labour law (see chapter 12), they have an increasingly prominent role in general enterprise policies. Wage differentials are being encouraged under restructuring to reward quality work results and higher skills, and the enterprise has greater latitude to determine its own manning requirements and levels, work hours, leave policy, and the like. The brigade system is being encouraged, together with the 'independent-work contract' system, the latter encouraging shops, sectors, and other subdivisions of an enterprise to contract with management for the performance of particular activities. Where appropriate, independent-work contracts may be concluded with families.

In a sharp departure from previous practice, the Soviet enterprise is being encouraged to become directly involved in foreign economic relations (see chapter 19).

Within the framework of restructuring legislation, considerable innovation and adaptation of corporate, co-operative, employment, contract, and other legal models and institutions is in evidence. Unlike the sponsored experimentation of the early 1980s, much of this activity is spontaneous as emphasis shifts to the principle 'that not expressly prohibited is permitted.' The tensions between centralised direction and enterprise autonomy will persist, however, and it remains to be seen how the balance successively adjusts.

Chapter 14

Collective farm law

Although in 1917 some of his colleagues counselled a prompt transition to State-owned and managed agriculture, Lenin successfully advocated an intermediate approach: the nationalisation of land and confiscation of large land-holdings, redistribution of land use to favour the poor and middle peasants, and the encouragement of co-operative farms. Three co-operative models of farming were authorised by Soviet legislation in the early years. The lowest form was the 'Association for the Social Working of Land' (TOZ), wherein members worked collectivised land but owned their own livestock and equipment. The most radical form, the 'commune,' entailed members working together without pay, dining at a common table, living in communal housing, and regarding all or virtually all personal property as belonging to the collective.[1] The medium and ultimately preferred model was the 'artel', which required members to work principally the social sector of the farm while retaining a personal plot, livestock, and implements for their own use. All three models were structured as voluntary self-governing entities that divided, after meeting obligations to the State or creditors, their proceeds (or losses) among the members. State farms (*sovkhoz*) were and are something quite different, for they hire workers for wages and share neither profits nor losses; they represent an attempt to industrialise agriculture.

HISTORICAL BACKGROUND

The first Decree 'On Land' adopted 26 October 1917 referred to the possibility of transition to the social cultivation of land, somewhat elaborated in the Decree 'On the Socialisation of Land' of 19 February 1918.[2] The Law of 14 February 1919 'On Socialist Land Tenure and On Transition Measures to Socialist Land Cultivation' made provision for a variety of legal arrangements: State farms, communes, social land cultivation, and artels.[3] Associations of specialised interest were encouraged, for example, for farm machinery, livestock farming, soil conservation. Limitations were removed during the NEP era on the right of collective farms to dispose of their produce, but although one-quarter of the

---

1 See R. G. Wesson *Soviet Communes* (1963).
2 *SU RSFSR* (1917) no. 1, item 3; (1918) no. 25, item 346.
3 *SU RSFSR* (1919) no. 4, item 43.

peasantry were said to work on one type or another of collective farming in 1922, most land throughout the 1920s remained in the use of family units. Soviet land policy (see chapter 15, below) underwent a variety of changes during this period to encourage agricultural production and improve the lot of the poor and middle farmers. By a Law of 16 March 1927 tax and financial incentives were accorded to collective farms in order to expand the general agricultural movement.[4] The legal structure of collective farms was developed in a Statute on the Agricultural Cooperative confirmed on 30 October 1927.[5]

For political and economic considerations, still much debated, the Party authorities decided to embark upon mass collectivisation of agriculture. A veritable revolution in the countryside commenced from summer 1929 at enormous human cost. The number of peasants in collective farms increased from less than half a million households in 60,000 collective farms as of September 1928 to more than 14 million households in over 200,000 collective farms by 1932. The economic strength of the wealthy peasant family (kulaks) was broken by this policy, the poor and middle peasants being organised into collective units with priorities for obtaining machinery, seeds, and housing, and credit. Of the three models of collectivisation, the artel became the preferred scheme. A Decree of 17 March 1931 required the artel to be used.[6] Model artel charters of 1 March 1930 and especially 17 February 1935 laid down the basic structure.

The details of agricultural organisation during the next five decades underwent repeated modifications. The 1935 Model Charter remained on the statute books until the Model Charter of 28 November 1969 was confirmed, but in actuality many of its provisions were made obsolete by subsequent legislation. For decades the basic organisational link for labour within collective farms was the brigade, and farm members were paid in kind or cash for labour contributed to the farm on the basis of accounting units called labour-days. From 1929–58 collective farms contracted with outside organisations called Machine-Tractor Stations (MTS) to supply and repair major farm machinery as required. Party and State organs created to assist collective farms were reorganised time and again; from 1964 collective farmers were brought within the State pension system.

Throughout their existence collective farms have lived under the theoretical threat of ultimate abolition and absorption into State farms. They are regarded as a transitional form of agricultural organisation that at some future stage will pass on to a higher level of industrialised agriculture. The extent of social disruption ensuing if such a policy were

4 *SZ SSSR* (1927) no. 15, item 161.
5 *SZ SSSR* (1927) no. 109, item 736.
6 A. K. R. Kiralfy 'The History of Soviet Collective Farm Legislation' in W. E. Butler (ed) *Russian Law* (1977) p 194.

pursued at the moment is impossible to foresee, but there is little doubt that even though the system has succeeded in providing a basic food supply, for sundry reasons plan targets for agricultural production have fallen short more often than they have been met. Experiments continue with legal means to improve collective farm efficiency—joint inter-farm enterprises, larger personal plots, expanded credit facilities, more flexible procurement contracts—but none has proved to be wholly effective.

The modern collective farm system

MODEL CHARTER

Every collective farm has its own charter that defines its legal capacity, structure, functions, and duties. The charter is adapted from the Model Charter adopted in 1988 by the Fourth All-Union Congress of Collective Farmers and confirmed by joint decree of the CPSU and the USSR Council of Ministers. To become valid, the charter and all amendments must be registered at the executive committee of the district or city soviet of people's deputies after being accepted by the general meeting of collective farm members. Collective farms enjoy legal capacity under Soviet civil legislation as juridical persons: they own the social property of the collective, which is distinct from property belonging to other socialist organisations or to individual collective farm members or households. They are liable for obligations out of their own assets and within the powers conferred by their charters enter into civil law transactions, for example, contracts for the acquisition of machinery or procurement of agricultural produce, but may not conclude transactions contrary to their charter, for example, acting as a commercial intermediary or transport expediter, or buying agricultural produce for resale. Many collective farms have joined with others to form subsidiary enterprises for the purpose of using by-products or employing labour during slack periods. Collective farms also employ individuals, that is, conclude labour contracts to perform certain services, for example, teach in schools, provide legal aid, and the like. In the course of apportioning work assignments to members and others, the collective farms lay down legally enforceable normative rules affecting the organisation and planning of labour, work norms and scales for remuneration, safety requirements, and the settlement of labour disputes.

MEMBERSHIP

Collective farms are under their charters a type of 'co-operative organisation voluntarily uniting peasants' in order jointly to carry on large-scale socialist agricultural production. Labour relations as between the farm and its members are regulated not by the labour codes but by the farm charter and the rules for internal order. The right to become a collective farm member is open to any able-bodied citizen 16 years of age or above. Members may not be employed simultaneously in other institutions nor be a member of two or more collective farms.[7] There are no membership fees or dues, but entering members who have a personal plot must conform to the norms for such plots laid down by the collective farm.

Membership applications may be oral or written and must be considered by the collective farm board within one month. The final decision rests with the general meeting or, on large farms, the council of plenipotentiaries. The same bodies consider applications for withdrawal. Membership may be terminated by reason of transfer to permanent work in industry or another branch of the national economy, transfer from one collective farm to another, transformation of the collective farm into a State farm, expulsion, or death. An application for withdrawal must be considered within three months and a final account settled within a month of confirmation of the annual report. If a collective farm is transformed into a State farm, the members may either choose to be employed on the State farm or join a neighbouring collective farm. Members called up to active military service, elected to office in a local soviet or other bodies, or commencing studies while continuing to work, or seconded to employment elsewhere are allowed to retain their membership.

So few individual farm units remain in the Soviet Union that in the strict sense the notion of co-operatively pooling resources to form a collective farm has become obsolete. Nevertheless, the concept of the labour relationship is different. Members pool their labour for their common benefit, have a voice in determining work assignments, and probably have a larger appreciation of their interdependence than ordinary urban employees. Some of the rigours of co-operative independence have been ameliorated. Pensions are linked to the State scheme, and standard labour law requirements regarding safety, arduous labour, liability for damage done while at work, and wage scales are being incorporated by reference or analogy. On the other hand, collective farms tend to reinvest a greater share of their proceeds in activities and amenities that reinforce the attractiveness of the farm as a unit, for example, housing, advanced training, and incentives of various types.

State and Party guidance of collective farms

Historically, the collective farms have had a close and sometimes difficult relationship with State and Party agencies. In some periods the Soviet press indicated that local officials illegally diverted collective

---

7 G. V. Ivanov (ed) *Kolkhoznoe pravo* (1973) pp 58–61.

farm resources or acted contrary to decisions of general meetings. The CPSU determines on a broad scale the basic provisions of agricultural policy, and primary Party organisations within each collective farm exercise a right of control of the economic activity of farm organs. The Party treats the office of farm chairman as a *nomenklatura* post.

Collective farms just as other organisations are obliged to respect State legislation. Plans for the State procurement of agricultural produce are confirmed by the respective levels of Government. Local soviets especially are much concerned with collective farm matters: the fulfilment of plans, the observance of charters, the range and scale of State assistance to farms, the precise amounts of agricultural procurement per farm, the allocation of land to farms, various agronomy measures, credit plans, the acquisition of agricultural machinery and equipment, the legality of collective farm decisions, contributions to social security funds, observance of labour legislation, weed control, labour productivity and discipline, comrades' courts, and cultural amenities. The State Agro-Industrial Committee of the USSR and all its administrative sub-divisions likewise have jurisdiction over many facets of a collective farm, including its financial plans, accounts, capital construction, balance sheets, irrigation, sowing practices, soil erosion, land use, and proper distribution of collective farm revenues. In recent years State and Party organs have been instructed to exercise these functions in ways compatible with collective farm democracy. The State in particular is not to prejudice or diminish their rights and should operate through the governing bodies of the farm rather than around them.

COLLECTIVE FARM MANAGEMENT

The highest organ of a collective farm is the general meeting, composed of all collective farm members, or on very large farms a meeting of authorised representatives elected in collective farm brigades and other sub-divisions. It convenes at least four times a year and takes decisions by simple majority vote, a quorum being two-thirds of all members. The general meeting elects the collective farm board, a chairman, and an auditing commission, the board and chairman acting in the intervals between sessions of the meeting and serving a three-year term of office. The board meets at least once a month and operates on the basis of majority decision. The chairman carries on the day-to-day direction of collective farm activity with the aid of one or two deputies and represents the farm juridically in relations with State agencies or other organisations. A bookkeeper and specialists are either appointed by the farm board from among members of the farm or hired on the basis of a labour contract; large farms hire a jurisconsult or contract with a local legal consultation office for legal services.

The infrequency and size of the general meeting makes it difficult for collective farmers to become involved directly in ordinary management matters. This problem is attenuated by utilising the brigades and other farm sub-divisions for more frequent sessions; each brigade elects its own council and 'brigadier,' the latter being subordinate to the chairman, the collective farm board, and specialists. The auditing commission elected for a three-year term oversees the economic and financial activity of the farm. Some collective farms create economic councils or bureaus for economic analysis to make recommendations for improving economic efficiency, agronomy councils to advise on technical matters, rationalisation offices to encourage the submission of appropriate proposals, cultural councils, women's councils, pensioners' councils, and advisory groups composed of senior or retired collective farmers.

COLLECTIVE FARM OWNERSHIP

Collective farm and co-operative ownership is a variety of socialist ownership under the 1977-78 Soviet constitutions. As a form of collective ownership it is superior to personal property, but as the ownership is vested in a juridical entity composed of collective farm members and not the State as a whole, it is an inferior category as compared to State ownership. Eventually collective farm ownership is to be transmuted into State; intercollective farm undertakings are seen as a step in this direction, the more so when joint enterprises are formed with State farms or organisations. The principal sources of collective farm property are the original contributions made by members upon joining, means of production granted without cost by the State, property purchased from supply or other organisations, and the proceeds of the farm's economic operations not distributed to members. Collective farms do not own land, which is allocated to them in perpetuity and free of charge; land holdings may be enlarged by State grant but may be reduced only in special circumstances for reasons of public domain. Short-term land grants may also be made to collective farms for special purposes. The Model Charter does not even make provision for new members contributing their property to the social sector of the farm.

Under Soviet civil law, collective farms have the right to possess, use, and dispose of their property so long as they do not divert assets for ultra vires purposes. Structural sub-divisions of collective farms may possess and use property allocated to them by the farm but may not dispose of or alienate it. Intercollective farm organisations are formed on the basis of share ownership based on contributions in kind or cash; the organisations have the right of operative management over their property as provided for by their charters. An association of collective farms, however, owns its own property outright and is not based on shared ownership.

The Soviet constitutions and the 1988 Model Charter specify what kinds of property a collective farm may own: enterprises, buildings, installations, farm machinery, means of transport, livestock, plantings, produce, cash, and more. Since 1958 collective farms have begun to purchase their own tractors, combines, harvesters, and other heavy equipment, although in some areas they depend on repair stations to service the equipment. Most farm assets make up the basic and circulating production funds, and these are not subject to distribution among collective farm members. If members damage, spoil, or lose collective farm property, they are obliged to pay compensation to the farm.

REMUNERATION FOR LABOUR

Every collective farm member must contribute his personal labour to the social economy of the farm. Workers may be hired from outside under contract only when seasonal work or lack of available specialists so requires. The social economy in turn provides the basic income for farm members in the form of an annual wage paid in monthly instalments and disbursements in kind to farmers from the gross harvest yield. Bonuses are paid for exceeding plan targets. Collective, family, individual, and other forms of independent-work contracts are now used to determine remuneration levels and bonuses. Income differentials exist, based on the principle that highest payment is to be made for the best quantity and quality of work. Several schemes are employed to measure output and productivity: piecework, job rate, time, or time-bonus being the chief among them. Female members have the right to pregnancy and birth leave, nursing breaks, and similar benefits. Adolescents work a shorter day. Systematic violations of labour discipline can result in expulsion from the farm. If crop failures so reduce collective farm revenues that the guaranteed wage payments cannot be met, the farm can obtain bank credits to cover the short-fall.

Under the 1988 Model Charter labour disputes of collective farmers are considered by labour dispute commissions created from representatives of the farm board and the farm trade union committee, unless the general meeting has exclusive jurisdiction. If the collective farmer does not agree with the decision rendered, he may apply either to the general meeting of the farm or to a people's court.

PROCUREMENT BY THE STATE

One of the considerations leading to mass collectivisation in 1928–29 was the desire of the State to ensure that food would be available for urban requirements and export. Various schemes have been devised over the years to encourage, require, or compel collective farmers to market minimum levels of produce to the State at stipulated prices. Under the present scheme the collective farm is to operate on principles similar in many ways to those applicable to State enterprises. Although its basic task is to produce and market agricultural products, a collective farm also may form production entities to process and store such products, to extract and manufacture construction materials, to produce consumer goods, to develop other subsidiary trades, and to contract with industrial enterprises, trade, supply, and other economic organisations regarding the formation on the collective farm of industrial units for the production of various manufactures and goods. Its mandate under the 1988 Model Charter extends to any production and economic activities, including beyond the district where the collective farm is located, providing the activities are consistent with the Charter and not contrary to legislation. Trade, economic, scientific-technical, and cultural links may be developed with agricultural co-operatives, firms, and other enterprises in COMECON member countries and in western and the third world States.

Just as a State enterprise, the collective farm is to draft and confirm its own five-year and annual plans. The base data in the plans includes the economic contracts for the delivery of agricultural products to the State and to other outlets, deliveries of centrally-distributed material resources, quotas for independent-work contracts, and long-term economic normative standards. Within the collective farm contracts are to be concluded between the farm and structural sub-divisions that incorporate economically-accountable planning tasks. Except for that portion of its production which is sold to the State under contract at procurement prices ('State orders'), the collective farm is free to fix its own prices for products sold through its own trade network, the collective farm market, consumers' co-operatives, or other organisations. The failure to meet obligations under contracts for the delivery of agricultural produce is regarded as a violation of State discipline for which guilty officials may be sanctioned. A standard form contract is used; field-crop contracts are concluded each year and contracts for fruit, vegetables, and potatoes concluded for a term of several years, subject to adjustment each year in light of current State procurement plans and production-finance plans. Procurement contracts are then augmented by delivery and transport contracts so that the produce is shipped expeditiously to a particular customer. Penalties are imposed for failure to perform in a timely way, but a farm is released from liability for failure to perform by reason of natural disaster or the fault of the procurement agency.

DISTRIBUTION OF REVENUES

The 1988 Model Charter places a number of requirements upon collective farms with respect to distributing their gross produce and revenues. The underlying principle is the proper combination of 'accumulation and consumption.' All products produced within a year by a collective farm are called the gross product. From this are subtracted expenses for amortisation of basic funds, seed, feed, fertiliser, petrol, current repairs, and the like. The balance is gross income, from which the labour payment fund and the State social security and insurance contributions are deducted. The remaining balance is net income, which the collective farm must use to pay taxes and make cash payments to the State, enlarge the basic and circulating funds, form funds for cultural amenities, social security, material assistance, incentives, and other reserves. Contributions to the basic and circulating funds are compulsory; other contributions depend upon investment choices. The collective farm likewise maintains a plant and livestock reserve for seed, feed, forage, insurance, farm consumption requirements, and the like.

If a collective and produces surpluses in excess of the State procurement plan minimums and above-plan requirements, these may be sold either in collective farm markets at prices determined by the farm or free-market prices or by concluding a commission contract with a consumer co-operative. These revenues are used in the same priority as other gross or net incomes.

SOCIAL SECURITY

A major disadvantage of the collective farm system had been its exclusion from the State social security system. Wealthy farms could provide for their aged or disabled members, whereas poor or medium farms experienced great difficulty in doing so. From 1965 collective farms were brought within the State pension scheme. Each farm makes payments into the centralised union social security and social insurance funds for collective farmers, who in turn are eligible for old age, disability, loss of bread-winner, pregnancy, birth, and poverty pensions or allowances, payments for temporary disability, sanatorium passes, or other types of social insurance. The farm may supplement these benefits from its own resources and make provision for individuals who did not qualify for support under them. Individuals employed under labour contracts by collective farms are covered by separate legislation.

TRADE UNIONS

For many years the co-operative nature of the collective farm appeared to preclude any role for the trade unions. In 1965 the VI Congress of Trade Unions made it possible for employees at collective farms under labour contracts to join trade unions. Their role has gradually expanded. On many farms the trade unions administer the social security scheme. Under the 1988 Model Charter, the collective farm board is to conduct its work 'in close contact with the collective farm trade union committee,' including the consideration of labour disputes by labour dispute commissions. On some farms the trade unions advise on housing, amenities, and labour protection measures.

COLLECTIVE FARM HOUSEHOLDS

Although the precise customary provisions varied from locality to locality, the Russian peasantry had for centuries held farmyards with some arable land attached in perpetuity as household plots. The Imperial Russian Government acknowledged their right of possession in legislation. The right of land use vested in households, not individuals, and consequently was not altered by the death of the head of the household. Some Russian jurists believed the law of succession was inappropriate for conceptualising the transfer of possession. The peasant household rather was a work community in possession of land and other goods; death of a member entailed a change in the work community rather than succession to property.[8]

Soviet agricultural policy adopted the concept of the peasant household, although from time to time it seemed fated to disappear. The 1977-78 Soviet constitutions, unlike their 1936-38 predecessors, omit to mention the collective farm household; indeed, nowhere in Soviet legislation is a formal definition to be found. Nevertheless, many provisions of Soviet civil, collective farm, family, and labour law regulate the household and enable us to deduce its principal legal characteristics. It is linked to the collective farm as an institution, a family labour community basically engaged in furthering the social economy of the farm. It owns property in common; at least one household member must be a collective farm member. Principally, although not exclusively, the household is a family unit. Subsidiary husbandry conducted by a household must be with its own labour and means, and the household is entitled by law to a personal land plot for that purpose. The collective farm household is independently a subject of legal rights; for example, it insures property, buys agricultural produce, uses collective farm pastures, and pays the agricultural tax as an entity. Family relationship is the basic criterion for household membership, but membership is contingent upon personally participating in the social and subsidiary husbandry of the farm and household. Marriage does not in and of itself mean household membership. The spouse must be registered also on the household list maintained by the local rural soviet. A newly born child becomes a member of the mother's household.

The property which may be owned by a collective farm household is defined in civil legislation and in the 1988 Model Charter as: a dwelling house, farm buildings, productive and working livestock, poultry, bees, rabbits, and minor agricultural implements and machinery for working the personal plot. The precise numbers and types of livestock vary from region to region and are fixed by union republic legislation. In the 1980s many republics increased livestock quotas in order to encourage

---

8 R. Beermann 'Pre-revolutionary Russian Peasant Laws' in note 6, above, p 189.

production and under the 1988 Model Charter the general meeting of the collective farm fixes quotas for livestock and poultry.

Under Soviet civil law the property of a collective farm household belongs to its members in joint ownership. As the number of household members changes, their respective shares change. If a member of the household leaves permanently, he may claim his share of the household property in kind or the value thereof. This is known as separation. A partition of property ensues if the household divides to form two or more, for example, if one member marries. The partition must be registered with the local soviet to be legally valid. A household member may not sell, exchange, or alienate his interest in a household. Just as in the old peasant customary law, the possible share of a household member does not pass by succession when he dies; the membership of the household merely changes. His personal belongings, however, for example, his clothing and other objects purchased for himself and not the household, do pass by way of succession in the ordinary way. It can sometimes be very difficult to ascertain whether property should be treated as household or personal property; for example, if a household sold a cow to the collective farm in order to buy a television set, the latter would be household property. If the television was purchased with the personal earnings of a household member, it would be his personal property. But property which may be owned only by a collective farm household, such as a dwelling house, livestock, etc, may not be personally owned by a collective farmer, although non-members of a collective farm might personally own such objects.

Personal plots under Soviet law are not restricted to collective farm households. Any Soviet citizen, even city- dwellers, may and do apply for one to be allocated. The 1977-78 Soviet constitutions guarantee every citizen the right to a personal plot. During the discussion preceding the adoption of the USSR Constitution, L. I. Brezhnev reaffirmed their usefulness and criticised those who urged their abolition. In 1981, after several years of harvest disappointments, the Soviet Government took measures to encourage this type of cultivation and facilitate the marketing of personal plot produce. More than one-quarter of all Soviet agricultural produce is produced on these plots; for intensively cultivated crops, the percentage is much higher. Each household may have up to one-half hectare of land for this purpose, including land occupied by buildings, although plots granted prior to 1969 need not be reduced in size. The precise plot dimensions within that limit are fixed by each collective farm charter, taking into account family size and participation in the social economy of the farm. A plot may not be transferred to other persons or worked by hired labour. Specialists employed by a collective farm also may be granted personal plots from collective farm land. Those who work personal plots are free to consume the produce or to sell it in collective farm markets at free-market prices or to the State at fixed prices.

Some farms allow members to borrow or hire farm machinery from the collective to use on personal plots. Under the 1988 Model Charter collective and State farms may contract with collective farmers or other citizens to raise livestock or poultry with guaranteed purchase by the State at prescribed intervals and prices and grant supplementary personal plots for this purpose.

Inter-collective farm enterprises and associations

Collective farms are encouraged to pool their resources with other farms or with State farms or enterprises in order to take advantage of economies of scale, joint construction, use of labour in the slack season, shared facilities, and the like. There are three types of arrangements: those jointly owned and administered, those jointly owned but administered by a State organisation, and those not jointly owned. Joint ownership is usually based on the share of assets contributed, and profits are divided accordingly. Most such enterprises have legal personality.

Specialisation, concentration, and production co-operation on another scale is encouraged through the production associations in agriculture formed pursuant to a Statute of 28 May 1976. Such associations are formed by collective farms, State farms, inter-farm enterprises, processing enterprises, transport, or other State and co-operative organisations either to specialise in a particular type of product within a designated territory or to provide several products to a specific territory. The association is an independent juridical person operating on the principle of economic accountability with its own charter. When collective farms are members of associations, the association property is held by right of common joint ownership.

In 1982 further steps were taken to stimulate agricultural production and co-ordinate agricultural administration. Collective farms operating at a loss or low profit margin were granted a variety of concessions and subsidies to improve their status. On 25 November 1982 the USSR Council of Ministers confirmed model statutes for agro-industrial associations at all levels from autonomous republic to district. Collective farms, State farms, inter-farm enterprises, and other entities comprising part of several ministries concerned with agriculture may become association members with a view to achieving a more proportional, balanced, and co-ordinated development of their respective activities. All enterprises and organisations retain their economic autonomy, legal personality, and departmental affiliation. The council of the agro-industrial association is an agency of State administration, subordinate to the respective soviet or republic, whereas the association itself is a juridical person with an independent balance sheet obliged to carry out its activity in accordance with the plan. Among the association's many functions are organising the conclusion of agricultural procurement contracts and promoting the development of personal subsidiary husbandry by citizens.

Other co-operative organisations

Collective farms are but one species of co-operative organisation under Soviet law. Fishing collective farms exist near many Soviet seaports. Their vessels fish the high seas and either sell their catch in foreign ports, transfer it to factory ships on the high seas, or land it themselves in port. Land-based co-operative members commonly engage in the normal collective-farm pursuits. Housing and dacha construction co-operatives are popular forms of organisation. At least ten citizens are required to form the co-operative, adopt a charter, and register the charter at the local soviet executive committee. Co-operatives also may be formed to carry on specialised activities, for example, gardening, bee-keeping, or raising rabbits. Also, under legislation introduced in 1987, co-operatives are being encouraged in the areas of consumer goods and services (see chapter 12).

The 1988 Law on Co-operative Societies in the USSR distinguishes between two basic types of co-operative: production co-operatives and consumer co-operatives. The production co-operatives produce goods, products, and services; that is, they may produce, procure, process, and realise agricultural products, consumer or producer goods, and secondary raw materials; extract minerals; repair and service equipment; engage in road, housing, and other building or in retail trade, operate public dining enterprises; arrange domestic or cultural services, medical care; or render legal, transport, research, design, management, or other services. Consumer co-operatives basically provide amenities or services to their members, but they are not precluded from becoming a 'mixed-type' of co-operative and doing both.

The collective farm, being itself a species of co-operative, is also governed by the 1988 Law on Co-operative Societies, and the 1988 Model Collective Farm Charter provisions reflect the more general provisions of that enactment.

Chapter 15

Natural resource law

Strictly speaking, there is no natural resource law in the Soviet Union. Legal science treats land, water, forestry, and mining as distinct branches of law, and appropriate sets of FPL have been enacted for each. Other types of natural resource legislation—hunting, flora and fauna, the atmosphere, sea resources, and the like—regulate individual resources. Environmental protection legislation has received enormous attention in the last two decades. Soviet jurists and policy-makers have debated strenuously the extent to which environmental regulation can be a part of branch legislation or requires a particularistic integrated approach. Those who stress the role of law in regulating the interaction of society with the environment as a whole prefer the term 'ecological law' to describe what they regard as a new branch of law. Economic, political, and environmental interests have contended for priority of place in environmental standards, disclosing a pattern of public dialogue and decision making that has illuminated the role of law as a mechanism for social engineering and the expression of policy preferences through interest groups.[1] As environmental protection has come to be acknowledged to be a global concern, the legal techniques and institutions fashioned by the Soviet legal system have come to be of interest both as a model whose effectiveness or failures are instructive to others and as an approach that must be taken into account when devising bilateral or multilateral measures to cope with nature conservation.

HISTORICAL BACKGROUND

Soon after coming to power, the Soviet governments of the several union republics nationalised all land, minerals, forests, water, and other natural resources in decrees expressly modelled upon or reproducing the essential provisions of the RSFSR 'Basic Law on the Socialisation of Land.'[2] Thereafter followed an assortment of additional normative acts regulating certain aspects of resource exploitation: fisheries, hunting, minerals, forests, waters, and land. Most of the legislation was of an

---

1 See M. Goldman *The Spoils of Progress: Environmental Pollution in the Soviet Union* (1972); P. Pryde *Conservation in the Soviet Union* (1972); C. E. Ziegler *Environmental Policies in the USSR* (1987).
2 A definitive text is given in *Dekrety sovetskoi vlasti* (1975) I pp 406–420.

ad hoc character; an integrated approach to resource exploitation seemed unnecessary in light of their limitless abundance. During the NEP era, considerable efforts were devoted to codification; land codes were in force in many union republics and forestry or water codes in a few. Some attention was given to all-union statutes or sets of basic principles for particular resources, land and mining law being examples. All of these enactments were quickly overtaken by the collectivisation of agriculture and the accelerated, planned industrialisation of the country, however, and though formally on the statute books, they were for the most part superseded by subsequent legislation.

The 1957 constitutional amendment effectuating a transition to FPL and respective union republic codes was extended in due course to natural resources. There are the 1968 Fundamental Principles of Land Legislation (FPLL), the 1970 Fundamental Principles of Water Legislation (FPWL), the 1975 Fundamental Principles of Minerals Legislation (FPML), and the 1977 Fundamental Principles of Forestry Legislation (FPFL). Between 1957-63 the respective union republics enacted nature conservation laws that laid down a basic framework of conservation policies and principles, most of which required further implementing legislation. Although these laws had considerable impact upon the legislation of other socialist countries, they proved by virtue of their generality to be unsatisfactory. The September 1972 session of the USSR Supreme Soviet devoted itself almost entirely to nature conservation and enacted a far-reaching decree 'On Measures to Further Improve Nature Conservation and Rational Utilisation of Natural Resources,' which in turn was elaborated by a decree of the USSR Council of Ministers 'On the Intensification of Nature Conservation and Improved Utilisation of Natural Resources.' In June 1980 the USSR enacted a Law on the Protection of the Atmosphere and a Law on the Protection and Use of the Animal World. These basic acts have been augmented by myriad edicts, decrees, statutes, and subordinate legislation regulating narrower issues in greater detail. In 1989 a draft Law of the USSR on Nature Conservation is to be submitted to the USSR Council of Ministers.

Soviet 'ecological law'

Much of what is discussed in this chapter would be central to 'ecological, or environmental, law.' Soviet jurists continue to debate whether there is or ought to be a branch of legal science or legislation designated by this appellation. The issue is partly terminological: the Russian expression widely used in this connection is *pravo okhrany prirody*, literally the law of nature protection. The term dates back to the era when nature conservation encompassed principally the creation of game reserves or parks, although it is increasingly accepted that the phrase embraces or should embrace the rational utilisation, renewal, increase, and protection of natural resources in the broadest meaning of that term. There has been some concern that the FPL governing particular natural resources and representing distinct and autonomous branches of law may inhibit an integrated approach to environmental regulation when choices, for example, among conflicting uses for different resources require resolution.[3]

National economic planning and natural resources

Contemporary Marxism-Leninism looks upon environmental regulation and protection as inextricably linked with the optimal harmonious relationship between man and nature. Environmental quality is regarded as a component of society's well-being, to be pursued with the same energy as other material values. In accord with the proposition that the proper relationship of productive forces can ensure environmental protection, the Soviet scientific community maintains that mankind does not face an inevitably irreversible deterioration of the environment and is capable of remedying or averting such depredation as had occurred or could do so.

National economic planning (see chapter 13, above) is a crucial element of this approach. The allocation on a more or less central basis of State-owned natural resources for exploitation as a part of planned economic development requires that environmental measures be integrated into the plan if they are to have any hope of realisation. Since 1974 Gosplan has been legally obliged to incorporate conservation indices and plans within both the long-term and current annual plans and when reviewing proposals submitted by all-union ministries or departments or by union republic councils of ministers from the standpoint of the efficient use of natural resources and nature conservation. In the realm of water resources, for example, Gosplan confirmation is required for schemes for the integrated use and conservation of water and for all-union water balance sheets drawn up in accordance with the FPWL and union republic water codes. And it is Gosplan that submits to the USSR Council of Ministers the proposals for determining those water resources whose use is to be regulated by all-union agencies, the said proposals having been agreed with union republic bodies. Gosplan is further charged with ensuring that general schemes for siting 'productive forces' in economic regions of the country provide for whatever

---

3 See O. S. Kolbasov 'The Concept of Ecological Law' in W. E. Butler and M. Grant (eds) *Environmental Law in the USSR and the United Kingdom* published as a special issue of the Connecticut Journal of International Law III (1988) no. 2.

special nature conservation measures may be needed and to co-ordinate with other ministries so that appropriate environmental equipment and resources are incorporated in plans as required.

The 1977–78 Soviet constitutions stipulate that 'necessary measures' are to be taken for the protection and scientifically well-founded, rational use of land and its minerals, water resources, flora and fauna, the preservation of air and water purity, for ensuring the production of natural wealth, and improvement of the human environment (Art 18). Soviet citizens have a constitutional duty to care for nature and to protect its wealth (Art 67).

The 1987 Law on the State Enterprise (Art 20) endeavours to integrate environmental concerns more directly into enterprise activities. In addition to general injunctions that the enterprise should use natural resources rationally and efficiently, prevent environmental pollution, undertake land reclamation and anti-erosion measures, and have regard to the environmental implications of new installations and construction, payments are to be made by enterprises for the use of natural resources, and nature conservation measures are to be effected at enterprise expense and exceptionally from centralised sources. In its environmental protection activities, an enterprise is under the supervision of the local soviet and relevant environmental protection agencies. If an enterprise causes pollution or uses natural resources irrationally, it is obliged to pay compensation and bear the responsibility provided by legislation. In the event of flagrant violations of the regime for nature use, the operation of the enterprise may be suspended until the violations are eliminated.

Natural resource regulation

The legal regulation of land, water, forests, minerals, the atmosphere, and the animal world follows, despite the differences peculiar to each resource, a basic pattern.

Land, water, minerals, and forests are under the 1977–78 Soviet constitutions in the exclusive ownership of the State. Surprisingly, early Soviet legislation which nationalised these resources, that is, confiscated them from private ownership, did not unequivocally vest ownership in the State. Soviet jurists for decades pointed this out in doctrinal writings.[4] The animal world is not mentioned in this respect in the Soviet constitutions, but is declared to be State property in the 1980 Law on the Protection and Use of the Animal World (Art 3). The atmosphere is not claimed to be in State ownership at all, merely the object of State concern and protection.

---

4 See W. E. Butler 'Land Reform in the Chinese Soviet Republic' in id (ed) *The Legal System of the Chinese Soviet Republic 1931–1934* (1983) p 84.

Those resources owned by the State may be granted only for use. Accordingly, a unified State fund is established for each resource embracing the multitudinous forms in which they exist. The unified State water fund, for example, embraces rivers, lakes, reservoirs, canals, ponds, and other surface waters; subterranean waters and glaciers; internal sea waters; and the territorial sea. Jurisdictional limits are prescribed for the disposition of resources from each fund, provisions for their respective use, pollution control, quality standards and balances; supervision over utilisation and conservation, and related matters. An enormous complex of State agencies are concerned with the conservation of each resource and employ hundreds of inspectorates at all levels of State administration. Social organisations such as trade unions, youth organisations, union republic nature conservation societies, and others and citizens are expressly authorised by legislation to assist State conservancy agencies by making proposals for improving resource utilisation and reporting breaches of the law. The various union republic codes lay down basic criteria to be met when siting, designing, building, or introducing into operation any enterprises, structures, or installations affecting the resource concerned or the surrounding environment.

Categories of use have been devised for each resource, and procedures for granting use and issuing permits. No charge traditionally has been made for resource use except in certain special instances, for example, special water use, but in 1987 the possibility of imposing use charges and differential rents for land, water, and mineral use on enterprises was introduced. The right to use a resource is usually granted for a specified term of years or in perpetuity. Water use, for example, may be granted for a term of from 3 to 25 years, or in perpetuity. Resource users assume certain legal duties, including that of resource protection. Failure to perform these duties can serve as grounds for terminating resource use rights or result in the imposition of administrative or criminal penalties. Detailed consideration is given in the codes to the utilisation of resources for particular purposes (consumption, agriculture, industry, hunting, fishing, leisure, among others).

All resources of the respective resource funds are subject to protection against pollution, depletion, or waste that may cause harm to public health, diminish fish or game stocks, reduce supplies, or otherwise induce undesirable changes in the physical, chemical, or biological properties of the resource. Enterprises, organisations, and institutions whose activity affects the state of a resource are legally required to carry out protective measures as may be instructed by or agreed with those State agencies or inspectorates having jurisdiction over such matters. Provision is specially made in the codes for including appropriate conservation measures in the national plans for economic and social development.

In the case of water, for example, the discharge of industrial, domestic, and other forms of waste into waters is prohibited; effluents may be discharged only if appropriate permits have been obtained from the State sanitary inspectorate. The pollution or obstruction of water (including glaciers and ice-covered waters) from losses of industrial products such as oil, timber, petrochemicals, fertilisers, toxic substances, and the like is similarly proscribed. Other code provisions treat resource depletion, flood control, and anti-erosion measures.

Vital components in the co-ordination of resource use and conservation are the State registers compiled for each resource which inventory the qualitative and quantitative data, the respective resource balance sheets compiled for territorial sub-divisions, and integrated resource utilisation and conservation schemes. Each of these is prepared according to a unified national model.

Comprehensive as the respective FPL and union republic codes regulating natural resources are, they leave much, either expressly or by omission, to be dealt with through subordinate or collateral legislation. The operation of the State registers, for example, is dealt with by separate statutes; individual rules and decrees lay down environmental standards, construction requirements, sanitation rules, and the like. Several large bodies of water—the Caspian Sea, Lake Baikal, Lake Ladoga, the Volga and Moscow rivers, the Arctic seas—have been the object of special pollution-control enactments, and the USSR continental shelf and exclusive economic zone are governed by particular regulations treating exploitation and conservation.

Institutional enforcement of natural resource legislation

A variety of institutions are involved in the enforcement of Soviet legislation concerning natural resources. Disputes over resource use are resolved administratively by agencies of State administration, usually the executive committees of local soviets of people's deputies. In the instance of water, for example, when water granted for solitary use is in dispute, the agency which granted the water use shall decide; if a special water use is in question, the permit-issuing agency shall judge. If water use disputes arise between different territorial sub-divisions, a joint commission is appointed to resolve the matter and, failing agreement, the matter is referred to a higher governmental instance.

The ministries of soil and water conservation, of public health, of fisheries, and the State Committee of the USSR for Nature Protection, the State Agro-Industrial Committee, and the hydrometeorological service, among others, maintain inspectorates to supervise the observance of pollution-control measures, use requirements, conservation standards, public health and sanitation rules, and the like. Their basic authority is to monitor the resource, notify serious instances of violation to higher officials, suspend in some cases the operations of offending plants or users, apply administrative sanctions, and bring criminal violations to the attention of the Procuracy. The Procuracy may issue an instruction (*predpisanie*) ordering a violation to cease, suspending if necessary, the operations of an enterprise.

The Procuracy itself has been instructed to display greater initiative in exercising its power of general supervision over compliance with environmental and natural resource legislation, and the USSR Supreme Court has issued decrees to inferior courts evaluating judicial practice in environmental cases and clarifying the law on several points. State Arbitrazh has issued an Instructive Letter to inferior arbitrazhes concerning the application of environmental legislation to disputes between State enterprises. Arbitrazhes are instructed when hearing pre-contractual disputes to amend contract provisions that are contrary to Soviet environmental decrees and to involve experts from organisations concerned with enforcing natural resource legislation in the actual hearing of disputes when environmental violations are concerned.

An extensive network of social nature conservation inspectorates assists State inspectorates in monitoring compliance with environmental legislation and alerting such bodies as the people's control agencies about material breaches.

Sanctions against breaches of natural resource legislation

The union republic criminal codes contain several articles specially punishing violations of natural resource legislation. These are treated principally as a type of economic crime: illegally engaging in fishing and other water-extractive trades, illegally hunting seals and beavers, floating timber or blasting in violation of rules for the protection of fish stocks, illegal hunting, violation of mining rules, violation of USSR continental shelf legislation, illegal felling of timber, polluting of waters or air, and pollution of the sea with substances harmful for human health or for living resources of the sea.

Minor violations by citizens are commonly punished by administrative fines; the fines may be payable on the spot to a duly authorised inspectorate official or imposed by an administrative commission attached to the executive committee of a local soviet of people's deputies. Corporate legal persons are no longer subject to administrative fines. Managers and officials also are subject to disciplinary responsibilities by their superior agencies, all of which are bound to observe environmental legislation. The failure of such officials to perform their tasks in this regard may result in a reprimand, demotion, or even dismissal. In

Moscow and other Soviet cities the local press has begun to publish the names of enterprises guilty of pollution, together with the names of the enterprise director and Party secretary and their addresses.

Both citizens and organisations are civilly liable on general tort principles laid down in the FPCivL and union republic civil codes for injury caused to another through their fault, and State institutions are liable for injury caused to citizens by improper official acts of their employees in the sphere of administrative management. Special rules apply in the event State institutions cause injury to a corporate legal person. In the case of forestry, fishing and hunting, Soviet legislation has fixed a monetary scale for compensating the State for the destruction or taking of designated quantities and species. The implements used for illegally felling timber or poaching are confiscated by the State together with whatever was unlawfully obtained with their use.

Finally, each branch of natural resource legislation contains its own sanction enabling the right of use to be terminated, although in many instances that is not a feasible alternative.

Sanctions in these branches of law pose unusual difficulties because the State is both the owner of the resource and, through the operations of its departments, officials, and State-owned enterprises, the principal violator of natural resource legislation. Fines ordinarily are effective only against individuals, but even in instances when State officials are at fault or when liability can be placed upon a juridical entity, responsibility in individual cases can be very difficult to determine. Consider the following hypothetical instance adapted from an actual situation:

A pulp-paper mill came into operation in 1983, having been accepted as conforming to State construction and design standards by a State committee assigned to ascertain these facts, without water purification equipment. Acceptance was confirmed by the RSFSR Council of Ministers. In 1986 the director of the mill was sentenced to one year correctional tasks because the plant unlawfully discharged effluents into an adjacent river. The court heard in evidence the absence of purification installations and the confirmation by the Council of Ministers that the plant met prevailing construction and design standards.

The issues posed by the case are not easy ones. In a planned economy an enterprise's capacity to obtain equipment often may be circumscribed by agencies or circumstances beyond its control, and this unavoidably has implications for traditional notions of criminal responsibility for an omission to act in instances such as the above.

Restructuring and Soviet environmental policy

During the 1980s, attention concentrated on the effective implementation of environmental legislation and appropriate readjustments to administrative responsibilities for environmental policies.[5] In January 1988 the Central Committee of the CPSU and the USSR Council of Ministers adopted a joint Decree 'On the Fundamental Restructuring of Nature Conservation in the Country' which introduced the most radical changes to date. Taken especially seriously was the complaint that the existing structure precluded an integrated approach to environmental protection and could not take adequate account of the newly-introduced economic methods of industrial and agricultural management.

The relevant State committees and other central economic agencies are instructed under the Decree to integrate the basic orientations for economic and social development of the USSR with the orientations of nature conservation measures and the contemplated scale of economic expansion. The appropriate indicators are to be incorporated into the control figures, State orders, long-term economic normative standards, and quotas issued to enterprises with due regard to the Long-term State Programme for Environmental Protection and Rational Use of Natural Resources of the USSR being developed for the thirteenth Five-Year Plan (1991–95) and up to the year 2005.

After years of discussion, the decision was taken in 1988 to create a 'super' environmental agency in the form of the union-republic State Committee for Nature Conservation (Goskompriroda SSSR). To the jurisdiction of Goskompriroda were transferred the relevant subdivisions of nearly a dozen ministries and departments. The principal functions of the new State committee include: effecting the integrated administration of nature protection activities in the country; developing and implementing a unified scientific-technical policy in nature conservation and the rational use of natural resources; co-ordinating the relevant activities of other ministries and departments; State control over the use and protection of all lands, waters, atmosphere, flora, fauna, minerals, and the marine environment; preparation and submission of proposals to the State Planning Committee for inclusion in the long-term environmental planning schemes; control over the implementation of planning tasks; confirmation of ecological normative standards, rules, and standards directed against pollution; performing State expert ecological evaluations of general schemes for developing and siting new plants and factories; control over the observance of ecological norms when new technology and materials are developed, as well as over the environmental impact of new construction; the issuance of permits for the burial of wastes, for discharges of harmful substances into the environment, for special use of water, wildlife, air, and land; direction of game preserves, hunting, and protected species, and co-operation with foreign countries and international organisations in environmental matters.

5 O. S. Kolbasov and N. I. Krasnov (eds) *Effektivnost' iuridicheskoi otvetstvennosti v okhrane okruzhaiushchei sredy* (1985).

Goskompriroda is advised by a council of scholars, public figures, representatives of local soviets, and enterprise directors. All levels of the Goskompriroda system have powers to impose prohibitions against the construction, renovation, or expansion of industrial or other objects or against the continuance of natural resource exploitation in violation of legislation; to suspend the operation of enterprises which flagrantly violate environmental norms, and to bring suit against enterprises, organisations, or citizens to recover compensation for damage caused to the State by environmental pollution or the irrational use of natural resources. In due course administrative violations relating to the environment are likely to be considered by organs within the Goskompriroda system. Decisions of Goskompriroda within its competence are binding upon all ministries, departments, associations, enterprises, and organisations.

The economic charges and rents introduced for resource use are to be fixed at levels that will encourage enterprises to conserve resources, and payments imposed on an enterprise for pollution violations will be set to deter such activities. Both types of payment will affect the economically-accountable income of the labour collective and are intended to serve as an economic stimulus to management consistent with the general policy of economic restructuring. Monies recovered from such violations are to be directed toward expenditures for improvement of the environment. Goskompriroda has responsibility for organising compliance in the Soviet Union with international treaties of the USSR relating to nature conservation and use.

Educational efforts will be intensified in the 1990s at all levels with respect to the environment. From 1989 a weekly newspaper, *Priroda*, is to be published and a Union of Nature Conservation Societies to be formed.

Chapter 16

Taxation

The economic policies of restructuring require, according to Party decrees and State legislation, 'a financial policy new in principle, the implementation of a radical reform' of the financial 'mechanism', and a greater appreciation of the role that financial levers can play in guiding economic behaviour. Taxation, consequently, will assume a more central role in ordering Soviet economic life, including Soviet citizens and, directly or indirectly, foreigners. The greater differentials in remuneration and in accumulation of wealth likely to accompany restructuring may see the reintroduction of an inheritance tax. And while foreign natural and juridical persons have been subject to Soviet taxation since 1978, western investment in joint enterprises and analogous ventures gives them a wholly new set of reasons for being conversant with the basic principles of Soviet domestic tax policy.

There is difficulty in applying western concepts of taxation to the Soviet system, for the notion of tax as an obligatory transfer of money from the private sector to the State treasury in order to finance State expenditure is not entirely apt in a society where the State is the principal owner of the means of production. Soviet works on financial law consequently speak of the 'concept of State revenues' which originate in 'compulsory payments' to the national budget by State enterprises and economic organisations and in 'taxes' of various types levied against collective farms, enterprises, social organisations, and citizens.[1]

Compulsory payments to the State budget

A key element of restructuring will be the extent to which the scheme of compulsory payments to the State budget introduced under the 1965 economic reform, as amended, is altered to further enterprise autonomy. Levels of profit under the 1965 reform were but one indicator of economic performance and certainly not the major indicator. As a rule, enterprises could expect to receive financial resources for planned activities, and profit in excess of plan indicators was mostly taken by the superior ministry and budget contributions. As profit is to become the

---

[1] The leading work in English is M. Newcity *Taxation in the Soviet Union* (1986).

central criterion for enterprise operations, the principles for and levels of payment will be decisive; for many enterprises a transition period will be in effect, perhaps lasting several years.

Under the pre-1988 system, the payment of first priority to be made by economically-accountable enterprises and organisations from profit is for production funds. Introduced by a Decree of the USSR Council of Ministers on 4 October 1965, the procedure for calculating the payment is governed by an Instruction of 30 November 1979 issued by the USSR Ministry of Finances and the State Planning Committee. The payment is not universally required—only those State production associations, enterprises, production construction-assembly associations, trusts, and certain other organisations which operate with a planned profit and whose financial plans call for the payment are liable.[2]

The payment is assessed as a percentage of: (1) the initial value of basic production funds (without regard to depreciation); (2) the value of above-norm or above-plan equipment not yet installed at operating enterprises; and (3) the value of circulating assets not obtained with bank credits. The rate as a rule is 6%, with a lower rate of 3% for associations, enterprises, and organisations with relatively low revenue levels; a scale of 2% to 6% is applicable to assembly and construction organisations. Payments are made on the tenth, twentieth, and twenty-eighth days of each month at one-ninth of the amount provided in the quarterly plan. At the end of each quarter the sum owed is recalculated to take into account the actual value of the funds.

There are exemptions for production funds created by borrowing from the bank, for new equipment and installations until the operation is fully mastered, for experimental production entities at enterprises, for buildings or installations used for design offices and research laboratories, and for installations and equipment used for production sanitation or labour safety. The rationale of levying payments against the initial value of basic funds is to induce enterprises to replace obsolete equipment more rapidly. No advantage is obtained from the declining actual value of used equipment. Uninstalled equipment in excess of norms or plan is levied against, so that enterprises will effect rapid installation. Circulating assets financed by the bank are excluded because bank interest is being paid. Certain enterprises which fulfil their production and profit plans using funds of a lower value than provided by the plan are allowed to retain those economies and their payments to the State budget are reduced accordingly.

Under restructuring this type of payment is to be extended gradually to a single rate of payment for all enterprises in a particular branch of industry and eventually to all branches, with exemptions or reductions

---

[2] On the pre-restructuring period, see G. S. Gurevich (ed) *Sovetskoe finansovoe pravo* (1985).

in the rate being permissible for enterprises with a low profitability rate or operating at a loss. As a 'priority' payment, the levy against production funds represents a payment from profit and not a tax on profit. The State is in effect being reimbursed for the use of its property made available to the enterprise by right of operative management.

Fixed payments (rents)

Fixed payments are payments from profit to the State budget by economically-accountable enterprises which have received supplementary incomes for reasons which have nothing to do with their activities, but which reflect natural, transport, geographic or other factors or conditions. Production technology, for example, may vary from one enterprise to another within the same industry because the quality of raw materials differs, or differential electricity rates or proximity to transport may give enterprises in one part of the country an advantage over others which is reflected in profit. These payments operate in effect as an equalisation device vis-à-vis less favoured enterprises in the same branch of industry. In the extractive industries the payments are linked to differences in the natural environment and hence are called 'rents'; in the processing and manufacturing industries the expression 'fixed payments' is used.

This type of payment also originated in the 1965 economic reforms and is governed by the Statute on Fixed Payments to the Budget of 11 November 1966. The group of enterprises levied with fixed payments is rather small, principally in the oil, gas, copper, and certain processing industries. The rates vary with the type of product and payment may be levied against units of production, weight, value or profit, or may be simply a lump sum. No exemptions are provided for by legislation. In certain industries the revenues received by the State from this levy exceed those obtained from payments for the production fund. In 1979 the fixed payment was extended to highly-profitable products which are produced for a long time, the object being to provide an additional incentive for improving quality and expanding the product range.

Under restructuring the principle of fixed payments and rents is to be extended considerably. The State is to be compensated for training the work force by a differential levy against labour resources, depending on the region of the country. Socio-cultural and municipal amenities also will be affected. Differences in the natural productivity of such resources as land, water, and minerals have become the object of differential rents. These components of restructuring are recited in the 1987 Law on the State Enterprise (Art 17(3)) and the Decree of 17 July 1987 'On Restructuring the Financial Mechanism and Enhancing the Role of the USSR Ministry of Finances Under the New Economic Conditions' (point 4) and appropriate amendments introduced in natural resource legislation.

Residual profits

For most enterprises the major contribution to State revenues takes the form of transferring residual profits. Profits are 'residual' in the sense that they remain after profits have been utilised for all other purposes provided for by plan. This type of payment was also introduced with the 1965 economic reform, but the procedure for calculating the amounts due is governed by a 1979 Statute on the Procedure for Distributing the Profits (Plan and Above-Plan) of Production Associations, Enterprises, and Organisations of Industry. The Statute extends to those entities which do not distribute profit under the 'normative method of profit distribution.'

The amount of the residual profit is confirmed by the superior organisation and incorporated into the enterprise financial plan. Payments are made quarterly at the same intervals as payments for production funds, with quarterly and annual recalculations based on the actual sums. In effect this payment represents the final balancing of accounts of the enterprise, and under the pre-restructuring philosophy represented the extent to which the financial resources of an enterprise exceeded its requirements. Unlike the payments above, however, residual profits assume that the enterprise profit plan itself has been fulfilled; if not, the enterprise pays in a lower sum to the State budget than was called for by the Plan and both State and enterprise interests are adversely affected. Hence there is a disposition to transfer enterprises to the normative method of profit distribution. Under restructuring residual profit payments will continue to be phased out in favour of the normative method.

In its present guise the normative method of profit distribution dates from 1979. The object of the method is to introduce a stable standard for deductions from profit by confirming a sum certain of profit deductions, calculated as the difference between payments for production and fixed payments on one hand, and the total amount of payments to the budget. With a view to tightening planning, the first 3% of above-plan profit is distributed half to the enterprise and half to the budget. Above-plan profit in excess of 3% is less advantageous to the enterprise. 25% remains with it and 75% goes to the budget. If the profit plan is not fulfilled, the profit deductions are reduced accordingly.

Deductions from profits

More than two decades after the 1965 economic reform, some State enterprises have still never been transferred to the reform system. Deductions from their profits for the State budget are governed by legislation dating from 1931 as amended. The enterprises and organisations under this system are primarily ones where operations are not based principally upon the utilisation of premises, machines, and equipment: design organisations, credit and insurance institutions, trade organisations, and the like. In effect the entities concerned pay into the State treasury all profits remaining after planned expeditures have been covered. The minimum payment to the budget is 10% of annual profit, even if enterprise expenditures comprise more than 90% of the planned profit, the deficit being made good by the superior organisation through profit redistribution.

Certain categories of enterprises or institutions pay profit deductions of 75% of balance-sheet profit. Specified types of enterprise are partially or wholly exempt from this type of payment, eg domestic service enterprises. Under restructuring this type of payment should be wholly phased out.

Turnover tax

Although its role in Soviet economic life is considerably less than when it was first introduced in 1930, the turnover tax nonetheless accounts for a significant share of State revenue. The general provisions for levying the tax, periods for payment, exemptions, and special applications to particular types of goods are set out in the Statute on the Turnover Tax of 30 June 1975, as amended, and the General Instruction on the Turnover Tax confirmed by the USSR Ministry of Finances on 31 December 1975, as amended; there are supplementary regulations applicable to special situations. In principle the tax varies with the price levels of individual products and is imposed on those goods whose price generates revenues that significantly exceed the profit required for the normal operation of the enterprise. Although various types of enterprise, organisation, and other entities pay the tax, the levy is against the goods and not the taxpayer. Furthermore, each good or product is levied against only once, even though it may pass through several links of the chain from producer to consumer. At precisely which point the levy is imposed, depends on the good concerned and the ways in which it is realised. Even certain co-operative and social organisations may pay the turnover tax.

The rate of turnover tax may fluctuate widely even on the same product, weight being given to regional or other considerations. In the interests of inducing enterprises to improve product quality or introduce new technology, the tax may be increased for obsolete goods or reduced for new products. Under the 1975 General Instruction the turnover tax may be levied as a lump sum or fixed amount per unit of product, as a percentage of sales revenue, or against the difference between the retail and wholesale prices of a product. The last method is employed most widely, especially in light industry and trading enterprises with an extensive assortment of goods. Various schemes for payment are utilised, including settlement of account, daily, five-day, ten-day, monthly, and quarterly payments. Sugar, vodka, liqueurs, and textiles are amongst the products where the tax is paid upon settlement of the account.

Exemptions from the tax are numerous, and the USSR Ministry of Finances has considerable discretion to reduce the rate for products or wholly exempt certain enterprises from payment. The great majority of enterprises that produce means of production, for example, are exempt. The tax also is used to influence consumer demand; consequently, rates may be high on goods deemed to be luxuries or socially harmful (eg alcoholic beverages) and nominal on objects whose use is to be encouraged (eg vitamins, children's toys, bread, etc). Under restructuring the role of the turnover tax is likely to diminish.

Other payments to the State budget

State social insurance is financed from contributions levied against enterprises, associations, and other economic organisations. These are paid into the State budget and spent on benefits established by law but administered by trade union agencies. The contributions are based on a percentage of the wage fund and vary from industry to industry, the precise levy being fixed by the Central Trade Union Council. Detailed regulations specify procedures for payment. Collective farm social insurance contributions are paid not into the State budget but into a special all-union social insurance fund.

Levies against industrial enterprises for water use were introduced with effect from 1 January 1982 and in 1987–88 were extended to land and minerals. These levies are intended to encourage the more rational use of natural resources and are paid into the State budget. They are regarded as part of the costs of production of an enterprise provided they are incurred within the quota of water use fixed by water conservancy agencies, usually at preferential rates. Excess use entails much higher rates and is treated as a 'non-production expenditure.'

Enterprises and social organisations which charge an admission fee to screen films pay a tax under a 1975 Edict. The rate varies from city to countryside and is levied against gross receipts. The top rate is 55% in the city down to zero for children's theatres and the like.

Other sources of revenue in the form of payments to the State budget include levies to cover geological survey work in certain industries, unused credits allocated to enterprises, amounts payable for exceeding price levels or failing to observe technical standards, cash penalties imposed by people's control committees, and the residual assets of institutions being wound up. Although in the western perception these would not be categorised as taxation, they are in the Soviet view a form of levy designed to ensure the observance of legality or guide economic behaviour without quite passing into the realm of a fine.

Income tax on collective farms

As a form of co-operative organisation possessing independent legal personality, collective farms are outside the State sector and are treated for revenue purposes as genuine taxpayers. Although collective farms have been subject to some sort of agricultural tax since their formation in the early 1920s, an income tax was first imposed in 1936. At present the relevant enactment is an Edict of 10 April 1965 'On the Income Tax from Collective Farms', as amended by the redaction of 10 June 1987.

The income tax is levied against revenues received by collective farms from all types of activities according to normative standards determined by taking into account the economic valuation of the land and the production potential of the farm. The fish tax was abolished with effect from 1 January 1988. Two facets of collective farm operations are subject to income tax: the net income of the collective farm obtained from the aforementioned sources; and the wage fund for the collective farmers. Net income is to be defined by normative standards devised in a procedure confirmed by the USSR Council of Ministers. Exemptions or reduced rates apply to collective farms accepting new settlers, to farms located in remote areas, and to farms experiencing economic difficulties or natural disasters, and to farms engaging in certain activities which the State wishes to encourage.

Quite independently of the tax on revenues, collective farms are liable for income tax on the wage fund. The tax is levied only on that portion of the fund exceeding average monthly earnings per working member of the collective farm equal to the minimum State wage for workers and employees. The rates are to be fixed by the USSR Council of Ministers. Inter-farm enterprises and organisations pay income tax on the same basis as the collective farms, that is, on their net profit after distributions to shareholders. The shareholders include their portion of the profit in their net income.

Income tax on co-operative and social organisations

The enterprises and subdivisions of consumer co-operatives, social organisations, and co-operatives for the production of products and rendering of services are subject to income tax under the Edict of 1 March 1979 'On the Income Tax From Co-operative and Social Organisations', as amended in 1987 and 1988. Such entities must operate on the principle of economic accountability, have an independent balance sheet and their own bank account, and possess the right independently to dispose of the profit earned. Agencies of such entities which have their own bank account but are not economically accountable are subject to income tax on revenues from their activities for which they receive compensation as well as on revenues received by their subordinate subdivisions that do not have an independent balance sheet. The tax rate is 35% on the profits of consumer co-operatives and enterprises of social organisations, with the exception that trade union enterprises pay 25%. The tax on product and service co-operatives is fixed by the USSR Council of Ministers.

The exemptions from this tax are numerous and significant. Trade union clubs, palaces and houses of culture, sanatoriums, resorts, and tourist institutions are exempt, as are many sport organisations and the principal unions of journalists, writers, cinematographers, and other professional or creative organisations, the enterprises and economic agencies of the Communist Party and the Komsomol, the Red Cross and Red Crescent societies, and the like. Special rates may be fixed to encourage co-operatives, and revenues donated by co-operatives to approved charities are exempt from income tax.

Income tax on individuals

Although income tax is the most significant tax imposed directly on individuals, it accounts for only about 7% of State revenue. As part of the transition to a communist society, Soviet policy has attempted to reduce the dependence of the State on revenues obtained directly from individuals with a view to ultimately abolishing income tax completely. Under restructuring, the role of income tax may increase in light of the greater differentials expected in individual incomes, though perhaps this end may be achieved by giving greater exemptions to lower-income families. Collective farmers do not pay income tax on their earnings from the collective farm.

All individuals—Soviet citizens, foreign nationals, and stateless persons—who have independent sources of income on Soviet territory are in principle liable for income tax in the Soviet Union. The liability of foreign citizens and stateless persons for income tax is governed by an

Edict of 12 May 1978 (see chapter 20). The income tax levied against Soviet citizens is regulated by an Edict of 30 April 1943 as approved in a consolidated version on 20 October 1983, with subsequent amendments and subsidiary regulations.

WORKERS AND EMPLOYEES

A progressive rate of income tax is levied against the earnings and other receipts in cash or in kind received by workers and employees at their principal place of work for the performance of labour duties. The rate is 25 kopecks on incomes of 71 rubles per month, rising to 8.20 rubles plus 13% of the amount exceeding 100 rubles. The average monthly wage of Soviet workers and employees at the beginning of 1988 was 201 rubles. Excluded from monthly earnings are: severance allowances payable in the event of dismissal, amounts paid as an extraordinary grant, certain compensatory payments, accommodation allowances, gifts, and other allowances. Equated to workers and employees for tax purposes are military servicemen with respect to cash allowances; students and postgraduates with respect to their stipends; advocates with respect to remuneration received from their legal consultation offices. Members of product and service co-operatives, with respect to incomes received for work in those co-operatives, are taxed under an Edict of 14 March 1988 at the same rates as workers and employees up to 500 rubles per month, then at 60.20 rubles plus 30% of the amount exceeding 500 rubles up to 700, rising to 620.20 rubles plus 90% of the amount exceeding 1500 rubles per month.

SECONDARY INCOME EARNERS AND SELF-EMPLOYED

Individuals who hold second jobs or who do one-off jobs, hunters and trappers, homeworkers, and temporary workers are amongst those who fall into this broad category. They are taxed progressively at rates from 1.5% on monthly incomes up to 100 rubles rising to 8.20 rubles plus 13% of the amount exceeding a monthly income of 100 rubles. The same rates are applicable to the authors of discoveries and inventions, rationalisation proposals and industrial models, who receive remuneration under their respective certificates exceeding 1,000 rubles for each discovery, invention, proposal, or model.

COPYRIGHT AND ROYALTIES

Remuneration for the publication, performance, or other use of works of science, literature, and art is subject to progressive taxation generally as follows. Amounts paid to Soviet and other authors for the use of their work in the Soviet Union and receipts from abroad for Soviet authors for works (including translations) specially done to be performed or published overseas are taxed at the rate of 1.5% on income up to 180 rubles rising to 92.40 rubles plus 13% of the amount exceeding 1,200 rubles per annum. The same rate is applicable to the incomes of writers and performers obtained from sources outside their principal place of work and to citizens who are not members of professional societies but who sell original paintings, sculpture, graphics and other types of art, including decorative and applied arts, through exhibitions or specially-founded State, co-operative, and other social organisations.

Royalties received from overseas by Soviet authors or other authors permanently resident in the USSR (excluding works mentioned above) are taxed at a rate of 30% up to 500 rubles per year, rising to 2,775 rubles plus 75% of the amount exceeding 5,000 rubles. However, if the royalties come from other socialist countries, the rates are reduced by one-half if the remuneration does not exceed 1,000 rubles per year. Above that the normal rates apply. The legal successors of authors pay income tax at the same rates, except for heirs who are taxed at the rate of 60% on annual royalties up to 500 rubles, rising to 11,725 rubles plus 90% of the amount exceeding 15,000 rubles per year. Lower rates are applicable to heirs who are under age 16, students, pensioners, disabled persons, or women above the age of 55 and men above 60.

OTHER TYPES OF ACTIVITIES

Soviet citizens who derive incomes from individual labour activity in the spheres of handicrafts, domestic services, folk arts and socio-cultural activities pay income tax at the rate equal to the amount levied against workers and employees at their principal place of work, being exempt up to the same minimum wage levels as workers and employees, up to 3,000 rubles per year. Above that amount the tax rises to 1,332.40 rubles plus 65% of the amount exceeding 6,000 rubles per year. For persons engaged in various forms of 'private practice' (doctors, architects, artists, teachers, and others not elsewhere enumerated) the progressive rate is from 15 rubles plus 10% of the amount exceeding 300 rubles, rising to 3,171.40 rubles plus 69% of the amount exceeding 7,000 rubles. The same rates extend to personnel of religious bodies in the Soviet Union. In all cases the taxable income is considered to be the difference between gross income less deductible expenses.

EXEMPTIONS

Soviet legislation enumerates broad categories of exempted individuals or sources of income. In addition the USSR, union republic, and inferior finance agencies have the power to exempt individual taxpayers or groups of taxpayers wholly or partially from income tax. Among incomes exempted from tax are State social insurance and security benefits, alimony, disability and loss of bread-winner benefits, the proceeds from the sale of subsidiary husbandry products, and a lengthy list of exempt incomes enumerated in a Decree of 29 September 1983 'On the Incomes of Citizens Not Subject to Income Tax'.

Tax on bachelors, single citizens, and citizens with small families

With a view to offsetting the tax concessions granted to large families and distributing more equitably the social costs associated with nurturing and educating children, Soviet legislation has since 1941 imposed a special tax on bachelors, single citizens, and citizens with small families. Foreigners are not subject to this tax, which is levied against Soviet citizens who are 20-years-old and have independent sources of income. Women are exempted when they reach age 45 and men upon attaining the age of 50. Essentially all incomes subject to income tax also attract the bachelors' tax. The rate of the tax is 6%.

Marriage is not a prerequisite for exemption, and all children are taken into account, whether natural or adopted, irrespective of their age. In some instances citizens who must pay the tax are exempted with respect to certain types of income.

Agricultural tax

In its present form the agricultural tax is governed by consolidated legislation enacted 22 December 1983. The tax is assessed against collective farm households and the households of other citizens who have land plots on the territory of rural soviets. Where applicable, the tax is assessed at stipulated rates per hundredths of a hectare. The rates vary widely from one locality to another, taking into account land fertility, household income and regional differences. Exemptions are numerous and sometimes structured to serve as an incentive or reward to categories of the general public. About one-third of all households potentially subject to the tax are wholly or partially exempted for one reason or another.

Vehicle tax

On 21 March 1988 the taxation of owners of automobiles, motorcycles, and other craft was removed from the category of 'local taxes.' The new legislation treats such revenues as all-union income and imposes the levy upon State, co-operative, and social enterprises and organisations which operate on economic accountability, Soviet citizens, stateless persons, and foreign natural and juridical persons who own automobiles, motorcycles, and other self-propelled vehicles or air-powered machinery (excluding caterpillar vehicles). The tax is based on horsepower or kilowatts and must be paid before registration, re-registration, or annual inspection. There are certain exemptions for public transport enterprises and disabled persons.

Local taxes

Taxes in this category, regulated by the Statute on Local Taxes of 26 January 1981 as amended, may extend both to individuals and to co-operative enterprises or organisations. The tax revenues go wholly to the budgets of local government, but broad powers exist at all levels to exempt individual taxpayers or groups of taxpayers.

LAND AND BUILDINGS TAX

Those who possess structures or plots of land are subject to a building or land tax. The buildings include dwelling houses or other structures and the land tax is imposed on land plots granted for use in perpetuity. The rate for buildings owned by co-operative enterprises, institutions, and organisations and by foreign legal persons is 0.5% of the value of the building; for buildings owned by citizens the rate is 1% of its value. The land tax depends on how the land is classified. There are six categories, reflecting the administrative stature of the community, size of population, and various economic considerations. The rates vary from 1.8 to 6.4 kopecks per year for each square metre of land.

In individual localities taxes and charges may be imposed in respect of tourism, sport fishing and hunting, excursions, and the like. Since 1981 an assessment has been made against collective farm markets with a view to financing the expansion and improvement of their premises.

SELF-ASSESSMENT

Under the Edict of 26 January 1981 'On Local Taxes and Charges' rural communities may voluntarily impose special assessments upon themselves for special purposes up to a maximum of four rubles annually per household. The decision, taken by a majority vote of a general meeting held by one or several settlements, is binding and the assessment, if not paid, may be recovered in the usual way applicable to State taxes. The proceeds, however, do not become part of the rural budget but are spent directly for the designated purpose in accordance with the estimate confirmed by the local soviet.

State and customs duties

Many functions performed by State agencies are subject to a charge called a State duty. These are enumerated in an Edict of 29 June 1979 'On State Duty' and include filing a petition to sue or a cassational appeal; issuing copies of documents; performance of various functions by ZAGS and notarial agencies; residence registration; remittance of money abroad; or the issuance of documents to travel abroad or invite a foreigner to visit the USSR privately.

The duty may be a lump-sum payment or represent a percentage of the value of the transaction. Certain exemptions are provided for by law.

Customs duties may be levied as prescribed against goods imported and exported.

Recovery of unpaid taxes

The procedures for recovering unpaid taxes are laid down in the 1981 Statute on the Recovery of Overdue Taxes and Non-Tax Payments unless special provision is made elsewhere. Statutory financial penalties are imposed for delays in payment. If formal proceedings are necessary, in the case of enterprises, institutions, and organisations the arrears will be recovered through a non-judicial administrative proceeding instituted by the finance agencies responsible for calculating and collecting the tax. Execution may be levied against the delinquent enterprise's bank accounts, accounts receivable, and certain other specified enterprise assets.

With respect to Soviet citizens, foreign juridical persons, foreign nationals, and stateless persons in arrears, a judicial proceeding is required. The procedures closely approximate those applicable to the enforcement of judgments under the union republic codes of civil procedure. The finance agencies prepare an inventory of property to be attached in the presence of the debtor and witnesses and publish a notice prohibiting the disposition of that property. The debtor then has ten days to pay before the court will hear the case. Certain property is excluded from attachment.

Chapter 17

Criminal law

The development of criminal law in the Soviet Union has been a barometer of both the degree of insecurity felt by the authorities toward forces within and without Soviet society who are perceived to represent a real or potential threat and of the extent to which the Soviet Union is believed to be maturing in the direction of a society where crime and punishment are obsolete.

HISTORICAL BACKGROUND

Even though many of its provisions were abhorrent, the Soviet authorities inherited in 1917 an Imperial Russian Criminal Code of 1903 that technically speaking was among the most advanced in Europe. An initial proposal to repeal at once the laws of the overthrown governments set out in a draft Decree 'On the Court' (prepared by P. I. Stuchka) was revised at Lenin's behest to provide that 'local courts shall decide cases in the name of the Russian Republic and be guided in their decisions and judgments by laws of the overthrown governments only insofar as these have not been repealed by the revolution and are not contrary to the revolutionary conscience and revolutionary legal consciousness' (Art 5). This provision extended only to courts and not to revolutionary tribunals.[1] Decree No 2 'On the Court' of 15 February 1918 established that 'the court shall be guided in civil and criminal cases by civil and criminal laws prevailing up to now only insofar as they have not been repealed by decrees of the Central Executive Committee and the Council of People's Commissars and are not contrary to socialist legal consciousness' (Art 36).[2] Decree No 3 'On the Court' of 20 July 1918 said nothing whatever about the old laws, requiring that the courts be guided 'by decrees of the workers' and peasants' government and socialist conscience.'[3] The RSFSR Statute on the People's Court promulgated 30 November 1918 forbade, in repeating the same language, 'references in judgments and decisions to laws of the overthrown governments.'[4]

Criminal offences and sanctions were in fact established piecemeal in

1 *SU RSFSR* (1917) no. 4, item 50.
2 *SU RSFSR* (1918) no. 26, item 347.
3 *SU RSFSR* (1918) no. 52, item 589.
4 *SU RSFSR* (1918) no. 85, item 889.

a number of early decrees, commencing with the decree on land. The 1918 Constitution conferred jurisdiction over '. . . criminal legislation, etc' on the All-Russian Congress of Soviets and All-Russian Central Executive Committee but did not call for the enactment of a criminal code. The first systematic attempt along these lines emanated from neither of those bodies, but from the RSFSR People's Commissariat of Justice, which on 12 December 1919 approved a set of Guiding Principles of Criminal Legislation of the RSFSR.[5] The Guiding Principles dealt cursorily in 27 Articles with the concept of crime and punishment, attempt, preparation, types of punishment, and related matters. In the opinion of many Soviet jurists, the Guiding Principles laid down the first definition of crime under Soviet law requiring the act be evaluated both formally (was it contrary to the law?) and materially (was it dangerous to society?).

The impetus to codification stimulated by the NEP led to the enactment of the 1922 RSFSR Criminal Code.[6] The formation of the USSR in December 1922 and adoption in 1924 of the USSR Constitution relegated the codification of criminal law to the constitutent union republics within the framework of Fundamental Principles laid down by the all-union authority. The Fundamental Principles of Criminal Legislation were enacted in October 1924.[7] Consisting of merely 39 articles, the Fundamental Principles required amendments to RSFSR criminal legislation, and on 22 November 1926 the RSFSR adopted a new criminal code that entered into force on 1 January 1927 and remained, as revised, the keystone of Soviet criminal policy for more than three decades.[8] The scheme of all-union codes of law contemplated by the 1936 USSR Constitution produced several drafts between 1939 and 1950, but none were given legislative endorsement. Soon after the 1957 amendment of the Constitution restoring the scheme of all-union fundamental principles and union republic codes, the USSR Supreme Soviet on 25 December 1958 confirmed the present FPCrimL, followed between 1959–61 by new criminal codes in each of the 15 union republics.

Criminal law: the General Part

The union republic criminal codes, reproducing, elaborating, and supplementing the imperative provisions of the FPCrimL, the Law on Crimes Against the State, the Law on Military Crimes, and certain other all-union criminal legislation, are divided into two parts: a General Part

---

5 *SU RSFSR* (1919) no. 66, item 590.
6 *SU RSFSR* (1922) no. 15, item 153.
7 *SZ SSSR* (1924) no. 24, item 205.
8 *SU RSFSR* (1926) no. 80, item 600.

containing general provisions applicable to the effect and operation of the codes as a whole and a Special Part containing definitions and punishments for each specific offence. Appended to the codes is a list of property not subject to confiscation by court judgment.

A. PURPOSE OF CRIMINAL LAW

Anglo-American criminal law is remarkable for the absence of a specific legislative statement of purpose. A leading English text declares simply: '. . . the primary objective of the criminal law is the punishment of the offender.'[9] In Soviet criminal law the statement of purpose has been central to the course of criminal policy. The 1959–61 criminal codes, as amended in 1982, provide as their tasks '. . . the protection of the social system of the USSR, of its political and economic system, of socialist ownership, of the person and the rights and freedoms of citizens, and of the entire socialist legal order, against criminal infringements,' (Art 1). It is for this purpose, the codes continue, that they determine which 'socially dangerous acts are criminal, and establish the punishments applicable to persons who have committed crimes.' The codes do not indicate whether their objects are to be accomplished by way of repression, example, prevention, or general education; that is, although they define their functions as codes, their larger role in criminal policy is left unarticulated. Soviet commentators make clear that this larger purpose is to be found in Party documents such as the 1961 Programme of the CPSU, which declares 'attention should be devoted principally to crime prevention.' Criminal repression consequently is regarded as having an auxiliary role in protecting the socialist legal order.[10]

B. OPERATION OF CRIMINAL CODE IN TIME AND SPACE

All persons, including foreign citizens and stateless persons, who commit crimes on the territory of a union republic are subject to responsibility in accordance with the union republic criminal code unless they enjoy diplomatic privileges and immunities or are otherwise exempted from jurisdiction by international treaties of the USSR. Territory for these purposes encompasses the land and subsoil thereof, internal waters, the territorial sea, and certain maritime zones beyond, frontier rivers and lakes up to the State frontier, Soviet-registered warships and non-military vessels, and Soviet-registered aircraft.

Soviet citizens as defined by the 1979 Law on Citizenship of the USSR and stateless persons are subject to criminal responsibility for criminal acts committed under Soviet laws outside the USSR and may be prosecuted even if they were convicted and served punishment for the

9 R. Cross and P. A. Jones *Introduction to Criminal Law* (6th edn, 1968) p 10.
10 Iu. D. Severin (ed) *Kommentarii k Ugolovnomu kodeksu RSFSR* (1980) p 6.

crime in a foreign jurisdiction. Soviet criminal legislation extends to foreigners who commit crimes outside the USSR only if international treaties so provide.

The criminality and punishability of an act are determined by legislation in force when the act was committed, except that a subsequent law reducing punishment or repealing an offence shall have retroactive force whereas a law increasing punishment or establishing a new offence shall not. Despite this clause on retroactivity, at least one case is known dating from 1961 when the Presidium of the USSR Supreme Soviet specifically authorised the retroactive application of the death penalty.[11]

C. DEFINITION OF CRIME

A crime is defined as a 'socially dangerous act (an action or omission to act)' that is expressly provided for by a criminal law. This definition represents a considerable advance upon the approach taken in the 1926 RSFSR Criminal Code, for the modern codes imposed two requirements: first, the act must be specifically stipulated in the law; and second, it must be 'socially dangerous.' Thus are the formal and material elements combined.[12] An act even if dangerous to society cannot be treated as a crime unless the law so provides. Moreover, even if an act is defined as a crime, it may be regarded as not a crime by virtue of its insignificance, since it does not represent a danger to society. Only a court, under the present codes, may determine that someone is guilty of committing a crime and assign criminal punishment, in accordance with law.

The 1926 Criminal Code created a very different equation between elements of formality and materiality. The code undertook to protect the socialist State against 'socially dangerous acts (crimes) by applying to persons committing the said acts the measures of social defence' provided for in the Code. There was no requirement that the law expressly prohibit such acts; social danger was the test. The flexibility (and therefore uncertainty of precisely what behaviour was criminal) of this approach was extended by the principle of analogy in the 1926 Code: 'if any other socially dangerous act is not expressly provided for by the present Code the grounds and limits of responsibility therefor shall be determined according to those articles of the Code which provide for crimes most similar in nature' (Art 16). The analogy principle was controversial among Soviet jurists and deeply criticised abroad. Some dismissed it as a purely 'technical' matter having no 'political or socially nurturing significance.' They regarded it as a method of interpretation, and more dangerously, as a means of filling gaps in the law or a transformation of

11 H. J. Berman *Justice in the USSR* (rev. edn, 1966) pp 86, 403.
12 See I. Lapenna *Soviet Penal Policy* (1968) pp 31-34, 67-71.

the Special Part into a 'model list' of crimes.[13] The omission of analogy in the 1958 FPCrimL was a major step forward in post-Stalin criminal law reform.

Certain acts under the 1959–61 criminal codes are believed to represent a heightened social danger. These are categorised as 'grave crimes' by virtue of amendments to the criminal codes in 1972–74 and 1982.

Amendments introduced in late 1982 to the RSFSR Criminal Code gave reason for some concern about the integrity of the Special Part. Under the 1960 redaction of the Code, all crimes were to be provided for in the Special Part; according to the 1982 amendments, merely by a criminal law [*zakon*]. This suggests the criminal codes may no longer be the sole repository of union republic criminal legislation, which if true will detract considerably from the unity of criminal law and accentuate certain other weaknesses of the criminal codes: the broad definitions of certain offences, the lack of definition for certain offences or constituent elements thereof, and the incorporation by reference of other legislation, often subordinate enactments, whose text is not readily available.[14] In some instances these weaknesses can be attenuated through the use of commentaries to the codes prepared by jurists or reference to supreme court guiding explanations and judicial practice. In others, the citizen confronts great difficulty in ascertaining the limits of legally admissible conduct.

D. INTENT AND NEGLIGENCE

The criminal law reforms of 1958 incorporated an element omitted in the 1926 RSFSR Criminal Code: the moral guilt or fault of an accused. Guilt may be manifested in two ways, by intent and through negligence. Intent may be direct or indirect. The FPCrimL provide that 'a crime shall be deemed to be committed intentionally if the person who commits it is conscious of the socially dangerous character of his action or omission to act, foresees its socially dangerous consequences, and desires those consequences or consciously permits them to occur' (Art 8). There is direct intent when a person is aware that his action and its consequences are socially dangerous and desires those consequences to happen. Indirect intent is present when a person is aware that from his action or omission to act a socially dangerous consequence may occur and he consciously will risk this possible consequence. The majority of intentional crimes require direct intent, some may be committed with

---

13 See V. G. Smirnov and M. D. Shargorodskii in O. S. Ioffe (ed) *Sorok let sovetskogo prava 1917–1957* (1957) I, pp 484–485, for an account of some of the early contending views.
14 Although subordinate legislation sometimes elaborates the definition of a crime, the Procuracy has repeatedly protested initiatives by local soviets which amount to the creation of new offences.

either direct or indirect intent, and a few only with indirect intent. In practice a distinction is drawn between situations when a person's intent was *definite*, that is, he foresaw a specific definite result arising from his socially dangerous act or omission to act, or was *indefinite*, that is, he foresaw socially dangerous consequences but not specific ones.

Likewise there are two forms of negligence. The first, sometimes called criminal presumptuousness, arises when a guilty person foresees the possibility of the occurrence of the socially dangerous consequences of his action or omission to act but frivolously counts on their being prevented or averted. The second variety of negligence is often termed criminal carelessness. It arises when a guilty person did not foresee the possibility that the socially dangerous consequences of his action or omission to act would occur, although he could and should have foreseen them.

Just as in all legal systems these distinctions can be difficult to draw in practice. The state of mind in direct and indirect intent and criminal presumptuousness of the guilty person is the foreseeing of the socially dangerous consequences of his act either as desired or possible. An element of will is present in all these instances, whereas in the instance of criminal carelessness, a failure of will occurred—to foresee socially dangerous consequences which should and could have been foreseen—although the guilty person intellectually should have been aware of his neglect of the requirements of the law or the rules of socialist community life or the interests of other persons.

Examples. The USSR Supreme Court considered the following to be a case of criminal presumptuousness: The custodian of a warehouse of combustible material, obliged to leave on business, wound the barbed wire fence surrounding the warehouse around the rosette of a 220 volt electrical connection. A passer-by touched the fence and was electrocuted. In convicting the custodian of negligent homicide, the Supreme Court pointed out that the warehouse was situated in an uninhabited area and approaches were fenced off on three sides; that on the fourth side the custodian erected a sign 'Attention Fence is Wired, Caution, Death,' and that before leaving the custodian had tested the current in the fence to be sure that no one approaching the fence would be injured.

As an instance of criminal carelessness, the USSR Supreme Court convicted a citizen who, noticing children picking berries from a mulberry tree while on a shed roof, threw a wooden stick at them and hit a 15-year-old girl, who jumped from the shed, ran about 45 yards, fell, and died from grave bodily injuries. The Plenum of the Court held that the citizen could and should have foreseen the consequences which occurred.

If a consequence causally linked with the actions of a person causes harm but the persons did not, could not, and should not have foreseen the occurrence of these consequences, no criminal responsibility under Soviet law would lie.

Example. Citizen K poured acid from a champagne bottle during a drinking bout, for all participants, including himself. No criminal negligence occurred, said the USSR Supreme Court, because K was mistaken in good faith about the contents of the champagne bottle and did not nor could not foresee that as a result of his actions he and everyone else might be gravely injured or die.

E. ATTENUATION OF CRIMINAL RESPONSIBILITY

Two factors may diminish or preclude criminal responsibility: age and mental illness. All Soviet criminal codes establish the age of 16 as the minimum for criminal responsibility. There is no maximum age. For certain crimes minors aged 14 to 16 may be prosecuted, for example, homicide, intentional infliction of bodily injury causing impairment of health, rape, assault with intent to rob, theft, robbery, malicious hooliganism, and others. Minors aged 16 to 18 who commit a crime which does not represent a great social danger and can be reformed without criminal punishment may be assigned compulsory measures of an educational character, just as minors aged 14 to 16. The court may take this action either in administrative or judicial session and ordinarily will refer the case to a commission for cases of minors.

Persons who are non-imputable, that is, at the time of committing a socially dangerous act could not realise the significance of their actions or control them because of chronic mental illness, temporary mental derangement, mental deficiency, or other condition or illness are not subject to criminal responsibility but may be subject to compulsory medical measures. The criteria for non-imputability may be medical (biological) or legal (psychological). The court must base its judgment on the expert opinion of a forensic psychiatrist and also determine whether the gravity of the illness was sufficient to establish legal non-imputability.

A person who committed a crime while in a state of intoxication is not relieved of criminal responsibility.

F. EXCULPATORY CIRCUMSTANCES

Even when an action falls within the constituent elements of a crime as defined by a criminal law, there are three types of exculpatory circumstances. The first has been noted above: an action or omission to act is not a crime if by reason of its insignificance it does not represent a social danger. Illegality is a legal expression of the social danger of an act. Each case must be judged on the basis of the factual circumstances: the character of the act, the situation and conditions under which it was committed, the lack of material harmful consequences or insignificance of harm caused, and the non-intention to harm socialist legal relations. Factors relating to the character of the individual are not weighed in this connection, for they affect only the assignment of punishment.

Necessary defence as a principle has been closely related in Soviet doctrine and practice to the concept of the ideal Soviet Man. Should a Soviet citizen be required to retreat when subjected to attack with a view to reducing personal injury at all possible cost or should he be resolute and stand up for his rights assertively? The commentators stress that necessary defence reflects the policy of the Party and Government to enlist citizens in the struggle against criminality. Accordingly, current judicial practice emphasises necessary defence as 'an important guarantee for realising the constitutional provisions concerning the inviolability of the person and of the dwelling and property of citizens and for ensuring the conditions for the fulfilment by citizens of their constitutional duty to protect socialist ownership and State and social interests.'[15] The criminal codes provide that an action shall not constitute a crime if it is committed while protecting the interests of the Soviet State, social interests, or the person or rights of the defender or of another person against a socially dangerous infringment by causing harm to the infringer, unless the defence is clearly disproportionate to the character or the danger of the infringement. The USSR Supreme Court has indicated that a person subjected to an attack has the right actively to defend himself even if he could flee, seek the aid of other citizens or State agencies, or choose some other means not directed against the infringer. A contrary view, the Court has declared, would be '. . . alien to principles of Soviet morality and socialist legal consciousness.' Necessary defence thus is a moral duty of every citizen and a legal duty for law enforcement officials, military servicemen, and the like.

Judicial practice has been important in fashioning the limits of necessary defence. The courts have required that an infringement must be socially dangerous, but necessary defence may legitimately be used against a minor or a non-imputable person, for example, unless the defender knows of the minority or non-imputability, in which event he must exhaust other means of defence unless the intensity of the infringement precludes this. Likewise, necessary defence may not be invoked if the defender knew the infringement had terminated or there was no real and direct threat of causing harm. Termination is not suspension, however; if an attacker withdraws to regroup or acquire better weapons, the infringement is considered to be a present one. The USSR Supreme Court has said that if an infringement has ended but the act of self-defence followed directly after the ended infringement and it was not clear to the defender that the infringement had ceased, necessary defence could apply.

In the event of an imagined infringement, the USSR Supreme Court reaffirmed in 1984 that, depending on the circumstances, an individual who had sufficient grounds to suppose an imaginary infringement were real and was not aware of his erroneous presupposition might either be

15 Decree of the Plenum of the USSR Supreme Court, 16 August 1984, No. 14.

exculpated from criminal responsibility or be charged with criminal negligence.

The proportionality of defence to attack is an issue of fact for the court, taking into account the degree and nature of the danger threatening the defender and his opportunity and strength to repulse the attack. The lower courts are instructed not to compare mechanically the equivalence of means for defence and attack, but to have regard for the number of attackers and defenders, their ages, physical condition, presence of weapons, place and time of infringement, mental state, and the like. The defence must be *clearly* disproportionate in order to override the right of necessary defence.

Extreme necessity is the third exculpatory circumstance: citizens who commit a criminal action in order to eliminate a danger which threatens the interests of the Soviet State, social interests, or the person or rights of the given person or of other citizens if under the particular circumstances this danger cannot be eliminated by other means and if the harm caused is less significant than the harm prevented. Examples of such dangers are flooding, earthquakes, avalanche, illness, starvation, a bull attacking a person, motor vehicle with faulty brakes, or a person who is causing or threatening to cause harm to legally-protected interests. The equation between the harm caused and the harm prevented is one of fact for the court, which is to be guided by its socialist legal consciousness. A crime against property, however, in order to save one's own life is always a legitimate use of extreme necessity.

Example. S stole a fire engine belonging to a State farm and caused damage to the vehicle in an amount of 611 rubles in order to deliver a hit-and-run victim to the hospital. The USSR Supreme Court held the theft of the fire engine was lawful.

Causing harm to avert equal harm is inadmissible. Saving one's own life by causing the death of another person is regarded as both amoral and criminal.

G. PUNISHMENT

According to the FPCrimL and union republic criminal codes, punishment serves three purposes: (1) chastisement for the crime committed; (2) reforming and re-educating the guilty person; and (3) preventing the commission of new crimes by the guilty person and others. Punishment may not, under the law, serve the purpose of causing physical suffering or debasing human dignity.

The FPCrimL provide a list of kinds of punishments which all the union republic criminal codes incorporate and to varying degrees augment. Certain punishments under the 1926 Criminal Code were abolished in the 1958 reforms: declaring an offender to be an enemy of the working people, with deprivation of Soviet citizenship and obligatory exile abroad; deprivation of freedom in special correctional-labour camps in remote areas of the USSR; removal of political and particular civil rights; and exile from the USSR for a designated term of years. The 1960 RSFSR Criminal Code lays down 12 punishments.

The death penalty is treated as an 'exceptional measure of punishment.' Capital punishment has been as controversial in the Soviet Union as in most other countries. Proponents believe it serves a deterrent purpose; opponents argue it is contrary to the Marxian explanation of crime and in any event its deterrent effects are doubtful and outweighed by considerations of humanity. Capital punishment was abolished in November 1917, restored in Spring 1918, abolished again in 1920, but again soon reinstated. The 1924 Fundamental Principles of Criminal Legislation included capital punishment as a 'provisional measure' pending complete abolition. In May 1947 the death penalty was abolished, reintroduced in 1950 for treason, espionage, and sabotage, enlarged in April 1954 to embrace intentional homicide under aggravating circumstances, and expanded again in the 1958 law reforms, with yet further additions in 1962. Crimes which might now entail the death penalty include currency speculation, counterfeiting, rape, stealing of State property, and others when committed on a large scale or causing grave injury. Individuals under 18 years of age and women who are pregnant when the crime was committed or when judgment was rendered or executed may not be condemned to death. The death penalty is carried out by shooting; most western estimates place the number of executions per year at about 200. Soviet sources in 1987 indicated that the death penalty is usually only assigned for intentional homicide under aggravating circumstances, rarely for rape and for stealing on a large scale, and since 1964 not applied at all for counterfeiting or violating rules on currency regulations.

Deprivation of freedom in a prison or correctional-labour colony (see chapter 17, below) may be assigned for a minimum of three months up to 15 years. This represents a reduction from the maximum under the 1926 RSFSR Criminal Code of 25 years. If the death penalty is commuted by a pardon, deprivation of freedom may be assigned for a term of up to 20 years. Exile or banishment may be assigned for a term of from two to five years. Correctional tasks without deprivation of freedom may be for a term of from two months to two years at the convicted person's place of employment or any other place in his district of residence. Deprivation of the right to occupy specified offices or to engage in a specified activity, for example, to drive a car, may be assigned for a term of from one to five years. A monetary fine is imposed by a court within the limits laid down in the Special Part for each offence. The court must have regard to the offender's financial status and may substitute correctional tasks if the fine cannot be paid in a lump sum. Dismissal from office may be imposed as a punishment when the character of a crime precludes the offender from continuing to hold a position of trust. The court may require a person to make amends for harm caused, either by directly reparating or compensating for harm caused or by a public apology to the victim or to the members of the collective in a form prescribed by the court. Compensation may not exceed 500 rubles, for otherwise it must be the object of civil proceedings. Social censure consists of a public expression by the court regarding the guilty person's improper conduct, which may be brought to public notice by various means, including publication in the press. Military servicemen may be assigned to a disciplinary battalion for a term of from three months up to two years. Correctional tasks without deprivation of freedom may for military servicemen be replaced by detention in a guardhouse for a term not exceeding two months. Confiscation of personal property owned by a convicted person may be imposed for certain crimes, but excluding items on the List appended to the Soviet criminal codes. Courts may deprive persons who have a military or special rank upon conviction for a grave crime and make recommendations to the appropriate bodies concerning the deprivation of an order, medal, or honorary title.

Some union republics impose penalties not found in other republics. The Ukrainian SSR, for example, authorises the deprivation of parental rights as a punishment.

Soviet law draws a distinction between 'basic' and 'supplementary' measures of punishment. Confiscation of property and deprivation of an order, medal, or honorary title may be applied only as supplementary punishments. Deprivation of freedom, correctional tasks, social censure, and assignment to a disciplinary battalion are basic measures of punishment. The others may be either basic or supplementary. The Special Part of the respective Soviet criminal codes determines for each crime the minimum and maximum range of a punishment and the particular types of punishment or refers the matter to the limits laid down in the General Part for the particular type of punishment.

H. ASSIGNMENT OF PUNISHMENT

When assigning punishment, the courts are required to work within the requirements of the types and limits imposed for each crime in the Special Part and to have regard to the character and degree of the crime committed, the personality of the guilty person, and any mitigating or aggravating circumstances. The codes list examples of each type of circumstance. Mitigating circumstances include the prevention of harmful consequences by the guilty person from the crime committed or voluntary compensation for the loss inflicted; committing a crime as a result of the concurrence of grave personal or family circumstances; committing a crime under threat or compulsion or by reason of material, occupational, or other dependence; commission of a crime by a minor or pregnant woman; sincere repentance; and others. Among the aggravating circumstances are the previous commission of a crime; commission of a crime by an organised group, or for mercenary or other base motives, or against a young, aged, or helpless person; causing grave consequences by the crime; denouncing a person known to be innocent; and if the court chooses, the commission of a crime by a person in a state of intoxication; and others.

In exceptional situations, a court may assign a milder punishment than that prescribed by law, but may not exceed the limits provided for by law. In recent years Soviet criminal legislation has encouraged sharper differentiation in assigning measures of punishment. A wider variety of possible punishments is available for first offenders, who for example may be assigned a conditional sentence on condition of good behaviour or a stay of execution of sentence on condition of exemplary conduct, or release on surety to a social organisation or collective of working people. When appropriate, conditional early relief from punishment may be granted or a milder punishment substituted. Persons sentenced to deprivation of freedom may be conditionally released and assigned to mandatory labour for a prescribed period. For minor infractions the case may be transferred for the instituting of administrative proceedings or be referred to a comrades' court.

Second offenders are being treated with increasing severity. Many qualify for being declared recidivists, which requires the imposition of harsher penalties, a more severe regime in correctional-labour institutions, and extended supervision upon release.

I. COMPULSORY MEDICAL AND EDUCATIONAL MEASURES

Compulsory medical measures arise when a person who has committed a socially dangerous act is non-imputable under the Soviet criminal codes or who committed such an act while imputable but before judgment was rendered or while serving punishment contracted a mental illness depriving him of the possibility of realising the significance of his actions or controlling them. The court must determine that the act committed was socially dangerous, was provided for by a criminal law, and would have entailed criminal responsibility if the act had been committed by an imputable person; the failure to so determine precludes the application of compulsory medical measures.

The application of compulsory medical measures is the right of a court, not a duty. The court must apply them in judicial session on the basis of evaluating all the circumstances of the case linked with the socially dangerous act and data relative to the personality of the mentally ill person. Under Soviet law, such measures are not a punishment; they are not a negative evaluation of an individual in the name of the State, do not contain elements of chastisement, and are not intended to reform or re-educate. Their object is to cure and socially rehabilitate the ill and protect society against dangerous conduct resulting from a deranged mind. The medical measures are compulsory in the sense that a court may apply them irrespective of the wishes of the mentally ill person, close relatives, or legal representatives, and only the court may modify or terminate them. Supervision over judicial rulings assigning, modifying, or terminating compulsory medical measures lies with the Procuracy, and supervision over the actual treatment with public health agencies.

A court may commit individuals to either a general or a special psychiatric hospital. The latter is used for an individual whose mental state and socially dangerous act means he represents a special danger to society. The procedure for applying compulsory medical measures is governed by an Instruction confirmed 14 February 1967 by the USSR Ministry of Public Health in agreement with the Procuracy, the USSR Supreme Court, and the Ministry for the Protection of Public Order.[16] In applying such measures the court will act on the basis of an expert opinion by a forensic psychiatrist evaluating the mental state of the individual concerned and recommending the type of hospital. The USSR Supreme Court has held that the expert's advice on type of hospital is not binding upon a court and, moreover, that a court may apply compulsory medical measures even if the forensic psychiatrist made no such recommendation provided that the individual committed a grave socially dangerous act as defined in the criminal codes.

The law places no time limit on the duration of compulsory medical measures, nor does a court when assigning such measures. Compulsory treatment under the 1967 Instruction continues until the individual so changes that he is no longer a danger to those around him or himself. Every six months at least a medical commission must recertify the need to continue compulsory treatment and, when appropriate, recommend to the court that the treatment be altered or terminated.

Soviet commitment procedures and forms of treatment of the mentally ill have caused grave disquiet among some specialists abroad who believe that certain commitments represented an effort to stifle discordant personal opinions rather than treat genuine mental illness.

On 5 January 1988 a Statute on the Conditions and Procedure for Rendering Psychiatric Care, confirmed by the Presidium of the USSR Supreme Soviet with effect from 1 March 1988, introduced standards intended to eliminate past abuses. The Statute governs all types of psychiatric committals, not merely compulsory measures applied by a court. Persons suffering mental distress are to be given qualified medical assistance without charge using humane methods of treatment authorised by the Ministry of Public Health and the least restrictive conditions of

---

16 Biulleten' verkhovnogo suda SSSR, no. 4 (1967) pp 37–39.

confinement necessary under the circumstances. Social and legal assistance, court protection, Procuracy supervision, and the aid of an advocate are guaranteed.

A psychiatrist is, when performing duties connected with rendering medical care to the mentally ill and preventing the possible commission of socially dangerous actions, to be independent in his judgments and guided solely by medical indicators and the law. The mental state of an individual is confidential; persons who in the course of their duties come to have such information may be prosecuted for divulging it. Committing an individual, who is known not to be mentally ill, to a psychiatric hospital is a serious criminal offence under amendments introduced into the union republic criminal codes in 1988. An individual who is placed under observation in a psychiatric hospital may not be deprived of his rights nor restricted in his legal interests.

Committals for psychiatric treatment are usually made by a commission of psychiatrists; upon the petition of the ill person, his relatives, or his legal representatives, any psychiatrist employed in public health institutions of the particular locality may be included on such a commission. If an individual has committed a socially dangerous act provided for by a criminal law, the normal procedures of a forensic psychiatric examination apply pursuant to the codes of criminal procedure.

The rights and duties of chief psychiatrists are clarified in the Statute. Appeals against the opinion of a psychiatrist or commission of psychiatrists may be lodged with the chief psychiatrist, and the latter's opinions or actions may be appealed to the superior public health agency or directly to a court. Under the Statute the treatment of mentally ill persons who have committed socially dangerous acts is to be effected in psychiatric hospitals of public health agencies, and not of other agencies.

Compulsory treatment of alcoholics and drug addicts must be considered by a court whenever assigning punishment to such persons for committing a crime. The court is not obliged to assign treatment, and may not do so if no crime was committed or the accused was acquitted; in every instance of assigning treatment, the court must have a medical opinion advising such treatment in the particular case and specifying there are no medical reasons not to apply compulsory treatment. The court may assign treatment upon its own initiative or upon the petition of a social organisation, collective of working people, comrades' court, or public health agency. Whether the crime was committed in a state of drunkenness is immaterial. The treatment continues until terminated by the court upon the recommendation of the medical institution giving the therapy. An alcoholic or drug addict is defined by the commentators as an individual who systematically abuses alcoholic beverages or narcotics, as a result of which there occurs the degradation of the individual so as to require compulsory treatment, but not to such an extent that the individual is mentally ill. Under measures adopted 7 January 1988, the police may deliver persons who abuse alcoholic beverages or narcotics to medical institutions in order to determine whether treatment is required, if such persons avoid a medical examination. Further, the police may visit such persons at their home or summon them for the purpose of carrying on educational work with them.

Compulsory educational measures have reference to minors when a court finds it appropriate not to assign criminal punishment. The Soviet criminal codes list seven such measures, ranging from an apology to the victim, a reprimand or warning, duty to pay compensation if the minor has independent earnings and the loss does not exceed prescribed amounts, to committing the minor to a special training-educational or medical-educational institution. In the latter event, the term, procedure, and conditions are determined by the union republic Statutes on commissions for cases of minors.

Criminal law: the Special Part

As noted above, the Special Part of the Soviet criminal codes defines individual offences and the particular punishments for each. The structure of the Special Part is not identical in all the union republic codes. Most follow the RSFSR model, beginning with crimes against the State, crimes against socialist ownership, crimes against the life, health, freedom, and dignity of the person, crimes against the political and labour rights of citizens, crimes against personal ownership, economic crimes, official crimes, crimes against justice, crimes against the administrative order, crimes against public security, public order, and public health, and military crimes. Several republics have a chapter on crimes constituting survivals of local customs.

All societies give expression to their philosophies or ideologies, objectives, prejudices, and problems in their criminal codes. Soviet law offers much by way of interesting contrast to Anglo-American criminal law in this respect. There are crimes in England, for example, which do not exist under Soviet law: blasphemy, foreign enlistment, trade disputes, among others of recent vintage. Many offences are common to both systems: homicide, rape, theft, robbery, and the like. But some are peculiar to the Soviet system and behaviour is punished that would under Anglo-American law be wholly lawful. The following are by way of example.

A. ANTI-SOVIET AGITATION AND PROPAGANDA

Article 70 of the RSFSR Criminal Code punishes by deprivation of freedom for a term of from six months to seven years, with or without additional exile for a term of from two to five years, or by exile for two to five years, agitation or propaganda carried on for the purpose of subverting or weakening Soviet power or of committing particular especially dangerous crimes against the State, or the circulation for the same purpose of slanderous fabrications which defame the Soviet State and social system, or the circulation or preparation, or keeping, for the same purposes, of literature of such content. Under Anglo-American law, criticism of the State and system is the very essence of the democratic process. The 1977–78 Soviet consitutions qualify the right of free speech, assembly, and press by requiring that these be exercised 'in accordance with the interests of the working people and with a view to strengthening the socialist system.' Trials of writers and others whose works or actions were deemed to violate Article 70 have aroused much attention and concern. The crime is classified as an especially dangerous crime against the State.

The commentators indicate that circulation may occur among a more or less broad group of persons by way of conversation, speeches, reports, cinema, displaying flags, emblems, and the like. The number of persons present affects only the gravity of the offence and not whether the offence was committed. Slanderous fabrications may be circulated orally or demonstratively; they must be proved to be knowingly false, to relate to the socialist way of life or to the Soviet form of government and not to a specific event or occurrence, nor to a particular State agency, nor to a particular individual. The information circulated must be defamatory, that is, must portray the socialist system in an unfavourable light. Anti-Soviet literature may take the form of books, pamphlets, articles, records, photographs, magnetic tapes, or others. Circulation may occur by showing, posting, marking, or otherwise distributing it. However, a person who shows anti-Soviet propaganda to others not for ideological motives but to boast of his access to such material is not deemed to have the requisite intent of circulating. The preparation of anti-Soviet material may take the form of authorship, editorship, or reproduction, and whether it was prepared for circulation is to be adjudged from the nature of the work, the number of copies, an attempt to conceal authorship, and the like. Keeping is a more difficult matter. Merely holding anti-Soviet literature for scholarly purposes or keeping diaries and personal memoranda containing anti-Soviet ideas is not sufficient if the diaries and memoranda were not intended for circulation to others.

B. LEAVING IN DANGER

Under Article 127 of the RSFSR Criminal Code, Soviet citizens have a legal duty to render necessary aid which is clearly required immediately to a person in danger of death if the aid can be rendered without serious danger to themselves or to other persons, or to notify appropriate

Criminal law: the Special Part 313

institutions or persons to render aid. Criminal liability also arises for knowingly leaving without aid a person in danger of death who cannot take measures for self-preservation by reason of youth, old age, illness, or general helplessness when the guilty person could render aid or is under an obligation to care for the victim, or placed the victim in danger. Sanctions range from correctional tasks up to six months or social censure to deprivation of freedom for two years.

Judicial practice has contributed significantly to the scope of the offence. A situation dangerous to life may include an earthquake, fire, childbirth, or unconsciousness. The RSFSR Supreme Court has held that leaving a two-year-old child in an uninhabited place late in the day on the edge of a deep ravine came within Article 127. On the element of risk, however, the courts have held that a person who knew how to swim but suffered from heart trouble was not liable to assist a drowning person. An obligation to care for someone may arise from a legal duty (parents toward their children), official functions (kindergarten teacher), contract (nurse attending a gravely ill person), or norms of socialist morality (leaving a disabled person with heart trouble who was invited to take part in a summer stroll), or because the victim was placed in danger by the guilty person (advising an inexperienced tourist on climbing a mountain). Hit and run drivers and kidnappers who abandoned a kidnapped child have been successfully prosecuted under this Article in conjunction with other Code provisions.

C. SPECULATION

A cornerstone of Anglo-American economic life, the buying up and reselling of goods or any other articles for the purpose of making a profit, is a serious economic crime under the RSFSR Criminal Code (Art 154), and if engaged in as a form of business or on a large scale shall be punished by deprivation of freedom for a term of from two to seven years with confiscation of property; or if committed on an especially large scale, from five to ten years with confiscation. The Soviet authorities regard these actions as representing a significant social danger in that they disturb the normal channels for distribution of goods in Soviet trade in an economy where goods shortages are considerable and thereby damage the material interests of citizens. The application of the article by the courts has engendered some interesting glosses on the scope and substance of speculation.

A good as an article of speculation may be any product intended to satisfy human requirements and having monetary value, including industrial or agricultural products or handicrafts, home or imported, including items whose circulation is illegal (weapons, ammunition, pornography). Narcotics are an exception; their purchase and resale for a profit is punished as a separate crime, as is speculation in currency or securities. 'Buying up' refers to the acquisition of goods or articles for resale by cash payment or in kind, and may consist of a single purchase or several from any source—State or co-operative organisations or individual persons—using one's own assets or those to whom the goods are being sold. The offence also may be committed abroad during business or tourist visits if foreign goods are imported and resold.

Certain actions have been excluded from speculation by the courts on the grounds there was no 'buying up.' Receiving goods as payment in kind for work, as a gift, by inheritance or lottery winnings, or by manufacturing or stealing them is not 'buying up.' Selling nominal rights to acquire goods unpaid for in the form of coupons and the like is not speculation but may be unlawful commercial middleman activity. Purchasing raw materials to manufacture and subsequently realise articles for the purpose of profit is not speculation, but the USSR Supreme Court has held that when goods are bought up for resale and merely modified in appearance without making a qualitatively new product the offence of speculation has been committed.

'Resale' means disposing of the good or article for money or other material remuneration. An unsuccessful effort to sell is regarded as attempted speculation. The place of resale is immaterial, and a purchaser may be either a private individual or a representative of a State, co-operative, or social organisation. 'Profit' means the receipt of money or goods which exceed the purchase price of the good or article sold. Speculation presupposes a direct intent and purpose to make a profit when the goods being resold are originally purchased. A person who resells goods at a higher price which originally were purchased for personal use and then no longer required is not guilty of speculation. Likewise, if the purpose to make a profit is manifest in the transaction, speculation is committed even if the goods are sold for less than the nominal price.

The law offers no guidance as to what is 'large-scale' speculation. The USSR Supreme Court has ruled that the courts are to proceed from the specific circumstances of each case, having regard to the amount of profit actually received or contemplated, the amount of goods bought up and resold and their value. The RSFSR Supreme Court has held that, as a general rule, profit exceeding 200 rubles is considered to be large-scale. Many prices of goods in the Soviet Union, it should be borne in mind, are fixed by the State Committee of the USSR for Prices. Enactments establishing prices are normative acts under Soviet law.

D. PARASITIC WAY OF LIFE

The 1977–78 Soviet constitutions prescribe that the 'avoidance of socially useful labour is incompatible with the principles of a socialist society.' Conscientious labour in socially useful activity and the observance of labour discipline is a 'duty and matter of honour' for every Soviet citizen. The present Soviet leadership has signalled its determination to reinforce that ethos. On 25 February 1983 the Soviet news agency TASS reported the case of a Soviet citizen sentenced under Article 209 of the RSFSR Criminal Code to one year's deprivation of freedom by a people's court on circuit. This individual, aged 45, had ceased working in December 1981 and become a burden to his aged mother, who was forced to return to work in order to feed him. Several times warned by the police to lead an honourable life, he protested that he was ailing and could not find work, but his claims were not supported by doctors.[17] Article 209 provides that systematically engaging in vagrancy or in begging, or leading any other parasitic way of life over a protracted period of time, may be punished by deprivation of freedom or correctional tasks for from one to two years. A second offence can result in from one to three years' deprivation of freedom.

Soviet anti-parasite legislation dates back to 1957, when several smaller union republics experimented with enactments that allowed, without judicial supervision, the direct resettlement of 'parasites' to other communities. A 1961 RSFSR Edict eventually set the standard.[18] Persons who avoided socially useful labour, derived 'non-labour incomes' from exploiting land plots, automobiles, or housing, or committed other 'antisocial acts' enabling them to lead a parasitic way of life could be subjected by a court or a collective of working people to 'settlement' in designated localities for a term of from two to five years with confiscation of property acquired by non-labour means and with the duty to work at the place of resettlement. Resettlement was treated as an 'administrative measure' and not considered to be a punishment. Decisions taken by collectives were subject to confirmation by the execution committee of a local soviet and could not be reviewed in a court.

The vague wording of the Edict led to judicial interpretations intended to curb abuses and eventual legislative amendment. On 12 September 1961 the USSR Supreme Court imposed certain procedural requirements for anti-parasite proceedings: open trials heard by a full court, adequate time to find work after being warned, and others. Certain classes of individuals were deemed to fall outside the Edict: pensioners, housewives, individuals living on inherited income, freelance translators, for example. Amendments to the Edict in 1965 provided that persons leading an antisocial parasitic way of life were subject to being assigned by the local soviet executive committee to employment in enterprises or construction sites within a territorial sub-division of their permanent residence, unless they resided in the city or region of

---

17 *Izvestiia* 25 February 1983, p 6, cols 7–8.
18 See H. J. Berman, in Berman and J. W. Spindler (transl.) *Soviet Criminal Law and Procedure: The RSFSR Codes* (2nd edn, 1972) pp 77–82.

Moscow or the city of Leningrad, in which event they could be resettled to another locality to work for a period of two to five years. Only a court could render a decree of resettlement if the person had not begun work within a month after being warned to do so by police agencies or a social organisation. Refusing to take up the employment assigned by the local soviet executive committee or evading resettlement became a criminal offence punishable by correctional tasks of 10% for up to one year. The 1965 reforms reportedly had the effect of virtually eliminating parasite cases from the courts.[19] The scope of the original edict had been narrowed, and the power of collectives to order resettlement was abolished. Nevertheless, there continued to be difficulties with administering the scheme. Communities to which people were resettled objected strenuously to being populated by ne'er-do-wells. Many enterprises and construction sites obliged to employ 'parasites' were content to see them depart after a brief period and did not inform the authorities. On the other hand, warnings given to find employment were not necessarily in writing, and the police were not necessarily fully informed about warnings issued by social organisations. Many proceedings involving parasites were subject to inordinate delays. On 14 February 1970, Article 209-1 was added to the RSFSR Criminal Code punishing the malicious evasion of performing a decision rendered by a local soviet for the arrangement of work and discontinuance of a parasitic existence. The illegal act consisted not of leading a parasitic existence, although that was essential to the crime, but of disobeying the local soviet's order; that is, the status of being a 'parasite' technically was not punished but rather the wilful disobedience of the local soviet. Resettlement as a sanction was entirely eliminated. Still the offence was a peculiar one, for it combined a status (leading a parasitic way of life) and a breach of constitutional duty (to work) culminating in a failure to carry out an administrative order. On 7 August 1975 Article 209-1 was repealed and parasitism incorporated in Article 209 treating vagrancy and begging.

Article 209 regards vagrancy, begging and other forms of parasitism as forms of avoiding socially useful labour. For criminal liability to attach, they must be 'systematically engaged in' for a protracted period. The commentators declare that 'other forms of parasitism' encompass a person capable of being employed living on non-labour income and avoiding socially useful labour despite an official warning that such a way of life is inadmissible. Socially useful labour includes permanent employment in State, social, or collective farm-co-operative organisations, work pursuant to labour contracts with various organisations and citizens, handicrafts, and other occupations not prohibited by law and paid in accordance with the quality and quantity of work expended. Non-labour income is not defined by law, but examples from judicial

[19] Ibid p 79.

practice embrace revenues from operating personally-owned vehicles, petty speculation, prostitution or gambling. In increasing the penalties for deriving non-labour income in legislation of May 1986, the enumerative approach was retained and no general definition of non-labour income attempted. The USSR Supreme Court has excluded from Article 209 minors, pensioners, disabled persons, pregnant women, housewives, and women with children under eight years of age.

E. SURVIVALS OF LOCAL CUSTOMS

Several union republic criminal codes, including the RSFSR, contain a chapter devoted to crimes constituting survivals of local customs: blood vengeance, bride price, compelling or obstructing marriage, arranging the marriage of a minor, bigamy, or polygamy. In the RSFSR these provisions extend only to those localities where these socially dangerous acts are survivals of local customs. Blood vengeance is said to be uncommon. Some local soviets have formed conciliation commissions consisting of the executive committee chairman, people's judge, two representatives of social organisations, and one representative of a local women's organisation.[20] The commission undertakes to reconcile the feuding parties and obtain a written agreement to that effect. A refusal to accept reconciliation or a failure to appear at the commission entails criminal liability under the code.

Bride price apparently does occur from time to time, and the courts are instructed to ascertain whether wedding presents are not concealed forms of bride price and the proper age of the bride.[1] Compelling a woman to marry may embrace, under judicial practice, either a registered marriage or a de facto marriage. The coercion may be physical or psychological; abducting a woman for entry into marriage may occur by force or deceit. The bride's subsequent consent to marriage after an abduction does not release the abductor(s) of responsibility.

Other union republic criminal codes

In this rather general presentation of Soviet criminal law we have referred to the Soviet criminal codes as though they were virtually identical. Although each of the 15 codes conforms to the FPCrimL, there are material differences both with regard to what is criminal and to

---

[20] See the RSFSR Decree of 5 November 1928 'On Conciliation Procedures in the Struggle Against the Custom of Blood Vengeance' *SU RSFSR* (1928) no. 141, item 927.

[1] The problems of proof are well illustrated in the case of Bulguchev, which originated in the Chechen-Ingush ASSR. Transl. in J. N. Hazard, W. E. Butler, and P. B. Maggs *The Soviet Legal System* (3rd edn, 1977) pp 484–485.

punishment. Some differences reflect cultural, religious, historical, or geographical factors; others originate in the sophistication and quality of legal science in the various republics. Some variations seem purely cosmetic, whereas others seem to detract from the unifying purpose of the FPCrimL.

Reference already has been made to crimes constituting survivals of local customs. Other differences will be found in provisions governing sex offences and family relations. The definition of crimes also can vary, for example in the requirement of malice. Certain terms, for example, 'recidivist' or 'official,' vary from one code to another. Punishments especially reflect substantial differences from republic to republic.

The rising generation of criminal codes

In January 1987 the Plenum of the Central Committee of the CPSU instructed that Soviet criminal legislation be revised. This decision followed more than a year of lively and sometimes savage criticism in the Soviet press and legal media of criminal law and policy. From 1985, moreover, it was evident that attitudes toward sentencing policy in Soviet courts were changing sharply against many practices of the early 1980s. The assignment of deprivation of freedom as a punishment, for example, in many people's courts was reportedly the practice in 70-80% of the criminal cases in 1982-83; by 1988 it reportedly had dropped to as little as 30%. The deterrent value of capital punishment was vigorously debated in the Soviet press and a broad range of opinion expressed. Articles 70 and 190-1 of the RSFSR Criminal Code, treating respectively anti-Soviet agitation and propaganda, and the circulation of fabrications known to be false which defame the Soviet State and social system, were deemed by many to be incompatible in their present formulation with the principle of *glasnost'*.

As it happened these debates and the deliberations of the law revision committees had available as a point of departure the 'Theoretical Model of a Criminal Code (General Part)' drafted by legal scholars at the Institute of State and Law of the USSR Academy of Sciences, circulated for discussion in 1985,[2] and published with detailed commentary two years later.[3] The principal ideas developed in the Theoretical Model are being incorporated in the new Fundamental Principles of criminal legislation and union republic criminal codes of 1988-90. These include a shorter Special Part in the criminal codes, reflecting the 'decriminalisation' and relegation of many types of unlawful behaviour to the categories

---

2 English translation in W. E. Butler (ed) *Justice and Comparative Law* (1987) pp 187-240.
3 V. N. Kudriavtsev and S. G. Kelina (eds) *Ugolovnyi zakon; opyt teoreticheskogo modelirovaniia* (1987).

of administrative, disciplinary, or moral offences; a significant reduction in the offences punishable by the death penalty and the abolition of exile; greater clarification of the constituent elements of individual crimes and of the boundaries between criminal and non-criminal behaviour; and a higher degree of legislative formalisation of judicial discretion.

Without precedent in Soviet legal writings from the standpoint of the socio-legal research underlying its formulations and the care with which a case is made for a particular formulation, the Theoretical Model offers unusual insight into the rationale of modern Soviet criminal policy. Two examples, one an innovation and the other a revision of existing practice, illustrate the range and style of change.

LAWFUL PROFESSIONAL RISK

Article 54 of the Theoretical Model proposes an innovation in Soviet criminal law which apparently over the years found support in judicial practice: the introduction of 'lawful professional risk' as a circumstance precluding criminal responsibility. The author of Article 54[4] proposed a formulation as follows:

Article 54. Lawful Professional Risk
(1) An action (or omission to act) which has caused harm to legally-protected interests, if it was committed under conditions of lawful risk for the purpose of achieving a socially useful result in professional activity, shall not be a crime.
(2) A risk shall be lawful if the actions committed do not violate an express prohibition established by law or a normative act, conform to modern scientific-technical knowledge and experience, and the socially-useful purpose pursued could not be achieved by other actions not linked with the risk, and the person undertaking the risk has taken all necessary measures to avert the ensuing of harmful consequences.
(3) If the conditions specified in paragraph two are present, criminal responsibility for harm caused as a result of professional risk shall not ensue even though the socially useful result being pursued is not achieved and the ensuing harm is more significant than the socially useful purpose being pursued.

Although doctrinal writings had supported the view that production risk was a circumstance precluding criminal responsibility for causing harm, the Soviet codes made no such provision. A Decree of 12 June 1929 'On the Financial Responsibility of Workers and Employees for Damage Caused by Them to the Employer'[5] precluded civil liability for damage originating in normal production and economic risk; a fortiori, it was argued, so too should criminal responsibility be excluded. Under modern conditions of innovative technology, scientific experiments might involve a considerable risk of material damage, including damage to the natural environment.

4 A. B. Sakharov, ibid, pp 133–135.
5 *SZ SSSR* (1929) no. 42, item 367.

The Theoretical Model deems professional risk to be lawful if the activities performed are of a socially-useful character and directed toward the resolution of long-term scientific-technical and production tasks, or the achievement of positive results or the elimination of negative consequences in a particular domain of professional activity. The individual concerned is aware that damage might be caused (hence the risk), but does not act with criminal frivolousness. The expression 'professional' risk is used in preference to 'production' risk in order to stress that the risk may arise in any sphere of professional activity, not merely production activity, and that only those who are professionally engaged in a particular activity and are capable of ensuring that the conditions laid down in the draft Article are observed, may invoke the principle of professional risk.

The activities of risk (scientific experiment, medical operation, new production method, etc) must not be contrary to express provisions of legislation, including safety rules and sanitary legislation. Further, they should conform to the level of scientific and technical knowledge and the practical experience available; innovations, which by definition exceed that standard, should not directly be contrary to such knowledge and experience. The socially useful purpose must not be attainable by activities without risk—a proposition that brings the concept of professional risk close to the notion of two legally protected interests juxtaposed, one being achieved at the expense of the other (extreme necessity). A refusal to assume a professional risk is not connected with the ensuing of socially harmful consequences.

Under the above circumstances, a professional risk is lawful if all measures have been taken to avert possible harmful consequences, both with regard to the actions themselves and safety measures (including the permission of competent persons, warnings of possible danger, removal of outsiders, installation of fall-back devices, etc). The harm may ensue either because the socially useful purpose was not achieved or as a concomitant to a successful undertaking, even though the harm caused may be more significant than the result achieved. The causal link between the professional risk and the consequent damage is regarded as having been without guilt. Should the circumstances be such that not all of the preconditions for lawful professional risk have been observed, the socially useful intentions of the guilty person would be treated under the Theoretical Model as a mitigating circumstance.

DEPRIVATION OF FREEDOM

Although the vagaries of sentencing policy in Soviet courts are not fully a matter of public record, the doctrinal literature has for some time given evidence of a sceptical disenchantment with deprivation of freedom in a correctional-labour institution as a punishment. While reports persist that courts relied extensively on this type of custodial sentence in the late 1970s and early 1980s, research studies done in the late 1960s and early 1970s suggested that it was possible to significantly reduce the assignment of this type of punishment. This finding led to the introduction of so-called 'intermediate' punishments, representing a 'restriction' rather than a 'deprivation' of freedom; for example, the conditional sentence to deprivation of freedom with compulsory enlistment for labour. The intermediate punishments did not involve confinement in special closed institutions but they nonetheless were more severe in restraining freedom than the other punishments not entailing deprivation of freedom.

The Theoretical Model proposes to enlarge the role of intermediate punishments as alternatives to deprivation of freedom and also introduces a new category of punishment, called 'arrest', for short-term isolation from society for up to six months. As regards deprivation of freedom itself, the author[6] proposed the following formulation:

Article 70. Deprivation of Freedom
(1) Deprivation of freedom consists of isolating the convicted person from society through placing him in a correctional-labour colony of general, reinforced, strict, and special regimes, or prison.
(2) Persons sentenced to deprivation of freedom for crimes they committed while under 18 years of age shall be placed in an educational-labour colony for minors.
(3) Deprivation of freedom shall be assigned by a court for a term of from one to 10 years.
(4) When assigning deprivation of freedom to a person who committed a crime while under 18 years of age, the term of punishment may not exceed seven years.
(5) A court may assign deprivation of freedom for a term of up to 15 years to persons for whom the death penalty has been replaced by deprivation of freedom.

This formulation differs from the 1958 FPCrimL in two material respects. First, it indicates that deprivation of freedom means isolation of the convicted person from society. Second, the great detail found in the 1960 RSFSR Criminal Code under the equivalent Article 24 has been relegated by the Theoretical Model to the correctional-labour codes. The maximum period of deprivation of freedom is fixed at ten years (compared with 15 years under the 1960 Criminal Code), and for those whose sentence of death is commuted to deprivation of freedom, the maximum is reduced from 20 to 15 years.

The argument on behalf of reducing the term of deprivation of freedom rests on a combination of social, psychological, and criminological considerations. 'Structural' changes are said to have occurred in the incidence of criminality, principally a reduction in what are regarded as the 'more dangerous forms of criminal phenomena'. While certain fluctuations are conceded to have occurred in particular periods or regions,

---

6 I. M. Gal'perin, note 3, above, pp 152–153.

the overall trend is believed to support a progressive lessening of the severity of punishments. At the individual level, the forces of socio-economic change are considered to be such that lower terms of deprivation of freedom will better serve the purposes of punishment. The minimum period of one-year deprivation of freedom is stipulated in light of the other 'intermediate' forms of isolation from society for a shorter period.

Chapter 18

Criminology and correctional-labour law

Soviet legal science distinguishes between the criminal law (to define and determine responsibility for crimes), criminology (to identify scientifically the causes of criminality and develop recommendations and methods for eradicating it), and correctional-labour law (to apply correctional policies to punish and reform offenders).

Criminology

Marxism-Leninism has emphasised the social factors that contribute to criminality. The individual has been regarded as a product of society; hence societal aberrations and conflict, such as class struggle, economic exploitation, and the like, have been looked upon as the causes of criminality, and it followed that the elimination of these under socialism and communism would lead to a crimeless society. During the 1920s, Soviet criminologists pioneered the investigation of the social causes of crime, influenced partly by the writings of Enrico Ferri in Italy. Numerous State institutes and centres performed empirical studies, published detailed and impressive statistical records of crime patterns, and developed interesting hypotheses about the origins of criminality. Their work contributed to a philosophy of crime and punishment that de-emphasised the moral guilt of the accused and genetic factors: the criminal personality. Law was to be simultaneously an instrument of social protection, of education in general, and of reform in particular.

In the mid-1930s criminological research was completely stopped for three decades.[1] The incidence of crime in absolute figures became a State secret. In 1963 criminology was formally reinstated with the formation of the All-Union Institute for the Study of the Causes of Criminality and the Elaboration of Preventive Measures as part of the Procuracy of the USSR (renamed in 1987; see chapter 7), followed by a host of lesser centres in university law faculties and other institutions.

As for the incidence of crime, there is conflicting data. Many Soviet

---

1 This is not to say criminologists did not continue to contribute to the formation of Soviet criminal policy. Their views were influential on drafts of the all-union criminal codes of 1939 and 1947, which were never enacted.

writers claim that crime is decreasing; be that as it may, it is equally evident that levels of crime are unsatisfactory. Certain periods since the mid-1950s have experienced a marked increase in crime, for example, 1958, 1962, and the late 1960s. Crimes against personal ownership and petty theft have increased as has criminal negligence, especially in traffic offences. Hooliganism is said to comprise about 30% of all crimes, and alcoholism or drunkenness is said to be a factor in two-thirds of all intentional homicides, three-quarters of grave bodily injuries, robbery, and assaults, and two-fifths of all traffic violations. Although the anti-alcohol campaign has had a marked effect on some types of crime, drunkenness remains a significant factor in the crime rate. The rate of juvenile crime is said to remain disturbingly stable. Criminological studies also suggest a high correlation between population migration, urbanisation, family instability, and population density, on one hand, and criminality on the other.[2] Even, however, if Soviet criminal statistics were published, meaningful generalisations could be drawn only if data were available about patterns of enforcement, reporting procedures, decisions not to prosecute, and the like. Above all, the trend of the 1970s to broaden the number of administrative offences and punish certain first offenders administratively would have been reflected in crime statistics but would not necessarily have meant the number of social infractions had diminished. The same will be true of 'decriminalisation' policies of the late 1980s.

Soviet criminology continues to stress in a more refined way than in earlier periods that all human behaviour is socially determined. Contradictions within socialism, for example, between consumption demand and inadequate production levels, or between manual and intellectual labour, are believed to contribute to criminality. So too do shortcomings in education, family upbringing, and material standard of living. The individual is not ignored in the emphasis upon social elements; Soviet criminology has been interested in the process of socialising the individual, especially his interaction with social groups. Marxism views social life as a dynamic relationship, a continual interaction of positive and negative social processes. If one can identify accurately the nature of their interrelationship, one ought to be able to predict the consequences that development and change will have upon that relationship. Criminology is also therefore a technique of social engineering. Defining the functions of social communities and institutions in regulating behaviour, in stabilising social relations, in enabling individuals or groups to accomplish their aims, in furthering social conformity, are among its

---

2 See M. C. Bassiouni and V. M. Savitskii *The Criminal Justice System of the USSR* (1979). For various extrapolations of crime statistics, see I. Zeldes *The Problems of Crime in the USSR* (1981); G. P. van den Berg *The Soviet System of Justice: Figures and Policies* (1985).

tasks; likewise, disfunctions of social institutions will contribute to aberrations and offences. Criminology is to identify disfunctions in a timely manner and offer remedial measures.

To the extent that Soviet criminology has observed that social processes such as migration, urbanisation, and industrialisation contribute to disintegration of the family, disruption of territorial communities, and alterations of the natural male/female balance, which then lead to a shattering of community identity and values and a decrease in behavioural standards, and a rise in aggressive, violent criminality, it has recommended a combination of general social and particular criminological responses. Normal social communities require stabilisation, higher social cohesion, and stronger mechanisms for formal and informal social control, the latter of both a positive (approval, incentive, prestige) and negative (censure, ostracism) nature. Income levelling, higher wages, larger social consumption funds, compulsory secondary education, a stronger family unit, a transition to more highly skilled and automated labour, and the democratisation of social control over officials all are believed relevant in a general way to crime prevention. Social development plans are regarded as an indispensable element of national economic planning; migration, urbanisation, and industrialisation, it is believed, should proceed by forecasting and by coping simultaneously with their impact on related social processes. On the family level, it would follow that parents who neglect their children or mistreat them might be deprived of parental rights. Commissions for cases of minors and for the struggle against drunkenness and the establishment of administrative supervision over recidivists after their release are among the particular measures designed to cope with the personality and special requirements of certain types of offender.

The most extensive western studies of Soviet criminology have concluded that criminologists have had considerable influence upon some policy deliberations in which they had taken part and a moderate impact upon the face of Soviet criminal policy as a whole. Such constraints as they experienced upon their capacity to influence criminal policy were not peculiar to Soviet society but rather were similar to limitations that affect criminologists at large.[3]

Correctional-labour law

Soviet correctional-labour legislation represents an application of Soviet criminology. It has perhaps been the object of greatest attention in

3 P. H. Solomon, Jr. *Soviet Criminologists and Criminal Policy: Specialists in Policy-Making* (1978); P. H. Juviler *Revolutionary Law and Order* (1976); W. D. Connor *Deviance in Soviet Society* (1972).

foreign writings touching upon the Soviet legal system, yet the full body of legislation is not a matter of public record. Official materials include the 1969 Fundamental Principles of Correctional-Labour Legislation (FPCorL), the 15 union republic correctional-labour codes, relevant provisions of the criminal, criminal procedure, labour, family, and other codes, the 1977 Rules for the Internal Order of Correctional-Labour Institutions which entered into force on 1 January 1978, and other departmental subordinate legislation, together with court reports and guiding explanations, commentaries, and legal doctrine. For more than 70 years official enactments have been augmented by a flow of memoirs written by those who were or are inmates and by a genre fictional literature based on personal experience. Despite individual shortcomings, the literature of this type as a whole offers much insight and detail into the operation of the institutions concerned.

A. HISTORICAL BACKGROUND

Early Soviet legislative provisions affecting the confinement of prisoners were scattered among a number of enactments. The emphasis was upon isolating elements hostile to the regime, not rehabilitation, and it required some years for a transition to a policy of reform through labour. The provisional Instruction of 23 July 1918 issued by the People's Commissariat of Justice 'On Deprivation of Freedom As a Means of Punishment and the Procedure for Serving Such' outlined in 31 brief articles the assignment of prisoners to various types of institutions, the kinds of work they were to do, the rules of internal order, disciplinary sanctions, and the structure of the Chief Administration for Places of Confinement (GUMZ).[4] Individuals sentenced by the CheKa were often sent to forced-labour camps under decrees of 15 April and 17 May 1919.[5] A substantial (232 articles) Statute on General Places of Confinement approved 15 November 1920 dealt only with places of confinement under the jurisdiction of the People's Commissariat of Justice.[6] Some provisions of the 1919 Guiding Principles Relating to Criminal Law, the 1922 RSFSR Criminal Code, and the 1924 all-union Basic Principles of criminal legislation were relevant. The respective penal institutions of the People's Commissariat of Justice were brought under a single regime by the RSFSR Correctional-Labour Code enacted 16 November 1924,[7] followed by other union republic codes in 1925–28.

4 *SU RSFSR* (1918) no. 53, item 598. See N. A. Struchkov (ed) *Sovetskoe ispravitel'no-trudovoe pravo* (1977). Local soviets also legislated widely on penal questions.
5 *SU RSFSR* (1919) no. 12, item 124; no. 20, item 235. These camps were operated by the CheKa. *SU RSFSR* (1919) no. 20, item 235.
6 *SU RSFSR* (1921) no. 23/24, item 141.
7 *SU RSFSR* (1924) no. 86, item 870. The administrative unification occurred by a departmental decree of 12 October 1922. See *Sbornik normativnykh aktov po sovetskomu ispravitel'no-trudovomu pravu (1917–1959 gg.)* (1959).

By a Decree of 7 April 1930 the camp system was divided so that persons sentenced to more than three years by courts or special boards of the OGPU served their terms in camps administered by the latter.[8] A new RSFSR correctional-labour code was adopted 1 August 1933.[9] A year later the People's Commissariat for Internal Affairs (NKVD) was created, absorbing the OGPU correctional-labour camps and those still under the People's Commissariat of Justice. For two decades the details of the penal system were regulated by subordinate legislation whose texts have never been fully accessible. In the post-Stalin era, the USSR Council of Ministers confirmed a Statute on Correctional-Labour Camps and Colonies of the Ministry of Internal Affairs on 10 July 1954, superseded on 8 December 1958 by another Statute. On 29 August 1961 the Presidium of the RSFSR Supreme Soviet adopted a Statute on the same subject, followed by the other union republics and signalling a greater role for the union republics in this branch of law. None of these enactments were published in full. On 26 June 1963 the union republics introduced a new penal institution, the colony-settlement, for persons well on the path to reform[10] and on 3 June 1968 a Statute on labour colonies for minors,[11] which provided for colonies of general and reinforced regimes.

B. CURRENT LEGISLATION

This account of current practice, it should be stressed, is based on the basic enactments and commentaries available. Departmental and interdepartmental acts whose texts are not available have come to play an increasingly influential role in governing the affairs of prisoners. The USSR Ministry of Internal Affairs (MVD) determines the procedure for sending convicted persons to correctional-labour institutions; the procedure for keeping such persons in mental institutions is from 1988 the responsibility of the public health agencies. The procedure for rendering medical care is determined jointly by the MVD and the Ministry of Public Health. The 1977 Rules for the Internal Order of Correctional-Labour Institutions were adopted by the MVD at the all-union level. Both decrees and regulations of the USSR and union republic councils of ministers, orders and regulations of the USSR and union republic

---

8 *SZ SSSR* (1930) no. 22, item 248. The policy change was prescribed by a Decree of 6 November 1929. *SZ SSSR* (1929) no. 72, item 686.
9 *SU RSFSR* (1933) no. 48, item 208. This Code did not regulate correctional-labour camps under the OGPU, only those within the jurisdiction of the People's Commissariat of Justice.
10 *Vedomosti RSFSR* (1963) no. 26, pp 591–592. Conditional early release was authorised by RSFSR edicts of 24 April and 14 July 1954; a Statute on Supervisory Commissions was enacted on 24 May 1957.
11 *Vedomosti RSFSR* (1968) no. 23, item 189. See F. J. M. Feldbrugge 'Soviet Penitentiary Law' Review of Socialist Law I (1975) 123–139.

Ministers of Internal Affairs, and their deputies may contain normative prescriptions. Soviet jurists have publicly warned against attempts to confer similar powers on the heads of internal affairs departments at intermediate levels and even on the heads of correctional-labour institutions.[12]

C. BASIC PRINCIPLES

Soviet textbooks postulate several principles underlying Soviet correctional-labour policy. These include the principle of 'socialist humanism,' expressed in concern for protecting society as a whole against criminal infringements, the multi-faceted activity to reform, re-educate, re-socialise, and return individuals to society, insistence upon respect for human dignity, the possibility of altering punishments in light of model conduct; the principle of 'combining persuasion and coercion;' the principle of 'differentiating in the execution of punishment' by separating convicted persons into appropriate categories of similar offenders and adjusting the severity of the punishment regime accordingly; the principle of 'individualisation,' adapting punishment and education measures to the personality and character of each prisoner; the principle that it is possible to 'reform every person who has committed a crime,' expressed in measures for lightening the punishment of persons who respond to educational measures; the principle of 'combining punishment with measures of correctional-labour influence,' requiring that rehabilitation is a joint punitive-educational process based on an integrated approach to reform and re-education; the principle that 'socially useful labour plays a leading role in the reform of convicted persons,' in the conviction that labour has a special role in the life of society and the 'formation of a new man' under present levels of societal development; and the principle that the norms of correctional-labour law must be 'psychologically and pedagogically well-founded.'

D. GENERAL PROVISIONS

Correctional-labour institutions are within the jurisdiction of the MVD. First offenders usually are sent to serve deprivation of freedom within the union republic where they resided or were convicted. Serious offenders and foreigners or stateless persons are sent to specially designated institutions. The basic means for reform and re-education are the regime of serving punishment, socially useful labour, political-educational work, general education, and vocational training, to be applied by taking into account the social danger of the crime committed, the personality of the convicted person, and his conduct and attitude

---

12 Struchkov, note 4, above, p 55.

towards labour. The Procuracy exercises supervision over the execution of criminal judgments and the administration of correctional-labour institutions.[13]

E. CORRECTIONAL-LABOUR INSTITUTIONS

There are three types of correctional-labour institutions: correctional-labour colonies, prisons, and educational-labour colonies.

(a) Correctional-labour colonies. This type of institution exists in six levels of regime: general, reinforced, strict, special, plus colonies and settlements for persons who committed crimes through negligence, and colonies and settlements. General regime is reserved for males sentenced for the first time for a crime that is not grave or for a grave crime but not exceeding three years' deprivation of freedom and for most females; reinforced regime is for males sentenced for the first time for a grave crime and exceeding three years. Strict regime is for males or females sentenced for especially dangerous crimes against the State, for males who have previously served punishment in the form of deprivation of freedom, and for females deemed especially dangerous recidivists or for whom the death penalty has been replaced by deprivation of freedom. Special regime applies to male especially dangerous recidivists or persons for whom the death penality has been commuted to deprivation of freedom. Persons who committed crimes through negligence and sentenced for the first time to not more than five years' deprivation of freedom serve punishment in special colonies and settlements. Ordinary colonies and settlements are reserved for persons whose model conduct justifies their transfer thereto from the other levels of regime.

(b) Prisons and educational-labour colonies. Prisons are for the most serious offenders, such as especially dangerous recidivists sentenced to more than eight years, and the like. There are two prison regimes: general and strict. Educational-labour colonies are for minors; they have two regimes for males, general and reinforced, but only a general regime for female minors.

F. REGIME OF CORRECTIONAL-LABOUR INSTITUTIONS

The day-to-day existence of inmates in correctional-labour institutions is governed by the 1977 Rules for the Internal Order of Correctional-Labour

---

13 Social control over correctional-labour institutions is exercised by Supervisory Commissions consisting of deputies from local soviets and representatives from trade union, Komsomol, and other social organisations and collectives of working people pursuant to the RSFSR Statute on Supervisory Commissions confirmed by the Presidium of the RSFSR Supreme Soviet on 30 September 1965, as amended.

Institutions.[14] The 1969 FPCorL and union republic correctional-labour codes outline in general some of the differences in levels of regime. Persons in places of deprivation of freedom, for example, are under constant supervision or isolation so as to preclude the commission of new crimes. They wear uniforms and are subject to search. Their correspondence is subject to censorship and packages and parcels to inspection. Those in special regime colonies are confined in ordinary dwelling premises or cell-type premises, depending on their crime, and wear special uniforms. Those serving punishment in either form of colony or settlement, on the other hand, are confined under supervision but without guard. During waking hours they enjoy the freedom of the premises, wear ordinary clothing, may use money without restriction, and even live with their families in the colony. Convicted persons in prisons are housed in common or individual cells and enjoy a daily walk of a prescribed duration. The extent to which inmates may receive or send post or packages, meet with relatives, and enjoy other privileges varies, depending on the level of regime. Complaints, applications, and letters addressed to a procurator, however, are not subject to inspection and must be sent within 24 hours.

All convicted persons are obliged to work. The administration of a correctional-labour colony must ensure that they are involved in socially useful labour taking into account their capacity to work and, if possible, their specialised training. Persons in correctional-labour colonies of special regime are to be used, as a rule, for arduous work. Most inmates are employed at enterprises formed within correctional-labour institutions. Reform and re-education are said to be the principal object of penal labour, but the goods or services produced form part of the social product and are calculated in national planning indicators. Convicts work six days per week, eight hours a day, with one rest day each week plus national holidays; the regime is less strenuous in colonies and settlements. Each convict is paid for the quality and quantity of his work at the rates applicable in the national economy generally, less partial reimbursement for expenses related to his confinement (food, ordinary clothing, alimony, sums due under writs of execution), but depending on the level of regime a certain percentage may be reserved in the convict's personal account to be spent on sundries. All convicts undergo 'political-

---

14 The importance of the 1977 Rules cannot be exaggerated. They lay down, for example, the requirement that the administration of a correctional-labour institution must notify the family of an inmate within ten days of his arrival about the address of the institution, his right to correspond, receive parcels, messages, packages, and to have visitors, the list of prohibited articles and the amounts of permitted articles, the work, leisure, and sleeping hours, and the basic outline for a model order of the day that varies from institution to institution. A brief account of the Rules is given in N. P. Mal'shakov (ed) *Kommentarii k ispravitel'no-trudovomu kodeksu RSFSR* (2nd edn, 1979).

educational work' to instill in them an honourable attitude toward labour, respect for law, useful initiative, and other desirable social values. Participation in such measures is weighed when assessing the extent of reform and re-education.

Convicts under age 40 who have not completed the minimum eight years of general education are required to do so, with released time to sit examinations and free food, but without wages. Compulsory vocational training is organised for convicts having no special skills.

A large variety of incentive and disciplinary measures are employed to reward convicts for good conduct and an honourable attitude toward labour and study and to penalise individuals who violate the rules. Incentives range from an announcement of gratitude to a reduction of sentence; penalties extend from a warning or reprimand to solitary confinement or transfer to a correctional-labour colony of harsher regime.

G. CONDITIONAL SENTENCES

As an alternative to deprivation of freedom, Soviet legislation allows courts to impose a conditional sentence that either exempts or releases persons from deprivation of freedom on condition that they report for work at a prescribed place and remain there until the sentence has been completed. They live in special halls of residence or rented accommodation and have the freedom of the administrative district; their families often may reside with them. The local internal affairs agencies supervise their activities. Such persons may be transferred to other localities but may not be dismissed.

H. EXILE AND BANISHMENT

Soviet criminal legislation authorises courts to exile or banish individuals for committing certain offences. Exile entails an individual being sent to a specific locality at State expense, where he may choose his own abode and is obliged to engage in socially useful labour. Local soviets are obliged to arrange employment. More often than not the localities selected are in remote regions of the country, whose residents have complained strenuously about being inundated with undesirables. Banishment requires an individual to move away from his place of residence. He may select a place of work and new abode anywhere except a place where the court judgment prohibits him from living. Local soviets again are required to arrange employment.

I. CORRECTIONAL TASKS

A penalty widely misunderstood and mistranslated in western reporting, correctional tasks do *not* entail confinement in a correctional-labour institution. An individual sentenced to correctional tasks continues to work at his regular place of employment or other employment assigned by agencies that supervise this penalty, but has a stipulated percentage of his earnings, from 5 to 20%, withheld to the benefit of the State for a prescribed period. Deductions are made from total earnings before taxes and irrespective of claims lodged under writs of execution.

J. RELEASE

Persons released from places of deprivation of freedom are provided with passage free of charge to their place of residence or work, a food allowance in cash or kind, appropriate seasonal clothing or footwear, and sometimes a lump sum cash allowance. Upon arrival home, they are entitled to housing if required and assistance with finding employment. Persons who are granted conditional early release are placed under the observation of social organisations and collectives of working people. Individuals who were especially dangerous recidivists or served deprivation of freedom for committing grave crimes and whose conduct suggests they have not reformed and are unlikely to join in an honourable working life may be placed under the administrative supervision of police agencies pursuant to a Statute of 26 July 1966. They are obliged to report to the police at prescribed times and may be restricted in their movements or residence.

Application of correctional-labour legislation

The unavailability of the texts of subordinate acts governing correctional-labour institutions makes it difficult to assess the extent to which complaints about penal administration may be exaggerated in accounts by inmates or former inmates. What is a stern but even-handed application of normative acts may strike outsiders as cruel or demeaning arbitrariness, and vice versa. It is clear that the Procuracy often plays a positive role in safeguarding prisoner rights, and inmates make frequent recourse to that office. On the other hand, there are frequent reports of violations of safety and health standards, that the right to 'censor' mail includes the right to withhold it, and that the letter of subordinate legislation sometimes seems to violate the spirit of the FPCorL and union republic correctional-labour codes.

The extent to which recidivism occurs evidently varies with the level of regime of the respective correctional-labour institution. Those harbouring hardened criminals have a higher incidence. One Soviet study suggests on the basis of data analysed over a ten-year period that an 'average' correctional-labour colony experienced an 8.4% rate of recidivism, a level that was reduced when former inmates were assigned someone to befriend and supervise them at the enterprise where they work.[15] Although Soviet criminology accepts in principle that any person is capable of being reformed, current legislation tends to look upon the recidivist as one who wilfully resists educational measures and therefore authorises the application of a larger dose of chastisement than is the case for first offenders.

Criminal punishments not connected with correctional-labour

The FPCorL provide that the procedure and conditions for executing criminal punishments not connected with correctional-labour are to be determined by USSR and union republic legislation. In pursuance thereof, the Presidium of the USSR Supreme Soviet enacted on 15 March 1983 a Statute regulating the legal status of convicted persons in respect of, Procuracy supervision over, and the procedure for executing punishments in the form of depriving individuals of the right to hold specified offices or engage in specified activities, fines, public warnings, confiscation of property, and deprivation of military rank or special title.

---

15 Individual guidance through 'patrons' and 'social educators' during and after inmates have completed their sentence is widely encouraged under Soviet law. Social councils for organising work by 'patrons' in correctional-labour are formed on the basis of an RSFSR Statute adopted 18 November 1968. The RSFSR Statute on Social Educators for Minors was confirmed on 13 December 1967. Those who are sentenced to correctional tasks without deprivation of freedom often are supervised by social inspectors pursuant to an RSFSR Statute confirmed on 23 August 1978.

Chapter 19

Civil and criminal procedure

Soviet civil and criminal procedure represent a model of procedure which has influenced many other socialist legal systems and embody a number of distinctive elements not found in the western European continental model to which the Soviet system is akin. In Soviet legislation and legal scholarship both types of procedure are regarded as parts of a larger whole rather than two distinct legal realms. Both rest on what the eminent Soviet proceduralist, M. S. Strogovich, called 'uniform and common fundamental principles' for effectuating justice.[1] The same courts (although at higher levels special divisions may be created for civil and for criminal cases) hear each type of proceeding. The Soviet constitutions and legislation on court organisation lay down procedural principles and guarantees that are applicable to both: the right to use national language, the independence of judges and their subordination only to law, the purposes of justice, equality of citizens before the court and law, effectuation of justice in exact conformity with the law, collegial consideration of cases in all courts, and the open examination of cases in all courts. Unlike Anglo-American proceedings, moreover, it is common under Soviet law for a civil suit to be dealt with simultaneously in a criminal proceeding. The victim of a crime is usually the plaintiff, but a third party may also have been injured by the offence and appear as civil plaintiff. So too may there be a civil defendant, for example, when an employer is liable civilly for an employee's criminal behaviour.

Notwithstanding these elements of unity, civil and criminal procedure are the object of individual codification and treated independently in textbooks and teaching. Accordingly, we shall treat them individually below.

Civil procedure

HISTORICAL BACKGROUND

Both the French Revolution of 1789 and the Russian Revolutions of 1917 harboured deep grievances against the respective pre-existing systems of

[1] M. S. Strogovich *Kurs sovetskogo ugolovnogo protsessa* (1968) I, pp 94–95.

civil procedure in their countries. The judicial systems were enormously over-burdened with cases; litigation was cumbersome, expensive, time-consuming, and favoured the wealthy classes; complex and incomprehensible procedures allowed cases to drag on for years, adding to the expense and contributing to nefarious practices within the court system and legal profession; and innocent people were ruined or degraded by unjust civil judgments against them. The celebrated judicial reforms of 1864 in Russia brought some relief, including a simplified Code of Civil Procedure, but patterns of thought and habit were not so readily transformed.[2]

The system of appellate procedure enacted by the Soviet Government on 24 November 1917 conformed in several essential respects to that introduced by the French Revolution in 1790.[3] For a very brief period Soviet courts were authorised to apply the 1864 Russian Imperial Code of Civil Procedure (2,175 articles) unless it was contrary to Soviet decrees, but soon any reference to the pre-1917 legislation was prohibited.[4] Not until 1923 was civil procedure the object of special legislation. Such regulations as existed were scattered amongst a plethora of acts on court organisation. In general the early legislation introduced greatly simplified court structures, a lay element in the disposition of civil cases, a system of cassational review of cases to replace the usual appellate process, and greater judicial initiative in ascertaining the facts in both civil and criminal cases. Civil litigation was not infrequent during these early years of revolutionary upheaval; by mid-1918 the Soviet courts were obliged to enlarge their staff in order to cope with a flow of civil cases which far outstripped the rate of criminal proceedings; most related to contract, tort, divorce, or maintenance.[5]

The decision of the Soviet leadership to restore the national economy, ravaged by the First World War and civil war, through the NEP had implications for civil procedure just as for other branches of legislation. The RSFSR People's Commissariat of Justice published a draft code of civil procedure in instalments between August 1922 and February 1923, inviting comments. Enactment of the code met with delays, however, largely attributed to apprehensions that civil procedure might become a weapon to be used by NEP-men against the working class or by moneylenders, and the like. An interim decree on civil procedure had to be adopted on 4 January 1923 pending a resolution of these apprehensions, and the full RSFSR Code of Civil Procedure ultimately was approved

[2] See S. Kucherov *Courts, Lawyers and Trials Under the Last Three Tsars* (1953); R. Wortman *The Development of a Russian Legal Consciousness* (1976).
[3] D. W. Chenoweth *Soviet Civil Procedure: History and Analysis* (1977) p 3.
[4] Statute on People's Courts of the RSFSR, adopted 30 November 1918. *SU RSFSR* (1918) no. 85, item 889.
[5] J. N. Hazard, W. E. Butler, P. B. Maggs *The Soviet Legal System* (3rd edn, 1977) p 133.

on 7 July 1923 and entered into force on 1 September 1923.[6] With amendments and sometimes de facto superseded in part by subsequent legislation, the Code remained in force until 1964 and served as a model for the civil procedure codes of other union republics.

The 1923 Code was only one-fifth as long as its Imperial predecessor. The 'return to law' epitomised by the NEP was reflected in the Code by omitting any reference to 'revolutionary consciousness' when deciding cases. Well-enshrined, however, was the principle that the State was entitled to take an active role in the settlement of civil disputes both through the initiative of the court and the intervention, when necessary, of the Procuracy in a civil proceeding. The Code impressed nearly all western observers as being a modification of the model used in European continental jurisdictions, a '. . . framework similar to that of any European country.'[7]

Although 'revolutionary consciousness' has been dispensed with, class attitudes were not irrelevant in civil procedure. Soviet commentators in the 1930s often looked upon civil procedure as an anachronistic borrowing from the capitalist world destined to disappear as law withered away and stressed the importance of a class approach to evidence and its evaluation (the Code gave no guidance to courts for weighing evidence). The adoption in 1936 of a new Constitution and transition to a 'restoration of stability of laws' entailed a new attitude toward civil procedure. Antagonistic classes were declared to have disappeared; the private sector of the economy stimulated by NEP policies had largely vanished with the collectivisation of agriculture and introduction of national economic planning. Civil procedure could now in principle be observed and enforced impartially, although its scope of operation would be reduced. As time passed, civil procedure '. . . provided an increasingly stable and important element in the system of Soviet socialist legality. . .'.[8] During the darkest days of Stalinist terror, when so many facets of human behaviour seemed to pose a threat in the minds of the regime, civil procedural relations would be singled out as an area of the legal order which surely must function in a more or less normal fashion in the daily life of people.[9]

Apart from certain individual all-union enactments, most notably the 1938 USSR Law on Court Organisation, civil procedure had been regulated until 1961 by legislation of individual union republics patterned chiefly upon the 1923 RSFSR Code of Civil Procedure. On 11 February 1957 the USSR Supreme Soviet introduced a constitutional amendment

[6] *SU RSFSR* (1923) no. 46–47, item 478.
[7] V. Gsovski *Soviet Civil Law* (1949) I, p 855. Gsovski added: 'The Soviet civil procedure is like a new building erected of old bricks' (p 856).
[8] J. N. Hazard, W. E. Butler, P. B. Maggs, note 5, above, p 135.
[9] See the preface and introduction by Harold J. Berman, editing B. A. Konstantinovsky *Soviet Law in Action: The Recollected Cases of a Soviet Lawyer* (1953).

placing, inter alia, civil procedure within the jurisdiction of the union republics while retaining for the all-union authority jurisdiction to enact Fundamental Principles of civil procedure; this amendment reversed the original intention of the draftsmen of the 1936 Constitution—never realised—to prepare an all-union code of civil procedure. On 10 December 1961 the USSR Supreme Soviet adopted the Fundamental Principles of Civil Procedure of the USSR and Union Republics (FPCivPL), which entered into force on 1 May 1962. These were followed in 1964-65 by the enactment of individual codes of civil procedure in the 15 union republics of the Soviet Union.[10]

SCOPE OF CIVIL PROCEDURE

The FPCivPL contain imperative provisions which are binding throughout the Soviet Union and incorporated verbatim into the union republic codes of civil procedure. Each union republic elaborates these provisions to suit its own circumstances. These circumstances include local or nationality considerations, but in the case of civil procedure more often than not reflect different models of structuring the codes or diverse approaches to the precision of legal formulations.[11] Each code contains three annexes: (1) a list of property which may not be levied against; (2) rules for reinstating a lost judicial or execution proceeding; and (3) a statute on mediation tribunals. The remarks which follow are based chiefly on the FPCivPL and RSFSR and Ukrainian codes of civil procedure, the latter two codes illustrating the different approaches to structure mentioned above.

The legal relationships directly regulated by the Soviet law of civil procedure are much more limited than in the Anglo-American legal system for two reasons. First, economic disputes between State enterprises, organisations, and institutions, except certain categories expressly in the jurisdiction of the courts, are considered in State Arbitrazh, which has its own simplified rules of procedure. State Arbitrazh organs dispose of more than one million cases annually. Second, many categories of cases under Soviet law are relegated for consideration to particular administrative bodies or social organisations and may not be considered by the courts. Jurisdiction of the courts consequently is a key issue in any civil proceeding. The civil procedure codes assign to the courts those cases which arise out of civil, family, labour, and collective farm legal relations if one party to the dispute is a citizen,

---

10 A full list of the respective dates of enactment and entry into force is given by Chenoweth, note 3, above, p 41. The RSFSR Code of Civil Procedure is translated in W. B. Simons *The Soviet Codes of Law* (1980).
11 The differences among union republic codes of civil procedure have been analysed exhaustively in L. F. Lesnitskaia and V. K. Puchinskii *Osobennosti GPK soiuznykh respublik* (1970).

collective farm, or inter-collective farm organisation (unless these have been relegated to other bodies) and cases arising out of contracts for the carriage of goods in direct international rail and air transport between State or social enterprises and organisations, on one side, and rail or air transport agencies, on the other, and governed by an international agreement. Among administrative cases within court jurisdiction are appeals against inaccuracies in the voters' lists and against the imposition of administrative penalties by agencies or officials, other cases arising out of administrative-law relations, and against the unlawful actions of officials which impinge on the rights of citizens and have been relegated to court jurisdiction. Certain categories of special proceedings fall within special provisions of the civil procedure codes. The courts also will hear cases in which foreign nationals, stateless persons, or foreign enterprises and organisations take part, although the latter most commonly stipulate contractually that the USSR Maritime Arbitration Commission or the Arbitration Court attached to the USSR Chamber of Commerce and Industry will resolve their disputes.

The types of cases excluded from judicial consideration in a civil proceeding are too numerous to enumerate here. Examples are labour disputes, which fall into three categories: (1) those within the jurisdiction of courts; (2) those which may be considered by courts only after a preliminary hearing by labour dispute commissions or trade union committees at plants; and (3) those not within court jurisdiction, such as certain categories of employees whose dismissal may not be challenged in court, disputes over fixing work norms, assignment of State social insurance pensions and benefits, computations of labour experience, housing distributions, and others.

Social organisations may preclude their members from having recourse to the courts. In a case much commented upon, a Soviet advocate, Murzin, brought a special appeal against the refusal of a people's court to consider his petition to sue the RSFSR College of Advocates for legal fees due him. The Judicial Division for Civil Cases of the RSFSR Supreme Court held that since colleges of advocates were voluntary unions of persons, not employed under labour contracts, whose rights and duties to practise law arose by virtue of their membership in the College, and that membership in the College and payment for services were governed by the Statute on the College, and that disputes on these matters were to be resolved by the College Presidium or the State body which supervised College activity, and the consideration of such disputes was not expressly relegated to the courts, the lower court properly rejected the petition to sue.[12]

Comrades' courts, which are not part of the State apparatus, have jurisdiction over certain categories of minor civil dispute. The technical-

---

[12] Biulleten' verkhovnogo suda RSFSR no. 5 (1970) p 13.

ities of the codes of civil procedure do not formally apply in comrades' courts, although the basic principles are relevant, and the ordinary State courts are prohibited from considering the same case if the comrades' court has decided a case within its competence.

Cases involving housing, family, collective farm, or inventions legislation are among those which require special reference to the appropriate codes in order to determine whether a civil court proceeding will lie.

PURPOSE OF CIVIL PROCEDURE

Soviet law has long since rejected the traditional private law concept of civil procedure as a mechanism for merely impartial State adjudication of disputes between persons or organisations.[13] The proper and rapid consideration and settlement of civil disputes is essential, the civil procedure codes declare, in order to protect the social and State system of the USSR, the socialist system of economy and ownership, and the rights of citizens and State, co-operative, collective farm, and social organisations. Civil procedure should promote 'the strengthening of socialist legality, the prevention of violations of law and the nurturing of citizens in a spirit of undeviating execution of Soviet laws and respect for the rules of socialist community life.'

Other recent basic enactments have underlined the importance of civil law protection of the rights and interests of citizens in this spirit. Commentators link to this purpose the language of Article 57 of the 1977 USSR Constitution, a view reinforced by Decree No 1 of the Plenum of the USSR Supreme Court adopted 3 February 1978 on the new Constitution.[14] Socialist ownership is protected by civil procedure insofar as the property of State, social, collective farm, and trade union organisations figure in civil cases.

From this statement of purpose flow certain other features of Soviet civil procedure which differentiate it from both the Anglo-American and Romanist models.

A. BROAD PARTICIPATION IN CIVIL PROCEEDINGS

The Soviet codes of civil procedure stipulate that 'any interested person' has the right to apply in the procedure established by law to a court for the protection of a violated or disputed right or an interest protected by law. 'Person' here refers to both natural and juridical persons, and the concept of 'interested' has been held to include the relatives of a deceased person: a daughter filed suit in Leningrad to seek retraction of

---

13 D. M. O'Connor 'Soviet Procedures in Civil Decisions: A Changing Balance Between Public and Civic Systems of Public Order' in W. R. La Fave (ed) *Law in the Soviet Society* (1965) p 52.
14 For the Plenum Decree, see Biulleten' verkhovnogo suda SSSR no. 2, (1978) p 9.

libels published in the press about her father, a victim of the purges, as he had been rehabilitated posthumously. The people's court refused to hear the case on the ground that only the person defamed could bring suit. The Presidium of the Leningrad City Court reversed that judgment, indicating that any interested person might defend the honour and dignity of an individual.[15]

The right to apply to a court may not be renounced. Commentators point to the case of a house-owner who concluded a lease with his tenant stipulating that the tenant would never be sued for eviction. The courts held the clause void.[16]

The filing of suit does not depend exclusively upon the individual seeking protection of his right or interest, although that is the most common situation. A procurator may initiate civil proceedings on behalf of another and in some instances State agencies, trade unions, collective farms, social organisations or citizens may file suit on behalf of others. Trade unions may represent workers and employees in matters of production, labour, and the like. Cases concerning the deprivation of parental rights may be brought by the procurator or by State or social organisations, as well as a parent or guardian. The correctness of an author's certificate may be contested by individual citizens or State, co-operative, or social enterprises, organisations, and institutions. The procurator is the most interesting figure in this connection, for he must bring a civil proceeding or intervene in a case when there is a violation of State, social, or citizens' interests, when any of these are unable for whatever reasons to protect their interests, or when there is an abuse of right (such as unlawful legal transactions).

Procuracy participation is almost always imperative in cases concerning the deprivation of parental rights, declaring a person to be missing or dead, the confiscation of structures erected by using non-labour income, reinstatement in work, eviction from housing, or whenever the court deems his participation to be essential.

The public is represented in other senses and at other levels as well. Civil cases in Soviet courts are heard 'collegially,' that is, by a bench composed of a judge and two lay assessors, which ensures a lay element in the proceedings. Both judges and lay assessors are enjoined by the USSR constitutions and codes to be 'independent and subordinate only to law,' to decide civil cases 'on the basis of law, in accordance with a socialist legal consciousness, in conditions precluding any outside influence on them.' Soviet commentators have construed this to mean:

> No person, institution, or organisation has the right to obstruct judges in the objective, comprehensive, and full investigation of the case, verification of

---

15 Biulleten' verkhovnogo suda RSFSR no. 4 (1965) p 14.
16 Cited in S. S. Kipnis and P. Ia. Trubnikov *Postateino-prakticheskii kommentarii k GPK RSFSR* (1971) p 11.

evidence, and decreeing of a legal and well-founded judicial decision ... The Soviet court as a State agency implements the policy of the Communist Party and Soviet State. Therefore, Party organs may hear reports of judges and render assistance to them in resolving the tasks of socialist justice. However, no organs or persons have the right to instruct a court how a civil cases should be decided. Such interference in the activity of judicial agencies is categorically prohibited.[17]

The general public is encouraged to be represented in civil proceedings as representatives of social organisations or collectives of working people. They are not parties to the dispute, but appear in order to give the view of the organisations they represent on the substance of the case. Public opinion in this form is felt to be especially important in labour, housing, tort, alimony, or deprivation of parental rights cases. The courts are to take the initiative in notifying social organisations and collectives of cases having a 'social' element. Social representatives who speak in court must be duly authorised by the sending organisation; failure to submit a proper power of attorney is grounds for reversal. In cases involving the compensation of a house illegally acquired by non-labour income, the law requires the participation of a social representative.[18]

Circuit sessions of courts held at enterprises, factories, or institutions are encouraged when a civil case involves issues of social or educational value for the general public.

Individually and together these requirements and occasions for public involvement in the disposition of civil cases reinforce what Soviet jurists and legislation call the 'nurturing' role of law, the function of law as an 'educator' or 'parent' in shaping the model Soviet citizen. The 'nurturing of a new man is one of the most important functions of State agencies, including judicial.' The significance of the 'educational function' of the court is said to be growing 'in the stage of developed socialism.' The courts are called upon 'actively to further the growth of the law-consciousness of the masses, nurture in them a communist attitude toward labour and social ownership and strengthen discipline ...'[19]. Constraints on party disposition of cases are an extension of this philosophy. A court may, if the rights or interests of a citizen or organisation are adversely affected, refuse to allow a plaintiff to modify or abandon a claim, or a defendant to concede a claim, or the parties to settle a claim. A

---

17 Ia. L. Shtutin and A. M. Fel'dman, in I. P. Konenko and A. M. Fel'dman (eds) *Grazhdanskii protsessual'nyi kodeks Ukrainskoi SSR. Nauchno-prakticheskii kommentarii* (1979) p 13.
18 See the case of Kazarian, where the Plenum of the USSR Supreme Court reversed for failure to invite a social representative to the proceeding. Biulleten' verkhnovnogo suda SSSR no. 5 (1965) p 9. Some union republics allow a social representative to be present also at the court of second instance, but they do not themselves have the right to appeal a decision.
19 S. S. Kipnis and P. Ia. Trubnikov, note 16, above, p 7.

suit brought by a State farm against a citizen, for example, was ordered to be reinstated after the State farm dropped proceedings on the grounds that State interests were affected.[20] The same principle applies to an appeal. Nor does the plaintiff's claim determine the limits of judgment; higher compensation may be awarded to protect the rights or legal interests concerned. Similarly, a decision in a civil case may be protested by a superior court or procurator irrespective of the will of the parties: 'once the dispute reaches the state of litigation it is treated as a symptom of social disorder. . . .'[1]

Civil proceedings can give rise to special rulings by courts directed to officials or organisations not before the court in an effort to eliminate the causes which contribute to the social disorder manifested by the civil dispute.

B. LEGAL COUNSEL

Civil matters engage the attention of lawyers and courts to a far greater extent than any other. Nevertheless, it is common for civil cases to be decided without a lawyer present; indeed the majority are so heard. The Soviet codes of civil procedure speak of 'representation in court.' There are in essence three types of representation: voluntary, legal, and statutory.

Citizens may conduct their own cases in court personally or through a representative, and a citizen's personal participation in a case does not deprive him of the right to also have a representative. When a representative is designated, more often than not he is an advocate. Frequently, representatives of trade unions or other organisations empowered by law or their constitutive instruments to protect their members' interests appear. 'Legal representatives' appear on behalf of adopted persons, minors, mentally retarded persons, and the like. 'Statutory' representatives usually are jurisconsults or officials duly authorised by the charters of their organisations to appear in court on their behalf.

Although advocates do not appear in the majority of civil cases heard by the courts, civil cases ordinarily being disposed of on the basis of the documentation submitted and the initiative of the court in ascertaining the facts, legal fees are a relatively minor consideration, for legal assistance rendered by Soviet advocates is regulated by an Instruction confirmed by the USSR Minister of Justice on 4 August 1977. For appearing in a court of first instance, for example, an advocate may charge up to 15 rubles for a suit without value and as much as 30 rubles for a suit valued between 50 and 100 rubles. Consultation on legal questions may cost up to two rubles; written information on legislation,

---

20 State Farm 'Molodinskii' v Karpacheva translated in J. N. Hazard, W. E. Butler, P. B. Maggs, note 5, above, p 140.
1 H. J. Berman 'The Educational Role of Soviet Criminal and Civil Procedure' in D. D. Barry, W. E. Butler, and G. Ginsburgs *Contemporary Soviet Law* (1974) p 7.

up to three rubles, and drafting complex legal documents, up to five rubles. Foreigners may avail themselves of the services of Iniurkollegiia (see chapter 6, above).

C. COURT COSTS AND FINES

Court costs and fines under Soviet law are the expenses incurred for conducting a civil case in court. They consist of State duty and actual expenditures incurred. Their object is not fully to reimburse the State for the costs of civil proceedings but rather to deter people from filing clearly unsubstantiated suits and to encourage the parties to perform their civil law obligations promptly.[2] State duty is regulated by an Edict of the USSR Supreme Soviet adopted 29 June 1979, which stipulates, inter alia, that State duty is to be recovered for 'petitions to sue, for applications (or appeals) regarding special proceedings filed in courts, for cassational appeals against court decisions, as well as for the issuance of copies of documents by courts.' The duty on a petition to sue, for example, is levied against the value of the suit. For suits in excess of 500 rubles, the duty is 6%. A petition to sue for divorce attracts a State duty of ten rubles.

The value of a suit is fixed by the plaintiff based on rules laid down in the civil procedure codes. If the sum he fixes is clearly unreasonable, the judge will determine the amount. Rights to property are valued for these purposes. Textbook examples are: A married to B petitions that half the property in a house be acknowledged to be hers and registered in her name; C petitions for a division of collective farm household property between himself and household member D. In both cases the value of the suit would be one-half the value of the entire property being contested.

Other court costs include amounts paid to witnesses or experts, expenses for conducting views on the spot or for searching for the defendant, and the like. Exemptions from paying court costs are given in certain instances—to plaintiffs suing to recover labour earnings (including collective farmers), for suits arising out of copyright, discoveries, inventions, or rationalisation proposals, for suits to recover alimony; for suits on compensation for harm causing injury or other impairment of health or death of a breadwinner, and others, and, in any event, a court may exempt a citizen from court costs in light of his financial need. Witnesses are entitled to retain their average salary for time missed and are paid at established rates for transport, per diem, and accommodation.

Experts and interpreters are paid, by court ruling, remuneration for their work and travel, per diem, and accommodation expenses at rates

2 M. A. Gurvich (ed) *Sovetskii grazhdanskii protsess* (2nd edn, 1975) p 83.

fixed by the union republic councils of ministers. In the Ukraine, for example, experts are paid at from 40 to 60 kopecks per hour, exceptionally up to two rubles per hour. For written translations, a translator is paid from 20 to 30 kopecks per thousand typed or written symbols and 30 to 40 kopecks per hour in court.[3] Translation costs arise with frequency in Soviet judicial practice and probably involve Soviet citizens more than foreigners because many union republic courts hear civil cases in languages other than Russian. In the Ukraine, for example, civil proceedings are conducted usually in the Ukrainian language, so that in many localities persons whose first language is Russian will be required to submit documentation and plead in Ukrainian or use a translator/interpreter.

As a general rule, Soviet courts award all court costs against the losing party even if the winning side's costs were paid by the State. If the plaintiff succeeds in part of his claim, he will bear that proportionate share of court costs. A superior court which modifies a lower court decision or decrees a new one must respectively alter the distribution of court costs. Legal fees are specially treated. The winning party is awarded from the losing side costs for representation by an advocate, but not exceeding 5% of the total amount recovered. If the advocate acted without fee as a form of legal aid, the court will nonetheless recover the costs of legal fees from the losing party for the benefit of the legal consultation office which made the advocate available.

A plaintiff who withdraws his suit will not be awarded costs against the defendant, but may petition for costs if the defendant voluntarily settles the claim. When the parties come to a friendly out-of-court settlement, the usual practice is to distribute court costs as part of the settlement. When a civil suit is filed by the procurator or another body or person on behalf of other interested persons and recovery is not awarded or only partially awarded, the defendant is compensated proportionately from the State budget for court costs. The rulings of courts fixing and distributing the value of a suit and court costs may be appealed, or be protested by the procurator, without payment of State duty for the appeal.

In certain instances a Soviet court or judge may impose fines for the failure to perform procedural actions in a timely manner. When such fines are imposed on officials, they must be paid from personal assets. Fines may be imposed, for example, for the failure to submit written evidence, for violating measures to secure a suit, for disturbing a court session, for the failure of a defendant to appear in an alimony case, for loss of a writ of execution by an official, and others.

D. PROCEDURAL ECONOMY

An enlightened system of civil procedure accepts as axiomatic that justice delayed by congested court calendars or procedural tactics of the parties

---

[3] Ia. L. Shtutin and A. M. Fel'dman, in I. P. Konenko and A. M. Fel'dman (eds), note 17, above, p 94.

is justice frustrated. The Soviet legal system attempts to cope with the matter by imposing strict procedural deadlines or time periods within which specified actions must be performed, documents submitted, or cases heard. Unless there are justifiable reasons, the penalties for failure to comply can be draconian: the action or suit is terminated to the benefit of the other party. In a bureaucratic society this approach is perhaps the best means of forcing the machinery of the system to work, although to be sure a system of procedure which limits party disposition of cases, places a premium upon the formalisation of documentation, and hears the majority of civil cases without counsel present, probably must bring pressure of this kind to bear. The Soviet codes of civil procedure impose various deadlines for different kinds of cases. Cases concerning alimony, compensation of damage which caused injury or impairment of health, or labour relations must be heard within ten days by the court of first instance, or 20 days if the parties live in different cities, from the date the petition to sue is accepted by the court. Otherwise, the period for considering a civil case is one month. The Ukrainian SSR is among the union republics that impose time periods for the preparatory stages of a civil proceeding. The preparation of a case for judicial examination must be completed within from 7 to 20 days, depending on its nature, and heard on the substance within from 7 to 15 days. All the civil procedure codes lay down designated periods for appeals of all types, protests, execution, and the like; if the law is silent on the matter, the court may assign the procedural period itself. Detailed formulas for calculating the running, suspension, extension, or reinstatement of the periods are given in each civil procedure code.

E. FILING SUIT

A civil proceeding is commenced in the Soviet Union through the filing of a written petition to sue by a person having dispositive legal capacity (or his legal representative) in the court of proper jurisdiction (only the Azerbaidzhan SSR retains the Tsarist and earlier Soviet practice of accepting an oral petition to sue). The petition to sue must contain information specified in the civil procedure codes and be signed by the plaintiff or a duly authorised representative. A properly drafted petition must be accepted by the judge unless it falls within certain specified criteria for rejection (not triable by a court, failure to exhaust preliminary extra-judicial procedures, res judicata,[4] same case already pending

---

[4] See the case of Abramenko v Ramensk Registration Bureau, translated in J. N. Hazard, W. E. Butler, P. B. Maggs, note 5, above, pp 142–143. Procedurally, the case is illustrative of: initial civil judgment, appeal by way of cassation; quashing of the initial judgment by the cassational instance; retrial; a new suit to establish a right to ownership; a refusal to accept the suit on grounds of res judicata; a protest by the Procuracy, and satisfaction of the protest with an explanation of why res judicata was not applicable.

in court, comrades' court decision already properly decreed, lack of jurisdiction, lack of dispositive legal capacity by plaintiff and others). An improperly drafted petition may be amended and proceedings stayed until that is done. A counterclaim may be brought by the defendant in the same way as an ordinary action at any time before the court renders judgment on the original claims. The counterclaim must be set off against the original claim, must wholly or partially exhaust that claim, and must be linked with the original claim, on condition that the civil dispute would be more expeditiously considered if the claims were heard together. A claim for damages arising out of a criminal act may be heard simultaneously with the criminal proceeding or separately.

Security for a suit may be required upon application of a party to the case or upon the initiative of the judge or the court.

F. PREPARATION FOR TRIAL

After a petition to sue is accepted, a judge acting alone takes a number of measures to guarantee an expeditious and proper decision. First, the judge questions the plaintiff about the substance of his case, explores possible defences which may support the defendant, requests additional evidence when necessary, and briefs the plaintiff on his procedural rights and duties. When necessary, the defendant will be similarly summoned for the same purpose. The judge decides the issue of joinder or intervention if there are co-defendants or third parties and briefs them as he has done the plaintiff and defendant.[5] To all the parties the judge explains other possible means of settling the dispute, including a comrades' court or arbitration, and the consequences of making use of these. Whether the procurator should be involved or a State organisation joined to the case, or a representative of a social organisation or collective of working people invited to participate or observe, are likewise matters for the judge to decide. He also resolves which witnesses are to be summoned, obtains documentary or real evidence, or authorises a search warrant to obtain such, resolves whether expert evidence must be obtained, may carry out an inspection on the spot and sends judicial commissions to other courts. The ultimate determination that a case is ready for trial belongs to the judge alone, and he, having made that determination, fixes the date of the trial.

G. TRIAL

As noted above, at trial the case is heard by a judge and two people's assessors. The proceedings are to be direct, oral, and uninterrupted; that

5 Failure to join parties can be reversible procedural error. See the case of the Leushkins, translated in J. N. Hazard, W. E. Butler, P. B. Maggs *The Soviet Legal System* (3rd edn, 1977) pp 144–145.

is: the court must personally examine the evidence, hear witnesses, experts, and trial participants, and consider the case with only the usual recesses until it is finished and before hearing another or until it has adjourned the case for reasons specified in the civil procedure code. The bench may not change during the trial; any changes require retrial from the beginning.

At the opening of the judicial session, the court verifies whether persons summoned to appear have done so, explains to interpreters, experts, and persons taking part in the trial their rights and duties, removes witnesses from the courtroom until questioned, and announces the composition of the court and the right of challenge. The judge or a people's assessor then formally opens the case by reporting on the case, asking whether the plaintiff persists in his claim, whether the defendant admits the claim in whole or in part, and whether the parties wish to conclude a friendly settlement. The court may refuse to accept a withdrawal by the plaintiff, admission of the claim by the defendant, or a friendly settlement of the parties but must give its reasons.

Explanations are then heard from all persons taking part in the case, who may put questions to one another. Written explanations are read out by the presiding judge. Once explanations are completed, the court determines in which order the witnesses, experts, and other evidence are to be heard. Each witness is questioned separately. Those who have not testified may not be present in the courtroom until they have done so, whereupon they must remain until the trial is concluded or leave only with permission from the court. After all the evidence is heard, the judge presiding invites those taking part to add in any way to the materials of the case if they wish. In the absence of such request, the court declares the judicial examination to be completed and proceeds to hear the pleadings.

The court pleadings consist of speeches by those taking part in the case summing up their position, emphasising relevant evidence and arguments to the court, and asking for judgment in their favour. The plaintiff and his representatives speak first, followed by the defendant and his representative, then any third party who has an independent claim, followed by any other independent party, the procurator or authorised representatives of State agencies, trade unions, State enterprises, or others acting to protect the rights and interests of other persons, followed by authorised representatives, if any, of State agencies joined to the case by the court or at their own initiative. Finally, representatives of social organisations or labour collectives may speak. All have a right of reply after they have spoken, the last word being the prerogative of the defendant. If a procurator is present, he gives his opinion on the substance of the case as a whole after the court pleadings.

The bench then retires to its consultation room to draw up its judgment. After the judgment is signed by all three members of the bench, or a dissenting opinion attached, the bench returns to the courtroom to announce its judgment and explain the procedure and the terms for appeal.[6]

H. EVIDENCE

Soviet courts have enormous latitude in admitting and evaluating evidence. The role of the judge in assembling the evidence already has been noted. In civil cases 'evidence' means any factual data on the basis of which the court establishes the presence or absence of circumstances supporting the claims or defences of the parties and other circumstances material to deciding the case correctly. Each party must prove those circumstances on which his claim or defence rests. In some instances there are statutory requirements about what type of evidence is necessary; otherwise the court is obliged to admit only relevant evidence. A court is required to weigh evidence according to its own inner conviction based on a comprehensive, full, and objective consideration of the case looked at as a whole and being guided by the law and its socialist legal consciousness. No kind of evidence is accorded any a priori established weight. The codes of civil procedure treat in detail the evidence of witnesses, documentary evidence, real evidence, and expert evidence.

I. APPEAL

The right of appeal or protest by way of cassation to the next higher court is available for ten days after judgment is pronounced. When that period has lapsed, the judgment enters into legal force. The cassational instance reviews the entire case and not merely the errors of law or fact alleged by the appellants. Its decision is not subject to appeal and enters into legal force as soon as it is pronounced. Thereafter, review of a civil judgment is possible only on the basis of a protest of the Procuracy or a higher judicial instance by way of judicial supervision.

Civil procedural rights of foreign citizens and stateless persons

Foreign citizens and stateless persons, under Soviet law, enjoy the same rights and freedoms and bear the same duties as citizens of the USSR unless provided otherwise by USSR legislation.[7] Procedural rights in

---

6 Certain categories of cases, for example, appeals against actions of administrative agencies or officials, cases concerning tax or compulsory insurance arrears, and cases treated as special proceedings (establishing legal facts, declaring property to be ownerless, and others) are dealt with specially in the civil procedure codes.

7 Article 3, Law on the Legal Status of Foreigners in the USSR, enacted 24 June 1981 and translated in International Legal Materials XX (1981) 1211.

court are expressly mentioned (Article 21) in this connection, as well as in the FPCivPL and union republic codes of civil procedure. These rights are accorded on the national regime principle irrespective of whether other countries grant analogous rights, although the USSR Council of Ministers may establish reciprocal restrictions.

The principle of national regime for these purposes means that all norms of the civil procedure codes extend to aliens, including those governing legal capacity and dispositive capacity. Foreigners may appear as both plaintiff, defendant, or third persons with or without independent claims. They bear the same rights and duties of persons who participate in a case and may conduct their case personally or through their representatives. On the basis of international treaties, consuls of a sending State often are empowered to defend the interests of their nationals in a Soviet court, sometimes without a special power of attorney.

These same procedural rights extend to foreign enterprises and organisations.

Neither the FPCivPL nor the union republic codes contain special rules treating territorial or generic jurisdiction for cases having a foreign element. Consequently, civil cases in which foreign citizens, stateless persons, foreign enterprises or organisations, and disputes in which one of the parties resides abroad, are dealt with in matters of court jurisdiction on the same principles used for allocating purely internal cases by way of analogy of law. The commentators lay down the general rules as follows:

(1) suits shall be filed in the court at the defendant's place of residence, or the place where the management body of a juridical person is located, or a branch of the latter;
(2) suits against a defendant who has no place of residence in the USSR may be filed at the place where his property in the USSR is located or his last known place of residence in the USSR;
(3) suits against a defendant whose permanent residence is unknown shall be filed at the place where his property or temporary residence is located, or the last known place of permanent residence or permanent occupation of the defendant;
(4) suits arising from contracts in which the place of performance is specified or which by reason of the contract can only be performed in a particular place may be filed at the place of performance.

In addition to these general provisions, those articles of the civil procedure codes which enable the plaintiff to select his jurisdiction in certain types of cases (alimony, tort, etc) would apply equally to foreigners.

Criminal procedure

HISTORICAL BACKGROUND

Distinctive elements in the development of Russian criminal procedure already have been discussed (chapter 2, above). In the early years after the October 1917 Revolution, criminal procedure was regulated haphazardly and incidentally by a profusion of individual enactments treating court organisation. For a brief period judges were instructed to apply the 1864 judiciary reform legislation unless expressly repealed together with the revolutionary consciousness of the working people. In July 1918 the People's Commissar of Justice issued basic guidelines to judges counselling them on how to acquaint themselves with the materials of the case, to evaluate the evidence, summon the parties, and witnesses, and on the order for conducting the proceedings. The legal press of the day debated whether criminal procedure rules were purely technical guidance or had a legally binding character and whether the element of controversiality was essential to a criminal proceeding or the court might act without prosecutors and defence counsel. Later in the 1920s some suggested there should be two criminal procedure codes: one based on 'socialist democratism' for the working people and another without procedural guarantees for elements of antagonistic classes. With the abolition of the VChKa, the creation of a unified judicial system early in the NEP, and the cessation of civil war, procedural due process was accorded greater priority. Demand intensified for a systematised procedural law that would regulate a proceeding from beginning to end. On 25 May 1922 the RSFSR enacted the first Code of Criminal Procedure, in effect as of 1 August 1922;[8] it was rapidly supplanted, on 15 February 1923, by a new RSFSR code[9] that survived with amendments until the present 1960 Code. Other union republics enacted their own criminal procedure codes—Belorussia (1923), Georgia (1923), Ukraine (1927), Uzbek SSR (1929), Turkmen SSR (1932), Armenia (1934), Azerbaidzhan SSR (1934), Tadzhik SSR (1935)—but often these were highly abbreviated versions which obliged those republics to fall back upon the RSFSR code. On 31 October 1924 the USSR enacted a set of Fundamental Principles of Criminal Procedure of the USSR and Union Republics which laid down certain all-union principles to which the union republics must conform.[10]

The codes of criminal procedure underwent some distressing amendments in the 1930s, for example, the additions on 10 December 1934 and 2 February 1938 allowing cases concerning terrorist organisations, terrorist acts, and counter-revolutionary wrecking and sabotage to

8 *SU RSFSR* (1922) no. 44, item 539.
9 *SU RSFSR* (1923) no. 7, item 106.
10 *SZ SSSR* (1924) no. 24, item 206.

be investigated within ten days, to be heard in absentia, to be not subject to appeal, and the death penalty, if assigned, to be carried out as soon as judgment was rendered. Many modifications of the criminal procedure codes, however, seem to have occurred through judicial interpretation or departmental legislation. The RSFSR Supreme Court, for example, issued a special decree in 1927 altering Article 10 of the Code of Criminal Procedure with respect to Procuracy participation in certain categories of cases. From 1929-33 the formalities of criminal procedure were abbreviated through circulars issued by the RSFSR People's Commissariat of Justice, a trend that was reversed from 1935-36 by the same process.

The 1936 USSR Constitution required the enactment of all-union legislation on court organisation and criminal procedure. The Law on Court Organisation adopted 16 August 1938[11] supplanted the 1924 Fundamental Principles of Criminal Procedure to some extent, but the various commissions appointed to draft an all-union code of criminal procedure never produced an acceptable redaction. A draft published in 1939 received brief comment in the Soviet legal media, and another of 1948 was limited to internal circulation only. The drafts were prepared by order of the People's Commissariat of Justice within the All-Union Institute of Legal Sciences. In the early 1950s several decrees of the Plenum of the USSR Supreme Court actually amended or repealed provisions of criminal procedure legislation, a display of judicial lawmaking that contributed in 1957 to giving the USSR Supreme Court an express right of legislative initiative. Discussions of new union republic codes of criminal procedure and a set of all-union Fundamental Principles (FPCrimP) were well underway when the constitutional amendment abandoning an all-union code was adopted in February 1957. The FPCrimP were enacted on 25 December 1958, followed by the RSFSR Criminal Code on 27 October 1960 (entered into force 1 January 1961) and those of the other union republics.

GENERAL PROVISIONS

Soviet criminal procedure is a variant of the inquisitorial model of continental Europe and very different from the Anglo-American adversarial model. The investigation of serious offences is entrusted to an official, called an investigator, who is required to conduct a comprehensive, balanced, exhaustive investigation of all the evidence and to prepare an opinion to indict or not. Unlike the French or German systems, the investigator is subject not to judicial control, but to that of the Procuracy or other State agencies. As noted previously, Soviet law encourages the joinder of civil suits to criminal cases when these are

---

[11] *Vedomosti SSSR* (1938) no. 11, p 2.

related. The absence of a jury system means a sharp distinction is not drawn between law and fact. Opportunities for defence counsel to participate at the investigative stage are very limited, although these are expected to be increased. The object of the proceedings likewise may differ; they are not merely to expeditiously expose crimes, convict the guilty, and ensure the proper application of the law, but also to strengthen legality, assist crime prevention, and help nurture or educate citizens to obey the law and respect the rules of socialist community life.

A Soviet court, procurator, investigator, and agency of inquiry is required to initiate a criminal case whenever the indicia of a crime are disclosed on the grounds and in accordance with the procedure established by law. This categorical requirement is ameliorated in the codes by a list of circumstances or situations in which criminal proceedings are precluded or may be terminated, for example, transfer of a case to a comrades' court or for the imposition of administrative penalties.

JURISDICTION

As has been noted (chapter 7, above), all levels of the Soviet judiciary have original jurisdiction. The codes of criminal procedure provide that people's courts have jurisdiction over all cases except those reserved to higher courts or military tribunals, the latter courts and tribunals being vested with jurisdiction over cases arising under specified articles of the criminal codes or the Law on military crimes. Moreover, a higher court always has jurisdiction at first instance over any case within a lower court's jurisdiction. Territorial jurisdiction is based in the place where the crime was committed or, if this is impossible to determine, the place where the preliminary investigation or inquiry is completed.

PRE-TRIAL PROCEEDINGS

A Soviet criminal proceeding may pass through several stages before trial.

A. INITIATION OF CRIMINAL CASE

A case may be initiated on the basis of statements or letters of citizens, communications from trade unions, the Komsomol, people's guards, comrades' courts, or other social organisations, enterprises, institutions, and organisations, officials, information published in the press, or of someone giving himself up, or through direct discovery of the indicia of a crime by a procurator, court, investigator, or agency of inquiry. A case may be initiated only when there is sufficient data pointing to the indicia of a crime. Any of the latter four bodies or officials may set the procedure for initiation in motion by issuing a formal decree to initiate the case, whereupon measures must be taken simultaneously to prevent or suppress the crime or preserve any traces. A refusal to initiate also must be by decree with reasons given and may be appealed to the appropriate procurator or a higher court. Initiation of a case is, as a procedural stage, subject to Procuracy supervision. Either an improper initiation or refusal to initiate may be vacated by decree of a procurator.

B. INQUIRY

When a decree to initiate a case is issued, the case is either referred by the procurator or judge for inquiry or preliminary investigation or an agency of inquiry sets about its respective task. 'Agencies of inquiry' under Soviet law are several. Most commonly they are police agencies, but commanders of military units, KGB agencies, heads of correctional labour or similar institutions, State fire supervision agencies, border guard agencies, captains of sea-going vessels, or heads of polar stations may act when necessary. An agency of inquiry undertakes the immediate steps to discover whether a crime has been committed and by whom. These include searches or other operational measures to gather evidence. Their activity differs, depending on whether the offence is one for which a preliminary investigation is obligatory or not. If not obligatory, the agency of inquiry initiates the case and takes all steps to establish the facts that must be proved in the case. Defence counsel may not participate in such an inquiry, and the victim or civil parties may not see the materials of the case until trial. An inquiry of this type may last up to one month, but that period is subject to extension. In those instances when a preliminary investigation is mandatory, the agency of inquiry initiates the case and carries out the most urgent investigative actions (view, search, seizure, the examination, detention, and interrogation of suspects, or the interrogation of victims and witnesses); these must be completed within ten days, whereupon the case is turned over to an investigator.

Soviet law draws distinctions, not observed in Anglo-American legal systems, between detention and arrest. The codes of criminal procedure authorise an agency of inquiry to *detain* a person suspected of committing a crime for which deprivation of freedom may be assigned as a punishment under certain circumstances, for example, a person caught committing a crime or immediately thereafter, or when eyewitnesses or the victim directly indicate a particular person, or when obvious traces of the crime are discovered on the suspect, his clothing, or dwelling. Otherwise he may be detained only if the individual attempts to escape, or he has no permanent place of residence or identification. Written notification indicating details, grounds, reasons, and the explanations of the person detained must be given to the procurator within 24 hours by the agency of inquiry. The procurator has 48 hours from receipt of notice within which either to sanction the detention (arrest) or to release the person detained. The Soviet constitutions do not employ the term 'detention' at all. They refer to 'arrest' only, stipulating that '. . . no one may be subjected to arrest other than on the basis of a judicial decision or with the sanction of a procurator.' An individual can therefore be held in custody for 72 hours plus the time for an agency of inquiry's notification to reach the procurator. 'Arrest' may arise under other circumstances. The FPLAdR provide for the imposition of 'administrative arrest' for a term of up to 15 days by a people's court or judge. In this instance 'arrest' is a penalty, not an investigative safeguard, but the constitutional phrase '. . . on the basis of a judicial decision' is intended to authorise such a measure. In the Theoretical Model of a Criminal Code (see chapter 17), the term 'arrest' is being proposed as a type of punishment. The arrest of property in connection with a civil or maritime proceeding is another matter. During the interwar and early post-war period the Soviet distinction between detention and arrest worked to the disadvantage of foreigners detained in the USSR for criminal investigation because applicable international treaties governing consular access to such individuals provided for access only in the event of their arrest. Detention in those days could be several days in duration, but because 'arrest' had not been imposed consuls sometimes found access delayed or denied. Current international practice is to refer to 'arrest or detention in other form' in order to surmount the divergent attitudes toward police custody in Anglo-American and continental or socialist legal systems. When it is necessary to keep an individual confined during an inquiry or preliminary investigation, the provisions of the 1969 USSR Statute on Preliminary Confinement Under Guard are applicable.

Soviet legal terminology, it should be observed, changes with respect to individuals at each stage of the pre-trial proceedings. An individual detained on suspicion of committing a crime or to whom a measure of restraint has been applied before an accusation is presented is called a 'suspect' (*podozrevaemyi*). Once the accusation is presented the individual is the 'accused' (*obviniaemyi*), and when the conclusion to indict is accepted by the court, he becomes the 'person brought to trial' (*podsudimyi*).

During an inquiry, a suspect is summoned and interrogated. He must be informed of his right to give explanations, submit, petitions, and appeal against the actions of the person conducting the inquiry, and he must be told what crime he is suspected of committing. When under detention, the suspect must be interrogated within 24 hours of being detained.

C. PRELIMINARY INVESTIGATION

The preliminary investigation may be conducted by investigators of the Procuracy, of the KGB, or of the agencies of internal affairs. The codes of criminal procedure stipulate which agencies are to investigate which crimes and under what circumstances a preliminary investigation is mandatory or not. In general the KGB investigates serious crimes against the State; most major crimes require a preliminary investigation, which also is compulsory for all crimes committed by minors or persons mentally or physically incapable of exercising their right of defence.

Unless the law requires the sanction of the Procuracy, the investigator takes all decisions regarding the course and performance of the investigation independently. He may appeal to a higher procurator against instructions of a procurator with which he disagrees. In cases when a preliminary investigation is mandatory, the investigator may commence at once without waiting for agencies of inquiry to act, but he may instruct the latter to undertake certain actions on his behalf. In addition to the Procuracy, an investigator is supervised by the chief of an investigative department, who may check criminal cases, give instructions on how to conduct the investigation, how to refer a case, how to classify a crime, and more. Appeal against the chief of an investigative department also lies with the Procuracy. When an investigator initiates and accepts a criminal case, he renders a single decree to that effect; if the case is initiated by another official or agency, the investigator issues a decree to accept the case. Complex cases may be accepted by several investigators.

The investigator, just as the court, procurator, or person conducting an inquiry, is obliged to take all measures provided by law for a 'thorough, complete, and objective analysis' of the circumstances of a case and to elucidate those that both tend to convict or acquit the accused or to aggravate or mitigate his guilt. Ordinarily, the investigator will begin by interrogating the accused, who has the right to remain silent without any implications being drawn. The investigator is forbidden to use threats or force to obtain a confession, and even if a confession is given, it has no evidentiary value. Perhaps with an eye to past history, Soviet criminal procedure places no value on confessions and requires that the crime be proven by independent evidence. Although in most criminal cases defence counsel is not admitted to the preliminary investigation—a policy to be changed under *perestroike*—the suspect, accused, defence counsel, victim, or civil plaintiff or defendant may not be denied the right to interrogate witnesses, conduct an expert examination, or perform other investigative actions to collect evidence if the circumstances they petition to establish may be of significance for the case. A petition denied must be justified with reasons. The investigator for his part may engage an interpreter or summon specialists or witnesses to assist him. If in the course of an investigation the investigator discovers moral, physical, or material harm has been caused, he may involve individuals in the proceedings as a victim, civil plaintiff, or civil defendant. The preliminary investigation must be completed within two months from the date of initiating the case until the case is referred with a conclusion to indict, transferred to a court in order to consider the possible application of compulsory measures, or terminated or suspended. Extensions of a further two months are possible, and thereafter exceptionally only by the union republic procurator, Chief Military Procurator, or USSR Procurator General. Supplementary investigations should be completed within one month, with extensions possible on the same grounds. Although the law imposes no ultimate maximum limit for the preliminary investigation, confinement under guard during the investigation of a case may not exceed nine months even in the most exceptional instances.

If the investigator concludes there is sufficient evidence, he renders a decree to prosecute a person as an accused. This decree must be presented within 48 hours of being rendered or the date fixed for compulsory appearance. The accused must be informed of his rights to know of what he is accused, to offer explanations, present evidence, submit petitions, familiarise himself with the materials of the case and have defence counsel as provided in the Code of Criminal Procedure, among others. Interrogation may begin at once, but not at night except in urgent situations. Witnesses and victims likewise are interrogated, and searches, views, and expert examination conducted. An accused or suspect may even be committed by the investigator to a medical institution for observation. If the investigator decides there is no basis for prosecution, the accused is released; otherwise, the investigator draws up the conclusion to indict. At that point he must invite the victim, civil plaintiff, or civil defendant, or their representatives to acquaint themselves with the materials of the case; they may petition for further investigation, which must either be done or a reasoned refusal given. Then the accused is advised that the evidence will support a conclusion to indict and he too has the right to examine the materials of the case. In most instances the defence counsel retained by the accused enters the case at this point of the proceedings. The accused or his counsel may request further investigation, which must be granted or a reasoned refusal given.

By Anglo-American standards, the proceedings now move very rapidly. The accused may not have retained defence counsel yet, or his counsel may be occupied with other matters. Not more than five days may elapse before defence counsel appears, and if he cannot, other counsel may be arranged by the investigator. Defence counsel has the right to meet with the accused alone, to acquaint himself with all materials of the case and copy necessary information, to discuss the filing of petitions with the accused, to file petitions or challenge officials who took part in the investigations, to appeal to the procurator against investigative actions that prejudice or violate the rights of the accused or defence counsel, and to be present during requested supplementary investigative actions with the investigator's permission. A formal record is kept of the presentation of the materials of the case.

When the offence committed is not serious, the investigator may with the procurator's consent decide not to prosecute and hand the individual over to a collective on condition of good behaviour, or transfer the case to a comrades' court or to a commission for cases of minors, or refer the case to a court for compulsory medical measures. If the case is to be pursued, the conclusion to indict is issued containing the substance of the case, the place and time of committing the crime, the methods, motives, consequences, and other relevant circumstances, the evidence confirming the existence of a crime and the guilt of the accused, mitigating or aggravating circumstances, arguments put forward by the accused and the verification thereof. Page references must be given to relevant passages in the file of the case. Information also must be given about the personality of the accused and the specific article(s) of the criminal code which provide for the crime cited. The case must be referred immediately to the procurator.

The procurator has five days to consider the conclusion to indict and either to confirm it and refer the case to a court, to return the case for supplementary investigation, to terminate the proceedings, to request a proper conclusion to indict be drafted if it is defective, or to draw up a new conclusion to indict and return it to the agency of inquiry or investigator, specifying the errors discovered. The procurator may strike out sections of the conclusions to indict or apply provisions for a less grave crime, but if a more serious crime is called for, the case must be returned for the preparation of a new accusation. If the procurator confirms the conclusion to indict or draws up a new one, he refers the case to the appropriate court.

D. ADMINISTRATIVE SESSION

When the conclusion to indict is received by the court, it is received in an administrative session consisting of a judge, two people's assessors, and the procurator, unless the judge himself accepts there are sufficient grounds to bring the accused to trial. Whether to bring to trial must be resolved within 14 days from the moment the case comes to the court. Without predetermining guilt, the court or judge examines a variety of issues, from jurisdiction to the sufficiency of evidence to securing property. A court in administrative session may rule to bring an accused to trial, return the case for supplementary investigation, suspend proceedings, refer the case to the proper jurisdiction, or terminate the case. The court also may alter the conclusion to indict by inserting a less grave crime or excluding individual sections, giving reasons. Certain matters concerning the conduct of a trial are decided in administrative session, for example, whether to allow State or social accusers, whether to allow defence counsel selected by the accused or to appoint defence counsel, whether the case is to be heard in open or closed session. Once the judge or the court decides to bring a person to trial, the judicial consideration of the case must commence within 14 days.

Trial

A. JUDICIAL EXAMINATION

The judicial examination of a case at first instance usually takes place in open court and must proceed continuously, except for rest, until completion. Other cases may not be interposed. A court secretary keeps a record of the judicial session. All trial participants—an accuser, person brought to trial, defence counsel, victim, civil plaintiff, civil defendant, and their representatives enjoy equal rights in presenting and analysing evidence or submitting petitions. Trials of persons in absentia may occur only at their request or if the person is abroad and evades appearance in court. The procurator supports the State accusation in most cases, but in minor offences a trade union official, inspector, or even the victim may prosecute. Social accusers or defenders may appear by ruling of the court. Unless the accused expressly refuses counsel, he must be represented by defence counsel if the procurator appears in the case or the law requires defence counsel.

When the judge and people's assessors enter the courtroom, all rise. Trial participants stand when addressing the court or giving testimony. The person presiding opens the judicial session by announcing which case is being examined, verifying whether anyone has appeared in court and reading out the accusation. Witnesses are removed from the courtroom until they have been questioned by the court. The person brought to trial is asked his full name, date and place of birth, residence, occupation, education, family status, and whether and when he was handed the conclusion to indict. The composition of the court is announced and the right of challenge explained. Then each trial participant's rights are explained. The court inquires whether any trial participant has petitions to summon new witnesses, experts, and specialists, or to acquire real evidence and documents; the court must rule on petitions at once, giving reasons for refusal. Should some trial participants not be present, the court must decide whether the case may proceed in their absence. If so, the judicial investigation commences.

B. JUDICIAL INVESTIGATION

This phase begins by publicly disclosing the conclusion to indict and any changes introduced in the administrative session of the court. The person brought to trial must be asked whether he has understood the accusation and acknowledges his guilt or not, with reasons if he wishes. Acknowledgment of guilt does not alter the court's responsibility to investigate the case fully. The court next entertains proposals about the sequence in which the evidence shall be heard and evaluated. Ordinarily the person brought to trial will be invited to give testimony regarding the accusation and circumstances of the case. Thereafter the court, accuser, victim, civil plaintiff or defendant, and defence counsel are invited to put questions, which the person presiding may not allow if they are not germane. The court may put questions at any time, and in practice the judge is usually active in doing so, playing a leading role in adducing testimony and evidence. Any testimony given in court is compared with that recorded during the preliminary investigation, and substantive contradictions may be disclosed publicly.

The court then hears witnesses, who appear not for prosecution or defence but in order to assist the court in finding the whole truth. Each witness is explained his duty to tell the truth, warned of criminal responsibility for perjury, or refusing to testify, and obliged to sign a statement confirming that his duties have been explained to him. The witness does not swear an oath. Each witness is interrogated separately and in the absence of those not yet questioned. His relationship to the person brought to trial and the victim is ascertained and he is invited to impart everything known to him in the case. All trial participants as above are then invited to ask their questions. The victim usually is interrogated before the witnesses in the same procedure. The sequence of examination and cross-examination is rather flexible, and the questioning may continue until all the trial participants have no further questions.

The person brought to trial is treated differently from ordinary witnesses. He is not bound to testify, although a refusal to do so will result in public disclosure of his statements, if any, during the preliminary investigation. Neither is he required to sign the statement regarding the duty to tell the truth in court. Nor must he confine himself to the facts of the case. He may advance arguments and explanations at any time during the proceedings and the court is obliged to consider them when coming to a decision.

Expert opinion may be introduced when necessary. Evidence of this nature relates not to the facts of the case but to the qualifications and experience of the expert. All trial participants may suggest questions to be put to an expert. The questions must be publicly disclosed and the opinion of all trial participants and the procurator heard concerning them. Irrelevant questions may be excluded. The expert prepares a written opinion and may treat issues relevant to the case but not expressly asked. The opinion is read out in court and the expert then interrogated in the usual way by all trial participants.

When all evidence has been considered, the judge invites petitions from trial participants to supplement the judicial investigation. When these are disposed of or if there are none, the judicial investigation is declared to be completed.

C. ORAL ARGUMENT

The court then passes to oral argument. The oral argument consists of speeches to the court by the accuser, civil plaintiff, civil defendant, or their representatives, sometimes the victim, and defence counsel or the person brought to trial if there is no defence counsel. The sequence of addresses is determined by the court. Participants in oral argument may refer only to evidence considered in the judicial investigation. The court may not restrict the duration of oral argument but may stop persons if they touch upon irrelevant circumstances. After all participants have given their speeches, they may each speak in rebuttal, the right of last rebuttal always belonging to the defence counsel and the person brought to trial.

When oral argument is completed, the person brought to trial has the right of the last word; he may be neither questioned nor limited in time, so long as he speaks about circumstances relating to the case. All trial participants are then invited by the court to make non-binding suggestions concerning the substance of the accusation. The court then retires for conference to decree judgment. The judgment must be based on evidence considered in the judicial session, be well-founded and reasoned, and be rendered in complete privacy. The three-person bench resolves all questions it must decide by simple majority vote, without abstention. The presiding person votes last. Any member of the court who holds a dissenting opinion may set it out in writing. In this event the dissent is not disclosed when judgment is proclaimed but is attached to the file of the case, where it may be considered by a higher court during an appeal or review. The judgment must be either of conviction or acquittal, with disposition of any civil claim being jointly considered. After the judgment is signed, the bench returns to the courtroom. All stand, including the court, while hearing the judgment. Within three days of proclamation, a copy of the judgment must be handed over to the convicted or acquitted person. If an advocate has appeared in the case upon assignment by the court, the latter shall when decreeing judgment render a ruling regarding his remuneration for legal services.

Presumption of innocence

The main outlines of a Soviet criminal proceeding are wholly familiar to anyone brought up in continental Europe. To the Anglo-American lawyer, many aspects of the inquisitorial model are disturbing, and none more so than the relationship between the preliminary investigation and the trial. This model is not interested in probabilities; it requires certainties and, ultimately and ideally, absolute truth. From the agency of inquiry onward, the officials who perform investigative actions, the procurator, and ultimately the court must be absolutely convinced of the guilt of the accused. At all stages they are required by law to examine and weigh all circumstances of the case, favourable and unfavourable, before forming their opinion. Unlike the 'adversary' system of Anglo-American law, where the judge acts as 'referee' between two contending sides in the presence of a jury, carefully monitors the rules of evidence and admissibility so the jury is not prejudiced, and instructs the jury about the applicable law, the entire proceeding being the first full disclosure of evidence and argument, the Soviet trial seems in some respects more in the nature of a review of the preliminary investigation than a trial in the proper sense. Although the percentage of convictions in Soviet criminal proceedings is not published, one would suppose a figure below 90-95% would suggest grave shortcomings in the quality of investigations.

A more serious concern is the extent to which, if at all, the Soviet model of investigation may prejudice the trial court, consciously or unconsciously. The court knows that the investigator and the procurator are absolutely convinced of the guilt of the accused else the case would not have been referred for trial. Moreover, the court has briefly glanced at the file of the case while sitting in administrative session and allowed the case to go forward for trial. Serious doubts arise in the minds of some Anglo-American lawyers whether under such circumstances there is a presumption of innocence under Soviet law.[12]

Soviet jurists have themselves debated for decades whether the presumption operates in Soviet law. The expression was denounced during the parliamentary debate preceding the adoption of the 1958 FPCrimL as a 'worm-eaten dogma of bourgeois doctrine' by one Supreme Soviet deputy. But many Soviet proceduralists favour the term and in any event believe that the substance of the presumption of innocence is firmly embodied in the Soviet law of criminal procedure. It is certainly clear that Soviet legislation does not place the burden of proving innocence on the accused. The codes of criminal procedure require that the court, procurator, investigator, or agency of inquiry may not transfer the obligation of proof to the accused, that the accused may present evidence but may not be forced to do so or punished for refusing to do so, that the court judgment may be based only on evidence considered during the judicial investigation, that unless participation in the commission of a crime is proved, the accused must be acquitted, that a conviction may not be based on presuppositions, and that on appeal a judgment of conviction shall be quashed if the judgment is not confirmed by evidence in the judicial investigation.[13]

---

12 For contending views, see G. P. Fletcher 'The Presumption of Innocence in the Soviet Union' UCLA Law Review XV (1968) 1203-1229, with replies by H. J. Berman, J. B. Quigley, Jr., and G. Ginsburgs.
13 Berman 'Major Changes Reflected in the 1960 Code of Criminal Procedure' in Berman and Spindler (transl.) *Soviet Criminal Law and Procedure: The RSFSR Codes* (2nd edn, 1972) pp 57-65.

The fact that the codes contain the essence of what is meant by presumption of innocence does not fully dispose of the concern that the trial is merely a review of the investigative stage, and it is perhaps surprising that Soviet draftsmen have not employed greater rhetorical reinforcement for the notion that only a trial court can determine guilt and must do so independently of the views of the investigator and procurator. Notwithstanding the objectivity required of the investigator, there is a strong body of opinion in the Soviet legal profession that the quality of preliminary investigations could be improved if an adversarial element were introduced more widely into the investigation, that is, if defence counsel were admitted earlier in most if not all cases in order to raise pertinent issues.

Reliance upon an investigative apparatus to conduct a complete and impartial investigation and assemble all the evidence has implications for the rules of evidence. By Anglo-American standards, the Soviet rules of evidence are remarkably flexible and permissive. Witnesses may be questioned about any circumstances to be established in a given case, including the personality of the accused and victim and his relationship with them. Hearsay evidence is admissible only if the witness can indicate the source of his information.

Experience with forced confessions during the Stalinist era, when under the 1923 RSFSR Code of Criminal Procedure the court would dispense with further proof in any case if the accused admitted his guilt, convinced Soviet draftsmen not to place reliance on confessions. Even when voluntary, people are known to confess to offences mistakenly or for other ulterior motives. Similarly, the evidence of an accomplice is not sufficient for a conviction under Soviet law unless confirmed by other evidence. The codes of criminal procedure require that there be subject to proof: (1) the occurrence of the crime; (2) the guilt of the accused in committing the crime and his motives; (3) circumstances which influence the degree and character of responsibility of the accused, or his personality; and (4) the nature and extent of loss caused by the crime. Evidence, defined as 'any factual data' on the basis of which the presence or absence of a socially dangerous act is established, the guilt of the person who committed the act, and any other relevant significant circumstances, must be evaluated by a court, procurator, investigator, or agency of inquiry in 'accordance with their inner conviction, based on a thorough, complete, and objective consideration of all the circumstances of the case in their totality, being governed by law and by socialist legal consciousness.' No evidence has any a priori force.

Appeal and review

Soviet criminal procedure distinguishes between appeals against court judgments that have entered into force and those that have not. Appeals against or protests of a judgment of a court of first instance (except of a union republic supreme court, which may not be appealed or protested by way of cassation) must be filed within seven days from the date judgment is proclaimed or a convicted person under guard is handed a copy of the judgment. The seven-day period may be extended for valid reasons. The filing of an appeal, called a cassational appeal, has the effect of suspending execution of the judgment. The cassational instances must hear the appeal in open session within ten days, and in the supreme court, within 20 days, from receiving the case in open judicial session. The court is not bound by the grounds of the appeal, but is obliged to verify the legality and well-foundedness of the judgment with respect to all persons in the case. A cassational instance may reject the appeal, refer the case for new investigation or judicial consideration, vacate the judgment and terminate the case, or change the judgment. However, a punishment assigned may not be increased nor the law of a more serious crime applied.

Soviet appeal procedures are unusual in that appeals may be lodged not merely by the convicted person or his defence counsel but also by the victim, and by the civil plaintiff or defendant with regard to the civil claim. Moreover, the procurator must protest against any illegality in the trial proceedings, even on behalf of the accused. This means that an acquitted person may appeal, for example, on the grounds that he was acquitted for the wrong reasons (which may leave him open to civil liability), and likewise that a procurator may protest acquittal or conviction because it was contrary to the evidence, or the sentence was too severe, or socialist legality has otherwise been violated. Procedural violations are grounds for reversal if they are substantial; for example, the case is considered without defence counsel when his participation is required by law, or the court judgment has not been signed properly.

Allowing all the parties to a Soviet criminal proceeding to appeal by way of cassation, in contrast to the Anglo-American practice of allowing an acquittal to stand, has been attributed to the fact that until recently the Soviet people's courts were staffed by judges without a higher legal education. It was thought desirable, 'under Soviet conditions, to get as many cases as possible into the appellate courts, staffed by trained professional judges. . . .'[14] In fact, many superior court judges did not have a higher legal education, but in any event the review powers of higher courts would have accomplished the same end. A more likely explanation lies in the Soviet concept of objective truth in the judicial process. If the object is to acquit the innocent and convict the guilty, then no first instance court's decision should be irrevocably final; an unjustified acquittal is as reprehensible as an unwarranted conviction.

---

14 E. L. Johnson *Introduction to the Soviet Legal System* (1969) p 129.

In the Soviet view a criminal trial is not a contest between rival parties, but an impartial inquiry into precisely what occurred and why.

A judgment takes legal effect when either the time for bringing a cassational appeal has lapsed or the cassational appeal has been decided. Review by way of judicial supervision is still possible, but only upon protest of a procurator, a court chairman, or their deputies as specified in the codes of criminal procedure. Even a judgment of acquittal may be reviewed by supervision within a year of entering into legal force. Those entitled to bring a protest may do so on the basis of their own analyses of lower court decisions or by virtue of representations from an aggrieved person, who has the right to petition for review. Courts maintain regular office hours to receive such petitions. Much of the work of the supreme courts consists of reviewing cases. Many are reviewed upon the initiative of the higher courts, who regularly survey inferior court practice in selected areas of the law to hunt for judicial error or ascertain whether the law is being uniformly applied. A case reviewed on protest must be considered within 15 days or, in the supreme courts, within a month from receiving the protest. A procurator must take part and the court may summon a convicted or acquitted person or his defence counsel. Cases also may be reopened on the basis of newly discovered circumstances.[15]

The theoretical possibilities of appeal and review are virtually unlimited under the codes of civil and criminal procedure.

Special proceedings apply in cases involving minors, the application of measures of a medical character, and cases of hooliganism or the petty stealing of State property. In general, special proceedings are more expeditious and require the court to weigh heavily the personal circumstances of the individual. Defence counsel is mandatory in cases of persons who have committed socially dangerous acts while in a state of non-imputability or who contracted a mental illness after committing a crime.

Restructuring and the law of procedure

The decision taken in January 1987 by the Plenum of the Central Committee of the CPSU to reform the criminal law also had implications for the law of procedure. It was acknowledged that the time has come to admit the advocate to the preliminary investigation in all cases. The remaining issue was at what stage—the presentation of the accusation or the time of arrest or detention under guard.

Most of the other major criticisms have been levelled at the failure to implement the procedural model properly. The courts in particular are

---

15 On the tactics of appeals, see W. E. Butler 'Criminal Appeal Practice and The Soviet Advocate' *Yearbook on Socialist Legal System 1987* (1988) pp 357–385.

being expected to be more demanding in their evaluations of the preliminary investigation and of evidence presented in court. The rate of acquittals reportedly increased in 1986–87 in consequence. There is some discussion of removing the preliminary investigation service away from the Procuracy, of increasing the numbers of people's assessors, of protecting the independence of the judiciary, and of enhancing the elements of contentiousness, that is, of accentuating the adversarial factors, in proceedings.

As for the codes of criminal procedure as such, in the three decades of their existence they have grown considerably in size, the number of sections increasing by 50%, and dozens of other amendments have produced a 'mass of inconsistencies, contradictions, and gaps that have reached a critical level and begin to tell on the effectiveness of the law.'[16] A Theoretical Model of a Code of Criminal Procedure being developed at the Institute of State and Law of the USSR Academy of Sciences would, in its preliminary form, consist of General and Special Parts divided into 15 sections containing 75 chapters. A number of matters would be regulated in detail for the first time, including exhumation, the procedures for rehabilitation and private prosecutions, whereas others treated in passing and sometimes cryptically would be elaborated within the Code itself: detention of a suspect, confinement in a medical institution, evidence and proof, compensation to victims of crime, crime prevention measures, pre-trial proceedings, and others.

---

16 See V. M. Savitskii (ed) *Problemy kodifikatsii ugolovnoprotsessual 'nogo prava* (1987) p 7 (A. M. Larin). The draft structure of the Theoretical Model is reproduced at pp 126–129.

Chapter 20

Foreign relations law

The conduct of foreign relations in the broadest sense of the term by the Soviet Union is governed by several thousand normative acts. Some are directly concerned with foreign relations, for example, claims to sovereign rights, nationality, the procedure for concluding international treaties, whereas others touch upon foreign relations in passing, for example, statutes on ministries, family, civil, criminal, or other branches of legislation.[1] Departmental legislation in practice has had a large role in foreign relations law, often apparently supplanting long obsolete legislative acts. The USSR Ministry of Foreign Affairs, for example, evidently continues to be governed by its 1923 Statute, although in almost all respects that document is woefully inadequate and may have been amended by unpublished legislation in the 1940s. Soviet legal doctrine does not look upon foreign relations law as a separate branch of law as yet,[2] and there are no efforts underway comparable to those in the United States to systematise the core principles in the *Restatement of Foreign Relations Law*. Soviet law reform in this realm has proceeded by examining individual areas of foreign relations legislation and consolidating or unifying the relevant acts.

Legal status of foreign citizens in the USSR

The 1977-78 Soviet constitutions guarantee to 'foreign citizens and stateless persons' the rights provided by law including 'the right to have recourse to a court and other State agencies in order to defend their personal, property, family, and other rights.' In turn, these persons are obliged to respect the USSR Constitution and to observe Soviet laws. On 24 June 1981 the USSR Supreme Soviet adopted the Law on the Legal Status of Foreigners in the USSR (in effect as from 1 January 1982). The Law is the first of its kind in Soviet history and gives legislative sanction for the first time to a number of rules previously existing only as administrative practice.

1 The only Soviet study, indispensable for the early years, is N. V. Mironov *Pravovoe regulirovanie vneshnikh snoshenii SSSR* (1971).
2 K. K. Sandrovskii *Pravo vneshnikh snoshenii* (1986), is essentially a study of diplomatic and consular law.

A. GENERAL PROVISIONS

Foreign citizens under Soviet law are persons who are not citizens of the USSR and who have evidence of their being a citizen of a foreign state. Their legal status is governed by the Soviet constitutions, the 1981 Law mentioned above, all relevant legislative acts, and international treaties of the USSR. The basic principle is that foreign citizens enjoy the same rights and freedoms and bear the same duties as citizens of the USSR unless Soviet legislation or international treaties of the USSR provide otherwise. The 1981 Law stipulates foreign citizens shall be equal under Soviet law irrespective of origin, social and property status, racial and national affiliation, sex, education, language, attitude towards religion, nature and character of occupation, and other circumstances. Reciprocal limitations may be placed on the exercise of these right and freedoms by the USSR Council of Ministers if Soviet citizens are restricted in their rights in the particular foreign country. The 1981 Law further adds that foreign citizens in the USSR may not exercise their rights and freedoms to prejudice the interests of Soviet society and the State nor the rights and legal interests of Soviet citizens and other persons. The duty to respect Soviet laws likewise encompasses an obligation to respect the rules of socialist community life and the traditions and customs of the Soviet people.

The particular rights enjoyed by foreign citizens in the USSR depend partly on whether they are permanently or temporarily resident. Those who have an authorisation for permanent residence and a residence permit issued by internal affairs agencies are deemed to be permanently resident; all others are deemed to be temporarily in the country and obliged to register their foreign passports or documents replacing them and to leave the country when their period of stay has expired. Health care, for example, is extended to foreign citizens permanently resident in the USSR on the same basis as Soviet citizens, whereas for foreign citizens temporarily resident special regulations issued by the USSR Ministry of Public Health are applicable and, in the absence of bilateral treaty arrangements, charges imposed at established rates.

B. CITIZENSHIP AND ASYLUM

A single union citizenship exists in the Soviet Union; each citizen of a union republic is simultaneously a USSR citizen. The 1978 Law on Citizenship of the USSR was adopted on 1 December and entered into effect as from 1 July 1979; bilateral international treaties modify its provisions under certain circumstances. The 1978 Law on Citizenship applies the criteria of both *jus soli* and *jus sanguinis* for the acquisition of Soviet citizenship. A child born of parents who at the time of birth were both Soviet citizens is regarded as being a USSR citizen irrespective of the place of birth. If the parents were of different citizenship when the child was born, the child is a Soviet citizen provided it was born on Soviet territory or, if born elsewhere, one parent had a permanent place of residence in the USSR. However, if both parents, one of whom is a Soviet citizen, give birth to a child abroad and neither has a permanent residence in the USSR, the agreement of the parents is decisive for the citizenship of the child.

Persons may be admitted to Soviet citizenship by application irrespective of racial and national affiliation, sex, education, language, and place of residence. No formal requirements for application—age, period of residence, language, or whatever—are stipulated by the 1978 Law. If both parents take Soviet citizenship, the citizenship of their children under age 14 automatically changes. If only one parent becomes a Soviet citizen, children under age 14 become Soviet citizens only if the parent becoming a Soviet citizen expressly so petitions. For children between ages 14 and 18 whose parents change citizenship the written consent of the children is required. Marriage to a Soviet citizen does not automatically change the citizenship of the foreign spouse. The position of stateless persons often is decided on the basis of different considerations. Individuals from territories which became part of the USSR after 1917 may be affected in citizenship matters by international treaties for choice of nationality. Special rules govern adopted children.

A person who has lost Soviet citizenship may upon his petition be restored to citizenship by decision of the Presidium of the USSR Supreme Soviet. Changes in citizenship take effect from the date the respective Edict is enacted unless the text provides otherwise and, being personal Edicts, are not normally published in the official gazette.

Asylum has been provided for in all Soviet constitutions since 1917. The present Soviet constitutions authorise the USSR and union republics to grant asylum to foreign citizens who are being persecuted for defending the interests of the working people and the cause of peace, for participation in a revolutionary or national liberation movement, or for progressive socio-political, scientific, or other creative activity. The Presidium of the USSR or union republic supreme soviet decides whether to grant asylum or not. Individuals granted asylum enjoy certain rights not accorded to other foreigners. They are not subject to extradition or exile abroad, they enjoy those rights on Soviet territory needed to live a normal existence, and they may arrive on Soviet territory without a visa, although Soviet legislation does not expressly so provide. They may continue to engage in the activity on Soviet territory for which they were persecuted abroad only if their activity does not harm the interests of Soviet society and the State or the rights of other citizens.[3]

3 L. N. Galenskaia *Pravovoe polozhenie inostrantsev v SSSR* (1982) pp 31–34.

C. ENTRY AND EXIT

Foreign citizens entering the Soviet Union require valid foreign passports or documents replacing them and an authorisation or visa of a competent Soviet agency. As a rule, visas are obtained by application to Soviet diplomatic or consular representations abroad; the Soviet Union has bilateral treaty arrangements with some countries allowing simplified procedures, or multiple entry-exit visas. Entry or exit-entry visas likewise may be issued when foreigners resident in the USSR travel abroad for a specified period, pursuant to the Statute on Entry into the USSR and on Exit from the USSR confirmed on 22 September 1970. The 1981 Law on the Legal Status of Foreign Citizens in the USSR enumerates five grounds on which a foreign citizen may be refused entry: (1) in the interests of State security or public order; (2) if this is necessary to protect the rights and legal interests of USSR citizens and other persons; (3) if during a previous vist to the USSR a violation of legislation on the legal status of foreign citizens in the USSR, or of customs, currency, or other Soviet legislation has been established; (4) if when applying for a visa the applicant has disclosed false information or has not submitted the necessary documents; (5) on other grounds established by Soviet legislation. This provision is broad and seems to embody pre-existing practice.

Transit passage is allowed without a visa on Soviet territory to the frontier point of exit if the established route is observed. Air passengers, for example, may transit in Soviet airports if they have entry documents to their destination, an airplane ticket, and their stay in the airport does not exceed 24 hours. Under international treaties crew members of foreign merchant ships are allowed visa-free entry to Soviet ports under special passes; analogous arrangements are made for foreign airline personnel. Tourists on cruise or excursion vessels constantly cruising between adjacent states may be allowed up to 48 hours on shore without a visa.

Foreign citizens also require a valid passport and a Soviet authorisation or visa to leave the USSR. Exit may be refused if: (1) there are grounds for initiating a criminal prosecution, until the proceedings have ended; (2) the person has been convicted for committing a crime, until the sentence is served or he is relieved from punishment; (3) his exit is contrary to the interests of State security, until the said circumstances cease; or (4) there are other grounds provided for by USSR legislation. Exit may be postponed until a foreign citizen has executed any financial obligations with which the essential interests of Soviet citizens or other persons, or State, co-operative, or other organisations are linked. In one incident in the 1960s a foreign vessel was pursued and fired at when the master attempted to sail without authorisation and had failed to settle his financial affairs with the Soviet port authorities.

D. CUSTOMS RULES

Foreigners who cross the Soviet frontier are subject to customs control. When entering the USSR, foreigners complete a customs declaration in which they must itemise all currency, precious metals or stones, manufactures therefrom, weapons, hand luggage, works of art, and the like. An identical form is completed upon departure. Soviet currency may not be imported or exported, but there is no restriction upon foreign currency in the possession of foreign citizens provided it is declared upon entering. Expeditious customs procedures and special exemptions are provided for in bilateral treaties especially with other socialist countries.

E. POLICE REGISTRATION

Within 24 hours of arrival in the Soviet Union foreigners must register with a visa section or local police administration. Tourists register with Intourist, Sputnik, and trade union hotels and individuals who arrive for work or study usually with the administration of their respective institution or enterprise. Individuals visiting the Soviet Union on the basis of private invitations must appear in person for registration. An appropriate identification document is submitted in all cases, usually the foreign passport. Foreigners who intend to reside permanently in the USSR must obtain in addition a residence permit.

Foreign citizens under the 1981 Law on the Legal Status of Foreign Citizens in the USSR may move about on Soviet territory and choose their place of residence in accordance with the procedure established by Soviet legislation. Limitations may be imposed in the interests of State security, public order, health, and morality or to protect the rights and legal interests of USSR citizens and other citizens. Certain areas of the country are closed to all foreigners and other areas to foreign nationals of certain countries. Many countries have introduced reciprocal limitations upon the movement of Soviet citizens.

F. ADMINISTRATIVE RESPONSIBILITY

Foreign citizens are bound under the Soviet constitutions to respect and obey Soviet legislation, and likewise are subject to administrative responsibility just as is every Soviet citizen (see chapter 7, above). Certain administrative sanctions are applicable only to foreigners. Under the FPAdR a warning might, for example, be issued as an administrative sanction to a foreigner who has violated the rules for stay in the USSR by failing to obtain residence documents, to register his passport, departed from his prescribed itinerary, or violated transit rules. Fines may be imposed for certain violations, in exceptional instances up to 200 rubles, for flagrant violations of customs regulations, for intruding into a frontier zone, breaches of the 1983 USSR Air Code, and others. Administrative sanctions such as confiscation or deprivation of a special right (eg fishing licence) apply in the ordinary way. Correctional tasks could be applied only to foreigners employed in the Soviet Union. Administrative arrest is wholly applicable to foreigners when provided for by law, in which case consular access may be allowed by treaty or at the discretion of the Soviet authorities.

The two administrative sanctions applicable only to foreigners are: (1) reduction of period of stay; and (2) deportation. The former may be imposed by internal affairs agencies on a foreign citizen who has violated legislation on the legal status of foreigners or if the reasons for his continued presence have lapsed. Deportation may be imposed if a foreign citizen's actions are contrary to the interests of State security or public order, if deportation is necessary to protect the health and morality of the populace or to defend the rights and legal interests of USSR citizens and other persons, and if a foreign citizens flagrantly violates legislation on the legal status of foreign citizens, or customs, currency, or other Soviet legislation. 'Competent agencies' take decisions regarding deportation. The foreign citizen is obliged to depart within the period designated and may, with the sanction of a procurator, be detained and deported in a compulsory manner. Detention in this event is permitted only for the term required for deportation. More than 50 foreigners were deported in 1976 for transporting anti-Soviet or pornographic literature. An Italian was deported in 1979 instead of being prosecuted for currency smuggling. The 1981 Law on the Legal Status of Foreign Citizens clarifies again what seems to have been administrative practice.

Foreigners may be detained by other duly authorised Soviet officials, including hunting or fishing inspectors, frontier guards, masters of ships or river vessels, aircraft commanders, and others, for particular infringements. The procedures for boarding or arresting foreign non-military vessels in waters under Soviet jurisdiction are laid down in the 1982 Law on the State Boundary of the USSR.

G. CIVIL LAW RIGHTS

The FPCivL provide that foreign citizens enjoy civil legal capacity (see chapter 18, above) in the USSR equally with Soviet citizens, although individual exceptions may be established. Among the exceptions or limitations are the following: minerals may be granted for use to foreigners only in specified instances or pursuant to treaty obligations; foreigners may not explore or exploit the USSR continental shelf unless a special permit has been obtained or an international agreement so provides; foreign vessels may not fish within 200 miles of the Soviet coast unless international agreements so allow, or fish Soviet internal waters for commercial purposes. The USSR Council of Ministers has from time to time imposed retaliatory restrictions on foreign citizens whose countries limit the civil legal capacity of Soviet citizens.

H. SUCCESSION

Under the 1981 Law on the Legal Status of Foreign Citizens in the USSR foreign citizens may inherit or bequeath property in accordance with Soviet legislation. A decree of the USSR Council of Ministers of 21 April 1955 provides that inherited sums due to foreigners are transferred from the USSR abroad without hindrance if there is reciprocity on the part of the respective foreign state, unless other arrangements are provided by international treaties of the USSR. 'Reciprocity' for these purposes Soviet commentators believe should contain two elements: (1) allowing Soviet citizens in the respective foreign State to transfer inherited monies to the USSR, and (2) the possibility of effectuating that right. The actual receipt of inherited monies is widely regarded as decisive for reciprocity. A foreign heir is not obliged to prove reciprocity. This determination is at the disposal of banks through which foreign remittances are transferred. In the absence of reciprocity the monies are kept in the Soviet bank in an account for the foreign heir until reciprocity is established, that is, the foreign heir does not lose the inheritance purely by virtue of a temporary absence of reciprocity.

Unless international treaties establish otherwise, the FPCivL provide that legal relations respecting inheritance are determined by the law of the country where the testator had his last permanent place of residence. When Soviet law is applicable, the group of heirs under intestate succession is governed by the union republic civil codes (see chapter 10, above). Foreigners who are heirs of either priority take equally with Soviet citizens of the same priority. Last place of permanent residence is crucial. In the absence of treaty provisions, where the inheritance is to be opened under Soviet law, most commentators suggest, the basis for deciding the applicable law is determined by residence. Some Soviet treaties invoke the distinction between movable and immovable property as the basis for deciding the applicable law. This distinction is not drawn in Soviet legislation, and Soviet courts are instructed to treat any type of structure as immovable.

As for wills, the FPCivL provide that the legal capacity of a person to draw up and retract a will, the form of the will, and the document retracting it are determined by the law of the country where the testator had his permanent place of residence when drawing up the particular document, but the failure to observe the form of the country is immaterial if the form meets the requirments of Soviet law. Bilateral treaties of the USSR with certain socialist countries follow a different principle, and most consular conventions concluded by the USSR allow consuls of the sending State to draw up, certify, and keep wills under the laws of the

State, sometimes specifying precisely where the consul may perform these activities.

Foreign heirs by will or by operation of law must accept an inheritance either at the notarial office where the inheritance was opened or at a consular representation of the USSR within the usual six-month period. Foreigners may inherit either movable or immovable property owned by a Soviet citizen, but of course the scope of ownership is limited to what a Soviet citizen may lawfully hold in personal ownership. The fact a foreign citizen resides permanently abroad is no bar to his inheriting structures in the Soviet Union. Shares in a housing construction or dacha construction co-operative pass to foreign heirs as the value of the share-accumulation and not in kind unless the foreign citizen resides permanently in the USSR and requires better living accommodation in the particular locality and is over 18 years of age, in which case he may be admitted to the respective co-operative.

I. COPYRIGHT

Foreigners may have copyright in the USSR and inherit copyright. The FPCivL provide that copyright in a work first issued on the territory of the USSR or not issued but situate on Soviet territory in any objective form shall be recognised for the author and his heirs irrespective of their citizenship, and likewise for the author's legal successors. Under the union republic civil codes 'issuance' means publication, public performance, public showing, transmission by radio or television, and others. So long as issuance of a foreigner's work first occurs in the USSR, protection is accorded irrespective of whether the foreign citizen's country is party to international copyright conventions. Otherwise, the work is protected in the USSR only if the state where the work first appeared has ratified the conventions.

Under Soviet civil law an author may publish, reproduce, and disseminate his work under his own name, pseudonym, or anonymously, but only by legally admissible means, that is, by concluding a contract with a publishing house. Although Samizdat is not permitted, an author may publish at his own expense and take advantage of the State distribution network under an arrangement introduced in 1988. Most publishing contracts with foreigners are concluded through the All-Union Copyright Agency (VAAP), specially empowered to represent the interests of authors and their legal successors and to act as intermediary in preparing and concluding publishing contracts with foreigners. Royalties are paid at Soviet rates for various categories of printed material and print runs either in foreign or Soviet currency. If the latter, the currency must be used in the Soviet Union. Foreigners are subject to income tax on royalties at the same rate as Soviet authors are taxed in the foreigner's country unless exemption is provided for by international treaty. Under certain circumstances provided in the FPCivL a foreign work may be used without permission and with or without payment of royalties, for 'social needs.'

Foreigners not infrequently work as translators either as employees of Soviet publishing houses or on contract. The translator has copyright in his translation under Soviet law for his lifetime and 25 years thereafter. Some union republics reduce the copyright period for photographs and applied art to 10 or 15 years.

Copyright passes upon the author's death to his heirs, except, however, that the author's right to the name and integrity of the work does not pass but vests either in a person designated by the author or, in the absence of such, in the heirs and VAAP. An author may bequeath his copyright to any person; payments of royalties to heirs are made through VAAP and not directly.

J. INVENTIONS

Under the Statute on Discoveries, Inventions, and Rationalisation Proposals of 21 August 1973, foreign citizens who make inventions or rationalisation proposals, and their legal successors (including juridical persons), enjoy the same rights thereto as Soviet citizens and may be issued a patent or author's certificate as appropriate. The 1973 Statute as amended in 1979 allows the issuance of a patent in the names of a Soviet and foreign organisation for an invention resulting from economic and scientific-technical co-operation in performing an official planning task.

Discoveries are treated somewhat differently. A foreigner's discovery is protected by Soviet law only if a Soviet citizen is a co-author, in which case the whereabouts or residence of the foreigner is immaterial, or if the discovery was made on Soviet territory while the foreigner was working at a Soviet enterprise (see chapter 10, above).

The Soviet Union is party to the 1883 Paris Convention on Industrial Property, the 1970 Treaty on Patent Co-operation, the 1971 Strasbourg Agreement on International Patent Classification, and others. Fees for issuing patents are laid down by the USSR Council of Ministers. Foreign applicants residing or permanently resident abroad must remit these in foreign currency. Multilateral and bilateral patent co-operation agreements within COMECON and bilateral agreements with certain advanced Western industrial powers (France, Italy, and others) enable inventions to be protected more readily and make special provision for jointly developed inventions.

K. LABOUR ACTIVITY

The 1981 Law on the Legal Status of Foreign Citizens in the USSR distinguishes between the labour rights of foreigners permanently resident in the USSR and those temporarily resident. The former category may work as workers or employees at enterprises, institutions, or organisations or engage in other labour activity on the grounds and in the procedure established for USSR citizens. The commentators understand this to mean that foreigners have a right to work and to choose their profession just as Soviet citizens, with the same 41-hour work week, days off, annual leave, and earnings scale, and the duty to fulfil their labour contract and observe the rules for internal labour order.

Foreigners may not hold offices or employment which by law are linked with being a Soviet citizen. Foreigners consequently may not hold elective office, serve as a crew-member on a Soviet-flag vessel or aircraft, engage in commercial fishing or mining, or serve in law enforcement agencies. Individuals trained in medicine or pharmacy outside the USSR may be admitted to their profession in the USSR by special permission; foreigners who receive such training in Soviet institutions may practise in accordance with their degree and title.

Foreign citizens and their families may count up to one-third of their foreign work experience toward the minimum level required for assignment of a State pension under Soviet law unless provided otherwise in bilateral treaties.

Foreign citizens temporarily in the USSR may engage in labour activity if this is compatible with the purposes of their stay in the Soviet Union. Many visit the USSR as a form of 'business trip' or 'secondment' to carry on work while remaining in the employ of their sending organisation, for example, to assemble machinery, to lecture, to perform concerts. The terms of work are commonly stipulated in inter-State or interdepartmental agreements, which make provision for travel expenses, accommodation, per diem stipend, access to needed facilities or amenities, medical care, work load, and tax relief. Unless such matters are dealt with by special agreements, Soviet legislation applies. Persons temporarily resident do not qualify for pensions. However, foreigners in the USSR to study may be allowed to be gainfully employed with the permission of their host institution. Labour conditions for specialists from COMECON countries often are regulated by particular multilateral agreements.

Employees of inter-State international organisations in the USSR are not governed by Soviet legislation. Usually the international organisation itself adopts enactments governing these matters, for example, the Rules Concerning Labour Conditions of Personnel of the COMECON Secretariat, as amended.[4] Foreign personnel of international economic associations formed pursuant to COMECON recommendations and situations in the USSR are governed by a combination of their constitutive instrument, special regulations for their personnel, and Soviet legislation.

4 Translated in W. E. Butler *A Source Book on Socialist International Organisations* (1978) pp 192–204.

L. FINANCIAL ACTIVITY

The Soviet State has enjoyed a monopoly over currency operations ever since the banks were nationalised in 1917. Two banks exercise this monopoly: the State Bank of the USSR (Gosbank) and the Bank for Foreign Economic Activity of the USSR (Vneshekonombank), under the supervision of the USSR Ministry of Finances. Gosbank has the exclusive right to perform transactions on Soviet territory in gold, silver, platinum, and platinum-group metals in coin, bullion, or raw form, in foreign currency or payment documents in foreign currency, bond coupons, joint-stock shares, and the like. Vneshekonombank grants foreign trade credits, carries on currency operations, maintains settlement accounts for the import and export of goods, accepts funds for demand deposit from foreign citizens, banks, institutions, representations, firms or other organisations, remits and receives monies to and from other countries, opens and confirms letters of credit, issues and cashes traveller's cheques, and accepts for safekeeping foreign currency, precious metals, or securities, among other functions.

An Edict of 30 November 1976 governs the procedure for purchasing, selling, exchanging, giving, inheriting, keeping, transferring, or making payments in 'currency valuables' on the territory of the USSR. 'Currency valuables' are defined as foreign currency (banknotes, treasury notes, coins), payment documents (cheques, bills of exchange, letters of credit) and shares, bonds, etc in a foreign currency, bank payment documents in rubles which were acquired for foreign currency and may be converted back, precious metals in any form or state excluding jewellery or other manufactures of precious metals or fragments thereof, and natural precious stones, raw or processed (diamonds, sapphires, pearls, etc). Bank payment documents in rubles are issued by Vneshekonombank in the form of cheques that may be used to purchase goods in special stores and may be converted back into foreign currency upon departing the country if unused. Lottery tickets, Vneshposyltorg cheques, synthetic precious stones, and jewellery are not considered to be 'currency valuables.'

Individuals may engage in operations with 'currency valuables' on Soviet territory only as follows without special permission of the USSR Ministry of Finances: (1) by gift to a spouse, children, parents and grandchildren, grandparents, or natural brothers or sisters; (2) by will or intestate succession; (3) by concluding a legal transaction for purchase-sale, exchange, or gift for the purpose of collecting single examples of coins; and (4) as payment for goods and services in stores or other organisations which have the right to accept payment in foreign currency. The store most often encountered by tourists is the 'Beriozka' chain situated in most cities open to travellers.

Violation of currency regulations on a small scale (not exceeding

25 rubles at the official rate of exchange) entails an administrative fine of up to 50 rubles and confiscation of the currency or payment documents. On a larger scale the provisions of the union republic criminal codes become applicable.

Foreigners may open savings accounts in State Labour Savings Banks on the same basis as Soviet citizens. These banks accept deposits in rubles only.

Foreigners in the USSR are liable for income tax on revenues obtained from carrying on activity authorised in the established procedure on Soviet territory at the same rates levied on Soviet citizens, except, however, that if a foreign State taxes Soviet citizens at higher or lower rates, these rates will apply to citizens of that State in the USSR. Exemptions are granted on the basis of reciprocity to amounts paid to foreign firms by Soviet foreign trade organisations, to earnings paid to foreign employees of foreign organisations sent to work in the USSR, and to performers for concerts and the like. Foreigners permanently resident in the USSR pay income tax on royalties received from abroad, and likewise taxes are withheld from Soviet royalties paid to foreigners irrespective of their place of residence; several countries have concluded double taxation and other treaties to ameliorate the effect of tax obligations.

Local taxes and fees are applicable to foreigners permanently resident unless specially exempted. Foreign natural and juridical persons must pay the motor vehicle tax if they own automobiles or motorcycles in the Soviet Union. State duty is imposed on Soviet and foreign citizens for the performance of certain actions, for example, filing a petition to sue in court, performing notarial functions, or registering acts of civil status. Foreigners may incur State duty for registering or extending the registration of foreign passports, the issuance or extension of residence permits, or applying for USSR citizenship. Duties are waived on the basis of reciprocity in some cases, and foreign tourists are exempt from State duty for registering their foreign passports.

The import, export, and transfer of Soviet and foreign currency and other valuables is governed by a consolidating Statute confirmed on 6 April 1982. Powers of attorney for the disposal of assets in Soviet and foreign currencies, other 'currency valuables,' and other property also come within the purview of the Statute. For the most part the Statute concerns situations under which remittances may be made to or from Soviet citizens, but foreign citizens who reside permanently abroad are particularly singled out with respect to the right to receive inherited sums of money and sums obtained from the realisation of inherited property, on the basis of reciprocity as noted above. In all instances not covered by the Statute, currency movements must be with the authorisation of the USSR Ministry of Finances.

M. CRIMINAL LAW AND PROCEDURE

The scope of Soviet criminal law extends fully to foreigners on Soviet territory (see chapter 17, above). Certain articles of the union republic criminal codes extend only to foreigners, for example, espionage, illegally flying the USSR or a union republic State flag on a merchant vessel, and violation of the rules for stay or transit in the USSR.

Under the 1981 Law on the Legal Status of Foreign Citizens in the USSR, foreign citizens enjoy procedural rights in court on the same basis as USSR citizens (see chapter 19, above). The USSR is a party to the 1963 Vienna Convention on Consular Relations, and the 1976 Consular Statute of the USSR and all bilateral consular conventions to which the USSR is party make provision for consular access to and defence of the rights of citizens who may be arrested or detained in other form. The consular conventions differ in the specificity and time limits within which consular access must be granted, and whether a consul may visit persons serving sentence. Some socialist countries are party to a Convention enabling foreign citizens sentenced to deprivation of freedom to serve the sentence in their own country.

N. OTHER RIGHTS AND FREEDOMS

Marriage and family relations have been treated in chapter 11, above. The 1981 Law on the Legal Status of Foreign Citizens enables foreigners to receive education on the same basis as USSR citizens in accordance with the procedure laid down by legislation, to use 'the achievements of culture,' to exercise freedom of conscience, and to enjoy inviolability of the person and dwelling. Foreigners may participate in social organisations and trade unions if they reside permanently in the USSR provided that the charters of these organisations do not make provision to the contrary. Foreigners do not enjoy the right to vote in elections for State office or in all-people's referendums, and they are exempt from the duty to perform military service in the USSR Armed Forces.

Foreign economic relations

On 22 April 1918 the RSFSR Council of People's Commissars adopted the Decree on the Nationalisation of Foreign Trade, which continues in force throughout the entire USSR by virtue of an all-union decree of 13 July 1923.[5] The State monopoly of foreign trade has been maintained in each series of Soviet constitutions to date, despite some momentary second thoughts at the highest level in 1923–24. The 1977 USSR

5 *SU RSFSR* (1918) no. 33, item 432; *Vestnik TsIK, SNK i STO SSSR* (1923) no. 1, item 12; transl. in Butler *Commercial, Business and Trade Laws: Soviet Union and Mongolia* (1982-).

Constitution relegates to all-union jurisdiction '... foreign trade and other types of foreign economic activity on the basis of the State monopoly' (Art 73(10)).

Until mid-1986 principal responsibility for administering foreign trade had rested with the USSR Ministry of Foreign Trade for more than half a century. On 19 August 1986 the Central Committee of the CPSU and the USSR Council of Ministers adopted two joint Decrees: 'On Measures Relating to the Improvement of the Administration of Foreign Economic Relations' and 'On Measures Relating to the Improvement of the Administration of Economic and Scientific-Technical Co-operation with Socialist Countries'. The two decrees introduced several fundamental policy changes. The direction and co-ordination of Soviet foreign economic activities was placed in the hands of a newly-formed State Foreign Economic Commission of the USSR Council of Ministers (SFEC). The formation of joint enterprises with non-socialist firms was approved. The monopoly rights of Soviet foreign trade organisations (FTOs) were curtailed and dispersed; a list of ministries, departments, economic associations, and enterprises (initially 91) authorised to engage in export-import operations directly from 1 January 1987 was confirmed. Financial measures were introduced to give associations and enterprises a direct involvement and interest in foreign currency transactions. The scheme of direct links and joint enterprises with other COMECON member countries on Soviet territory was to be expanded. In principle and in law foreign economic activity is to become a part of all Soviet State enterprise activity.

On 13 January 1987 legislation was enacted to elaborate the formation of joint enterprises with firms in 'capitalist' and third world countries. Further administrative reform was introduced in January 1988 when the USSR Ministry of Foreign Trade and the State Committee of the USSR for Foreign Economic Relations were abolished and an all-union Ministry of Foreign Economic Relations created in their stead.

A. DIRECTION AND GUIDANCE OF FOREIGN ECONOMIC ACTIVITIES

The SFEC, formed in October 1986, is intended to co-ordinate what previously had become a highly dispersed and fragmented State monopoly of foreign trade. It directs the work of the USSR Ministry of Foreign Economic Relations, the State Committee of the USSR for Foreign Tourism, the USSR Bank for Foreign Economic Activity, the Chief Administration of State Customs Control attached to the USSR Council of Ministers, all ministries and departments with respect to their foreign economic activities, and the Soviet portions of inter-governmental commissions for economic and scientific-technical co-operation with foreign countries. Its particular functions include the development of a strategic overview of foreign economic activity, the implementation of fundamental improvements in foreign economic activity, and the continued pursuance of socialist economic integration with COMECON member countries.

The SFEC is to ensure that ministries, departments, associations, and enterprises take an active part in foreign economic activity; is itself to improve foreign economic planning, incentives, and management and to expand the export potential of the country; and should carry on work to fundamentally alter the structure of Soviet imports and exports. Responsibility for co-ordinating Soviet obligations under the COMECON Comprehensive Programme for Scientific-Technical Progress up to the Year 2000 rests with the SFEC, as does the duty to ensure that foreign economic obligations of the Soviet Union generally are met. More particularly, the SFEC is empowered to consider and draft long-term and current plans for foreign economic relations and control the conformity of such plans to the overall strategic development of foreign economic relations, to supervise the foreign economic activities of all ministries and departments, to decide which economic associations and State enterprises are to have the right to conduct export-import operations directly, and to take 'decisions in the form of regulations of the USSR Council of Ministers'. The SFEC also has some role in approving the creation of joint enterprises with foreign firms and in authorising the transfer of shares in a joint enterprise to third persons.

B. ADMINISTRATION OF FOREIGN ECONOMIC RELATIONS

The former USSR Ministry of Foreign Trade and the former State Committee for Foreign Economic Relations, abolished in January 1988, had each received a new Statute on 22 December 1986. The new USSR Ministry of Foreign Economic Relations (MFER) has inherited their respective functions and responsibilities.[6] These include foreign trade planning: the composite export and import plans for goods submitted to the State planning and supply committees and the summary data on receipts and payments in foreign currency submitted to the State planning committee. The MFER also considers the draft plans of all ministries, departments, associations, and enterprises which have the right to engage in export-import operations. Inter-State foreign trade negotiations continue to be the responsibility of the MFER with both socialist and capitalist countries, but involving the supply and planning organisations and those ministries, departments, and organisations which are concerned with export and import activities. Export and import permits, re-export permits, and transit permits for goods are issued by the Ministry.

6 On the period 1986–88, see W. E. Butler 'The State Monopoly of Foreign Trade and the Family of Socialist Legal Systems' Connecticut Journal of International Law II (1987) 215–260.

The MFER has responsibility for the operation of FTOs within its jurisdiction and for their economic expenditure of material resources and hard currencies. Opportunities for export and import, foreign trade legislation and policies of other countries, and the state of international markets are studied by the Ministry, which also negotiates and concludes international treaties of the USSR or proposes the conclusion or accession to such treaties. State control over the quality of export goods is effected by the Ministry at those associations and enterprises where there is no State Acceptance Centre. The MFER maintains a role in working out the principles and method for fixing foreign trade prices and tariffs and in improving the carriage of foreign trade goods or expediting foreign shipments in transit. The Ministry helps to organise trade fairs and exhibitions in the Soviet Union, co-ordinates the participation of Soviet entities in such arrangements abroad, and organises the participation of its own FTOs in trade fairs. Through its Academy of Foreign Trade the MFER trains foreign trade personnel for all entities involved in foreign economic relations.

Together with the SFEC, the Ministry is charged with protecting Soviet State interests on the foreign market and conducting uniform commercial, economic, currency, and price policies. To this end the MFER is empowered to verify the export-import operations of ministries, departments, associations, enterprises, and organisations, and to obtain from them or make available to them necessary materials, proposals, and opinions on foreign trade matters, reporting to the SFEC about the results of such control.

With regard to FTOs within its own system, the Ministry may create, reorganise, or liquidate them, authorise FTOs to form branches, offices, divisions, representations, or joint-stock societies in the USSR or abroad, and allow FTOs to take part in any organisations whose activities are consistent with the FTO Charter. The MFER retains its function of issuing permits to foreign firms that wish to open representations in the Soviet Union.

By absorbing the functions of the former State Committee for Foreign Economic Relations, the MFER also is concerned with the Soviet foreign aid programme abroad and the commercial import and export of complete plants, including gas pipeline projects and nuclear power plants, from and to other socialist countries, developing nations, and advanced western industrial powers. The Ministry is closely involved in working out the long-term and short-term State plans for economic and technical co-operation, draft currency plans, design, construction, and assembly plans, and specialist personnel plans with the ministries and departments concerned, and has the right to submit proposals on a vast range of foreign economic matters to other bodies. Foreign governments, organisations, and firms may apply directly to the MFER regarding proposals to build or convert enterprises or other installations abroad.

C. FOREIGN TRADE REPRESENTATIONS

Outside the Soviet Union the Ministry of Foreign Economic Relations operates through trade representations. These are defined by the 1982 Statute on Trade Representations of the USSR Abroad as 'agencies of the USSR effectuating abroad the rights of the USSR in the realm of foreign trade and other types of foreign economic activity, including trade, economic, and industrial co-operation on the basis of the State monopoly.' They occupy a peculiar status administratively. Although 'being constituent parts of embassies of the USSR in receiving countries and enjoying the privileges and immunities of the latter,' according to the 1982 Statute, they are simultaneously subordinate to the Ministry of Foreign Economic Relations, which determines the structure and personnel establishment of the trade representations. International treaties govern the status of the Soviet trade representation in the receiving country and in some cases accord less than full diplomatic privileges and immunities to them. Trade representations engage the responsibility of the Soviet State and are not liable for the obligations of FTOs or other economic organisations, or vice versa. They may perform legal transactions and other legal acts in their own name and in the name of the USSR which are necessary to carry out their tasks, appear as plaintiff or representative thereof in court, but appear as defendant in court only with regard to disputes arising from the trade representation's legal transactions or other legal acts in the receiving country and then only if by virtue of an international treaty or unilateral declaration the USSR has consented to the trade representation being under the jurisdiction of the court for the said category of disputes. Otherwise, the trade representation will invoke State immunity.

The functions of the trade representation are many. They oversee Soviet foreign trade policy in the receiving country, protect Soviet interests, study economic and market trends and developments and inform Soviet institutions about these, and likewise advise organisations in the receiving country about economic and commercial conditions in the USSR, undertake to improve the structure and efficiency of foreign trade, supervise the activities of FTOs in the receiving country, assist in commercial negotiations and the conclusion and execution of foreign trade transactions, issue import, transit, and re-export permits, certificates of origin, and other documents, take part in the work of intergovernmental commissions and committees formed with many receiving countries, and promote participation in Soviet and foreign trade and industrial exhibitions. In countries where the Soviet Union does not have a trade representation, commercial counsellors at the respective Soviet embassy perform these functions.

D. FOREIGN TRADE ORGANISATIONS AND ASSOCIATIONS (FTOs)

Under the restructuring of Soviet foreign economic relations, there are two types of FTOs: those within the system of the MFER and other non-branch ministries or State committees, and those formed within the system of a branch ministry or department. The legal status of the first group appears still to be governed by the 1978 Statute on the All-Union Economically-Accountable Foreign Trade Association Within the System of the Ministry of Foreign Trade, whereas the last group is regulated by the 1986 Statute on the All-Union Economically-Accountable Foreign Trade Organisation (or Association) of a Ministry or Department. To both groups apply the relevant provisions of the FPCivL and union republic civil codes, the Charter of each individual FTO, and other foreign economic legislation.

The 1978 Statute (which is likely to be changed in the light of restructuring) authorises an FTO to carry on export and import operations in accordance with the five-year and annual State plans and the contracts concluded pursuant thereto within the ambit of goods and services which the FTO may engage in. The FTO participates in those plans, assists branch ministries and departments in increasing exports and improving the competitiveness of goods, studies markets and submits annual situation surveys to the respective ministries and departments.

The FTO Charters are confirmed by the Ministry of Foreign Economic Relations. Each Charter follows a basic pattern, contains the official name and location of the FTO, the object and purposes of the FTO, the amount of stated capital of the FTO, a list of firms and other organisations comprising the FTO, the system of management, property, accounts and profit distribution, and liquidation or reorganisation. Within each FTO is a Board composed of the FTO officers and officials from the Ministry of Foreign Economic Relations, branch ministries, and other agencies which meets at least once quarterly. A major innovation of the 1978 Statute, the introduction of the Board was intended to involve branch ministries, departments and industrial enterprises and associations directly in FTO management with a view to meeting export and import commitments more efficiently. The Boards carry on the commercial activity of the respective FTOs through firms that are a constituent part thereof. The FTOs within the Ministry of Foreign Economic Relations system contain about 300 firms. Each firm deals directly as necessary with Soviet and foreign organisations or citizens but does not enjoy legal personality and acts only in the name of the FTO itself.

The FTO in one sense is a legal artifice intended to enable State trading to be conducted in a world of mixed economies where the private sector still enjoys a predominant role. An FTO is a juridical person under Soviet law. The Soviet State allocates State property for the operative management of the FTO. The FTO may possess, use, and dispose of this property in accordance with its Charter and Soviet legislation, sue and be sued, conduct in the USSR and abroad all kinds of legal transactions and legal acts, build, acquire, alienate, or lease enterprises subsidiary to its activity in the USSR or abroad or any movable or immovable property, and establish its branches, divisions, etc as may be necessary. As an 'economically accountable' association, it keeps accounts on a profit and loss basis and is expected to meet or exceed all performance indicators laid down for it; in this respect an FTO is analogous to most Soviet enterprises (see chapter 13, above). The Soviet State is not liable for FTO obligations, and vice versa. Each FTO is apportioned, so to speak, a component of the State foreign trade monopoly, that is, it specialises in certain goods or serves a particular geographic area or type of activity.

Despite its independent legal existence, an FTO is closely linked to the superior ministry or State committee which created it and confirmed its Charter. The superior ministry or State committee appoints the director-general to office and may dismiss him 'in the established procedure.' The director-general organises the work of the FTO and has full responsibility for its activity, operating on the principle of 'one-man leadership.' The FTO Board elects the deputy chairmen, but the director-general is ex officio the chairman of the Board. The superior ministry or State committee may liquidate, reorganise, merge, or divide FTOs, and this happens from time to time. Portions of an FTO's net profit are paid in to the national treasury as State revenues, just as with other State enterprises. The dual character of an FTO as an instrument for managing the State monopoly of foreign trade and as an independent legal person have given rise to legal difficulties in some countries, for some have sought to pierce the corporate veil by alleging that the latter personality is but a mask for what in reality is a State agency. English courts have accepted to date the view that an FTO is an independent legal entity. The stated capital of an FTO varies but is usually modest in size befitting its function as a trading body rather than an association directly providing goods or services. In principle only certain assets including cash may be levied against in a legal proceeding; a list of property owned by socialist organisations against which execution may not be levied, and the priority for satisfying claims when assets are insufficient, is provided for in Soviet legislation.

The FTO of a branch ministry or department is, unlike the FTOs discussed above, more closely linked with the production of the particular goods or services of its ministry. It operates under the direction of its own ministry but with respect to the State interests of the Soviet Union on the foreign market it is supervised by the MFER. Being fully economically accountable for its operations, the FTO has an independent balance sheet and is a juridical person. Its Charter follows a Model Charter for this type of FTO, is confirmed by its own ministry or department by agreement with the MFER, and is to be published in *Vneshniaia torgovlia*. The enumeration of its powers conforms essentially to the FTOs of the MFER, but it also is given the right to build, acquire, alienate, and rent subsidiary enterprises, as well as movable and immovable property, both in the USSR and abroad. It may take part in joint enterprises and international associations.

Economic contracts for the delivery of export or import products are concluded with Soviet enterprises, associations, and organisations, and, with foreign firms or organisations, export and import contracts. These are negotiated by the FTO itself; it may advertise, arrange exhibitions, send specialists abroad and receive foreign specialists, and perform similar functions.

The FTO is headed by a director-general and his deputies, but there also exists a 'council' of the FTO whose competence is determined by the ministry or department. The profit of the FTO comprises the excess of revenues over expenses connected with effecting foreign economic activities. Depreciation, economic incentive, and foreign trade activity funds are to be formed from the FTO revenues.

E. FOREIGN TRADE FIRMS

Specialised foreign trade firms exist within both types of FTOs and within a scientific-production or a production association, enterprise, or organisation. Irrespective of where they are formed, they are governed by the Model Statute on an Economically-Accountable Foreign Trade Firm of a Scientific-Production or Production Association, Enterprise, or Organisation, confirmed by the USSR Council of Ministers on 22 December 1986. Such firms effect export and import operations with regard to their designated products and services, but they are not juridical persons even though they may have a separate balance sheet. The name of the firm must incorporate in some way the name of the entity to which it belongs.

A foreign trade firm concludes foreign trade legal transactions on behalf of the association or entity to which it belongs, in the name of that entity. Such legal transactions are to be signed in the procedure established by Soviet legislation. In virtually all other respects the foreign trade firm performs functions and duties and exercises powers and competence within its sphere of activity in a manner analogous to the FTOs, except that the firm cannot act in its own name. In individual instances by decision of the ministry or department of which it is a part, a foreign trade firm may be a juridical person, but in that event its activities are governed by the Statute on the FTOs of a ministry or department.

F. ENTERPRISES, COLLECTIVE FARMS, AND OTHER STATE ORGANISATIONS

Although the early practice under restructuring has been to list those ministries, departments, and enterprises having direct access to western and third world markets, all others being expected to trade through other FTOs, these are not being regarded as exceptions. The 1987 Law on the State Enterprise provides that foreign economic activity is an 'important integral part of all the enterprise's work (Article 19)'. Such activity is to be effected, as a rule, on the basis of 'hard currency, non-subsidy and self-financing', and the results are an organic part of enterprise performance indicators, economic incentive funds, and hard currency proceeds. An enterprise is required to give priority to export deliveries and preference to co-operation with socialist countries.

Within COMECON the Soviet enterprise is encouraged to establish direct links, conclude economic contracts, determine the conditions for economic co-operation (including contract prices), agree the types and volume of export and import deliveries, carry on construction design and experimental work, and take part as appropriate in joint enterprises, international associations, and organisations created on the basis of international treaties of the USSR. Enterprise relations with firms of capitalist and developing countries are to take the form of production and scientific-technical co-operation on a long-term and balanced basis or joint enterprises and production entities.

The economically accountable dimension of foreign economic activity is stressed in the Law on the State Enterprise. Co-operation with foreign partners is to be based on economic contracts. Each enterprise should have a hard currency fund formed from export proceeds of all types, including the sale of licences. Bank credits in hard currency may be obtained to found or develop export production entities provided that the credit can be repaid from export earnings. Losses that may be incurred because export planning tasks have not been fulfilled or by reason of other contractual violations are to be borne by the enterprise from its hard currency resources. The enterprise may use its hard currency resources to import items needed for conversion or experimental work. Superior agencies may not remove an enterprise's hard currency fund, and the latter may accumulate from year to year.

The 1988 Model Collective Farm Charter authorises collective farms to take part in the activities of international co-operative organisations, to establish and develop trade, economic, scientific-technical, and cultural links and co-operation with agricultural co-operatives and other enterprises of COMECON member countries and with enterprises and firms of capitalist and developing countries. Just as enterprises, collective farms bear full responsibility for the results of their foreign economic activities.

A major factor in the great expansion of Soviet entities authorised to engage in foreign transactions has been the development of COMECON. Under a decree of 9 July 1981 concerning co-operation between Soviet entities and those of other COMECON countries, all-union industrial associations, chief administrations for deliveries abroad ('Zagranpostavka'), and industrial, scientific, production and agricultural associations, enterprises, and organisations may conclude, with the permission of their superior ministry, production specialisation and co-operation agreements and contracts jointly with the revelant FTOs. The actual delivery contracts of various types are then concluded within the Ministry of Foreign Economic Relations system by the FTOs. Little is known to date of the 'Zagranpostavka' associations; each has its own Statute and is an independent legal person operating on economic accountability with funds transferred by the FTOs.

G. SOCIAL ORGANISATIONS

The USSR Chamber of Commerce and Industry, founded in 1932 and presently operating on the basis of a Charter adopted 12 September 1974, is a social organisation under Soviet law. It has legal personality and its own assets, formed principally from dues and proceeds from its economic activities. Like chambers of commerce elsewhere, the USSR Chamber promotes foreign trade through contacts with business circles abroad, exchanges delegations, and organises exhibitions. On behalf of the persons concerned the Chamber will handle trademark and patent applications respectively in the Soviet Union or abroad. The Chamber will issue certificates of origin for goods exported from the USSR, perform expert examinations for quality of goods at the request of Soviet or foreign organisations, certify the existence of port or commercial customs and conditions of force majeure, and through two arbitration tribunals attached to it, settle disputes referred to them. Foreign trade transactions are entered into by the Chamber principally when organising fairs and exhibitions or acting in the registration of patents and trademarks.

The Chamber membership consists chiefly of State, co-operative, and social organisations and has grown substantially in recent years; more than 3,000 industrial enterprises alone are said to belong. Three all-union associations, Expotsentr, Sovintsentr and Soiuzpatent, are attached to the Chamber and operate on the basis of their own Charters. A Consultation Centre offering economic and legal advice on joint ventures has been set up within the Chamber.

The All-Union Copyright Agency (VAAP) has the exclusive right to grant on behalf of an author or his successor the use outside the Soviet Union of a work by a Soviet author, whether published or not, unless provided otherwise by law. Also a social organisation with its own

Charter, VAAP protects the interests of Soviet authors against infringements of copyright and acts as intermediary in the purchase and sale of foreign rights. In some western countries VAAP has established permanent representations or concluded agency agreements with foreign partners.

H. CO-OPERATIVE ORGANISATIONS

Since the early years of Soviet power the Central Union of Consumers' Societies of the USSR has engaged in export and import operations on behalf of the consumer's co-operatives. 'Soiuzkoopvneshtorg' is the present name of the association performing that function; it is an independent co-operative enterprise with its own balance sheet and assets wholly owned by the Central Union. Under the 1988 Law on Co-operative Societies in the USSR, all co-operatives including collective farms, are encouraged to engage in foreign economic activity.

I. JOINT-STOCK SOCIETIES

Three legal entities engaged in foreign trade are organised as joint-stock societies: the USSR Bank for Foreign Economic Activity, Intourist, and the agency specialising in foreign insurance, Ingosstrakh. Since the legislation governing joint-stock societies has been repealed, their legal status is governed by the FPCivL, union republic civil codes, and their respective charters.

J. FOREIGN CORPORATE ENTITIES

The Soviet Government operates commercial banks, insurance companies, and a variety of concerns and joint ventures incorporated under the laws of the country where they are situate. In England the Moscow Narodny Bank Ltd, founded in 1919 and owned by Gosbank, Vneshekonombank, and certain FTOs, is actively involved in financing East-West trade and other international commercial banking operations. The Russian Wood Agency Ltd has been operating since 1923; in the United States the Amtorg Trading Corporation incorporated in the State of New York in 1924 has handled appreciable portions of Soviet-American trade.

K. JOINT ENTERPRISES AND OTHER PRODUCTION ENTITIES

Although western firms operated 'concession agreements' on Soviet territory during the 1920s and early 1930s, joint equity ventures on a substantial scale were introduced in 1971 within COMECON in pursuance of the 1971 Comprehensive Programme for socialist economic integration. Acting under the Model Rules for the creation of international economic associations within COMECON, the Soviet Union concluded international treaties to establish such entities and nominated

Soviet economic associations to be members. On 26 May 1983 basic legislation defining the procedure for the creation and activities of 'joint economic organisations' on Soviet territory was enacted.

The restructuring of foreign economic relations that commenced in August 1986 has proceeded along two parallel lines: within COMECON and outside COMECON. The Decree of 19 August 1986 on improving economic and scientific-technical co-operation with socialist countries called for a shift in emphasis from principally trade relations to extensive production specialisation and co-operation in the institutional form of joint enterprises, joint organisations, and international associations. The creation of those entities in the USSR is regulated by a Decree of the USSR Council of Ministers adopted 13 January 1987 'On the Procedure for the Creation on the Territory of the USSR and the Activities of Joint Enterprises, International Associations, and Organisations of the USSR and Other COMECON Countries'. Direct links between Soviet production associations and enterprises with their counterparts in other COMECON member countries are governed additionally by a normative document, undated and of undesignated origin, called the 'Procedure for the Effectuation by Associations, Enterprises, and Organisations of the USSR of Direct Production and Scientific-Technical Links With Enterprises and Organisations of Other COMECON Member Countries'.

The restructuring of foreign economic relations and the introduction of joint enterprises and other production entities on Soviet territory is part of a larger economic strategy applicable to COMECON and non-COMECON relations alike. Within COMECON, the production specialisation and co-operation is in furtherance of the Comprehensive Programme for Scientific-Technical Progress Up to the Year 2000.

In the case of direct foreign investment by firms of western and developing countries, the Soviet Union has in its Decree of 13 January 1987 had regard to the policies of Eastern European countries and China. Under legislative acts of 13 January and 17 September 1987, joint enterprises in which Soviet organisations and firms participate with firms of capitalist and developing countries on the territory of the USSR are juridical persons formed on the basis of a contract between the parties. A proposal to form a joint enterprise is, in practice, usually reduced to a Protocol of Intent concluded by the parties without obligation. A thorough feasibility study is undertaken, and after further negotiations a contract is concluded and the draft charter of the joint enterprise prepared.

The charter recites the legal capacity of the joint enterprise to conclude contracts in its own name, acquire personal and non-property rights, bear duties, and be a plaintiff or defendant in a court or arbitration tribunal. The joint enterprise has an independent balance sheet and operates on the economic principles of restructuring: 'full economic accountability, non-subsidy, and self-financing.' The charter further defines the object and purpose of joint economic activities, the location of the enterprise and identity of its participants, the amount of charter capital and respective share of each participant, how the charter fund is to be formed (Soviet currency, foreign currency, contributions in kind), the structure, competence, and composition of those organs that manage the enterprise, the procedure for adopting decisions and the range of issues for which unanimity is required, and the procedure for liquidating the enterprise. Other provisions not contrary to Soviet legislation and relating to the distinctive aspects of joint enterprise activities may be included in the charter.

Once the contract and draft charter are agreed, the Soviet side submits them together with the feasibility study to its superior ministries and departments. The superior agencies in turn will seek the agreement of the USSR State Planning Committee, the USSR Ministry of Finances, and other interested ministries and departments, including the MFER. Once these approvals are secured, the final decision to create the joint enterprise may be taken by a union republic council of ministers or by the relevant USSR ministry or department. Should the decision be favourable, the constitutive documents of the joint enterprise enter into force and the charter must be registered at agencies of the USSR Ministry of Finances, whereupon the joint enterprise acquires the rights of a juridical person.

In addition to cash in rubles or foreign currency, capital contributions may take the form of buildings; installations; equipment; other material valuables; the right to use land, water, or other natural resources, buildings, installations, equipment; or property rights (including inventions and 'know-how'). The parties may agree to value their contributions respectively in either Soviet or foreign currency at contract prices, but with regard to world market prices. Any equipment, materials, and other property imported by foreign partners as capital contributions are exempt from customs duties. All property of a joint enterprise is subject to compulsory insurance by Soviet insurance companies.

As a juridical person under Soviet law, the joint enterprise enjoys the right to possess, use, and dispose of property in accordance with the purposes of its activities and of the property itself. Its property may not be administratively requisitioned or confiscated and may be protected in the same manner as the property of Soviet State organisations; execution may be leved against the property of a joint enterprise only by those agencies empowered under Soviet law to consider disputes in which a joint enterprise participates. However, a joint enterprise is liable for its obligations with all the property which belongs to it, but not for the obligations of the Soviet State or of its participants, and vice versa. Should the joint enterprise create branches on Soviet territory which are juridical persons, then the same principles apply.

Disputes of joint enterprises with other joint enterprises, or with

Soviet State, co-operative, and other social organisations, or with the participants of the joint enterprise may be heard either in Soviet courts or in an arbitration tribunal. The latter formulation excludes the State Arbitrazh but would encompass the permanent foreign trade and maritime arbitration bodies in the Soviet Union or abroad, or ad hoc arbitration under Soviet law, per agreement of the parties.

The highest agency of a joint enterprise is the Board, consisting of persons appointed by the partners in the enterprise. However, the chairman of the Board and the director-general of the joint enterprise must be Soviet citizens, although foreigners may be represented on the directorate formed to direct the current operations of the enterprise.

The joint enterprise is free to work out and confirm its programme of economic activities independently; it is not subject to State planning tasks, nor on the other hand, does it enjoy a guaranteed sale of its products. It may conduct export and import operations independently which are necessary for its economic activities, including operations on the markets of COMECON member countries. If the joint enterprise chooses, those operations may be effected through Soviet FTOs of either type or through the sales network of the foreign participants on the basis of respective contracts. Export and import permits must be obtained if required.

Soviet legislation contemplates that the foreign aspects of joint enterprise activities should be more or less self-financing; that is, expenditures of the joint enterprise in hard currency, including repatriation of profits and any other amounts due to foreign partners, specialists, or personnel, should be covered from hard currency earnings of the joint enterprise on the foreign market. Under certain circumstances, however, sales to the Soviet market may generate foreign currency; a joint enterprise may determine, by agreement with Soviet organisations and enterprises, the type of currency for settlements with respect to products realised and goods purchased.

The joint enterprise is required to make provision from its profits for a reserve fund (that fund not to exceed 25% of charter capital), a social development fund, and any other funds required by enterprise activities. After all expenses, obligations to the State budget, and fund contributions have been met, the profit is to be distributed to each participant in accordance with his share participation. The joint enterprise is subject to a 30% tax on profits remaining after payments to the reserve funds; however, they are exempt from tax on profits during their first two years of operations at a declared profit and the Ministry of Finances has the right to further reduce the tax on profits or wholly exempt the joint enterprise from any tax. In addition, unless provided otherwise by an international treaty, the profit repatriated by a foreign participant will, when transferred abroad, be taxed at the rate of 20%.

Soviet citizens will make up most of the joint enterprise personnel, and Soviet labour legislation extends in full to their wages or salaries, work and leisure regime, social security, and social insurance. There is to be a collective contract between the joint enterprise management and the employees. In the case of foreigners, wages, leave, and pensions are a matter for individual negotiation and contract, but otherwise Soviet legislation applies. The unspent portion of earnings received by a foreign worker may be transferred abroad in foreign currency.

L. SIGNING FOREIGN TRADE TRANSACTIONS

Under the union republic civil codes and a USSR Decree of 14 February 1978 on the procedure for signing foreign trade legal transactions, certain mandatory formalities must be observed for such transactions to be valid: they must be in writing and they must be signed by two duly authorised persons. The names of persons who ex officio have the right to sign foreign trade transactions, bills of exchange, and other monetary obligations are published in the journal issued by the agency within whose system the particular organisation is situate. Foreign trade legal transactions concluded at auctions and exchanges by Soviet organisations follow the rules prevailing at the respective auction or exchange. Obligations signed on behalf of Gosbank, Vneshekonombank or foreign insurance operations follow the procedure laid down in the charters of the respective organisations.

M. FOREIGN TRADE AND MARITIME ARBITRATION

Attached to the USSR Chamber of Commerce and Industry are two arbitration tribunals, the Arbitration Court attached to the Chamber (fomerly the Foreign Trade Arbitration Commission) founded in 1932 and the Maritime Arbitration Commission (MAC) created in 1930. The Arbitration Court presently operates under a Statute of 14 December 1987 and a Reglament confirmed in 1988. The MAC functions under a Statute confirmed 9 October 1980 and Rules of Procedure confirmed 13 January 1982. Both tribunals were established in a period when ordinary Soviet courts lacked experience in adjudicating complex foreign trade disputes involving a knowledge of foreign and international law and were desperately short of trained legal personnel. By the same token, it was desirable to avoid the expense and complications of litigation in western countries, many of whose courts at the time were hostile to the Soviet socio-political and legal order. Arbitration offered the prospect of voluntary, expeditious, expert, and impartial dispute settlement in a forum where due account could be taken of the need to adopt and accommodate Soviet legal concepts and practices to those of the international trading community.

Between 1934–87, the Arbitration Court issued more than 3,600 awards, and from 1930–87 the MAC, more than 3,000 awards. The most important are published from time to time in collections by each tribunal. The Arbitration Court is considering about 300 cases a year at present, nearly 90% of which are between organisations from socialist countries and concern disputes arising out of purchase-sale contracts; MAC currently decides about 100 cases a year. Between 1959-74 The Arbitration Court published 18 awards in which British firms were parties, as plaintiffs in 16 and as defendants in two. The Arbitration Court found in favour of the British firms in eight of the 18 cases. Although western traders and lawyers have held deep reservations about certain aspects of the links between the Arbitration Court, MAC, their parent chamber, and the State, the relationship with the MFER, and the alternative occupations of Soviet arbitrators, both tribunals have acquired an excellent reputation for independence and impartiality and have been increasingly accepted by the international community.

There are minor differences in the procedures of the two tribunals particularly as regards appeal. Arbitration Court awards are final and not subject to appeal, whereas MAC awards may be appealed within a month to the USSR Supreme Court or within the same period the Procurator General of the USSR or his deputies may bring a protest to the same Court.

In 1987 the Arbitration Court considered 220 cases, of which 60 involved a party from a western country and 10 were cases in which both parties were non-Soviet. Forty cases concerned amounts of less than 1,000 rubles. Under its 1987 Statute and 1988 Reglament, the Arbitration Court may resolve disputes between any two foreign firms (not necessarily from different countries) and between joint enterprises and a foreign party or a Soviet FTO. The scale of arbitration fees was increased in January 1987 to reflect amendments to the Uniform Reglament for Arbitration Tribunals attached to Chambers of Commerce of COMECON member countries. About 60% of the cases heard by MAC in 1987 concerned charters of vessels or carriage of goods by sea, and about 20% dealt with marine insurance. Awards are published only with the consent of the parties and may be edited to delete confidential information.

N. FOREIGN FIRMS IN USSR

The expansion of Soviet commercial links in the 1970s led to many western corporations and banks opening their own offices in the Soviet Union. In 1988 the first foreign law firm opened a Moscow office. Many have taken accommodation in the Moscow World Trade Centre, a purpose-built complex containing all types of amenities for conducting business with Soviet clients. However, not any firm may open offices in Moscow. A formal procedure must be gone through as laid down in a

Decree of 23 May 1977 on the procedure for opening and for the activity in the USSR of representations of foreign firms. Special permits for opening a representation are obtainable from a variety of Soviet ministries or State committees provided that the foreign firms are well-known on the world market, have concluded large-scale commercial transactions or have a large goods turnover with the respective Soviet organisation, or carry out industrial co-operation with Soviet enterprises and organisations, or have concluded very important scientific-technical co-operation agreements with the respective Soviet organisations, or seek a permit pursuant to an intergovernmental agreement with the Soviet Union.

Representatives of foreign firms do not enjoy independent legal personality under Soviet law. Permits are issued usually for two years and are subject to renewal if advisable. The permit specifies the purposes for which the representation is opened, any applicable conditions, the expiration date, and the number of employees of the firm who may be foreign citizens. Housing, office premises, telephone, telex, and, if required, Soviet employees as personnel, are supplied by local Soviet agencies through the Administration for Services to the Diplomatic Corps. Relations with Soviet organisations in furtherance of the purposes of the representation are carried out through the ministry or department which issued the permit.

Public policy (ordre publique)

The FPCivL, union republic civil codes, FPMarL, union republic family codes, and MShC all contain public policy clauses. The FPCivL provide: 'A foreign law shall not be applied if the application thereof would be contrary to the basic principles of the Soviet system.' The FPMarL contain a variant formulation. Soviet commentators stress the legislator has in view not a contradiction between a foreign law and the Soviet system, but an application of that law. The classic textbook example is a foreign law permitting polygamous marriage. Even though polygamy is illegal in the USSR, Soviet law would not deny alimony to the members of a polygamous marriage on the grounds of public policy. Nor may the simple socio-economic and political differences between laws of socialist and non-socialist countries serve as the basis for applying public policy. The commentators require exceptionally serious grounds for each particular instance. In practice, there have been few cases where public policy has been invoked under Soviet law.[7] Invoking public policy in the positive sense, Soviet textbooks stress there are certain rules of Soviet law which may not be attenuated by

7 L. A. Lunts *Mezhdunarodnoe chastnoe pravo; obshchaia chast'* (1973) p 327.

reference to foreign law, for example, the signature requirements for foreign trade legal transactions or the currency monopoly. Trade treaties concluded by the USSR with some East European countries have included public policy clauses relative to the execution of arbitration awards.

International treaties

The 1977 USSR Constitution (Art 29) provides that 'Relations of the USSR with other States shall be built on the basis of . . . good faith fulfilment of obligations arising from generally recognised principles and norms of international law and from international treaties concluded by the USSR.' Soviet international legal doctrine has since 1917 given priority to international treaties as the principle source of international law. On 6 July 1978 the USSR enacted a Law on the Procedure for the Conclusion, Execution, and Denunciation of International Treaties of the USSR. This Law does not define a treaty. It merely provides that treaties shall be concluded 'with foreign States, and also with international organisations' and that the 1978 Law shall extend to 'all international treaties of the USSR irrespective of their form and appellation (treaty, agreement, convention, pact, protocol, exchange of letters or notes, or other forms and appellations of international treaties).' The expression 'international treaty' is a new terminological standard introduced by the 1978 Law; all Soviet legislation is being amended to incorporate that term in place of the expression previously employed, 'treaties and agreements.' The Soviet Union ratified the 1969 Vienna Convention on the Law of Treaties in 1986, and most of the provisions in the 1978 Law are modelled upon the Convention.

The 1978 Law distinguished between three categories of international treaties: inter-State, intergovernmental, and interdepartmental. Inter-State treaties seem to embrace those concluded in the name of the highest agencies of State power—the State in the person of the USSR Supreme Soviet or its Presidium. The 1978 Law offers no guidance as to what types or subject matter of international treaties should fall into the inter-State category; rather this is a matter for political decision, tempered perhaps by the jurisdiction of the bodies concerned and the importance—symbolic or substantive—attached to the international treaties.

Intergovernmental international treaties are those concluded in the name of the Government of the USSR, that is, the USSR Council of Ministers, whereas interdepartmental international treaties constitute those contracted by central agencies of State administration of the USSR—ministries, State committees, and other entities attached to the USSR Council of Ministers—or by agencies of administration, such as chief administrations, which are subordinate to ministries, State committees, or departments of the USSR. The number of interdepartmental international treaties is believed to be very substantial, by far the largest category, the majority probably concluded within the COMECON framework in pursuance of socialist economic integration. On 28 August 1980 the USSR Council of Ministers adopted a decree elaborating the procedures for concluding, executing, and denouncing interdepartmental international treaties of the USSR. A variety of State agencies under this decree are responsible for receiving and co-ordinating proposals to conclude such treaties, depending on their subject matter. All such treaties engage the State responsibility of the USSR and must be observed in accordance with the rules of international law. The USSR Ministry of Foreign Affairs exercises general supervision over the execution of all treaties of whatever category.

The 1978 Law gives union republics the right of 'treaty initiative,' that is, the right to propose that international treaties be concluded on a certain matter. The powers of particular legislative and governmental organs to conduct treaty negotiations, sign treaties, and the occasions and procedure for ratification, confirmation of treaties not subject to ratification, and decisions to accede to treaties are given in greater detail than in any prior Soviet legislation.

The publication of international treaties always has been a matter of more than passing concern to the Soviet international lawyer, for the 1917 October Revolution was founded in part upon exposing the perfidious secret diplomacy engaged in by the Imperial Russian Government and publishing the treaty archives, to the considerable discomfiture at the time of those Powers involved. Unlike legislation in many national legal systems, the publication of international treaties is not a precondition under international law for their validity. Neither publication in official gazettes nor registration with, and subsequent publication by, an international organ is essential from the standpoint of international law unless the treaty expressly so stipulates. On the domestic level, the 1978 Law enumerates types of inter-State international treaties which, upon the recommendation of the USSR Ministry of Foreign Affairs, are to be published in the weekly official gazette of the USSR Supreme Soviet, *Vedomosti verkhovnogo soveta SSSR*. Treaties whose authentic texts do not include Russian are now sometimes printed in an official foreign language text. Intergovernmental international treaties are published also upon recommendation of the USSR Ministry of Foreign Affairs in a special separate section of the *Sobranie postanovlenii Pravitel'stva SSSR*. A unified procedure for the publication of interdepartmental international treaties has yet to be publicly disclosed, but some departmental media, such as the monthly journal of the Ministry of Foreign Economic Relations, already publish treaties. The USSR Ministry of Foreign Affairs publishes a serial collection, now in its 43rd volume, of international treaties which have entered into force for the Soviet Union within a designated time period.

The 1978 Law lays down the procedure for denouncing international treaties. Ordinarily, denunciation occurs pursuant to the treaty provisions themselves, but the same international procedures apply in the USSR if a treaty is to be abrogated or terminated by reason of a material breach of the treaty by another party or in other instances provided for by rules of international law, for example, changed circumstances.

Relationship between international treaties and Soviet law

Few questions of law have engendered wider differences of opinion and approach in Soviet legal doctrine than the relationship between international treaties and Soviet legislation. In recent years the subject has engaged not merely international lawyers, but also constitutional lawyers, comparatists, and specialists in the theory of law. Most Soviet jurists accept that the relationship between a national law and an international treaty is not one of subordination, but of co-ordination, by virtue of the fact that each appertains to a different legal system; they have equal legal force, are mutually linked, influence one another, and should not be contrary to one another.[8] Some argue that an international treaty ratified by the USSR passes directly into Soviet law:

> a national law and an international treaty have equal force on the territory of a State, and citizens, juridical persons, and institutions are obliged to execute, and national courts are obliged to apply the international treaty just as a national law on the territory of the State.[9]

In the event of a conflict between national legislation and an international treaty, under this view, the enactment last in time governs. Other Soviet jurists see this view as approximating the United States concept of self-executing treaties. They believe when an international treaty contains rules regulating relations or imposing duties upon citizens, organisations, State agencies, and the like, a further act of transformation is required to implement them, unless the treaty as a whole becomes transformed by its terms into national legislation upon notification. Transformation, in this view, is essential whenever national legislation must be amended or augmented in order to achieve a particular legal result called for by the treaty.[10] Another Soviet jurist has suggested

---

8 V. G. Butkevich *Sovetskoe pravo i mezhdunarodnyi dogovor* (1977) p 66.
9 I. P. Blishchenko *Mezhdunarodnoe i vnutrigosudarstvennoe pravo* (1960) p 230. Also see A. N. Talalaev *Mezhdunarodnye dogovory v sovremennom mire* (1973) p 64, where it is insisted that ratification edicts of the Presidium of the USSR Supreme Soviet are special normative acts imparting municipal legal force to international treaty norms.
10 S. L. Zivs *Istochniki prava* (1981) p 226. Also see D. B Levin *Aktual'nye problemy teorii mezhdunarodnogo prava* (1976) p 252.

that international treaties ratified by the USSR become binding upon State agencies not by virtue of ratification but rather because of Article 21 of the 1978 Law on the procedure for the conclusion of international treaties, which provides that the State agencies enumerated are to ensure the fulfilment of obligations accepted under treaties by the Soviet side. Accordingly, many international treaty obligations automatically become binding internally by reference pursuant to Article 21.[11]

The question also has arisen in connection with other Soviet legislation. The FPCivPL, for example, provide that 'if other rules have been established by an international treaty of the USSR than those which are contained in Soviet legislation on civil procedure, then the rules of the international treaty shall be applied.' Under the Blishchenko approach, this provision according priority to international treaty provisions over inconsistent national legislation would seem to represent a general statement of principle in Soviet law. Similar provisions are to be found in the FPCivL, Customs Code, MShC, FPMarL, FPPubH, FPPubEd, FPML, among others. Other legislative acts omit this provision, however, for example the FPCrimL and the FPAdR, and some Soviet jurists believe this clause represents a reserve guarantee in certain specific types of social relations rather than a universal rule in Soviet law. The ultimate course of the debate has implications for all branches of international law, in the 1980s especially for Soviet obligations under human rights covenants and treaties and under the large numbers of interdepartmental international treaties being negotiated within COMECON.

Territory

The spatial limits of Soviet frontiers are defined in the 1982 Law on the USSR State Boundary, which entered into force on 1 March 1983. The boundary under the 1982 Law is the line which determines the extent of Soviet land and water territory; the perpendicular surface passing along this line is the boundary of air space (upwards) and subsoil (downwards). Unless provided otherwise by international treaties, the land boundary is demarcated along characteristic relief points and lines or clearly visible orientation points; the boundary at sea is the outward limit of territorial waters or the territorial sea of the USSR; on navigable rivers, along the middle of the principal channel or thalweg; and detailed provisions cope with non-navigable rivers, border lakes, hydro-installations, rail and road bridges, and the like. The Soviet Union has a territorial sea of 12 nautical miles calculated from the lowest-ebb tide line on the mainland

---

11 R. A. Miullerson *Konstitutsiia SSSR i voprosy sootnosheniia mezhdunarodnogo i natsional'nogo prava* (1980) p 42.

and around islands or from straight baselines joining appropriate points whose geographic co-ordinates were confirmed by the USSR Council of Ministers in Decrees of 7 February 1984 and 15 January 1985. In individual instances, for example, with Finland, the breadth of territorial waters is determined by an international treaty or, in the absence thereof, in accordance with generally recognised principles and norms of international law. Geographic co-ordinates have been prescribed by the USSR Council of Ministers to clarify the boundaries of time zones in a Decree adopted 24 October 1980 on the procedure for calculating time on the territory of the USSR.

Also part of Soviet territory are internal waters, which under the 1982 Law encompass sea waters situated landward of straight baselines for calculating the territorial sea; port waters; the waters of bays, inlets, coves and estuaries whose entire shore belongs to the USSR up to a straight line drawn from shore to shore in a place where, seaward, one or several passages are first formed, if the breadth of each of these does not exceed 24 nautical miles; the waters of bays, inlets, coves, and estuaries, seas, and straits historically belonging to the USSR; and the waters of rivers, lakes, and other waters whose shores belong to the USSR. Soviet legislation has designated certain specific waters to be historic bays or straits, and Soviet international lawyers sometimes have mentioned others.[12]

Soviet legislation lays down neither an upward boundary for airspace nor a downwards boundary for subsoil. Jurisdictional rights beyond the Soviet territorial sea are provided in Soviet legislation for the continental shelf, installations affixed thereto, economic zone (two hundred nautical miles), and environmental protection measures. The legal status of foreign warships and non-military vessels, including the right of innocent passage, is governed by the 1982 Law on the USSR State Boundary. Violations of State boundary regime can result in administrative or criminal sanctions which, in the instance of illegal fishing, for example, may entail large fines commensurate with those levied by other coastal countries.

Diplomatic and consular law

The specialised central Soviet State agencies concerned with conducting foreign relations are several. The USSR Supreme Soviet has the power to decide all matters relegated by the 1977 USSR Constitution to all-union jurisdiction. Its Presidium may ratify and denounce international treaties, grant asylum, appoint and recall plenipotentiary representatives of the USSR to foreign States and international organisations,

---

12 See W. E. Butler *Northeast Arctic Passage* (1978); id (ed) *The USSR, Eastern Europe, and the Development of the Law of the Sea* (1983–).

accept credentials and letters of recall of accredited foreign diplomatic representatives, or declare a state of war. The Government (USSR Council of Ministers) exercises general direction over relations with foreign States, foreign trade, economic, scientific-technical, and cultural co-operation with foreign countries, ensures the fulfilment of international treaties, and may confirm or denounce intergovernmental international treaties. Ministries, State committees, and departments conduct foreign relations as determined by their respective statutes, and virtually all have some foreign relations function. The principal entities concerned, however, are the USSR Ministry of Foreign Affairs, the USSR Ministry of Foreign Economic Relations, and the State Foreign Economic Commission. Within the powers conferred by their respective constitutions, the 15 union republics also are involved in foreign relations.

The structural framework for the foreign relations functions of some of these entities has not been comprehensively altered since the 1940s and in some key respects since the early 1920s. The relations between Soviet institutions and officials of foreign States are governed by a Decree of 16 December 1947 as amended. As a general rule, the 1947 Decree requires that relations be carried on through the USSR Ministry of Foreign Affairs and, when relevant, by the USSR Ministry of Foreign Economic Relations. Special procedures are laid down for the USSR Ministry of Defence, consular relations, journalists, and others. Everyday matters, including post and telegraph, railway, urban, water, and air transport, customs, police, notarial offices, housing administrations, fire departments, first-aid stations, stores, kiosks, restaurants, museums, exhibits, and information offices are exempted from this requirement.

Of Soviet foreign relations institutions abroad, consular establishments and trade representations have been the object of recent legislation. Diplomatic representations evidently still function on the basis of legislation dating from the 1920s. Ranks for diplomatic representatives were abolished in 1918 by the Soviet Government and restored in 1941 for USSR diplomatic representations and in 1943 for workers in the Ministry of Foreign Affairs, embassies, and missions abroad. The 1923 Statute on the USSR People's Commissariat for Foreign Affairs remains in force but has been altered by departmental legislation.[13] Other regulations affecting Soviet diplomatic personnel are scattered throughout various statutes and codes, including the 1964 Customs Code and passport regulations.

The Soviet consular service is governed by the 1976 Consular Statute of the USSR, other Soviet legislation, and an extensive network of bilateral consular treaties. The USSR has signed but not ratified the

---

13 For English translations of the principal acts, see 'Diplomatic and Consular Law' Soviet Statutes and Decisions II, no. 2–3 (1967) transl. by W. E. Butler.

1963 Vienna Convention on Consular Relations. Soviet consular establishments are subordinate to the USSR Ministry of Foreign Affairs and operate under the general political guidance of the head of the USSR diplomatic mission in the receiving country. Only a Soviet citizen may be a consular officer, but with the consent of a receiving State a foreign citizen may be appointed an honorary consul. With respect to Soviet citizens a consul may protect their rights and interests when infringed, register them for military service, fulfil commissions of USSR investigative or judicial agencies, perform an adoption or take steps to establish a guardianship or trusteeship, protect and transmit property left by a deceased Soviet citizen, assist citizens who may be arrested or detained by local authorities, issue or extend passports and visas, deal with citizenship matters, and register acts of civil status. Under the Law on the State Notariat and the Consular Statute, a consul may certify an extensive number of legal transactions and documents and perform other notarial actions. The consul likewise has functions in regard to Soviet vessels, aircraft, rail transport, and motor transport. In the absence of a trade representation or a commercial counsellor, a consul sometimes may be concerned with commercial matters.

The status of foreign diplomatic and consular representations on USSR territory is governed principally by a Statute confirmed by Edict of the Presidium of the USSR Supreme Soviet on 23 May 1966. The 1966 Statute draws substantially on the 1961 Vienna Convention of Diplomatic Relations, which the USSR ratified in 1964. Premises occupied by a diplomatic representation are inviolable. Access requires the consent of the head of the representation or the person replacing him, and no enforcement actions, including search, seizure, and attachment, may be performed with respect to the premises, the property therein, or transport belonging to the representation. The right of communication is guaranteed, including by post or courier. On the basis of reciprocity a diplomatic representation and staff are exempt from all general State and local taxes and assessments. Customs exemptions are granted on items required for personal use. Diplomatic staff enjoy personal inviolability and may not be subjected to detention or arrest, and immunity from the criminal, civil, and administrative jurisdiction unless the immunity is expressly waived by the accrediting State. Civil immunity does not extend to instances when diplomatic staff enter into civil law transactions as private persons concerning structures belonging to them on Soviet territory, inheritance, or activity beyond their official functions. Diplomatic staff may not be obliged to give testimony as witnesses nor be summoned for judicial or investigatory agencies. Family members of diplomatic staff who are not Soviet citizens and reside together with the said staff enjoy the same privileges and immunities. Administrative and technical personnel enjoy more limited privileges and immunities unless special reciprocal arrangements are made.

Consular premises and the residence of the head of the consular respresentation enjoy inviolability on the basis of reciprocity. The personal immunity of consuls is limited. They may be detained or arrested in connection with a prosecution for a grave crime, for example, and are subject to civil suit for harm caused by road transport accidents. Their immunity against giving testimony appertains solely to matters connected with their official duties. Reciprocal exemptions are granted regarding payment of taxes and customs duties. By special agreement other diplomatic privileges and immunities may be extended to consular personnel.

Representatives of foreign States and members of parliamentary and government delegations which arrive in the Soviet Union to participate in international talks, conferences, or meetings or on other official missions are accorded full diplomatic privileges and immunities. The privileges and immunities granted to international intergovernmental institutions and their foreign representatives and officials are determined by international treaties governing these matters.

Chapter 21

Note on additional reading

This chapter draws the reader's attention to resource materials that develop or provide legislation or documentation for observations made in the main text in addition to items cited in the footnotes. References are confined to those in the English language a reader is likely to find of immediate interest and relevance.

BIBLIOGRAPHY

An extensive not surveying the principal bibliographies treating Russian and Soviet law is found in W. E. Butler (ed) *Russian and Soviet Law: An Annotated Catalogue of Reference Works, Legislation, Court Reports, Serials, and Monographs on Russian and Soviet Law (including International law)* (1976, Zug, IDC) with supplements. The catalogue itself is a considerable bibliography of immediately obtainable material. A bibliography of books in English on the Soviet and East European legal systems since 1945 and a checklist of Soviet normative acts available in English translation are appended to J. N. Hazard, W. E. Butler, and P. B. Maggs *The Soviet Legal System* (3rd edn, 1977, Dobbs Ferry, Oceana Publications); the bibliography is updated in J. N. Hazard, W. E. Butler, and P. B. Maggs *The Soviet Legal System: The Law in the 1980s* (1984, Dobbs Ferry, Oceana Publications) and the checklist of legislation in the *Yearbook on Socialist Legal Systems 1986* (1986, Dobbs Ferry, Transnational Publishers). For an annotated guide, selective, with a sometimes quixotic introduction, see I. I. Kavass *Soviet Law in English: Research Guide and Bibliography 1970-1987* (1988, Buffalo, W. S. Hein). Selected Soviet official publications are annotated by Mrs J. Brine in G. Walker (ed) *Official Publications of the Soviet Union and Eastern Europe 1945-1980* (1982, London, Mansell). Also see P. M. Leideritz *Key to the Study of East European Law* (1973, Deventer, Kluwer).

ENCYCLOPEDIAS

The leading reference is F. J. M. Feldbrugge (ed) *Encyclopedia of Soviet Law* (1973, Leiden, A. W. Sijthoff; 2nd edn, 1985, Dordrecht, Martinus Nijhoff).

403

YEARBOOKS

The *Yearbook on Socialist Legal Systems* (1986–, Dobbs Ferry, Transnational Publishers) is edited at the Centre for the Study of Socialist Legal Systems, University College London, by W. E. Butler. Its contents treat all branches of socialist law, comparative law, legal history, and public international law and commonly contain numerous contributions by jurists from the socialist legal systems.

CASEBOOKS

Structured in the classical American casebook tradition, the standard work is *The Soviet Legal System* ((1962–77, Dobbs Ferry, Oceana Publications). The first edition was written by John N. Hazard and Isaac Shapiro (1962), joined in the second edition by Peter B. Maggs (1969), and in the third edition W. E. Butler replaced Shapiro (1977). The casebook is organised around legal issues and melds commentary, reported cases, extracts from doctrinal writings and legislation, and legal forms, all chosen for pedagogical purposes. The three editions are cumulative, building one upon the other. A 'fourth edition', although not designated as such, was prepared by Hazard, Butler and Maggs under the title *The Soviet Legal System: The Law in the 1980s* (1984, Dobbs Ferry, Oceana Publications). Also see B. A. Konstantinovsky *Soviet Law in Action: The Recollected Cases of a Soviet Lawyer* ed H. J. Berman (1953, Cambridge, Mass., Harvard University Press).

JOURNALS

Dozens of law reviews and journals publish articles from time to time on Soviet law. The leading specialist law review is the *Review of Socialist Law*, published quarterly by Martinus Nijhoff for the Documentation Office for East European Law at the University of Leiden. The leading journal of translations is *Soviet Statutes and Decisions*, published quarterly by Myron B. Sharpe in White Plains, New York. Each volume is devoted to a particular topic or branch of Soviet law.

LEGISLATION

Current all-union, union republic, and departmental legislation is translated and updated as amended in a looseleaf service published by Oceana Publications since 1979, *Collected Legislation of the USSR and Constituent Union Republics* ed. W. E Butler. The set includes all 36 Soviet consitutions. Each enactment is preceded by a brief legislative history. Foreign trade legislation is treated specially in another looseleaf series published by Oceana and edited by Butler, *Commercial, Business and Trade Laws: The Soviet Union and Mongolia* (1982–). For maritime legislation, see Butler (ed)*The USSR, Eastern Europe, and the Development* of the Law of the Sea (1983–, Dobbs Ferry, Oceana Publications), also in looseleaf. Selected enactments appear in *Legislative Acts of the USSR* (1981–, Moscow, Progress Publishers), covering the period from 1977. Six volumes have appeared.

Soviet legislation in effect on the eve of the 1977–78 Soviet Constitutions is translated in Butler *The Soviet Legal System: Contemporary Legislation and Documentation* (1978, Dobbs Ferry, Oceana Publications). For Soviet legislation as of 1 October 1968, see H. J. Berman and J. B. Quigley Jr., *Basic Laws on the Structure of the Soviet State* (1969, Cambridge, Mass., Harvard University Press).

All the RSFSR codes as of 1 August 1980 are translated in W. B. Simons (ed) *The Soviet Codes of Law* (1980, Alphen aan den Rijn, Sijthoff and Noordhoff).

ARBITRATION AWARDS

Selected awards issued by the USSR Foreign Trade Arbitration Commission (now the Arbitration Court attached to the USSR Chamber of Commerce and Industry) and Maritime Arbitration Commission are reproduced with translations of relevant legislation in W. E. Butler *Soviet Commercial and Maritime Arbitration* (1980–, Dobbs Ferry, Oceana Publications), issued in looseleaf.

COURT REPORTS AND STATE ARBITRAZH AWARDS

Soviet court reports are not systematically translated into English. The best selection of cases in translation is to be found in the editions of *The Soviet Legal System* cited under 'Casebooks' above. Court decision and State Arbitrazh awards appear from time to time in *Soviet Statutes and Decisions*. See 'Journals' above.

DICTIONARIES

Only one legal dictionary has been published which is accessible from both English and Russian. Containing about 11,000 terms, it was compiled by W. E. Butler and A. J. Nathanson *Mongolian-English-Russian Dictionary of Legal Terms and Concepts* (1983, The Hague, Martinus Nijhoff). An introductory article discusses the history of legal dictionaries in the Soviet Union. Also see N. P. Prishchepenko *Russian-English Law Dictionary* (1969, New York, Praeger), and for English-Russian, see S. N. Andrianov and A. S. Nikiforov *Anglo-russkii iuridicheskii slovar'* (1964, Moscow, IMO).

Special glossaries have been published: for criminal law, in H. J. Berman and J. W. Spindler *Soviet Criminal Law and Procedure: The RSFSR Codes* (1965, Cambridge, Mass., Harvard University Press); for maritime law, in W. E. Butler and J. B. Quigley Jr. *The Merchant Shipping Code of the USSR (1968)* (1970, Baltimore-London, The Johns

Hopkins Press); for public international law, in G. I. Tunkin *Theory of International Law* transl. W. E. Butler (1974, Cambridge, Mass., Harvard University Press). Early issues of *Soviet Statutes and Decisions* usually contained extensive translation notes.

On the language of Soviet codes, see the relevant chapter by H. J. Berman in the introduction to Berman and Spinder *Soviet Criminal Law and Procedure: The RSFSR Codes* (2nd edn, 1972) and literature cited therein; also Berman 'A Linguistic Approach to the Soviet Codification of Criminal Law and Procedure' in F. J. M. Feldbrugge (ed) *Codification in the Communist World* (1975, Leiden, A. W. Sijthoff). On the Soviet constitutions, see Feldbrugge (ed) *The Constitutions of the USSR and Union Republics* (1979, Alphen aan den Rijn, Sijthoff and Noordhoff).

For pre-revolutionary Russian terms, see S. G. Pushkarev (comp.) *Dictionary of Russian Historical Terms From the Eleventh Century to 1917* (1970, New Haven, Yale University Press).

GENERAL WORKS

The best study to the end of the Khrushchev period is H. J. Berman *Justice in the USSR* (rev edn, 1963, Cambridge, Mass., Harvard University Press). Also useful is E. L. Johnson *An Introduction to the Soviet Legal System* (1969, London, Methuen). A learned critique by a former Leningrad professor is O. S. Ioffe and P. B. Maggs *Soviet Law in Theory and Practice* (1983, Dobbs Ferry, Oceana Publications), enlarged upon in O. S. Ioffe *Soviet Law and Soviet Reality* (1985, Dordrecht, Martinus Nijhoff). The relationship of Soviet Law to other socialist legal systems is explored imaginatively and authoritatively in J. N. Hazard *Communists and Their Law* (1969, Chicago, University of Chicago Press). Also see K. Grzybowski *Soviet Legal Institutions: Doctrines and Social Functions* (1962, Ann Arbor, University of Michigan Press).

COLLECTED ESSAYS

Soviet law specialists have collaborated to produce several collections of essays devoted to particular aspects, developments, or periods of the Soviet legal system. Among the more substantial collections are: D. D. Barry, W. E. Butler, and G. Ginsburgs *Contemporary Soviet Law: Essays in Honor of John N. Hazard* (1974, The Hague: Martinus Nijhoff); a three-volume collection developed at conferences supported by the Ford Foundation and under various editorships published in the Law in Eastern Europe Series by the Documentation Office for East European Law *Soviet Law After Stalin* (1977-79, Leiden, A. W. Sijthoff); Feldbrugge (ed) *Codification in the Communist World* (1975, Leiden, A. W. Sijthoff); Feldbrugge and Simons (eds) *Perspectives on Soviet Law for the 1980s* (1982, The Hague, Martinus Nijhoff);

O. S. Ioffe and M. W. Janis (eds) *Soviet Law and Economy* (1986, Dordrecht, Martinus Nijhoff); F. J. M. Feldbrugge (ed) *The Distinctiveness of Soviet Law* (1987, Dordrecht, Martinus Nijhoff); W. E. Butler, P. B. Maggs and J. B. Quigley (eds) *Law After Revolution* (1988, Dobbs Ferry, Oceana Publications). Also see the special issue of the *Columbia Journal of Transnational Law* XXIII (1985) no. 2.

The collected papers of H. J. Berman, W. E. Butler, and J. N. Hazard, Rudolf Schlesinger, and M. M. Wolff are available on microfiche, published by IDC with full bibliographies. An absorbing memoir has been penned by J. N. Hazard, *Recollections of a Pioneering Sovietologist* (1984, Dobbs Ferry, Oceana Publications; 2nd edn, 1987).

THE PRE-REVOLUTIONARY HERITAGE

In addition to the works cited in chapter 2, above, a useful two-volume collection of Catherinean documents has been translated and introduced by P. Dukes *Russia Under Catherine the Great* (1977–78, Newtonville, Oriental Research Partners). Richard Hellie has produced monumental studies of Russian slavery and serfdom *Enserfment and Military Change in Muscovy* (1971, Chicago, University of Chicago Press) and *Slavery in Russia 1450–1725* (1982, Chicago, University of Chicago Press). N. M. Korkunov's *General Theory of Law* transl. W. G. Hastings (1909, Boston, The Boston Book Co) is an instructive précis of the early twentieth-century Russian approach. *The Lithuanian Statute of 1529* (1976, Leiden, E. J. Brill) by K. van Loewe treats a document widely considered to have been influential in drafting Russian legislation. M. Szeftel has written extensively on medieval Russian law. See his papers in *Russian Institutions and Culture Up to Peter the Great* (1975, London, Variorum Reprints). Studies by historians and political scientists of the Russian bureaucratic tradition have great implications for our understanding of the legal process in its broadest sense. In addition to R. Wortman on the development of a Russian legal consciousness, see G. L. Yaney *The Systematization of Russian Government* (1973, Urbana, University of Illinois Press). An excellent evaluation of nineteenth-century legal philosophy is A. Walicki *Legal Philosophies of Russian Liberalism* (1987, Oxford, Clarendon Press). A fine biography of a preeminent Russian legal statesman is M. Raeff *Michael Speransky* (2nd edn, 1969), The Hague, Martinus Nijhoff). The practitioner's perspective during the 'Golden Age' of Russian law is given in O. O. Gruzenberg's autobiography *Yesterday: Memoirs of a Russian-Jewish Lawyer* (1981, Berkeley, University of California Press).

IDEOLOGICAL FOUNDATIONS OF SOVIET LAW

The works of Karl Marx, Friedrich Engels, V. I. Lenin, J. Stalin, M. S. Gorbachev, and others are widely available in English translations, and there are innumerable critiques and commentaries of every hue and variety. The jurisprudential writings of Soviet jurists are less accessible, but some invaluable anthologies have been prepared. The first, introduced by J. N. Hazard and translated by H. Babb, *Soviet Legal Philosophy* (1951, Cambridge, Harvard University Press) contains selections by Lenin, P. I. Stuchka, M. A. Reisner, E. B. Pashukanis, I. V. Stalin, A. Ia. Vyshinskii, P. Iudin, S. A. Golunskii, M. S. Strogovich, and I. P. Trainin. Pashukanis' *General Theory of Law and Marxism* has appeared in two new translations, the first by Barbara Einhorn and introduced by Chris Arthur, *Law and Marxism: A General Theory* (1978, London, Ink Links), and another by P. B. Maggs containing other selections as well, introduced by Piers Beirne and R. Sharlet with a foreword by J. N. Hazard, *Pashukanis: Selected Writings on Marxism and Law* (1980, London, Academic Press). A broad spectrum of views from 1917–61 is given in translation by M. Jaworskyj *Soviet Political Thought: An Anthology* (1967, Baltimore, The Johns Hopkins Press). For a Soviet critique of western jurisprudence, see V. A. Tumanov *Contemporary Bourgeois Legal Thought: A Marxist Evaluation of the Basic Concepts* (1974, Moscow, Progress Publishers). Three useful Soviet textbooks on legal theory have been translated: L. S. Jawitsch [Iavich] *The General Theory of Law* (1981, Moscow, Progress Publishers); *Theory of State and Law* (1987, Moscow, Progress Publishers); V. Chirkin, Yu. Yudin, O, Zhidkov *Fundamentals of the Socialist Theory of the State and Law* (1987, Moscow, Progress Publishers).

SOURCES OF LAW

Nearly all of the essays in F. J. M. Feldbrugge (ed) *Codification in the Communist World* (1975, Leiden, A. W. Sijthoff) are relevant. All of *Soviet Statutes and Decisions* XII (1975/76) is given over to techniques of law reform. Also see P. P. Gureyev and P. I. Sedugin (eds), *Legislation in the USSR* (1977, Moscow, Progress Publishers).

SOVIET LEGAL EDUCATION

Correspondence and lecture notes from 1934–37 belonging to J. N. Hazard while a student at the Moscow Juridical Institute have been published on microfiche with an introduction by W. E. Butler. Uniquely valuable for their insight into Moscow student life and for recording lectures in a period when legal textbooks were few, the materials were published as *Law Student Life in Moscow: The Letters and Course Notes of John N. Hazard, 1934–1939* (1978, Zug, IDC). For an account of law student life by an exchange postgraduate, see L. Robinson *An American in Leningrad* (1982, New York, W. W. Norton). On Soviet experimentation with Anglo-American instructional methods, see W. E. Butler 'The American Case Method and Soviet Legal Education' *The International Lawyer* XI (1977) 206–209.

LEGAL PROFESSION

Valuable data is to be found in S. Kucherov *The Organs of Soviet Administration of Justice: Their History and Operation* (1970, Leiden, E. J. Brill). For a Soviet perspective, See Y. Zaitsev and A. Poltorak *The Soviet Bar* (1959, Moscow, FLPH).

ADMINISTRATION OF SOCIALIST LEGALITY

On the Soviet judicial system, see V. Terebilov *The Soviet Court* (2nd edn, 1986, Moscow, Progress Publishers). Exceptionally well-written and sometimes poignant glimpses of actual court proceedings are given by G. Feifer *Justice in Moscow* (1964, London, Bodley Head). An admirable distillation of Soviet legal statistics is G. P. van den Berg *The Soviet System of Justice: Figures and Policy* (1985, Dordrecht, Martinus Nijhoff).

The educational or parental role of Soviet law has been explored principally by H. J. Berman in *Justice in the USSR* (rev edn; 1963, Cambridge, Harvard University Press) and the earlier edition of 1950 and numerous articles, all reproduced in the microfiche edition of his *Collected Papers*. Berman also introduced a substantial collection of Soviet articles translated in a special issue of *Soviet Education* XIV, no. 11-12 (1972), published in New York by the International Arts and Sciences Press. The notion of a special Soviet ideal personality and how it is fashioned is treated by G. Smirnov *Soviet Man* (1973, Moscow, Progress Publishers). Also see A. Vengerov and A. Danilevich *Law, Morality and Man: The Soviet Legal System in Action* (1985, Moscow, Progress Publishers).

CONSTITUTIONAL FOUNDATIONS

The Soviet constitutions have produced a massive body of commentary. The texts are available in several translations. A succinct commentary on the four stages of constitutional developments with texts is provided in A. L. Unger *Constitutional Development in the USSR: A Guide to the Soviet Constitutions* (1981, London, Methuen). Seventeen essays by Soviet jurists are collected in P. N. Fedoseev (ed) *The Fundamental Law of the USSR* (1980, Moscow, Progress Publishers). A recent Soviet study is V. Chirkin *Constitutional Law and Political Institutions* (1985, Moscow, Progress Publishers). The Soviet model and its relationship to other socialist constitutions is analysed in O. Bihari *The Constitutional Models of Socialist State Organisation* (1979, Budapest, Akademiai kiado). Stimulating parallels between British and Soviet concepts of parliamentarianism are explored in J. M. Gilison *British and Soviet Politics: Legitimacy and Convergence* (1972, Baltimore, The Johns Hopkins Press) and in W. E. Butler and A. D. H. Oliver (eds) 'Law, Policy and Administration' *Coexistence* XXV (1988) no. 1 (special issue). Also see T. Friedgut *Political Participation in the USSR* (1979,

Princeton, Princeton University Press). The policy role of Soviet parliamentary institutions has begun to attract investigators. Two useful studies are R. W. Siegler *The Standing Commissions of the Supreme Soviet: Effective Co-operation* (1982, New York, Praeger) and P. Vanneman *The Supreme Soviet: Politics and the Legislative Process in the Soviet Political System* (1977, Durham, Duke University Press). For the Stalin era, see A. Ia. Vyshinskii *The Law of the Soviet State* transl. H. Babb (1948, New York, Macmillan). On local government, see C. Ross *Local Government in the Soviet Union* (1987, London, Croom Helm) and E. S. Savas and J. A. Kaiser *Moscow's City Government* (1985, London, Praeger). For Soviet views and documents on civil liberties, see A. Barmenkov *Freedom of Conscience in the USSR* (1983, Moscow, Progress Publishers), and *Rights of Soviet Citizens: Collected Normative Acts* (1987, Moscow, Progress Publishers).

COMMUNIST PARTY AND THE LEGAL SYSTEM

Some discussion of the role of the Party is to be found in G. Antalffy *Basic Problems of State and Society* (1974, Budapest, Akademiai kiado) and A. Kh. Makhnenko *The State Law of the Socialist Countries* (1976, Moscow, Progress Publishers). Also see Ts. Yampolskaya *Socialist Organisations in the Soviet Union* (1975, Moscow, Progress Publishers).

For Party constitutive documents, see W. B. Simono and S. White (eds) *The Party Statutes of the Communist World* (1984, The Hague, Nijhoff). All are analysed in D. A. Loeber (ed) *Ruling Communist Parties and their Status Under Law* (1986, Dordrecht, Nijhoff).

CIVIL LAW

A standard Soviet text is O. I. Sadikov (ed) *Soviet Civil Law* (1986, White Plains, M. Sharpe). For a critical view, see O. S. Ioffe *Soviet Civil Law* (1988, Dordrecht, Nijhoff). A useful survey of the union republic civil codes is given in E. Fleishits and A. Makovskii *The Civil Codes of the Soviet Republics* (1976, Moscow, Progress Publishers). Also see G. Eorsi *Comparative Civil (Private) Law* (1979, Budapest, Akademiai kiado). On ownership, see G. M. Armstrong *The Soviet Law of Property* (1983, The Hague, Nijhoff). Brief commentary on the Soviet law of contract is to be found in R. B. Schlesinger (ed) *Formation of Contracts: A Study of the Common Core of Legal Systems* (1968, Dobbs Ferry, Oceana Publications). Also see V. S. Pozdniakov (ed) *USSR Contract law* (1982, Helsinki, Union of Finnish Lawyers). On copyright law, see M. A. Newcity *Copyright Law in the Soviet Union* (1978, New York, Praeger); S. L. Levitsky *Copyright, Defamation and Privacy in Soviet Civil Law* (1979, Alphen aan den Rijn, Sijthoff & Noordhoff); and M. M. Boguslavskii *The USSR and International Copyright Protection* (1979, Moscow, Progress Publishers).

FAMILY LAW

Also see R. Schlesinger *Changing Attitudes in Soviet Russia: The Family in the USSR* (1949, London, Kegan Paul) for selections and an analysis of Soviet family law doctrine. A useful overview of Soviet family policy is H. K. Geiger *The Family in Soviet Russia* (1968, Cambridge, Mass., Harvard University Press). For an assessment of an experienced practitioner, see Y. I. Luryi *Soviet Family Law* (1980, Buffalo, W. S. Hein).

LABOUR LAW

V. Gsovski *Soviet Civil Law* (1948, Ann Arbor, University of Michigan Law School) contains extensive labour law materials. A standard Soviet text of the early post-Stalin era was translated in India: N. G. Aleksandrov *Soviet Labour Law* (1961, Delhi, University Book House). A recent conspectus is R. Livshitz and V. Nikitinsky *An Outline of Soviet Labour Law* (1977, Moscow, Progress Publishers). On trade unions see E. C. Brown *Soviet Trade Unions and Labor Relations* (1966, Cambridge, Mass., Harvard University Press). The Soviet model is explored in A. Weltner *Fundamental Traits of Socialist Labour Law* (1970, Budapest, Akademiai kiado). Recent developments are treated in W. E. Butler, B. Hepple and A. Neal (eds) *Comparative Labour Law* (1987, London, Gower) and in Butler, Hepple and R. W. Rideout (eds) 'The Right to work under British and Soviet Labour Law' International Journal of Comparative Labour Law and Industrial Relations III (1987), no. 3 (special issue).

ECONOMIC LAW

Soviet economic law up to the 1987 restructuring is treated with authority in O. S. Ioffe and P. B. Maggs *The Soviet Economic System: A Legal Analysis* (1987, Boulder, Westview) and in V. Lapter *Economic Law* (1987, Moscow, Progress). The introduction to and major portions of the draft economic code are translated by W. E. Butler in *Soviet Statutes and Decisions* XII (1976) 433–483. The relationship between law and economic reform is discussed in G. Eorsi and A. Harmathy (eds) *Law and Economic Reform in Socialist Countries* (1971, Budapest, Akademiai kiado) and in L. Ficzere *The Socialist State Enterprise* (1974, Budapest, Akademiai kiado). Standard economic texts on the Soviet economy will provide useful background. Also see O. Kuschpeta *The Banking and Credit System of the USSR* (1978, Leiden, Nijhoff).

COLLECTIVE FARM LAW

Invaluable for an impression of collective farm life in the early days is F. Belov *The History of a Soviet Collective Farm* (1956, London, Kegan Paul). The history of the machine-tractor stations is treated comprehensively in R. F. Miller, *One Hundred Thousand Tractors: The MTS and the Development of Controls in Soviet Agriculture* (1970, Cambridge, Mass., Harvard Univ. Press). For the modern period, see C. Humphrey *Karl Marx Collective: Economy, Society and Religion in a Siberian Collective Farm* (1983, Cambridge, Cambridge University Press). On the communes, see D. Atkinson *The End of the Russian Land Commune, 1905-1930* (1983, Stanford, Calif., Stanford University Press).

NATURAL RESOURCE LAW

Also see N. Syrodoyev *Soviet Land Legislation* (1975, Moscow, Progress Publishers); I. K. Fox (ed) *Water Resources Law and Policy in the Soviet Union* (1971, Madison, University of Wisconsin Press); O. S. Kolbasov *Ecology: Political Institutions and Legislation* (1983, Moscow, Progress); W. E. Butler and M. Grant (eds) 'Anglo-American and Soviet Concepts of Environmental Law' Connecticut Journal of International Law III (1988) no. 2 (special issue). A general comparative introduction to policy issues is D. R. Kelly, K. R. Stunkel, and R. R. Westcott *The Economic Superpowers and the Environment* (1976, San Francisco, W. H. Freeman).

CRIMINAL LAW

The General Part of the criminal law is treated thoroughly in F. J. M. Feldbrugge *Soviet Criminal Law: The General Part* (1964, Leiden, A. W. Sijthoff). A recent account by Soviet jurists is M. C. Bassiouni and V. M. Savitskii (eds) *The Criminal Justice System of the USSR* (1979, Springfield, C. C. Thomas). Also see R. W. Makepeace *Marxist Ideology and Soviet Criminal Law* (1980, London, Croom Helm). An extensive selection of Soviet criminal cases is translated in *Soviet Statutes and Decisions* I, no. 4 (1965).

CRIMINOLOGY AND CORRECTIONAL-LABOUR LAW

A standard Soviet textbook translated by J. B. Quigley Jr., and edited by G. V. Morozov and Ia. M. Kalashnik introduced the basic elements of the approach to mental illness, *Forensic Psychiatry* (1970, White Plains, IASP). An enormous body of memoirs and Samizdat literature has accumulated over the years offering insight into the penal system from the inmate's perspective for both the pre-revolutionary and post-revolutionary periods. A useful analysis of Samizdat materials from a juridical perspective is provided in F. J. M. Feldbrugge *Samizdat and Political Dissent in the Soviet Union* (1975, Leiden, A. W. Sijthoff). Several trial transcripts have appeared. Among those most interesting for the constitutional and substantive issues raised is M. Hayward (ed) *On Trial: The Soviet State versus 'Abram Tertz,' and 'Nikolai Arzhak'* (rev edn, 1967, New York, Harper & Row). Literary portrayals of this dimension of Soviet life have drawn on the colloquial terminology of the penal institutions. See M. Galler and H. E. Marquess (comps.) *Soviet Prison Camp Speech* (1972, Madison, University of Wisconsin). On alcoholism, see V. G. Treml *Alcohol in the USSR: A Statistical Study* (1982, Durham, Duke Press Policy Studies).

CIVIL AND CRIMINAL PROCEDURE

An extensive collection of Soviet writings on the role of defence counsel in criminal proceedings is translated in *Soviet Law and Government* IX (1971) pp 295–391. The law of evidence in criminal cases is discussed in A. Trusov *An Introduction to the Theory of Evidence* (circa 1961, Moscow, FLPH). Criminal procedure, evidence, civil procedure and sentencing policy are treated by Soviet jurists in W. E. Butler (ed) *Justice and Comparative Law* (1987, Dordrecht, Nijhoff). Forensic investigative techniques are treated in R. Belkin and Yu. Korukhov *Fundamentals of Criminalistics* (1987, Moscow, Progress).

FOREIGN RELATIONS LAW

Soviet foreign relations law as such has never been dealt with in a single work. For a general introduction to private international law, see M. M. Boguslavskii *Private International Law: The Soviet Approach* (1988, Dordrecht, Nijhoff); K. Grzybowski *Soviet Private International Law* (1964, Leiden, A. W. Sijthoff). Outdated but still helpful is M. Boguslavskii and A. Rubanov *The Legal Status of Foreigners in the USSR* (1962, Moscow, FLPH). On citizenship, see G. Ginsburgs *Soviet Citizenship Law* (1968, Leiden, Sijthoff) and V. Shevtsov *Citizenship of the USSR* (1969, Moscow, Progress Publishers). Ordre publique is treated in A. Garnefesky *Public Policy in Soviet Private International Law* (1968, Groningen, V. R. B.).

The literature on foreign trade law is extensive, but because of restructuring is mostly of historical interest. A useful bibliography has been edited by J. D. M. Lew, C. A. Rathkopf Jr., and R. Starr *Selected Bibliography on East-West Trade and Investment* (1976, Dobbs Ferry, Oceana Publications). For legislation, see the section above on looseleaf services. The best account of the foreign trade system is J. B. Quigley Jr. *The Soviet Foreign Trade Monopoly* (1974, Columbus, Ohio State University Press). Two collections of essays treating problems of East-West trade with particular reference to Anglo-American law have been edited by R. Starr *Business Transactions With the USSR* (1975, Chicago, ABA) and *East-West Business Transactions* (1974, New York, Praeger). An excellent general work is S. Pisar *Coexistence and Commerce* (1971, London, Allen Lane). Issued with pocket supplements is D. Campbell (ed) *Legal Aspects of Doing Business in Eastern Europe and the Soviet*

Union (1986, Deventer, Kluwer). Government departments and chambers of commerce publish a variety of manuals, handbooks, and hints to assist the lawyer and businessman. An especially helpful guide is D. Winter *Contracts With Eastern Europe* (2nd edn, 1980, London, EETC). The English-language monthly journal *Foreign Trade* published in Moscow contains much of legal interest, as does *The Journal of The British-Soviet Chamber of Commerce*, issued since 1983 in London.

COMECON and its sister institutions have an increasingly predominant role in foreign relations law. The standard reference is W. E. Butler *A Source Book on Socialist International Organizations* (1978, Alphen aan den Rijn, Sijthoff and Noordhoff) and supplements. For introductions to the institutions, see G. Schiavone *The Institutions of Comecon* (1981, London, Macmillan), and R. Szawlowski *The System of the International Organizations of the Communist Countries* (1976, Leiden, A. W. Sijthoff). On foreign trade, see T. W. Hoya *East-West Trade: Comecon Law, American-Soviet Trade* (1984, Dobbs Ferry, Oceana).

For the history of Soviet treaty policy, see J. F. Triska *The Theory, Law and Policy of Soviet Treaties* (1962, Stanford, Stanford University Press). An index to Soviet treaties from 1917–80 has been compiled by G. Ginsburgs and R. Slusser *A Calendar of Soviet Treaties*. The first volume was published by Standford University Press in 1959 and the second and third by Martinus Nijhoff in 1981 and 1988. Diplomatic and consular law is treated in G. I. Tunkin (ed) *International Law* (1986, Moscow, Progress).

Index

Academy of Sciences
  legal—
    education in, 19, 65
    research in, 76
Acts
  issue of, 45, 46, 47, 48
  military commands, of, 50
  social organisations, of, 48–50
  State Arbitrazh, of, 50
Administration of legality
  administrative commissions, 126–130. *See also* ADMINISTRATIVE COMMISSIONS
  arbitration procedure, 141, 142
  citizen initiative, role as to, 132, 133
  comrades' courts. *See* COMRADES' COURTS
  CPSU, role of, 171, 172
  judicial systems, 98–107. *See also* JUDICIAL SYSTEM
  meaning of, 96
  ministries of justice—
    functions of, 96, 97
    history of, 96
  Notariat. *See* NOTARIAT
  people's control commissions—
    functions of, 131, 132
    history of, 130, 131
  people's guards. *See* PEOPLE'S GUARDS
  police agencies. *See under* POLICE
  Procuracy. *See* PROCURACY
  Registry for Acts of Civil Status (ZAGS). *See* ZAGS
  social centres for the protection of order, 141
  State Arbitrazh, 121–126. *See also* STATE ARBITRAZH
Administrative commissions
  alcoholics, duties as to, 129, 130
  composition of, 127
  functions of, 126–130
  minors, duties as to, 128, 129
  procedure at, 127

Adoption
  legislation as to, 217, 220
Advocates
  all-union organisation for, 90
  college of—
    definition of, 83
    general meeting, 84
    legal consultation offices, role as to, 85
    membership of, 84
    presidium of, 85
  current legislation, 83
  disciplinary sanctions, 88
  fees, 85, 86
  foreign citizens, role as to, 89, 90
  history of, 80–82
  legal—
    consultation offices, 85
    ethics of, 87, 88
  national economic planning, at time of, 81, 82
  numbers of, 83
  scope of activity of, 89
  supervision of, 87
Agriculture. *See also* COLLECTIVE FARMS
  tax, 294
Alcoholism
  alcoholic—
    compulsory treatment of, 310, 311
    definition of, 310
  Commissions for the Struggle Against Drunkenness, 129, 130
  division of spouses' property, effect on, 210
  divorce, ground for, 212
  parental rights, effect on, 216
Alimony
  foreign citizens, obligations of, as to, 219, 220
  payment of, 211, 213, 216, 217
Animal world. *See also* NATURAL RESOURCE LAW
  legal regulation of, 277–279

416 Index

Anti-Soviet agitation and propaganda
  punishment for, 311, 312, 318
Appeals
  adoption of—
    Communist Party organs, by, 49
    supreme soviets by 43, 44
  arbitrazh decisions, against, 126
  citizen initiative, 132, 133
  civil proceedings, following, 348
  comrades' courts, from, 138
  criminal proceedings, following, 362–364
Arbitration
  Arbitration Court, 141, 142, 392, 393
  Maritime Arbitration Commission, 141, 142, 392, 393
  procedure, 141, 142
Arbitrazh. *See* STATE ARBITRAZH
Armed forces. *See* MILITARY LAW
Arms, State
  provision for, 162
Arrest
  meaning of, 321, 353, 354
  sanction of procurator for, 113
Artisans
  personal ownership by, 187
Asylum
  foreign citizens, for, 368
Atmosphere. *See also* NATURAL RESOURCE LAW
  legal regulation of, 277–279

Banishment
  punishment of, 306, 331
Begging
  crime of, 316
Brigades
  functions of, 231, 232
Buildings tax
  liability for, 295

Canon law. *See* ECCLESIASTICAL LAW
Capital punishment
  penalty of, 300, 306, 318
Catherine II
  reforms of, 20, 107
Chamber of Commerce
  foreign trade and, 142, 387
Children. *See* FAMILY LAW; MINORS
Citizens
  acquisition and loss of citizenship, 150, 151
  criminal resposibility of, 299, 300
  equality of, 151
  foreign. *See* FOREIGN CITIZENS

Citizens—*cont.*
  initiative, administration of legality, in, 132, 133
  rights, freedoms and duties of, 151–153
Civil law. *See also* PROCEDURE
  civil codes—
    general principles of, 178–180
    organisation of, 177, 178
  collective farms, as to—
    households, 270, 271
    ownership, 266, 267
    See also COLLECTIVE FARMS
  contemporary—
    general principles, 178–180
    obligations, law of—
      contract, 188–191. *See also* CONTRACT
      duty to rescue, 195–197
      generally, 188
      tort, 191–195. *See also* TORT, LAW OF
  organisation of civil codes, 177, 178
  ownership, law of. *See* OWNERSHIP
  copyright, as to, 197, 198, 373, 374
  discoveries, as to, 198, 199, 374
  economic law and, 242–244, 254, 255
  foreign citizens, rights of, 177, 371, 372
  generally, 175
  historical background, 175–177
  inheritance, 199–202. *See also* INHERITANCE; WILLS
  inventions, as to, 197, 198, 199, 374
  legal transactions, 179, 180
  patents, as to, 197, 199
  'persons' under Soviet Law, 178, 179
  wills. *See* WILLS
Civil procedure. *See* PROCEDURE
Collective contracts
  form of, 226, 227
Collective farms
  agricultural tax, 294
  All-Union Congress of Collective Farmers, 49
  contracts—
    procurement, 268
    sale, of, as to surplus produce, 190
  credit facilities for, 191, 267
  disputes procedure, 267
  foreign economic activities of, 386
  General Meeting of, 265, 266, 267
  households, 270–272, 294
  income tax on, 290
  inter-collective farm enterprises and associations, 272, 273

Collective farms—*cont.*
law as to—
generally, 261
historical background, 261–263
management of, 265, 266
membership of, 263, 264
Model Charter of 1988 . . . 49, 263, 266, 267, 268, 269, 270
modern system, 263, 264
ownership of, 266, 267, 270, 271
personal plots, 271, 272
plans, 268
procurement by the State, 267, 268
property rights of, 169, 181, 266, 267
remuneration for labour, 267
revenue, distribution of, 268, 269
social security for, 236, 269
State and Party guidance of, 264–273
trade unions at, 269

COMECON
Comprehensive Programme for Scientific-Technical Progress, 380
countries, foreign citizens from, 375
development of, 387
enterprises, Soviet economic relations with, 379, 386, 387, 388, 389, 391

Commissions
administrative, 126–130. *See also* ADMINISTRATIVE COMMISSIONS
people's control—
functions of, 131, 132
history of, 130, 131

Communist Information Bureau (Cominform)
role of, 173

Communist International (Comtern)
role of, 173

Communist Party of the Soviet Union (CPSU)
All-Union Leninist Communist Youth League (Komsomol), 167
All-Union Party Conference, 167
armed forces, Party organisations in, 167
Central Audit Commission of, 167
Central Committee of, 166, 167, 171, 172
Congress, 166
XXVII Party Congress, importance of, 39
constitutions, role under, 147, 167–169
Control Committee, 167
elections, introduction of, 40
enactments of, as source of law, 49
generally, 163

Communist Party of the Soviet Union (CPSU)—*cont.*
guidance of—
legal system, as to, 171–173
legislation, as to, 171
legal—
education of Party personnel, 173
status of—
international, 173, 174
within USSR, 167–169
Lenin's concept of role of, 163, 170
membership—
candidate members, 164
legal importance of, 169–171
numbers, 164
requirements, 164
structure, 164
Party—
committees, 165, 166, 172
Programme and Rules, 164, 165
Politburo, 166, 167
primary Party organisations, 164, 165
revision of 1961 Party Programme and Party Rules, 39

Comparative law
bilateral symposia, 8
study of, in Soviet Union, 3, 8, 9

Compensation
employee, by, for damage caused to enterprise, 236–239
harm, for, under law of tort, 193–195
rescuing life or property, in connection with, 195–197

Comrades' courts
appeals from, 138
direction of, 138, 139
history of, 136, 137
introduction of, 36, 137
jurisdiction of, 137, 138, 338, 339

Confessions
criminal proceedings, in relation to, 362

Conservation. *See* NATURAL RESOURCE LAW

Constitutional foundations of Soviet legal order
amendment of constitutions, 162
arms, State, provision for, 162
citizens—
citizenship and equality, 150, 151
rights, freedoms and duties of, 151–153
Communist Party role, as to, 147, 168
defence, national, 149
development, continuity of, 145, 146

Constitutional foundations of Soviet legal order—*cont.*
economic system, 147, 148
electoral system, 154
flag, State, provision for, 162
foreign policy, 148, 149
generally, 143, 144
judicial review, 161
legislative and executive agencies—
  councils of ministers, 45, 158, 159
  local agencies of state power and administration, 159, 160
  supreme soviets, 155-158. *See also* SUPREME SOVIETS
See also ADVOCATES; JUDICIAL SYSTEM; PROCURACY; STATE ARBITRAZH
national and State structure, 153, 154
national anthem, provision for, 162
personal ownership under, 148, 182-187. *See also* OWNERSHIP
political system, 146, 147
social development and culture, 148
State, the, and the individual, 149, 150

Consular law. *See also* FOREIGN RELATIONS LAW
provisions as to, 399-402

Consumer goods
co-operatives for production of, 239-241, 273

Contract
collective, 226, 227
economic—
  form of, 249, 250
  role of, 248-250
labour. *See also* LABOUR CONTRACTS
law of—
  features of, 188, 189
  non-performance of obligation, as to, 189
  Pashukanis' theory as to, 33
  Plan, governed by, 189
procurement, with collective farms, 267, 268
sale, of, 118, 190, 191
writing, to be in, 188

Control Commissions. *See* PEOPLE'S CONTROL COMMISSIONS

Co-operatives
Central Union of Consumers' Co-operatives, 49, 388
collective farms. *See* COLLECTIVE FARMS
definition of, 240
foreign trade and, 388
generally, 273
individual labour activity—
  encouragement of, 239, 273

Co-operatives—*cont.*
individual labour activity—*cont.*
  income tax, 241, 291
  legislation relating to, 239, 241
  numbers engaged in, 240
  organisation of, 239, 240
1988 Law on Co-operative Societies in the USSR, 240, 241, 238

Copyright
All-Union Copyright Agency (VAAP), 387, 388
civil law as to, 197, 198
foreign citizens, law as to, 373, 374
income tax liability, 292, 293
inheritance of rights as to, 198, 374

Correctional-labour law. *See also* CRIMINAL LAW; CRIMINOLOGY
application of, 332, 333
basic principles of, 328
colonies, 306, 329, 330. *See also* institutions, *below*
conditional sentences, 331
correctional tasks, 306, 307, 311, 312
criminal punishment not connected with, 333
current legislation as to, 327, 328
educational-labour colonies, 329. *See also* institutions, *below*
exile and banishment, 306, 331
general provisions as to, 328, 329
historical background, 326, 327
institutions—
  clothing worn in, 330
  education in, 331
  general provisions, 328, 329
  regime of, 329-331
  types of, 329
  work in, 330
prisons, 306, 329. *See also* institutions, *above*
purpose of, 323, 325, 326
release procedure, 332

Correctional tasks
punishment, as, 306, 307, 311, 312

Costs
civil cases, for, 343, 344

Councils of ministers
functions of, 45, 158, 159
membership of, 158, 159

Counsel
civil cases, for, 342, 343
defence, Party membership of, 172

Courts
compensation for harm caused by, 193, 194
comrades'. *See* COMRADES' COURTS
cost, civil cases, for, 343, 344

Index 419

Courts—*cont.*
development of, 36, 37
divorce procedure in, 211–213
labour disputes, 232–234
people's, 102, 138, 232–234, 237
post-revolutionary development of, 36, 37
pre-revolutionary restructuring of, 22, 23
Procuracy supervision in, 113, 114
sources of Soviet law, as—
  doctrine, 53, 54
  judgments, 51–53
structure of, 102–104
Supreme, 99, 104–106
tort, law of, as to, 193, 194
CPSU. *See* COMMUNIST PARTY OF THE SOVIET UNION
Credit facilities
collective farms for, 191, 267
sale of goods, for, 191
Criminal law. *See also* CORRECTIONAL-LABOUR LAW; CRIMINOLOGY
Anglo-American—
  compared with Soviet, 311
  examples of differences, 311–317
anti-Soviet agitation and propaganda, 311, 312, 318
crime, definition of, 300, 301
criminal codes—
  other union republic, differences of, 317, 318
  Theoretical Model of a Code of Criminal Procedure, 365
  Theoretical Model of a Criminal Code, 318–322
criminal responsibility—
  attenuation of, 303
  foreign citizens, of, 299, 300
  minimum age of, 303
danger, leaving in, liability for, 312, 313
deprivation of freedom, 320–322
educational measures, compulsory, 311
exculpatory circumstances, 303–305
extreme necessity, circumstance of, 305
foreign citizens, as to, 369, 378
General Part, 298–311
historical background, 297, 298
intent, 301–303
lawful professional risk, 319, 320
local customs, survivals of, under, 317, 318
medical measures, compulsory, 308–311
necessary defence, 303–305
negligence, 301–303

Criminal law—*cont.*
operation of criminal code in time and space, 299, 300
parasitic way of life, 314–317
punishment—
  anti-Soviet agitation and propaganda, for, 311, 312, 318
  assignment of, 307, 308
  banishment, by, 306, 331
  capital, 300, 306, 318
  deprivation of freedom, by, 306, 307. *See also* CORRECTIONAL-LABOUR LAW
  exile, by, 306, 331
  fine, by, 306
  kinds of, 305–307
  leaving in danger, for, 312, 313
  minors, of, 306, 307, 311
  not connected with correctional-labour, 333
  prison or correctional—labour colony, in, 306, 329
  reasons for, 305
  speculation, for, 313, 314
purpose of, 299
Special Part, 299, 311–317
speculation, crime of, 313, 314
vagrancy, begging, 316
Criminology. *See also* CORRECTIONAL-LABOUR LAW; CRIMINAL LAW
meaning of, 323
study of, 323–325
Curatorship
law as to, 217, 218
Currency
operations, 376, 377
valuables—
  definition of, 376
  foreign citizens and, law as to, 376, 377
Customary law
collective farm households, 270
crimes constituting survivals of local customs, 317, 318
pre-revolutionary tolerance of, 24, 25
Soviet attitudes to, 54, 55
Customs
duties, levy of, 296
rules, foreigners subject to, 369, 370

Dacha
contract of sale for, 190
division of property in relation to, 210
ownership of, 185
Damages. *See* COMPENSATION; TORT, LAW OF

Danger
  leaving in, criminal offence of, 312, 313
Death. *See also* INHERITANCE; WILLS
  penalty, 300, 306, 318
  property of spouses in cases of, 210, 211
Debts
  contract, notaries' functions as to, 118
Defence
  counsel, Party membership of, 172
  national, 149
  necessary, under criminal law, 303, 304
Deportation
  foreign citizens, of, 371
Deprivation of freedom
  sentence of, 320–322
Detention
  meaning of, 354
Diplomatic law. *See also* FOREIGN RELATIONS LAW
  provisions as to, 399–402
Discovery
  civil law as to, 198, 199
  definition of, 198
  foreign citizens, law as to, 374
  inheritance of rights as to, 199
Divorce. *See also* FAMILY LAW
  alimony, 211, 213, 216
  children, care of, 213
  court procedure, 212
  foreigners, legislation as to, 219
  grounds for, 212
  post-revolutionary background, 204, 205
  pre-revolution, 203
  property of spouses, 209–211
  registration of, 212, 213, 214
  Second World War, following, 206, 212, 213
  stateless persons, legislation as to, 219
  support in case of, right to, 211
  ZAGS agencies, through, 206, 211, 212
Documents
  notarial certification of, 117, 118
Drugs
  abuse of, effect on parental rights, 216
  addict—
    compulsory treatment of, 310, 311
    definition of, 310
    purchase and resale of, 313
Dwelling house
  contract of sale for, 190, 191
  division of property in relation to, 210
  duty to maintain, 186, 187
  inheritance of, 199, 202
  ownership of, 184, 185
  purchaser to support seller for life, where, 119, 191

Ecclesiastical law
  Kievan Rus, of, 12
  marriage and divorce, as to, 203
  modern law, in, 10
  Russian Empire, during, 18
Ecological law. *See also* NATURAL RESOURCE LAW
  generally, 275, 276
Economic law
  agencies of economic direction, 252, 253
  civil law and, 242–244, 254, 255
  competition, 256
  concept of, 252–254
  draft economic code, 243, 244, 254
  economic—
    contracts—
      form of, 249, 250
      role of, 248, 250
    legislation, restructuring. *See* restructuring economic legislation, *below*
    management—
      from NEP to 1965 . . . 244, 245
      from 1965 to 1987 . . . 245–252
    obligations, 254
    system, nature of, 147, 148
  foreign economic relations, 378–394. *See also* FOREIGN TRADE
  generally, 242
  planning—
    indicators, 246, 247
    introduction of, 33, 34, 242, 243
    legal aspects of, 5, 6
    natural resources and, 276, 277
    principles of, 253, 254
    restructuring economic legislation in, 258
    1965 reform, following, 245, 247, 248
  prices and finance, 258–260
  production—
    associations, 250–252
    entities, 245–247
  reforms since 1965, generally, 245
  restructuring economic legislation—
    concept of State enterprise, 255, 256
    documents of reform, 255
    environmental policy and, 281–283
    planning, 258
    prices and finance, 258–260
    procedure, law of, and, 364, 365
    protection of enterprise autonomy, 256, 257
    taxation in relation to, 284–286. *See also* TAXATION
    wages, 260
  sanctions, 254

Index 421

Education
compulsory, for minor offenders, 311
correctional-labour institutions in, 331
educational-labour colonies for minors, 329
foreign citizens, of, 378
legal. *See* LEGAL EDUCATION; LEGAL RESEARCH

Electoral system
experiment of 1987 . . . 40, 154
workings of, 154

Engels
writings of, 30, 31

Environmental law. *See also* NATURAL RESOURCE LAW
generally, 275, 276
restructuring and environmental policy, 281-283

Equality
women and men, of, 207, 208

Evidence
civil cases, in, 348

Exile
punishment by, 306, 331

Family law
adoption, 217, 220
basic principles of, 207, 208
birth, registration of, 215
children. *See* MINORS
Commissions for Cases of Minors, functions of, 128
curatorship, 217, 218
customs, 55
divorce. *See* DIVORCE
equality of women and men, 207, 208
foreigners, as to, 218-220
generally, 203
guardianship, 217, 218
historical background, 203-207
illegitimacy—
historical attitudes to, 204
parental duties in cases of, 214, 215
marriage. *See* MARRIAGE
minors. *See* MINORS
parents—
children's support of, 216
parental rights, 215, 216
support, duties as to, 214, 215, 216
paternity proceedings, 215
property of spouses, 209-211
separation, right to support in case of, 211
spouses—
property of, 209-211
support, duty to, 211

Family law—*cont.*
stateless persons, as to, 218-220
support—
parents' duties as to, 214, 215, 216
spouse, duty of, as to, 211
tax on small families, 294

Farms. *See* COLLECTIVE FARMS

Fees
advocates', 85, 86
agreement for, 85, 86
not charged, where, 85
notaries, charged by, 117
Registry for Acts of Civil Status, charged by, 120
scale of, 86

Fines
civil procedural action, for failure as to, 344
contractual obligations, for non-performance of, 189
criminal offences, for, 306
currency violations, for, 377
foreign citizens, imposed on, 370
natural resource regulations, for breaches of, 280

Flag, State
provision for, 162

Foreign citizens
administrative responsibility of, 370, 371
adoption, rights as to, 220
alimony obligations of, 219
asylum for, 368
citizenship of, 367, 368
civil law and procedural rights of, 177, 348, 349, 371, 372
copyright, law as to, 373, 374
criminal—
law and procedure as to, 369, 378
responsibility of, 299, 300
customs rules, as to, 370
damages of, under Soviet law of tort, 194, 195
deportation of, 371
discoveries, law as to, 374
divorce procedure for, 219
education of, 378
entry and exit by, 369
family law as to, 218-220
financial activity of, 376, 377
fines imposed on, 370
income tax, liability for, 377
inventions, law as to, 374
labour activity of, 374, 375
legal—
consultation offices for, 89, 90

Foreign citizens—*cont.*
  legal—*cont.*
    status of, 366–378
  marriage of, 218
  notarial offices, application to, of, 120
  passport requirements as to, 369
  patents, law as to, 374
  personal property rights of, 182
  police registration by, 370
  rights and freedoms of, generally, 378
  royalties, subject to income tax on, 373
  sanctions against, 370, 371
  social organisations, joining, 378
  Soviet law, position under, 151
  succession, law as to, 372 , 373
  taxation of—
    income tax, liability for, 291, 293, 373, 377
    local taxes, liability for, 377
    motor vehicle tax, liability for, 377
    recovery of unpaid taxes, 296
    State duty, liability for, 377
  trade unions, joining, 378
  visas for, 369

Foreign relations law. *See also* FOREIGN CITIZENS; FOREIGN TRADE
  All-Union Copyright Agency (VAAP), 387, 388
  CPSU, international legal status of, 173, 174
  diplomatic and consular law, 399–402
  economic. *See* FOREIGN TRADE
  generally, 366
  international—
    legal arrangements, 7
    treaties—
      CPSU, role of, as to, 174
      meaning of, 56
      ministries of justice, role of, as to, 97
      provisions as to, 56, 57, 395–397
      publication of, 396, 397
      Soviet law and, relationship between, 397, 398
  policy—
    basic aims of, 148, 149
    public, 394, 395
  territory, as to, 398, 399

Foreign trade
  administration of, 379, 380, 381
  Arbitration Court, 141, 142, 392, 393
  Chamber of Commerce and, 387
  collective farms and, 386
  co-operative organisations and, 388

Foreign trade—*cont.*
  direction and guidance of foreign economic activities, 379, 380
  enterprises and, 386, 387
  firms, 385
  foreign—
    corporate entities and, 388
    firms in the USSR, 393, 394
  investment, direct, 389
  generally, 378, 379
  joint enterprises—
    effect of, 89, 90, 187, 389
    other socialist countries, with, 187, 388, 389
    western and third world countries, with—
      activities of, 391
      Board of, 391
      Charter, 389, 390
      disputes, 390, 391
      finances, 391
      introduction of, 6, 187, 389
      legal advice to, 90
      personnel, 391, 392
      procedure for formation of, 389, 390
      rights under Soviet law, 390
  joint-stock societies engaged in, 388
  maritime arbitration and, 392, 393
  Ministry of Foreign Economic Relations (MFER), role of, 380, 381
  organisations (FTOs), 379, 381, 382, 383–385, 387, 388, 391
  representation, 382
  social organisations and, 387, 388
  State Foreign Economic Commission of the USSR Council of Ministers (SFEC), 379, 380
  transactions, signing, 392
Forests. *See also* NATURAL RESOURCE LAW
  legal regulation of, 277–279
Forfeits
  contractual obligations, for non-performance of, 189
Freedom
  deprivation of, 320–322

Goods
  sale of. *See* SALE
Goskompriroda SSSR
  functions of, 282, 283
Guardianship
  law as to, 217, 218

Heirs. *See* INHERITANCE

Index   423

History of Soviet law. *See also* PRE-REVOLUTIONARY LEGAL HERITAGE
advocates, of, 80–82
civil—
   law, of, 175–177
   procedure, of, 334–337
collective farms, of, 261–263
comrades' courts, of, 136, 137
constitutional development, of, 145
correctional-labour law, of, 326, 327
courts, development of, 36, 37
criminal—
   law, of, 297, 298
   procedure, of, 350, 351
economic management from NEP to 1965 . . . 244, 245
family law, of, 203–207
inheritance, law of, 199, 200
international legal status, of, 173, 174
judicial system, of, 98–100
juriconsults, of, 90–92
KGB, of, 134
labour law, of, 221–223
legal—
   education, of, 64–68
   system—
      dismantling of, in 1930s, 34
      restoration of, 34–40
Marxist-Leninist theory of State and law, 27–30
ministries of justice, of, 96
national economic planning, introduction of, 32, 33, 34, 242–244
natural resource law, of, 274, 275
new economic policy (NEP), introduction of 81, 99, 176
Notariat, 116
ownership, of, 37–39, 175–177
Pashukanis, influence of, 32, 33, 34, 35, 66, 67, 68, 243
people's—
   control commissions, of, 130, 131
   guards, of, 139
post-revolutionary period, 30–32
post-Stalin era, 35
Procuracy, of, 18, 107–109
Registry for Acts of Civil Status (ZAGS), of, 120
State Arbitrazh, of, 121, 122
Vyshinskii, influence of, 35, 36, 67
1920s, in, 32
House. *See* DWELLING HOUSE
Human rights
standards of, 150

Illegitimacy
historical attitudes to, 204
parental duties in cases of, 214, 215
paternity proceedings, 215
Income. *See also* PAY
non-labour, 186, 316, 317
personal ownership and, 186
tax. *See* TAXATION
Industry. *See* ECONOMIC LAW; LABOUR LAW
Inheritance
copyright, of rights as to, 198, 374
discovery, rights as to, 199
dwelling house, of, 199, 202
foreign citizens, law as to, 373
heirs—
   absence of will, in cases of, 201
   compulsory share for certain, 200
   procedure for acquisition of estate, 201, 202
history of, 199, 200
intestacy, in event of, 201
invention, rights as to, 199, 374
minors, by, 200
opening of an, 200, 201
rationalisation proposal, rights as to, 199
restrictions on—
   post-revolutionary, 199, 200
   removal of, 200
wills, 200, 201, 202. *See also* WILLS
Inquiry, agencies of. *See* INVESTIGATIVE AGENCIES
Institutions
corrctional-labour. *See* CORRECTIONAL-LABOUR LAW
International law. *See* FOREIGN RELATIONS LAW
Inventions
civil law as to, 197, 198, 199
foreign citizens, law as to, 374
inheritance of rights as to, 199, 374
Investigative agencies
compensation for harm caused by officials of, 193, 194
criminal proceedings, for, 353
Party control of, 172
Investigators
criminal proceedings, role in, 354–356

Joint enterprises. *See* FOREIGN TRADE
Judges
election of, 101
Party membership of, 172
recall of, 102

Judges—*cont.*
role of—
civil case trials, in, 346, 347
generally, 100, 101
Judicial system
court structure, 102–104
current legislation, 100
history of, 98–100
judges. *See* JUDGES
military tribunals, 99, 106, 107
people's assessors, 101, 102, 172
recall of judges and people's assessors, 102
supreme courts, 99, 104–106
Juriconsults
current legislation as to, 92
employees, as, 93
functions of, 93, 94
future role of, 95
generally, 90
history of, 90–92
methods assistance to, 94, 95
Juridical persons
Soviet law, under, 178, 179, 255, 377

KGB (Committee of State Security)
role of, 133–135
Kievan Rus
devastation of, 13
law of, 10–12
Komsomal (All-Union Leninist Communist Youth League)
operation of, 167

Labour contracts
dissolution of—
management, by, 229, 230
workers, by, 229
form of, 227, 228
labour book, submission of, 230
Labour law
brigades, 231, 232
codes as to, 230
contracts—
collective, 226, 227
labour. *See* LABOUR CONTRACTS
co-operatives and individual labour activity, 239–241, 273
damage caused to enterprise—
employee compensation for, 236–239
legislation as to, 236
discipline, 222, 232
disputes, 232–234
foreign citizens, as to, 374, 375
generally, 221

Labour law—*cont.*
historical background, 221–223
labour book, submission of, 230
regulation of labour, generally, 223, 224
State social insurance, 236
trade unions, 230, 231, 232, 234, 235.
See also TRADE UNIONS
wages, 223, 226
Land. *See also* NATURAL RESOURCE LAW
legal regulation of, 277–279
tax, 295
Law reform
restoration of legal institutions, 34–40
revisions of XXVII Party Congress, following, 39, 40
techniques of, 61–63
Lawful professional risk
criminal responsibility in relation to, 319, 320
Legal education. *See also* LEGAL RESEARCH
Academy of Sciences, in, 19, 65
expansion of, 75, 76
generally, 64
historical background, 64–68
junior lawyer's schools, 75
modern—
admission, 69
assessment, 70, 71
career placement, 71
course of study, 69, 70
generally, 68, 69
post-graduate studies, 71–74
teaching, 70, 71
Party personnel, of, 173
pre-revolution, 19, 20, 21, 22
reforms in, 74
types of, 75, 76
1930s, in, 34
Legal history. *See* HISTORY OF SOVIET LAW; PRE-REVOLUTIONARY LEGAL HERITAGE
Legal profession
advocates, 80–90. *See also* ADVOCATES
counsel. *See* COUNSEL
development of, in pre-revolutionary Russia, 22, 23
ethics, 87, 88
fees, 85, 86
generally, 80
judges. *See* JUDGES
juriconsults, 90–95. *See* JURICONSULTS
legal consulataion offices, 85
Party membership in, 171, 172

Index 425

Legal research
Academy of Sciences, in, 76, 77
All-Union Scientific Research Institute for Problems of Strengthening Legality and Legal Order, 78
All-Union Scientific Research Institute of Soviet Legislation (VNIISZ), in, 77, 78
generally, 75, 76
number of personnel, 78, 79
organisations, generally, 78, 79
Union Republic Academies of Sciences, in, 76, 77
Legal system
study of—
history of, 1–4
reasons for, 1, 4–7
Legal transactions
definition of, 179
form of, 179, 180
invalidity of, 179, 180
purpose of, 180
Legislation
details of types of, 42–48
economic, restructuring. *See* ECONOMIC LAW
entry into force of, 57–59
publication of, 57–59
source of Soviet law, as, 41–48
Lenin
Communist Party, concept of role of, 163, 170
Marxist-Leninist theory of State and law, 27–30
Life
danger, in, duty to render aid where, 312, 313
duty to rescue, compensation in connection with, 195–197
Local taxes. *See* TAXATION

Maritime Arbitration Commission
role of, 141, 142, 392, 393
Marriage. *See also* DIVORCE; FAMILY LAW
age at which allowed, 204, 205, 209
bride price, 317
de facto, 204, 205, 206, 209
foreigners, legislation as to, 218, 219
legal requirements for—
current, 209
historical background, 204, 205
local customs, survivals of, 317
nullity of, 214
post-revolutionary background, 203–207

Marriage—*cont.*
pre-revolution, 203
property of spouses, 209–211
registered—
foreigners, with, 218
post-revolutionary period, in, 204, 205
procedure as to, 208, 209
property acquired during, 209
religious, 203, 204, 208
stateless persons, legislation as to, 218, 219
support, duty of spouse as to, 211
Marx
theory of State and law, 27–30
Mental health
compulsory medical measures, 308–310
criminal responsibility where mental illness, etc., 303
Military law
acts of military commands, 50
national defence, under the constitution, 149
Party organisations in armed forces, 167
procuracy, military, 99, 115, 116
reforms of Peter the Great, 18, 19
tribunals, military, 99, 106, 107
Minerals. *See also* NATURAL RESOURCE LAW
legal regulation, of, 277–279
Ministries of justice
functions of, 96, 97
history of, 96
Minors. *See also* FAMILY LAW
adoption of, 217, 220
age of criminal responsibility of, 303
alimony for, 213, 216, 217, 219, 220
birth, registration of, 215
Commissions for Cases of, functions of, 128, 129
compulsory educational measures for, 311
curatorship of, 217, 218
divorce, in cases of, 213
educational-labour colonies for, 329
emigration of, 207
foreign citizens' obligations and rights as to, 219, 220
guardianship of, 217, 218
illegitimate, 214, 215
inheritance by, 200
labour colonies for, 327
marriage of, 317
neglect or abuse of, 128, 129, 216
parental rights as to, 215, 216

Minors—*cont.*
parents' property, rights as to, 210
paternity proceedings, 215
punishment of, 306, 307, 311
support of—
  parents' duties as to, 216
  temporary benefits where parents not paying alimony due, 21
Mongol subjugation
effect of, on law, 12, 13
Muscovite law
influence of, 14–16
MVD. *See* POLICE, agencies

Narcotics. *See* DRUGS
National anthem
provision for, 162
National economic planning. *See also* ECONOMIC LAW
indicators, 246, 247
introduction of, 33, 34, 242–244
natural resources and, 276, 277
principles of, 253, 254
Natural resource law
ecological law, 275, 276
generally, 274
Goskompriroda SSSR, 282, 283
Gosplan, 276
historical background to, 274, 275
institutional enforcement of, 279, 280
regulation of natural resources, 277–279
restructuring and environmental policy, 281–283
sanctions against breaches of, 280, 281
State Committee for Nature Conservation, 282, 283
Negligence
criminal offence, causing, 301–303
New economic policy (NEP)
advocacy and, 81, 82
introduction of, 81, 99, 176
views as to, 32
Notariat
history of, 116
role of, 116–120
wills, activities as to, 117, 118, 119, 200, 202

Ownership
collective farm, 266, 267, 270, 271
historical background, 37–39, 175–177
juridical persons, 179
law of, generally, 180
meaning of, 38

Ownership—*cont.*
personal—
  artisans, by, 187
  collections, of, 185
  constitutions, under, 148, 182–187
  cultural value, items of—
    acquisition of, 185
    duty to maintain, 186, 187
  dacha, of, 185
  disposing of, 186, 187
  dwelling house—
    constitutions, under, 184, 185
    duty to maintain, 186, 187
    meaning of, 184
  income and, 186
  legal limits as to, 186
  'monuments of history and culture', of, 185
  permitted items, 183–187
  private, distinguished from, 182
  rights as to, 182
  Soviet and Western concepts compared, 182
  special authorisation, articles requiring, 185
  status of, 37–39
  subsidiary household husbandry, articles of, 183, 184
  use of, 185, 186
private, distinguished from personal, 182
socialist—
  developments in law of, 187, 188
  law as to, 180, 181
  primacy of, 147, 148

Party. *See* COMMUNIST PARTY OF THE SOVIET UNION
Pashukanis, E. B.
influence of, on Soviet law, 32, 33, 34, 35, 66, 67, 68, 243
Passport
requirements for foreign citizens, 369
Patents
civil law as to, 197, 199
foreign citizens, law as to, 374
Pay
brigades and, 231, 232
collective farms, on, 267
co-operatives, of members and individuals working in, 240
court experts and interpreters, of, 343, 344
joint enterprises, in, 392
provisions as to, 223, 226, 227

Pay—*cont.*
  restructuring economic legislation, under, 260
People's assessors
  Party membership of, 172
  recall of, 102
  role of, 101, 102
People's control commissions
  functions of, 131, 132
  history of, 130, 131
People's court
  damage caused to enterprise, cases of, 237
  labour law disputes, 232–234
  role of, 102, 138
People's guards
  history of, 139
  introduction of, 36
  powers of, 139–141
Personal property. *See* OWNERSHIP
Peter the Great
  reforms of, 18, 19, 107
Planning. *See* ECONOMIC LAW; NATIONAL ECONOMIC PLANNING
Police
  agencies—
    inquiries for criminal cases, as to, 353
    KGB (Committee of State Security), 133–135
    Ministry of Internal Affairs (MVD), 133, 135, 136
    Party control of, 172
  people's guard, role of, 139–141
  registration with, of foreign citizens, 370
Politburo
  role of, 165–167
Pre-revolutionary legal heritage. *See also* HISTORY OF SOVIET LAW
  Byzantine influence, 10, 12, 17, 18, 24
  canon law. See ecclesiastical law, *below*
  Catherine II, under, 20, 107
  Christianity, influence of, 10, 12, 16
  continuity and change, 25, 26
  customary rules, tolerance of, 24, 25
  ecclesiastical law, 10, 12, 18
  ethnic groups, systems in different, 10, 24, 25
  Islamic influence, 24
  Kievan Rus—
    devastation of, 13
    law of, 10–12
  late sixteenth and early seventeenth centuries, in, 17–19
  law codes, 14, 17–19, 21, 23, 24, 25

Pre-revolutionary legal heritage—*cont.*
  legal education, 19, 20, 21, 22
  legal profession, 22, 23
  legal texts—
    Book of the Pilot, 12, 13, 18
    Complete Collected Laws of the Russian Empire, 21
    Digest of Russian Laws, 21, 22
    Nakaz by Catherine II, 20
    Pravda Russkaia, 11, 12, 13, 17
  Mongol subjugation, effect of, 12, 13
  Muscovite law, 14–16
  nineteenth century, in, 20–23
  Peter the Great, under, 18, 19, 107
  procuracy, 18, 107, 108
  reconstruction of, 10
  Russian Empire, 17–25
  twentieth century, in, 23
Press
  Party control of, 172
Prices
  restructuring economic legislation, under, 258–260
Prisons. *See also* CORRECTIONAL-LABOUR LAW
  deprivation of freedom in, 306, 329
Procedure
  civil—
    appeal, 348
    broad participation in proceedings, 339–342
    court costs, 343, 344
    evidence, 348
    filing suit, 345, 346
    fines for failure as to procedural action, 344
    foreign citizens, rights of, 348, 349
    generally, 334
    historical background, 334–337
    legal counsel, 342, 343
    procedural economy, 344, 345
    purpose of, 339
    scope of, 337–339
    stateless persons, rights of, 348, 349
    trial, 346–348
      preparation for, 346
  criminal—
    appeal, 362–364
    arrest, distinguished from detention, 353, 354
    confessions, 362
    detention, distinguished from arrest, 353, 354
    foreign citizens, as to, 369, 378

Procedure—*cont.*
  criminal—*cont.*
    generally, 334, 351, 352
    historical background, 350, 351
    jurisdiction, 352
    pre-revolutionary Russia, in, 22, 23
    presumption of innocence, 360–362
    pre-trial proceedings—
      administrative session, 357, 358
      initiation of criminal case, 352, 353
      inquiry, 353, 354
      preliminary investigation, 354–357
    restructuring and, 364, 365
    review, possibility of, 364
    Theoretical Model of a Code of Criminal Procedure, 365
    trial—
      examination, judicial, 358
      investigation, judicial, 358, 359
      oral argument, 360
    See also pre-trial proceedings, *above*
Procuracy
  criminal proceedings, role as to, 354–357, 358, 363, 365
  establishment of, 18, 25, 91, 107, 108
  functions of, 37, 109, 110
  history of, 18, 107–109
  investigators of, 354, 355
  membership of, 109, 172
  military, 115, 116
  Party membership in, 172
  structure of, 110, 111
  supervision, branches of, 111–115
Production associations
  functions and jurisdiction of, 250, 251
  meaning of, 250
  reforms, of, 251, 252
Production entities
  features of, 245, 246
  financial position of, 246
  plan indicators, 246, 247
Propaganda
  anti-Soviet, punishment for, 311, 312, 318
Property. *See also* OWNERSHIP
  collective farms, of, 181
  duty to rescue, compensation in connection with, 195, 196
  personal. *See* OWNERSHIP
  social organisations, of, 181
  socialist—
    damage to, 236–239
    execution against, 181
    ownership of. *See* OWNERSHIP
  spouses, of, 209–211
  trade unions, of, 181

Publication
  legislation, of, 57–59
  indigenous languages, in, 59–61
Punishment
  criminal law, under. *See* CORRECTIONAL-LABOUR LAW; CRIMINAL LAW

Rationalisation proposal
  civil law, under, 198, 199
  inheritance of rights as to, 199
  meaning of, 198, 199
Registration
  birth, of, 215
  divorce, of, 212, 213, 214
  marriage, of. *See* MARRIAGE
  police, by foreign citizens, 370
Registry for Acts of Civil Status (ZAGS). *See* ZAGS
Remuneration. *See* PAY
Rescue
  duty to, compensation for, 195–197
Restructuring economic legislation. *See* ECONOMIC LAW
Royalties
  income tax in relation to, 292, 293, 373
  payment of, 373

Sale
  contract of, 118, 190, 191
  goods, of—
    contracts as to, 118, 190, 191
    credit facilities for, 191
    quality, provisions as to, 190, 191
    speculation, crime of, 313, 314
Sanctions
  collective farm procurement contract offences, for, 268
  economic, 254
  foreign citizens, against, 370, 371
  labour disciplinary, 222, 232
  natural resource regulation, for breaches of, 280, 281
  non-labour income, against, 186
Scientific advisory councils
  function of, 53
Services
  co-operatives for rendering, 239–241, 273
Social centres for the protection of order
  role of, 141
Social insurance
  collective farms, for, 236, 269
  State scheme for, 236

Social organisations
  acts of, 48–50
  foreign—
    citizens joining, 378
    trade and, 387, 388
  income tax on, 291
Social security. *See* SOCIAL INSURANCE
Socialist community life
  rules of, 55, 56
Sources of Soviet law
  acts—
    military commands, of, 50
    social organisations, of, 48–50
    State Arbitrazh, of, 50
  Communist Party enactments, 49, 50
  court judgments, 51–53
  custom, 54, 55
  doctrine, 53, 54
  generally, 41
  guiding explanations, 51–53
  international treaties, 56, 57
  legislation, details of types of, 41–48
  publication and entry into force of legislation, 57–59
  rules of socialist community life, 55, 56
  techniques of law reform, 61–63
  translation of enactments into indigenous languages, 59–61
Soviet legal system(s)
  model, as, 5
  operating simultaneously, 10, 24, 25
Speculation
  crime of, 313, 314
State
  arms, provision for, 162
  flag, provision for, 162
  ownership. *See* OWNERSHIP
  social insurance, 236
  tort liability of, 193
State and law
  theory of—
    Marxist-Leninist, 27–30
    Soviet era, in, 30–40
State Arbitrazh
  acts, of, 50
  appeals of decisions, 126
  educational functions, 126
  fees, 86
  functions of, 122, 123
  history of, 121, 122
  introduction of, 34
  jurisdiction, 123–125
  legislative functions, 125
  role, of, 34, 92, 122, 123
  structure, 123

State Committee for Nature Conservation
  functions of, 282, 283
State duty
  levy of, 295, 296, 377
State enterprises
  economic law in relation to. *See* ECONOMIC LAW
  environmental protection and, 277
Stateless persons. *See also* FOREIGN CITIZENS
  civil procedural rights of, 348, 349
  criminal responsibility of, 299
  divorce procedure for, 219
  family law as to, 218–220
  legal status of—
    citizenship, as to, 368
    constitutions, under, 366
  marriage of, 218, 219
  notarial offices, application to, of , 120
  personal property rights of, 182
  Soviet law, position under, 151
  taxation—
    income tax, liability for, 291
    recovery of unpaid taxes, 296
Succession, law of. *See* INHERITANCE; WILLS
Supreme Attestation Commission (VAK)
  role of, 73, 74
Supreme courts
  history of, 99
  operation of, 104–106
  structure of, 104
Supreme soviets
  convocation of, 157
  election of, 154, 155
  enactment of legislation by, 43, 44
  functions of, 155–158
  government, election of, by, 45
  powers of, 155

Taxation
  agricultural tax, 294
  bachelors, tax on, 294
  customs duty, 296
  deductions from profits, 288
  fixed payments, 286, 287
  generally, 284
  income tax—
    collective farms, on, 290
    co-operatives, on 241, 291
    copyright, in relation to, 292, 293
    employees, liability of, 292

Taxation—*cont.*
  income tax—*cont.*
    exemptions, 293
    foreigners, liability of, 377
    individual activities, citizens engaged in, 293
    individuals, on, 291–293
    royalties, in relation to, 292, 293, 373
    secondary income earners, liability of, 292
    self-employed, liability of, 292
    social organisations, on, 291
    workers, liability of, 292
  local taxes—
    foreign citizens, liability of, 377
    generally, 295
    land and buildings tax, 295
    self-assessment, 295
  residual profits, 287
  restructuring, under, 284–286, 287
  single citizens, tax on, 294
  small families, tax on, 294
  State budget—
    compulsory payments to, 284–286
    other payments to, 289, 290
  State duty, 295, 296, 377
  turnover tax, 288, 289
  unpaid taxes, recovery of, 296
  vehicle tax, 294, 377
Territory
  law as to spatial limits, 398, 399
Tort, law of
  causation, liability founded on, 191, 192
  compensation for harm, 192–195
  court, compensation for harm caused by, 193, 194
  fault, basis of, for causing harm, 192, 193
  foreign citizens, damages payable to, 194, 195
  'heightened danger', liability for, 192
  inquiry agencies, etc., compensation for harm caused by officials of, 193, 194
  liability of State, 193
Trade unions
  acts relating to, 48, 50
  All-Union Central Trade Union Council (VTsSPS), 231, 234, 235
  collective—
    contracts and, 227
    farms, at, 269
  foreign citizens in, 378
  labour—
    disputes, role as to, 233
    law, as to, 230, 234, 235

Trade unions—*cont.*
  membership of, 234
  property rights of, 181
  role of, 234, 235
  State social insurance scheme, and, 236
Translation
  enactments into indigenous languages, of, 59–61
  foreign legal literature of, pre-revolution, 20
Trial
  civil case procedure, 346–348
  criminal. *See under* PROCEDURE

Union Republic Academies of Sciences
  legal research in, 77
USSR Academy of Sciences. *See* ACADEMY OF SCIENCES
USSR Chamber of Commerce. *See* CHAMBER OF COMMERCE

VAAP (All-Union Copyright Agency)
  role of, 387, 388
Vagrancy
  crime of, 316
VAK (Supreme Attestation Commission)
  role of, 73, 74
Vehicle tax
  levy of, 294, 377
Visas
  foreign citizens, for, 369
Vyshinskii, A. Ia.
  influence of, on Soviet law, 35, 36, 67

Wages. *See* PAY
Water. *See* NATURAL RESOURCE LAW
  legal regulation of, 277–279
Wills. *See also* INHERITANCE
  executors, 200, 201
  functions of notaries as to, 117, 118, 119, 200, 201, 202
  procedure as to drawing up, 200
  where none, 201
Women
  equality with men, of, 207, 208
Workers. *See* LABOUR LAW

ZAGS (Registry for Acts of Civil Status)
  history of, 120
  role of, 120, 121, 204, 205, 206, 208, 209, 212, 213, 218